N·I·N·T·H E·D·I·T·I·O·N

INTERNATIONAL ECONOMICS

Peter H. Lindert
University of California at Davis

IRWIN

Homewood, IL 60430
Boston, MA 02116

Sponsoring editor: Gary L. Nelson
Project editor: Waivah Clement
Production manager: Carma W. Fazio
Designer: Stuart Paterson
Artist: John Foote
Compositor: Arcata Graphics/Kingsport
Typeface: 10/12 Times Roman
Printer: R. R. Donnelley & Sons Company

Library of Congress Cataloging-in-Publication Data

Lindert, Peter H.
    International economics / Peter H. Lindert.—9th ed.
      p.   cm.
    Includes bibliographical references and index.
    ISBN 0-256-07900-5
    ISBN 0-256-09957-x INTERNATIONAL EDITION
    1. International economic relations.   2. Commercial policy.
3. Foreign exchange.   I. Title.
HF1411.L536   1991
337—dc20   90–44740
                                             CIP

Printed in the United States of America
1 2 3 4 5 6 7 8 9 0 DOC 8 7 6 5 4 3 2 1

Preface

Keeping a textbook abreast of new events and changes in theory is a welcome challenge for any scholar dedicated to learning and to teaching. The challenge has been posed anew since 1986, more by changing events than by changing theories. The economic revolutions of 1989–90 have shaped much of the fresh material of this edition, with an important supporting role being played by new theories of modern trade, exchange-rate theory, and the theory of international debt problems. While there are thousands of micro-revisions that defy summary, a few themes stand out.

- The trade-bloc revolution of the late 1980s and early 1990s now has its own chapter. Chapter 9 combines the breakup of the Eastern bloc with the European Community's march to 1992, the North American Free Trade Treaty, and the economics of blockades and embargoes. Far from being just a repository for recent newsclippings, Chapter 9 uses frugal economic theory to interpret the prospects for both trade blocs and trade blocks.

- The struggle for economic leadership among leading industrial nations is the dominant theme of the new Chapters 5 and 10. Chapter 5, on Alternative Theories of Modern Trade, finds a unity in the diverse economies-of-scale theories. All take aim at Part I's over-arching issues of what explains our trade patterns and who gains or loses from them. All focus on modern trade in knowledge-intensive products, with a high share of ''intra-industry'' trade. Their appeal and their limitations are weighed without undue complexity. Chapter 10 shows the potential and the limitations of strategic trade policy, with application to the race to capture high-definition television markets in the mid-1990s. Chapter 10's harvest is far richer than just a presentation of strategic trade policy, however. It offers the lessons recently learned about the international competitive races for leadership in steel, autos, and electronics. The lessons about the role of government policy and the role of private industrial performance differ among these key sectors.

- Sometimes events vindicate an old decision instead of calling for a new one. The sixth through eighth editions have given OPEC and the economics of international cartels their own chapter, even when the oil price decline of 1985–86 made them less topical. I have long felt that this material was crucial to international economics, and that American policy is a key force holding up the cost of energy. Iraq's invasion of Kuwait in 1990 makes the material in Chapter 11 all the more compelling.

- The three lead chapters of Part III have been overhauled and rearranged, both to simplify their logical flow and to bring order to the turbulence of payments flows and exchange rates in recent years. Chapter 14, Payments among Nations, now stands at the gateway to the unbroken path of chapters (15–18) on the economics of exchange rates. The reader can take in this clear view of the basic flows between nations before heading in any traditional direction, whether into the foreign exchange market in Part III, or into the macroeconomics of Part IV, or even into the trade side in Parts I and II. The introduction to exchange-rate economics has some fresh updates and a candor that I hope will be welcome. Candor is essential in reporting the track record of our models for explaining exchange-rate movements. A key innovation here is Chapter 16's map of how model errors rise and fall with the time-span of the forecast. Our strength and our weakness appear side by side: our insights have greatest power in the long run and in hyperinflations, yet fail to illuminate short-run movements (except for the relationship of spot and forward rates to each other and to interest rates).

- A new compromise has been struck in Part IV regarding the diagrams of the IS-LM-FE analysis built on the ISLM of intermediate macroeconomics. Teaching opinions differ sharply on this diagrammatic tool. Some like it not, some like it bold. The sixth edition appeased the faction wanting the diagrams, while the seventh and eighth dispensed with them. They now reappear in Chapter 20 in the limited role they play best: policy analysis under fixed exchange rates. The text flows in such a way, however, that the IS-LM-FE diagrams are discussed in discrete sets of paragraphs that instructors can place in quarantine if they wish.

- Fresh material also dominates Chapter 24 on international capital flows and the debt crisis. The continuing debt crisis of developing countries needs a careful survey and interpretation, of course, as does America's switch from top creditor to top debtor. The theoretical slant on the debt crisis is my own.

  Clarity and honesty are the stylistic goals throughout. Even more than in earlier editions, abundant road signs show where the argument is going. The signs are unmistakable at the start of each chapter, often helped by a schematic sketch. Almost every paragraph also leads off with its keynote sentence pointing the way. Summaries recap every chapter. As in the first five editions by Charles Kindleberger, I try to be candid about which tools and which facts are more important than which others. The undeniable power of some of the economist's tools is applied repeatedly to recent events, without apology. Tools that fail to improve on common sense and intuition are not over-sold. Truth in packaging also holds for empirical trends and patterns. Some facts are weightier than others, and I have tried to order them carefully. As a result, the book has more empirical material than most competing texts, yet avoids presenting masses of facts as if they could speak for themselves. Data sources are cited: a textbook has no excuse for hiding the untidy facts behind the shiny displays. The sceptical reader who wants to track down the messier and deeper truth must be rewarded, even if twenty others don't want to know where the Received Truth came from.

The format of the book has been fine-tuned for better teaching. Most (though still not all) exam-worthy **definitions** appear in boldface in the text, and are distinguished from words of *special emphasis,* which appear in italics. For further visual contrast,

> Some *key points or results* with a high probability of being covered on the exam are block-indented, like this.

Shaded boxes appear in different type with a different right edge format, unlike the main text. It should be easy to see that they offer extensions and case studies of a different character, to be emphasized more or less, at the instructor's discretion.

By popular demand, the questions for review at the ends of chapters have been expanded. They vary in character. Some are frontal prods, asking the student "Did you remember this? If not, look back and memorize." Some are numerical exercises. Others pose open-ended conceptual challenges to tackle in section or seminar. About half the review questions were born as exam questions at UC–Davis. Many invite longer answers than exam questions, however, because time is less scarce during review than in the exam room.

STUDY GUIDE AND INSTRUCTOR'S MANUAL

Also by popular demand, the *Study Guide* and *Instructor's Manual* have been expanded. Again, the exercises vary in character and length. It is a pleasure to have Professor Osman Suliman of Grambling State University take the lead on writing both. We began working together in much the same way that Charles Kindleberger and I first teamed up for the sixth and seventh editions. Professor Suliman sent a letter ''over the transom'' with friendly criticisms of the flow of my argument in a few parts of the eighth edition, especially in Chapter 2. Students and I are in his debt.

ACKNOWLEDGMENTS

For the ninth edition I received more help than usual from users of earlier editions. I have been guided by the abundant written suggestions and criticisms of Paul Cantor (Herbert H. Lehmann College, CUNY), D. J. Daly (York University), Henry N. Goldstein (University of Oregon), Jacqueline E. Gosline (New York University), Louis Johnston (Bowdoin College), Philip G. King (San Francisco State University), Pamela Langlais (New York University), Kathy A. Lindert (American University of Paris and U.S. Department of Agriculture), Nolin Masih (St. Cloud University), Thomas A. Pugel (New York University), Joseph T. Salerno (Pace University), John Sheahan (Williams College), Howard Stein (Roosevelt University), Osman Suliman (Grambling State University), Harold R. Williams (Kent State University), and Susan J. Ye (George Washington University). Excellent suggestions were also given in conversation by Professors Ali Fatemi, Farhad Nomani, and Ali Rahnema and their students at the American University of Paris, and from my colleagues Terry Alexander, Maite Cabeza-Gutés, Robert Feenstra, and Wing Thye Woo and a host of students at the University of California–Davis. In the background there is the perennial help from my whole family. This edition is dedicated to them, especially to my father on his 80th birthday and to Lin on our 25th anniversary.

Peter H. Lindert

Contents in Brief

ix

Contents

PART V   Factor Movements

APPENDIXES

▼

International Economics Is Different

•

Nations are not like regions or families. They can put up all sorts of barriers between their members and the outside world. Being sovereign, nations can be more indifferent to the interests of others. A region or family must deal with the political reality that others within the same nation can out-vote it, and therefore coerce it or tax it. They have to compromise with others who have political voice. Nations feel little such pressure, and often ignore the interests of foreigners. They use policy tools that are seldom available to regions and never available to families: their own currencies, their own trade barriers, their own fiscal policies, and their own laws of citizenship and residence.

As long as nations exist, international economics will always need a separate body of analysis distinct from the rest of economics. The special nature of international economics makes its study fascinating and sometimes difficult. Future events are sure to keep reminding us of what is special about this field. To see why, let's look at five recent events that have been shaping this book.

FIVE EVENTS

The American Import Invasion and Protectionism

Since the early 1970s the United States, Canada, and other countries have debated a kind of policy move that is unique to the international side of economics: measures to clamp down on the import of foreign goods. The main target is Japan.

The pressure has been building for some time mainly because of the rising intensity of industrial competition from Japan, South Korea, Taiwan,

Angry members of the United Auto Workers protest unrestricted auto imports in March 1981 by smashing a Toyota car near the Ford Motor Company stamping plant in Chicago Heights, Illinois. Soon thereafter, Japanese auto firms agreed to voluntary export restrictions. These restrictions have since been eased, but remain informally in effect. (Courtesy United Auto Workers, Local 588)

and Brazil. The United States has been importing larger and larger shares of its clothing, steel, automobiles, motorcycles, and consumer electronic products. Even strong sectors like aircraft and agriculture have faced tougher competition in home and foreign markets. The U.S. trade surplus (the value of exports minus imports) disappeared, and a yawning trade deficit (imports exceeding exports) opened up.

The U.S. auto industry has become the main arena for the trade wars. Early warnings were sounded when Volkswagen "bugs" began to creep across North America in the late 1950s. By 1985 imports accounted for nearly a third of U.S. new car sales, with Japan alone taking a quarter of the U.S. market. The invasion of cheap and efficient cars has been an undeniable boon for most households. It has been a disaster in eastern Michigan and other auto-making regions. There the unemployment rate remains stubbornly high, General Motors has at times been a nonprofit organization, and Chrysler was pushed to the brink of extinction before getting government emergency loans in the late 1970s. The United States has imposed new restrictions on imports of textiles, autos, steel, motorcycles, and other products. Special resentment has been building against Japan, whose demand for free access to foreign markets has clashed with its own import barriers. In 1989, polls showed that a majority of Americans felt Japan's trade policies were unfair and would support boycotting Japanese goods if Japan does not do more to open its markets to American and other imports.

The issue of protection against imports requires a specifically international analysis. Within nations, such protection is illegal, except in subtle and slight forms. California cannot impose, say, a 50 percent tax on all products imported into that state from the rest of the United States. Nor can British Columbia put up such a barrier against products from the rest of Canada. Doing so to protect jobs against "unfair" Eastern competition would destroy Eastern jobs in companies that had counted on being able to sell to California or British Columbia. The interests of the rest of the nation cannot be ignored. The U.S. Constitution explicitly defends against state or local trade barriers. Yet truly foreign interests can be more easily ignored, and any analysis of the likely effects of protectionist laws must explicitly distinguish between effects within the nation and effects on foreigners. Such analysis is offered in Parts One and Two of this book.

The Trade Bloc Revolution

In the 1990s the world does business between giant trade blocs, large international economies acting more and more like nations. We are approaching a true world economy, but are not there yet. Governments still restrict the international flow of people, firms, goods, and money. Now, however, they do so largely as groups of nations acting together, not just as individual nations. More than anytime in history, there is something approaching a West European economic nation and a North American economic nation. These, together with Japan, now account for 70 percent of the world's product. East Asia and the Third World face the challenge of dealing with the new blocs. Eastern Europe, with revolutions of its own, scrambles to realign its trade with Western Europe as the previous socialist trade bloc comes apart.

The West Europeans led the way. Since World War II, nations with a history of bitter warfare have integrated their economies ever more closely together. With the 1957 Treaty of Rome as a landmark, the nations of the growing European Community (EC) have removed all the usual taxes (tariffs) on trade among themselves. In 1986 they passed the Single European Act, pledging to become virtually a single economic nation by 1992. Policies toward business practices, jobs, safety standards, and private finance will be uniform EC policies, not differing policies of 12 nations. Even their national moneys may stand in new fixed equivalence to each other in 1993, according to an agreement signed in 1989 despite British opposition. What will be left of national economic policies (some, but not all, tax policies

THREE ECONOMIC GIANTS

	Data for 1987			
	Population (millions)	GDP Per Capita	Total GDP ($ billions)	Share of World GDP (percent)
1. Canada–U.S. free trade area:	270	$18,397	4962	33%
Canada	(26)	($17,140)	(444)	(3)
United States	(244)	($18,530)	(4518)	(30)
2. European Community (10 nations)	340	$11,744	3998	27
3. Japan	122	$13,249	1618	11
World:	4987	$ 2,985	14,884	100

Notes: GDP = gross domestic product per year.

The GDP's of countries in the three giants are adjusted for international price differences, from the University of Pennsylvania's International Comparisons Project. Those for the whole world are just crude exchange-rate conversions into U.S. dollars. In this example, the "world" equals the world minus Albania, Angola, Mongolia, Namibia, North Korea and 55 nations and territories each with populations less than 1 million.

The figures for the European Community include East Germany, with an estimated GDP of $190 billion and a population of 17 million in 1987.

Sources: Summers and Heston (1988); World Bank, *World Development Report 1989*, Tables 1 and 30, Box A.2.

and most government expenditure decisions)? Meanwhile, countries outside the EC must bargain with an economic unit that has the second highest GNP, gross not-just-national product, of any free-trade unit in the world, larger than Japan and approaching that of the United States (see the box on ''Three Economic Giants'').

North America followed suit. The EC's clear determination to form a giant almost national market by 1992 may have given new urgency to the movement to make Canada and the United States a single market. Certainly the timing suggests that Europe forced the hands of the North Americans. On October 4, 1987, less than a year after the EC passed the Single European Act, Prime Minister Brian Mulroney and President Reagan initialed a free-trade pact that seemed politically dangerous. The idea of free trade between Canada and the United States was already a century old, but it had always met with protectionist opposition in one or both countries. To make matters worse, the two countries had just waged a trade war in 1986. The United States slapped a tax on Canadian lumber sold to the United States, and Canada retaliated with a tax on U.S. corn, citing the same argument about export subsidies that the United States had used in the lumber case. In this troubled setting, Prime Minister Mulroney gambled on making the free-trade pact a central issue in his bid for reelection in November of 1988. Amazingly, it worked at the last minute: though polls had shown the pact trailing and Mulroney in trouble, the public mood swung around and brought him victory on both fronts. The two nations formalized a free-trade agreement effective January 1, 1989. The political climate warmed up so much, in fact, that the two nations agree in December 1989 to speed up the process of removing trade barriers between them, instead of waiting for the scheduled final date of 1999. What they created was less of a unified economy than the Europeans planned for 1992, in that Canada and the United States kept the right to set separate trade policies vis-à-vis third countries, and they also kept very separate tax policies. Quebec may also break some ties with the rest of Canada. But North America was moving closer to unity. Figuring out which country gains how much and whether third countries will be harmed calls for a special kind of analysis (Chapter 9).

The Gyrating Dollar

On August 15, 1971, President Nixon ended one era and began another with a few terse sentences announcing that the value of the U.S. dollar must be changed in terms of other nations' currencies and gold. Soon the exchange rates between the dollar and other currencies were drifting toward higher values for other currencies and lower values for the dollar. Suddenly international travelers, long accustomed to fixed exchange rates between dollars and other currencies, found that their dollars exchanged for fewer German marks, Japanese yen, and other currencies. The change also affected firms and individuals trading goods between countries. Firms in the United States such as Boeing found it easier to sell their aircraft and other products abroad now that foreigners felt that they could afford more dollars and more U.S. goods priced in dollars. Foreign firms who were used to selling large amounts of goods to the United States felt a new kind of pressure. Volkswagen found that the same dollar prices for VWs in North America brought it fewer West German marks with which to pay West German workers and shareholders. It soon had to raise its car prices in dollars, losing some business to its U.S. and Canadian competitors.

Since then, the fluctuations in exchange rates have shocked most observers. The fact that the dollar sank about 20 percent in its ability to buy other currencies between mid-1971 and mid-1973 might have been dismissed as a temporary adjustment to regain equilibrium exchange rates from which the previously fixed rates had departed. But the gyrations didn't stop there. The value of the dollar in terms of other currencies rose about 16 percent between mid-1973 and mid-1976, fell back 16 percent between 1976 and 1978, and stayed at its lower value into 1980. Next the dollar amazed everybody by rising 83 percent between mid-1980 and early 1985, ending up stronger (more valuable) than it had been when its weakness forced Nixon's hand in 1971. A whole new chorus of complaints was heard. Now it was American firms that had more trouble competing because their dollar prices looked so expensive to foreigners. Scholarly writings (including the eighth edition of the textbook) questioned if the dollar hadn't risen beyond what fundamental forces could explain. Starting from that peak in early 1985, the dollar fell 39 percent by early 1988, and it has risen slightly since.

Why should the value of a large nation's currency swing so widely, as widely as more traditional objects of speculation, such as stock market prices or real estate values? This question is not simply academic. Think, for example, of the fact that the dollar fell 39 percent in the three years after early 1985, when there was not much price inflation within the United States. One could have reaped a gain of 39 percent (or about 11.6 percent each year) just by exchanging dollars for other currencies in early 1985 and exchanging them back again three years later. Why didn't the financial market experts foresee that?

Explanations of these movements and whether the new system of fluctuating exchange rates is better or worse than the system it replaced are very complex issues to be pursued in Parts Three and Four of this book. These issues are clearly unique to the international sphere in economics. Exchange rates do not change between Kansas and Missouri or between Alberta and British Columbia. The usual tools that economics applies to domestic issues must be modified and extended if one is to make sense of what changes in exchange rates mean to ordinary people.

The Lingering World Debt Crisis

In August of 1982, Mexico warned the International Monetary Fund (IMF) that it could not repay its debts to private foreign banks. A flurry of negotiations and special missions led to a remarkable agreement in November. Private foreign banks and the IMF would give Mexico new loans to pay off part of the old loans in exchange for a Mexican belt-tightening program.

The belt was indeed tightened: across 1983, the Mexican economy sank further into depression for the third year in a row, unemployment soared, and as much as 12 percent of Mexican national product went to paying creditors in the United States and other wealthy countries.

Mexico was not alone. Over a dozen other countries, most notably Brazil, Argentina, and Poland, were also deeply in debt and also had to negotiate with the IMF later in 1982. The IMF demanded such severe cutbacks in government spending, money supply, and wages that riots against the fund broke out in Brazil and Argentina. Since 1982, the results have not comforted anyone. The debtor countries in Latin America and elsewhere continued to suffer widespread unemployment and stagnation partly because of their reluctant belt-tightening and partly because the flow of international lending suddenly stopped. The major banks that lent to them were still not being repaid all the interest they were promised in the original loan contracts. Worse yet, the threat of wholesale default (refusal to repay at all) continued to hang over the lenders. Nine leading U.S. banks, for example, would be bankrupt as a group if Latin America's governments defaulted on their foreign debts.

The international debt crisis is different from a wave of domestic bankruptcy. Its effects are truly macroeconomic, involving at least massive unemployment if not financial panic. The size of the problem is rooted in strictly international considerations. What makes the threat of default so credible is that the lenders have no way of forcing the borrowers to repay. The borrowers either are, or are backed by, sovereign governments. If Argentina refuses to repay its debts, there is no court it can be tried in and no way to seize its land or capital as partial repayment. The existence of separate nations helps explain not only the vulnerability of the creditors but also their gullibility in lending so much in the first place. Many banks happily joined the ill-starred rush to lend to Latin America, other developing countries, and Poland between 1974 and 1982 on the argument that national governments "will never go out of business," as if their ability to tax their citizens guaranteed a willingness to do so. It is a different kind of finance from the domestic finance studied in other fields of economics, as we shall see in more detail in Chapter 24.

Ironically, the lending country whose banks will suffer most if Third World governments do not repay has itself become by far the world's greatest international debtor, that is, the United States. Starting with the tax cuts of 1981, the U.S. federal government has run huge budget deficits, and by the beginning of 1990 owed about $400 billion, or about a fifth of the federal public debt, to foreigners. That foreign public debt easily eclipses the largest external debt in the Third World, the $113 billion owed to foreigners by Brazil. How will the United States pay it back? Will it have to go hat in hand to its main creditors, Japan, Germany, and the international agencies? If we think the United States can borrow forever without paying its foreign debt, what happens to the debt when "forever" comes? Chapter 24 explores the possibilities.

THE WORLD'S BIGGEST BANKS

(as measured by total assets and by market value, June 1990)

Rank	Bank	Nation	Total Assets ($billions)	Market Value of Equity ($billions)
1	Dai-Ichi Kangyo Bank	Japan	406	50
2	Sumitomo Bank	Japan	371	56
3	Fuji Bank	Japan	365	53
4	Mitsubishi Bank	Japan	362	47
5	Sanwa Bank	Japan	356	46
6	Industrial Bank of Japan	Japan	249	68
7	Credit Agricole	France	242	nt
8	Banque National de Paris	France	231	5
9	Citicorp	U.S.	231	8
10	Tokai Bank	Japan	229	24
11	Norinchukin Bank	Japan	221	nt
12	Credit Lyonnais	France	211	4
13	Barclays	Britain	205	10
14	Mitsui Bank	Japan	205	27
15	Bank of Tokyo	Japan	202	19
16	Deutsche Bank	Germany	198	19
17	National Westminster Bank	Britain	186	9
18	Societe Generale	France	176	7
19	Long-term Credit B. of Japan	Japan	175	32
20	Mitsubishi Trust & Banking	Japan	175	15
21	Taiyo Kobe Bank	Japan	174	17
22	Sumitomo Trust & Banking	Japan	152	14
23	Dresdner Bank	Germany	144	9
24	Mitsui Trust & Banking	Japan	142	12
25	Paribas	France	139	8

(nt = equity shares of this bank are not publically traded.)

Source: William Glasgall, "International Bank Scorecard: Happy Days Aren't Here Again," *Business Week*, July 2, 1990, pp. 80–85.

Japan, the World's Banker

Japan has bought more foreign assets than just U.S. government debt. In the late 1980s, Japan accelerated its purchases to include assets all over the globe. Japanese firms have built most of the new auto plants in North America and Britain. Rockefeller Center in New York City belongs to Japan.

In 1989, Sony paid $3.4 billion to buy Columbia Pictures and its properties, ranging from the film "When Harry Met Sally" to the TV show "Jeopardy." Sony also bought CBS records, including Michael Jackson's CBS releases. Although such direct-ownership investments are presently much smaller in value than Japan's holding of U.S. government debt and ordinary deposits in U.S. banks, they are highly visible signs that America is selling off her icons.

Japan has taken over world banking. As the box on "The World's Biggest Banks" shows, the top six commercial banks (ranked by total assets) are all based in Japan. The largest U.S. banks have been held back by state restrictions on branch banking. They have also made bad investments on loans to the Third World, farming, and energy. Citicorp is only ninth in the asset ranks, and has sold its New York headquarters to Dai-ichi Seimei. Meanwhile, U.S. taxpayers will have to spend hundreds of billions on America's failed savings and loan banks and their deposits.

The main reason for the surge of Japan into the number one position in world finance is no mystery. Japan saves a much higher share of its income than the United States does. Between 1975 and 1987, gross national saving averaged 32 percent of Japan's GNP, versus only 15 percent in the United States. The difference in *net* saving, after subtracting depreciation, was slightly greater. Savings means accumulating assets or reducing debts. Japan's asset accumulation has been so extraordinary that its domination of world finance was inevitable. The financial home base is where the wealth is.

The meteoric rise of Japan, and fall of the United States, in the world financial ranks, calls for a different kind of analysis from domestic financial economics. Exchange rates, like the yen/dollar rate, become crucial. So does U.S. trade policy, since the fear of U.S. protectionism might drive more Japanese firms to set up their own plants within the United States. And because nations are involved, military issues and foreign policy issues unavoidably arise. Chapter 25 develops these themes.

ECONOMICS AND THE NATION STATE

It should be clear from such events that international economics has to be a separate area of study as long as nations are sovereign. For every country there is a whole set of national policies. And for every country, those policies will always be designed to serve some part of the national constituency. Remember that nations almost never give the interests of foreigners the same weight as domestic interests. Think of any recent debate over restricting cheap imports from Asia and Mexico into the United States or Canada (or Europe or Japan). How loudly have the North Americans spoken out to defend the Asian and Mexican jobs and incomes that would be lost if North American jobs and firms were protected? Similarly, the United States or Canada can decide which immigrants to keep out without asking what such a policy will do to the well-being of people who want to migrate to the United States or Canada. Although we, as students of international economics, need not share the usual indifference to other countries, we do need to weigh separate national interests in order to understand and shape national policy debate.

DIFFERENT MONEYS

To many economists, and especially to the average person, the principal difference between domestic and international trade is that the latter involves the use of different moneys. That is, of course, very different from trade within a country, where everybody uses the same currency. You cannot issue your own currency, nor can your roommate, nor the state of Ohio.

The existence of separate national currencies means that the price ratio between them can change. If a dollar were worth exactly 10 francs for 10 centuries, people would certainly come to think of a franc and the U.S. dime as the same money. Yet, if the price ratio between the two currencies can change, everyone will have to treat them as different moneys. And since 1971, as we have seen, the price ratios between major currencies have been fluctuating.

The variability of exchange rates has necessitated a modification of monetary economics, one that has seemed more and more urgent to economists since 1971. It is hard to talk about "the money supply" for the whole world in the same way we traditionally use that phrase in basic macroeconomics or in courses on money and banking. If a person in any country could hold any of several currencies whose relative prices can change by the minute, what is the world's money supply? Supply of which currencies? Supplied by whom? Held by whom? Parts Three and Four explore the special relationships between national moneys.

DIFFERENT FISCAL POLICIES

For each sovereign nation there is not only a separate currency, but also a separate government with its own public spending and power to tax. Differences in national tax policies are as a rule more pronounced than differences between the tax policies of states, provinces, or cities. Thus, in the international arena tax differences can set off massive flows of funds and goods that would not have existed without the tax discrepancies. Banks set up shop in the Bahamas, where their capital gains are less taxed and their books less scrutinized. Shipping firms register in Liberia or Panama, where registration costs very little and where they are free from other nations' requirements to use higher-paid national maritime workers. Sovereignty in tax policies and government spending also leads to lobbying and bribery on an international scale. Korean agents have bribed U.S. officials to continue subsidizing the export of U.S. rice to Korea. Aircraft manufacturers in the United States have bribed several foreign governments to favor their products. At a more mundane level, each country's array of export subsidies and duties and import barriers is a separate fiscal policy. The contrasts among the fiscal regimes of states, provinces, and localities are usually not so sharp.

FACTOR MOBILITY

In differentiating international from domestic trade, classical economists stressed the behavior of the factors of production. Labor and capital were mobile within a country, they believed, but not internationally. Even land was mobile within a country, if we mean occupationally rather than physically. The same land, for example, could be used alternatively for growing wheat or raising dairy cattle, which gave it a restricted mobility.

The importance of this intranational mobility of the factors of production was that returns to factors tended to equality within countries but not between countries. The wages of French workers of a given training and skill were expected to be more or less equal; but this level of wage bore no necessary relation to the level of comparable workers in Germany or Italy, England or Australia. The same equality of return within a country, but inequality internationally, was believed to be true of land and capital.

This distinction of the classical economists is *partly* valid today. Factors do move internationally, in response to opportunities for economic gain. It is accurate to say that there is a difference of degree in labor mobility interregionally and internationally and that people usually migrate within their own country more readily than they will emigrate abroad. This is true in part because identity of language, customs, and tradition are more likely to exist within countries than between countries. Capital is also more mobile within than between countries. Yet it is partially mobile over both kinds of boundaries. We shall see in Part Five what happens when capital moves from country to country.

THE SCHEME OF THIS BOOK

This book deals first with international trade theory and trade policy, asking in Part One how trade seems to work and in Part Two what policies toward trade would bring benefits and to whom. This essentially microeconomic material precedes the macroeconomic and financial focus of Parts Three and Four. In places this approach involves some momentary inconvenience, as when we look at an exchange-rate link between cutting imports and cutting exports in Chapter 4 or when we note in Appendix D that changing a tariff affects the exchange rate and therefore welfare. Yet there are gains in logic in proceeding from micro to macro, as in the way that the demand and supply analysis of trade in individual markets sets the stage for the use of the same tools at a more aggregate level in the treatment of international finance. It is in Part Three that we enter the world of currencies, examining foreign exchange markets, the balance of payments, and exchange rates. Part Four surveys the policy issue of how nations are affected by, and can best respond to, changing pressures regrading their currencies. Part Five examines the special problems raised by the partial international mobility of humans and other assets.

The Theory of International Trade

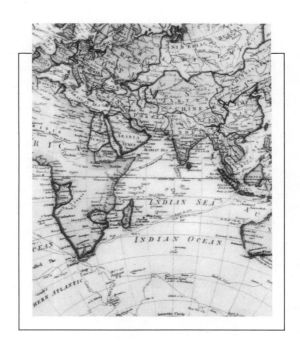

▼

The Basic Theory of International Trade: Supply

•

THE TWO TRADE ISSUES

1. How does international trade really work?
2. How should it work?

With international trade, as with so many other human studies, we want quick answers to the second of these two questions. Yet today, as in the past, the first question must be answered first.

For at least three centuries, ideas about international trade have been prompted by policy debates over what trade should be allowed. The study of trade emerged in the mercantilist era (roughly the 16th century through the 18th century in Europe) as a crude set of arguments about how a nation should trade. Writers and politicians felt that each nation's self-interest was best served by encouraging its exports and discouraging imports—a view that is common again today. After the late 18th century, the mercantilist view began to yield to a free-trade view, arguing that just letting people trade as they saw fit was the best way to serve both the nation and the whole world. Yet the free-traders, led by Adam Smith and David Ricardo, had trouble pressing their case without a convincing story of why it was that nations traded the way they did. If you don't know how people decide what goods to trade, it is hard to say who gains and who loses from trade, or whether trade should be restricted by governments. Even today, concern over whether or not governments should restrict foreign trade leads us to ask what forces make countries trade in the first place.

The answer to the first question might seem obvious: people will trade in whatever way they find privately profitable. That answer doesn't take us very far. Who ends up making the profits, or gains, from trade? Everybody? If not everybody and if some are hurt by trade, then how do we know who is who, and whether the gains to some are bigger than the losses to others? If one country gains from trade, must the other countries trading with it lose? Should trade be restricted for any of these reasons? These immediate questions show how tightly the two trade issues are tied together.

A LOOK AHEAD

This chapter and the rest of Part One tackle the first issue, and Part Two tackles the second.

Our *basic theory of trade* says that trade results from the interaction of competitive supply and demand. This chapter begins on the supply side, looking at what lies behind the supply curves used in analyzing international trade. We will look at different theories of why costs of the same good can differ between countries (when trade is not perfect). Chapter 3 adds the demand side and the incomes and tastes that lie behind demand curves. Chapter 4 explores who wins and who loses from international trade, according to the basic theory. First, this chapter asks how the gains from trade are divided between nations. Next, it asks why some sectors within a nation's economy decline when trade expands other sectors. Finally, it explores who are the winning and losing economic groups within a trading country: are they workers, capitalists, managers, farmers, miners, or landlords? Chapter 5 asks what is different about modern international trade, trade in higher-technology manufactured goods and services that may reflect different economic forces from the simpler trade observed by Adam Smith and his 19th-century successors.

Part One explores a diverse set of leading theories. Fortunately, the basic theory of competitive supply and demand serves many purposes fairly well. But the basic theory includes some special cases and some extensions designed to get at deeper explanations. It also has been challenged by new views, about which economists are still debating. Figure 2.1 offers a guide to this diversity. It lists the forces that each theory considers crucial in explaining the direction and amount of trade between nations, and it also lists the key assumptions that each theory makes in order to simplify things. You will probably want to refer back to this figure when reviewing all of the theories in Part One.

Part Two uses the theories of Part One to explore a broad range of policy issues. Chapters 6 through 8 set out on a journey to map the border between good trade barriers and bad ones. This journey turns out to be intellectually challenging, calling for careful reasoning. Chapter 9 switches to the economics of economic blocs like the European Community, the Canada-U.S. free-trade area, and the socialist bloc. Chapter 10 questions both what role policies have played and what role other economic forces have played in causing world trade leadership to change hands. In this chapter, we examine particular case studies, such as the steel industry, in which America (and Germany) overtook Britain early in the 20th century, Japan overtook America

FIGURE 2.1   A Guide to the Trade Theories of Part One

Name of Theory	What Forces Determine Trade Flows?	Some Key Assumptions
A. The basic theory (Chapters 2–4)	Productivities Factor supplies Product demands	Competition in all markets Constant or increasing costs Any number of factors (types of labor, land, etc.)
B. Supply-oriented theories of trade (special cases of the basic theory):		
1. Absolute advantage (in Chapter 2)	Absolute productivities	Competition in all markets Ignore demand side Constant marginal costs Only one factor (labor)
2. Comparative advantage (Ricardo, in Chapter 2)	Relative productivities	('')
3. Factor-proportions (Heckscher-Ohlin theory in Chapters 2,4)	Relative factor supplies	Competition in all markets Ignore demand side Ignore technology Increasing marginal costs Small number of factors
C. Alternative theories of modern trade (Chapter 5):		
1. Economies of scale theory (Krugman and others)	History, luck, and market power of industry leader Government "strategic trade policy"	Imperfect competition Ignore demand side De-emphasize factor supplies
2. Product cycle theory (Vernon)	Technological innovation Technological "age" of industry	Competition Vague about demand and factor supplies

since the 1950s, and Korea and other countries are now challenging Japan's leadership. Chapter 11 considers the biggest triumph of a monopoly in all history, the pair of giant oil price hikes imposed by the Organization of Petroleum Exporting Countries (OPEC). Chapter 12 looks at Third World trade and what developing countries can do about it and Chapter 13 tries to explain the special international policy puzzles relating to agricultural trade.

ADAM SMITH'S THEORY OF ABSOLUTE ADVANTAGE

The way in which trying to make a welfare judgment about international trade quickly leads to a search for the causes of trade was neatly illustrated first by Adam Smith and next by David Ricardo when they struggled to convince their fellow Britons of the virtues of free trade in the late 18th and early 19th centuries. In their effort to make a case for free trade, they came up with simple classic statements about how both sides are likely to gain from international trade. Their classic theories swayed policy makers for a whole century, even though today we view them as only special cases of a more basic, and more powerful, theory of trade.

It was not easy to advocate completely free trade in the late 18th century, even for so persuasive a writer as Adam Smith. Trade was hobbled by an elaborate array of taxes and prohibitions on imports and exports. Equally elaborate was the set of arguments that mercantilist writers had developed as excuses for those taxes and prohibitions. Taxing imports was often defended as a way to create jobs and income for the nation. Imports were supposed to be bad because they had to be paid for, which might make the nation lose specie (gold and silver) if it imported a greater value of goods and services than it sold to foreigners. A dependence on imports was also feared because those same foreign goods might not be available in time of war.

In his *Wealth of Nations* (1776), Adam Smith ridiculed the fear of trade by comparing nations to households. Since every household finds it worthwhile to produce only some of its needs and to buy others with products it can sell, the same should apply to nations:

> It is the maxim of every prudent master of a family, never to attempt to make at home what it will cost him more to make than to buy. The taylor does not attempt to make his own shoes, but buys them from the shoemaker. . . .
>
> What is prudence in the conduct of every private family, can scarce be folly in that of a great kingdom. If a foreign country can supply us with a commodity cheaper than we ourselves can make it, better buy it of them with some part of the product of our own industry, employed in a way in which we have some advantage.

Smith's reasoning can be illuminated with a numerical example. Let us look at the kind of example used by David Ricardo in the early 19th century, that will bring out a key difference between Smith's idea and later ideas about what made trade profitable. To see the effects of trade, begin with a situation in which nations do not trade with each other. Without trade, what would determine the relative prices of the two goods? Smith thought that all economic "value" was determined by, and measured, in hours of labor. The labor cost of producing a unit of a good was the value, or price, of that unit. In this respect he was imitated by Ricardo and by Karl Marx, who also believed that labor was the basis for all value. Let us suppose that the United States has an *absolute advantage* in producing wheat, meaning that we can produce it at an absolutely lower labor cost. And let us suppose that the rest of the world has an absolute advantage in producing cloth. Specifically, we have:

	When Each Country Is Absolutely Better at Making Something = A Case of Absolute Advantage:		
	In the United States		*In the Rest of the World*
Labor cost required to make:			
1 bushel of wheat	2 hours	<	2.5 hours
1 yard of cloth	4 hours	>	1 hour

If there is no trade between nations, the relative prices of the two goods will be dictated by conditions within each country (calling the rest of the world a country). Smith thought that labor costs alone determined how much wheat it took to buy a yard of cloth, or how much cloth it took to buy a bushel of wheat, without considering the strength of demand for each good. People would only trade equal labor values of wheat for cloth. So within the United States, with each bushel of wheat requiring only 2 hours of labor, one would have to give up two bushels of wheat, made with 4 hours of labor to trade for one yard of cloth, which also took 4 hours to make. Correspondingly, in the rest of the world, where it takes two and a half times as much labor to grow a bushel of wheat as it takes to make a yard of cloth, Smith's labor theory of value says that people would have to offer 2.5 yards of cloth to get others to give up a bushel of wheat, which cost the same labor to make. The underlying idea was reasonable: if individual households and businesses had the choice of switching their own labor between growing wheat and making cloth, this choice would tend to dictate the prices at which they were willing to trade wheat for cloth in their nation's marketplace.

So, because of relative labor costs, it would turn out that people's desire to consume mixtures of wheat and cloth would make these prices prevail in the separate national marketplaces:

	In the United States	*In the Rest of the World*
With no international trade		
Price of wheat	0.5 yards/bushels	2.5 yards/bushels
Price of cloth	2.0 bushels/yard	0.4 bushels/yard

Each nation has its separate price ratio between wheat and cloth. There is really only one ratio, because the price of wheat and the price of cloth are just the reciprocals of each other, just the same thing stated two ways. If you are wondering what happened to prices denominated in money, such as dollars per bushel or dollars per yard, economists tend to put such money prices, or nominal prices, aside when looking at the effects of trade on real values. It's as if we were in a world without money, a world of pure barter between real goods like wheat and cloth.[1]

Now let trade be opened up between the United States and the rest of the world, and let us follow the reasoning by which Smith and others felt trade would reshape economies and bring gains to both sides. Somebody will notice the difference between the national prices of the same good and will think of a way to profit from that difference. The first person to notice, perhaps some merchant, will think of sending wheat from the United States in exchange for foreign cloth. Consider the profits that person could make on each bushel of American wheat sent abroad in exchange for cloth. Each bushel could be obtained by giving up 0.5 yards of cloth in the United States. But the same bushel would be sold for 2.5 yards of cloth in that other "nation," the rest of the world. Let us assume that the cost of transporting goods between nations is zero.[2] Therefore, with each 0.5 yards of cloth given up, the merchant can end up with more of the very same good— with 2.5 yards of cloth. Somebody else could profit by starting with a bushel of hard-to-grow wheat in the rest of the world, getting cloth, and selling the cloth in the United States in exchange for still more wheat. This person could start with a bushel of wheat and trade it outside the United States for 2.5 yards of cloth, then ship the cloth to the United States and get 2.5 times 2.0 bushels per yard, or 5.0 bushels of wheat, having started with only one bushel. The principle is simple and universal: as long as prices differ in two places (by more than any cost of transportation between the places), there is a way to profit by trading.

The opening of trade would do more than make new exchanges profitable. It would also affect what people decide to produce with their labor. Alert traders who first figure out that wheat and cloth should be traded internation-

---

[1] We keep money hiding in the wings throughout Parts One and Two and Five of this book, allowing it to take center stage only in the more macroeconomic Parts Three and Four. It appears briefly in the box later in this chapter entitled "What if Trade Doesn't Balance?" and again in Chapter 4, both times in order to think about how exchange rates relate to real prices like the bushels/yard prices used here. Part Two switches to what look like ordinary money prices, such as dollars per bicycle in Chapter 6. Even there, however, the prices do not have much to do with money: the dollars are simply units of all real goods other than the one being pictured (e.g., bicycles).

[2] The assumption of zero transport costs is relatively harmless. Recognizing that transport costs are positive merely reduces the gains from trading, but does not reverse any of our major conclusions.

ally would want to get each nation to follow its absolute advantage in deciding what to make. That is, nations would *specialize* in their production. Sooner or later labor in the United States would be shifted toward making more wheat, which has a higher value abroad, and less cloth, which is cheaper to import from abroad. Meanwhile, in the rest of the world, people would stop making wheat, which is cheaper to import from the United States, and instead they would make more cloth, which is getting a higher price in the United States. As long as the unit labor costs stay at the levels shown above—and Smith's reasoning assumed they would—the United States would keep shifting its labor from cloth to wheat, and the rest of the world would keep shifting its labor from wheat to cloth, until at least one side was completely specialized and could not shift its production any more.

Thus countries would gain by trading and specializing according to their absolute advantages, the United States in wheat and the rest of the world in cloth. But where would the shifting stop? At what price would they finally trade, and which country would get the greater gains? Smith did not say. In thinking about cases like this one, he was content to show that both nations must be at least as well off as before. We cannot exactly say when that will be because the simple labor-cost example hasn't told us how strongly the two nations demand each of the two goods. We know the cost and supply side, but not the demand side; therefore, we can't be sure exactly what price the Americans will end up getting for their wheat and what the rest of the world will get for each yard of its cloth.

We are not completely without information about the new international price ratio, however. It must lie somewhere between the no-trade price ratios in the United States and the rest of the world, that is, somewhere between 0.5 yards per bushel and 2.5 yards per bushel. To see why, suppose that the United States was asked to consider trading at the ratio of only 0.2 yards of cloth for each bushel of wheat. The United States would certainly not export wheat abroad in exchange for the same bushel in the United States. Indeed, at 0.2 yards per bushel the United States might offer to export *cloth*. But the rest of the world would have none of that. They would not want to give up five bushels of wheat (1/0.2) to get a yard of cloth they could make or buy in their own markets for only 0.4 bushels. Similar reasoning applies to the other extreme, with a price of wheat higher than 2.5 yards per bushel. In that price range, both the United States and the rest of the world would want to be the exporters of wheat and the importers of cloth. The only way the two sides could agree to have one of them export wheat and the other export cloth is for the international price to settle somewhere in the range where:

$$0.5 \leq \text{international price of wheat} \leq 2.5 \text{ (yards/bu.)},$$

i.e., where

$$2.0 \geq \text{international price of cloth} \geq 0.4 \text{ (bu./yard)}.$$

WHAT IF TRADE DOESN'T BALANCE?

You may be struck by a contradiction between the spirit of the trade theory and recent headlines about international trade.

The theory implies that trade balances. In diagrams like Figure 2.2, the theory seems to imply a perfect balance between the value of exports and the value of imports. The balance seems guaranteed by the absence of money from the diagram, as noted in footnote 1. As long as countries are just bartering wheat for cloth, they must think U.S. wheat exports must have exactly the same value as U.S. cloth imports. Export value equals import value. Trade must balance.

Yet the news media have been announcing huge U.S. trade deficits every year since 1975. Imports keep exceeding exports. (Conversely, Canada and Japan have been running trade surpluses since that time). What's going on? How can the basic theory of trade be so silent about the most newsworthy aspect of international trade flows? Isn't the theory wrong in its statements about the reasons for trade or the gains from trade? Maybe Ricardo was too optimistic about every country's having enough comparative advantage to balance its overall trade.

These are valid questions, and they deserve a better answer than simply, "Well, the model assumes balanced trade." In later chapters, we will add details about how trade deficits and surpluses relate to exchange rates and

Suppose that the strengths of demand, which we introduce in Chapter 3, are such that the ratio settles at the price of 1 bushel = 1 yard. Then, in the end, both countries end up getting gains (1) from trading and (2) from specialization in their production, just like the gains we started to imagine when thinking about what would happen at first, when the first merchants began the international trade. The United States gains from the chance to trade at 1.0 yards per bushel. Again, the United States can get each bushel of wheat by giving up only 0.5 yards of cloth, yet trades it internationally for 1.0 yards. The rest of the world makes each extra yard of cloth by only giving up the production of 0.4 bushels of wheat, then trades that extra yard for 1.0 bushels of wheat.

Smith's reasoning was fundamentally correct, and it helped to persuade

CONTINUED

money. But the real answer is more fundamental: the model is not really wrong in assuming balanced trade, even for a country with a huge trade deficit or trade surplus!

Take the case of the U.S. trade deficit. It looks as though exports are always less than imports. Well, yes and no. Yes, the ordinary trade balance (more precisely the "current-account" balance of Chapter 14) has stayed negative for over a decade. But a country with a current-account deficit pays for it by either piling up debts or giving up assets to foreigners. Such a country is *exporting* paper IOU's, such as bonds, that are a present claim on future goods. The value of these net exports matches the value of the ordinary current-account deficit.

There is no need to add paper bonds to our wheat-and-cloth examples because the bonds are a claim on future wheat and cloth. Today, the United States may be importing more cloth than it is exporting wheat, but this deficit is matched by the expected value of its net exports of extra wheat someday when it pays off the debt. Trade is expected to balance over the very long run. That expectation could prove wrong in the future: maybe the United States will default on some of its foreign debts, or maybe price inflation (deflation) will make it give up less (more) wheat than expected. But today's transactions are based on the *expectation* that trade will balance.

some governments to dismantle inefficient barriers to international trade over the 100 years after he wrote the *Wealth of Nations*.

Yet his argument failed to put to rest a fear that others had already expressed even before he wrote. What if we have no absolute advantage? What if the foreigners are better at producing everything than we are? Will they want to trade? If they do, should we want to? That fear persisted in the minds of many of Smith's English contemporaries, who feared that the Dutch were more efficient than they at making anything. It persists in this century, too. In the wake of World War II many nations thought they could not possibly compete with the efficient Americans at anything and wondered how they could gain from free trade. Today, some Americans have the same fear in reverse: aren't the Japanese getting more efficient at making everything that enters international trade, and won't the United States be hurt by free trade? The question deserves an answer. We turn next to the theory that first answered it satisfactorily and established a fundamental principle of international trade.

RICARDO'S THEORY OF COMPARATIVE ADVANTAGE

David Ricardo's main contribution to our understanding of international trade was to show that countries gain from trade whether or not they have any absolute advantage. His writings in the early 19th century demonstrated what has become known as:

> the **principle of comparative advantage:** a nation, like a person, gains from trade by exporting the goods or services in which it has its greatest comparative advantage in productivity and importing those in which it has the least comparative advantage.

The key word here is comparative, meaning relative and not necessarily absolute. Even if one nation were the most productive at producing everything and another were the least, they would both gain by trading with each other and with third countries as long as their (dis)advantages in making different goods were different in any way.

Ricardo drove this point home with a simple numerical example of gains from trading two goods between two countries.[3] Here is a similar illustration, again using wheat and cloth in the United States and the rest of the world:

	Even if One Country Is Absolutely Worse at Producing Everything, We Still Have a Case of Comparative Advantage:		
	In the United States		*In the Rest of the World*
Labor costs required to make:			
1 bushel of wheat	2 hours	>	1.5 hours
1 yard of cloth	4 hours	>	1 hour

Here, as in Ricardo's original illustration, a nation has inferior productivity in both goods: the United States requires more labor hours to produce either wheat or cloth. The United States, in other words, has no absolute advantage.

---

[3] His famous illustration showed the gains from trading English cloth for Portuguese wine. He assumed that Portugal was relatively better at making both wine and cloth, but especially better at making wine. After a demonstration like that in the text above, he went on to show that adding money to the analysis had no long-run effect on the gains from trade. See David Ricardo, *On the Principles of Political Economy and Taxation* (1817), pp. 133–49 of the 1951 edition of his collected works.

What goods will the United States trade, and how do we know that trade will bring net national[4] gains to both sides?

As in the absolute-advantage case, we begin by imagining the two economies separately with no trade between them. Ricardo, like Smith, felt that labor costs dictated economic value and prices, as long as there was no international trade. In the United States, people would tend to buy or make each yard of cloth, worth four hours of labor, by giving up two bushels of wheat, which would also take four hours to make. In the rest of the world, exchanging equal labor values would mean giving up a yard of cloth for each 2/3 bushel (= 1/1.5) of wheat. Thus, within the two isolated economies, national prices would tend to follow the relative labor costs of wheat and cloth:

	In the United States	In the Rest of the World
With no international trade		
Price of wheat	0.5 yard/bushel	1.5 yards/bushels
Price of cloth	2.0 bushel/yard	0.67 bushel/yard

Opening up trade brings the same opportunities for profit and the same pressure on prices to equalize internationally, as in the case of absolute advantage. Somebody will notice the international price difference and trade profitably. Perhaps they will acquire wheat in the United States, by giving up only 0.5 yard of cloth, and sell the same wheat abroad for 1.5 yards of cloth, ending up with a yard of cloth in pure gain. Or perhaps they will acquire cloth in the rest of the world, giving up only 0.67 bushel of wheat for each yard, and sell it in the United States in exchange for 1.5 yards, ending up with 0.83 bushel of wheat in pure gain. One way or the other, they will gain.

The opening of profitable international trade will start pushing the two separate national price ratios into a new worldwide equilibrium. The more people start removing wheat from the American market for export, the more expensive wheat will start to become relative to cloth in the United States. Meanwhile, wheat starts to become cheaper in the rest of the world, thanks to the new supply of wheat from the United States. So wheat tends to get more expensive where it was cheap at first, and cheaper where it was more expensive at first (and this is true in reverse for cloth). The tendencies will continue until the two prices become one world price. Again,

[4] Throughout this chapter we treat each nation as a unitary optimizing individual, rather than as a collection of individuals. Beginning in Chapter 3, we focus on the fact that trade brings clear net losses to some people while bringing gains to others in the same country. Even if this happens, however, we will find that entire nations gain, in the sense that the economic value of the gains to some outweigh the value of losses to others in the same country.

we cannot say exactly how many yards per bushel that final international price ratio will be, but we do know that it must settle between the two price ratios that prevailed in each country before trade. Why? Because if the cloth/wheat price ratio were outside that range, both countries would want to be sellers of the same good and buyers of the same (other) good. This is impossible because the two countries add up to the entire world, and trade must balance for the planet Earth. Thus, the international price ratio will settle somewhere in the range where:

$$0.5 \leq \text{international price of wheat} \leq 1.5 \text{ (yards/bushels)},$$

i.e., where

$$2.0 \geq \text{international price of cloth} \geq 0.67 \text{ (bushel/yard)}.$$

Let us again say that the demand forces bring the international price ratio to rest at that same convenient value of 1 bushel = 1 yard. Both countries gain from trade and from specialization. To see how, repeat the same argument that was given for the absolute-advantage case when the international price ratio had settled at 1.0 bushel per yard.

Comparing the absolute-advantage and comparative-advantage cases reveals a startling fact that Ricardo was trying to emphasize: the two cases show the gains from trade in exactly the same way. What matters is that before trade the two countries had different price ratios. It didn't matter why they differed. The absolute labor costs (or their reciprocals, the average labor productivities) were irrelevant to the fact that countries gained from trade. The gains from trade, and the direction of trade, arose from differences in the **opportunity costs** of each final good—that is, the amount of the other good you gave up to get more of this one. What mattered was that without international trade, the opportunity cost of a bushel of wheat in the United States (give up 0.5 yards of cloth) differed from its opportunity cost in the rest of the world (give up 2.5 yards in the first example, or 1.5 yards in the second). Labor costs in a given country could be multiplied by, say, 10, and the direction of trade and the gains from trade would still be the same. In this way, Ricardo advanced thinking by laying to rest the fear that trade would work only if everyone had an absolute advantage in something.

RICARDO'S CONSTANT COSTS AND THE PRODUCTION-POSSIBILITIES CURVE

Ricardo's numerical illustration succeeded in proving the principle of comparative advantage. Yet it also had some limitations. A minor limitation is that it demonstrated the gains from trade using only marginal changes at the lowest level (what if we exported one more bushel, etc.), without an explicit look at the aggregate activity of the nation and the rest of the world. A more serious limitation is that Ricardo's example assumed that marginal costs stay constant, and this assumption violates some known facts. To see the larger second point, let us turn first to the task of showing how Ricardo's comparative advantage case looks in a diagram showing what whole nations can produce and consume.

Figure 2.2 portrays comparative advantage at the level of whole nations. Each nation can produce only so much because its labor force and productivity are limited. To show what a nation can produce requires more than a single number. It requires a whole curve. The United States, for example, could make 50 billion bushels of wheat a year if it did nothing but produce wheat— or it could made 25 billion yards of cloth a year if it made only cloth. The United States also could produce of mix of wheat and cloth, say 20 billion bushels of wheat and 15 billion yards of cloth, at Point S_0. The curve showing all the combinations of wheat and cloth that the United States could produce if it used all its resources at maximum efficiency is a curve often used in economics:

the **production-possibilities curve** (ppc) shows all the combinations of outputs of different goods that an economy could produce with full employment and its maximum productivity.

The solid lines in Figure 2.2 are the ppc's for the United States and the rest of the world. Note that each is a straight line, with a constant slope (steepness). This slope is the cost of extra cloth, the number of bushels of wheat the United States would have to give up to make each extra yard of cloth. In this case, it is always $50/25 = 2$ bushels per yard, the same marginal cost of cloth as in the Ricardian example of the principle of comparative advantage. For the rest of the world the cost of extra cloth is $67/100 = 2/3$. The ppc's in Figure 2.2 are drawn as straight lines to reflect Ricardo's belief that the marginal or opportunity cost of each good was constant in any economy.

To set the stage for the more modern portrayals of the basis for trade, let us use Figure 2.2 to restate the gains from trade and specialization. If neither country traded, each could only consume and enjoy combinations of wheat and cloth that are on (or below) its ppc, combinations like those shown as S_0 in Figure 2.2. When trade is opened, each nation can trade at a price between 2/3 and 2 bushels per yard. Again, let us suppose that demand conditions would make the free-trade price equal 1 bushel per yard. To show how each nation gains from trade at this price, using Figure 2.2, we need to consider how trade should be drawn on the diagram. When a nation sells its exports to get imports, it ends up consuming a different set of goods. How different? In a diagram such as Figure 2.2, the line connecting where a nation produces and where it consumes is a line along which wheat trades for cloth at the world price ratio, 1 bushel per yard. Two trade lines are shown in Figure 2.2.

To see the gains from trade and to understand the trade lines, let us

FIGURE 2.2 The Gains from Trade, Shown for Ricardo's Constant-Cost Case

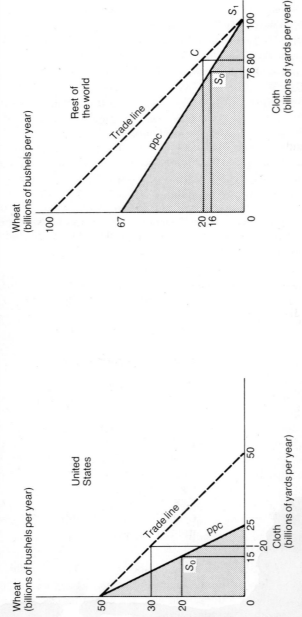

Here the solid lines are the production-possibility curves (ppc's), showing what each nation can produce. Once each specializes in producing only one good, at S_1, it can reach the highest possible levels of consumption (consuming at C) by trading along the dashed trade line.

Result: both sides gain from trade. For any no-trade point like S_0 on the ppc, specializing and trading make it possible to consume more of both goods at C.

again imagine that each nation discovers the benefits of specializing its production while trading, using the previous reasoning about the principle of comparative advantage. If the United States again specializes in making only wheat, at S_1, it can sell wheat for cloth at the world price ratio, moving along the trade line. Giving up wheat and gaining cloth means moving southeast along the trade line. The United States could consume anywhere along this line. Clearly, this is a better set of consumption options than if the United States did not trade. For each point like S_0, where the nation consumes what it produces, there are better consumption points like *C,* where it can end up consuming more of everything by specializing and trading. The United States gains from trade. It is equally clear that the rest of the world also gains from specializing in cloth production (at S_1) and trading some of that cloth for wheat, moving northwest along its trade line to consume at some point like *C.* Thus, Figure 2.2 is a different way to view the workings of comparative advantage with Ricardian constant costs.

Later writers challenged Ricardo's simple assumption of constant marginal costs. First, they noted empirically that many industries seemed to be characterized by rising, rather than constant, marginal costs, so that more and more of other goods had to be given up to produce each succeeding extra unit of one good. Second, they thought of some good theoretical reasons for expecting that marginal costs would rise when one industry expanded at the expense of others. One obvious possibility is that each individual industry, contrary to the assumption of Ricardo's trade example, may itself have diminishing returns, or rising costs. Even if every industry has constant returns to scale, the shift from one industry to another may involve increasing marginal costs because of subtle effects stemming from the fact that different goods use inputs in different proportions, a point that will be discussed below.

Perhaps the most damaging objection to the assumption of constant marginal costs is that it implied something that failed to fit the facts of international trade and production patterns. The constancy of marginal costs in Figure 2.2 led us to conclude that each country would maximize its gain by specializing its production completely in its comparative-advantage good.[5]

The real world fails to show total specialization. In Ricardo's day, it may have been reasonable for him to assume that England grew no wine grapes and relied on foreign grapes and wines, but even with cloth imports from England, the other country in his example, Portugal, made most of its own cloth. Specialization is no more common today. The United States and Canada continue to produce some of their domestic consumption of goods they partially import—textiles, cars, and TV sets, for example.

---

[5] With constant costs one of the two trading countries can fail to specialize completely only in the special case in which the international terms of trade settle at the same price ratio prevailing in that country with no trade.

INCREASING MARGINAL COSTS

Facts like these led economists to replace the constant-cost assumption with the assumption about marginal costs that is likely to hold in most cases. They have tended to assume *increasing marginal costs:* as one industry expands at the expense of others, increasing amounts of the other goods

---

FIGURE 2.3   Production Possibilities under Increasing Costs

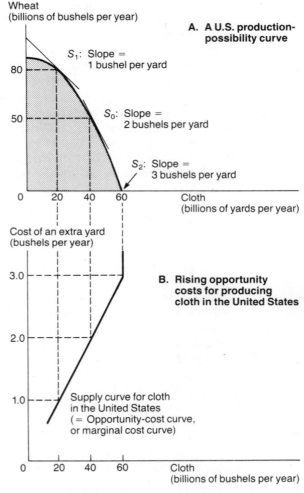

Increasing opportunity costs can be shown in either of two equivalent ways: as changing slopes along a convex production-possibilities curve or as a rising supply (or marginal cost) curve.

must be given up to get each extra unit of the expanding output. Figure 2.3 shows a case of increasing marginal costs. This can be seen by following what happens to the marginal cost of producing an extra yard of cloth as we shift more and more resources from wheat production to cloth production. When the economy is producing only 20 billion yards of cloth, the slope of the production-possibility curve at Point S_1 tells us that an extra yard could be made each year by giving up a bushel of wheat. When 40 billion yards are being made each year, getting the resources to make another yard a year means giving up two bushels of wheat, as shown at Point S_0. To push cloth production up to 60 billion yards per year requires giving up wheat in amounts that rise to three bushels for the last yard of cloth. These increasing costs of extra cloth also can be interpreted as increasing costs of producing extra wheat: when one starts from a cloth-only economy at Point S_2 and shifts increasing amounts of resources into growing wheat, the costs of an extra bushel mount (from one-third yard at S_2 to one-half yard at S_0, one yard at S_1, and so forth).

The increasing marginal costs reappear in a familiar form in the lower half of Figure 2.3. Here the vertical axis plots the marginal costs of extra cloth, which were the slopes in the upper half of the figure. The resulting curve is properly called a supply curve for cloth since the marginal costs of producing extra cloth are just the marginal costs that a set of competitive U.S. cloth suppliers would bid into equality with the price they receive when selling the cloth. Although this reexpression adds no new information by itself, it helps set the stage for converting the entire basic model of trade into familiar supply and demand curves, a task to which we return in the next chapter.

Trade with Increasing Costs

Under conditions of increasing costs, trade has the same basic effects as when constant costs were assumed. Both sides still stand to gain from trade in the aggregate, and both tend to respond to trade opportunities by specializing more on producing their comparative-advantage products. The two changes caused by assuming increasing rather than constant costs are both changes in the direction of realism: countries tend to specialize incompletely, and marginal costs are bid into equality between countries.

The effects of opening trade with increasing costs are shown for one country in Figure 2.4. (A similar diagram and results could be shown for the rest of the world.) Without trade, the United States must consume its own production. Let us say that U.S. production possibilities and taste patterns (tastes are not shown on the diagram) are such that the economy settles at Point S_0, where the price (and marginal cost) of cloth is two bushels per yard and the economy is producing 50 billion bushels and 40

FIGURE 2.4   The Effects of International Trade under Increasing Costs

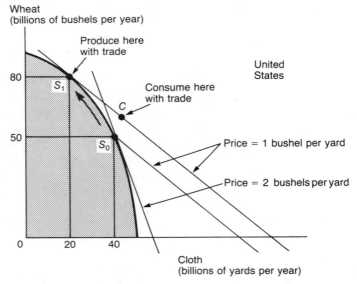

With increasing costs as with Ricardo's constant costs, a country gains from trade as long as the outside world's price ratio (terms of trade) differs from the country's price ratio before trade. Trade again lets the country consume more by specializing its production somewhat (at S_1) and exporting some of its specialty product to enjoy a better consumption mix (at C).

billion yards a year. Opening trade gives the United States the opportunity to exchange wheat for cloth at a new price. As with our earlier examples, let's say that the pretrade price of cloth is lower abroad than in the United States, so that the United States ends up exporting wheat in order to import the cheaper cloth. Once again, we cannot say exactly what the new international-trade price of cloth will be or how much the United States will trade at that price until we have added the demand side of the trade model in the next chapter, but the direction of effects from trade is already clear.

Even if the United States continues to produce S_0, it stands to gain from trading. The nation still has the option of refusing to trade and being no worse off than before at S_0. Yet it can also exchange wheat for cloth at some new international price ratio, such as the one bushel per yard price shown in Figure 2.4. At this price the United States would certainly not want to export cloth and import wheat since it could get two bushels of wheat for each yard of cloth forgone just by shifting resources from cloth to wheat in U.S. production. By exporting wheat at the international price, however, the United States could reach consumption points that were unattainable without trade. These are the points on the international price line extending southeast from S_0. At least one of these previously unattainable points will be better than S_0.

Yet the United States stands to gain even more from trade by changing its output mixture. U.S. producers will soon realize that if foreigners are willing to pay one yard of cloth for each bushel of exported wheat, it is a bargain to shift more resources out of cloth production and into wheat, losing only half a yard of cloth for each extra bushel grown. They will shift more resources into wheat, causing a movement from S_0 to S_1. In this increasing-cost case, unlike the less realistic constant-cost case, they will not specialize completely, however. Under increasing-cost conditions, the more resources they shift into wheat, the higher the cost of producing extra wheat. Specialization will be profitable only up to the point where the marginal cost of extra wheat has risen to meet the price received for wheat on world markets. This will be at Point S_1, where both the marginal cost and the world price of wheat are one yard per bushel. The result, then, is that under increasing costs, nations are still likely to gain from trade, especially if they specialize more in their comparative-advantage export lines, but find it best to specialize only incompletely.

What's behind the Production-Possibility Curves?

It is clear that the shapes of production-possibility curves are key to explaining how supply conditions can create a basis for trade. This observation leads immediately to three other questions:

1. What information do we need to derive the production-possibility curve of each country?
2. Why are increasing-cost curves so likely to occur?
3. What makes for differences in comparative costs? That is, why do the production-possibility curves have different shapes in different countries?

A country's production-possibility curve, or transformation curve, is derived from information on both total factor supplies and the production functions that relate factor inputs to output in various industries. In Appendix A we show how the production-possibility curves are derived under several common assumptions about production functions in individual industries.

The answer to the second question emerges from the formal derivation of the transformation curves, yet we can sketch the explanation for the prevalence of increasing costs even without a rigorous demonstration. The key point is that different products use inputs in very different proportions. To stay with our wheat-cloth example for a moment, wheat uses relatively more land and less labor than cloth, whether the yarn for the cloth comes from synthetic fibers or from natural fibers such as cotton or silk. This basic variation in input proportions can set up an increasing-costs transformation curve even if constant returns to scale exist in each industry. When resources are released from cloth production and are shifted into wheat production, they will be released in proportions different from those initially prevailing in wheat production. The cloth industry will release a lot of labor and not much land relative to the labor and land use pattern in wheat. To employ these factors, the wheat industry must shift toward using much more labor-intensive techniques. The effect is close to that of the law of diminishing returns (which, strictly speaking, refers to the case of adding more of one factor to fixed amounts of the others): adding so much labor to slowly changing amounts of land causes the gains in wheat production to decline as more and more resources, mainly labor, are released from cloth production. Thus, fewer and fewer extra bushels of wheat production are gained by each extra yard of lost cloth production.

The third question takes us to the core of the supply side. Of all the possible reasons why comparative costs might differ between countries, perhaps the most important is a subtle point about relative factor supplies and demands, a point that has become the basis for the orthodox modern theory of comparative advantage.

THE HECKSCHER-OHLIN (H-O) THEORY: FACTOR PROPORTIONS ARE KEY

The leading theory of what determines nations' trade patterns emerged in Sweden. Eli Heckscher, the noted Swedish economic historian, developed the core idea in a brief article in 1919. A clear overall explanation was developed and publicized in the 1930s by Heckscher's student, Bertil Ohlin. Ohlin, like Keynes, managed to combine a distinguished academic career— professor at Stockholm and later a Nobel Laureate—with political office (Riksdag member, party leader, and government official during World War II). Ohlin's persuasive narrative of the theory and the evidence that seemed to support it were later reinforced by another Nobel Laureate, Paul Samuelson, who derived mathematical conditions under which the Heckscher-Ohlin (H-O) prediction was strictly correct.[6]

---

[6] Ohlin backed the H-O theory with real-world observation and appeals to intuition. Samuelson took the mathematical road, adding narrow assumptions that allowed a strict proof of the theory's main prediction. Samuelson assumed (1) that there are two countries, two goods, and two factors (the frequent ''2 x 2 x 2'' simplification, which will be used again in Appendix C); (2) that factor supplies are fixed for each country and mobile between sectors within each country, but immobile between countries; (3) that the two countries are identical except for their factor endowments; and (4) that both countries share the same constant-returns-to-scale technology. The H-O predictions follow logically in Samuelson's narrow case and seem broadly accurate in the real world.

The Heckscher-Ohlin theory of trade patterns says, in Ohlin's own words, that:

> Commodities requiring for their production much of [abundant factors of production] and little of [scarce factors] are exported in exchange for goods that call for factors in the opposite proportions. Thus indirectly, factors in abundant supply are exported and factors in scanty supply are imported. (Ohlin, 1933, p. 92)

Or, more succinctly,

> **The H-O theory predicts that countries export the products that use their abundant factors intensively** (and import the products using their scarce factors intensively).

To judge this plausible and testable argument more easily, we need definitions of factor abundance and factor-use intensity:

> A country is **labor-abundant** if it has a higher ratio of labor to other factors than does the rest of the world.

> A product is **labor-intensive** if labor costs are a greater share of its value than they are of the value of other products.

The Heckscher-Ohlin explanation of trade patterns begins with a specific hunch as to why prices might differ between countries before they open trade. In the example we have been using above, why was cloth so expensive in the United States (2 bushels per yard of cloth) and so cheap in the rest of the world (2/3 bushel per yard of cloth) before trade?

In principle, any of several things *might* cause such a price gap. Demand patterns might differ: maybe Americans demand more clothing, due to a harsher climate or religious convictions or more expensive fashions in clothing. Technologies might differ: perhaps the Americans have learned how to grow wheat better, the foreigners have learned how to make cloth better, and each side somehow keeps its secret from the other.

But Heckscher and Ohlin doubted that demand or technology explains much of the international differences we observe in the real world. Rather, they predicted, the key to comparative costs lies in factor proportions. If cloth costs two bushels a yard in America and less than a bushel a yard elsewhere, it must be primarily because America has relatively more of the factors that wheat uses intensively, and relatively less of the factors that cloth uses intensively, than does the rest of the world. Let us say that *land* is the factor that wheat uses more intensively and *labor* is the factor that cloth uses more intensively. Let all costs be decomposable into land and labor costs (e.g., it takes certain amounts of land and labor to make fertilizer for growing wheat and certain other amounts of land and labor to make cotton inputs for cloth making). Therefore, the H-O theory would predict that if the United States exports wheat and imports cloth, it is because wheat is land-intensive and cloth is labor-intensive *and:*

$$\frac{(America's \ land \ supply)}{(America's \ labor \ supply)} > \frac{(Rest \ of \ world's \ land \ supply)}{(Rest \ of \ world's \ labor \ supply)}$$

Under these conditions[7] (with other things equal), land should rent more cheaply in the United States than elsewhere, and labor should command a higher wage rate in the United States than elsewhere. The cheapness of land cuts costs more in wheat farming than in cloth making. Conversely, the scarcity of labor should make cloth relatively expensive in America. This, according to H-O, is why the prices differed in the direction they did before trade began. And, the theory predicts, it is the difference in relative factor endowments and the pattern of factor intensities that make America export wheat instead of cloth (and import cloth instead of wheat) when trade opens up.

DOES H-O EXPLAIN ACTUAL TRADE PATTERNS?

To know if the Heckscher-Ohlin hunch is correct and useful, we must go beyond abstract models of barter involving only two countries and two goods and two factors of production. Merely traveling further down the road of theory—introducing more countries, goods, and factors into the same abstract model—will not tell us whether the theory is correct or useful. The job of theory is to help us interpret real-world data.

Economists have tested the H-O theory in several ways. The upshot of their tests can be seen through a simple direct look at some recent trade patterns.

Broad Patterns in 1980

Let us compare relative factor endowments with actual trade patterns. Figure 2.5 shows six leading countries' shares of the (non-Soviet-bloc) world supplies of certain factors of production in 1980. To recognize the patterns here, many of them familiar, contrast the endowments of each individual factor with the endowments of all factors together (all GNP).

Nonhuman *capital,* in the first pie, is slightly skewed toward the richer

---

[7] Take care not to misread the relative factor endowment inequality. It does not say America has more land than the rest of the world. Nor does it say that America has less labor. In fact, America really has less of both. Nor does it say America has more land than it has labor—a meaningless statement in any case (how many acres are ''more than'' how many hours of labor?).

Rather it is an inequality between *relative* endowments. Here are two correct ways of stating it: (1) there is more good land per laborer in America than in the rest of the world and (2) America's share of the world's land is greater than its share of the world's labor (as is shown directly in Figure 2.5).

countries. Capital is slightly more abundant, relative to other factors, in five of the six leading countries shown here (e.g., the United States has 33.6 percent of the world's estimated capital, a bit over its 28.6 percent share of all factors contributing to national income). The rest of the world, accordingly, is slightly capital-poor (27.3 percent of world capital versus 39.3 percent of all factors).

Much more concentrated is the distribution of *scientists* engaged in research and development (R&D), a key input into high-technology goods. If we had data on the numbers of R&D scientists in all countries, the six nations shown here would have over 85 percent of all scientists in the non-Soviet-bloc world. In particular, scientists are relatively abundant (relative to other productive inputs) in the United States, Japan, West Germany, and Britain.

Moving down the ranks of *labor* inputs, we see a familiar pattern emerging. The concentration of R&D scientists in a few leading countries is completely reversed when it comes to unskilled labor, represented here by its lowest-skill stratum, illiterate workers. Unskilled workers supplying only manual labor and basic ground-level skills are concentrated, of course, in the populous poor countries of the world. As for the groups in between, the nonscientific skilled and the semiskilled workers, the international contrasts are not nearly so sharp. Every country has them in shares that do not depart too much from the same countries' shares of all productive factors.

Finally, Figure 2.5 confirms what we know about the distribution of the world's *arable land*. This land is relatively concentrated in North America and certain countries grouped into the rest of the world (Latin America, China, India, the Soviet Union). Europe and Japan are notoriously poorly endowed with arable land. If there were convenient world data on *other natural resources*—minerals, forests and fishing rights—these data would show slightly different patterns. Canada would again be relatively abundantly endowed, though the United States would not. Other leading resource-abundant countries are the oil producers and the metal-ore producers (Australia, Bolivia, Chile, Jamaica, Zaire, Zambia).

If Heckscher and Ohlin have given us the right prediction, the unequal distribution of factors should be mirrored in the patterns of trade, with each country exporting those goods and services that use its abundant factors relatively intensively.

The trade patterns of six leading countries broadly confirm the H-O prediction that nations tend to export the products using their abundant factors intensively. Japan is crucially dependent on imports of natural-resource-intensive primary products (agriculture, fishing, forestry, and minerals) since it cannot begin to produce enough of these products internally to satisfy the high demand that goes with its high standard of living. Without trade, Japan would be a far poorer nation. To pay for such imports, Japan has a particular export advantage in technology-intensive products, as H-O would predict on the basis of the country's abundant supply of scientific personnel. Contrary to a once-common belief that is now obsolete, Japan does not

FIGURE 2.5   Shares of the "World's"[a] Factor Endowments, 1980

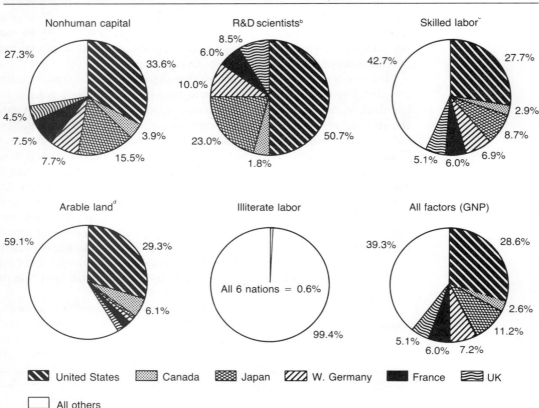

Nonhuman capital
27.3%
33.6%
4.5%
3.9%
7.5%
15.5%
7.7%

R&D scientists[b]
8.5%
6.0%
10.0%
50.7%
23.0%
1.8%

Skilled labor[c]
42.7%
27.7%
2.9%
8.7%
5.1%   6.0%   6.9%

Arable land[d]
59.1%
29.3%
6.1%

Illiterate labor
All 6 nations = 0.6%
99.4%

All factors (GNP)
39.3%
28.6%
2.6%
11.2%
5.1%
6.0%   7.2%

** United States   **▓ Canada   **▓** Japan   **///** W. Germany   **■** France   **≋** UK

☐ All others

Note: All estimates are rough approximations.

[a] Here the "world" GNP excludes the Soviet Union, Eastern Europe, and Kampuchea for want of comparable data. For the individual factors, it also excludes other small countries that account for less than 15 percent of market-economy gross product.

[b] From data provided by the U.S. National Science Foundation. It is an exaggeration to show, as here, that these six countries had 100 percent of the R&D scientists. Had data been available for other countries, however, the six countries would still have accounted for at least 85 percent of the "world" total.

[c] Workers in professional and technical categories (ILO data).

[d] Based on land area measurements adjusted for different productivity in different climatic zones, for 1975.

Source: For individual factors, Mutti and Morici (1983, p. 8) drawing in turn on Bowen (1980). For GNP, World Bank, World Development Report 1984 (Washington, D.C., 1984), Appendix Table I.

have a comparative advantage in labor-intensive manufactures. Now that its living standards and wage rates are near those of North America, Japan has lost its earlier comparative advantage in labor-intensive lines.

The United States has a comparative advantage based on certain skills and certain natural resources. The net exports in technology-intensive manufactures reflect America's relative abundance of scientific and related personnel. Part of the comparative advantage in exporting services also reflects these skills, plus prior accumulations of capital. America is a net exporter of marketing services, patent licensing, and managerial services. These particular services are somewhat technology-intensive and somewhat capital-intensive. Finally, America retains a comparative advantage in temperate-zone agricultural products favored by its abundant farmland, but these exports are swamped by heavy net imports of other primary products (especially oil, other minerals, and tropical crops.)

The comparative-advantage patterns for other countries are more muted. The West European countries have comparative advantages like those of Japan but with more balance in the export/import ratios. Canada tends to export primary products in exchange for services and labor-intensive manufactures. Even its exports of manufactures tend to be natural-resource-intensive manufactures, such as petrochemicals, metals, wood products, and paper. Given Canada's abundant natural resources per capita, Ohlin was not surprised by Canadian trade patterns, and neither are we.

In general, recent trade patterns fit the H-O pattern, but only roughly.[8]

Changes in Manufacturing Competition since the 1960s

Both the power and the limits of the H-O theory are suggested by trends in international manufacturing competition since the 1960s, as shown in Figure 2.6.

The H-O theory is able to suggest a link between two trends in the relative position of the United States. The United States has been slower to raise its capital stock and skills per member of the labor force than have competitors such as Japan and the newly industrializing countries (or NICs). Correspondingly, the United States' trade position has slipped in technology-intensive and capital-intensive manufactures. H-O theory would predict that these two trends should go together.

On the other hand, trends since the 1960s also show the limits of the H-O theory. First, some of the data in Figure 2.6 fail to show trends in comparative advantage correlating with trends in factor abundance, as

[8] A systematic study by Leamer (1984) found that the H-O theory correctly predicted correlations between countries' net factor flows through trade and their relative factor endowments, though with modest significance. A tougher test by Bowen, Leamer, and Sveikauskas (1987) measured the ability of factor endowments and U.S. input-output patterns to predict the net factor flows through trade in 1967. Out of 324 cases, defined by 12 factors and 27 countries, H-O correctly predicted the sign of net exports in 61 percent of the cases. This share was better than a coin-flip, but only modestly so.

FIGURE 2.6   Differences in Factor Growth and Changes in Manufacturing Trade
Patterns, 1963–1985

A. Differences in relative factor growth, 1963–1984 (growth in each factor *per
member of the entire national labor force,* in percent per annum)

	Nonhuman Capital (1963–1980)	R&D Scientists and Engineers (1965–1984)	All Skilled Labor (1963–1984)
Japan	8.3	5.0	2.6
United States	1.4	0.1	0.9
Canada	2.0	2.4	1.1
West Germany	3.0	4.1	2.4
France	4.9	3.6	1.9
United Kingdom	3.3	3.0	3.4
Six NICs*	6.2	n.a.	2.6

B. Changes in manufacturing competitiveness: Export/Import ratios, 1969–1985

	Technology-Intensive Manufacturing 1969	1985	Capital-Intensive Standardized Manufactures 1969	1985	Labor-Intensive Manufactures 1969	1985
Japan	3.41	6.67	1.50	1.04	14.92	1.32
United States	1.78	0.75	0.53	0.31	0.33	0.13
Canada	0.78	0.81	1.29	1.41	0.22	0.20
West Germany	3.04	2.19	0.71	0.89	0.73	0.69
France	1.13	1.22	0.83	1.02	1.31	0.79
United Kingdom	3.16	1.04	0.60	0.66	1.22	0.55

* NICs = newly industrializing countries. The term usually applies to Brazil, Mexico, and
the East Asian five tigers: South Korea, Taiwan, Hong Kong, Singapore, and Thailand. In
this figure, however, the NICs are Argentina, Brazil, Hong Kong, India, South Korea, and
Mexico.

Technology-intensive manufactures = transport equipment (autos, planes, ships, motorbikes,
etc.), machinery, chemicals, and professional goods.

Labor-intensive manufactures = Textiles, apparel, footwear, and leather goods.

Source: Morici (1988a, p. 49; 1988b, p. 32).

Since the 1960s, some changes in comparative advantage in manufacturing lines have
followed changes in relative factor endowments, as predicted by the H-O theory. In technology-
intensive lines, the rise of Japan relative to the United States parallels the growth gap in
scientific personnel. But one other change has contradicted an H-O prediction. Changes in
X/M for capital-intensive manufactures do not correlate with rates of accumulation of capital
per worker.

In general, North America's relative abundance of science, skills, and capital has eroded,
bringing the industrialized countries, and soon also the NICs, closer together in their overall
factor proportions.

H-O would predict. Why, for example, should Britain and West Germany lose gound in technological manufacturing trade when they have had such a rapid growth of scientific personnel? Why should France, with mediocre scientific expansion, have gained greater technology-intensive comparative advantage?

Second, the factor growth trends in the top half of Figure 2.6 portend a new kind of trade pattern, a pattern suggesting less future relevance for the contrasts in factor supplies featured in the H-O theory. There are signs of international convergence among industrialized and industrializing countries. Those that led in science, skills, and capital abundance in the 1960s are being caught by others. The part of the slow-growing early leaders in these factor endowments is being played by Canada and especially the United States. West Europe is a bit less slow in these respects. Both groups are being overtaken in their endowments of science, skills, and capital per worker by Japan and the NICs. To the extent that such a pattern continues, the industrialized countries will become more and more similar in their broad factor endowment patterns, while the contrast between all industrialized countries and the lesser developed countries of the Third World will remain as strong as ever. If so, the H-O theory would predict: (1) less and less reason for trade among the industrialized countries and (2) a continued expansion of "North-South" trade between the industrialized countries (North) and the underdeveloped world (South).

So far, these H-O predictions have not yet been borne out by the facts. On the contrary, a high and rising share of international trade takes place between countries with high and similar incomes. A further difficulty regarding H-O theory is that a high and rising share of international trade consists of two-way trade in similar manufactured products. These facts about today's international trade lead to an alternative theory, discussed in Chapter 5.

SUMMARY

The **basic theory of trade** (Chapters 2–4) explains trade patterns in terms of competitive supply and demand. This chapter focused on the supply side. Three variants of the basic theory emphasizing the supply side are Adam Smith's **theory of absolute advantage,** David Ricardo's **principle of comparative advantage,** and the **Heckscher-Ohlin (H-O) theory** stressing factor proportions.

The principle of **comparative advantage** says that it will pay the country to produce more of those goods in which it is relatively more efficient and to export them in returns for goods in which its relative advantage is least. Trade is not a zero-sum game, in which one side gains only what the other loses. The whole world gains from trade, and both sides are at least as well off with some trade as with no trade. A country can gain from trade even if it is worse at everything, or better at everything, than the rest of the world.

The principle of comparative advantage, as first successfully argued by Ricardo in the early 19th century, assumed constant marginal costs. Dropping his constant-cost assumption to allow for increasing marginal costs makes it easier to explain why countries do not specialize completely. It does not overturn the principle of comparative advantage, however.

International differences in the shape of the **production-possibility curves** (ppc's) stem largely from the facts that (1) different goods use the factors of production in different ratios and (2) nations differ in their relative factor endowments. Building on these two facts, the **Heckscher-Ohlin (H-O)** explanation of trade patterns predicts the nations will tend to export the goods that use their relatively abundant factors more intensively in exchange for the goods that use their scarce factors more intensively.

The Heckscher-Ohlin theory explains some trade patterns quite well. Countries tend to export goods that intensively use their relatively abundant factors. The postwar erosion of the American comparative advantage in technology-intensive products also parallels a trend toward faster accumulation of scientific inputs and capital in Japan and other countries.

Other facts do not square so easily with H-O. Some recent changes in competitive position, especially in Europe, do not fit the available data on what is happening to factor endowments. Recent trends hint that the industrial countries are becoming more similar in their endowments, suggesting that the H-O theory, which emphasizes international contrasts in endowments, may slowly become less relevant. Meanwhile, international trade has been slowly drifting toward trade among similar countries and toward trade in similar goods rather than trade between very different industrial sectors. The recent trends have prompted a search for new theories (see Chapter 5).

SUGGESTED READING

See suggested reading for Chapter 3 and Appendixes A and B.

QUESTIONS FOR REVIEW

1. Which of the following pretrade cost ratios was crucial to the existence of a basis for gainful trade: *(a)* the ratio of the input (e.g., labor) cost of U.S. wheat to the input cost of foreign wheat, *(b)* the ratio of the input cost of U.S. wheat to the input cost of U.S. cloth, or *(c)* the ratio of the cost of U.S. wheat in yards of cloth to the cost of other countries' wheat in yards of cloth?

2. You are given the following information about production relationships in Burma and the rest of the world:

	Inputs per Bushel of Rice Output	*Inputs per Yard of Cloth Output*
Burma	75	100
Rest of the world	50	50

You may make several Ricardian assumptions: these are the only two commodities, there are constant ratios of input to output whatever the level of output of rice and cloth, and competition prevails in all markets. *(a)* Does Burma have an absolute advantage in producing rice? Cloth? *(b)* Does Burma have a comparative advantage in producing rice? Cloth? *(c)* If no international trade were allowed, what price ratio would prevail between rice and cloth within Burma? *(d)* If free international trade is opened up, what are the limits of the international ''terms of trade'' (the international price ratio between rice and cloth)?

3. The United States has an endowment (total supply) of 20 units of labor and 3 units of land, whereas the rest of the world has 80 units of labor and 7 units of land. Is the United States labor abundant? Is the United States land abundant?

4. To test your understanding of how the supply curve for one group is derived from the production-possibilities curve, sketch the U.S. supply curve for wheat that derives from Figure 2.4.

5. Extending what you know about production-possibility curves, try to draw the production-possibility curve (ppc) for a nation consisting of four individuals who work separately. The four individuals have these different abilities:

Person A can make 1 unit of cloth, or 2 units of wheat, or any combination in between (e.g. can make 0.5 cloth and 1 wheat by spending half time on each).

Person B can make 2 cloth, or 1 wheat, or any combination in between.

Person C can make 1 cloth, or 1 wheat, or any combination in between.

Person D can make 2 cloth, or 3 wheat, or any combination in between.

What is the best they can all produce? That is, draw the ppc for the four of them. Try it in these stages:

a. What is the most wheat they could grow if they spent all of their time growing wheat only? Plot that point on a cloth-wheat graph.

b. What is the most cloth they could make? Plot that point.

c. Now the tricky part: find the best combinations they could produce when producing some of both, where *best* means they could make that combination but could not make more of one good without giving up some of the other.

(Answer: *a.* They could make 7 wheat, with no cloth production. *b.* They could make 6 cloth, with no wheat production. *c.* The ppc is *not* a straight line between (6 cloth, 0 wheat) and (0 cloth, 7 wheat). Rather it has four parts with different slopes. Here is a tour of the ppc, starting down on the cloth axis (x axis). They could produce anything from (6 cloth, 0 wheat) up to (5, 2) by having A shift between cloth and wheat while the others make only cloth. Then they could make anything from (5, 2) up to (3, 5) by keeping A busy growing wheat and B and C busy at cloth, while D switches between the two tasks. Then they could make anything from (3, 5) up to (2, 6) by choosing how to divide C's time, keeping B in wheat making and A and D in cloth. Finally, they could make anything between (2, 6) and 0, 7) by varying B's tasks while the others make cloth.

Study this result to see how the right assignments relate to people's comparative advantages. Note that with four different kinds of comparative advantage, there was a convex curve with four slopes. In general, the greater the number of different kinds of individuals, the smoother and more convex the curve. Therefore, we get an increasing-cost ppc for the nation, even if every individual is a Ricardian constant-cost type.)

▼

The Basic Theory of International Trade: Demand

•

Knowing supply without knowing demand accomplishes little, like one blade of a scissors or one hand clapping. Chapter 2 focused on supply alone. Each of its examples of the effects of opening trade had to say something vague and unsatisfactory, such as "*Suppose* that demand conditions were such that the new price is one bushel per yard and that at this price exports and imports are," and so on. There is a temptation to be more concrete in linking trade flows to the supply side alone. Some economic literature comes close to saying that the law of comparative advantage determines what commodities will be exported or imported by each country, whereas demand conditions set the prices at which they will be traded. Yet this is not correct. In the marketplace, demand and supply *together* determine *both* the quanitities of goods bought and sold *and* their relative prices. Demand and supply interact just as simultaneously in international trade as in local domestic markets.

The importance of having a complete explicit model of both prices and quantities in international trade can be quickly appreciated by remembering the importance of the international price in the examples of Chapter 2. In order to describe the gains and effects of trade, we had to know where the international price settled. In the Ricardian constant-cost example of comparative advantage, the price had to be somewhere in between the U.S. pretrade price ratio of two bushels of wheat per yard of cloth and the foreign pretrade price ratio of two-thirds bushel per yard. But where in between? It does matter. If the world price ended up equaling the pretrade U.S. price, trade would be a matter of indifference to the United States and any gains from trade would accrue to the rest of the world, whose prices changed with trade. Conversely, if the price in the rest of the world remains unaffected by trade, only the United States will gain from being able to trade at prices different from those dictated by pretrade conditions. The important matter of how the gains from trade are divided clearly hangs on what the new price will be, and we cannot answer this question by referring to supply alone.

TRADE WITH DEMAND AND SUPPLY

The demand side of any marketplace is dictated by the tastes and incomes of the users of final products (plus the cost conditions facing the suppliers of a final product, if we are discussing the demand for an intermediate product). These tastes and incomes constrain how the quantity demanded will react to changes in price.

Once we know the demand curves relating the quantity demanded to price, we can combine them with the supply curves derived from cost conditions (in Chapter 2) to show the production, consumption, and price effects of international trade. The demand-and-supply-curve framework is the main geometric tool that will be used in analyzing trade policy options. Let's begin by examining what answers the demand-supply framework yields once the shapes of the curves are known and then look at how the relevant demand curves could be derived from underlying information about tastes and incomes.

Figure 3.1 summarizes the impact of trade on production, consumption, and prices in the United States and the rest of the world. The national supply curves, or marginal cost curves, are derived from the production-possibility curves (as in Figure 2.3 in Chapter 2), which in turn come from production technology and factor-supply conditions (as shown in Appendix A). The demand curves can be derived as shown in the next section.

If no trade is allowed, the United States and the rest-of-world markets for cloth clear at different prices. Cloth costs two bushels of wheat per yard in the United States at Point *A* as it did in the examples of the last chapter. In the absence of any trade with the United States, the rest of the world finds its demand and supply matching at the lower price of two-thirds bushel per yard at Point *H*.

Opening up trade frees people in both the United States and the rest of the world from the necessity of matching national demand with national supply. This presents a new opportunity for U.S. cloth buyers and foreign cloth sellers. Buyers in the United States will soon find that they can get cheaper cloth from abroad, where cloth had been selling at only two-thirds bushel per yard. And the foreign sellers will find that they need not settle for this low price of two-thirds bushel when they can sell to the United States for more. The two groups will increasingly get together and start transacting to exchange U.S. wheat for foreign cloth at prices somewhere in between two-thirds of a bushel and two bushels per yard.

The final price that results in world trade can be determined now that our analysis contains the demand curves as well as the supply curves. There

FIGURE 3.1 The Effects of Trade on Production, Consumption, and Price, Shown with Demand and Supply Curves

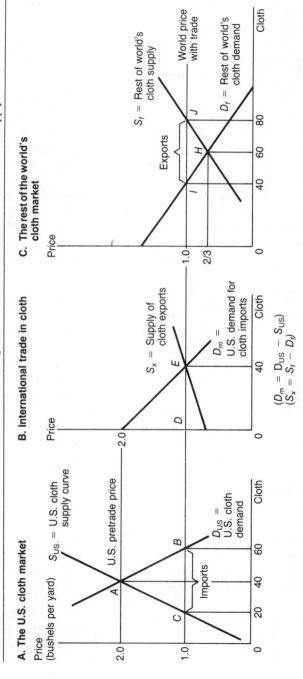

In the market for cloth, the desire to trade is the (horizontal) difference between national demand and supply. The difference between U.S. cloth demand and supply, on the left, is graphed in the center diagram as the U.S. demand for imported cloth (the D_m curve). The difference between foreign supply and demand for cloth, on the right, is graphed in the center diagram as the foreign supply of cloth exports (the S_x curve). The interactions of demand and supply in both countries determine the price of cloth and the quantities produced, traded, and consumed.

Results of trade	Price	Quantity Supplied	Quantity Demanded
United States	Down	Down	Up
Rest of the world	Up	Up	Down

is only one price ratio at which world demand and world supply are in balance. To find this price one can compare the first and third diagrams of Figure 3.1. The excess of U.S. demand over U.S. supply matches the excess of foreign supply over foreign demand at only one price: the price of one bushel per yard. At this price the U.S. excess demand, or *CB*, equals the foreign excess supply, or *IJ*. At a slightly higher price, say at 1.2 bushels per yard, the U.S. excess of demand over supply would be less than 40 (billion yards a year), whereas the rest of the world's excess supply would be above 40. This imbalance would force the price to fall back to the equilibrium value of one bushel per yard. Conversely, a price below unity would not last because world (U.S. plus foreign) supply would be below world demand.

The balancing of world demand and supply also can be seen in a single diagram showing international trade in cloth, as in the middle diagram of Figure 3.1. The two curves shown there are trade curves derived from the national demand and supply curves. The curve showing U.S. demand for cloth imported from other countries in an excess demand curve, showing the quantity of cloth demand minus cloth supply in the United States for each price level. Similarly, the supply curve of the rest of the world's cloth exports is an excess supply curve, plotting the quantity gaps between cloth supply and demand in the rest of the world. The trade demand and supply curves cross at *E*, yielding exactly the same international flow of cloth *(DE = CB = IJ)* and the same world price as the other diagrams. In what follows, the middle diagram of Figure 3.1 will be used when it is desirable to focus on international exchanges, and diagrams like those to the left and right will be used when it is important to focus on the effects of trade and trade restrictions on domestic producer and consumer groups. Either set of curves has the advantage of being not only familiar to anyone introduced to the demand-supply basics but also empirically measurable.

BEHIND THE DEMAND CURVES: INDIFFERENCE CURVES

In using the demand curves now introduced, it helps to know what behavior and what welfare meaning might lie behind them.

Very few assumptions are strictly necessary to derive the main empirically observed features of demand curves from underlying behavior. The mere fact that consumers face income constraints can explain why demand curves usually slope downward, why goods tend on the whole to be substitutes for each other, and why demand rises with income on the average. The existence of demand curves is thus easily understood. The welfare meaning of demand curves remains more controversial.

To derive demand curves, economists traditionally begin with the notion that each individual derives utility from consuming goods and services (including experiences). Figure 3.2 shows the usual way of relating an individu-

FIGURE 3.2 Indifference Curves Relating an Individual's Utility Levels to Consumption of Two Goods

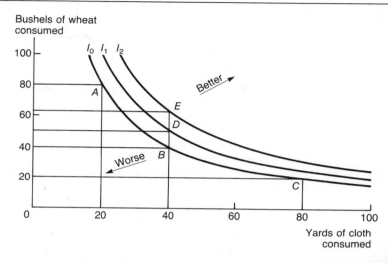

al's utility to amounts of two goods, again wheat and cloth, that the individual consumes. Instead of drawing utility in a third dimension rising out of the printed page, economists draw contours called indifference curves. An **indifference curve** shows all the consumption points at which utility equals some constant. For example, the indifference curve I_0 shows that the individual is *indifferent* between Points A, B, and C, each of which gives the same utility. Any consumption point below and to the left of I_0 is worse than A or B or C in the eyes of this individual. Points above and to the right of I_0 are better. For example, Point D, on the better indifference curve I_1, yields a higher level of utility than A or B or C. Point E, on I_2, is even more preferred. With a family of such curves one can portray how the individual would react to any change in income or price.

When exploring trade issues, though, we will want to judge which situations are better for large groups, not just for an individual. How could we use indifference curves to shown what makes all consumers of cloth, or an entire nation, or the whole world better off? Do such large groups also have indifference curves? Yes, we will say they do. We will use **community indifference curves,** which purport to show how utility or welfare of a whole group depends on the whole group's consumption of wheat and cloth. In what follows, we look at sets of indifference curves like those in Figure 3.2 as if they were community indifference curves for millions or billions of people.

The higher branches of economic theory raise difficult questions about community indifference curves. How can we say whether the community is better off with an average of 40 bushels less and 40 yards more? Some members of the community may lose, while others gain. Who can say that the increase in satisfaction of the one is greater than the decrease in satisfaction of the other? Also, if the changes are evenly distribued, there is still a problem if some vastly prefer cloth over wheat and others have opposite tastes. In this case it is impossible to say that the gain of the wheat devotees outweighs the loss of the cloth addicts. Levels of satisfaction or welfare cannot be compared from one person to another.

These examples are real difficulties. The community indifference curve thus will be used only with caution and, as we shall see, with the reminder that it is based on value judgments that could yield the same policy conclusions without its use. Yet the community indifference curve is a neat schematic device. Among other things, it provides one way of deriving demand curves and therefore determining the prices and quantities that will be involved with or without trade. Let's look first at its use in portraying situations without and with trade and next at its ability to yield demand curves.

PRODUCTION AND CONSUMPTION TOGETHER

Without Trade

Figure 3.3 uses community indifference curves to summarize information about tastes in an economy that does not trade with the rest of the world. (**Autarky** is another name for such a no-trade situation.) In this illustration the United States must be self-sufficient and must find the combination of domestically produced wheat and cloth that will maximize community material well-being. Of all the points at which the United States can produce, only S_0 can reach the indifference curve I_1. A point such as S_1 can only yield a lower indifference curve, such as I_0. At S_1 either consumers or producers or both will find the prevailing price ratio allows them to be better off by moving toward S_0. If the price ratio is temporarily tangent to the production-possibility curve at S_1, consumers will find that this makes cloth look so cheap that they would rather buy more cloth than 20 billion yards and less wheat than 80 billion bushels. Their shift in demand will cause producers to follow suit and shift more resources into cloth production and out of wheat. The tendency to move along the production-possibility curve will persist until the economy produces and consumes at S_0.

As long as increasing costs exist, there will be one and only one such optimizing point. Although there is only one production-possibility curve (ppc), an infinite number of indifference curves can be drawn, representing infinitesimally small increases in real income. If these indifference curves do not intersect, as we assume they do not, any production-possibility curve must produce one point of tangency to a family of indifference curves. At

FIGURE 3.3   Indifference Curves and Production Possibilities without Trade

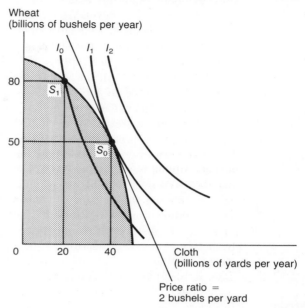

Without trade, the best an efficient economy can do is to move to the production point that touches the highest consumption indifference curve, just as an individual does. This best no-trade point is S_0, where the nation both produces and consumes, reaching indifference curve I_1.

the equilibrium point S_0, the price ratio is such as to bring both producers and consumers into equilibrium.[1]

With Trade

When trade is opened, a nation no longer has to settle for a consumption point on its ppc, as it had to do under autarky. Figure 3.4A shows how a nation can have a higher indifference curve by trading with other nations.

---

[1] In the jargon often used in advanced microeconomic theory, three slopes are equal at S_0:

The trade line's price slope = The marginal rate of transformation (slope of the ppc)
                            = The marginal rate of substitution (slope of the indifference curve).

(continued)

Starting from any production point on the ppc, the United States could trade at international prices and consume at some point above its ppc. So can the rest of the world. The trade gains awaiting them are especially large if they decide to specialize their production. Of course, the United States cannot reach just any higher point by trading: there can only be one point like C_1, where the amounts of U.S. cloth imports and wheat exports are also what the rest of the world wants to trade at the same price.

To see this, imagine the possibility of a price even flatter (making cloth even cheaper) than the price of one bushel per yard. The United States would be able to reach an even higher (undrawn) indifference curve at such a price by producing above and to the left of Point S_1 and trading large volumes in order to consume out beyond C_1. The catch, however, is that the rest of the world would not want to trade so much at a price ratio that made their cloth look cheaper than one bushel per yard. This can be seen by finding the tangency of the new flat price line to the rest of the world's production-possibility and indifference curves on the right-hand side of Figure 3.4A. The result of a price ratio making cloth cheaper than one bushel per yard is closer to S_0, the no-trade point. With the rest of the world wanting so little trade at such a price, the United States would soon have to yield in the marketplace to bring into line the trade desired by both sides. The only equilibrium price would be the unitary price shown in Figure 3.4.

The community indifference curves also can be combined with the production-possibility curves to plot out demand curves for cloth or wheat. A demand curve for cloth is supposed to show how the quantity of cloth demanded responds to its price. To derive the United States demand curve for cloth, start in Figure 3.4A with a price ratio and find how much cloth the United States would be willing and able to consume at that price. At two bushels per yard, the United States is willing and able to consume 40 billion yards a year (at S_0). At one bushel per yard, the United States would consume 60 billion yards (at C_1). These demand points could be replotted in Figure 3.4B, with the prices on the vertical axis. Point S_0 above becomes Point A below; Point C_1 above becomes Point B below;

The *marginal rate of transformation* between two goods, or the slope of the production-possibilities curve, is defined as the rate at which production of the first good must be cut in order to free enough inputs to produce one more unit of the second. (It could be measured either as bushels of wheat per yard of cloth or as yards of cloth per bushel of wheat.)

When the marginal rate of transformation equals the prevailing price ratio, as it does at S_0, producers are in equilibrium.

The *marginal rate of substitution* between two goods is the largest amount of the first good that a consumer would willingly give up in order to get one more unit of the second. (Again, it could be the largest number of bushels of wheat willingly given up for an extra yard of cloth, or the most yards of cloth willingly given up to get an extra bushel of wheat.)

When the marginal rate of substitution equals the prevailing price ratio, as it does at S_0, consumers are in equilibrium.

FIGURE 3.4   Two Views of the Effects of Trade

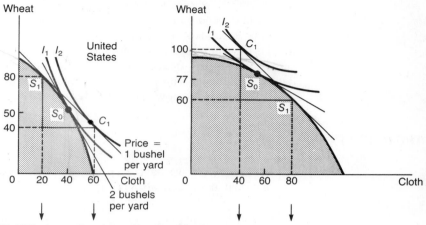

A. With indifference curves and production-possibility curves

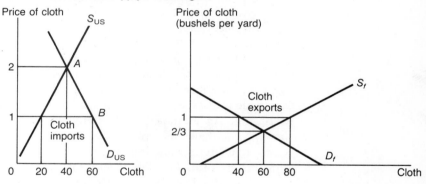

B. With demand and supply curves again

There are two convenient ways to portray how trade allows both sides to reach better consumption points. The upper panels show how trade lets both countries reach beyond their production-possibility curves to consume at Points C_1, reaching indifference curves I_2. The lower panels show the same thing in terms of familiar demand and supply curves, preparing the way for Figure 3.5's measurement of gains from trade.

and so forth. The same could be done for the rest of the world. (The demand-curve derivation is like that found in ordinary price-theory textbooks, except that the nation's income constraint takes the form of a production-possibilities surface instead of a fixed-income point.) In this way the handy demand-supply framework can be (though it need not be) derived from community indifference curves plus production-possibility curves.

The theoretical literature on international trade often uses the indifference and production-possibility curves to derive not demand and supply curves but an equivalent known as an *offer curve*. An offer curve is another way of showing how a nation's offers of exports for imports from the rest of the world depend on international price ratios. A nation's offer curve shows the same information as its export supply or import demand curve. Even though the offer curve adds nothing not already embodied in demand and supply curves, its frequent use by trade theorists makes it an important device for anyone who has a special interest in the theory of international trade. Appendix B shows how an offer curve can be derived and used.

THE GAINS FROM TRADE

All of the devices we have used to show the price and quantity effects of international trade can also be used to show what both sides gain from trade. The community indifference curves in Figure 3.4A allow us to point directly at the gains from trade by comparing indifference curves. We can say that both the United States and the rest of the world get whatever gain in utility a group gets when moving from I_1 to I_2. This is not very helpful by itself since levels of community utility are unmeasurable. As long as we rely on the indifference curves themselves to tell us about the gains, we can only make qualitative statements about whether a country gains or loses, not quantitative statements of how much they gain or lose.[2]

Another shortcoming of using the indifference curves to show the gains from trade is that they can only claim to show an effect on aggregate national well-being. As we noted when introducing the indifference curves, this simplification hides the crucial fact that opening trade actually hurts some economic interests while bringing gains to others. Even the quickest glance at the history of trade policy reveals that freer trade is consistently opposed by groups who fear that imports will compete away their incomes and jobs. Any theory of the gains from trade must, at a minimum, contain a way of quantifying the stake of import-competing groups to see how their stakes compare with the effects of freer trade on other groups.

The demand-supply framework allows us to look separately at the effects of freer trade on import-competing producers and on groups who consume

---

[2] More concrete measures of the gains can be made on the basis of Figure 3.4A itself. One can convert the gains into units of wheat or cloth by using price ratios to put a nation's consumption into a single dimension. In Figure 3.4A this can be done by extending price lines from Points S_0 and C_1 to either axis and comparing the total values in wheat or cloth. For the United States, this procedure shows that at the pretrade price ratio (two bushels per yard), the gains from trade equal 30 billion bushels of wheat a year on the vertical axis, while at the free-trade price of one bushel per year the U.S. gains in units of wheat come to 10 billion bushels a year. The gains at the average price come to 20 billion bushels a year, the same figure we will get from demand-supply analysis in the text.

but do not produce import goods. In practice, of course, many people belong to both groups. Cloth producers in the United States also consume cloth, and foreigners who produce wheat in competition with U.S. wheat exports also consume some wheat themselves. Yet people do specialize in production, and nothing is lost by talking as though the producer and consumer groups were separate.

Figure 3.5 shows what trade means to U.S. cloth producers and to U.S. cloth consumers separately. To understand either set of effects, one must begin by remembering how to interpret demand and supply curves as measures of (private) marginal benefits and costs.

Consumers' Stake in Trade

Turning first to cloth consumers, recall that their cloth demand curve shows for any level of cloth purchases per year the maximum amount (of wheat) that somebody in the nation would be willing and able to give up to get an extra yard of cloth per year. At point *A*, with 40 billion yards being bought a year, the demand curve is telling us that somebody would be willing to pay as much as two bushels of wheat to get another yard of cloth. That person would not be willing to pay any more than two bushels, and at any higher price of cloth even some of the buyers of the first 40 billion yards would decide that cloth isn't worth the price to them and would stop buying. In this way the demand curve revealed by people's behavior is a private marginal benefits curve, plotting marginal benefits from extra cloth on the vertical axis against the cloth of cloth purchases on the horizontal axis. Therefore, we can interpret the whole area under the demand curve up to the point of consumption as a measure of what it is worth to cloth consumers to be able to buy cloth at all.

The marketplace does not give cloth away for free, of course. The buyers of cloth must pay the market place, thus losing part of the gains they get from buying cloth. Yet paying the price will not take away all of their gains, except in the case of a price so high that nobody buys. At Point *A*, without international trade, consumers must pay 80 billion bushels of wheat each year to buy their 40 billion yards of cloth. This means that their net consumer gain from being able to buy cloth is not the whole area under the demand curve, but this minus the 80 billion bushels below the price line paid out to get the cloth. Thus consumers' net gain from buying cloth at all is only area *c* without international trade. This area of net gain below the demand curve but above the price line is called the **consumer surplus.** The area measures what it is worth to consumers to be able to buy a product at a price lower than the prices some of them would be willing and able to pay.

The opening of international trade brings a net gain to cloth consumers. Common sense says that, since trade means a lower price for cloth. The

FIGURE 3.5   The Welfare Effects of Trade on Import Consumers, Import-
Competing Producers, and the Nation as a Whole

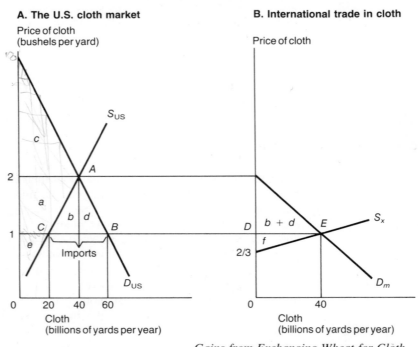

A. The U.S. cloth market

Price of cloth
(bushels per yard)

S_{US}

D_{US}

Imports

Cloth
(billions of yards per year)

B. International trade in cloth

Price of cloth

S_x

D_m

Cloth
(billions of yards per year)

Group	Gains from Exchanging Wheat for Cloth		
	With International Trade	− Without International Trade =	Net Gain from International Trade
U.S. cloth consumers	$a + b + c + d$	c	$a + b + d$
U.S. cloth producers	e	$a + e$	$-a$ (i.e., a loss)
U.S. as a whole (cloth consumers plus cloth producers)	$a + b + c$ $+ d + e$	$c + a + e$	$b + d$
Rest of the world	f		f

Note: All of these areas of gain or loss are measured in bushels of wheat per year.

concept of consumers' surplus allows us to quantify what the better price
is worth to cloth consumers. At Point *B* consumers enjoy all the gains
from cloth purchases represented by the whole area under the demand curve
out to Point *B* and pay only the area under the lower price line, or 60
billion bushels of wheat a year, to get the cloth. This means that, with

free international trade, the consumers' surplus equals areas $a + b + c +$ d. Thus, the opening of trade brings consumers of cloth a net gain of areas $a + b + d$ (worth 50 billion bushels a year). Remember that this is a gain spread over many people, many of them producers of wheat but some of them producers of cloth.

Producers' Stake

The effect of opening trade on cloth producers is quite different. To see why, let's first return to the supply curve and recall that it is a measure of the (private) opportunity cost of producing and selling an extra yard of cloth, as explained in Chapter 2. At Point A without trade, producers are making 40 billion yards a year, and the supply curve tells us that making an extra yard a year would require giving up two bushels of wheat (on the vertical axis) to provide the extra resources for cloth production. What is true of an extra yard at the 40-billion-yard level of production is also true of each earlier yard: if we add up all of the supply-curve heights to get the total area under the supply curve between 0 and 40 billion, we would have the total variable cost of all cloth production.

When selling the cloth at Point A without trade, the producers receive revenues equal to price times quantity, or 2 bushels per yard $\times$ 40 billion yards = 80 billion bushels per year. After the producers have paid the costs under the supply curve out of these revenues, they are left with the area above the supply curve and below the price line, or areas $a + e$, without trade. This net gain in producer revenue minus cost is often referred to as the **producer surplus.** It is meant to be a measure of what it is worth to producers to be able to sell cloth for wheat.[3] These producers are themselves consumers of both wheat and cloth, and their producer surplus is intended to be added to the consumer surplus in order to judge the net effects of some market change on the two groups together.

As a result of the opening of trade, cloth producers are faced with a lower price for their product. Our theory agrees with common sense that this must mean a loss of income for some people who were producing cloth when trade opened up. The reduction in the income gains from producing cloth is likely to cause some resources to be shifted out of cloth production (and into wheat production). At Point C in Figure 3.5 less cloth is being produced than at Point A. The reason is that the lower price makes it unprofitable to produce the extra yards that added a cost of more than one bushel of wheat for each yard of cloth produced. So at Point C with trade, producers

---

[3] The producer surplus areas are, more accurately, intended to measure net gains from being producers and sellers of cloth minus some fixed costs of being sellers of cloth at all. These fixed costs generally are ignored, except in our discussion of displacement costs at the end of Chapter 8 and in Chapter 11's treatment of cartels.

of cloth end up with lower quantities produced and sold as well as with lower prices and lower marginal opportunity costs. Their producer surplus is reduced to area *e* alone. Allowing free international trade has cost them area *a*. Area *a* is a loss of producer surplus on both the 20 billion yards of cloth that are still produced and on the 20 billion yards that were produced profitably without trade but are now imported instead of being produced domestically. (The loss of area *a* costs cloth producers 30 billion a year.)[4]

National Gains

If consumers gain areas *a* + *b* + *d* from the opening of trade and producers lose area *a*, what can we say about the net effect of trade on the United States, which comprises cloth consumers and cloth producers? There is no escaping the basic point that *we cannot compare the welfare effects on different groups without imposing our subjective weights to the economic stakes of each group.* Our analysis allows us to quantify the separate effects on different groups, but it does not tell us how important each group is to us. For example, we can tell from Figure 3.5 that cloth consumers gained 50 billion bushels of wheat (or its cloth equivalent at average prices), the value of the rectangle and triangle that equal areas *a* + *b* + *d*. We can also say that the cloth producers lost 30 billion bushels when losing area *a*. Yet how much of the consumer gain does the producer loss of 30 billion

---

[4] Figure 3.5 does not enable us to identify the "producers" who are experiencing these losses of producer surplus from the opening of international trade and the new competition from foreign cloth. If one views the supply curve as the marginal cost curve facing competitive entrepreneurs who face fixed prices for both outputs and inputs, then it is natural to talk as though whatever changes producer surplus affects just these entrepreneurs' profits and not the incomes of the workers or the suppliers of capital in the cloth industry. Taking this approach implicitly assumes that workers and suppliers of capital are completely unaffected by the fortunes of the cloth industry because they can just take their labor and capital elsewhere and earn exactly the same returns. Yet this kind of microeconomic focus is not justified, either by the real world or by the larger model that underlies the demand and supply curves.

Though the present diagrams cannot show the entire model of international trade at once, they are based on a general-equilibrium model that shows how trade affects the rates of pay of productive inputs as well as commodity prices and quantities. As we shall see in Chapter 4 and Appendix C, anything that changes the relative price of a whole sector in our examples, such as the cloth industry, must also change the whole distribution of income within the nation. If, for example, cloth is a labor-intensive industry, then opening trade will tend to bid down the wage rate on labor, since large numbers of cloth-released workers can find work in the less labor-intensive wheat industry only by bidding down the wage rate of workers in that industry. To repeat, the issue of how trade affects the distribution of income will be taken up later. Now the key point is simply that as the price of cloth drops and the economy moves from Point *A* to Point *C*, the producer surplus being lost is a loss to workers and other input suppliers to the cloth industry, not just a loss to cloth-firm entrepreneurs. To know how the change in producer surplus is divided among these groups, one would have to consult the full model that will be completed by the end of Chapter 4 and Appendix C.

bushels offset in our minds? No theorem or observation of economic behavior can tell us. The result depends entirely on our value judgments. This basic point came up when community indifference curves were introduced, and it returns here in the demand-supply context.

Economists have tended to resolve the matter by imposing the value judgment that we shall call the *one-dollar, one-vote yardstick* here and throughout this book:

> The **one-dollar, one-vote** yardstick says that one shall value any dollar of gain or loss equally, regardless of who experiences it.

The yardstick implies a willingness to judge trade issues on the basis of their effects on aggregate well-being, without regard to their effects on the distribution of well-being. This does not signify indifference to the issue of distribution. It only means that one considers the distribution of well-being to be a matter better handled by compensating those hurt by a change or by using some other non-trade-policy means of redistributing well-being toward those groups (for example, the poor) whose dollars of well-being seem to matter more to us. If the distribution of well-being is handled in one of these ways, trade and trade policies can be judged in terms of simple aggregate gains and losses.

You need not accept this value judgment. You may feel that the stake of, say, cloth producers matters much more to you, dollar for dollar or bushel for bushel, than the stake of cloth consumers in international trade. You might feel this way, for example, if you knew that cloth producers were, in fact, poor unskilled laborers spinning and weaving in their cottages, whereas cloth consumers were rich wheat farmers. And you might also feel that there is no politically feasible way to compensate the poor clothworkers for their income losses from the opening of trade. If so, you may wish to say that each bushel of wheat lost by a cloth producer means five or six times as much to you as each bushel given to cloth consumers, and taking this stand allows you to conclude that opening trade violates your conception of the national interest. Even in this case, however, you could still find the demand-supply analysis useful as a way of quantifying the separate stakes of groups whose interests you weight unequally.

If the one-dollar, one-vote yardstick is accepted, it gives a clear formula for the net national gains from trade. Let's use bushels of wheat here to measure what will later become "dollars" of purchasing power over all goods and services other than the one being discussed (cloth here). It is clear that if cloth consumers gain areas $a + b + d$ and cloth producers lose area a, the net national gain from trade must be areas $b + d$, or a triangular area worth 20 billion bushels per year [$= \frac{1}{2} \times$ (imports of 60 $-$ 20 billion yards) $\times$ (2 $-$ 1) bushels per yard]. It turns out that very little information is needed to measure the net national gain. All that is needed is an estimate of the amount of trade (here represented by the amount of cloth imports) and an estimate of the change in price brought about by trade. With these data, one can measure areas *b* + *d* on either side of Figure 3.5.

Effects on the Rest of the World

One can use the same tools to show that the net gains from trade to the rest of the world will equal area *f* in Figure 3.5B, an area measuring the difference between foreign cloth producers' gains from selling at the higher world price and foreign cloth consumers' losses from this same increase in cloth price. All that is needed to quantify this net effect on the rest of the world is the amount of trade and the effect of trade on foreign prices. The same results can be obtained either from a study of trade in cloth, as here, or from a study of trade in wheat. Since the rest of the world gains area *f* and the United States gains areas *b* + *d*, it is clear that the world as a whole gains from trade.

In addition to showing that both sides gain in the aggregate from trade, Figure 3.5B shows how the gains are divided internationally. It turns out that the division of the gains depends only on whose prices changed more since the gains on both sides are tied to the same quantity of trade. In our example, the United States gained more (areas *b* + *d* are greater than area *f*) because trade cut the U.S price of cloth by a greater percentage of its average level than it raised the foreign price as a percentage of its average level. To know how the gains from international trade are being divided, one should therefore start by investigating whose prices were more affected. Studying Figure 3.5 yields a useful rule on *how the gains are split:*

> The gains from opening trade are divided in direct proportion to the price changes that trade brings to the two sides. If a nation's price ratio changes *x* percent (as a percent of the free-trade price) and the price in the rest of the world changes *y* percent, then
>
> $$\frac{\text{Nation's gains}}{\text{Rest of world's gains}} = \frac{x}{y}$$

The side with the less elastic trade curves will gain more.

In Figure 3.5B, it was the United States that gained more. The United States, whose price dropped by 100 percent of the new free-trade price (from 2 to 1), gained 20 billion bushels a year (area *b* + *d*); the rest of the world, whose price rose by 33⅓ percent of the free-trade price (from ⅔ up to 1), gained 6⅔ billion bushels a year.

We return to this point in Chapters 9 and 12.

DIFFERENT TASTES AS A BASIS FOR TRADE

With the demand side now added to the basic model of international trade, it is easy to see how differences in tastes by themselves could create a basis for mutually advantageous trade, even in a world in which there were no differences among nations in the production possibilities, that is, no differences in supply conditions. This can be shown either with community indifference curves or with demand and supply curves.

Figure 3.6 shows a case in which two countries can produce wheat or rice equally well, having the same production-possibility curves, but having different tastes in grain foods. In the absence of international trade, the preference for bread in Country A (the *A* indifference curves) leads to a higher price for wheat, through the interaction of demand and supply, than will prevail without trade in the rice-preferring country. The pretrade positions are represented by Points *R* and *S,* respectively. Opening trade makes it profitable for somebody to ship wheat to the bread-preferring country in exchange for rice. When a new equilibrium price ratio is reached through international trade, producers in both countries will shift their production so as to make their marginal costs equal the same international price ratio. Since both countries are assumed to have the same production possibilities, they will both produce at the same point, *T.* The bread-preferring country will cater to its greater taste for wheat-based bread by importing wheat

FIGURE 3.6   Trade Based Solely on Differences in Tastes

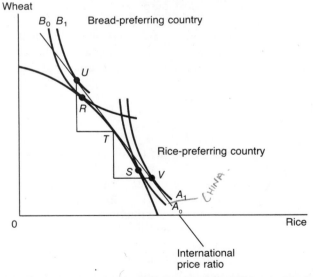

Even if all countries were identical in their production abilities and had identical production-possibility curves, there would be a basis for trade as long as tastes differ. They could produce identical bundles (at Point *T*) but trade so that they end up consuming different bundles (at *U* and *V*).

and reaching the higher indifference curve at Point *U*. The same trade allows the rice-preferring country to reach higher satisfaction at Point *V*. In this case, with tastes but not supply differing, trade leads to greater specialization in consumption but less specialization in production. The same result could be shown using demand and supply curves by giving both countries the same supply curves for production but different demand curves.

MORE COMMODITIES, MORE COUNTRIES

The analysis of this chapter has been limited to two countries and two commodities. Yet the two-by-two analysis is capable of extension, using a variety of techniques, to higher-dimensional models.

Given, say, five commodities produced in each of two countries, these can be ranked in order of relative productivity advantage in each country. Initially one can say only that a country will export the commodity in which it has the largest advantage and import the commodity in which its disadvantage is greatest. The question of whether it will export or import the three commodities between these limits will then depend on the balance of trade. If the demand for imports of the commodity offering a large disadvantage is very great, the country may have to export all four of the other commodities, given the nature of the foreign demand for them, to balance its accounts.

For most purposes our aggregating all countries but one into "the rest of the world" will serve well enough. Yet sometimes this may obscure certain problems rather than illuminate them. Chapter 9 deals with three or more countries in exploring the economics of trade discrimination by country through customs unions and free-trade areas.

SUMMARY

The main effects of international trade can be determined once information about tastes and the demand side has been combined with information about supply. One way of portraying the importance of tastes is to use community indifference curves. Another is to use demand curves, which can be, but need not be, derived from community indifference curves.

Both sides are likely to gain in the aggregate from opening up international trade. Community indifference curves imply this by showing that trade allows each side to reach a higher level of aggregate satisfaction. Demand and supply curves reach the same result in a more measurable way, one that shows us the separate effects of trade on consumers and producers of the importable good in each country. These welfare effects can be measured by using the devices of consumer and producer surplus, with the warning that it is hard to associate either kind of surplus with a fixed set of people. It turns out that what consumers of the importable good gain from opening trade is clearly greater in value than what the import-competing producers lose. If one is willing to weigh each dollar of gain or loss equally, regardless of who experiences it, then the net national gains from trade equal a simple measurable function of the volume of trade created and the change in prices caused by trade.

Differences in tastes can themselves be a basis for mutually advantageous trade. If a country differs from the rest of the world in taste patterns but not in production capabilities, trade will lead to some international specialization in consumption but not in production.

SUGGESTED READING (FOR CHAPTERS 2 AND 3)

The technical literature is vast, and cannot be cited at length here. For advanced technical surveys, see Chapters 1–3, 7, and 8 of the Jones-Kenen *Handbook of International Economics,* vol. I (1984). See also the works cited in Appendixes A to C.

A recent advance by Roy Ruffin (1988) has improved the Ricardian model of comparative advantage so that it generates the predictions of the Heckscher-Ohlin model. It does so by interpreting productivity differences in the one-factor Ricardian approach as differences in relative factor endowments.

For an excellent survey of empirical tests of trade theories, see Deardorff (1984). Tougher judgments of the Heckscher-Ohlin theory in its narrower forms appear in Leamer (1984) and Bowen, Leamer, and Sveikauskas (1987).

For empirical summaries of how the trade competition between the United States, Canada, Japan and other leading industrial economies is evolving, see the books by Morici cited in Figure 2.6, and Wright (1990).

QUESTIONS FOR REVIEW

1. Important: be sure you know how to interpret exports and imports as the flows that separate what a nation produces from what it consumes. In diagrams like those in Figure 3.4A, make sure that you can point to the exports and imports of each country at each price ratio. Note the "trade triangles" showing exports, imports, and the price ratio between production points and consumption points like $S_1 C_1$.

2. On graph paper derive the demand and supply curves for *wheat* from the diagrams in Figure 3.4A.

3. Explain what is wrong with the following statement: "Trade is self-eliminating. Opening up trade opportunities bids prices and costs into equality between countries. But once prices and costs are equalized, there is no longer any reason to ship goods from country to country, and trade stops."

4. What is consumer surplus? What is producer surplus? List the minimum set of information you would need to measure each of these concepts from real-world data.

5. Using Figures 3.1 and 3.5, identify the areas measuring the effects of trade on producers and on consumers of cloth in the rest of the world, and show how to measure the net gains from trade from the rest of the world as a whole.

6. To review how diagrams like Figure 3.4 are affected by a host of forces, consider this review table. Study the cases (rows) that have been filled in, and fill in the others:

	What Curves to Shift in Diagrams with		Effects of Shifts On
Shift	*. . . Indifference Curves & PPC's*	*. . . Supply and Demand Curves*	*Prices and Trade*
Our tastes shift toward wheat	Our indifference curves up and left	Our domestic wheat demand to right	Wheat price up, we trade less
Their tastes shift toward wheat	Their indifference curves up and left	Their domestic wheat demand to right	Wheat price up, we trade more
Our tastes shift toward cloth	_____	_____	_____
Their tastes shift toward cloth	_____	_____	_____
Our wheat-making productivity up	Our ppc up	Our domestic wheat supply to right	Wheat price down, we trade more
Our cloth-making productivity up	Our ppc to right	Our domestic cloth supply to right	Cloth price down, we trade less
Their wheat-making productivity up	_____	_____	_____
Their cloth-making productivity up	_____	_____	_____
Our land supply up (wheat is land-intensive)	Our ppc up, and a little to the right	Our supply cuves and demand curves for both goods (especially wheat supply) to right	Wheat price down, we trade more
Our labor supply up (cloth is labor-intensive)	_____	_____	_____
Their land supply up	_____	_____	_____
Their labor supply up	_____	_____	_____

▼

Who Gains and Who
Loses from Trade
and Specialization?

•

If it seems so likely that nations gain from opening trade, why should free-trade policies have so many opponents year in and year out? We shall return to this question repeatedly here and in Part Two. The answer does not lie mainly in public ignorance about the effects of trade. Trade *does* typically hurt large groups within any country, and many of the opponents of freer trade probably perceive this point correctly. To make our analysis of trade an effective policy guide, we must be able to show just who stands to be hurt by freer trade.

This is the task of the present chapter. We explore three ways in which large groups can lose from more trade. First, we look at an exception to the rule that nations gain from trade, a plausible case in which an entire nation can become worse off by expanding its ability to produce its comparative-advantage exportable good. Next, we explore the gains and losses for product sectors of the economy. Then we turn to gains and losses between factors of production such as land, labor, or capital.

MORE TRADE AND SPECIALIZATION COULD HURT A WHOLE NATION: THE CASE OF "IMMISERIZING GROWTH"

In one plausible situation, specializing more in producing goods for export can work so badly as to make a whole nation worse off. This perverse result can arise from export-oriented productivity improvement, or from accumulating factors of production used mainly in exports, or just from removing barriers to trade.

The possibility of immiserizing growth, which was underlined by Jagdish Bhagwati, is not a reference to the neo-Malthusian vision of the ecological limitations of economic growth. Rather, it hinges on the simple fact that improvements in the ability to supply some goods already being exported tend to lower their price on world markets, perhaps badly enough to make the growth damaging.

Figure 4.1 illustrates the case of immiserizing growth. It imagines that Brazil has expanded its capacity to grow coffee beans more rapidly than it has expanded its manufacturing capacity.[1] For any given terms of trade (international price ratio), this would make Brazil desire to supply much more coffee in exchange for more manufactures. But because Brazil already has a large share of the world coffee market and because the demand for coffee in other countries is price inelastic, Brazil's expansion of coffee supply bids down the world price. And the way Figure 4.1 shows it, this adverse effect on Brazil's terms of trade is so severe that Brazil's own improvements in supply capacity actually make it worse off, dropping it to a lower indifference curve at the consumption Point C_1. It may seem foolish for a nation to undergo an expansion that makes it worse off. Yet it must be remembered that the expansion was undertaken, both in this model and in Brazilian history, by many small competitive farmers, each of whom rightly assumed that *his own* coffee expansion had no effect on the world price. Individual rationality can add up to collective irrationality.

What conditions are necessary in order for immiserizing growth to occur? Three seem crucial:

1. The country's growth must be biased toward the export sector.
2. The foreign demand for the country's exports must be price inelastic, so that an expansion in export supply leads to a large drop in price.
3. The country must already be heavily engaged in trade for the welfare meaning of the drop in the terms of trade to be great enough to offset the gains from being able to supply more.

Brazil may have been in this situation with its coffee expansion before the 1930s, when it already had a large enough share of the world coffee market to face an inelastic demand for its exports, although this possibility has not been tested quantitatively. It is not likely that many other lesser developed countries face the same case, especially where their exports of modern manufactures are concerned, since they typically have too small a share of world markets to face inelastic demand curves for their exports. Immiserizing growth is a possibility, though, and it brings an extreme result: not only does export expansion bring a lower rate of return to the nation than do other kinds of growth, but it even brings a negative national return.

---

[1] The example of Brazilian coffee is convenient because it involves a large exporter of a product with a low price elasticity of demand. It is a dated example, however. Brazil has shifted away from reliance on coffee exports. Today, Brazil exports a far greater value of manufactures, and even of soybeans, than of coffee. Its share of the world coffee market has also been shrinking due to rising competition from dozens of countries on three continents.

FIGURE 4.1   A Case of Immiserizing Growth in a Trading Country

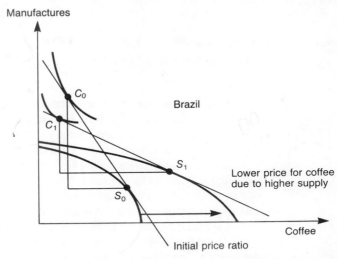

Yes, growth can make a country worse off—even without pollution and other ecological side effects. Before growth, Brazil produces at S_0 and consumes at C_0. Growth makes it possible for Brazil to produce much more coffee. But Brazil is (or was before the 1970s) a large seller on the world market, and its farmers' extra supply lowers the world price of coffee. The price ratio tilts so badly against coffee that the best Brazil can consume is the combination C_1, worse than its initial consumption (C_0).

WHEN SECTORS DECLINE

Having one factor grow relative to others does not just raise the output shares of the sectors using it intensively. It actually *reduces* the outputs of the other sectors if world prices remain the same. This strong effect has already been drawn in Figure 4.1. There the expansion of Brazil's ability to grow coffee caused an absolute drop in her manufacturing sector. Must it be this way? Must the other sector absolutely decline? Yes, because the sector with the expanding potential out-competes the other sector for mobile factors in general, as long as the terms of trade are fixed internationally. This is the **Rybczynski theorem:**

In a two-good world, the growth of one factor of production actually cuts the output of one good if prices are constant.[2]

---

[2] Rybczynski (1955) went beyond this proof to explore the changes in the terms of trade that were likely to accompany such factor growth. (You may abbreviate his name as "Ryb" when answering exam questions.)

For an algebraic proof, see Appendix C.

THE "DUTCH DISEASE" AND DEINDUSTRIALIZATION

Developing a new exportable resource can cause problems. One, mentioned in the text, is the problem of "immiserizing growth": if you are already exporting and your export expansion lowers the world price of your exports, you could end up worse off. Another problem has been called the "Dutch disease," after a situation perceived by the Netherlands following the development of new natural gas fields under the North Sea.

It seemed that the more the Netherlands developed its natural gas production, the more depressed its manufacturers of traded goods became. Even the windfall price increases that the two oil shocks offered the Netherlands (all fuel prices skyrocketed, including that for natural gas) seemed to add to industry's slump. The "Dutch disease" has been thought to have spread to Britain, Norway, Australia, Mexico, and other countries that have newly developed natural resources.

The main premise of this fear is correct: under many realistic conditions, the windfall of a new natural resource does indeed erode profits and production in the traded industrial-good sector. Deindustrialization occurs for the same reason that underlies the Rybczynski theorem introduced in this chapter: the new sector bids resources away from the industrial sector. Specifically, it bids away labor by putting upward pressure on wage rates, and it bids away capital by putting upward pressure on interest rates. The industrial sector tends to contract under such cost pressures.

Journalistic coverage of the apparent link between natural-resource development and deindustrialization tends to discover the basic Rybczynski effect in a very different way. The press tends to notice that the development of the

The Rybczynski result suggests that the development of a new natural resource, such as oil or gas in Canada or Britain, may retard the development of other lines of production, such as manufactures. (See the box on "The 'Dutch Disease' and Deindustrialization.") Conversely, the rapid accumulation of new capital and skills in a fast-growing trading country can cause a decline in domestic production of natural-resource products and make the country more reliant on imported materials. This happened to the United States, which was transformed from a net exporter to a net importer of

---

CONTINUED

---

exportable natural resource causes the nation's currency to rise in value on foreign exchange markets, by letting the nation earn more foreign exchange. A higher value of the nation's currency makes it harder for international customers to buy the whole range of the nation's tradable goods and services. To the industrial sector this feels like a drop in demand, and the sector contracts. The foreign exchange market, in gravitating back toward the original balance of trade, is simply producing the same result we would get from a barter trade model: if you export more of a good, you'll end up either exporting less of another good or importing more. Something has to give so that trade will return to the same balance as before.

So far, it looks as though the disease really does imply deindustrialization. That seems realistic to economists who have studied this issue. We should note, though, two ways in which industry could actually expand. First, if the price of the natural resource does drop, contrary to the terms of the example just presented, and the resource is a major industrial input (such as oil), then profits and production in the industrial sector could be raised instead of cut. Second, the new natural resources could be taxed and the tax proceeds given out according to industrial production in such a way as to bring net stimulus to industry (e.g., as direct output subsidies or as generous tax breaks for such things as real industrial investment or export sales).

We should also note that merely shifting resources away from industry into natural resources is not necessarily bad, despite a rich folklore assuming that industrial expansion is somehow key to prosperity. But bad or not, it is a very likely side effect of gaining new natural resources.

---

minerals as it grew relative to the rest of the world, perhaps partly because of the accumulation of skills and capital.

WHO GAINS AND WHO LOSES WITHIN A COUNTRY

A virtue of the Heckscher-Ohlin (H-O) theory of trade patterns is that it offers realistic predictions of how trade affects the distribution of income between groups representing different factors of production (e.g., landlords, capitalists, managers, technicians, farmers, and unskilled workers). The H-O theory and the facts agree on a key point: international trade is almost sure to divide society into gainers-from-trade and losers-from-trade because changes in relative commodity prices are likely to raise the rewards of some factors of production at the expense of others. To see how, we need to follow a whole chain of influence laid out in Figure 4.2, which returns to the "2 × 2 × 2" example used in Chapters 2 and 3: wheat and cloth, land and labor, the United States and the rest of the world.

Short-Run Effects on Prices and Outputs

Any move toward freer trade makes different nations' price ratios converge. The mere fact that they differ, after allowing for transport costs, makes merchants act in a way that eliminates the differences. So if the land-rich United States starts with cheaper wheat and the labor-rich rest of the world starts with cheaper cloth, somebody will make a profit by exporting wheat from the United States in exchange for cloth, to exploit the price differences. Such trade will expand until the price difference is gone. Wheat will become more expensive in the United States but less expensive in the rest of the world (relative to cloth).

New prices mean new signals to producers. As stated in Figure 4.2, American producers will rethink their previous decisions about how much wheat and how much cloth it pays them to produce. At the margin, they will try to shift some resources into wheat and out of cloth. The opposite shift will occur in the rest of the world, with some producers deciding to raise cloth production and cut wheat production.

Factor Demands Change

Shifts in output mean shifts in the demand for factors of production. The expanding sectors (here, U.S. wheat and foreign cloth) will try to hire more labor and land. The contracting sectors (U.S. cloth and foreign wheat) will lay off workers and rent less land.

The changes in factor demands have one meaning in the short run, another in the long run.

In the short run, when laborers, plots of land, and other inputs are still tied to their current lines of production, factor markets are out of balance. Some people will enjoy higher demand for the factors they have to offer. U.S. landlords in wheat-growing areas can charge much higher rents because their land is in excess demand. U.S. farm workers in wheat-growing areas are likely to get (temporarily) higher wages. Foreign clothworkers can also demand and get higher wage rates. Foreign landlords in the areas raising cotton and wool and other fabrics for clothmaking can also get higher rents.

FIGURE 4.2   How Freer Trade Affects the Income Distribution: The Whole Chain
of Influence

	In the United States	**In the Rest of the World**
Initial prices:	Wheat cheap, cloth expensive	Wheat expensive, cloth cheap
	Trade opens: —— wheat ——▶ ◀—— cloth ——	
Prices respond to trade	P_{wheat} up, P_{cloth} down	P_{wheat} down, P_{cloth} up
Production responds to prices:*	Produce more wheat Produce less cloth	Produces less wheat Produce more cloth
Crucial step — Factor demands change:	For each yard of cloth sacrificed, many workers and few acres laid off; extra wheat (at first, 2 bushels for each lost yard) demands few workers and much land.	For each bushel of wheat sacrificed, much land and few workers laid off; extra cloth (at first, 1.5 yards for each lost bushel) demands many workers little land.
(See Figure 4.3:)	* * * * * * * * * * *	* * * * * * * * * * *
Factor price response	Wage rates fall and rents rise (in both sectors)	Wage rates rise and rents fall (in both sectors)
Final results:	Prices equalized between countries. Countries specialize more. Net gains for both countries. Winners: U.S. landowners, foreign workers. Losers: U.S. workers, foreign landowners	

* The effects of price changes on national *consumption* patterns are ignored here. The more consumption responds to price, the greater the specialization and the effects on factor prices.

Meanwhile, the sellers of factors to the declining industries—U.S. clothworkers, U.S. landlords in areas supplying the cloth making industry, foreign wheat-area landlords and farm hands—lose income through unemployment and reduced prices for their services.

For the short run, then, gains and losses divide by output sector: all groups tied to rising sectors gain, and all groups tied to declining sectors lose. One would expect employers, landlords, and workers in the declining sectors to unite in protest. This is the state of affairs at the line with the asterisk in Figure 4.2, reexpressed as a short-run set of results in Figure 4.3.

FIGURE 4.3   Winners and Losers: Short Run versus Long Run

Effects of freer trade in the short run
(At * * * in Figure 4.2; before factors move between sectors)

	In the United States		*In the Rest of the World*	
	On Landowners	*On Laborers*	*On Landowners*	*On Laborers*
In wheat	Gain	Gain	Lose	Lose
In cloth	Lose	Lose	Gain	Gain

Effects of freer trade in the long run
(After factors are mobile between sectors)

	In the United States		*In the Rest of the World*	
	On Landowners	*On Laborers*	*On Landowners*	*On Laborers*
In wheat	Gain	Lose	Lose	Gain
In cloth	Gain	Lose	Lose	Gain

Reminder: The gains and losses to the different classes do not cancel out leaving zero net gain. In the long run, both countries get net gains. In the short run, net national gains or losses depend on the severity of the unemployment of displaced factors, an issue we return to in Chapter 8.

The Long-Run Factor Price Response

But sellers of the same factors will eventually respond to the gaps that have been opened up. Some U.S. clothworkers will find better-paying jobs in the wheat sector, bidding wages back down in the wheat sector while bidding them back up in the cloth making sector. Some U.S. cotton- and wool-raising land will also get better rents by converting to wheat-related production, bringing rents in different areas back in line. Similarly, foreign farmhands and landlords will find the pay better in the cloth-related sector, bringing down cloth-related pay and bringing up wheat-related pay.

When the factors respond by moving to the better-paying sectors, will all wages and rents be bid back to their pretrade levels? No they will not. In the long run, wage rates end up lower for all U.S. workers and higher for all foreign workers, while land rents end up higher everywhere in the United States and lower in the rest of the world, as stated in Figures 4.2 and 4.3.

What drives this crucial result is the imbalance in the changes in factor demand. Wheat is more land-intensive and less labor-intensive than cloth making. Therefore, the amounts of each factor being hired in the expanding sector will fail to match the amounts being released in the other sector— until factor prices adjust. In the United States, for example, expanding wheat production will create a demand for a lot of land and very few workers, whereas cutting cloth production will unemploy a lot of workers and not so much land.[3] Something has to give. The only way the employment of labor and land can adjust to the available national supplies is for factor prices to change. The shift toward land-intensive, labor-sparing wheat will raise rents and cut wages *throughout* the United States. The rise in rents and the fall in wages will continue until producers come up with more land-saving and labor-using ways of making wheat and cloth. Once they do, the rise of rents and the fall of wages will subside—but U.S. rents will still end up higher and wages lower than before trade opened up. The same kind of reasoning makes the opposite results hold for the rest of the world.

Trade, then, makes some absolutely better off and others absolutely worse off in each of the trading countries. It does so for the reasons sketched here and in Figure 4.2.

THREE IMPLICATIONS OF THE H-O THEORY

Three results that have been suggested so far have been rigorously proved by adding special assumptions to the Heckscher-Ohlin model.

The Stolper-Samuelson Theorem

Wolfgang Stolper and Paul Samuelson proved that trade does split a country into clear gainers and clear losers, under certain assumptions:

Assumptions: A country produces two goods (e.g., wheat and cloth) with two factors of production (e.g., land and labor); neither good is an input into the production of the other; competition prevails; factor supplies are given; both factors are fully employed; one good (wheat) is land-intensive and the other (cloth) is labor-intensive with or without trade; both factors are mobile between sectors (but not between countries); and opening trade raises the relative price of wheat.

The Stolper-Samuelson theorem: Under the assumptions just stated, moving from no trade to free trade unambiguously raises the returns to the factor used intensively in the rising-price industry (land) and lowers the returns to the factor used intensively in the falling-price industry (labor), regardless of which goods the sellers of the two factors prefer to consume.

---

[3] This passage uses convenient shorthand that is quantitatively vague: "a lot of" land, "very few" workers, and so on. These should give the right impressions with a minimum of verbiage. For more precision about the implied inequalities, see either the numerical example in the box on "A Factor-Ratio Paradox" or the explicit (advanced and technical) algebra of Appendix C.

A FACTOR-RATIO PARADOX

The effects of trade on factor use have their paradoxical side. By assumption, the same fixed factor supplies get reemployed in the long run. But everything else about factor use changes. To deepen understanding of several subtleties that help explain how trade makes gainers and losers, this box poses a paradox:

> In one country, trade makes the land/labor ratio fall in both industries—but this ratio stays the same for the country as a whole. In the rest of the world, the same kind of paradox holds in the other direction: trade makes the land/labor ratio rise in both industries—but this ratio again stays the same overall.

How, in one country, could something that falls in both industries stay the same for the two industries together? How, in the rest of the world, could it rise in both yet stay the same for the two together?

The explanation hinges on a tug-of-war that is only hinted at in the main text of this chapter. Here is what the tug-of-war looks like for the United States in our ongoing example: trade shifts both land and labor toward the land-intensive wheat sector, yet rising rents and falling wages induce both sectors to come up with more labor-intensive ways of producing. The two effects just offset each other and remain consistent with the same fixed factor supplies.

Let's look at a set of numbers illustrating how our wheat-cloth trade might plausibly change factor-use ratios in the United States and the rest of the world:

Aside from establishing this point rigorously instead of with casual illustrations, Stolper and Samuelson rendered a further service by showing that the result did not depend at all on which goods were consumed by the households of landowners and laborers. This result clashed with an intuition many economists had shared. It seemed that if laborers spent a very large

CONTINUED

	United States Before (with less trade)				Rest of the World Before (with less trade)			
Sector:	Output	Land Use	Labor Use	Ratio	Output	Land Use	Labor Use	Ratio
Wheat	50	20	40	0.500	77	28.75	77	0.373
Cloth	40	10	60	0.167	60	10	128	0.078
Whole economy		30	100	0.300		38.75	205	0.189

◇
                                       ◇

	United States After (with more trade)				Rest of the World After (with more trade)			
Sector:	Output	Land Use	Labor Use	Ratio	Output	Land Use	Labor Use	Ratio
Wheat	80	25	60	0.417 (down)	60	18.75	45	0.417 (up)
Cloth	20	5	40	0.125 (down)	80	20	160	0.125 (up)
Whole economy		30	100	0.300 (same)		38.75	205	0.189 (same)

Here we have both the factor-ratio paradox and its explanation. The paradox shows up in both countries. In the United States something has induced both wheat producers and cloth producers to come up with production methods having lower land/labor ratios (more labor-intensive techniques). Yet the same fixed factor supplies are employed.

One can see that the key is the shift of U.S. output toward land-intensive wheat. If it had been the only change, the aggregate land/labor would have risen. This is what induced the rise in rents and the fall in wages, and they in turn induced the shift toward labor-intensive techniques in both industries. (The same point again applies in mirror image for the rest of the world.)

share of their incomes on cloth, they might possibly gain from free trade by having cheaper cloth. Not so, according to the theorem. In fact, the theorem says the results have to be magnified: opening trade must enable one of the two factors to buy more of either good, and it will make the other factor poorer in its ability to buy either good.

Some simple reasoning can show why. Under competition, the price of each good must equal its marginal cost. In our wheat-cloth economy, price must equal the marginal land and labor costs in each sector:

$$P_{\text{wheat}} = \text{marginal cost of wheat} = ar + bw$$

and

$$P_{\text{cloth}} = \text{marginal cost of cloth} = cr + dw,$$

where the prices are both measured in the same units (e.g., units of a commodity, or dollars), r is the rent earned on land, and w is the wage rate paid to labor. The coefficients a, b, c, and d are physical input/output ratios; let them either be constant or vary only in response to r and w. Suppose that the price of wheat rises 10 percent and the price of the cloth stays the same. The higher price of wheat will bid up the return to at least one factor. In fact, it is likely to raise the rental price of land, since growing wheat uses land intensively. So r rises. Now look at the equation for the cloth sector. If r rises and the price of cloth stays the same, then the wage rate w must fall absolutely. It must be harder for workers to buy even the stable-price cloth, let alone the rising-price wheat. Next take the fall of w back to the equation for the wheat sector. If w is falling, and P_{wheat} is rising 10 percent, then r must be rising *more* than 10 percent to keep the equation valid. So if wheat is the land-intensive sector,

P_{wheat} ↑ by 10% and P_{cloth} steady means r ↑ more than 10% and w ↓.

Thus a shift in relative prices brings an even more magnified response in factor prices: a factor more closely associated with the rising-price sector will have its market reward (e.g., r or w) rise even faster than the price rise, while a factor more closely associated with other sectors will have its real purchasing power cut.

The same principle emerges no matter how we change the example (e.g., even if we let the price of wheat stay the same and change the price of cloth instead, or even if we let producers change the input/output coefficients a, b, c and w)[4] It really just follows from the fact that price must equal marginal cost under competition, both before and after trade has changed the price ratio between wheat and cloth. (Appendix C gives an alternative proof.)

---

[4] For a numerical example, let both prices start at 100, let r and w both start at 1, and let $a = 40$, $b = 60$, $c = 25$, and $d = 75$. Let the price of wheat rise by 10 percent to 110. Your task is to deduce what values of r and w could satisfy the new wheat equation $110 = 40\,r + 60\,w$, while still satisfying the cloth equation $100 = 25\,r + 75\,w$. You should get that r rises to 1.50 and w falls to 5/6.

The text says that the result still holds even if a, b, c and d change. To be more precise, the result still holds if a or c falls when r rises, or if b or d falls when w rises. These are the economically plausible directions of response, so the result holds in all plausible cases.

The Specialized-Factor Pattern

The Stolper-Samuelson theorem is a special case using only two factors and two commodities in two countries. Its results are part of a broader pattern, one that tends to hold for any number of factors and commodities and countries:

> The more a factor is specialized, or concentrated, into the production of exports, the more it stands to gain from trade. Conversely, the more a factor is concentrated into the production of the importable good, the more it stands to lose from trade.

This pattern should seem plausible. You may wonder whether it is meant as a pattern for the short run, when factors are immobile, or for the long run. The answer is both. As long as a factor continues to be associated with producing exportables, the greater its stake in freer trade. As long as it is associated with production threatened by imports, the more it gains from trade barriers. In the extreme case, a factor that can be used only in one sector has a life-long or permanent stake in the price of that sector's product. A good example of such an immobile factor is farm land, which is hard to convert to other uses. There is little difference between the short run and the long run, when it comes to farm land. If the land is of a type that will always be good for growing import-competing crops, there is nothing subtle about the landowner's stake in policies that keep out imports of those crops.

The Factor-Price Equalization Theorem

The same basic $2 \times 2 \times 2$ trade model (two factors, two commodities, two countries) that predicts the Stolper-Samuelson result also makes an even more surprising prediction about the effects of trade on factor prices and the distribution of income. Beginning with a proof by Paul Samuelson in the late 1940s, a theorem was established about the effect of trade on international differences in factor prices:

> *Assumptions:* (1) There are two factors (for example, land and labor), two commodities (wheat and cloth), and two countries (the United States and the rest of the world); (2) competition prevails in all markets; (3) each factor supply is fixed, and there is no factor migration between countries; (4) each factor is fully employed in each country with or without trade; (5) there are no transportation or information costs; (6) governments do not impose any tariffs or other barriers to free trade; (7) the production functions relating factor inputs to commodity outputs are the same between countries for any one industry; (8) the production functions are functions are linearly homogeneous (if all factors are used 10 percent more, output will be raised by exactly 10 percent) and (9) not subject to "factor intensity reversals" (if wheat is land intensive at one factor-price ratio, it remains so at

any factor-price ratio); and (10) both countries produce both goods with or without trade.

The factor-price equalization theorem: Under the long list of assumptions above, free trade will equalize not only commodity prices but also factor prices so that all laborers will earn the same wage rate and all units of land will earn the same rental return in both countries regardless of the factor supplies or the demand patterns in the two countries.

This is a remarkable result. It implies that laborers will end up earning the same wage rate in all countries, even if labor migration between countries is not allowed. Trade makes this possible, within the assumptions of the model, because the factors that cannot migrate between countries end up being implicitly shipped between countries in commodity form. Trade makes the United States export wheat and import cloth. Since wheat is land-intensive and cloth is labor-intensive, trade is in effect sending a land-rich commodity to the rest of the world in exchange for labor-rich cloth. It is as though each factor were migrating toward the country in which it was scarcer before trade.

The theorem is more than just remarkable. It is also wrong. Even the most casual glance at the real world shows that the predictions of the factor-price equalization theorem are not borne out. One of the most dramatic facts of economic development is that the same factor of production, for example, the same labor skill, does not earn the same pay in all countries. The international pay gaps for comparable work are wide and perhaps widening. Hair stylists do not earn the same pay in Mexico or India as in the United States or Canada. Nor do household help. It seems clear that the assumptions made in proving the theorem must be the cause of the discrepancy between model prediction and fact. It is hard to say which assumptions are most "at fault." A true believer in free trade might be tempted to argue that factor prices have not been equalized between countries because we do not have free trade. Yet even in the freer-trade era of the 19th century, English unskilled workers earned noticeably more than did their Irish or Indian counterparts, despite fairly free trade and unprohibitive transportation costs. It must be that the whole set of assumptions contains many crucial departures from reality. Yet the factor-price equalization theorem remains an interesting exercise in the use of rigorous models of trade and is proved (given its assumptions) in Appendix C.

WHO ARE THE EXPORTING AND THE IMPORT-COMPETING FACTORS?

The analysis of the effects of trade on factor groups' incomes and purchasing power makes it clear that we need measures of export orientation versus import orientation. Such indicators help identify the groups that are likely to gain and lose from liberalizing or restricting foreign trade. Knowing who these groups are, national policy makers can better anticipate their views on trade and can plan ahead for ways to compensate the groups likely to be injured, if society wishes to compensate them. Knowing the patterns of export orientation and import orientation also helps interest groups to know their own stakes in the trade issue. There is a rich literature estimating such factor contents from elaborate input-output tables, especially for the United States.

The U.S. Pattern

At a minimum, a correct anatomy of the factor content of U.S. exports and of U.S. imports competing with domestic production must distinguish the factor contributions of farmland, minerals, skilled labor, unskilled labor, and nonhuman capital. Figure 4.4 does so, giving a rough picture of how

FIGURE 4.4   A Schematic View of the Factor Content of U.S. Exports and Competing Imports

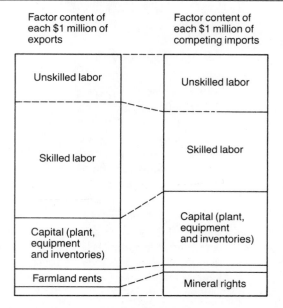

Note: Vertical distances are meant to give rough impressions of factor-content proportions in U.S. exports and the set of outputs that would replace the U.S. imports which compete with domestic products. The estimates must be rough since we lack correct calculations of the rents earned by farmland, mineral depletion, and plant and equipment. The proportions here are meant to represent postwar U.S. conditions.

THE LEONTIEV PARADOX

What we now know about the mixtures of productive factors that make up the exports and imports of leading nations has been learned largely because Wassily Leontiev was puzzled in the 1950s. Leontiev, who was later awarded the Nobel Prize in Economics, set off a generation of fruitful debate by following the soundest of scientific instincts: testing whether the predictions of a theory really fit the facts.

What Leontiev decided to test was the Heckscher-Ohlin theory that countries will export those products that use their abundant factors intensively and import products that use these factors less intensively. More precisely, he wanted to test two propositions at the same time: (1) H-O was correct, and (2) the United States economy was more capital-abundant than the countries with which it traded, as everybody assumed.

Leontiev's K/L Test

Leontiev computed the ratios of capital stocks to numbers of workers in the U.S. export and import-competing industries in 1947. This computation required figuring out not only how much capital and labor was used in each of these several-dozen industries but also the capital and labor their products embodied by using products purchased from other industries. As the main pioneer in input-output analysis, he had the advantage of knowing just how to multiply the input-output matrix of the U.S. economy by vectors of capital and labor inputs, export values, and import values to derive the desired estimates of capital-labor ratios in exports and import-competing production. So the test was set: if the H-O prediction was correct, and the United States was more capital-abundant, the U.S. export bundle should embody a higher capital-labor ratio (K_x/L_x), when all the contributions of input industries were sorted out, than the capital-labor ratio embodied in the U.S. production that competed with imports (K_m/K_m).

Leontiev's results posed a paradox that puzzled him and others: in 1947, the United States was exporting labor-intensive goods to the rest of the world in exchange for relatively capital-intensive imports! The key ratio $(K_x/L_x)/(K_m/L_m)$ was only 0.77 when H-O said it should be well above unity.

CONTINUED

Other K/L Studies

Leontiev and others wrestled with this result in many ways. His method was rechecked several times and found essentially correct. There could be no questioning that the United States was capital-abundant relative to the rest of the world. Other studies confirmed the bothersome Leontiev paradox for the United States between World War II and 1970. Here are some of the results:

Scholar	Data from	$(K_x/L_x)/(K_m/L_m) = >$ (H-O predicts: > 1)
Whitney (1968)	1899	1.12
Leontiev (1954)	1947	0.77
Leontiev (1956)	1947/51	0.94 (or 1.14 excluding natural-resource industries)
Baldwin (1971)	1958/62	0.79 (or 0.96 excluding natural-resource industries)
Stern and Maskus (1981)	1972	1.05 (or 1.08 excluding natural-resource industries)

The results break down as follows. For 1899 or for 1972, there is no paradox. The key ratio is above unity, as H-O and U.S. capital abundance would predict. For the postwar era before 1970, however, the paradox generally persisted. The ad hoc device of excluding natural-resource industries sometimes made the paradox go away, but this result was easily reversed. One cannot shrug off the early postwar results as a temporary oddity: a whole generation of wrong predictions is damaging to any theory. A narrow version of H-O remains guilty of a wrong prediction. As posed by Leontiev, the paradox remains.

Broader and Better Tests

The most fruitful response was to introduce other factors of production besides just capital and labor. Perhaps, reasoned many economists (including Leontiev himself), we should make use of the fact that there are different kinds of

CONTINUED

labor, different kinds of natural resources, different kinds of capital, and so forth. Broader calculations of factor content have paid off in extra insights about gains and losses from trade, as noted in this chapter. In a sense, this by-product of the Leontiev-paradox debate limits the damage done to H-O. True, the United States was somewhat capital-abundant yet failed to export more capital services than it imported. But the post-Leontiev studies also showed that capital was not the resource of greatest relative American abundance. The top rankings in this respect go to farmland and scientific-professional labor. And the United States is indeed a net exporter of products that use these factors intensively, as H-O would predict.

So far, the results of the Leontiev-paradox debate are:

1. The narrow prediction that $(K_x/L_x)/(K_m/L_m) > 1$ for the United States is wrong for at least the whole generation starting in 1947. In this sense, the Leontiev paradox remains.
2. The less narrow Heckscher-Ohlin prediction that comparative advantage follows factor endowments cannot be rejected (may be correct), once we recognize that there are many factors of production.
3. The standard trade model, which allows demand conditions and technology, as well as factor proportions, to affect trade, may still be correct. It was not even tested in the Leontiev debate.

the total value of exports and the total value of competitive imports are probably divided among these factors. Labor incomes account for a greater share of the value of exports than of the value of imports that compete with domestic production. This labor-intensiveness of exports is due in part to the fact that there are more jobs associated with exports than with an equal value of imports, as we shall see for the postwar period. At the same time it is due in part to the greater average skill and pay levels on the export side. If an arbitrary division were made between the pay of skilled labor and that of unskilled labor, it would turn out that exports embodied more skilled labor but slightly less unskilled labor than did imports, using the factor contents of import-competing U.S. industries to decompose the value of imports. Note that nonhuman capital is not an export-oriented factor in the U.S. case. As surprising as this result was to economists a generation ago (see the box on "The Leontiev Paradox"), it is consistent with H-O theory and with Chapter 2's finding that capital is not the most abundant factor in the United States relative to the rest of the world. Rather, as we saw in Chapter 2, the factors most abundant in the U.S. relative to the rest of the world's endowments are highly skilled labor and farmland.

The Canadian Pattern

Canada, by contrast, implictly exports and imports the factor mixtures sketched in Figure 4.5. About the only similarity to the U.S. pattern is that both countries are net exporters of the services of farmland through their positions as major grain exporters. Otherwise, the export-import patterns of the United States are reversed in Canada, in large part because the heavy bilateral trade between the two countries casts them in complementary roles. Canada is a net importer of labor, much of it embodied in U.S. exports to Canada. It is a slight net exporter of nonhuman capital (some of it owned, however, by U.S. subsidiaries in Canada). Finally, Canada is a heavy net exporter of mineral-right services through its exports of mineral products.

FIGURE 4.5   The Factor Content of Canada's Exports and Competing Imports

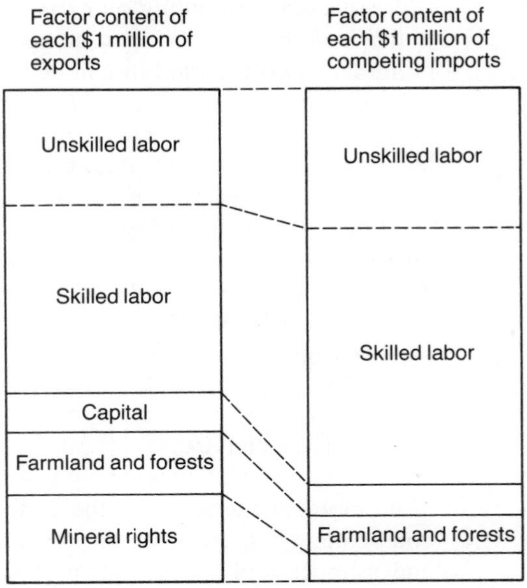

Factor content of each $1 million of exports

Factor content of each $1 million of competing imports

Unskilled labor

Unskilled labor

Skilled labor

Skilled labor

Capital

Farmland and forests

Mineral rights

Farmland and forests

Patterns in Other Countries

The patterns of factor content have also been roughly measured for other countries. Three such results deserve quick mention here.

The foreign trade of the Soviet Union has fit the Heckscher-Ohlin pattern to a degree that might seem surprising for a state-run trade monopoly. In its trade with lesser developed countries, both inside and outside the socialist-European (CMEA) bloc, the Soviet Union tends to export capital-intensive products and import labor-intensive ones. In its trade with more advanced countries, both outside the bloc (e.g., with Japan) and within (with East Germany), there is more labor-intensity to Soviet exports and more capital-intensity to Soviet imports. The H-O theory also correctly predicts the main comparative-advantage export line of the Soviet Union: mineral and forest products.

The factor content of *oil-exporting countries* is not surprising. They explicitly export mineral rights in large amounts, of course. The less populous oil exporters, particularly the oil nations of the Arabian peninsula, also export capital services through the interest and dividends they earn (the ''lending services'' they provide) on their still-extensive foreign wealth. The same countries implicitly import just about every other factor: all human factors and farmland rents. As noted in connection with the ''Dutch disease,'' there is tension between their attempts to earn more by exporting oil and their desire to develop new industries that are labor-intensive (including skilled-labor). Expanding oil exports makes it harder for the new industries to thrive in the face of import competition, since whatever promotes exports promotes imports, often in competition with domestic products.

The *oil-importing Third World* implicitly imports capital and human skills along with the oil. It exports unskilled labor, the services of agricultural land, and minerals other than oil. Here lies an important comment on the distributional effects of trade in the Third World. For many developing countries, lower-income groups selling unskilled labor or working small farm plots have the greatest positive stake in foreign trade since their products are the exportable ones. Protection against trade often widens the income gaps between rich and poor in developing countries. We return to this pattern, noting exceptions and complications, in Chapter 13.

U.S. LABOR'S STAKE IN FOREIGN TRADE

The empirical literature on the factor content of U.S. exports and import-competing production yields key insights into the question of what jobs and incomes U.S. workers stand to gain or lose from foreign trade or from policies to cut off that trade.

Several times since 1970 the U.S. Congress came close to passing comprehensive bills to slash U.S. imports with tariffs or other barriers. So far, those wanting protection against imports have had partial success in the form of ad hoc restrictions on several kinds of imports. Yet the pressure continues for more protection, especially for a comprehensive bill that would reduce imports on a broad front.

Each attempt to cut U.S. imports has been defended as something necessary to protect U.S. jobs against unfair foreign competition. Setting the issue of fairness aside until Part Two, we can nonetheless comment on the basic premise that more trade means less U.S. jobs (i.e., that cutting trade means more U.S. jobs). On this question, economists have developed a relatively clear answer.

To appraise the net effects of trade restrictions or freer trade on the number of jobs available at given wage rates, it is necessary to proceed in two steps: (1) to recognize and quantify the extent to which cutting imports would also cut the value of exports and (2) to multiply the changes in import value and export value by the ratios of jobs per dollar that seem to characterize the export and import-competing industries.

Cutting Imports = Cutting Exports

The first crucial step in judging the impact of new trade barriers is to recognize that *cutting the value of imports is likely to cut the value of exports by the same amount.* This is not obvious, yet there are four reasons for expecting this result:

1. *Exports use importable inputs.* Barriers that make importable goods more costly in the domestic market raise the cost of producing for export. Examples would be the tendency of the U.S. import quotas on oil (1959–73) to raise the cost of U.S. chemicals sold on world markets and the tendency of U.S. restrictions on steel imports to raise the prices of U.S. autos. To this extent, import barriers tend to price U.S. exportable-good industries out of some export business.

2. *Foreigners who lose our business cannot buy so much from us.* If higher import barriers deny sales and income to foreign exporters, foreign national incomes may sag. This is especially likely if our country is a large part of world trade and we cut imports severely. The impoverishment of foreigners will cut the value of the exports they buy from us.

3. *Foreign governments may retaliate.* All national governments are subject to pressure from individual industry groups wanting protection against import competition. If the United States were to impose severe restrictions on imports, it would become harder for foreign governments to resist raising their own import barriers, especially those on U.S. exports. The retaliation would be likely to cut U.S. export values further.

By themselves, these first three arguments have an uncertain quantitative importance. It is not clear, though very possible, that they imply export value cuts equal to the import value cuts. But whatever slack they leave between the import and export value cuts is likely to be taken up by the fourth argument:

4. *Cutting imports will bring the same net cut in export value through an exchange-rate adjustment.* Here it is necessary to step ahead of our survey of international trade to pick up a basic point of international finance from Part Three. Our trade models have ignored just how it is that export goods and import goods are exchanged between countries. They are not bartered but are bought and sold in exchange for national currencies, and persons wanting to swap currencies after trading goods do so in a foreign exchange market. Demand and supply for any national currency on international markets must retain a rough balance. If the exchange rates between the U.S. dollar and other currencies are flexible and are determined by demand and supply in the marketplace, then the supply of dollars (to buy foreign goods, services, and assets) will roughly match the demand for dollars (to buy U.S. goods, services, and assets) even in the very short run. If officials try to keep the exchange rates fixed, demand and supply for the dollar will be balanced only over the long run. But they will be balanced.

Putting up import barriers will cut the value of dollars that are being supplied in order to demand foreign currencies to import foreign goods. With the United States not demanding so much foreign currency as before, the value of the dollar will tend to rise and the value of foreign currencies will tend to fall in foreign exchange markets. Now that each dollar costs foreign buyers more, any given dollar price of a U.S. export looks more expensive to foreign buyers. They will therefore tend to cut their purchases of U.S. exports. To what extent? Roughly until the value of the dollars they demand to buy our exports has dropped by the same amount as the dollars we are willing to give up to buy imports (which are subject to the new extra import barriers). In other words, the workings of the foreign exchange market are likely to make our export values drop by as much as our import values drop, though the effects of exchange-rate changes on foreign ability to buy our exports. The conclusion, then, is that cutting imports is likely to bring roughly a dollar-for-dollar cut in export value.

The Job Content of Imports and Exports

If imports and exports decline by the same dollar value per year in response to the new import barriers, what, then, do we know about the net job effect? We can see that on the one hand jobs are being protected or created in import-competing industries that are now shielded from import competition, yet on the other hand it seems clear that jobs may be lost in export lines. To see which job effect is likely to prevail, let's now turn to the evidence on the job content of exports and imports.

FIGURE 4.6   Number of U.S. Jobs Tied to a Billion Dollars of Exports and a Billion Dollars of Import-Replacing Production

Year for Estimate	Source	Jobs per $1 Billion of Exports	Jobs per $1 Billion of Import Replacement
(1) 1899	Whitney	1,122,500	1,240,000
(2) 1947	Leontiev	182,000	170,000
(3) 1958/62	Baldwin	131,000	119,000
(4) 1970/71	Krause	111,000	88,600
(5) 1971	Brimmer	66,000	65,000
(6) 1972	Stern and Maskus	99,000	96,000
(7) 1978	U.S. I.T.C.	38,000	33,000
(8) 1981	U.S. I.T.C.	29,100	23,100
(9) 1984	U.S. I.T.C.	25,100	23,100

Note: All estimates except those of Krause measure average jobs per dollar of trade value. Krause estimated the more relevant ratio of *changes* in jobs to *changes* in exports or imports. Sources: (1) Whitney (1968, calculated from Table V-3); (2) Leontiev (1956); (3) Baldwin (1971); (4) Krause (1971, pp. 421–25); (5) Brimmer (1972); and (6) Stern and Maskus (1981); (7) through (9): U.S. International Trade Commission (1986).

Figure 4.6 gives some of the estimates of export and import-competing job content. These figures and others like them make it clear that since World War II there have been more jobs tied to a billion dollars of exports than to a billion dollars of import-competing production. This is the main policy message that can be gleaned from the literature on the Leontiev paradox. To that message we can add another point: it is also true that the average wage rate for workers tends to be higher in export industries than in import-competing industries. So the estimates imply that more wages (jobs times average rate of pay) are tied to exports than to imports. It must be stressed that these job-effect estimates are very rough, as their authors point out. Yet it does seem that all the studies that have confronted the comparison do find exports more job-intensive and wage-intensive. It is hard, then, to argue that a balanced cut in exports and imports, which a comprehensive import-cutting bill would produce, will bring a net gain in U.S. jobs. The evidence is clearly leaning toward the opposite conclusion that jobs and wages would be cut by such import cuts.

If a sweeping cut in imports would end up costing jobs rather than adding jobs, why would labor groups favor such import cuts? To arrive at an answer, it helps to note which labor groups have favored a major increase in import protection. The largest lobbyist for protection against imports is the AFL-CIO. It so happens that this organization has its membership concentrated in industries that are more affected by the import competition than is the economy as a whole. That is, AFL-CIO membership is heavily concentrated in the most import-threatened industries, the only exception being the heavily AFL-CIO populated tobacco industry, which is an export industry for the United States. It is thus quite practical for the AFL-CIO to lobby for protectionist bills that would create and defend the jobs of AFL-CIO members and their wages, even if the same bills would cost many jobs and wages outside this labor group. To understand who is pushing for protection, it is important to know whose incomes are most tied to competition against imports.

The analysis so far has argued that a large and balanced raising of *new* U.S. import barriers would bring a net loss in jobs and wages. It does not follow that the *existing* import barriers have the same job effect. On the contrary, a study by Robert E. Baldwin for the U.S. Labor Department has shown that the U.S. barriers against imports have been made most restrictive on goods that have higher than average job content, especially in the nonfarm unskilled job categories. The more protected industries also tend to be technologically "older" (more stagnant) and slightly more concentrated in the urban Northeast. The U.S. political process thus far has been somewhat selective in giving protection against imports, favoring industries that make fairly heavy use of lower-skilled workers, such as cotton textiles and footwear. Thus, it turns out that eliminating the existing U.S. import barriers would bring a very slight net job loss, even though raising new barriers against all imports also would cost U.S. jobs. Raising new barriers to imports could result in a net gain in U.S. jobs and wages only if the import barriers were confined to those industries with especially high job content per dollar of output value.

SUMMARY

A nation already engaged in foreign trade can be made worse off by export-biased economic growth. Expanding its ability to produce exports (e.g., by accumulating more of a factor of production that is used mainly in export-good production) will raise its export supply. Raising export supply may bid down the world price of its export good. We have a case of **immiserizing growth** if the export-biased growth lowers the price of exports enough to make the nation worse off. Immiserizing growth is more likely (1) the more the growth is biased toward supplying exportable goods, (2) the less elastic is the world's demand for its exports, and (3) the more heavily the country is already involved in trade.

The **Rybczynski theorem** says that in a two-good world, the growth of one factor of production actually cuts the output of one good if prices are constant. While the theorem is narrow and dry by itself, it rightly suggests a broader real-world tendency. When a nation becomes better at producing one good, typically the production of something else will decline. A case in point is the so-called **Dutch disease,** in which expanding production of a natural-resource export causes deindustrialization. That could be bad, but is not necessarily so.

To understand whom trade helps and whom it hurts within a nation, it is essential to comprehend how relative output prices affect factor incomes. In a simple two-factor, two-commodity model, the **Stolper-Samuelson theorem** has shown that opening trade and raising the relative price of the exportable good bring clear income gains to the factor of production used intensively in the exportable industry; they also bring clear income losses to the factor used intensively in the import-competing industry. Within the same model, adding a few extra (unrealistic) assumptions, the **factor-price equalization theorem** has shown that free trade gives each factor of production the same material reward in each country.

To apply the theory of how trade and product prices affect the distribution of income among factors, it is necessary to go beyond the simple two-factor, two-product model. More general analyses have yielded fewer clear mathematical proofs but some useful principles. One such principle is that the shares of their incomes that the members of a factor group spend on exportables and importables matter to their stake in foreign trade. Another is that the factors most extremely specialized in exportable and importable production will still clearly gain and lose, respectively, from expanded trade.

Economists have devoted considerable energy to finding out who the exporting and import-competing factors of production are. Their efforts centered on the **Leontiev paradox,** which showed that the United States was exporting less capital-intensive and more labor-intensive goods than it was producing in competition with imports. The paradox led to a more careful and elaborate view of the factor content of foreign trade, especially for the United States.

The factor-content calculations have revealed what factors are implicitly exported or imported via trade in goods they produce. The United States has recently been a net exporter of skills and farmland services and a net importer of mineral rights (mainly through oil imports) and unskilled labor. Canada has also been a net exporter of farmland services, but there the similarity to the United States ends. Canada is a net exporter of mineral rights, unskilled labor, and capital; it is a net importer of skills.

It turns out that U.S. export industries involve more jobs than do U.S. import-competing industries. Since a general cut in U.S. imports is likely to bring an equal cut in the value of U.S. exports, it appears that cutting imports would bring a net loss of U.S. jobs and wages, contrary to the frequent argument for shutting out imports to save jobs. On the other hand, eliminating *existing* U.S. import barriers also might bring about a slight job and wage loss since existing barriers are to be concentrated in the most labor-intensive of the import-competing industries.

SUGGESTED READING

For a technical proof of several results, including the Stolper-Samuelson and factor-price-equalization theorems, see Appendix C.

The contrast between factors' short-run and long-run fortunes from expanded trade was explicitly derived by Mussa (1974).

For a recent sampling from the vast literature on the factor content of U.S. foreign trade, see Harkness (1978), Leamer (1980), Stern and Maskus (1981), Brecher and Choudhri (1982), and the survey by Deardorff (1984). On Canada's foreign trade, see Postner (1975). On Soviet comparative advantage and factor content, see Rosefielde (1974). For multinational tests of the H-O factor proportions hypothesis and the Leontiev Paradox, see Leamer (1984) and Bowen, Leamer, Sveikauskas (1987).

QUESTIONS FOR REVIEW

1. From the following information calculate the total input shares of labor, land, and capital in each dollar of cloth input:

	For Each Dollar of		
	Cloth Output	*Synthetic Fiber Output*	*Cotton Yarn Output*
Direct labor input	.40	.50	.50
Direct land input	.02	.00	.20
Direct capital input	.20	.50	.30
Synthetic fiber input	.18	.00	.00
Cotton yarn input	.20	.00	.00
All inputs	$1.00	$1.00	$1.00

2. You are given the following input cost shares in the wheat and cloth industries in the United States:

	For Each Dollar of		
	Wheat Output	*Cloth Output*	*Overall National Income*
Total labor input	.60	.59	.60
Total land input	.15	.06	.10
Total capital input	.25	.35	.30
	$1.00	$1.00	$1.00

Suppose that a move toward freer trade (e.g., due to reductions in international transport costs) tends to raise the price of wheat relative to cloth, and the

United States responds by exporting more wheat and importing more cloth.
   a. If the factors were each completely *immobile* between the wheat and cloth sectors, who would gain from freer trade? Who would lose?
   b. If the factors were each completely *mobile* between sectors, who would gain from freer trade? Who would lose?
   3. Essay question: "Opening up free trade does hurt people in import-competing industries in the short run. But in the long run, when resources can move between industries, everybody ends up gaining from free trade."
   Do you agree or disagree? Explain.

▼

Alternative Theories of Modern Trade

•

When the facts change, theories often need to change with them. The facts of international trade seem to be moving in directions that will force us either to expand on the standard theory of Chapters 2 through 4 or to replace it with new theories. Here we explore where the facts about world trade seem to be moving, what changes they demand of the standard theory, and the leading theories that try to explain what is different about today's international trade.

MODERN TRADE FACTS IN SEARCH OF BETTER THEORY

The Rise of Knowledge-Intensive Trade

International trade, like peoples' living standards, reflects the advance of human knowledge. The goods and services that nations trade, like peoples' careers, embody more and more productive human knowledge. Figure 5.1 shows this trend indirectly, by tracing the shares of different kinds of products in world merchandise exports over a recent 34-year span.[1] From 1963 to 1987 world trade drifted toward engineering products—autos, planes, scientific instruments, electronic goods, and other machinery and equipment. The rise in their share from 27 percent to 39 percent is a rise in *knowledge-intensive sectors*—the sectors of the economy making the heaviest use of

---

[1] The total value of all countries' exports can be called "world trade" because it should match the total value of all countries' imports. In practice, official data miss many exports, implying that the world as a whole is a net importer of merchandise. *Merchandise,* here and in Figure 5.1, refers to visible goods only, not services. For more on the measurement of trade flows, see Chapter 14.

FIGURE 5.1   The Rise of Engineering Products and other Manufactures as a Share of World Trade, 1963–1987.

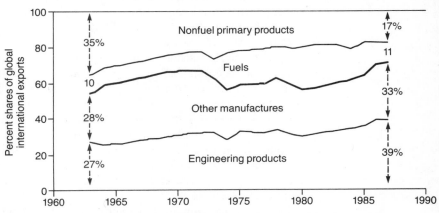

Source: General Agreement on Tariffs and Trade, *International Trade,* annually.

knowledge and of the scientists and technicians that create and apply it. The next most knowledge-intensive of the four categories shown here also rose as a share of world trade: "other manufactures" (e.g., textiles, clothing, and processed foods) advanced slightly from 28 percent in 1963 to 33 percent in 1987. The trend has been steadily toward manufacturers, especially those engineering products, despite brief drops in their trade shares during the oil crises of 1973–74 and 1979–80, when a greater share of world trade had to go to paying higher fuel bills.

How can we explain the move toward knowledge-based trade, and who gains or loses from it? To answer such questions, we must pay more attention to what is special about how knowledge becomes translated into traded commodities. The process that creates and applies knowledge involves schooling, science, research and development (R&D), and the conversion of knowledge into property rights and monopolies (e.g., through patents). It is a process that cannot necessarily be trusted to the unregulated marketplace, and it cannot necessarily be explained through our standard model of market competition. In what follows we must explore both the "externalities" of knowledge, their public-goods quality, and the problem of monopolies on knowledge.

Convergence among Industrial Countries

Comparative advantage in modern knowledge-intensive products is more dynamic, and less reliable, than comparative advantage in natural resource products like cocoa or lumber or oil. Some nations can acquire new knowledge faster than other nations, and become exporters of goods they previously imported. The dominant competitive event of the last quarter-century has been Japan's rise to export leadership, overtaking the United States in knowledge-intensive (and capital-intensive) product trade. Trade theory must try to predict when leadership will change and when it will not.

Part of the explanation for changes in knowledge-industry leadership fits easily into the Heckscher-Ohlin theory. America's loss of comparative advantage in knowledge-intensive exports seems to have followed a slower growth in human skills, per member of the labor force, in America than in other countries. Chapter 2 noted that between 1963 and 1984 the United States had the slowest growth rates for R&D scientists and for all skilled labor among major industrial countries. There are signs that the trend might continue.[2] Whatever its causes, the trend fits Hechscher-Ohlin: as a country falls back in its human-skills endowment, the H-O theory would predict that it will lose comparative advantage in skills-intensive (i.e., knowledge-intensive) products.

Part of the explanation is less convenient for standard theories, however. The rise of Japan's comparative advantage in knowledge-intensive, especially "high-tech," exports did not simply follow the changes in its relative skills. Rather, comparative advantage *preceded* the catch-up in human skills and may have been deliberately fostered by far-sighted government policy. A study by Peter Heller (1976), in the spirit of the factor-content studies of Chapter 4, found that Japan began developing comparative advantages in capital-intensive high-tech products already in the 1950s and 1960s, when it was still a labor-abundant, capital-poor nation relative to its top trading partners. The government of Japan explicitly encouraged the strategy of reaching ahead of current factor endowments to plan on a future Japan that would be rich in capital and skills, not labor as such. Miyohei Shinohara,

---

[2] To understand the sources and likely future trends in human skills, it helps to watch trends in schooling and educational test scores. Trends in educational attainment measures, such as school attendance or median years of schooling for young adults, do not show the United States falling behind. On these measures, the United States has advanced just as fast as other industrial countries, including Japan, since the 1950s.

More ominous is the trend in test scores reflecting on the quality of knowledge for given years of schooling. Between 1967 and 1980, the achievement test scores of U.S. twelfth-grade students dropped about 1.25 grade-year equivalents, though much of the lost ground was regained later in the 1980s. The decline showed up in compulsory tests (e.g., the Iowa test), and not just in tests like the college boards, where a rise in the test-taking share could have lowered average scores. Its effect on subsequent adult productivity may have accounted for a large share of the slowdown in U.S. productivity growth (Bishop 1988). By the mid-1980s U.S. twelfth-graders scored lower on standardized math tests than the industrial-country norm, and much lower than Japanese students (Morici 1988, p. 39, citing the Council on Competitiveness). The differences seem to arise somewhere between third grade and twelfth grade, and may relate to the shortness of the U.S. school year. Given these results and other supporting clues, it is no longer valid to speak of the United States as *the* leader in education and in economically relevant knowledge.

former head of the Economics Section of Japan's Economic Planning Agency, described Japan's strategy for dynamic comparative advantage as an improvement over standard theories:

> In modern economics it has been considered that in an economy of abundant labor and scarce capital, the development of labor-intensive production methods would naturally bring about a rational allocation of resources. . . . It has also been assumed that any measures taken contrary to this theorem would be going against economic principles, thus distorting resource allocation.
>
> If this reasoning is correct, the industrial policies adopted by MITI [Japan's Ministry of International Trade and Industry] in the mid-1950s were wrong. Ironically, however, Japan's industrial policies achieved unprecedented success by going against modern economic theory.
>
> The problem of classical thinking undeniably lies in the fact that it is essentially 'static' and does not take into account the possibility of a dynamic change in the comparative advantage of industries over a coming 10- or 20-year period. To take the place of such a traditional theory, a new policy concept needs to be developed to deal with the possibility of intertemporal dynamic development.

It may be that a consistent policy strategy can create a whole new comparative advantage in high-technology and capital-intensive products. But how? And can any nation do it? Answering such questions again requires thinking about what might be the special attributes of modern industrial sectors.

The Rise of Intra-Industry Trade

By itself, the convergence in industrial nations' human resources per capita would lead us to expect less and less trade among the industrial countries. If they are becoming more similar in their relative skills, the Heckscher-Ohlin theory would predict less and less basis for international trade. In fact, we observe the opposite. Trade is growing fastest among the industrial countries. From 1963 through 1987, trade between industrial nations rose from 45 percent to 55 percent of all world trade.

To add to the puzzle, trade has grown fastest *within* industrial categories, turning economists' attention to the phenomenon of **intra-industrial trade.** Economists coined this term in the 1970s to describe two-way trade within industries (e.g., trading Hondas for Volkswagens, French wines for Italian wines, Canadian skis for Swiss skis, or Boeing planes for Airbus planes). To describe the phenomenon more carefully, specialists measure intra-industry trade for a nation (or region) as the opposite of inter-industry trade:

$$\frac{\text{Trade between industries as a share of all trade}} {} = \frac{\text{Sum of the nation's trade imbalances}}{\text{Sum of its trade flows}} = \frac{\text{Sum of } |X\text{'s} - M\text{'s}|}{\text{Sum of } X\text{'s} + M\text{'s}}$$

$$\frac{\text{Intra-industry trade (IIT) share}}{} = \frac{100\% \text{ minus trade between industries}}{} = \frac{\text{Sum of } |X\text{'s} - M\text{'s}|}{\text{Sum of } X\text{'s} + M\text{'s}}$$

FIGURE 5.2   Intra-Industry Trade (IIT) as a Share of All Trade, for 62 Countries, 1978

Group of Countries	GNP Per Capita ($)	Intra-Industry Trade as a Percent Share of All Trade
15 low-income countries	261	21.4
18 middle-income countries	1273	25.7
6 newly industrializing countries (NICs)	1466	36.6
23 high-income countries	7722	60.3
All 62 countries	2909	55.7

Sources: O. Havrylyshyn and E. Civan (1983, p. 118) for IIT; World Bank, *World Development Report 1980* for GNP per capita.

The low-income countries are those with GNP per capita below $600, and the high-income countries are those with GNP per capita above $2,400. The six NICs are Brazil, Mexico, Hong Kong, Singapore, South Korea, and Taiwan.

Every sum here is a sum over the industrial sectors given in a nation's official trade data. The IIT share is a number between zero and 100 percent. If all trade were between industries, like the trade of wheat for cloth in Chapters 2–4, then for each sector either exports *(X)* or imports *(M)* would be zero. In this extreme case, the top ratio is one, and the IIT share is therefore zero, as it should be. If all trade were intra-industry trade, trade would balance for every industry *(X = M* every time). In this extreme case, the top ratio is zero and the IIT share is one (100 percent).

Specialists find clues to the nature of modern trade in their measures of IIT. Figure 5.2 reveals that IIT is more characteristic of high-income industrial countries. In Europe, North America, and Japan, IIT accounts for more than 60 percent of all trade, whereas it is only 21 to 26 percent in low- and middle-income countries that are not rapidly industrializing. This snapshot taken in 1978 suggests that IIT may grow throughout the world as incomes rise and industrialization spreads. Economists have also found that IIT is more prevalent when trade barriers and transport costs are low, and within free-trade blocs like the European Community, other things equal. Each of these associations again warns us to expect intra-industry trade to become gradually more dominant, since trade barriers and transport costs are dropping, especially within the free-trade blocks.

Intra-industry seems to call for a different kind of analysis from the standard trade models of Chapters 2–4. Economists have found that the two-way trade within each modern industry is an exchange of slightly different goods that use the same mixtures of those broad factors of production—unskilled labor, versus skilled labor, versus capital versus natural-resource endowments. The Heckscher-Ohlin theory seems to have little to say here. Why should trade involve swapping goods with the same factor intensities? The suspicion that we need a different kind of analysis gains further support from another finding of the studies of intra-industry trade: IIT is significantly more prevalent in industries with economies of scale and in industries dominanted by a few large firms. The link to economies of scale and to concentration warns that we need to deal with cases of imperfect competition (e.g., monopoly, monopolistic competition, or oligopoly), and not just assume atomistic competition, as was assumed in Chapters 2 through 4.

To summarize this section, we have gathered three kinds of clues suggesting a need for new kinds of trade theory:

- The rise of trade in knowledge-intensive products hints that trade theory needs to have a closer look at the development of new knowledge, with its characteristic potential for monopoly and economies of large scale.
- Comparative advantage in knowledge-intensive industries is dynamic. Leadership, which shifted toward the United States earlier during this century, has shifted to Japan, though Japan too faces competitive threats from newcomers. Part of this dynamic can be explained in terms of differences in the rate of knowledge buildup, the sort of factor-endowment growth that the Heckscher-Ohlin theory has already featured. But there are strong hints that new strength in knowledge-intensive industries has been, and can again be, shaped in advance by far-sighted government policy.
- Even though the leading industrial nations have become increasingly similar in their factor endowments, their trade consists more and more of intra-industry trade (IIT) among themselves. Why?

Let us turn to some preliminary answers offered by recent theories of modern industrial trade.

THE DEMAND SIDE: PART OF THE STORY

Part of the rise of knowledge-intensive trade and of IIT is explained by a simple two-part formula: income growth shifts demand toward luxuries, and knowledge-intensive goods and product variety are both luxuries.

Average incomes have kept growing since World War II, despite depressions like the oil shocks of 1974–75 and 1979–80 and the brief depression of 1982. From 1965 through 1986, for example, GNP per capita grew 2.8 percent a year on the average for developing countries, and 2.3 percent a year on the average for the industrial market economies. If these rates continue, average incomes will double every 25 years in the Third World as a whole, and every 30 years in the industrialized nations. Economists have long known that income growth shifts demands from some kinds of goods toward others. To investigate the effects of income growth on demand, they measure the income elasticity of demand:

$$\eta = \frac{\text{Income elasticity}}{\text{of demand for a good}} = \frac{\text{The percent change in demand for that good}}{\text{The percent change in income causing it}}$$

Goods for which $\eta > 1$ are called **luxuries.** As income rises by, say, 10 percent, the demand for luxuries goes up by more than 10 percent. The richer the consumers, the greater the share of their budget devoted to luxuries (holding many other things equal). Goods for which $\eta < 1$ are called **staples.** A 10-percent rise in income raises the demand for them by less than 10 percent. The richer the consumers, the lower the share of their budgets devoted to staples (other things again being equal). Food is a staple, and there are especially low income elasticities for such staples as grains.[3] The demand for housing is near the margin, with η near one, so that the share of expenditures devoted to housing changes little.

Knowledge-intensive goods, like the engineering products featured in Figure 5.1, are luxuries. World income growth has been pushing demand toward luxuries for at least a century, and the trend is sure to continue. An easy part of the explanation for a shift toward knowledge-intensive products in world trade is simply that these products are destined to rise as a share of overall consumption. So unless there is an even stronger antitrade bias in the way production grows, we should expect more international trade in knowledge-intensive products.

Another luxury is product variety. The higher the incomes of consumers, the greater the proliferation of near-substitute varieties of goods and services. Higher incomes make it possible to value variety for its own sake. Thus, affluent people vary their choices of wines, beers, automobiles, music, clothing, travel experiences, and so on. An immediate consequence is two-way trade, or IIT. Even if all nations had the same factor endowments and same income level, the higher that common income level, the more they would buy each others' versions of similar product so that each nation can have variety in its consumption. Thus IIT, like the rise of knowledge-intensive trade, can be based partly on a rising demand for luxuries.

Yet demand effects cannot be the whole story. If they were, the shift toward luxuries would raise their relative price forever. To draw on a point that will be made in Chapter 12, it is not really true that luxury goods have had strongly rising price trends over the long run. We therefore have a minor puzzle: how can demand shift toward luxuries without their rising much, if at all, in relative price?

ECONOMIES-OF-SCALE THEORIES OF MODERN TRADE

The modern knowledge-intensive sectors can expland faster than the rest of the economy without rising in relative price partly because of economies

---

[3] The fact that food is a staple is known as Engel's Law. It plays an important role in Chapters 12 and 13.

of scale. Economists define **economies of scale** as the percent reduction in average costs achieved by expanding all inputs by a given percentage. Or, in a related use of the term, they say that economies of scale exist whenever a balanced expansion of all inputs causes a drop in average costs.[4] Such economies are hard to measure precisely, but we can use a simple survival test to decide where they exist. Industries in which only very large firms or plants survive are ones probably characterized by economies of scale. This is true of many capital-intensive sectors, including some that are also knowledge-intensive, such as aircraft manufacture. When demand for such products rises (e.g., due to rising incomes), their prices can actually decline. Paul Krugman, Elhanan Helpman, and others have used different models with economies of scale to broaden our view of the effects of opening or expanding trade. We now turn to two key variants, one with external economies in highly competitive markets, and one with that is called monopolistic competition. There are also pure-monopoly variants, but these are not discussed until Chapter 8 (on dumping) and Chapter 10 (on strategic trade policy).

External Economies

The first kind of economies of scale is external to each firm but internal to the industry. In knowledge-intensive industries, new knowledge spills over from firm to firm either as direct information or as knowledge carried by skilled workers. The more contact any one firm has with others in the same industry, the greater the transmission of knowledge among them, as they hear about each other's techniques and as skilled labor migrates from firm to firm. One example is New York's historic garment district, where firms seem to gain from being near their competitors. Another is California's Silicon Valley, in which semiconductor producers and computer industries swap ideas, workers, and even factories at a rapid rate.

To analyze such gains from agglomerating together, economists define **external economies** as productivity gains and cost reductions that an individual firm reaps from the expansion of *other* firms in the same industry. The more a whole industry expands its scale of production, the more contact each firm has with others, and the lower each firm's costs fall. In other words, external economies mean that while each firm's average and marginal costs may be raised by expanding its own output, they are lowered by expanding the output of its competitors in the same industry.

When an expansion of the industry lowers costs for each firm, new export opportunities have a more dramatic effect than we would otherwise expect. Figure 5.3 imagines that a national semiconductor (computer-chip-unit) indus-

---

[4] Alternatively, such a situation is said to be one in which there exist "increasing returns to scale."

FIGURE 5.3   External Economies Magnify an Expansion in a Competitive Industry

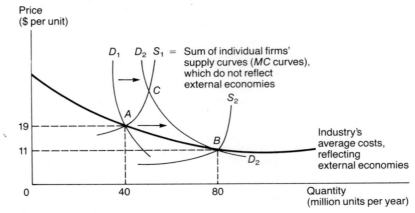

Results:

- In industries that can reap external economies (e.g., knowledge spillovers from firm to firm), a rise in demand triggers a great expansion of supply and even lowers costs and price.
- Therefore expanding trade brings gains to all consumers, home-country and foreign, as well as to the exporting producers.
- Corollary: Among nations having the same initial factor endowments, cost curves and demand curves, whichever nation moved first to open its export market would capture a comparative advantage in this product.

try is competitive, but characterized by economies of scale. There is an initial equilibrium at Point *A*, with many firms competing to sell 40 million units at $19 a unit. Here the usual short-run supply and demand curves intersect in the usual way. What is new in the diagram is the coexistence of the upward-sloping supply curve S_1 with the downward-sloping average cost curve. The upward-sloping supply curve is the sum of small individual firms' views of the market. Each firm operates at given levels of industry production, which it cannot affect very much. It reacts to a change in price according to its own upward-sloping supply curve, and the sum of these supply curves is shown as S_1.

The industry's downward-sloping average cost curve comes into play as soon as demand shifts. To bring out points about international trade, let us imagine that opening up a new export market shifts demand from D_1 to D_2. Each firm would respond to the stronger demand by raising output. If each firm were acting alone and affected only itself, the extra demand would push us up the supply curve S_1 to a point like Point *C*. Yet the new export business raises the whole industry's output and employment, bringing each producer into more contact with the others. There is more exchange of useful information, which raises productivity and cuts costs throughout the industry. This means, in effect, a sustained rightward movement of the industry supply curve. To portray the cost-cutting more conveniently than with multiple shifts of the supply curve, Figure 5.3 shows the average cost curve reflecting external economies, a curve that could in principle be measured from economic behavior. The external economies are likely to be exhausted at some high rate of output, so that the process of expansion will come to an end. As Figure 5.3 is drawn, we imagine that demand and supply expansion catch up with each other at Point *B*, a new equilibrium.

Comparing the new and old equilibria, we can judge who gains and who loses from the opening of trade for an industry with external economies. Everybody whose stake can be seen in Figure 5.3 is a gainer. The semiconductor firms themselves reap producers' surpluses above the now-lower marginal cost curve (= supply curve) S_2, though entry of new firms will limit such gains and leave the average firm with price equal to average cost. Foreign competitors, not pictured but netted out in drawing the D_2 demand curve, lose because of the new competition from imported semiconductors. The new foreign buyers, whose demand is the difference between D_1 and D_2, can buy from these suppliers for the first time, so apparently they gain. In fact, even the semiconductor buyers in the exporting country benefit from a lower price, thanks to the external economies sparked by the expansion. Here is a definite contrast to the standard case (e.g., Figure 3.1), where the buyers suffer from a price rise on goods that can suddenly be exported.[5]

How can the existence of external economies help us explain comparative advantage? How does it improve over the modest empirical success of the Heckscher-Ohlin theory? We can see in Figure 5.3 that some country gained new access to export markets and that external economies magnified its success. But which country is likely to be the new exporter when a new market opens up somewhere in the world? The external-economies model passes over this issue. It says that whichever country is favored by historical luck or a far-sighted government's initial push will become a seller of semiconductors to the world. The first country to set the new markets and supply them captures a big expansion of exports and production and lowers its

---

[5] With external economies, it is at least possible to get a result that is a paradoxical extreme case of "immiserizing growth": expanding foreign export demand for this country's semiconductors could actually make this country worse off!

To see how, imagine three things about Figure 5.3. First, imagine that our "home" demand D_1 is really an old, established export demand, with D_2 playing the role of a new export demand that has just opened up. Second, redraw the diagram with the average cost curve sloping steeply downward from Point *A* to Point *B*. Third, draw the supply curve S_2 very flat (elastic) to the left of Point *B*, unlike the more vertical S_1. In this situation, having the new export market open up makes our semiconductor industry cut its costs and its price so much that we now get a much worse (lower) price on our old export business (the D_1 curve). The terms-of-trade loss on the old business can outweigh the gain of producer surplus on the new, leaving us worse off because the world wanted more of our product.

costs. The outcome is analogous to the production of pearls. Which oysters produce pearls depends on either luck or outside human intervention. An oyster gets its pearl either from the accidental deposit of a grain of sand or from a human's introducing a grain of sand in order to cultivate a pearl. The external economies case is one in which a lasting comparative advantage is acquired from luck or policy, even if there is no difference in nations' initial comparative advantages.

The key role of historical luck or of initial policy in fact transcends the opening-of-trade example we have just considered. The same point emerges whatever the cause of the expansion of demand. Figure 5.3 need not refer to the initial opening of trade, though that is a main focus here in Part One. It could also tell a story of how a particular region developed a comparative advantage by having the luck or foresight to be the first to meet the rising demand for a knowledge-intensive luxury good, without reference to international trade.

Economies of Scale with Monopolistic Competition

Economies of scale can also be internal to the firm. In the case of **internal economies,** expanding *the firm's own* scale of production raises its productivity and cuts its average cost. This attribute has long been observed in capital-intensive, and often knowledge-intensive, industries like steel, electrical power, and the manufacture of transport equipment (e.g., planes, trains, and automobiles). To survive in such an industry, a firm must produce above a certain minimum scale. How many firms can do that depends on how the *maximum* efficient scale compares to the size of the market. In many industries, internal economies are such a strong force that a single firm, or even a single plant, can capture more than half the total demand.

If the size of the market does not make room for many firms to produce above their minimum efficient scale of production, we should not expect atomistic competition among the many. Industries that have internal economies therefore tend to be industries with imperfect competition of some form. The forms featured in microeconomic theory are monopolistic competition, oligopoly, and pure monopoly. We shall look at pure monopoly in Chapters 8 and 10. Let us turn to the case of monopolistic competition here, first in a closed economy and next in an economy open to trade.

To set the stage for the effects of more trade under monopolistic competition, we turn first to monopolistic competition within a closed national economy, using a model pioneered by Edward Chamberlin in the 1930s. As its hybrid name suggests, **monopolistic competition** is somewhat like monopoly and somewhat like competition. It is like monopoly in that the individual firm has some control over the price it charges, and that firm can maximize profits by producing less than it would under perfect competition. Yet, it is like competition in that the entry and exit of other firms in

FIGURE 5.4   A Monopolistic-Competitive Firm in a National Market, before Export Markets Open

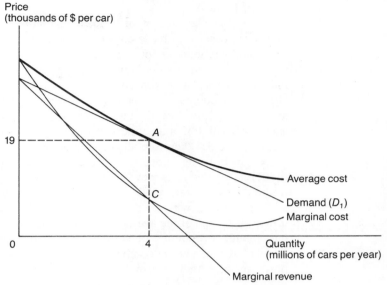

the industry eventually pushes each firm toward zero pure profit. Two market features seem to breed such a hybrid condition. One is the proliferation of differentiated products. When each firm in an industry produces a unique good that consumers consider a partial substitute for other goods in the same industry, the firm faces an intermediate kind of competition. It has a monopoly on its own product. But its product competes so closely with other products that it cannot extract pure profits above all costs, at least not for very long. The other condition breeding monopolistic competition is internal economies of scale, which keep out small firms and prevent perfect competition.

Figure 5.4 imagines a firm, says Honda, facing monopolistic competition in Japan's national market for subcompact cars. Like a monopolist, Honda does not expand its production out to the point where marginal cost rises to meet price on the demand curve at the far right side of the diagram. Rather the firm stops its production at an earlier point, as a monopolist would, because it is aware that expanding its own production and sales requires lowering price, which eats into its total revenue. It will only expand its product out to a point where the marginal revenue it gets from extra cars, taking the price cutting into account, falls to meet the marginal cost of making and selling them. That point, where profits are maximized and stop rising, is the output of 4 million cars a year, where marginal revenue equals marginal cost at point *C*. To get that many cars sold, it charges "what the traffic will bear," the price of $19,000 dictated by the demand curve at Point *A*.

So far our description of Honda's situation sounds just like the pure monopoly case from basic courses in microeconomics. Honda could indeed be a pure monopolist for a while, after first entering a market where its unique product had some advantages. After a while, though, there will be indirect competition from competing cars even if they are not identical to Honda's subcompact car. Honda may continue to find its maximum profits at optimal points like *C,* but eventually the entry of new firms into the subcompact automobile industry will drive Honda's pure profits down to zero. Figure 5.4 therefore shows an equilibrium in which the demand curve is kept from being above the average cost curve by the entry, or even just the threat of entry, of new competing firms. At point *A*, with output at 4 million cars a year, price just equals, and cannot exceed, average cost, leaving the firm with no pure profits.[6] Point *A*'s equilibrium is still on the downward slope of the average cost curve, though, because the auto industry has enough economies of scale to make small firms unprofitable, giving Honda less than perfect competition. This departure from perfect competition plays an important role in shaping the effects of foreign trade on such an industry.

The Effects of New Trade under Monopolistic Competition

If new trade opportunities open up for a monopolistic competitor, how will it behave? Who will gain, and who will lose? Figure 5.5 sketches an answer. Suppose that previously closed export markets opened up for Honda, say in Eastern Europe or the United States. There would be a new demand curve out to the right of the old demand curve D_1. At first, the new demand would probably allow Honda monopoly profits. Eventually, though, monopolistic competition would take its toll. Lured by Honda's monopoly profits, new firms would enter with partial-substitute car models, pushing the demand for Honda's back down and to the left. The process of new entry would continue until the price of a Honda no longer exceeded its average cost (i.e., Honda no longer made pure profits). Figure 5.5 has economized on

---

[6] One might wonder now we know that the equilibrium at Point *A* (price = average cost) occurs at exactly the same output as the optimization at Point *C* (marginal revenue = marginal cost), as drawn in Figure 5.4. One can use differential calculus to prove that both outputs must be the same. At Point *A* we know not only that price equals average cost, but also that the demand curve and the average cost curve are tangent to each other. These two pieces of information are enough to prove that marginal cost must equal marginal revenue at that same output.

FIGURE 5.5   The Same Monopolistic Competitor in an Automobile Market after Opening Trade

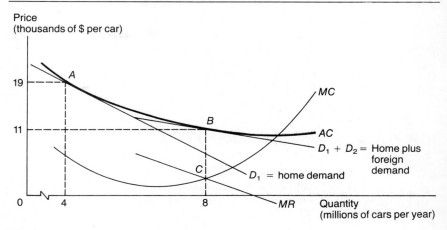

Results:

- Under monopolistic competition, as with external economies, opening an export market leads firms like this one to lower home-country prices.
- The gains from opening trade go to consumers in both countries, while export-country producers like this firm gain only temporarily, until the entry of new firms makes price = average cost again at B.

geometry by drawing only the start and finish of this competition. It compares the initial Point A (the same as Point A in Figure 5.4) only with the final equilibrium at Point B. Because of other firms' responses, Honda finds its price equal to average cost, as mentioned. The tangency of the average cost curve and the demand curve $(D_1 + D_2)$ at Point B shows that Honda could not do any better at any other level of output. The net result of opening up the new export market is that output is greater and price lower at Point B.

The gains from the opening of trade are curiously distributed. In this monopolistic-competition case, as with the external-economies case, consumers gain in both countries, thanks to economies of scale. In fact, Figure 5.5 even implies that a producer like Honda does not gain at all so that the consumers get all the gains. In long-run equilibrium, this may be so. We would certainly expect, though, that in the long transition between A and B, Honda would earn some pure profits before the entry of new competitors pushed those profits back to zero.

What was the basis for Honda's new comparative advantage in exporting autos? At first glance, one might think the economies of scale were the key. Yet that downward slope of the average-cost curve was presumably not special to Honda. The internal economies presumably stem from engineering realities common to the whole auto industry. Any other firm could have faced a similar downward slope in its average-cost curve. So the real key to Honda's capturing export markets was only that those markets happened to open up for Honda, due to either historical luck or government policy intervention. With internal economies and monopolistic competition as with external economies, economies of scale do not dictate each country's comparative advantage, but instead translate any given comparative advantage into lower prices and greater expansion of output and trade.

NEW PRODUCTS AND THE PRODUCT CYCLE

A different trade theory offers a dynamic theory of changes in comparative advantage in knowledge-intensive products.

Raymond Vernon and others have emphasized a *product cycle* through which *individual products* typically pass. It is analogous to the human life cycle. When the product is first invented (born) it must still be perfected. It needs advanced technological inputs and tends to do better when produced in the countries of its inventors and its initial customers—high-income countries usually, since most recent products are luxuries in the economist's sense. After a while, the product's design and production technology is worked out so that fresh knowledge plays less of a role in cutting costs. Once the product starts to become more standardized and familiar (mature), there is less reason to produce it in the country that has a comparative advantage in technology. The industry producing that product begins to migrate to other countries, countries that can easily apply the now-standard technology. Ultimately, its technology may become so embodied in purchasable equipment that it requires very little skill and migrates to developing countries that are abundant in cheap labor.

The trade patterns one might expect over the life cycle of a new product are illustrated in Figure 5.6. In the early stage of development with time measured along the horizontal axis, the innovation and production begin in, say, the United States (the invention may have occurred anywhere; what counts is the first commercial production). Soon, at t_0, the United States begins to export some of the new product to other industrial countries. Yet, after a lag these countries develop their own ability to produce the new good, perhaps with the help of subsidiaries set up abroad by U.S. producers. What makes this shift to production outside the United States possible is the assumed fact that the initial technological advantage of the United States erodes. This is a plausible assumption for many new manufactures, for which production technology becomes more standardized and learnable. Increasing imitation by other industrial countries makes them net exporters of the product, as at time t_1 in Figure 5.6. As the technology in this product line ages and becomes increasingly standardized, the United

FIGURE 5.6 How Trade Balances Might Evolve over the Product Cycle of a New Good

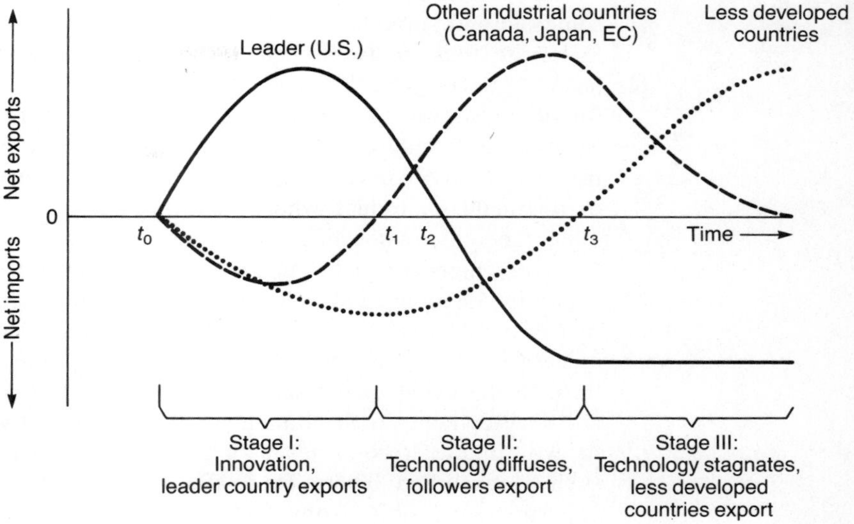

States loses its comparative advantage and becomes a net importer of this good (at t_2). Yet it is also reasonable to expect that the rest of the world can also catch up in time with the technological knowledge of Canada, Europe, and Japan in this aging product line. At time t_3, the product cycle enters its final phase as far as trade is concerned, with the product being exported from the rest of the world (for example, from less developed countries) to the United States and the other higher-income countries. What makes the mature product settle in less developed countries is the fact that sooner or later their wage-rate advantage will outweigh the dwindling gap in knowledge and make this product line a comparative-advantage export item for less developed countries.

What gains and losses from international trade does the product-cycle theory predict? The theory is vague on this subject, perhaps because Vernon was more interested in predicting the dynamic of comparative advantage than in weighing how welfare is affected by the technological life cycle. Compared with no trade at all, trade that follows the product cycle probably brings gains to all sides. It is not likely to bring immiserizing growth. To get immiserizing growth like that shown in Chapter 4, we would have to have an expansion in trade that already existed. But to weigh the welfare effects of trade in a new product, one must compare it with no trade at all in that product. Therefore having new-product trade follow the product cycle cannot spoil any country's terms of trade (there was no previous export price to lower).

The product-cycle hypothesis does fit the experience of many industries, some old and some new. Industries launched before World War I, such as factory textiles, footwear, leather goods, rubber products, and paper, also have migrated to the Third World, where they are likely to be concentrated for the foreseeable future. Hand-held calculators were pioneered in the United States with Texas Instruments leading the way in 1972 and Hewlett-Packard in 1973. Soon Sharp and the other Japanese consumer electronic firms began to dominate a product whose characteristics had begun to stabilize. By 1988 the only major line still produced within the United States was a relatively high-priced calculator made by Hewlett Packard at its plant in Corvallis, Oregon. Studies have found the same migration-with-standardization in petrochemicals, office machinery, and semiconductors.

Yet there is no iron law dictating that every product must pass irreversibly through the cycle. What the hypothesis says is that *when and if* research and development stop becoming crucial to comparative advantage, the industry will migrate to countries having a comparative advantage in other inputs, such as unskilled labor. Thus, the Third World *might* become the area exporting automobiles someday, but it also might end up at an even greater disadvantage in auto production if that industry gets a new wave of high-tech breakthroughs (and, unlike the human life cycle, actually becomes technologically "younger" again).

SUMMARY: HOW DOES TRADE REALLY WORK?

This chapter examined two kinds of theories that have broadened our answers to two sides of the question, How does trade really work? The two theories are (1) variations on the economies-of-scale theory, and (2) the product-cycle theory. They help us to answer the questions, What forces best predict nations' comparative advantage? and, Who gains from trade? Their predictive strength relates to the kind of modern trade most closely tied to new knowledge and new technology.

Increasingly, we live in a world of trade in knowledge-intensive products, a world in which comparative advantage is dynamic and leadership is increasingly shared among many industrial countries with similar incomes and similar factor endowments. The similarity of the industrial economies would suggest that there is less reason for trade among them. Yet we observe the opposite. Trade has not declined as a share of world product. A greater and greater share of world trade consists of **intra-industry trade (IIT),** or two-way trade within industrial categories. A challenge for trade theory is to explain what is special about knowledge-intensive trade, why we have so much IIT, and whether the standard model's conclusions about the gains from trade still hold in a world of IIT in knowledge-intensive goods.

Part of the reason we have so much intra-industry trade in modern knowledge-intensive products is that they are luxuries in a prospering world. Raising per-capita incomes causes an even faster rise in the demand for luxuries. Yet by itself, a shift of demand toward luxuries would raise their prices, something that is not usually observed. To put the rise of such trade into proper perspective, we need to think of special features on the producers' side of the same expanding markets.

Economies of scale and imperfect competition help to explain the rise of modern knowledge-intensive trade and intra-industry trade. Knowledge-intensive trade is given a boost by the fact that such products often show external economies, which convert a rise in demand into a magnified expansion of output and even a drop in price. Intra-industry trade in differentiated products is also easier to understand and portray when one recognizes that many such products are subject to economies of scale and monopolistic competition. Yet economies of scale and imperfect competition do not directly predict which countries will export which goods. Instead, they say that historical luck and government policy determine which countries will be the first to capitalize on economies of scale.

Thinking about economies of scale and imperfect competition also reinforces our appreciation of the gains from trade. It does not contradict the main welfare conclusions of the standard competitive-market analysis of Chapters 2 through 4. Rather, it broadens the set of conditions under which we can see the world gains from trade, with some changes in who receives those gains. Figure 5.7 gives a quick summary of the welfare gains and losses in four kinds of trade, the standard competitive trade of Chapters 2 through 4, two kinds of trade analyzed in this chapter, and an export-monopoly situation to be explored in Chapter 10. Relative to standard competitive trade, this chapter's external economies case pushes export-country consumers over to the winner's side. The monopolistic-competition case also gives them gains, while predicting only temporary gains for the monopolistically competitive exporters themselves. In all cases, each nation gains as a whole, as does the world.

Raymond Vernon's **product-cycle hypothesis** predicts that as the technology of a product becomes more standardized and static, labor costs become a more important basis for comparative advantage than do research and development. The world's production of this good migrates toward lower-income, lower-wage countries. Such links between trade and technology can be incorporated into the Heckscher-Ohlin framework emphasizing factor endowments, though only when one defines all specific technological advantages as relative endowments of knowledge and skills. The product-cycle hypothesis does not directly say who gains and who loses from opening trade in the new product, but implies that both sides gain.

Where then does the theory of trade patterns stand?

The standard models of Chapters 2–4, complete with both demand and supply sides, has the virtue of breadth. We can use it to predict most

FIGURE 5.7   Summary of Gains and Losses from Opening Up Trade in Four Cases.

Kind of Trade: Group:	Chapters 2–4 Standard Competition	This Chapter External Economies	This Chapter Monopolistic Competition	Chapter 10 Export Monopoly†
Exporting country	Gain	Gain	Gain	Gain
Export producers	Gain	Gain	Temporary gain*	Gain
Export consumers	Lose	Gain	Gain	Depends‡
Importing country	Gain	Gain	Gain	Gain
Import-competing producers	Lose	Lose	Lose	Lose
Import consumers	Gain	Gain	Gain	Gain
Whole World	Gain	Gain	Gain	Gain

* The gain is eventually bid down to zero by the entry of new firms into the industry. While the usual textbook presentations have been followed here, we should note that producers' profits are equally temporary in the pure competition case, again due to entry of new firms. In both cases, gains also tend to be passed forward to consumers, and back to suppliers of inputs in the form of higher prices for their services.
† See the private leadership case in Figure 10.7.
‡ In the constant-marginal-cost case of Chapters 8 and 10, consumers in the exporting country are unaffected by the opening of the new export market. If marginal costs declined (rose) with output, consumers in the exporting country would gain (lose from the opening of an export market.

trade patterns correctly, as long as we equip it with a long list of explanatory variables. Its weakness lies in that same breadth, that same ability to expand to explain any case: the problem is that we *need* to equip it with a long list of explanatory variables in order to explain all the real-world trade patterns. That gets cumbersome. For example, to explain why Toyota Corporation developed a comparative advantage in exporting automobiles to the whole world, one has to start with the personal entrepreneurial vision of Eishi Toyoda and call it a "factor endowment" of Toyota Corporation and of Japan. This is a valid way to use our standard model in explaining Toyota's success, but it does not give us any predictive power, any ability to forecast.

The Heckscher-Ohlin variant of the standard model makes the stronger assertion that the way to explain who exports what to whom is to look at factor proportions alone, concentrating on a few main factors of production. That has the scientific virtue of giving more testable and falsifiable predictions than the broadest standard model (of which it is a special case). But, as we saw in Chapter 2, the tests of the Heckscher-Ohlin model give it only a middling grade. It predicts the correct direction of trade better than a coin-flip, but only modestly better.

Our ability to predict (explain) trade patterns remains just as modest after we have added the economies-to-scale model and the product-cycle model. The economies-of-scale model helps describe the mechanism of trade in knowledge-intensive sectors, and adds an interesting twist about who gains from trade, but it does not identify a new source of comparative advantage. Rather, it says that which country reaps the economies of scale available to many countries depends on historical luck and perhaps on early government policy. The product-cycle model is more concrete about the sources of comparative advantage, but is useful only for products that actually pass through such a cycle of sudden breakthrough and gradual technological stagnation.

The most promising direction for improving the predictive power of our trade theories lies in the direction of (1) developing a better theory of how new technologies, and new knowledge in general, arise and (2) giving the theory an historical dynamic, so that we can be more systematic about how the past determines the accumulation of new knowledge.

SUGGESTED READING

Intra-industry trade is measured and interpreted in Grubel and Lloyd (1975), Tharakan (1983), Greenaway and Tharakan (1986), and Greenaway and Milner (1988).

The economies-of-scale and imperfect-competition models of trade were launched independently by Dixit and Norman (1980), Krugman (1979), and Lancaster (1980). A readable semitechnical catalogue of the many imperfect-competition variations and their policy implications is Helpman and Krugman (1989).

The product-cycle hypothesis of trade is put forth in Vernon (1966) and tested in many works, including Keesing (1967), Gruber, Mehta and Vernon (1967), Hufbauer (1970), and Stern and Maskus (1981). Doubts are voiced by Vernon himself (1979).

When you feel you are nearing mastery of the theoretical material in Chapters 2–5, give yourself a test by looking at the first 10 paradoxes in Magee (1979). First look at Magee's listing of the paradoxes on his pp. 92–93 and try to prove them before looking at the answers.

QUESTIONS FOR REVIEW

1. The measurement of intra-industry trade can be understood more firmly with a numerical example. Consider the "North-South" trade between the industrial countries and the rest of the world (developing countries plus Eastern bloc) in 1987, which looked something like this:

	Billions of Dollars	
Product Category	*Exports* (X) *from the Industrial Area to the Rest of the World*	*Imports* (M) *into the Industrial Area from the Rest of the World*
Primary products	67	209
Manufactures, etc.	341	199
	408	408

Use the formula in the text to compute the ITT trade share from the X's and M's.

> Answer: For primary products, $|X - M| = 142$ and $X + M = 276$. For manufactures, etc., $|X - M| = 142$ again, because we have only two product categories, and $X + M = 540$. So the overall share of in*ter*-industry trade is $(142 + 142)/(276 + 540)$, or 34.8 percent. That leaves 65.2 percent of this trade as in*tra*-industry trade (IIT).

2. Under perfect competition, in Chapters 2–4, opening trade generally brought net gains to both countries. Does the same result occur when production of a traded good is characterized by external economies? Does it occur with monopolistic competition?

3. To fit the material of this chapter together with the rest of Part One, review Figure 2.1, "A Guide to the Trade Theories of Part One," in Chapter 2.

4. If every new product goes through the product cycle, will the technological initiator (e.g., the United States or Japan) fall behind and develop chronic trade deficits?

5. Discussion question: why does the United States retain a comparative advantage in jet aircraft, yet is losing it in autos and possibly blue jeans?

Trade Policy

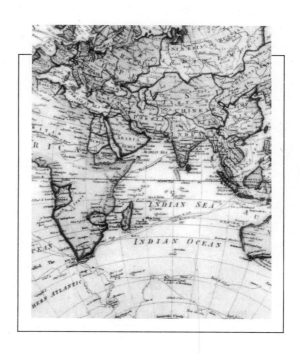

▼

The Basic Analysis of a Tariff

•

Before I built a wall I'd ask to know
What I was walling in or walling out,
And to whom I was like to give offense.

Robert Frost

A majority of economists has consistently favored letting nations trade freely with few tariffs or other barriers to trade. Indeed, economists have tended to be even more critical of trade barriers than have other groups in society, even though economists have taken great care to list the exceptional cases in which they feel trade barriers can be justified. Such agreement among economists is rare.

The presumption in favor of free trade is based primarily on a body of economic analysis demonstrating that there are usually net gains from freer trade both for nations and for the world. We caught an initial glimpse of this analysis in Chapters 3 and 4, which showed that free trade brings greater aggregate well-being than no trade. The main task of this chapter and the following chapters of Part Two is to compare free-trade policies with a much wider range of trade barriers, barriers that do not necessarily shut out all international trade. It is mainly on this more detailed analysis of trade policies that economists have based their view that free trade is generally better than partial restrictions on trade, with a list of exceptions. Once this analysis is understood, it is easier to understand what divides the majority of economists from groups calling for restrictions on trade.

The economic analysis of what is lost or gained by putting up barriers to international trade starts with a close look at the effects of the classic kind of trade barrier, a tariff on an imported good. This chapter and the next spell out who is likely to gain and who is likely to lose from a tariff, and they also explain the conditions under which a nation or the world

115

could end up better off from a tariff. Later chapters take up other kinds of barriers to trade.

A **tariff,** as the term is used in international trade, is a tax on importing a good or service into a country, collected by customs officials at the place of entry. Tariffs come in two main types. A **specific** tariff is stipulated as a money amount per physical unit of import, such as dollars per ton of steel bars or dollars per eight-cylinder two-door sports car. An **ad valorem** (on the value) tariff is a percentage of the estimated market value of the goods when they reach the importing country. We will talk mostly about ad valorem tariffs, though in this chapter it makes no difference.

A PREVIEW OF CONCLUSIONS

Our exploration of the pros and cons of a tariff will be detailed enough to warrant listing its main conclusions here at the outset. This chapter and the next will find that:

1. A tariff almost always lowers world well-being.
2. A tariff usually lowers the well-being of each nation, including the nation imposing the tariff.
3. As a general rule, whatever a tariff can do for the nation, something else can do better.
4. There are exceptions to the case for free trade:
   a. The "nationally optimal" tariff: When a nation can affect the prices at which it trades with foreigners, it can gain from its own tariff.
   b. "Second-best" arguments for a tariff: When other incurable distortions exist in the economy, imposing a tariff *may* be better than doing nothing.
   c. In a narrow range of cases with distortions specific to international trade itself, a tariff can be better than any other policy, and not just better than doing nothing.
5. A tariff absolutely *helps* groups tied closely to the production of import substitutes, even when the tariff is bad for the nation as a whole.

THE EFFECT OF A TARIFF ON CONSUMERS

Intuition would suggest that buyers of a good that is imported from abroad would be hurt by a tariff. The very fact that some of the good is imported means that consumers have found buying the foreign product to be a better bargain than confining their purchases to the domestic product. If the government charges a tariff on imports of this product, consumers will end up paying higher prices, buying less of the product, or both. The tariff, by taxing their imports, should make them worse off.

FIGURE 6.1   The Effect of a Tariff on Consumers

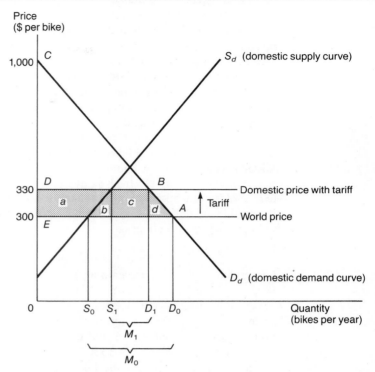

Shaded area = Cost of the tariff to consumers.

An import tariff of $30 raises the price consumers must pay for either imported or domestic bikes. This costs them the full $30 on every bike they continue to buy (D_1), plus smaller net enjoyment (area d) on bikes they would have bought at the lower tariff-free price but will not buy at the higher price including the tariff.

The demand and supply analysis of a tariff agrees with our intuition. It goes beyond intuition, though, by allowing us to quantify in dollars just how much a tariff costs consumers.

Figure 6.1 gives the basic demand-supply diagram of a tariff, here a tariff on bicycles.[1] If there were no tariff, bicycles would be imported freely

---

[1] The U.S. bicycle example is realistic. The industry has been petitioning for tariff protection. In 1985, for example, the Bicycle Manufacturers Association began lobbying Congress for an increase in bicycle tariffs from 5 to 11 percent (depending on wheel size) up to 19 percent, to stem import competition, which had risen to 42 percent of the U.S. market. The market struggle continues, with Cannondale and Trek, and some Schwinn bikes, still made in the United States.

at the world price of $300. Competition between foreign bikes and comparable domestic bikes would make the domestic bikes also settle at a price of $300. At this price consumers would buy S_0 bikes a year from domestic suppliers and would import M_0 bikes a year, buying $D_0 = S_0 + M_0$ bikes in all.

We can quantify what consumers gain from being able to buy bikes, and how much a tariff would cut their gains, if we understand the meaning of their demand curve. The demand curve can be interpreted in either of two ways, as we noted in Chapter 3. It tells us how much would be demanded at each price. It also tells us, for each quantity bought each year, the highest price that some consumer would be willing to pay to get another bike. The demand curve in Figure 6.1 tells us that at the free-trade price of $300, somebody in our country is just willing to pay that $300 for the last bike bought at Point A. It also says that at Point B somebody was willing to pay $330 for a bike that made total purchases come to D_1 a year. Similarly, if no bikes were being sold for some reason, there is apparently somebody willing to pay a high price, such as $1,000, to get the first bike, up at Point C.

This view of the demand curve allows us to add up dollar measures of how much consumers are gaining from being able to buy bikes at all. The very first bike each year brings $700 in net gains to somebody who would have paid up to $1,000 to get it (Point C) but who gets it at the world price of only $300. Similarly, as we go down the demand curve from Point C toward Point A, we find that the vertical gap between the demand curve and the world price of $300 shows us that somebody is getting another bargain by paying less for the bike than the maximum amount that person would have been willing to pay for a bike. So summing up the entire area between the demand curve and the $300 price line tells us the amount of "consumer surplus" from buying bikes, the amount by which what consumers would have been willing to pay as individuals exceeds what they end up paying. This consumer surplus area, triangle ACE, is an approximation to what being able to buy bikes is worth to consumers.

A tariff of $30, or 10 percent, raises the price of bicycles and cuts the gains that are represented by the consumer surplus. By raising the price to $330, the tariff in Figure 6.1 forces some consumers to give up an extra $30 per bike to get the same D_1 bikes they would rather have bought at $300, while it makes other consumers decide that a bike is not worth $330 to them, so that total demand drops back from D_0 to D_1. The net loss to consumers from the tariff is the total shaded area, or areas $a + b + c + d$. This is the amount that consumers lose by having their consumer surplus from bicycle purchases cut from triangle ACE to triangle BCD.

The cost of a tariff to consumers can be measured, and it can turn out to be large. It can be large partly because the tariff makes consumers pay more on the domestic product as well as on imports. When the tariff is first imposed, individual consumers will try to avoid paying the extra $30 by buying more domestic bikes. But the domestic supply cannot be increased without bidding up marginal costs above \$300 (if it could, then domestic suppliers could have outcompeted foreign suppliers even with no tariff). So the sales by domestic suppliers expand only up to S_1, at which level of output their marginal costs and their price also equal \$330, making the consumers pay more on all bikes, not just on foreign bikes. To measure the shaded area of consumer loss, one needs to know the prices of bikes with and without the tariff and the amounts that consumers would buy with and without the tariff (D_0 and D_1). Knowing these, one can compute the areas of the rectangle $a + b + c$ and the triangle area d. Even if one does not know the exact slope of the demand curve, one could approximate the amount of consumer loss: it would be slightly underestimated by multiplying the tariff gap (\$30) by the number purchased with the tariff (D_1), or slightly overestimated by multiplying the tariff gap by the number purchased without the tariff *(D_0)*.

THE EFFECTS ON PRODUCERS

A tariff brings gains for domestic producers who face import competition, by taxing only the foreign product. The more it costs consumers to buy the foreign product, the more they will turn to domestic suppliers, who get the benefit of extra sales and higher prices thanks to the tariff.

The producer gains from the tariff can be quantified with the help of Figure 6.2, which portrays from a producer's point of view the same bicycle market as is shown in Figure 6.1. As we have seen, the tariff drives up the price of domestic bikes from \$300 to \$330. Domestic firms respond by raising their output and sales as long as that is profitable. They will expand from S_0 to S_1. It is at output S_1 that their costs of producing each extra bike, shown by the supply curve, rise as high as the tariff-ridden market price of \$330. It is not profitable for them to raise their output any higher, because doing so would raise their marginal costs above \$330, the price they receive when selling bikes in competition with foreign firms in the domestic market.

The profits that producers make are the difference between their total revenues and their costs. In Figure 6.2, these profits, or more accurately, economic surpluses for those who produce and sell bicycles in order to consume other goods and services, take the form of a triangular area between the price line and the marginal cost curve. To see why, focus first on how total revenues for producers are represented in Figure 6.2. Total revenues equal price times quantity sold, or \$300 times S_0 without the tariff and \$330 times S_1 with it. The tariff has clearly raised the total sales revenues of the domestic producers. But not all of the revenues are profits. The part of total revenues lying below the supply curve, or marginal cost curve, represents the variable costs of producing bicycles. Only the part lying

---

FIGURE 6.2   The Effect of a Tariff on Producers

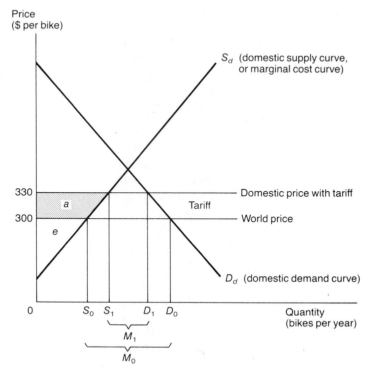

Shaded area a = Producer's gain from tariff.

The $30 bike tariff gives domestic producers extra profits on all the bikes they would have produced even without the tariff (an extra $30 \times S_0$) plus smaller net profits on additional sales [profits equaling $\frac{1}{2} \times \$30 \times (S_1 - S_0)$].

---

above the marginal cost curve and within the total-revenue area represents profits above costs. Thus, the tariff raises profits in the domestic bicycle industry only by the amount of area a, from area e to areas $a + e$.

What domestic producers gain from the tariff is smaller than what the tariff costs consumers. The reason is straightforward: producers gain the price markup on only the domestic output, while consumers are forced to pay the same price markup on both domestic output and imports. Figures 6.1 and 6.2 bring this out clearly for the bicycle example. The tariff brought bicycle producers only area a in gains, but cost consumers this same area a plus areas $b + c + d$. As far as the effects on bicycle consumers and bicycle producers alone are concerned, the tariff is definitely a net loss.

THE EFFECTIVE RATE OF PROTECTION

Clearly, the higher the percentage tariff on a good is, the more protection the tariff gives to the domestic firms producing in that industry. Yet to understand just who is being protected by a tariff or by a set of tariffs, one needs to take a closer look at the industrial structure.

A tariff on the product of an individual industry protects more than just the firms producing that product domestically. It also helps protect the incomes of workers and others whose inputs are counted in the "value added" in that industry. Beyond these groups, the firms in the industry and their workers, the tariff also protects the incomes of other industries that sell material inputs to that specific industry. Thus, our tariff on bicycles may help not only bicycle firms but also bicycle workers and firms selling steel pieces, rubber, and other material inputs to the bicycle industry. This slightly complicates the task of measuring how much the bicycle tariff helps bicycle firms.

Firms in a given industry are also affected by tariffs on their inputs as well as tariffs on the products they sell. The firms selling bicycles, for example, would be hurt by tariffs on steel or rubber. This again complicates the task of measuring the effect of whole sets of tariffs, the whole tariff structure, on an individual industry's firms.

To give these points their due requires a more elaborate portrayal of supply-demand interactions in many markets at once. To cut down on the number of such elaborate investigations, economists have developed a simpler measure that does part of the job. The measure quantifies the effects of the whole tariff structure on one industry's value added per unit of output, without trying to estimate how much its output, or other outputs and prices, would change:

> The **effective rate of protection** of an individual industry is defined as the percentage by which the entire set of a nation's trade barriers raises the industry's value added per unit of output.

The effective rate of protection for the industry can be quite different from the percentage tariff paid by consumers on its output (the "nominal" rate of protection). This difference is brought out clearly by Figure 6.3, which shows the effective rate of protection of a 10 percent tariff on bicycle imports and a 5 percent tariff on imports of steel, rubber, and all other material inputs into the bicycle industry. The 10 percent tariff on bicycles by itself would raise their price, and the value added by the bicycle industry, by $30 per bike, as before. The 5 percent tariffs on bicycle inputs would cost the bicycle industry $11 per bike by raising the domestic prices of inputs. The two sets of tariffs together would raise the industry's unit value added by only $19 per bike. But this extra $19 represents a protection of value added (incomes) in the bicycle industry of 23.8 percent of value added, not just 10 percent or less as one might have thought from a casual look at the nominal tariff rates themselves.

FIGURE 6.3   Illustrative Calculation of an Effective Rate of Protection

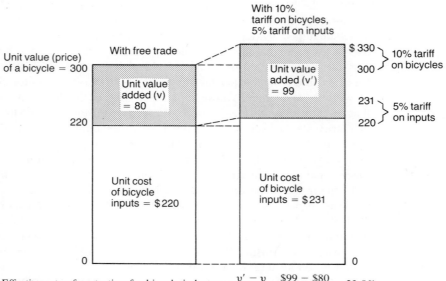

Effective rate of protection for bicycle industry $= \dfrac{v' - v}{v} = \dfrac{\$99 - \$80}{\$80} = 23.8\%.$

   To see who is getting protected by trade barriers, it helps (1) to distinguish between an industry and its suppliers and (2) to look at the effects of the whole set of barriers, not just the one directly protecting the industry. In this case, the bicycle industry's 10 percent tariff raises its value added per bike by more than 10 percent. On the other hand, the tariffs on the inputs the bicycle industry buys hurt it. The net result in this case is an "effective rate of protection" of 23.8 percent.

   The example in Figure 6.3 illustrates two of the basic points brought out by the concept of effective rate of protection: a given industry's incomes, or value added, will be affected by trade barriers on its inputs as well as trade barriers on its output, and the effective rate of protection will be greater than the nominal rate when the industry's output is protected by a higher duty than its inputs. (On this point and other aspects of the effective rate of protection, see Appendix D.) Thus, to get an accurate picture of just who is being protected by either a single tariff or a whole tariff structure, one needs to watch the input-output relationships of the economy.

THE TARIFF AS GOVERNMENT REVENUE

   The effects of a tariff on the well-being of consumers and producers do not exhaust its effects on the importing nation. As long as the tariff is not so high as to prohibit all imports, it also brings revenue to the government.

This revenue equals the unit amount of the tariff times the volume of imports with the tariff, or area *c* back in Figure 6.1.

The tariff revenue is a definite gain for the nation, since it is collected by the government. This gain could take any of several forms. It could become extra government spending on socially worthwhile projects. It could be matched by an equal cut in some other tax, such as the income tax. Or it could just become extra income for greedy government officials.[2] Although what form the tariff takes can certainly matter, the central point is that it represents revenue that accrues to somebody within the country, and thus it counts as an element of gain to be weighed in with the consumer losses and producer gains from the tariff.

THE NET NATIONAL LOSS FROM THE TARIFF

By combining the effects of the tariff on consumers, producers, and the government, we can determine the net effect of the tariff on the importing nation as a whole. To do so, we need to impose a further value judgment. We need to state explicitly how much we care about each dollar of effect on each group. That is unavoidable. Indeed, anybody who expresses an opinion on whether a tariff is good or bad necessarily does so on the basis of personal value judgments about how important each group is.

The basic analysis starts out by using a *one-dollar-one vote* yardstick: *Every dollar of gain or loss is just as important as every other dollar of gain or loss, regardless of who the gainers or losers are.* Let's use this welfare yardstick here just as we did in Chapter 3. Later we discuss what difference it would make it we chose to weigh one group's dollar stakes more heavily than those of other groups.

If the one-dollar-one vote yardstick is applied, then a tariff like the one graphed in Figures 6.1 and 6.2 brings a clear net loss to the importing nation, as well as to the world as a whole. This can be seen by studying Figure 6.4, which returns to the bicycle example used previously. We have seen that the dollar value of the consumer losses exceeded the dollar value of the producer gains from the tariff. We have also seen that the government collected some tariff revenue, an element of national gain. The left-hand side of Figure 6.4 makes it clear that the dollar value of what the consumers lose exceeds even the sum of the producer gains and the government tariff revenues.

The same net national loss can be shown in another way. The right-hand side of Figure 6.4 shows the market for imports of bicycles. Our demand curve for imports of bicycles is a curve showing the amount by which our demand for bicycles exceeds our domestic supply of bicycles at

---

[2] Part of it might be lost to the nation and the world as real resource costs of administering and enforcing the tariff, as noted in Appendix D.

FIGURE 6.4   The Net National Loss from a Tariff, in Two Equivalent Diagrams

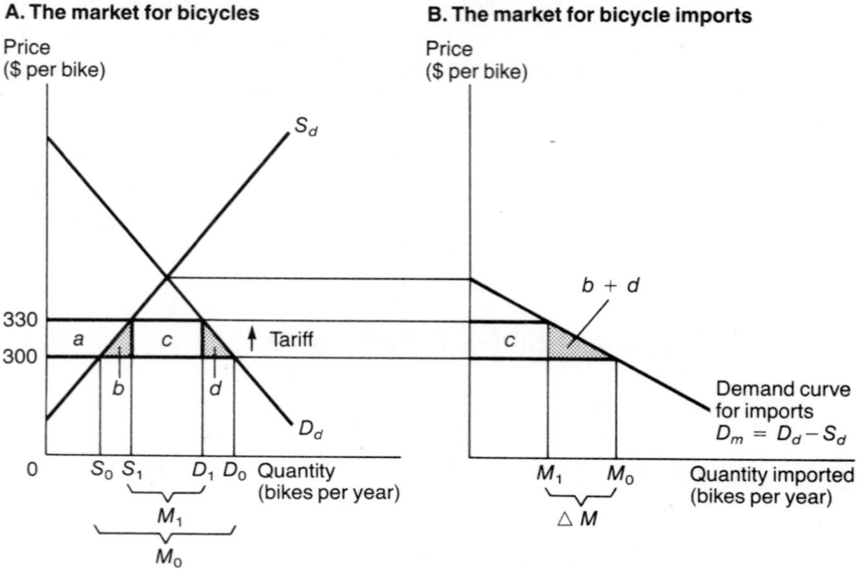

A. The market for bicycles

B. The market for bicycle imports

Consumers loss	Area $a + b + c + d$
Producers gain	Area a
Government collects	Area c in tariff revenue
Net national loss from the tariff =	Area b + d

Under the assumptions of this chapter, a tariff brings a net national loss. What it costs consumers is greater than what it brings producers plus the government's tariff revenue. The two reasons for the net loss are summarized in the areas b and d. Area b (the production effect) represents the loss from making at higher marginal cost what could have been bought for less abroad. Area d (the consumption effect) represents the loss from discouraging import consumption that was worth more than what it cost the nation.

---

each price. It is thus a curve derived by subtracting our domestic supply curve from our domestic demand curve for bicycles at each price (horizontally), since imports equal demand minus domestic supply. This allows us to show the net national loss, or area *(b + d)*, on the right-hand side of Figure 6.4 as well as on the left. Since area b and area d have the same tariff height and relate, respectively, to the net shift from imports to domestic supply and the total decline in demand, area *(b + d)* is a triangle with the tariff as its height and the total cut in imports as its base, as shown in the right-hand side.

The net national loss from the tariff shown in Figure 6.4 is not hard to estimate empirically. The key information one needs consists only of the height of the tariff itself and the estimated volume by which the tariff reduces imports, or ΔM. The usual way of arriving at this information is to find out the percentage price markup the tariff represents, the initial dollar value of imports, and the percentage elasticity, or responsiveness, of import quantities to price changes. It is handy, and perhaps surprising, that the net national loss from the tariff can be estimated just using information on imports, as on the right-hand side of Figure 6.4, without even knowing the domestic demand and supply curves.

What logic lies behind the geometric finding that the net national loss equals areas $b + d$? With a little reflection, it is not hard to see that these areas represent gains from international trade and specialization that are lost because of the tariff. **Area d**, sometimes called the **consumption effect** of the tariff, shows the loss to consumers in the importing nation that corresponds to their being forced to cut their total consumption of bicycles. They would have been willing to pay prices up to $330 to get the extra foreign bicycles lost in area d, yet the tariff prevents their being able to get them for less than $330, even though the extra bicycles would have cost the nation only $300 a bike in payments to foreign sellers. What the consumers lose in area d, nobody else gains. Area d is a "deadweight" loss, an element of overall inefficiency caused by the tariff.

Area b is a welfare loss tied to the fact that some consumer demand is shifted from imports to more expensive domestic production. The tariff is raising domestic production by S_0S_1 at the expense of imports. The domestic supply curve, or the marginal cost curve, is assumed to be upward sloping, so that each extra bicycle costs more and more to produce, rising from a resource cost of $300 up to a cost of $330. Yet society is paying more for the bicycles than the $300 price at which the bicycles are available abroad. This extra cost of shifting to more expensive home production, sometimes called the **production effect** of the tariff, is represented by area b. Like area d, it is a deadweight loss. It is part of what consumers pay, but neither the government nor producers gain it. It is the amount by which the cost of drawing domestic resources away from other uses exceeds the savings from not paying foreigners to sell us the extra S_0S_1. Thus, the gains from trade lost by the tariff come in two forms: the consumption effect of area d plus the production effect of area b.

The basic analysis of a tariff identifies areas b and d as the net national loss from a tariff only if certain assumptions are granted. The clearest key assumption is that the one-dollar-one vote yardstick is an appropriate common measure of different groups' interest. It was by using this yardstick that the analysis above was able to imply that consumers' losing areas a and c were exactly offset, dollar for dollar, by producers' gaining area a and the government's collecting area c. That is what produced $(b + d)$ as the net loss for the nation. Suppose that you personally reject this yardstick. Suppose, for example, that you think that each dollar of gain for the bicycle producers is somehow more important to you than each dollar of consumer loss, perhaps because you see the bicycle consumers as a group society as pampered too much. If that is your view, you will not want to accept areas *b* and *d* as the net national loss from the tariff. The same basic analysis of the tariff is still useful to you, however. You can stipulate by how much you weigh each dollar of effect on bicycle producers and government more heavily than each dollar for consumers, and you can apply your own differential weights to each group's dollar stake to see whether the net effect of the tariff is still negative.

Other assumptions have been made which also affect one's view of the tariff. Here are some of the most important ones:

1. It has been assumed that the importing nation is a "price taker," a country that is unable to affect the world price by its own actions.
2. The analysis so far has ignored the balance of payments between countries; we have not taken any note of the fact that the tariff will cut the amount being paid to foreigners. This drop in expenditures on imports will either affect the exchange rate or shift the balance of payments toward surplus. These balance-of-payments effects have implications that are not spelled out here.
3. The analysis has been implicitly assuming that we live in a "first-best" world in which the gains and losses for individual decision makers are also society's gains and losses without the tariff. Only the tariff itself is allowed to enter here as a factor that makes social costs and benefits different from private ones.

We return to these assumptions later in this and the next chapter, asking in each case what difference it would make if the assumption were thrown out in ways that make the analysis more realistic.

PAST MEASUREMENTS OF THE NATIONAL LOSS

Since the late 1950s several economists have made empirical estimates of the net national welfare losses from tariffs and other trade barriers. Their estimates often take account of refinements that will be introduced only later in this chapter and in Chapter 7. Yet basically their procedure has been simply to estimate the sizes of areas *b* + *d* in Figure 6.4 for several internationally traded commodities. They have used information on the extent of imports and the height of the tariff or other price-raising import barrier, and an estimate of the price elasticity of import demand for each product.

The correct way to measure the deadweight loss was spelled out in 1960 by Harry G. Johnson, who went on to argue that the value of the loss from tariffs had to be a positive but trivial share of a nation's gross national product. Johnson noted that for any commodity:

Net national loss from the tariff / GNP = ($\frac{1}{2}$) × (tariff rate)
$$\times (\% \text{ change in import quantity}) \times (\text{Import value} / \text{GNP})$$

By studying these fractions, one can see why this kind of measure of net loss from a tariff might easily look like a small fraction of GNP. Suppose, for example, that a nation's import tariffs were all 10 percent tariffs and that they caused a 20 percent reduction in import quantities. Suppose the total imports of all commodities were 10 percent of GNP. In this realistic case, the net national loss from all tariffs on imports equals ½ × 0.10 × 0.20 × 0.10, or only 0.1 percent of GNP. Johnson thus argued that the net national loss from tariffs is not likely to be great, at least for a large country that is not totally dependent on foreign trade, such as the United States.

Other empirical studies more or less confirmed Johnson's hunch. The first wave estimated Marshallian surpluses—triangles of net national gain like those shown in Figure 6.4. Then, from the mid-1970s on, more complex "computable general equilibrium" (CGE) methods were applied to the same task of welfare estimation. The CGE estimates were based on large computer-solved models of the economy that could pick up subtle income and price repercussions that are hidden by diagrams like those in this chapter. With either method, Marshallian or CGE, the range of welfare gains from freer trade was between −1 percent of GNP and +10 percent of GNP. The largest gains came when the barriers were (1) high and (2) to be removed completely, as in the studies of Brazil and Canada. Some of the authors of the studies concluded that the effects they measured were "small" shares of GNP. Yet, as argued in Appendix D, there are several ways in which these studies underestimate the costs of protection.

THE TARIFF AGAIN, WITH PRODUCTION AND INDIFFERENCE CURVES

Throughout Part Two we shall be using the demand-supply framework to bring out basic points about the pros and cons of trade barriers. This section will show that the results already established with the use of the demand-supply framework are consistent with the use of the production and indifference curves discussed in Part One.

Figure 6.5 shows how the effects of a tariff are portrayed using a nation's production and indifference curves. The free-trade position is represented by Points P_0 and C_0. The nation is producing more wheat and fewer bicycles at P_0 than it is consuming at C_0. By consuming at C_0, it is achieving a higher level of utility (I_0) than it could achieve if it had to consume only what it produced, along the production curve. This higher level of well-being is made possible by trading at the world price ratio, at which the country exports some wheat in exchange for its M_0 imports of bicycles.

Imposing a tariff on bicycles makes the domestic price of bicycles higher in terms of wheat than the world price. In terms of Figure 6.5 this means that the domestic price ratio is represented by a flatter line (it takes more wheat to buy a bicycle) than the world price line. The tariff makes both

FIGURE 6.5   The Effects of a Tariff, Portrayed with Production and Indifference Curves

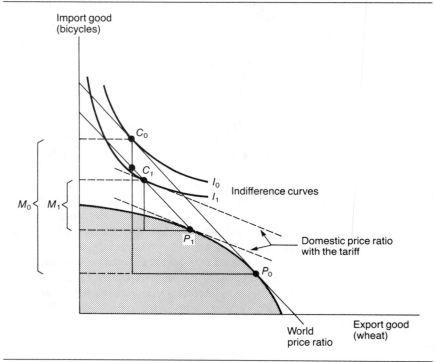

domestic producers and domestic consumers respond to the new price ratio, just as in the demand-supply framework above. Domestic producers shift resources out of the wheat industry into the now-protected bicycle industry until the marginal costs of producing each are brought into line with the tariff-ridden price ratio at Point P_1. Meanwhile, consumers also adjust, by setting their consumption at a point (C_1) where the marginal utilities of the two goods are in the same ratio as the domestic prices. In the process trade has shrunk, from imports of M_0 to imports of M_1.

The tariff has clearly lowered welfare, in Figure 6.5 as in the figures above. At Point C_1 the nation is enjoying only the level of utility represented by the indifference curve I_1, which is inferior to the I_0 enjoyed with free trade. The tariff cuts welfare in two ways, both analogous to welfare effects introduced earlier in this chapter. The fact that domestic production is shifted from wheat toward bicycles costs the nation something, since in moving from P_0 to P_1 the nation incurs production costs on bicycles exceeding what these bicycles cost on the world market. This "production effect," like its counterpart in Figure 6.4 is part of what the nation loses. It is a welfare loss represented by the fact that when producing at P_1, the nation is constrained to find its best consumption point somewhere on the world price line running northwest from P_1. The nation further loses by having the tariff distort its consumption pattern. The tariff makes consumers find a consumption point where the indifference curve is tangent to the domestic price ratio, even though this fails to correspond to the nation's trading opportunities at the world price ratio. This "consumption effect" on welfare is represented by the fact that private consumer decisions will leave us at Point C_1 instead of the nationally better range of points just to the northwest of C_1.

The national loss from the tariff thus equals the sum of a production effect and a consumption effect on national well-being, just as the national loss from the tariff equaled the sum of the same two effects (areas b and d again) in the earlier sections of this chapter.

SUMMARY

Under the assumptions of this chapter, a tariff on imports clearly lowers national well-being. It costs consumers more than it benefits producers and the government, which collects the tariff revenue. The tariff thus redistributes income from consumers of the imported product toward others in society.

To reinforce your understanding of the different welfare effects of a tariff, think about how you might describe each of them to legislators who are considering a tariff law. No legislator will be impressed by an abstract diagram or by algebra. What follows are concise verbal translations of each of the four lettered areas shown in Figures 6.1, 6.2, and 6.4:

a. "By raising the price on strictly domestic sales, a tariff redistributes incomes from consumers to producers. The amount redistributed is the price markup times the average quantity of domestic sales." (Describes Area a.)

b. "A tariff shifts some purchases from foreign goods to home goods. This costs more resources to make at home than to buy abroad." (Describes Area b, the protection effect.)

c. "A tariff makes consumers pay tax revenue directly to the government." (Describes Area c.)

d. "A tariff discourages some purchases that were worth more than they cost the nations." (Describes Area d, the production effect.)

e. "By both shifting some purchases toward costly home goods and by discouraging some purchases worth more than they cost the nation, the tariff costs the nation as a whole. The cost equals the price markup times the drop in our imports." (Describes Areas $b + d$, the net national loss.)

The effects of tariffs on producer interests are further clarified by the concept of the effective rate of protection, which measures the percentage effect of the entire tariff structure on the value added per unit of output in each industry. This concept incorporates the point that one industry's tariff affects a number of industries; also incomes in any one industry are affected by the tariffs of many industries.

SUGGESTED READING

For a good example of practical estimates of the welfare effects of recent trade barriers, see the estimates for U.S. automobiles, steel, sugar, and textiles in Tarr and Morkre (1984) and Tarr (1989). See also the discussion in Appendix D of the large amount of empirical literature on such welfare effects.

QUESTIONS FOR REVIEW

1. You have been asked to quantify the welfare effects of the U.S. sugar duty. The hard part of the work is already done: Somebody has estimated how many pounds of sugar would be produced, consumed and imported by the United States if there were no sugar duty. You are given the following information:

	Situation with Import Tariff	Estimated Situation without Tariff
World price (delivered in New York)	$0.10 per pound	$0.10 per pound
Tariff (duty)	$0.02 per pound	0
Domestic price	$0.12 per pound	$0.10 per pound
U.S. consumption (billions of per year)	20	22
U.S. production (billions of per year)	8	6
U.S. imports (billions of per year)	12	16

Calculate the following measures:
   a. The U.S. consumers' gain from removing the tariff.
   b. The U.S. producers' losses from removing the tariff.
   c. The U.S. government tariff revenue loss.
   d. The net effect on U.S. national well being.

Answers: *(a.)* U.S. consumers gain $420 million per year, *(b.)* U.S. producers lose $140 million per year, *(c.)* the U.S. government loses $240 million per year, and *(d.)* the U.S. as a whole gains $40 million a year.

2. Effective rate of protection problem—with free trade, each dollar of value added in the cloth making industry is divided as follows: 40 cents value added, 30 cents for cotton yarn, and 30 cents for other fibers. Suppose that a 25 percent ad valorem tariff is placed on cloth imports and a ⅙ tariff (16.7 percent) on cotton yarn imports. Work out the division of the tariff-ridden unit value of $1.25 (the old dollar plus the cloth tariff) into value added, payments for cotton, and payments for other fibers. Then calculate the effective rate of protection.

Answer: the $1.25 is made up of 60 cents of value added, 35 cents of cotton payments, and 30 cents payments for other fibers. The effective rate is (60¢ − 40¢)/40¢ = 50%.

3. Suppose that the United States produces 1.4 million bicycles a year and imports another 1 million; there is no tariff or other import barrier. Bicycles sell for $400 each. Congress is considering a $40 tariff on bicycles like the one portrayed in Figures 6.1, 6.2, and 6.4. What is the maximum net national welfare loss that this could cause the United States? What is the minimum national welfare loss? (Hint: draw a diagram like Figure 6.4 and put the numbers given here on it. Next, imagine the possible positions of the relevant curves.)

4. What is the minimum quantitative information you would need to calculate the net national welfare loss from a tariff?

▼

Arguments for and against a Tariff

•

The basic analysis of a tariff seemed to prove that free trade was better than any tariff, by showing that the tariff brought net losses to the nation as a whole. The empirical attempts to measure the net welfare effects of trade barriers also showed national losses in most cases. Yet the assumptions underlying the basic analysis and the usual empirical measurements are not always valid. The arguments for and against a tariff are subtler and more varied than those presented in Chapter 6. Both critics and defenders of tariffs need to know just where the limits to the case for free trade lie.

This chapter explores those limits, identifying the conditions under which a tariff can be better than doing nothing, or better than any other policy. We shall establish some of the policy conclusions previewed at the start of Chapter 6: there are valid "optimal tariff" and "second-best" arguments for a tariff, yet some other policy is usually better than the tariff in the second-best cases. It turns out that the valid arguments for a tariff are quite different from the usual defenses of a tariff.

THE NATIONALLY OPTIMAL TARIFF

One of the underpinnings of the conclusion that we are hurt as a nation by our own tariff is the assumption that we cannot affect the world price of the imported good. The basic analysis in Chapter 6 assumed this when it implied that the tariff on bicycle imports did not affect the world price of bicycles, which stood fixed at $300, tariff or no tariff. In other words, the basic analysis assumed that we are competitive *price takers* in the world markets for the goods we import.

This assumption is often valid. Trade between nations is frequently very competitive, often even for commodities for which trade within a nation is dominated by a few sellers. Moreover, individual nations usually control smaller shares of world markets for individual commodities as importers than they do as exporters, since nations tend to specialize more as exporters than as importers. Thus, in most cases an importing nation cannot force foreign suppliers to sell for less by trying to strike a tougher bargain. If Canada tried to demand a lower import price for bicycles by taxing foreign sales of bicycles to Canada, the foreign suppliers might simply decide to avoid sales to Canada altogether and sell elsewhere at the same world price. Similarly, Britain could not expect to force foreign sellers of rice to supply it more cheaply: any attempt to do so would simply prove that Britain was a price taker on the world market by causing rice exporters to avoid Britain altogether with little effect on the world rice price.

Yet in some cases a nation has a large enough share of the world market for one of its imports to be able to affect the world price unilaterally. A nation can have this **monopsony power** even in cases in which no individual firm within the nation has it. For example, the United States looms large enough in the world market for automobiles to be able to force foreign exporters like Toyota to sell autos to the United States at a lower price (or to move their plants to the United States) by putting a tariff on foreign autos. The United States probably has the same monopsony power to some extent in the world market for many goods.

A nation with such power over foreign selling prices can exploit this advantage with a tariff on imports, even though no competitive individual within the nation could do so. Suppose that the United States were to impose a small tariff on bicycles. Imposing the tariff markup would make the price paid by U.S. consumers exceed the price paid to foreign suppliers, as shown in Chapter 6. Now, however, the markup is likely to lower the foreign price as well as raise the domestic price a bit. As long as they can produce and sell to the United States smaller amounts at a lower marginal cost, foreign suppliers are likely to prefer to cut their price to the United States a bit in order to limit the drop in their sales to the United States. This is what makes it possible for the United States to gain as a nation from its own tariff. On all the bicycles that continue to be imported, the United States succeeds in paying a lower price to foreigners, even though the tariff-including price to U.S. consumers is slightly higher. To be sure, there is still a deadweight loss in economic efficiency for both the United States and the world on the imports prevented by the tariff. In discouraging some imports that would have been worth more to buyers than the price being paid to cover the foreign seller's costs, the tariff still has its costs. But as long as the tariff is small, those costs are outweighed for the United States by the gains from continuing most of the previous imports at a lower price. So there is some positive level of the tariff, perhaps a low level, at which the United States as a nation is better off than with free trade.

This same point can be made more fully using the illustration given in Figure 7.1, which shows the same diagram of the market for bicycle imports

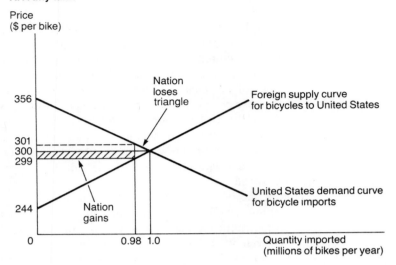

A. A tiny tariff

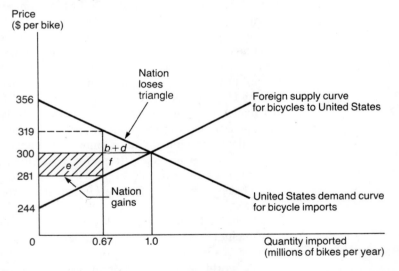

B. A nationally optimal tariff

If the foreign supply curve slopes up, an importing nation has some power over the price it pays foreigners for imports, even if individual importers have no such power. The importing nation can exploit this national monopsony power. In the top panel (A.), it imposes a slight ($2) tariff and gains slightly because competition makes foreign suppliers pay part of the $2. It can gain more by raising the tariff further—up to a point. The lower panel (B.) shows the nationally optimal use (or abuse) of this power in which the maximum national gains have been squeezed, with a tariff of $38 (= 319 − 281).

as in Figure 6.4B, except that now the foreign supply curve slopes upward instead of being flat at a fixed world price. Suppose again that the United States imposes a very small tariff, say a $2 tariff, on bicycles, driving up the domestic price to $301 and lowering the foreign price to $299. Figure 7.1A shows that the United States loses a bit on the 0.02 million bicycles that consumers decide not to buy each year now that they must pay the extra dollar. This loss is very small, however. It is easily outweighed by the gain reaped by the United States at the expense of foreign suppliers on the remaining 0.98 million bicycles imported each year. By getting the foreigners to sell those bicycles at a dollar less, the United States has made them pay for part of the tariff. This national gain ($1 × 0.98 million bikes a year) easily outweighs the small triangle of deadweight loss on discouraged imports.

If a tiny tariff works for the nation with power over prices, higher tariffs work even better—but only up to a point. To see the limits to a nation's market power, we can start by noting that *a prohibitive tariff cannot be optimal.* Suppose that the United States were to put a tariff on bicycle imports that was so high as to make all imports unprofitable, as would a tariff of over $112 a bike in Figure 7.1, driving the price received by foreign suppliers below $144. So stiff a tariff would not be successful in getting the foreigners to supply the United States at low prices, since they would decide not to sell bicycles to the United States at all. Lacking any revenues earned partly at the expense of foreign suppliers, the United States would find itself saddled with nothing but the loss of all gains from trade in bicycles. The optimal tariff must be somewhere in between no tariff and a prohibitively high one.

The optimal tariff can be derived in the same way as the optimal price markdown for any monopsonist, any buyer with market power. Appendix E derives the formula for the optimum tariff rate from static analysis. It turns out that:

> the **optimal tariff rate**, *as a fraction of the price paid to foreigners,*
> = *the reciprocal of the elasticity of foreign supply of our imports.*

It makes sense that the lower the foreign supply elasticity, the higher our optimum tariff rate: the more inelastically foreigners keep to supplying a nearly fixed amount to us, the more we can get away with exploiting them. Conversely, if their supply is infinitely elastic, facing us with a fixed world price as in Chapter 6, then we cannot get them to accept lower prices. If their supply elasticity is infinite, our own tariffs hurt only us, as in Chapter 6, and the optimal tariff is zero.

Figure 7.1B shows such an optimal tariff. The nation gains the markdown on foreign bicycle imports, represented by area *e,* which considerably exceeds what the nation loses as a net consumer of bicycles in area *b* + *d.* The national gain, $e - b - d$, is greater than the national gain at any other tariff rate.[1]

For the world as a whole, however, the nationally optimal tariff is still unambiguously bad. What the nation gains is less than what foreigners lose from our tariff. Figure 7.1B shows this. The United States gained area e only at the expense of foreign suppliers, dollar for dollar, leaving no net effect on the world from this redistribution of income through price. But foreign suppliers suffered more than that: they also lost area f in additional producer surplus on the imports discouraged by the tariff. Therefore, the world loses areas $b + d$ and f, which are the gains from trade caused by the fact that U.S. consumers value foreign bicycles more highly below the level of imports of 1.0 million a year than it would cost foreign suppliers to make and sell them. The tariff may be nationally optimal, but it still means a net loss to the world.

RETALIATION

The optimal tariff argument assumes that the foreigners do not retaliate, either by taxing their exports to us or by taxing their imports from us. This assumption may not be valid. They may respond to our import tariffs with import barriers of their own. Exactly this fear has beset U.S. farmers as a result of U.S. import barriers on industrial products from Asia. As the United States built a higher wall against Asian steel and textiles in the early and mid-1980s, China, Japan, and other Asian nations retaliated by cutting down on their imports of U.S. soybeans and other farm products. U.S. farmers have complained that they are being sacrificed for industrial jobs. If the mutual retaliation escalates into an all-out trade war, both sides suffer serious losses. That happened in the tariff war between France and Italy in the late 1880s, and to all major countries with the beggar-my-neighbor trade barriers of the 1930s. Knowing this, free-trade advocates stress that a seemingly optimal tariff can backfire.

THE TROUBLED WORLD OF SECOND BEST

To discover where the boundaries to the free-trade argument lie, it is necessary to go beyond another simplifying assumption made in the basic analysis of a tariff. So far we have been assuming that any demand or supply curve could do double duty, representing both private and social benefits or costs.

---

[1] As Figure 7.1 is drawn, the tariff rate does fit the optimal-tariff formula. The rate equals (\$38/\$281), or 13.5 percent. The elasticity of foreign supply works out to be about 7.5 at this point on the foreign supply curve. So the tariff rate of 13.5 percent is approximately the reciprocal of 7.5. This would not be true for any other tariff rate.

Our demand curve was supposed to represent not only marginal benefits of an extra bicycle to the private buyer but also the net benefits of another bicycle to society as a whole. Our supply curve was supposed to represent not only the marginal cost to private producers of producing another bicycle at home but also the marginal cost to society as a whole. That is, we assumed that there were no **distortions**, no gaps between the private and social benefits or costs of any activity, in the absence of the tariff. In this Garden of Eden the tariff was the original sin, introducing a distortion between the marginal cost of a bicycle to consumers (the tariff-including domestic price) and the marginal cost to society of buying another bicycle abroad (the world price).

It is often not realistic to assume that the distortions in our domestic economy are either zero or happen to cancel each other out. Distortions are widespread, and they pose some of the most intriguing policy problems of economics. Distortions include the wide range of effects that economists have also called "externalities" or "spillover effects": net effects on parties other than those agreeing to buy and sell in a marketplace. Pollution is a classic example: the buyers and sellers of paper products do not reckon the damage done by the paper mills' river pollution into the price of paper unless special action is taken, nor do the buyers and sellers of petroleum fuels reckon the social cost of pollution from consuming those fuels into the prices of the fuels. Such distortions between the interests of private parties and the net interests of society as a whole occur in many other spheres as well, for a host of reasons. We live in a **"second-best"** world, one riddled with gaps between private and social benefits or costs. As long as these gaps exist, private actions will not lead to a social optimum.

In a second-best world, a tariff can be justified by the existence of a domestic distortion. The easiest way to see how this can be true is to consider an example to which we shall return more than once. Suppose that jobs in a certain import-competing domestic sector will generate greater returns for society than are perceived by the people who are deciding whether or not to take those jobs. This can happen if the sector is a modern one in which jobs bring gains in knowledge and skills plus changes in attitudes, benefiting persons other than the workers and employers in that sector. Or perhaps the short-run costs of moving to jobs in a high-paying sector seem higher to the workers outside this sector than they do to society as a whole. For any of these reasons, the social cost of attracting workers into this sector may be a lot lower than the wage rate the firms in the sector would pay their workers. If so, there is a case for policy devices to attract workers to the sector.

Such a gap between the private and social costs of creating jobs in a sector can make a tariff beneficial on balance. Tariff protection can encourage firms in this sector to expand output and hire more labor. The social side benefits of creating the extra jobs can outweigh the losses caused by the fact that consumers and domestic firms are paying more to get extra units at home than they would cost to buy abroad if there were no tariff. The fact that such side benefits can exist complicates the task of judging whether a tariff is good or bad for the nation as a whole. Realizing this, some scholars have stressed that trade policy has to be agnostic in a second-best world. Once you realize that domestic distortions are common, there is little you can say in the abstract about the net gain or loss from a tariff. Each case must be judged on its own merits.

The Specificity Rule

In the world of second best we are not cast totally adrift. It is often possible to gather information on a case-by-case basis to quantify the various benefits and costs of an individual tariff, given what is known about relevant distortions in the home economy. Furthermore, there are some general rules that are valuable, even when one lacks detailed information about the situation of each industry. Here is one rough rule that serves well for policy-making in a distortion-riddled economy:

> The **specificity rule:** Intervene at the source of the problem. It is usually more efficient to use those policy tools that are closest to the sources of the distortions separating private and social benefits or costs.

The specificity rule applies to all sorts of policy issues. Let us illustrate it first by using some examples removed from international trade. Suppose that the most serious distortion to be attacked is crime, which creates fear among third parties as well as direct harm to victims. Since crime is caused by people, we might consider combating crime by reducing the whole population through compulsory sterilization laws or taxes on children. But such actions are obviously very inefficient ways of attacking crime, since less social friction would be generated (per crime averted) if we fought crime more directly through greater law enforcement and programs to reduce unemployment, a major contributor to crime.

A less extreme example of the specificity rule brings us back to the paper mills polluting rivers. To attack this problem, we could tax all production of paper products or we could subsidize the installation of a particular waste treatment device where the mills' pipes meet the river. But the specificity rule cautions us to make sure that we are as close as possible to the source of the problem. Taxing all paper products is likely to be too broad an instrument since it discourages the consumption and production of all paper without regard to the extent of pollution. The paper manufacturers would get the signal that society wants them to make less paper, but not the signal to look for less polluting ways of making paper. On the other hand, subsidizing the installation of a waste treatment device may be too narrow an instrument. Nothing assures us that the waste treatment approach is the cheapest way to reduce pollution. Perhaps a change in the internal production processes of the paper mills could cut down on the load of waste needing any pipeline treatment more cheaply than the cost of the waste treatment equipment. The problem arose from the failure to provide the paper manufacturers with incentives for cutting pollution, not from their failure to adopt a particular method. The specificity rule thus directs us to look at incentive policies geared to the act of pollution itself: such policies as taxes or quantitative limits on the amount of pollution discharged (effluent charges and environmental quality standards).

The specificity rule tends to cut against the tariff. Although a tariff can be better than doing nothing in a second-best world, the rule shows us that some other policy instrument is usually more efficient than the tariff in dealing with a domestic distortion. To see how, let us begin with the domestic target at which a tariff is most often aimed.

A Tariff to Promote Domestic Production

Debates over trade policy often come up with reasons for giving special encouragement to the domestic production of a commodity that is currently being imported. These reasons are varied. In fact, most of the popular second-best arguments for tariff protection can be viewed as variations on the theme of favoring a particular import-competing industry. The infant-industry argument is one variant. A tariff to create jobs at the expense of imports is another. Most of the "noneconomic" arguments for a tariff such as the national defense and national pride arguments, are also of this type. Each argument stresses that there are social benefits to domestic production in this particular import-competing industry that cannot be captured by the domestic industry unless it is given tariff protection. We shall take up these arguments in the following section. First, let us examine the general pros and cons of a tariff to promote domestic production, setting aside for the moment the reasons for thinking that there are social side benefits to domestic production.

A nation might want to encourage domestic production of bicycles, either because it thought the experience of producing this manufactured good generated modern skills and attitudes or simply because it took pride in producing its own modern bikes. It could foster this objective by putting a $30 tariff on imported bicycles, as shown in the diagram of the national bicycle market in Figure 7.2A. The tariff brings the nation the same elements of net loss that it did back in Chapter 6 (and Figure 6.4A): the nation loses area *b* by producing at greater expense what could be bought for less abroad, and it loses area *d* by discouraging purchases that would have brought more enjoyment to consumers than the world price of a bicycle. But now something is added: the lower part of the diagram portrays the social side benefits from home production, benefits that are not captured by the domestic bicycle producers. By raising the domestic price of bicycles, the tariff has encouraged

FIGURE 7.2   Two Ways to Promote Import-Competing Production

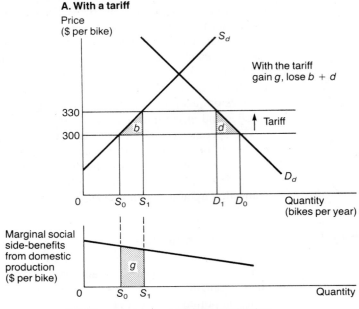

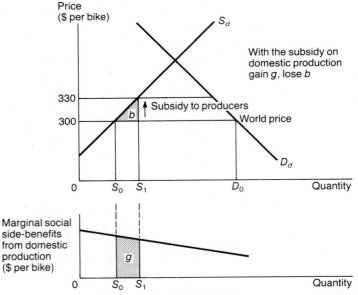

Compare the side effects of two ways of getting the same increase in domestic output $(S_0 - S_1)$ and in domestic jobs. Both the $30 tariff and the $30 subsidy to domestic production encourage the same change in domestic production. But the tariff also needlessly discourages some consumption of imports (the amount $D_1 - D_0$) that was worth more to the buyers than the $300 each unit of imports would have cost the nation. The subsidy is better than the tariff because it strikes more directly at the task of raising domestic production of this good.

more production of bicycles. This increase in domestic production, from S_0 to S_1, has brought area g in extra gains to the nation.

The tariff in Figure 7.2A could be good or bad for the nation, all things considered. The net outcome depends on whether area g is larger or smaller than the areas b and d. To find out, one would have to develop empirical estimates reflecting the realities of the bicycle industry. One would want to estimate the dollar value of the annual side benefits to society and also the slope of the domestic supply and demand curves. The net national gain $(g - b - d)$ might turn out to be positive or negative. All that one can say in the abstract is that the tariff might prove to be better or worse than doing nothing.

We should use our institutional imagination, however, and look for other policy tools. The specificity rule prods us to do so. The locus of the problem was domestic production, not imports as such. What society wants to encourage is more domestic production of this good, not less consumption or less imports of it. Why not encourage the domestic production directly by rewarding people on the basis of the amount of this beneficial good they produce?

Society could directly subsidize the domestic production of bicycles either by having the government pay bicycle firms a fixed amount or by having it lower their taxes by a fixed amount, for each bicycle produced and sold. Doing this would probably encourage them to produce more bicycles. Any increase in production that a given tariff could coax out of domestic firms could also be yielded by a production subsidy. Figure 7.2B shows such a subsidy, namely, a $30 subsidy per bicycle. This subsidy is just as good for bicycle firms as the extra $30 in selling price that the tariff made possible. Either tool gets the firms to raise their annual production from S_0 up to S_1, giving society the same side benefits.

The $30 production subsidy in Figure 7.2B is definitely better than the $30 tariff in Figure 7.2A. Both generate the same social side benefits, and both cause domestic firms to produce $(S_1 - S_0)$ extra bicycles each year at a higher direct cost than the price at which the nation could buy foreign bicycles (in both cases this extra cost is area b). Yet the subsidy does not discourage the total consumption of bicycles by raising the price above $300. It only enables domestic firms to capture part of the same total consumption for foreign competition at the same world price of $300. Consumers do not lose the additional area d. This is a clear net advantage of the $30 production subsidy over the $30 tariff.

What made the production subsidy better was its conformity to the specificity rule: since the locus of the problem was domestic production, it was less costly to attack it in a way that did not also affect the price at which consumers bought from foreigners.[2]

---

[2] Although this conclusion is broadly valid, it should be noted that a special assumption was needed to make the net advantage of the production subsidy exactly equal area d. It has been assumed here that no other distortions between private and social incentives result

If our concern is with expanding jobs, rather than output, in the import-competing industry, the same results hold with a slight modification. A production subsidy would still be preferable to the tariff, since it still achieves any given expansion in both bicycle production and bicycle jobs at lower social cost. We could come up with even better alternatives, however. If the locus of the problem is really the number of jobs in the bicycle industry, it would be more efficient to use a policy tool that not only encouraged production but also encouraged firms to come up with ways of creating more jobs per dollar of bicycle output. A subsidy tied to the number of workers employed might be better than a subsidy tied to output. (Alternatively, if the object is to create jobs and cure unemployment throughout the entire domestic economy, then it is logical to look first to economywide expansionary policies, such as fiscal policy or monetary policy, and again not to the tariff.)[3]

The Infant-Industry Argument

The analysis of the use of a tariff to promote domestic production helps us judge the merits of many of the most popular and time-honored arguments for protection. Of all the protectionist arguments, the one that has always

---

when the government comes up with the revenues to cover the production subsidies to the bicycle firms. That is, it has been assumed that there is no net social loss from having the government either raise additional taxes or cancel some spending to pay this subsidy to bicycle producers.

This assumption is strictly valid if the tax revenues going into the subsidy come from a head tax, a tax on people's existence, which should only redistribute income and not affect production and consumption incentives. Yet head taxes are rare, and the more realistic case of financing the production subsidy by, say, raising income taxes or cutting other government spending programs is somewhat murkier. If the income tax already exists, raising it further might or might not affect people's incentives to earn income through effort. Or if the government spending reallocated to the production subsidy had previously been providing some other public goods worth more than their marginal cost, there is again an extra loss that can attend the production subsidy. These possible source-of-subsidy distortions would have to be considered in policy-making. Yet it seems reasonable to presume that they are less important than the distorting of consumption represented by area *d*.

We return to this issue of how alternative policy tools are to be financed when discussing the infant-government argument below.

[3] So why do governments so often prefer import barriers instead of the less costly direct production subsidies? Once an industry's political lobby is strong enough to get government help, it uses its influence to get a kind of help that is sheltered from political counterattacks. The production subsidy favored here provides no such shelter. The subsidy is a highly visible target for budget-cutters. Every year it has to be defended again when the government budget is under review. A tariff or other import barrier, however, gives much better shelter to the industry that seeks government help year after year. Once it is written into the law, it goes on domestic prices without being reviewed. In fact, it might even generate government revenue (e.g., tariff revenue), giving it a better political appeal.

enjoyed the most prestige among both economists and policymakers is the infant-industry argument, which asserts that in less developed countries a temporary tariff is justified because it cuts down on imports of modern manufactures while the infant-domestic industry learns how to produce at low enough costs to compete without the help of a tariff. The argument stresses that industries learn by doing and that their cost curves will fall if they can gain experience. Tariff protection gives them this chance by keeping manufacturing competition from more advanced countries at bay while they incur the high initial costs of getting started. The infant-industry argument differs from the optimal tariff argument in that it claims that in the long run the tariff protection will be good for the world as well as the nation. It differs from most other tariff arguments in being explicitly dynamic, arguing that the protection is needed only for a while.

The infant-industry argument has been popular with developing countries at least since Alexander Hamilton used it in his *Report on Manufacturers* in 1791. America followed Hamilton's protectionist formula, especially after the American Civil War, setting up high tariff walls to encourage the production of textiles, ferrous metals, and other industries still struggling to become competitive against Britain. Similarly, Friedrich List reapplied Hamilton's infant-industry ideas to the cause of shielding nascent German manufacturing industries against British competition in the early 19th century.

The government of Japan has believed strongly in infant-industry protection, sometimes, but not always, in the form of import protection. In the 1950s and 1960s in particular, Japan protected its steel, automobile, shipbuilding and electronics industries before they became tough competitors and the import barriers were removed. Today, Japan still uses official roadblocks against IBM computer hardware to develop the already-mature "infant" Japanese computer hardware industry.

The infant-industry argument will continue to deserve attention because there will always be infant industries. The development of new products with new technologies will continue to contribute a growing share of world production and trade, and nations will have to consider time and again what to do about the development of new industries in which other countries have a current, comparative advantage.

How strong is the infant-industry argument? Three conclusions emerge in most cases:

1. There can be a case for some sort of government encouragement.
2. A tariff may or may not help.
3. Some other form of help is clearly a better infant-industry policy than the tariff.

To the extent that infant-industry concerns call for encouraging current domestic production, the analysis of the previous section applies. If the infant home industry will bring side benefits by causing the labor force and other industries to develop new skills, subsidizing production can achieve this more cheaply than can taxing imports. If the extra foreseen benefits take the form of future cost reductions for the *same* industry, through learning by doing, then there is another alternative more appropriate than either the tariff or the production subsidy. If an industry's current high costs are outweighed by the later cost cutting that experience will allow, then the industry can borrow against its own future profits to make it through the initial period in which costs are higher than the prices being charged on imports. Our bicycle industry, for example, could survive its youth by borrowing and then repaying the loan out of the profits it will make as a healthy competitor later on. Also, if defects in lending markets prevent such action, the government could advance loans to new industries—still not using the tariff.

If the need for help is truly temporary, there is another argument against using the tariff to protect the infant. Tariffs are not easily removed once they are written into law, and there is the danger that an infant that never becomes efficient will use part of its tariff-bred profits to sway policymakers to make a bad tariff immortal.[4] A production subsidy, by contrast, has the economic advantage of being subject to more frequent public review as part of the government's ordinary budget review process. It can be removed in cases in which the earlier help to an infant industry has proved to be a mistake.

More sophisticated versions of the infant-industry argument give more complicated defenses, yet each of these is better viewed as a defense of some policy other than protection against imports. Consider, for example, the correct point that workers trained in modern manufacturing skills in a firm struggling to compete against imports may leave that firm and take their skills to a competing firm. This threat is likely to make new firms underinvest in training their workers. A tariff to protect modernized firms is not quite on target, though, since the tariff will not keep workers from taking their new skills from firm to firm in the same protected industry. More appropriate is a subsidy on training itself, compensating the firm giving the training for benefits that would otherwise accrue largely to others. (Or the private firms could simply take more care to keep the wage lower during training, but with a commitment to paying much higher wages for workers who stay with the same firm after training.) Again, the specificity rule cuts against the tariff: although protecting an infant industry and its skill creation with a tariff on imports may be better than doing nothing, some other method can get at the problem more efficiently than the tariff.

This line of reasoning can be applied to the case of computer manufacture and computer services as an infant industry. Should the governments of Canada and Japan protect their computer industries against competition from

---

[4] In a study of Turkish protection, Krueger and Tuncer (1982) found no evidence that protected industries cut costs faster than unprotected ones.

IBM and other U.S. firms? If so, how? There is abundant evidence that the benefits of an expanding computer sector spill over to many industries and are not fully appropriated by computer firms (remember the external-economies argument of Chapter 5). These side benefits in the form of new productive knowledge are generated both by the industry that produces computers and by the industries that use computer services. The gains and losses from any one policy can be quantified only through a detailed investigation of the alternatives for developing these industries in Canada and Japan. Yet, the tariff is likely to be especially inferior to direct subsidies to production, training, and research in a technologically complex industry like computers, where many of the gains in knowledge occur in the consuming industries. If the encouragement is to be extended to the total use of computer services as well as to the domestic production of computers, it will not help to retard the use of computers with a tariff. This point seems reflected in the approach of Japan's Ministry of International Trade and Industry. MITI has indeed protected the Japanese computer industry against imports, but it has leaned increasingly on other forms of assistance—loans, patents, tax breaks, and so forth.

The Infant-Government, or Public Revenue, Argument

Import tariffs can still be justified by another second-best argument relating to conditions in less developed countries. In a newly emerging nation, the tariff as a source of revenue may be beneficial and even better than any alternative policy, both for the new nation and for the world as a whole.

For a newly independent nation with low living standards, the most serious "domestic distortions" may relate to the government's inability to provide an adequate supply of public goods. A low-income nation like Mauritania would receive large social benefits if it expanded such basic public services as the control of infectious diseases, water control for agriculture, primary schooling, and national defense. Yet, the administrative resources of many poor nations are not great enough to capture these social gains (others, of course, have the necessary administrative resources and use them inefficiently).

In such nations the import tariff becomes a crucial source, not of industrial protection but of public revenue. With severe limits on the supply of literate civil servants and soldiers, Mauritania will find tariffs efficient: revenue can be raised more cheaply by simply guarding key ports and borders with a few customs officials who tax imports and exports than with more elaborate and costly kinds of taxes. Production, consumption, income, and property cannot be effectively taxed or subsidized when they cannot be measured and monitored.

The infant-government argument is a valid reason why many low-income countries receive between one quarter and three fifths of their governmental revenue from customs duties, a higher dependence on customs than is found in equally trade-oriented high-income countries such as Canada. In principle, a new government can use the tariff to maximize social gains, gains that may even make the world as a whole benefit from tariffs in low-income countries. This is *not* to say that every Third World government that heavily taxes foreign trade is using the money to fund socially worthy investments. Foreign trade has also been heavily taxed by the likes of Bokassa, Ceausescu, Louis XIV, Marcos, or Mobuto.

NONECONOMIC ARGUMENTS

The other leading arguments for tariff protection relate to the national pursuit of "noneconomic" goals. Although aggressive economists may insist that nothing lies outside their field, these arguments do relate to points that are not usually thought of as part of standard economic analysis. The potential range of such arguments is limitless, but the view that man does not live by imported bread alone usually focuses on three other goals: national pride, income distribution, and national defense.

National Pride

Nations desire symbols as much as individuals do, and knowing that some good is produced within our own country can be as legitimate an object of *national pride* as having cleaned up a previous urban blight or winning Olympic medals. And as long as the pride can be generated only by something collective and nationwide, and not purchased by individuals in the market-place, there is a case for policy intervention. In fact, the above analysis still applies to a country seeking to derive national pride from home production. If the pride is generated by domestic production itself, then the appropriate policy tool seems to be the domestic production subsidy (setting aside the infant-government cases). Only if the pride comes from autarky itself is the tariff the best policy approach.

Income Redistribution

A second noneconomic objective to which trade policy might be addressed is the *distribution of income* within the nation. Often one of the most sensitive issues in national politics is either "What does it do to the poor?" or "What effect does it have on different regions or ethnic groups?" A tariff might be defended on the grounds that it restores equity by favoring some wrongly disadvantaged group, even though it may reduce the overall size of the pie to be distributed among groups. It is certainly important to know the effects of trade policy on the distribution of income within a country, a subject already treated in Chapter 4 and one to which we return in Chapter 13. It is fair to ask, though, whether the specificity rule should not be reapplied here. If the issue is inequity in how income is distributed within our country, why should trade policy be the means of redressing the inequity? If, for example, greater income equality is the objective, it could well be less costly to equalize incomes directly through taxes and transfer payments than to try to equalize them indirectly by manipulating the tariff structure. Still, if political constraints were somehow so binding that the income distribution could be adjusted only through tariff policy, then it is conceivable that tariffs could be justified on this ground.

National Defense

The *national defense argument* says that import barriers would help the nation accumulate more crucial materials for future economic or military welfare in the form of either stockpiles or emergency capacity to produce. It has a rich history and several interesting twists to its analysis. English mercantilists in the 17th century used the national defense argument to justify restrictions on the use of foreign ships and shipping services: if we force ourselves to buy English ships and shipping, we will foster the growth of a shipbuilding industry and a merchant marine that will be vital in time of war. Even Adam Smith departed from his otherwise scathing attacks on trade barriers to sanction the restrictive Navigation Acts where shipping and other strategic industries were involved. The national defense argument remains a favorite with producers who need a social excuse for protection. In 1984, the president of the Footwear Industry of America, with a straight face, told the Armed Services Committee of Congress:

> In the event of war or other national emergency, it is highly unlikely that the domestic footwear industry could provide sufficient footwear for the military and civilian population. . . . We won't be able to wait for ships to deliver shoes from Taiwan, or Korea or Brazil or Eastern Europe . . . improper footwear can lead to needless casualties and turn sure victory into possible defeat. (As quoted in *Far Eastern Economic Review*, October 25, 1984, p. 70.)

The same smell pervaded the U.S. oil industry's national-defense argument used to justify oil import limits from 1959 through 1973.

The importance of having strategic reserves on hand for emergencies is clear. Yet a little reflection shows that none of the popular variants of the national defense argument succeeds in making a good case for a tariff. A peacetime tariff does not stockpile goods for use in war. Instead, it merely makes us buy and use up more home-produced goods instead of foreign goods. The national defense argument presumes that this creates more productive capacity by encouraging the domestic industry. Yet, the industry will install only as much capacity as seems adequate to meet the peacetime needs, not any extra emergency capacity. If that is to be created, it is best subsidized directly.

The possibilities of storage and depletion also argue against the use of a tariff to create defense capability. If the crucial goods can be stored inexpensively, the cheapest way to prepare for the emergency is to buy them up from foreigners at the low world price during peace. Thus the English mercantilists might have given more thought to the option of stockpiling cheap and efficient Dutch-made ships to use when war later broke out between the English and the Dutch, while concentrating England's own resources on its comparative-advantage products. Similarly, the United States could stockpile low-cost imported footwear instead of producing it domestically at greater cost. And if the crucial goods are depletable mineral resources, such as oil, the case for the tariff is even weaker. Restricting imports of oil when there is no foreign embargo causes us to use up our own reserves faster, cutting the amount we can draw upon when an embargo or blockade is imposed. It is better to stockpile imports at relatively low peacetime cost as the United States has done with its Strategic Petroleum Reserve since the mid-1970s. To believe that restricting imports would increase our untapped reserves, we would have to accept two doubtful propositions: (1) protecting domestic oil producers makes them discover extra reserves faster than it makes them sell extra oil for peacetime consumption and (2) there is no more direct way to encourage further oil exploration within the country.[5]

SUMMARY

There are valid arguments for a tariff, though they are quite different from those usually given. One way or another, all valid defenses of a tariff lean on the existence of relevant **distortions**, or gaps between private and social costs or benefits.

When a nation as a whole can affect the price at which foreigners supply imports, a positive tariff can be nationally optimal. This national monopsony power is equivalent to a distortion, since there is a gap between the marginal cost at which society as a whole can buy imports and the price any individual would pay if acting alone without the tariff. The **nationally optimal tariff** rate equals the reciprocal of the foreign supply elasticity. If the foreign supply curve is infinitely elastic, and if the world price is fixed for the nation, the optimal tariff rate is zero. The less elastic the foreign supply, the higher the optimal tariff rate. The tariff is only optimal, however, if

---

[5] We will take a closer look at the case against using import barriers to prepare for national emergencies in Chapter 12's discussion of ''The Food Security Issue.''

foreign governments do not retaliate with tariffs on our exports. And with or without retaliation, the nationally optimal tariff is still bad for the world as a whole.

In a second-best world where there are distortions in the domestic economy, imposing a tariff may be better than doing nothing. Whether or not it is better will depend on detailed empirical information. Yet, when imposing the tariff is better than doing nothing, something else is still often better than the tariff. The **specificity rule** is a rough guideline that says: use the policy tool that is closest to the locus of the distorting gap between private and social incentives. This rule cuts against the tariff, which is usually only indirectly related to the source of the domestic distortion. Thus, many of the main arguments for a tariff, such as the infant-industry argument or the national defense argument, fall short of showing that the tariff is better than other policy tools. Although the tariff is sometimes better than doing nothing, it is usually inferior to some other policy tool.[6]

The case for a tariff is most secure in the infant-government setting, in which the country is so poor and its government so underdeveloped that the tariff is a vital source of government revenue to finance basic public investments and services.

SUGGESTED READINGS

An articulate plea for protectionism has been made by William B. Hawkins (1984, with rejoinders by Galbraith and Friedman). A protectionist argument has been given by a spokesman of organized labor, Rudy Oswald (1984).

The theory of trade policy in a second-best world beset with domestic distortions was pioneered in large degree by Nobel Laureate James Meade (1955). Major contributions were made by Harry G. Johnson (1965) and Jagdish N. Bhagwati (1969). The specificity rule is forcefully applied to the case of infant-industry protection by Robert E. Baldwin (1969). Excellent recent literature surveys, with varying degrees of technicality, are found in Baldwin (1984), Corden (1984), Dixit (1985), and Krueger (1984).

QUESTIONS FOR REVIEW

1. As in the question at the end of Chapter 6, you have been asked to quantify the welfare effects of removing an import duty, and somebody has already estimated the effects of U.S. production, consumption, and imports. This time the facts are different. The import duty in question is

---

[6] At this point you may wish to review the part of Chapter 6 entitled "A Preview of Conclusions," noting how each case discussed in Chapter 7 fits that preview.

the 5 percent tariff on motorcycles, and you are given the following information:

	Current Situation, with 5 Percent Tariff	Estimated Situation, without Tariff
World price of motorcycles (landed in San Francisco)	$2,000 per cycle	$2,050 per cycle
Tariff at 5 percent	$100 per cycle	0
U.S. domestic price	$2,100 per cycle	$2,050 per cycle
Number of cycles bought in U.S. per year	100,000	105,000
Number of cycles made in U.S. per year	40,000	35,000
Number of cycles imported by U.S. per year	60,000	70,000

Calculate (a.) the U.S. consumer gain from removing the duty, (b.) the U.S. producer loss from removing the duty, (c.) the U.S. government tariff revenue loss, and (d.) the net welfare effect on the United States as a whole.

Why does the net effect on the nation as a whole differ from the result in the question at the end of Chapter 6?

Answers: (a.) U.S. consumers gain $5,125,000 (b.) U.S. producers lose $1,875,000, (c.) U.S. government loses $6,000,000 in tariff revenue, and (d.) the United States as a whole loses $2,750,000 each year from removing the tariff. The U.S. national loss stemmed from the fact that the U.S. tariff removal raised the world price paid on imported motorcycles. In the Chapter 6 question, it was assumed that removing the duty had no effect on the world price (of sugar).

2. a. The minister for labor of the small nation of Pembangunan is anxious to encourage domestic production of digital clocks. A small clock industry exists, but only a few producers can survive foreign competition without government help. The minister argues that helping the industry would create jobs and skills that will be carried over into other ndustries by workers trained in this one. He calls for a 10 percent tariff to take advantage of these benefits. At the same cabinet meeting, the minister for industry argues for a 10 percent subsidy on domestic production instead, stating that the same benefits to the nation can be achieved at less social cost. Show the following diagramatically:

(1) The effects of the tariff on domestic output and consumption.
(2) The beneficial side effects of the tariff described by the minister for labor.
(3) The net gains or losses for the nation as a whole.

(4) All the same effects for the case of the production subsidy. Identify the differences in the effects of the two alternatives on the government's budget. Which policy would appeal more to a deficit-conscious minister for finance?

b. Can you design a policy that captures the alleged benefits of worker training better than either the 10 percent tariff or the 10 percent production subsidy?

3. A small price-taking nation imports a good that it could not possibly produce itself at any finite price. Can you describe plausible conditions under which that nation would benefit from an import tariff on that good?

4. Can you describe plausible conditions under which a nation would benefit from subsidizing imports of a good?

CHAPTER
8

▼

Other National Policies Affecting Trade

Modern governments have dreamed up hundreds of ways to restrict foreign trade without using a tariff. At times, the United States has molded its sanitary standards so that Argentine beef could not meet them. Colombia has used "mixing requirements," forcing steel importers to buy so many tons of more expensive domestic steel for each ton imported. Many governments put up a host of other nontariff barriers to trade: state monopolies on foreign trade, buy-at-home rules for government purchases, administrative red tape to harass foreign sellers, complicated exchange controls, and so forth. Many of these barriers relate to legitimate regulatory functions which happen to interfere with trade, while others are transparent manipulations of rules for the primary purpose of discriminating against foreign trade.

In the postwar era, the importance of nontariff barriers to trade has been on the rise. In the late 1940s and early 1950s many countries used them to keep tight control over their international payments while recovering from either World War II or longer-term underdevelopment. Since the 1950s, nontariff barriers have been reduced only a little, while multilateral negotiations have succeeded in cutting tariffs significantly. By the time the Kennedy Round of tariff cuts was consummated in 1967, nontariff barriers had emerged as the main roadblocks in the way of trade. Since the early 1970s, nontariff barriers have been getting even more formidable.

This chapter examines some of these barriers. Many of them are aimed at keeping out imports. Others restrict or subsidize exports. One, adjustment assistance, does not restrict trade at all but, instead, softens the harmful effects of freer trade on import-competing workers and firms. A guide to this chapter's variety of trade policy tools is offered in Figure 8.1. We have already started on the journey around this table. Chapters 6 and 7 related to the upper left-hand corner of this figure, considering the basic

FIGURE 8.1   A Catalogue of Some National Trade Policy Tools

	Tax or Subsidy	*Quantitative Restriction*
On Imports	Tariffs: Chapters 6 and 7 gave the basic analysis. Special cases in Chapter 8: countervailing duties, anti-dumping duties.	Import quotas. Important special cases: import embargoes, restrictions on government purchases from foreign suppliers.
On Exports	Export taxes and export subsidies, including dumping as a form of export subsidy.	Export quotas. Important cases include export embargoes, state export monopolies.

Other Policies
- Adjustment assistance to those injured by foreign competition is a domestic policy that can be viewed as a substitute for import restrictions.
- Many exchange-rate policies treated in Part Three are equivalent to trade barriers and trade subsidies.

analysis of taxes (tariffs) on imports. Now we set out on a clockwise journey around the top four squares of Figure 8.1. Moving across to the upper right square, we will continue to look at import barriers, but this time we will cover quantity restrictions rather than a tariff. Next, we turn briefly to quantitative restrictions on exports (embargoes, state export monopolies), and we will cover export taxes and subsidies, including dumping. Adjustment assistance rounds out this chapter's tour of nontariff trade policies.

THE IMPORT QUOTA

The most prevalent nontariff trade barrier is the import quota, a limit on the total quantity of imports allowed into a country each year. One way or another, the government gives out a limited number of licenses to import items legally and prohibits importing without a license. As long as the quantity of licensed imports is less than the quantity that people would want to import without the quota, the quota not only cuts the quantity imported but also drives the domestic price of the good up above the world price at which the license holders buy the good abroad. In this respect, it is similar to the import tariff.

Reasons for Quotas

There are several reasons why governments have often chosen to use quotas rather than tariffs as a way of limiting imports. The first is as insurance against further increases in import spending when foreign competition is becoming increasingly severe. In the wake of World War II, many countries found their competitive position weak and deteriorating at official exchange rates, and their governments tried stringent measures to improve the balance of payments. Quotas help government officials who are trying to improve the balance of payments; they ensure that the quantity of imports is strictly limited. If increasing foreign competitiveness lowers the world price of imports, that action will simply hasten the reduction in the total amount spent on imports. A tariff, by contrast, allows later foreign price cuts to raise import quantities and values if our demand for imports is elastic, thus complicating the planning of the balance of payments.

Quotas are also chosen in part because they give government officials greater administrative flexibility and power. International trade agreements have limited the power of governments to raise tariff rates. If import-competing industries mount greater protectionist pressures, the government cannot legally comply with higher tariffs, except where certain escape clauses permit. But the government is freer to impose more restrictive import quotas. Government officials also find that import quotas give them power and flexibility in dealing with domestic firms. As we shall discuss below, these officials usually have discretionary authority over who gets the import licenses under a quota system, and they can use this power to their advantage. For their part, protectionist interests also see in a quota system an opportunity to lobby for special license privileges, whereas a tariff is a source of government revenue to which they do not have any easy access.

These are some common reasons why government officials and protectionist industries often prefer quotas. Note that these are not arguments showing that quotas are in the interest of the nation as a whole.

Quota versus Tariff, with Competition

When we analyze the welfare effects of an import quota, we find that the quota is no better, and in some cases it is worse, than a tariff for the nation as a whole. To compare the two, let us compare an import quota with an equivalent tariff; that is, a tariff just high enough to make the quantity of imports equal to the amount allowed by the quota if the quota is used.

The effects of a quota on bicycles are portrayed in Figure 8.2. It is assumed here that the domestic bicycle industry is competitive and not monopolized with or without the quota; it is also assumed that the quota is binding enough to be less than what people would want to import at the

FIGURE 8.2 The Effects of an Import Quota under Competitive Conditions

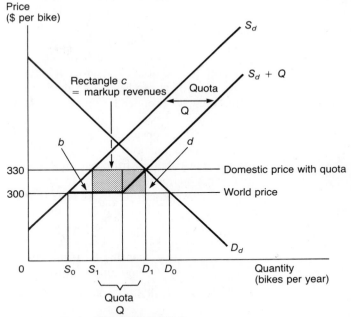

A. The U.S. market for bicycles

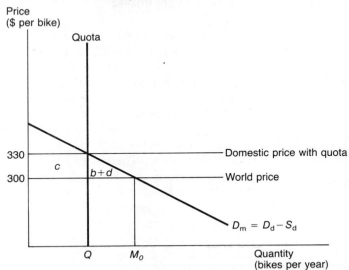

B. The market for U.S. bicycle imports

A quota cuts off the supply of imports by placing an absolute limit (Q) on what can be bought from abroad.

Under the competitive conditions shown here, the effects of an import quota are the same as those of a tariff that cuts imports just as much. The quota shown here has the same effects on everybody as the $30 tariff shown in Figure 6.4, as long as the government turns over the revenue from selling import licenses (area c in either half of the diagram) to the same residents as those that would get the tariff revenues.

world price. Domestic buyers as a group face a supply curve that equals the domestic supply curve plus the fixed quota, at all prices above the world price. Their inability to buy as much as they want at the world price drives up the domestic price of bicycles, in this case to $330.

The welfare effects of the quota are equivalent to those of a tariff under competitive conditions. The quota in Figure 8.2 has induced domestic producers to raise their production from S_0 to S_1, costing the nation area b by having bicycles produced at home at marginal costs rising up to $330 when they could have been bought abroad for $300 each without the quota. At the same time, consumers lose area d without its being a gain to anyone else. The price markup on the allowed imports, or the rectangle c, is an internal redistribution from consumers to whoever commands the licenses. So the net national loss is again areas b and d. This is the same set of results that we got with a $30 tariff (back in Figure 6.4), the tariff that let in the same amount of imports as the quota.

The import quota looks best, or least bad, under these competitive conditions, which make it no better or worse than the equivalent tariff. The quota looks worse than the tariff under either of two sets of conditions: (1) if the quota creates monopoly powers or (2) if the licenses to import are allocated inefficiently. Let us look at these two situations in order.

Quota versus Tariff, with Monopoly Power

The import quota turns out to cost the nation more than the equivalent tariff if the quota creates a domestic monopoly. It may do so. A dominant domestic firm cannot get much monopoly power from a nonprohibitive tariff, because it faces an elastic competing supply at the world price plus the tariff. With a quota, however, the domestic firm knows that no matter how high it raises its price, competing imports cannot exceed the quota. So a quota gives the dominant domestic firm a better chance of facing a sloping demand curve, and thus a better chance to reap monopoly profits with higher prices. Therefore, with the monopoly-creating quota we get even higher prices, lower output, and greater national losses than from a tariff that would have given us the same amount of imports. Appendix F shows this result geometrically, and it shows how to quantify the extra losses from a monopoly-creating import quota.

The quota can also harm the nation more than a tariff by giving monopoly power to foreign exporters. This odd result has occurred in the case of the **voluntary export restraint** quotas (VERs), which the United States has forced on Asian and other foreign suppliers of U.S. imports since the early 1960s. First in textiles, and later in steel and other products, the U.S. government found itself seeking a quota or its equivalent in order to ease protectionist lobbying pressures. Yet, the U.S. government wanted to avoid the embarrassment of imposing import quotas itself while still professing to be leading the world march toward free trade. It thus intimidated foreign suppliers into allocating a limited quota of exports to the U.S. market among themselves. The result was a quota on U.S. imports—but the foreign suppliers pocketed windfalls from the price markup, windfalls that more than compensated them for the profits they lost on the cutback in sales to the United States. The result: the same U.S. losses as with an equivalent tariff plus the failure to keep the price-markup revenues within the United States. Appendix F also shows this result geometrically.

Ways to Allocate Import Licenses

The welfare effects of an import quota further depend on how the government allocates the legal rights to import. Whoever gets these rights without paying for them captures the gains represented by area *c* in Figure 8.2 at the expense of consumers. Here are the main ways of allocating import licenses:

1. Competitive auctions.   (The best and rarest way.)
2. Fixed favoritism.   (The most arbitrary way.)
3. Resource-using application procedures.   (The least efficient way.)

The government can *auction* off import licenses on a competitive basis, either publicly or under the table. The public auction might work as follows. Every three months the government announces that licenses to import so many tons of steel or so many bicycles or whatever will be auctioned off at a certain time and place. Such a public announcement is likely to evoke a large enough number of bidders for the bidding to be competitive, especially if bid-rigging is a punishable crime. The auction is likely to yield a price for the import licenses that approximately equals the difference between the foreign price of the imports and the highest home price at which all the licensed imports can be sold. Returning to Figure 8.2, we can see that such an auction would tend to yield a price of $20 per imported-bicycle license, since that is the price markup at which all competitive license holders can resell imported bicycles in the home market. In this case of a public auction, the quota system does not cost the nation any more than an equivalent tariff. The proceeds of the quota, or area *c* in Figure 8.2, amount to a redistribution of income within the country, with bicycle consumers implicitly paying for the proceeds in the higher home price of bicycles and the proceeds being distributed by the government either as a cut in some other kind of tax or as spending on public goods worth this amount to society. The public auction revenues are essentially just tariff revenues under another name. The public auction, although the least costly way to allocate import licenses, is not used in the real world.[1]

---

[1] Robert Feenstra has estimated that auctioning off the U.S. import quota rights to steel, textiles, apparel, machine tools, sugar and dairy products could bring the government about $5 billion a year around 1987 (Feenstra, 1989, p. 246).

Some use is made of a variant on the competitive auction. Government officials can be corrupt and do a thriving business of auctioning import licenses under the table to whoever pays them the highest bribes. This variant entails some obvious social costs. Such blatant and persistent corruption can cause talented persons to become bribe-harvesting officials, instead of productive economic agents. Public awareness of such corruption also raises social tensions by advertising injustice in high places.

Import licenses adding up to the legal quota can also be allocated on the basis of *fixed favoritism* with the government simply assigning fixed shares to firms without competition or applications or negotiations. One common way of fixing license shares is to give established firms the same shares they had of total imports before the quotas were imposed. This is how the U.S. government ran its oil import quotas between 1959 and 1973. Licenses to import, worth a few billion dollars a year in price markups, were simply given free of charge to oil companies on the basis of the amount of foreign oil they had imported before 1959. This device served the political purpose of compensating the oil companies dependent on imports for their cutbacks in allowed import volumes so that they would not lobby against the import quotas designed to help oil companies selling U.S. oil in competition with imported oil. Income was redistributed, of course, toward oil companies and away from the rest of the United States, which could have benefited from the proceeds of a public auctioning of import licenses, instead of this fixed distribution of free licenses.

The final way of allocating import licenses is by *resource-using application procedures*. Instead of holding an auction, the government can insist that people compete for licenses in a nonprice way. One common, but messy, alternative is to give import licenses on a first-come, first-served basis each month or each quarter. This ties up many people's time in standing in line, time which they could have put to some productive use. Another common device for rationing imports of industrial input goods is to give them to firms on the basis of how much productive capacity they have waiting for the imported inputs. This policy also tends to foster resource waste because it causes firms to overinvest in idle capacity in the hope of being granted more import licenses. Any application procedure forcing firms or individuals to demonstrate the merit of their claim to import licenses will also cause them to use time and money lobbying with government officials. This cost is augmented by the cost of hiring extra government officials to process applications.

Anne Krueger has estimated that import-rationing procedures have cost the economies of Turkey and India large shares of their gross national product (7.3 percent for India in 1964, 15 percent for Turkey in 1968). As a rough rule of thumb, she suggests that the resource cost will approximate the amount of potential economic rents being fought for, or something like area c in Figure 8.2. This will tend to be the result since firms will tie up more resources in expediting their applications for import licenses up to the point where these resource costs match the expected economic rents from the licenses, or area *c*. Note that this is quite different from the result of the public auction. The auction caused area *c* to be redistributed within society, from consumers of the importable good through the government to the beneficiaries of the government's auction revenues. The application procedures tend to convert area *c* into a loss to all of society by tying up resources in red tape and expensive rent-seeking. Thus, the public auction emerges as the least costly way of administering an import quota system.

EXPORT BARRIERS

Nations can restrict their foreign trade by erecting barriers to exports as well as imports. It is intuitively clear that the analysis of export barriers should be a mirror image of the analysis of import barriers, and so it turns out, both for quantitative restrictions on exports and for export taxes.

Export quotas are rarer, but tend to be more severe, than import quotas. The usual export quota is zero (i.e., exporting any amount is a criminal offense). For example, governments have banned food exports during national famines in order to maximize the domestic food supply. More frequently, there is a complete ban on exports to *a particular country or set of countries,* a form of economic warfare. The United States is the principal peacetime user of the export ban, or export embargo.[2] Because an embargo discriminates between foreign nations, we defer treatment of embargoes to Chapter 9, which deals with trade discrimination more generally.

More common is the **export tax**, which has effects that are symmetrical to those of an import tax. Figure 8.3 shows the effects of an export duty on wheat from Canada under the assumption that Canada's policies cannot affect the world price of wheat. This diagram and its results are analogous to the case of a tariff on bicycle imports in Figure 6.4 in Chapter 6. The export duty of $1 a bushel causes exporters to receive a lower return on wheat exports, and they respond by shifting some of their wheat back to the domestic market. This action bids the domestic price of wheat back down to $4 a bushel from the world price of $5 a bushel. At the new equilibrium, wheat farmers will have shifted resources to some extent out of wheat growing and into other pursuits, while domestic consumers will have raised their consumption of wheat somewhat.

The welfare effects of the export duty are clear and quantifiable. Wheat farmers in the prairie provinces lose heavily by receiving only $4 a bushel

---

[2] The United States seems to contemplate export bans and quotas more often than other industrial nations for a special legal reason. The U.S. Constitution prohibits the taxing of exports. Any export restriction must therefore take the form of a quantitative control, not a tax.

FIGURE 8.3   The Effects of an Export Duty

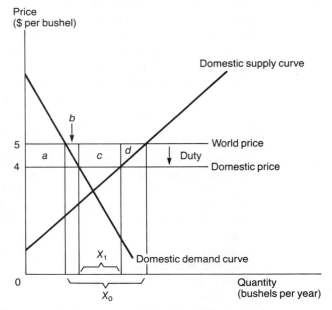

An export duty, in the face of a fixed world price, discourages exports and directs supplies back onto the home market, driving down the domestic price. Here a $1 export duty on Canadian wheat drives the domestic Canadian price of wheat down to $4. Domestic buyers benefit from the lower price, gaining consumer surplus equal to trapezoid *a*. Domestic growers are hurt by the lower domestic price, losing trapezoid *(a + b + c + d)*, and shift resources out of wheat production. The government collects the duty, rectangle *c*, leaving the same kinds of net national losses (triangles *b* and *d*) as in the import duty case (Figure 6.4).

instead of $5 a bushel. Their losses of net income add up to areas *a* + *b* + *c* + *d*. Consumers of wheat, concentrated in urban areas, gain area *a* through the reduction in wheat prices. The government collects and somehow redistributes area *c* in export duty revenues on the X_1 of exports that continue despite the duty. The nation as a whole loses areas *b* and *d*, the areas lost by exporters but gained by nobody.

If the exporting nation possesses some monopoly power in the world market, it could use the export duty to exploit this power to national advantage. Just as there was an optimal import tariff for the nation with monopsony power in Chapter 7, so there is a nationally optimal export duty, one that increases with the increase in the number of foreigners who are dependent on exports from the exporting nation. It is the hope of exploiting national monopoly power and getting the foreigner to pay more that prompts many export duties. Rice exports have been taxed in Thailand and Burma in part because these countries have some limited ability to get other Southeast Asian nations to pay them a higher price for rice given the duty (and in part simply to raise government revenues, albeit partly at the expense of rice-growing farmers). As we shall see in Chapter 11, the most important example of an export duty is the duty levied simultaneously by several nations joined in an international cartel. Here again, the main objective is the pursuit of monopoly profits by restricting exports. Canada may possess some small amount of this national monopoly power over world prices on wheat and minerals.

A different kind of export monopoly is the **state export monopoly**, in which the government gives itself the sole national right to export a good, whether or not it has any monopoly power in world markets. Examples are the "marketing boards" for such export crops as cocoa and coffee, and the state monopoly on foreign trade in socialist countries up to 1989. To analyze the welfare effects of such a state monopoly, we could simply use Figure 8.3 again. The only twist is that the government often has the objective of maximizing only its own profits, not national gains, from its monopoly. In terms of Figure 8.3, the state export monopoly is often a case in which the government seeks to maximize just area c, not the national gain $b + c + d$. Having a narrower objective, it ends up taxing and discouraging exports more than it would if it sought to maximize national welfare.

EXPORT SUBSIDIES AND COUNTERVAILING DUTIES

Exports are actually subsidized more often than they are taxed. This is curious and potentially controversial. It is curious because the same countries restrict imports without noting that subsidizing exports implicitly subsidizes imports by raising the country's exchange rate slightly, making it easier for others in the same country to buy foreign goods. It is potentially controversial because subsidizing exports violates international agreements. One of the provisions of the nearly worldwide postwar General Agreement on Tariffs and Trade (GATT) proscribes export subsidies as "unfair competition," and allows importing countries to retaliate with protectionist "countervailing duties."

Governments subsidize exports in many ways, even though they do so quietly to escape indictment under the GATT. They use taxpayers' money to give low-interest loans to either exporters or their foreign customers. An example is the U.S. Export-Import Bank, or Eximbank, founded in the 1930s, which has compromised its name by giving easy credit to U.S. exporters and their foreign customers but not to U.S. importers or their foreign suppliers. Governments also engage in direct promotional expenditures on behalf of exporters, advertising their products abroad and supplying cheap information on export market possibilities. Income tax rules are also twisted so as to give tax relief based on the value of goods or services each firm exports.

Export subsidies are very small on the average but loom large in certain products and for certain companies. For manufactured goods as a whole, they probably do not reach 1 percent of the value of exports for any major country even with a generous definition of what constitutes a subsidizing policy. Thus, one could not point to Japanese government subsidization of exports as a major explanation of the Japanese success in invading European and North American auto and electronics markets (though the United States might enter a self-righteous footnote pointing out that the U.S. industrial export subsidies are even smaller than the small ones of other industrial countries). On the other hand, export subsidies are large in certain cases. Most Eximbank loans have been channeled toward seven large U.S. firms and their customers, and Boeing in particular has been helped to extra foreign aircraft orders by cheap Eximbank credit. The biggest percentage export subsidies apply to agricultural products. All major countries have committed themselves to government programs that raise farmers' incomes by artificially using tax money to buy up (and to pay farmers not to plant) "surplus" farm products. To cut taxpayers' losses on these accumulated surpluses, the governments of Western Europe and North America sell the extra products at a loss abroad, sometimes with additional subsidies, offering a bargain to the Soviet Union and others who are able to buy at the relatively low world price.

If a foreign government is subsidizing exports into your national market, should you relax and enjoy the bargain on imports or should you retaliate by imposing **countervailing import duties** protecting the domestic industry in a way sanctioned by GATT? Officials may make up their minds on this issue partly with an eye to politics: those feeling intense lobbying pressure from the threatened domestic industry are more likely to seize the chance to impose duties, with fanfare about defending the industry from unfair foreign competition, whereas officials sensitive to antiinflation sentiments of consumers may avoid imposing the duty.

The economic pros and cons of countervailing duties against subsidized exports can be shown with the help of Figure 8.4, which can serve as a rough portrayal of the market for imported Korean steel shapes on the West Coast of either Canada or the United States. With free trade and no subsidy the market tends to the equilibrium at Point A. As usual, this maximizes world gains from trade in this market, since the marginal value of an extra ton, represented by the height of the demand curve, just matches the price P_0, which represents the marginal resource cost of supplying an extra ton of Korean steel.

The Korean government's export subsidy lowers the supply curve (here assumed perfectly elastic) to P_1 and raises West Coast imports to M_1. From a world point of view this is too much trade. North American firms are being encouraged to use Korean steel up to Point C where the value to

FIGURE 8.4 A Case of Export Subsidies and Countervailing Duties

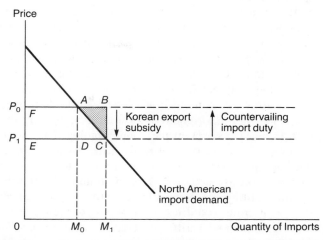

This diagram gives the effects of *(a)* a Korean export subsidy on steel to North America (either Canada or United States, say); *(b)* a North American countervailing duty against Korean steel, as allowed by GATT; and *(c)* the two together. An odd pattern results: each policy brings net losses to the country adopting it (so why do they do it?), yet for the world as a whole the countervailing duty undoes the harm done by the Korean export subsidy.

To harvest these results from the diagram, trace these steps and results:

	Moves Equilibrium		Welfare Effects on		
Policy	*From Point*	*To Point*	*North America*	*Korea*	*Both ("World")*
Korea's export subsidy	A →	C	gains *ACEF*	loses *BCEF*	lose *ABC*
North America's coun-tervailing duty	C →	A	loses *ACD*	gains *ABCD**	gain *ABC*
Both together	A back to A		gain *ADEF*	lose *ADEF*	zero

(Korean taxpayers implicitly pay
North American taxes)

* There are less exports to waste the subsidy on.

them of the last ton is only P_1, yet it costs the world P_0 in Korean resources to supply the last ton. This excess trade costs the world as a whole the shaded area *ABC* in the form of wasted resources. For the importing country, however, this is a bargain. Area *ACEF* represents the importing country's net gain from the cheaper steel imports.

If the United States or Canada were to apply a countervailing duty on Korean steel, one just large enough to offset Korea's export subsidy, we would return to the same price *(P_0)* and volume of trade *(M_0)* as with free trade and no subsidy at Point *A*. This makes good sense in terms of world efficiency since it eliminates the waste represented by area *ABC*. The countervailing duty in Figure 8.4 represents a successful application of Chapter 7's specificity rule: in this case the problem was indeed excess exports from Korea to North America and the countervailing duty taxes exactly that activity to the extent of the distorting subsidy. The net result of the subsidy plus the countervailing duty is interesting: trade ends up being unaffected (still at Point *A*), but Korean taxpayers unknowingly send invisible checks to North American taxpayers, to the tune of the area *ADEF*, each year. Yet the importing country would be serving the world interest at its own expense (to look at the countervailing duty alone) since it would lose area *ACD* by denying steel-using firms the better bargain. Export subsidies thus set up a curious division of national and world welfare stakes.[3]

Who typically accuses whom of unfair export subsidies? The left-hand columns of Figure 8.5 show the plaintiff (importing) countries and the defendant (exporting) countries in the antisubsidy cases reviewing under the General Agreement on Tariffs and Trade (see box) from 1980 through the middle of 1986. Just two plaintiff nations account for virtually all the cases: the United States and Chile. Setting aside the brief rash of Chilean accusations against Latin American neighbors and Spain between 1980 and 1983, we find that retaliation against export subsidies is essentially a tool of U.S. policy alone. Most of the accusations are aimed at the European Community and at the newly industrializing countries (NICs), such as Argentina, Brazil, Korea, Mexico and Taiwan, with almost none of them aimed at Canada or Japan.

DUMPING

The next dimension of government trade policy is quite similar to the case of policies dealing with export subsidies. Again the problem is specific to trade and again we get an unusual result.

Dumping is international price discrimination in which an exporting firm sells at a lower price in a foreign market than it charges in other (usually its home-country) markets. **Predatory dumping** occurs when the firm temporarily discriminates in favor of some foreign buyers with the purpose of eliminating some competitors and of later raising its price after the competition

---

[3] The reader may wish to diagram a different case, in which the importing nation has some monopsony power in the world market, facing an upward sloping foreign supply curve both before and after the fixed foreign subsidy. In this case, there are some rates of countervailing duty that would benefit both the importing country and the world. However, the rate of duty that was nationally optimal ($t^* = 1/s_m$ in Appendix E) usually would not equal the rate that maximized world gains by just offsetting the export subsidy. This hypothetical case might apply to, say, imports of autos into the United States.

FIGURE 8.5 Antisubsidy and Antidumping Rulings under GATT, 1980–1986

	Antisubsidy Cases		Antidumping Cases	
	Affirmative	Negative	Affirmative	Negative
Nation Acting as Plaintiff:				
United States	181	130	195	137
European Community	3	0	213	74
Australia	13	2	219	175
Canada	8	3	140	88
Chile	1	139	0	0
All nations	209	278	775	477
Nation accused of violation:				
United States	0	1	64	40
EC (or an EC member)	67	26	131	104
Japan	0	2	61	39
Canada	6	5	19	14
All industrial nations	107	101	397	308
Argentina	5	27	5	3
Brazil	23	63	31	12
Mexico	19	9	10	3
South Korea	8	13	76	40
Taiwan	1	6	24	23
All developing nations	101	173	122	111
Nonmarket economies	1	4	n.a.	n.a.

Note: Affirmative = Violation found; Negative = No violation

Source: Finger and Olechowski 1987, pp. 258–69. For antidumping cases, the international aggregate numbers are not fully comparable with those for individual nations.

the competition is dead. **Persistent dumping**, as its name implies, goes on indefinitely.

It is easy to conclude that *predatory* dumping is bad. It is practiced for the sole purpose of reaping monopoly gains and restricting trade over the long run. True, some buyers get a bargain on the dumped goods in the short run, but the practice would only continue if these were outweighed by the long-run damage to other buyers. Predatory dumping of manufactured goods was widely alleged during the international chaos of the 1920s and 1930s. Fortunately, predatory dumping is likely to become increasingly rare in modern competitive markets. A firm that tries to scare away all competitors with temporarily lower prices will find, once it has raised prices again, that many multinational enterprises can re-enter as competitors at an efficiently large scale of production.

While predatory dumping seems to have been fading, *persistent* dumping seems to have been on the rise since the early 1970s. In the early 1970s, as part of a larger campaign for relief against foreign competition, the

U.S. government charged firms in several countries with dumping their products in the U.S. market. By the 1980s, the number of affirmative (guilty) findings in dumping cases exceeded 100 per year. As shown in the right-hand columns of Figure 8.5, the battles over dumping involve many of the same nations as those over export subsidies. Again, the United States is a top plaintiff and the European Community and the NICs are frequently accused and found guilty. Japan has not brought formal antidumping charges, just as she has refrained from being an antisubsidy plaintiff. In other respects, though, the dumping battles are less one-sided than the export subsidy battles. The EC, Australia, and Canada are frequent antidumping plaintiffs, and the United States is a major offending (dumping) nation. The issue of dumping promises to remain at the center of the heated trade competition among the leading industrial nations and their newly industrializing challengers.

To judge whether persistent dumping is good or bad and whether or not retaliation against it is in order, it is first necessary to understand what makes some firms charge foreign buyers less. A firm will maximize profits by charging a lower price to foreign buyers if it has greater monopoly power in its home market than abroad and if buyers in the home country cannot buy the good abroad and import it cheaply. When these conditions hold, the firm is able to exploit home-country buyers more heavily.

Figure 8.6 shows such a case of profitable price discrimination, under the simplifying assumption that the firm faces a constant marginal cost of production. The illustration is based on a real case that surfaced in 1989. The U.S. government determined that firms in Japan, Korea, and Taiwan were all guilty of dumping telephones in the U.S. market, causing injury to AT&T (the plaintiff) and other U.S. firms.[4] We illustrate with the case of a single Japanese firm (e.g., Matsushita).

What makes the dumping profitable is that the firm faces a less elastic (steeper) demand curve in its home market than in the more competitive foreign market. Sensing this, the firm will charge prices so as to maximize profits. In any one market, profits are maximized by equating marginal cost and marginal revenue. In the U.S. market the profit-maximizing price is $25, which makes U.S. consumers buy X_1 telephones a year, at which marginal revenue just equals marginal cost. In the Japanese home market, where consumers see fewer substitutes for the major Japanese brands, the profit-maximizing price is $60, which causes consumers to buy S_1 phones a year, again equating marginal costs and revenues. This price discrimination is more profitable for the firm than charging the same price in both markets

---

[4] The actual dumping case involved phone equipment for small businesses, though here we illustrate with the case of cheap personal phones from Japan. The U.S. International Trade Commission estimated dumping margins (home-market markup above price on sales to the U.S.) of 120 to 180 percent for major firms in Japan and Taiwan, but only trivial markup for Korean firms. The Asian exporters had raised their share of the U.S. phone market for small businesses to 60 percent by 1989.

FIGURE 8.6 Dumping

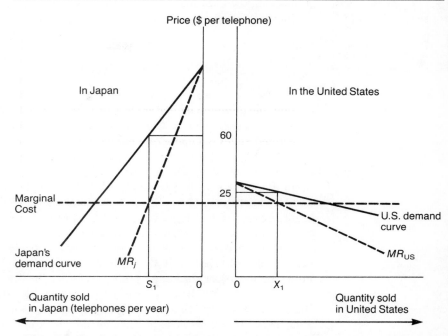

The price-discriminating monopolist maximizes profits by equating marginal revenue (MR) in each market with marginal cost. The firm will charge a higher price in the market where the demand curve it individually faces is less elastic (steeper). In this case, that is the home market in Japan. In the more elastic-demand, more competitive U.S. market, it charges less. It can get away with such discrimination only if there is no way for buyers in the high-price country to be served with output from the other country, and if policymakers do not retaliate.

which would yield lower marginal revenues in Japan than in the United States. As long as transport costs and import barriers make it uneconomical for Japanese consumers to import Japanese-made telephones all the way from the United States, the firm continues to make greater profits by charging a higher price in the Japanese market.

RETALIATION AGAINST DUMPING

Under pressure from import-competing firms, the governments of importing countries have often levied antidumping tariffs when given evidence that the foreign supplier is dumping. Such duties are sanctioned under the International Antidumping Code signed by most parties to the GATT. In the United

GATT: UNENFORCEABLE BUT SOMETIMES FORCEFUL

The first law of international law is that it does not exist. All the righteous international "laws" passed by international organizations and the moral pronouncements of religious leaders lack a firm enforcement mechanism to back them up. They are just international public opinions, which are enforced only if the balance of power allows. Nations large and small have ignored decrees from so-called international courts. Often, though, the international pronouncements do seem to show force. They shine a spotlight on violations of international norms. As long as a nation's own reaons for violating the norms are weak enough, the glare of the spotlight can make it conform.

Vague pressure is the key to the limited success of GATT, the General Agreement on Tariffs and Trade, a voluntary international code of conduct first signed by major industrial nations in 1947. Over the years, GATT's membership (number of "contracting parties") has expanded to about 100 nations. The agreement boils down to three principles: (1) liberalized trade, (2) nondiscrimination, and (3) no unfair encouragement for exports. On each front, it has had successes and failures.

Multilateral Trade Liberalization

It is never easy to get governments to overthrow their own protectionist lobbies, even though removing their own trade barriers unilaterally would raise national well-being. From the start, GATT agreements had to excuse some of the least reformable trade barriers, to lend credibility to its pressure for removal of others. Agricultural protection and subsidies have been exempted from the agreements, though serious efforts to reform agricultural trade have gained momentum in the late 1980s. Developing countries are also allowed to be heavily protectionist, though some have unilaterally liberalized their trade in the 1980s.

Meanwhile, tariff barriers among the industrial countries have been greatly reduced in eight rounds of multilateral negotiations: Geneva 1947, Annecy 1949, Torquay 1951, Geneva 1956, The Dillon Round 1960–61, The Kennedy Round 1964–67, The Tokyo Round 1973–79, and the Uruguay Round since 1987. The average tariffs of industrial countries, which were about 40 percent of import value in the 1940s, were less than 5 percent after the Tokyo Round in 1979. Part of the credit for this liberalization goes to the negotiating procedures set up under GATT. Each nation's government is able to defend its tariff-

CONTINUED

cutting "concessions" against its domestic protectionists as a price it must pay to gain better export access to other markets.

The toughest liberalization task now, however, is to deal with nontariff barriers (NTBs), which do not lend themselves as easily to reduction formulas as tariffs. As noted at the start of this chapter, NTBs are now the main form of protection, and have become slightly more serious since the early 1970s, often in violation of GATT.

Nondiscrimination

A second principle is that trade barriers should be lowered equally and without discrimination for all foreign trading partners. The GATT espouses the **Most Favored Nation** (MFN) principle. The MFN, dating back to the mid-nineteenth century wave of free trade led by Britain, stipulates that any concession given to any foreign nation must be given too all nations having MNF stafus, and GATT says that all contracting parties are entitled to that status. This prohibits any trade preferences, including the customs unions and free trade areas to be discussed in Chapter 9. Yet the GATT has looked like a "paper mouse" when it comes to nondiscrimination. It has granted exceptions for all preferences in place before 1947, for the customs union of the EC, the European Free Trade Area, the Canada-U.S. free trade area, and other arrangements. Perhaps GATT's insistence that such areas keep from raising their common external barriers had some slight effect, but even this is doubtful.

No Export Subsidies or Dumping

The GATT also prohibits export subsidies and dumping as unfair trade practices, and it permits retaliatory duties against such exports (though agricultural products are again exempted). Here the GATT has had a large effect, in the sense that it has sanctioned hundreds of specific retaliations by importing countries. We cannot say that this is such a good thing, however. As we saw elsewhere in this chapter, the welfare economics of retaliation against export subsidies and dumping is tricky. GATT has probably promoted the rise of a new protectionism, in the name of punishing unfair exports. Debate continues over the wisdom of this effective tool of GATT ethics.

States firms may bring dumping charges against foreign competitors. If the Department of Commerce finds that dumping has occurred and the U.S. International Trade Commission finds that U.S. firms have been materially injured, the customs officials are instructed to levy an extra import duty equal to the proven price discrepancy.

Who gains and who loses from an antidumping tariff is a question with a subtle answer. The free trader's first instinct is that the importing country, the "dumpee," should not retaliate against persistent dumping but only against predatory dumping. After all, if the foreign firm wants to go on selling to us at a cheaper price year in and year out, why not relax and enjoy it. Won't the gains to our consumers outweigh the losses to our import-competing producers?

Under current policies we get this pair of results:

1. An antidumping duty is likely to lower world welfare.
2. It could raise or lower the net national welfare of the importing country, whose government is retaliating. A small antidumping tariff can bring national gains, but a large tariff is bad for the nation as well as the world—as in Chapter 7's analysis of nationally optimal tariff.

In Figure 8.6, a small amount of duty would shift the U.S. import demand curve (and the MR_{US} curve) slightly downward and put pressure on the dumper to reduce its export price below \$25. This policy can bring gains to the importing country itself, and in the right dosage, it is a nationally optimal tariff, as in the first part of Chapter 7. Yet, any size of tariff lowers world welfare by discouraging some U.S. purchases of telephones worth more to buyers than the cost of making them. Thus, the current GATT practice of approving retaliation against dumping is probably bad for the world, but it may be bad or good for the importing nation.[5]

ADJUSTMENT ASSISTANCE

The last policy relating to trade is not so much a policy affecting trade as a way of responding to trade competition. It is the policy, now being increas-

---

[5] If the dumper eliminates all price discrimination, continues to serve both markets, and is rewarded by getting the duty removed again, the world could end up better off and the importing country worse off from the temporary punitive use of the duty. The world is better off in the sense that output is re-directed to the home-country buyers who valued the good more highly at the margin. (Readers can work out this result by combining the two demand curves from Figure 8.6 into one with a single price and a single *MR* curve.) Or the dumper may move his export-market production to the importing country at some slight extra expense of world resources. Or he might abandon the controversial foreign market as not worth the bother if it is spoiled by an antidumping duty. In the last case, the importing country and the world both lose. The issue of dumping is thus complex. The text gives the welfare results that seem most likely, however.

ingly practiced, of compensating those whose jobs and investments are displaced by import competition.

As noted in Appendix D, greater import competition entails **displacement costs**, whether or not this extra competition is the result of tariff reductions. These displacement costs are real and measurable, even though the usual analysis often leaves the impression that anybody whose job or investment is displaced by import competition simply finds another opportunity that is just as rewarding. In some cases, these costs can outweigh the efficiency benefits of freer trade, making a particular tariff reduction inadvisable.

Where the displacement costs are significant yet not high enough to justify maintaining higher tariff levels, society can consider the option of compensating those hurt by the keener import competition. As long as the free-trade policy brings net gains to the nation, the gainers can compensate the injured while still retaining net gains from the free trade. The United States and other countries have adopted this policy of **adjustment assistance**, or government financial aid to relocate and retrain workers (and firms) for reemployment in sectors where employment is expanding.

The U.S. adjustment assistance program, launched by President Kennedy's Trade Expansion Act of 1962, has received criticism from two sides. Organized labor, which originally supported the idea under Kennedy, has felt betrayed by a program that has, in practice, provided very little support. In the 1960s the official standards for eligibility for assistance were so stringent that nobody received any aid. The standards were loosened up somewhat through the Trade Act of 1974, in response to complaints by labor groups, but in the early 1980s the authorized assistance was still running below $100 million a year.

Defenders of the free marketplace (generally those who have secure jobs and investments) question the whole concept of adjustment assistance for import-competing industries. They ask why society should single out this particular group for aid. Why don't we give equally generous aid to those whose incomes are lowered by technological change, or government rerouting of highways, or bad weather? If we care about people who suffer income losses, why not cushion the fall of all incomes, regardless of the cause? What is so special about people who are hurt by import competition? These are valid questions. Some countries, most notably Sweden, indeed apply their income-maintenance and personnel retraining programs across the board, without singling out those injured by trade changes.

There remains the delicate problem of preserving the incentive to move out of an industry with a bad future. On the one hand, adjustment assistance programs are laudably concentrated on supporting retraining and relocation. But there is a perverse incentive in the promise of getting such aid if you are hurt by imports: firms and workers may be implicitly encouraged to gamble on import-vulnerable industries if they know that relief will be given should things work out badly. Here is the classical social-insurance dilemma: the desire to be there with help if an activity works out badly, versus the desire to discourage people from getting into, or staying with, such activities. The social insurance dilemma plagues adjustment assistance trade policy just as it plagues disaster relief (e.g., helping flood victims versus discouraging them from settling in the flood-prone lowlands), farm support policy, and welfare programs.

Yet, in many countries there may be a practical political case for tying adjustment to import injury. Where foreign trade is involved, free-trade advocacy is weakened because many of its main beneficiaries, being foreigners, have no votes in national politics. With no votes for foreign workers or firms, there is an extra danger that uncompensated injured workers and firms in the importing country will join lobbying alliances for more sweeping protectionist legislation. More generous adjustment assistance for import-competing groups than for others might be one effective political step to forestall more protectionist policies.

The existence of displacement costs carries another important policy implication, one worth applying whether or not society decides to help the injured. Any removal of import protection should be done *gradually*. If firms in a protected industry have sufficient advance warning, they can cut back on their investments and jobs without scrapping good capital or laying off workers. Normal capital depreciation and voluntary retirements by workers can cause output to shrink in the face of stiffer import competition. Gradualism can, in other words, eliminate nearly all the displacement costs while postponing only a small share of the benefits from the ultimately cheaper imports.

SUMMARY

Nontariff policies affecting international trade have emerged as the more important kind of trade distortion as tariffs have been gradually lowered in the postwar era. Government officials have many reaons for turning to import quotas and other nontariff barriers. Whatever these reasons, the basic analysis of the main nontariff barrier to trade, an **import quota**, indicates that at its best it is no worse than a tariff. It is more costly than the tariff if it creates monopoly power or if resources are used up in the private pursuit of licenses to import items legally.

Barriers to exports are symmetrical with import barriers. An **export duty** hurts exporting producers more than it helps consumers or gives revenue to the government, leaving a net cost to the nation, if the nation faces a fixed world price for its exports. If the nation has some monopoly power over world prices, it can reap net gains from an export duty, just as the nation with some monopsony power can levy an optimal import duty.

Export subsidies are widespread, even though they are condemned by the General Agreement on Tariffs and Trade (GATT). By causing excessive trade, they bring losses to the country making the subsidy and to the world. A **countervailing import duty** against subsidized exports, a duty that GATT sanctions, brings a loss to the country levying it but brings gains to the world by offsetting the export subsidy. The combination of an export subsidy and a countervailing duty that just offsets its effect on price would leave world welfare unchanged, with taxpayers of the export-subsidizing country implicitly making payments to the taxpayers of the importing country.

Dumping, or international pricing discrimination in favor of foreign buyers, occurs when firms have greater monopoly power in one national market, usually their home country, than in others. Temporary and predatory dumping should be countered with a tariff in the importing country. Persistent dumping poses a different policy puzzle for the importing country. The usual free-trade prescription is simply to relax and enjoy the cheap imports because they bring more gains to consumers than losses of income to import-competing producers. The truth seems more complex. Retaliation against dumping is probably bad for the world as a whole, but it could be good in small doses for the importing country.

The fact that increased international trade competition displaces import-competing firms and workers can be an argument for **adjustment assistance**, or income support while they relocate or retrain. Adjustment assistance is preferable to preventing import competition with trade barriers if the displacement costs of the free trade are less than the efficiency gains. The existence of displacement costs also counsels gradualism in the removal of existing trade barriers.

SUGGESTED READINGS

Careful empirical studies on a host of nontariff trade barriers were edited by Jagdish Bhagwati and Anne O. Krueger (1973–76), with country volumes on Turkey, Ghana, Israel, Egypt, the Philippines, India, South Korea, Chile, and Colombia.

The analysis of resource-using application procedures in the pursuit of import quota licenses is given by Anne O. Krueger (1974). Interesting theoretical embellishments are added by Bhagwati and Srinivasan (1980).

For an analysis of dumping, see William A. Wares (1977) and Ethier (1982).

GATT's victories, defeats, and challenges are well surveyed in Finger and Olechowski (1987).

QUESTIONS FOR REVIEW

1. The Gordian minister of trade proposes that the export duty on hemp fibers (one of Gordia's main exports) be removed, so that producers of hemp can take full advantage of good world prices and earn more foreign exchange. He is opposed by the minister of finance, who argues that she needs the revenues, and by the minister of industry, who argues that it will hurt the domestic rug industry, which uses hemp for backing. Assuming that the price of hemp is tied up in large world markets and is not affected by Gordia's policies, show each of these effects diagrammatically:

  a. The extra exports attainable if the export duty is removed.
  b. The loss of revenue resulting from removal of the duty.
  c. The benefit to hemp producers.
  d. The losses to domestic buyers of hemp.
  e. The net social gain from removal of the duty.

  2. Which of the following three beverage exporters is guilty of dumping in the U.S. market?

	(a) Banzai Breweries (Japan)	*(b)* Tipper Laurie, Ltd. (United Kingdom)	*(c)* Bigg Redd, Inc. (Canada)
Average unit cost	$10	$10	$10
Price charged at brewery for domestic sales	$10	$12	$9
Price charged at brewery for export sales	$11	$11	$9
Price when delivered to United States	$12	$13	$10

Answer: *(b.),* because its at-brewery price is lower for exports to the United States than for domestic sales. Selling at a loss, as in *(c.),* is not in itself dumping by present official definitions.

  3. Diagram the case of a countervailing duty in a country with some monopsony power as discussed in footnote 3 above. Show how the duty could benefit both the importing country and the world in this case.

▼

Trade Blocs

•

The last three chapters looked at equal-opportunity import barriers, ones that tax or restrict all imports regardless of country of origin. But some import barriers are meant to discriminate. They tax goods, services or assets from some countries more than those from other countries. The European Community (or EC) has done that, allowing free trade between members while restricting imports from other countries. (Any national government does the same, letting goods enter a region freely from other parts of the same nation but not from other countries.) Some export barriers are also designed to discriminate, by denying the outflow of goods, services, or assets to a particular country while allowing free export to other countries. The analysis of Chapters 6 through 8 has to be changed if it is to explain the effects of today's trade blocs.

TYPES OF ECONOMIC BLOCS

Some international groupings discriminate in trade alone, while others discriminate between insiders and outsiders on all fronts, becoming almost like unified nations. To grasp what is happening in Western Europe and North America and may happen elsewhere, we should first distinguish among the main types of economic blocs. Figure 9.1 and the following definitions show the progression of economic blocs toward increasing integration:

1. A **free-trade area**, in which members remove trade barriers among themselves, but keep their separate national barriers against trade with the outside world. In such an area customs inspectors must still police the borders between members in order to tax or prohibit trade that might otherwise avoid some members' higher barriers by entering (or leaving) the area through

low-barrier countries. One example of a free-trade area, true to its name, is the European Free Trade Area formed in 1960 (see the chronology given later in this chapter). Another is the Canada–U.S. Free Trade Area, which formally began in 1989.

2. A **customs union**, in which members again remove all barriers to trade among themselves and adopt a common set of external barriers, thereby eliminating the need for customs inspection at internal borders. The European Economic Community from 1957 to 1992 has included a customs union, along with some other agreements.

3. A **common market**, in which members allow full freedom of factor flows (migration of labor or capital) among themselves, in addition to having a customs union. Despite its name, the European Common Market (EEC and later EC) was not a common market up through the 1980s because it still had substantial barriers to the international movement of labor and capital. The EC is scheduled to become a true common market, and more, by 1992.

4. Full **economic union**, in which member countries unify all their economic policies, including monetary, fiscal, and welfare policies as well as policies toward trade and factor migration. Most nations are economic unions. Belgium and Luxembourg have formed such a union since 1921. By 1992 the EC will have approached full unity, though governments will keep much of their tax autonomy and may not live up to the promise of full monetary union.

The first two types of economic bloc are simply **trade blocs** (i.e., they have removed all explicit trade barriers but keep their national barriers to the flow of labor and capital and their national fiscal and monetary autonomy). Trade blocs have proved easier to form than common markets or full unions among sovereign nations, and they are the subject of this chapter. Freedom of factor flows within a bloc is touched on only briefly here, and returns in Part Five. The monetary side of union, such as the emerging European Monetary System, enters in Part Three.

FIGURE 9.1   Types of Economic Blocs

	Free Trade among the Members	Common External Tariffs	Free Movement of Factors of Production	Harmonization* of all Economic Policies (Fiscal, Monetary, etc.)
Free trade area	✓			
Customs union	✓	✓		
Common market	✓	✓	✓	
Economic union	✓	✓	✓	✓

* If the policies are not just harmonized by separate governments, but actually decided by a unified government with binding commitments on all members, then the bloc amounts to full economic nationhood. Some authors call this "full economic integration."

IS TRADE DISCRIMINATION GOOD OR BAD?

How good or how bad is trade discrimination? It depends on what you compare it to. Compared to a free-trade policy, putting up new barriers discriminating against imports from some countries is generally bad, like the simple tariff of Chapter 6 through 8. But the issue of trade discrimination usually comes to us from a different angle: beginning with uniform tariffs (the same tariff regardless of country of origin), what are the gains and losses from removing barriers only between certain countries? That is, what happens when a customs union like the EC gets formed?

Two opposing ideas come to mind. One instinct is that forming a customs union or free-trade area must be good because it is a move toward free trade. If you start from a uniform set of trade barriers in each nation, having a group of them remove trade barriers among themselves clearly means lower trade barriers in some sense. Since that idea is closer to free trade, and Chapters 6 through 8 found free trade better with only carefully limited exceptions, it seems reasonable that forming a trade bloc allows more trade and raises world welfare. After all, forming a nation out of smaller regions brings economic gains, doesn't it?

On the other hand, we can think of reasons why forming a free-trading bloc can be bad, even starting from uniform barriers to all international trade. First, forming the trade bloc may encourage people to buy from higher-cost suppliers. The bloc would encourage costly production within the bloc if it kept a high tariff on goods from the cheapest source outside the bloc and no tariff on goods from a more costly source within the bloc. By contrast, a uniform tariff on all imports had the virtue that customers would still do a lot of their buying from the cheapest source. Second, the whole idea of trade discrimination smacks of the bilateralism of the 1930s, that is, when separate deals with individual nations destroyed much of the gains from global trade. Third, forming blocs may cause international friction, simply because letting someone into the bloc will shut others out. For all these reasons, the General Agreement on Tariffs and Trade (GATT) is opposed to trade discrimination in principle. True, GATT has had to retreat and allow exceptions whenever there was strong pressure to allow a trade bloc (e.g., the EC) to be formed. But the idea that discrimination is bad still has the status of international law.

THE BASIC THEORY OF CUSTOMS UNIONS: TRADE CREATION AND TRADE DIVERSION

In fact, trade discrimination can be either good or bad. We can give an example of this, and in the process discover what conditions separate the good from the bad cases.

It may seem paradoxical that the formation of a customs union (or a "free-trade area") can either raise or lower welfare, since removing barriers among member nations looks like a step toward free trade. Yet, the analysis of a customs union is another example of the not-so-simple theory of the second best, which we discussed in Chapter 7.

The welfare effects of eliminating trade barriers between partners are illustrated in Figure 9.2, which is patterned after Britain's entry into the EC. To simplify the diagram greatly, all supply curves are assumed to be perfectly flat.[1] In the absence of any tariffs, the British could buy Japanese cars at £5,000. The next cheapest alternative is to buy German cars delivered at £5,400. If there were free trade, at Point C, Britain would import only Japanese cars and none from Germany.

Before its entry, however, Britain did not have free trade in automobiles. It had a uniform tariff, imagined here to be £1,000, which marks up the cost of imported Japanese cars from £5,000 to £6,000 in Figure 9.2. No Britons buy the identical German cars because they would cost £6,400. The starting point for our discussion is thus the tariff-ridden Point A, with the British government collecting (£1000 times M_0) in tariff revenues.

Now let Britain join the European Community, removing all tariffs on goods from the EC while leaving the same old tariffs on goods from outside the EC. Under the simplifying assumptions made here, German cars would now cost only £5,400 in Britain (instead of that plus the £1,000 tariff), and would take over all the imports of compact cars into Britain. British buyers, seeing the price drop from £6,000 to £5,400, would buy more imported cars, the imports M_1 now coming from Germany (at Point B). Clearly, British car buyers have something to cheer about. They gain the areas a and b in extra consumer surplus thanks to the extra bargain. But the British government loses all its previous tariff revenue, the area a plus the area c (or, again, £1,000 times M_0). So, after we cancel out the gain and loss of a, Britain ends up with two welfare effects:

1. A welfare gain from trade creation $(M_1 - M_0)$. **Trade creation** is the volume of new trade created by forming the trade bloc.
2. A welfare loss from *trade diversion (M_0)*. **Trade diversion** is the volume of trade diverted from outside exporters to bloc-partner exporters.

This is the general result: the national and world *gains from a customs union are tied to trade creation, and their losses are tied to trade diversion.*

---

[1] There is an alternative analysis assuming upward-sloping supply curves for all three countries, with similar but more widely applicable results (e.g., Harry G. Johnson, 1962). One point revealed by the upward-sloping supply analysis is that trade diversion may bring terms-of-trade gains to the bloc partners at the expense of the rest of the world. Diverting demand away from outside suppliers may force them to cut their export prices (i.e., the bloc's import prices). On the export side, diverting bloc sales toward bloc customers and away from outside customers may raise the bloc's export-price index. Thus, the bloc may experience a higher terms-of-trade ratio (= export price/import price), a possibility assumed away by the flat outside-world supply curve in Figure 9.2.

The flat-supply-curve case is used here because its diagram (or its algebra) makes the basic points more clearly.

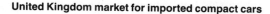

FIGURE 9.2   Trade Creation and Trade Diversion from Joining a Customs Union

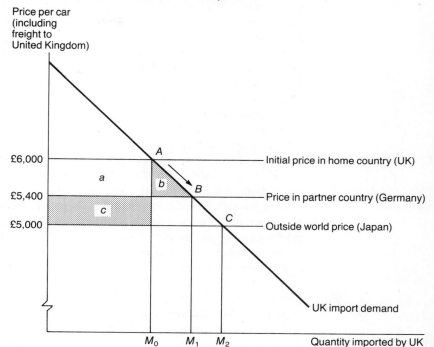

Starting from a uniform tariff on all compact cars (at *A*), Britain joins the EC customs union, removing tariffs on imports from EC but not on imports from the cheapest outside source, Japan. In this example, with flat supply curves, all the original imports from the cheapest outside source (M_0) are replaced with imports (M_1) from the new partner countries (e.g., Germany). The shift from *A* to *B* creates the new trade $(M_1 - M_0)$, bringing gains (area *b*) from the chance to buy the extra imports. It also *diverts* trade (M_0) from the cheapest supplier to the partner country, imposing extra costs (area *c*). The net welfare effect depends on whether the trade-creation gain exceeds the trade-diversion loss.

Studying the one-good case in Figure 9.2, you can discern what conditions dictate whether the gains outweigh the losses. Here are three tendencies that make for greater gains from a customs union:

a. The more elastic the import demand, the greater the gains.
b. The greater the difference between the home-country and partner-country costs (supply curves), the greater the gains.
c. The smaller the difference between the partner-country and outside-world costs (supply curves), the greater the gains.

So the best trade-creating case is one with highly elastic import demands, high preunion tariffs [allowing bigger cost differences in *(b.)*] and costs that are almost as low somewhere within the union as in the outside world [keeping the difference in *(c.)* small]. Conversely, the worst trade-diverting case is one with inelastic import demands and high costs throughout the new customs union.

What kinds of blocs are most likely to have these attributes? Although there is no simple answer, historical experience offers some clues. So far, economic unions between sovereign nations seem to have had the most success and longevity when they featured two-way trade in modern luxury-good manufactures rather than trade featuring agricultural products. Perhaps one reason why the EC and EFTA survived, and the idea of a Canada–U.S. free-trade kept reviving despite political opposition, was that the gains were perceived to be, and actually are, largest in such unions among major industrial countries. Both the demand for, and the supply of, agricultural productions are inelastic. The same should be true of import demands as well as overall demand and supply. Therefore, little net new trade would be created by a customs union featuring agricultural products. With modern manufactures, on the other hand, demand curves are more elastic (with respect to either price changes or income changes). Furthermore, intraindustry trade of the sort discussed in Chapter 5 is characteristic of modern manufactures, allowing previously competitive countries to reap large gains from specialization.[2] So, a good economic hunch is that the case for forming trade blocs will always look strongest among high-income industrial countries, especially ones starting from high initial trade barriers. To pursue this and other points, we can take a closer look at some experience that has already unfolded and has been studied by economists.

THE EC EXPERIENCE AND 1992

The formation of the EC's customs union has provided an experiment in the effects of trade integration. Numerous studies in the 1960s and 1970s

---

[2] Could it be that the net gains are especially large if the nations or blocs joining together are "large," in the sense that their union causes a great jump in the share of world manufacturing production that is within the union? Some economists have thought so, reasoning that the larger the jump in union size, the greater the chance that the world's lowest-cost producers in each industrial market will be captured and given a much wider market to work in. If this is true, then especially great gains can be reaped if the EC, North America, and Japan form a vast trade bloc, or even if they just agree to virtually free trade in GATT negotiations (to the possible detriment of Third World exporters of manufactures, of course).

We do not yet know that this is true, however. There is evidence that economies of scale and specialization are exhausted once industrial plants and industrial regions (e.g., Silicon Valley) reach a certain size; there is also evidence that minimum efficient scales of operation already seem to have been reached in most industries.

tended to conclude that the net gains from forming the EC (then the EEC) were small but positive. For example, net welfare gains on trade in manufactured goods calculated by Balassa (1975, p. 115) were a little under one tenth of one percent of members' total GNP. That tiny positive estimate overlooks some losses from the EC, but also overlooks some likely gains. By concentrating on trade in manufactured goods, the literature generally overlooked the significant social losses from the EC's Common Agricultural Policy. This policy protects and subsidizes agriculture so heavily as to bring serious social losses of the sort described in Chapter 12 below.[3] On the other hand, the studies of the 1960s and 1970s generally confined their measurements to static welfare measures like those in Figure 9.2, omitting possible gains from economies of scale or improved productivity incentives. Here, unfortunately, is a research frontier still unsettled: we know that economies of scale and productivity performance are key possible outcomes of economic union, but we still lack good estimates of them. For now, the empirical judgment is threefold: (1) on manufactured goods, the EC has brought enough trade creation to suggest small positive net welfare gains: (2) the static gains on manufactures have probably been smaller than the losses on the Common Agricultural Policy; but (3) the net judgment still depends on what one believes about the unmeasured dynamic gains from economies of scale and productivity stimuli.

What new effects should be expected from the formation of a truly common market in 1992? Here the empirical economist must exercise more imagination beyond the basic trade effects of Figure 9.2. The 1992 unification involves removing all sorts of nontariff trade barriers:

- No longer will truckers be irked by thousands of trade barriers within the EC, such as frontier checkpoint delays, paperwork, and freight-hauling restrictions.
- The common market means an end to product "quality" codes that were thinly disguised devices for protecting higher-cost domestic producers. Examples include German beer-purity regulations, Italian pasta protection laws, Belgian chocolate content restrictions, and Greek ice cream specifications.[4]

---

[3] Trade diversion on agricultural products is one reason why empirical studies find that joining the EC in 1973 may have cost Britain dearly. The Common Agricultural Policy meant that British consumers had to lose cheap access to their traditional Commonwealth food suppliers (Australia, Canada, New Zealand). They had to buy the more expensive EC food products and also had to pay taxes on their remaining imports from the Commonwealth, taxes that were turned over to French, Danish, and Irish farmers as subsidies. This cost Britain an estimated 1.8 percent of GNP in the 1970s, versus a static-analysis gain of less than 0.2 percent of GNP on manufactured goods (Miller and Spencer 1977). The Thatcher government later bargained for a fairer sharing of the burdens of farm subsidies.

[4] A controversial new quality code would regulate the entertainment industry uniformly after 1992. Though the details are still unresolved as of this writing, the EC may put a quota on TV and film imports from the United States and other outside suppliers. EC viewers

A CHRONOLOGICAL SKETCH OF POSTWAR TRADE INTEGRATION IN WESTERN EUROPE

1950–1952 Following the Schuman Plan, "the Six" (Belgium, France, West Germany, Italy, Netherlands, and Luxembourg) set up the European Coal and Steel Community. Meanwhile, Benelux is formed by *Be*lgium, *Nether*lands and *Lux*embourg. Both formations provide instructive early examples of integration.

1957–1958 The Six sign the Treaty of Rome setting up the European Economic Community (EEC, or "Common Market"). Import duties among them are dismantled, and their external barriers unified, in stages between the end of 1958 and mid-1968. Trade preferences are given to a host of third-world countries, most of them former colonies of EEC members.

1960 The Stockholm Convention creates the European Free Trade Area (EFTA) among seven nations: Austria, Denmark, Norway, Portugal, Sweden, Switzerland, and the United Kingdom. Barriers among these nations are removed in stages. 1960–1966. Finland joins as an associate member in 1961, Iceland in 1970.

1972–1973 Denmark, Ireland, and the United Kingdom join the EEC, converting the Six into nine. Denmark and the United Kingdom leave EFTA. The United Kingdom agrees to abandon many of its Commonwealth trade preferences.

1973–1977 Trade barriers are removed in stages, both among the nine EEC members and between them and the remaining EFTA nations. Meanwhile, the EEC reaches trade preference agreements with most non-member Mediterranean countries, along the lines of earlier agreements with Greece (1961), Turkey (1964), Spain (1970), and Malta (1970).

1978 The European Community (EC) is formed by the merger of the EEC (Common Market), the European Atomic Energy Commission, and the European Coal and Steel Community.

1979 European Monetary System begins to operate, based on the European Currency Unit. European Parliament first elected by direct popular vote.

1981 Greece joins the EC as its tenth full member.

1986 The admission of Portugal and Spain brings to 12 the number of full members in the EC.

1986–1987 Member governments approve and enact The Single European Act, which called for a fully unified market by 1992 and for weighted voting rules that no longer require unanimity in the European Council.

FIGURE 9.3   Potential Gains in Economic Welfare for the EC from Completing the Internal Market in 1992, as Forecast by the Cecchini Report (1988)

	As a Percent of GNP
Gains from removing trade barriers	0.2
Gains from removing barriers affecting overall production	2.2
Gains from exploiting economies of scale more fully	2.1
Gains from intensified competition, reducing business inefficiencies and monopoly profit	1.6
Total	6.1

Source: Cecchini 1988, p. 84. Cecchini somehow got a total of 5.3% from the same detail.

- Capital will be free to flow anywhere in the 12 countries.
- Workers from any of the 12 countries can practice their trades and professions anywhere.

How much benefit might such a miscellany of measures bring to the EC? It is hard to say, given the difficulty of measuring such key determinants as economies of scale. Despite the difficulty, the EC published a bold set of estimates of the gains to be expected. The welfare estimates from the 1988 Cecchini Report run around 5 to 6 percent of the EC's gross domestic product sometime in the 1990s, as shown in Figure 9.3. Note that half of the forecast gain relates to economies of scale and the benefits of increasing competition, two kinds of effects that are notoriously hard to quantify.

THE CANADA–UNITED STATES FREE-TRADE AREA

Unlike the attempts to measure the actual early effects of the EC, the studies of the North American bloc have all been counterfactual, estimating the effects of something that has not happened yet. The idea of a free-trade area between Canada and the United States has been debated since the 19th century, but is only now being enacted. As late as 1986, when the two countries had a minor trade war over lumber and corn, and another tiff over Arctic navigational rights, there seemed little chance of a free-trade area. But in 1987–88, as we saw in Chapter 1, the mood swung around and a pact was signed after all. Will the effects in the 1990s show more trade creation than trade diversion? Will Japan and other countries be harmed? Will Canada or the United States gain more?

may face a world with tighter restrictions on such programs as, in France, "Tom et Jerry," "Santa Barbara," and "Deux flics de Miami." Europe might reap cultural gains if such programming were replaced with test patterns. The plan, however, is to replace them with EC imitations, along the lines of the current "La roue de la fortune."

Our usual presumption is that the effects on Canada would be greater than the effects on the United States. That should be true on two levels. Less controversial is the point that the effects *as a share of GNP* should be stronger for Canada, since the Canadian economy is less than one-tenth the size of the next economy to the south. Beyond that, economists tend to expect even greater *absolute* effects on Canada than on the United States. The basic reasoning surfaced back in Chapter 3, where we reasoned that the absolute net national gains should be distributed in proportion to the two nations' price changes caused by the opening of new trade. We expect that Canada's elasticities of trade with the United States are the lower of the two sets of elasticities; therefore, opening new trade should shift Canadian prices more than U.S. prices. If so, the net national gains should be absolutely greater for Canada. So should the relative-price shock to different parts of the economy. Import-competing producers are likely to be hurt more, and consumers and exporters helped more, in Canada than in the United States, even in absolute dollar terms.

Suspecting as much, most studies of a proposed Canada–U.S. free-trade area have focused on Canada's stake in it. Canada stands to raise its GNP by 8 to 10 percent perennially thanks to the free-trade pact, a far larger gain than any EC country has ever gotten from the common market so far. More than half of Canada's prospective gain comes from the opening of U.S. markets, rather than from Canada's own removal of trade barriers. The importance of the better access to U.S. markets seems especially valid in studies that reckon there are economies of scale to be reaped by Canadian industry when faced with a much bigger market. The importance of access to U.S. markets seems like a reasonable justification for Canada's making a separate deal with the United States: global liberalization under the GATT approach would have done much less to give Canada foreign markets, given the dominant importance of selling to the United States.

OTHER TRADE BLOCS

European Free-Trade Area

In quick reaction to the formation of the EEC, seven other nations of Western Europe formed the European Free Trade Area (EFTA) in 1960. The EFTA was looser and less binding than the EEC in four respects. First, as its name implies, EFTA allowed each nation to keep its own separate tariff rates on goods and services from outside the area, unlike the common external tariff of the EEC. Second, the union was not geographically compact. Unlike the adjacent Six of the EEC (Italy, France, the three Benelux nations, and West Germany), the "outer Seven" of EFTA formed a trading bloc with probably higher transport costs: three Scandinavian countries (Denmark, Norway, Sweden); two landlocked alpine countries (Austria, Switzerland);

Portugal, and the United Kingdom. Third, the external tariffs of the Seven were already rather low, suggesting little effect from forming EFTA. Finally, on the positive side, EFTA was a loose unit in one beneficial way. The Seven wisely steered clear of developing a common agricultural policy, which would probably have ended up with all nations rising to the costly subsidies of the most protectionist members, as in the EC. All these dimensions of looseness would lead us to expect that the welfare effect of forming EFTA would be small but probably positive. That is indeed what the few estimates seem to suggest (Pomfret, 1988, p. 143). From these small positive effects, EFTA moved to zero effect in 1973–77, in the sense that EFTA and the EEC agreed to remove trade barriers between them on all manufactured goods.

Third World Trade Blocs

In several less developed settings, a different idea of gains from economic union took shape. The infant-industry argument held sway. It was easy to imagine that forming a customs union or free-trade area among Third World countries would give the union a market just large enough to support a large-scale producer in each modern manufacturing sector, without letting in manufacturers from the highly industrialized countries. With such a protected infancy, the new firms could eventually cut their costs through economies of scale, external economies, and learning by doing, until they could compete internationally, perhaps even without protection. A corollary about customs unions follows from this basic faith in infant-industry protection: countries can gain not only from trade creation but also from trade diversion. As long as the member countries can agree on which of them are assigned to which of the infant industries, the gains from the trade bloc could be great.

For all the appeal of the idea, its practice "has been littered with failures," as Pomfret has put it, and the life expectancy of an effective Third World trade bloc has been short. The Latin American Free Trade Area (Mexico and all the South American republics) lacked binding commitment to free internal trade even at its creation in 1960, and by 1969 it had effectively split into small groups with minimal bilateral agreements. The Central American Common Market, also created in 1960, scored some small victories for a decade, but fell apart in the 1970s. Other short-lived unions with only minimal concessions by their members included a chain of Caribbean unions, the East African Community (Kenya, Tanzania, and Uganda) disbanded in 1977, and several other African attempts. One centrifugal force was the inherent inequality of benefits from the new import-substituting industries. If economies of scale and external economies were to be reaped, the new industrial gains would inevitably be concentrated into one or a few industrial centers. Every member wanted to be the group's new industrial leader, and none wanted to remain more agricultural. No formula for gains-sharing could be worked out. Even the Association of Southeast Asian Nations (ASEAN), with its broader industrial base, was unable to reach stable agreements about comparative advantage when this was tried in the late 1970s and early 1980s.

The Socialist Trade Bloc

Between 1949 and 1989, socialist countries discriminated strongly against their trade with capitalist economies, in favor of trade among themselves. They faced a tough trade problem that has never been solved fully: How do centrally planned sovereign nations decide what to trade with each other? Each country's planners develop their own separate menus of desirable imports and surplus goods available for export. In practice, the result has tended to be bilateral barter, in which pairs of nations agree on long lists of exports and imports between each other with minimal use of money.

In the case of Eastern Europe, the institution charged with transforming bilateral barter into something more efficient and multilateral was the Council for Mutual Economic Assistance (CMEA), formed in January 1949.[5] It was not an easy assignment. The burden of setting up simultaneous bargained solutions among several countries, solutions that committed countries to a particular "socialist division of labor" for years to come, was a heavy one. Resistance was especially strong in countries like Romania, which wanted to develop their own import-competing manufacturing sectors instead of relying on exports of oil and other primary products to purchase manufactures. CMEA members reverted to separate bilateral deals with lip service to multilateralism.

Studies suggest that setting up the CMEA regime under Soviet tutelage actually lowered total trade volumes in Eastern Europe, at least up through the early 1980s. True, the trade among CMEA members was greater than one would have predicted given the members' GNP per capita, location, population size, natural resources, and trade propensities back in the 1920s. But given all the same factors, one would have predicted much greater trade with the West than was observed. The net result is that the total foreign trade of CMEA countries, with capitalist countries plus CMEA partners, was only 50 to 60 percent of that of comparable capitalist nations. Holzman's suggestion that CMEA might be called a "trade-destroying customs union" seems valid.

---

[5] The six original members of CMEA were all European: Bulgaria, Czechoslovakia, Hungary, Poland, Romania, and the Soviet Union. Late in 1949 Albania and East Germany joined. In 1962, Albania left and Mongolia joined. Cuba joined in 1972.

PROSPECTS FOR EAST-WEST TRADE

The Eastern European revolutions of 1989 changed the rules of East-West trade. East-West trade in the 1990s is destined to take a higher average share of world trade than its mere three percent share in the 1970s and 1980s.

Which side will gain more from the expansion of East-West trade? Our basic analysis of the gains from trade is potentially applicable here, despite the institutional differences between the trading regions. Since any trade bargains are entered voluntarily on both sides, it is likely that both sides will gain something. Which side gains more depends on how close the trading prices are to the prices that would prevail in West or East without East-West trade. Recall Chapter 3's simple formula for the international sharing of the gains from trade:

How the gains from opening trade are split between nations: The gains from opening trade are divided in direct proportion to the price changes that trade brings to the two sides. If a nation's price ratio changes x percent (as a percent of the free-trade price) and the price in the rest of the world changes y percent, then:

$$\text{Nation's gains} \,/\, \text{Rest of world's gains} = x/y$$

That is, the side with the less elastic trade curves will gain more.

Since expanding East-West trade has little effect on Western prices, it seems safe to guess that only a small share of the gains accrues to Western residents. The trade-expanding East Europeans on the other hand, will receive the greater net gains because their price structures are strongly affected by opening up more trade. Among East European countries, those likely to gain the most will be those with developed industrial sectors who are most willing and able to specialize more, to engage in intra-industry trade (see Chapter 5). East Germany stands to be a leading gainer by becoming a better industrial complement to West Germany. Czechoslovakia and Hungary are also likely to participate in heavy intra-industry trade in manufactures.

The prospects for expanded East-West trade in the 1990s are not all rosy, however. There will be basic problems if that trade does expand rapidly, and basic problems if it does not.

If East-West trade does expand rapidly, it will be based on major changes in the terms of trade, or price ratios, in the newly opening economies of the socialist bloc. Wide swings in relative prices do more than bring large net gains from trade. Within the national economy, they also bring sharp differences in the economic fortunes of different sectors. Recall from Chapter 4 that the greater the change in relative prices, the greater the economic *losses* to those who must compete against the newly cheap imports. While Chapter 4 presented that result in the context of market economies, the same point applies to a more state-directed economy opening itself up to world markets. Somebody gets hurt economically, and they are not likely to suffer in silence, that is, in countries where a strong social-protection ethic is combined with new-found political voice. Resentment is natural, whether the big gainers are private free-market enterpreneurs or whether they are officials with privileged access to foreign trade.

For a socialist country deciding to keep strong official control over foreign trade, there will be the old problem that the still-restricted trade may not balance well, as it did not in the four decades up through 1989. With exchange rates and trade prices officially fixed, it proved difficult to find enough exports from the socialist countries, or enough credit for them to borrow, at the officially quoted terms of trade. Although there must be some price ratios at which trade can be balanced, in practice socialist governments up through the 1980s maintained prices and exchange rates that offered the West few bargains on socialist goods. The trade imbalance raises the issue of credits that could finance it, allowing socialist countries to be persistent debtors. Yet political tensions put some limit on the amount of credit that Western lenders can prudently lend. With limited credit, the East's ability to buy Western manufactures is constrained by the problem of a trade deficit.

TRADE EMBARGOES

Trade discrimination can be more belligerent—a trade block, instead of just a trade bloc. A nation or group of nations can keep ordinary barriers on its trade with most countries, but insist on making trade with a particular country or countries difficult or impossible. To wage economic warfare, nations have often imposed **economic sanctions**, or embargoes, or boycotts. The term sanctions is the most general, referring either to discriminatory restrictions or to complete bans on economic exchange. **Embargoes** or boycotts both refer to complete bans. What is being restricted or banned can be ordinary trade, or it can be trade in services or assets, as in the case of a ban on loans to a particular country.

Waging economic warfare with trade embargoes and other economic sanctions has had a history dating back at least to the fifth century B.C. The American colonists boycotted English goods in the 1760s to protest against the infamous Stamp Act and Townsend Acts. In this case, the boycott succeeded: Parliament responded by repealing those acts. The practice of economic sanctions has become more frequent since the early 1970s than at any other peacetime era. Nobody practices such economic warfare nearly so readily as the United States. The United States was the prime initiator of about 54 out of the world's 89 major embargo episodes between 1945 and 1983, and has since continued the practice (against Nicaragua, South Africa, Panama, Iraq, etc.).

The effects of banning economic exchanges are easy to imagine. A coun-

FIGURE 9.4   Effects of an Embargo on Exports to South Africa

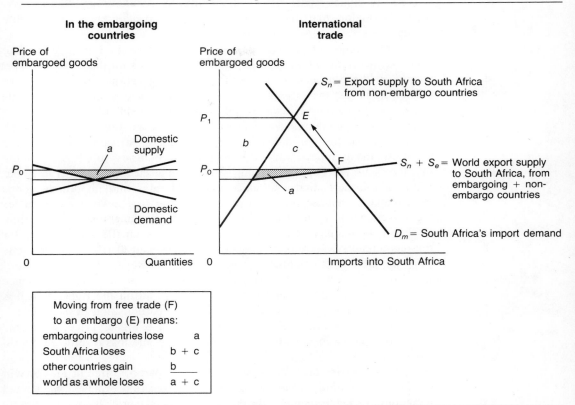

Moving from free trade (F)
to an embargo (E) means:

embargoing countries lose	a
South Africa loses	b + c
other countries gain	b
world as a whole loses	a + c

try's refusal to trade with a "target" country hurts both of them economically, and it creates opportunities for third countries. But who gets hurt the most? The least? Magnitudes matter because they determine whether the damage to the target rewards the initiating country enough to compensate for its own losses on the prohibited trade.

To discover basic determinants of the success or failure of economic sanctions, let us consider a particular kind: a total embargo (prohibition) on exports to the target country.[6] Figure 9.4 imagines a total embargo on

---

[6] The case of an embargo on imports from the target country is symmetrical to the export case studied here. In standard trade models, the symmetry is exact: as we noted in Part One, the net gains and losses on the export side and those on the import side are the same thing, in two guises. As an exercise at the end of this chapter, you are invited to diagram the import-embargo case and to identify the gains and losses and what makes them large or small.

exports to South Africa. The example is a caricature of the partial restrictions imposed on South Africa by many countries, particularly around 1986–87, when the major industrial economies stepped up their pressure on South Africa.[7]

Free-trade equilibrium is represented by Point F in Figure 9.4. Here South Africa's import demand is balanced by the rest of the world's export supply, at the price index P_0. For any exporting nation, the supply curve of exports is just the difference between its domestic supply curve and its domestic demand curve, as shown on the left-hand side of Figure 9.4.

When some countries decide to put an embargo on exports to South Africa, part of the world export supply to South Africa vanishes. Figure 9.4 shows the disappearance of the embargoing countries' supply S_e, meaning that the combined supply curve $S_n + S_e$ is replaced by the S_n curve alone. With their imports thus restricted, South Africans find importable goods more scarce, as represented by the price rise from P_0 to P_1, which accompanies the movement from the free-trade equilibrium F to the embargo equilibrium E. The new scarcity costs South Africa as a nation the area $b + c$, for reasons already described in Chapters 3 and 6–8. It also has its economic costs for the countries enforcing the embargo, however. They lose area a. The loss a is shown in two equivalent ways: on the left, as a difference between producer losses and consumer gains, and on the right, as a loss of profit on exports. Meanwhile, countries not participating in the embargo gain area b on extra sales to South Africa at a higher price. What the world as a whole loses is therefore areas $a + c$, the loss of efficient world trade.

Within countries on the two sides of the embargo, different groups will be affected differently. In the embargoing countries (e.g., Canada, the United Kingdom, the United States), the embargo lowers the price below P_0, slightly helping some consumers while hurting producers. Within South Africa, there might be a similar division (not graphed in Figure 9.4), with some import-competing producers benefitting from the removal of foreign competition, while others are damaged to a greater extent.

If the embargo brings economic costs to both sides, why do it? Clearly, the countries imposing the embargo have decided to sacrifice area a, the net gains on trade with South Africa, for some other goal, such as affecting South Africa's foreign policy or pressuring South Africa to abolish apartheid. By their actions the embargoing governments imply that putting the pressure on South Africa is worth more than area a. The lost area a is presumably not a measure of economic irrationality but, rather, a willing sacrifice for other goals, like the income sacrifices each of us makes for other goals

---

[7] In that particular case, the evidence suggests that the ban on loans to South Africa had more effect than embargoes on ordinary exports or imports, but the loans can in any case be viewed as an "export" of lending services.

ranging from simple leisure to moral principles. As Figure 9.4 is drawn, the hypothetical export embargo is imagined to have a good chance of success, since the economic damage to South Africa, areas $b + c$, looks large in relation to the embargoers' loss a.[8]

Embargoes can fail, of course. In a bare majority of cases, they fail to affect the policies of the target country, as Hufbauer and Schott have shown. The basic economics of embargoes can contribute part, though not all, of the explanation of why some attempts succeed while most others fail. Figure 9.5 leads us to the key points by showing two kinds of (export) embargoes that fail. In both cases, elasticities of supply and demand are the key.

In Figure 9.5A, the countries imposing the embargo have a very inelastic export supply curve, implying that their producers really depend on their export business in the target country. Banning such exports, and erasing the supply curve S_e from the marketplace, costs the embargoing nation(s) a large area a. The target country, by contrast, has a very elastic import demand curve D_m. It cuts its demand greatly when the price goes up even slightly, from P_0 to P_{1_p}. Apparently, it can do fairly well with supplies from nonembargoing countries (the S_n curve alone). Accordingly, it loses only the small areas $b + c$. Any nation considering an embargo in such a case must contemplate sustaining the large loss a in pursuit of only a small damage $(b + c)$ to the target country. What works against the embargo in Figure 9.5A is the low elasticity of the embargoing country itself and the high elasticities of either the target country's import demand or its access to competing nonembargo supplies.

Figure 9.5B shows a case in which the embargo "fails" in the milder sense of having little economic effect on either side. Here the embargoing country is fortunate to have an elastic curve of its own (S_e), so that doing without the extra trade costs it only a slight area a. On the other hand, the target country also has the elastic demand curve D_m and access to the elastic

---

[8] In the real-world debate over sanctions on South Africa, critics have consistently argued that the sanctions would lower incomes of "nonwhite" South Africans, the very groups the sanctions were supposed to help liberate. This is surely correct in the short run, as all sides of the debate have long known. To judge whether the sanctions were in the best interests of nonwhites, the best guide would be their own majority opinion. That opinion is not easily weighed in a context of disenfranchisement, press censorship, and tight police controls. The foreign governments imposing sanctions in the name of changing South African policy clearly imply that the policy gains are worth more than their own loss of area a *plus* the short-run losses that they believe nonwhite South Africans are willing to sustain for the cause.

If white South Africans stand by government policy despite their part of the economic losses, then their part of the losses is a lower-bound measure of what they thought the policies (apartheid, etc.) are worth to them. If they change the policies as demanded, then the policies were worth less to them than the implied costs.

What the economic analysis of the embargo adds is (1) reminders of the economic stakes involved plus (2) measures suggesting how the conflicting parties value the policies that are the target of the embargo.

FIGURE 9.5   Two Kinds of Unsuccessful Embargo

A. An Embargo that Backfires
The cost to the embargoers, *a*, is much larger than the damage *b* + *c* to the target country.

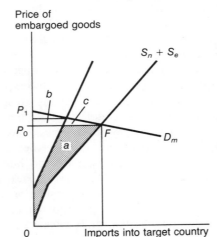

B. A Virtually Irrelevant Embargo
The costs to both sides are negligible because elasticities are so high.

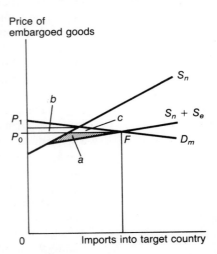

---

competing supplies S_n. Therefore it sustains only the slight damage $b + c$, and presumably can defy the embargo for a long time.

So, embargoes and other economic sanctions apply stronger pressure when the embargoing country or countries have high elasticities and the target countries have low ones. When is this likely to be true? Our simple analysis offers suggestions that seem to show up in the real world:

1. *Big countries pick on small ones.* A country (or group of countries) with a large share of world trade can impose sanctions on a small one without feeling much effect. In economic terms, the big country is likely to have highly elastic trade curves (like S_e in the examples here), because it can deal with much larger markets outside the target country. A small target country, on the other hand, may depend heavily on its trade with the large country or countries. Its vulnerability is summarized by low elasticities for trade curves like D_m and S_n. Little wonder that the typical postwar embargo is one imposed by the United States on smaller-trading nations like Cuba, Nicaragua, South Africa, and Iraq.

2. Sanctions have more chance of success if they are *extreme and sudden* when first imposed. Recall that the damage $b + c$ is larger, the lower the target country's trade elasticities. Elasticities are lower in the short run

than in the long run, and they are lower when a massive share of national product is involved. The more time the target country has to adjust, the more it can learn to conserve on the embargoed products and develop alternative supplies. Of course, quick and sudden action also raises the damage to the initiating country itself (area *a*), so success must be premised on the embargoing country's having alternatives set up in advance, alternatives that raise its elasticities and shrink area *a*.

SUMMARY

The trade bloc revolution of the late 1980s and 1990s has raised the importance of trade discrimination. The European Community is developing a true **common market**, with uniformity of virtually all regulations and taxes on trade and factor movements. From the Treaty of Rome in 1957 to 1992, the EC had adopted the less binding kind of economic bloc called a **customs union**, in which member countries adopted a uniform external tariff and removed all tariffs and quotas on trade among themselves.

The basic three-country model of a customs union shows that its welfare benefits for the partner countries and the world depend on its **trade creation**, the amount by which it raises the total volume of world trade. Its costs depend on its **trade diversion**, the volume of trade it diverts from lower-cost outside suppliers to higher-cost partner-country suppliers. Whether a customs union is good or bad overall depends on the difference between its trade creation effect and its trade diversion effect. In the case of the EC, most economists think that its trade creation has slightly outweighed its trade diversion up through the 1980s. EC enthusiasts predict larger gains from the 1992 market integration.

A lesser form of trade bloc is the **free-trade area**, in which member countries remove all tariffs and quotas on trade among themselves, but keep their separate barriers on trade with nonmember countries. In this case, member countries must maintain customs administration on the borders between themselves, to keep outside products from entering the high-barrier countries cheaply by way of their low-barrier partners. Two examples of free-trade areas are the European Free Trade Area created in 1960 and the Canada–U.S. Free Trade Area that began to take effect in 1989. Of all the participants in recent trade blocs, the one predicted to gain the largest share of GNP from bloc membership is Canada, who is expected to gain 8 to 10 percent of GNP from her free trade with the United States.

Elsewhere trade blocs have been less successful for various reasons. In the case of Eastern Europe, the socialist trade bloc arrangements of 1949–1989 seem to have destroyed more trade than they created. By leaving such trade arrangements, East Germany, Czechoslovakia, and Hungary are likely to reap particularly large gains.

Another form of trade discrimination is **economic sanctions**, such as a

trade embargo. Our basic analysis of an export embargo (which has effects symmetrical with those of an import embargo) reveals how the success or failure of such economic warfare depends on trade elasticities. Success is more likely when the embargoing countries have high trade elasticities, meaning that they can easily do without the extra trade. Success is also more likely when the target country has low trade elasticities, meaning that it cannot easily do without trading with the embargoing countries. As the simple theory implies, embargoes are typically imposed by large trading countries on smaller ones, and success is more likely the quicker and more extreme the sanctions.

SUGGESTED READINGS

The customs union literature is usefully surveyed in Corden (1984, pp. 114–24) and in Pomfret (1988).

On the economics of the European Community's customs union, see El-Agraa (1988), Calingaert (1988), Cecchini (1988), Hitiris (1988) and again Pomfret (1988). On the North American Free Trade area and Canada's stake in other trade liberalization, see Wonnacott and Wonnacott (1967, 1982), Weintraub (1984), Cox and Harris (1985), Whalley (1985), and Morici (1990).

On trade within the socialist bloc and on East-West trade, see Edward A. Hewett (1974) and Franklyn D. Holzman (1976, 1985).

The economics and the foreign-policy effects of trade embargoes are well analyzed in Hufbauer and Schott (1983, 1985) and U.S. Department of Agriculture, Economic Research Service (1986). A tentative judgment on sanctions against South Africa is rendered by Hayes (1987).

QUESTIONS FOR REVIEW

1. Homeland is about to join Furrinerland in a free-trade area. Before the union, Homeland imports 10 million transistor radios from the outside world market at $100 and adds a tariff of $30 on each transistor. It takes $110 to produce each transistor radio in Furrinerland and $130 in Homeland.

a. Once the free trade area is formed, what will be the cost to Homeland of the transistor-radio trade diverted to Furrinerland?

b. How much extra imports would have to be generated in Homeland to offset this trade-diversion welfare cost?

Answers: *(a.)* 10 million radios times ($110 − 100) = $100 million. *(b.)* To offset this $100 million loss, with linear demand and supply curves, the change in imports, ΔM, would have to be such that the trade-creation gains (the area *b* in Figure 9.2) had an area equal to $100 million.

So ½ × ($130 − $110) × ΔM = $100 million requires ΔM = 10 million, or a doubling of Homeland's radio imports.

2. Draw the diagram corresponding to Figure 9.4 for an embargo on *imports from* the target country. Identify the losses and gains to the embargoing countries, the target country, and other countries. Describe what values of elasticities are more likely to give power to the embargo effort and what values of elasticities are more likely to weaken it.

▼

Changing Leadership and Trade Policy

•

In newspapers and on television, international trade is cast as a race for leadership. North America is afraid of falling behind, and Japan is proud of taking the lead. The European Community feels both the potential for catching up to America and the threat of being overtaken by Japan. Korea and other NICs (newly industrializing countries) show signs of catching up to the leaders within a quarter-century. Trade policy issues from Chapters 6–9 have surfaced in a public debate over whether Japan has gained from "unfair trade," in the form of export subsidies, dumping, and informal barriers to the marketing of imports in Japan.

With the help of trade theories introduced in Part One and the policy analysis of Chapters 6–9, we can now judge what reshuffles the ranks of industrial nations, what role government policy has played, and what role it could play. The issues addressed here are:

- How have rising industrial nations, like Japan after World War II, overtaken the international leader?
- Are there inherent advantages in being a late starter?
- What role can government industrial targetting, or strategic trade policy, play in promoting comparative advantage in the most modern sectors? What role has it played so far?

THE MEANING OF INTERNATIONAL LEADERSHIP

For all the vast media coverage of international "leadership" and competition, one searches in vain for a clear definition of what the competition is about. Leadership in what dimension? Top exporter of high-technology goods? That is not a worthy object in itself, because selling things abroad is not inherently better than consuming them at home. Country using the latest equipment and techniques? They might not be worth their cost, especially when older equipment and techniques are a free gift from the past. Lowest-cost producer of high-technology goods or of manufactures in general? Under competition, everybody's costs may end up similar at the margin. Country with the largest export surplus? That's the country that has decided to postpone the most consumption to the future, but there is nothing inherently better or worse about doing so. Yet, all these notions get mixed into media accounts of competition among industrial nations, as if we all knew implicitly what leadership and competition were supposed to mean.

Living Standards

The most meaningful kind of leadership is to be ahead in something that is one step removed from international trade: material living standards, meaning the ability to get and consume. Living standards are what all the other dimensions of international competition were meant to secure for a nation. The definition of living standards starts with consumption or gross national product per capita, and then adds other dimensions that surely matter. Let us take a clear look at measures of material well-being, or living standards, before exploring trade-related indicators that may influence it. As it happens, each step of the measurement process brings up a striking contrast between the United States and Japan.

Economists start their measurement of material living standards with the value of goods and services a nation produces per person. While this first step is a perilous one, the best research comparing gross national product per capita across nations has produced sensible results. The leading nations, in terms of GNP per capita, are small ones peculiarly favored by geology (oil-rich Brunei, Kuwait, United Arab Emirates). These are less interesting for present purposes than the major industrial nations. Figure 10.1 gives estimates for some leading industrial nations since 1955.

The postwar rise of Japan stands out in Figure 10.1. Back in 1950, Japan, still under official American occupation, had a lower product per capita than at least 22 other countries, including all of Europe. By 1988 it ranked from 8th to 10th, depending on the exact measure, trailing only Switzerland, the United States, Canada, West Germany, Sweden, and a few tiny rich nations. While Japan apparently had not become "i chiban" (number one) by 1988, at the growth rates of the period 1980–87 it would pass Canada and the United States by 1996.[1]

---

[1] The statement that Japan is not yet ahead of North America in income per capita may clash with what you have heard or read. News coverage often presents figures showing a higher income per capita, or wages per capita, in Japan. Yet the figures usually cited are distorted by incorrect price comparisons. As elaborated in Chapter 16 below, the usual comparisons mislead readers by using market exchange rates to convert all national values into U.S.

FIGURE 10.1   GNP per Capita in Seven Leading Countries, 1950–1988

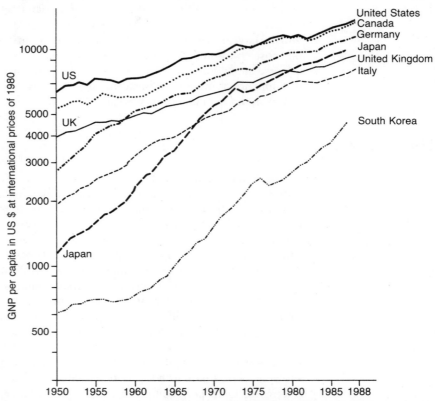

Sources: Summers and Heston (1985) for 1950–85. Estimates for 1986–88 were spliced onto the Summers-Heston series using real GNP per capita from International Monetary Fund, *International Financial Statistics*.

The most dramatic decline of an industrial leader is that of the United Kingdom. Figure 10.1 shows that Britain's income per capita was surpassed by that of Germany and Japan. In fact, Britain was overtaken by many

dollars. The market exchange rates are driven by relative prices for *internationally traded* goods and services and assets, not all goods and services that a nation would want to consume. They miss the influence of the prices of nontradables like local services and space to live or work in. Carefully comparing the right set of prices between countries reveals a higher purchasing power for residents of North America or the Third World, relative to Japan or Europe. Figure 10.1 uses figures adjusted for the prices of nontradables, based on the International Comparisons Project based at the University of Pennsylvania. Those figures showing Japan or Germany already well ahead of North America are based on exchange-rate conversions in years when the market exchange-rate value of the dollar happens to be lower than average.

countries in the same 38 years. Back in 1950, its income per capita ranked about eighth in the world. By 1988, Britain ranked about 20th. It is the poorest country in all of northwestern Europe except for Ireland.[2]

For North Americans, the figures on GNP per capita confirm that other countries are closing in, and much of Western Europe and Japan will have the same average incomes by the end of the century.

GNP is not happiness itself, however, and we must supplement the readily available GNP figures with impressions about important dimensions those figures omit. Incorporating some omitted aspects of well-being raises the standing of North America relative to, say, Japan, while others cast Japan's performance in better light. The North American lead in well-being is greater than the figures show to the extent that North Americans enjoy more free time. Their average work week is only 32–34 hours, and less than 40 hours for full-time employees, versus 47 hours for the nonagricultural labor force of Japan or Hong Kong or 52 hours for Korea. On the other hand, comparisons of GNP per capita overstate the North American advantage in several important ways. In the United States life is shorter, incomes are more unequally distributed, and crime is more widespread than in most other industrial countries, especially Japan. We should also note that North Americans get a boost in living standards from the abundance of living and working space. If we were interested in the overall productivity with which nations combine inputs to produce outputs, we must weigh the heavier use of land inputs in North America, leaving us more impressed with the productivity of crowded nations like Japan. When all these harder-to-measure aspects are given their due, the net result is still that the North Americans are in the process of losing their leadership to Japan in the 1990s.

What Is So Special about Manufacturing?

If the kind of leadership that really counts is something broader than GNP per capita, why does the public debate over international competition run along such narrow-gauged tracks? Why is the debate about costs of making manufactured goods, especially high-tech manufactures, in different countries? Why is trade in such goods the imagined arena of competition?

---

[2] In this sentence "northwestern Europe" includes all countries in, or northwest of, the chain of nations consisting of France, Switzerland, Austria, Germany, and Finland. It also includes Iceland.

Britain's dropping in the ranks does not mean that the postwar era was one of dismal growth by her own historical standards. On the contrary, British average incomes grew faster in the subperiod 1945–1973 than at any other time of equal length in British history, including the Industrial Revolution.

Britain was not alone in sliding down the international ranks. More serious declines in rank between 1950 and 1988 were experienced by Argentina and New Zealand, and Australia's average income also did not advance faster than Britain's.

WHOSE HIGH-TECH IS THE HIGHEST?
WHAT EUROPE'S EXECUTIVES THINK

The text of this chapter presents reasons why we should stick to the basics of living standards when defining international leadership, with only careful suggestions about how living standards may correlate with other measures. The media take little trouble with correct definitions, however. High technology, another term seldom defined, is considered a synonym for any kind of leadership a country could desire. One way to avoid having to define it is to ask "experts" what they think. Executives of over 200 West European firms surveyed by 1984 ranked national technological levels in "high-tech" sectors as follows (1 = top rank):

Industry	United States	Japan	West Germany	Scandi-navia	United Kingdom	France
Computing	1	2	3	4–5	6	4–5
Electronics	1–2	1–2	3	4	6–7	6–7
Telecommunications	1	2	3	4	5–6	5–6
Biotechnology	1	2	3	4	5	n.a.
Chemical	1	2	3–4	3–4	5	6–7
Metals/alloys	2	1	3	4	5–6	5–6
Engineering	1	2	3	4	5	6
Manufacturing	1–2	1–2	3	4	5	6
Robotics	2	1	3	4	6	5
Mean rank	1.3	1.7	3.0	4.2	5.4	5.8

As it happens, the rankings correlate almost exactly with the rankings of the same countries in terms of living standards. The only difference is that the United Kingdom ranked above France in the survey, yet below France in GNP per capita. *Why* the correlation is so good provides food for thought.

Sources: *The Wall Street Journal* (Europe) and Booz-Allen Hamilton, *Management and Technology—A Survey of European Chief Executives, 1984.* Reprinted in Kenneth Flamm, *Targeting the Computer* (Washington: Brookings Institution, 1987), p. 4.

The common intuitions may not be wrong. What the public implicitly assumes, most economists are willing to suspect, even though we cannot prove it. It is possible that manufacturing, especially high-tech manufacturing, deserves to be targeted as a key or leading sector in the process of economic growth. The manufacturing sector seems to have attributes that look special to economists. As a rule, economists avoid talking about key or leading sectors, since they feel that a market system usually can decide what needs to be expanded, without any special government aid. Yet, they recognize that the usual market institutions can make mistakes. When "externalities" like those described in Chapter 7 are present, or when economies of scale breed monopoly rents as in Chapter 5, there can be a case for active government encouragement.

Manufacturing, especially its technology-intensive lines, shows greater signs of external benefits and of economies of scale than the rest of the economy. The external benefits show up in the form of faster growth in outputs divided by inputs, or "total factor productivity," over long stretches of time. The manufacturing sector usually *seems to* show faster total factor productivity growth than the rest of the economy, though the estimates are shaky.[3] One suspected source of this extra productivity growth is the spillover of new knowledge from firm to firm within manufacturing. Given the likelihood of knowledge spillovers and of monopoly rents to be captured by whoever first exploits economies of scale in new manufacturing lines, there is great interest in the possibility that nations can grow faster than others by aggressively promoting manufactures.

The case for favoring manufactures draws additional, again shaky, support from a slight correlation between the expansion of manufacturing and overall success in economic growth. Figure 10.2 shows both the support and its shakiness. Between 1965 and 1987, 4 out of 24 industrial nations succeeded in raising their GNP per capita faster than four percent a year, a supergrowth rate that doubles the average income every 18 years. Three of these four supergrowth nations (Japan, Korea, Singapore) achieved that growth by shifting their economies toward manufacturing faster than most industrializing or industrialized countries; Brazil, on the other hand, did not. The three Asian experiences, plus a very slight correlation of income growth with the shift toward manufacturing within countries that did not have supergrowth, suggests that rising through the international income ranks *may* be tied to success in manufacturing, especially the knowledge-intensive manufacturing lines that all four of the super-growing nations have favored.

To pursue the role of manufacturing further, let us turn to case studies of manufacturing industries in which global leadership changed hands. Why did the initial leader fall behind in each of these cases? Did its government

---

[3] For a close look at the nasty conceptual and technical issues of measurement of a sector's total factor productivity growth, see Baily and Gordon (1988) and sources cited there.

FIGURE 10.2   Shifting toward Manufacturing versus Achieving Growth, 24
Countries, 1965–1987*

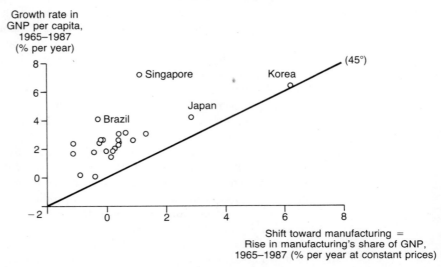

* The data refer to 24 countries with GNP per capita above $1,200 in 1987 that are not
heavily dependent on oil exports.

Source: World Bank, *World Development Report 1989.*

fail to help the industry against rising foreign competition? Did the government in the catching-up country give special aid to its own private industry?
Or are there more natural economic or social forces that bring changes in
leadership?

THE CASE OF STEEL

Changing Shares

The world steel market has changed almost beyond recognition over the
last 100 years. The technology of steelmaking has been transformed, and
each hour of labor now produces about five times as much steel as it did
in the 1890s. Steelmakers now get their iron ore from different places. A
century ago, the world's ore supply was dominated by Europe (Germany,
Britain, Sweden, Spain), North America, and Russia. Now the ore comes
primarily from (in order of volume produced since the mid-1970s): the
Soviet Union, Australia, and Brazil, followed at a distance by the United
States, China, and Canada.

With the changes in technology and ore supplies has come a new interna-

FIGURE 10.3   Leading Countries' Shares of World Steel Output, 1880–1987

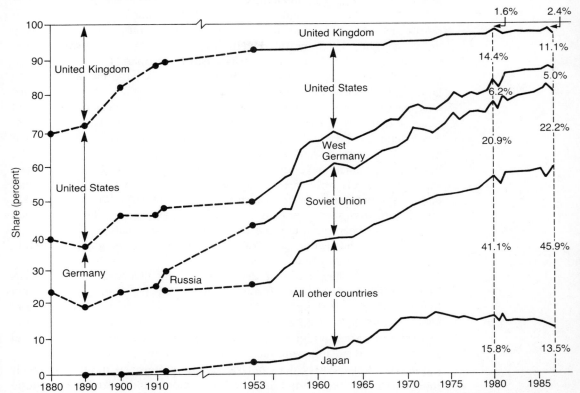

Sources: Temin (1966, p. 143), Svennilson (1954), UN *Statistical Yearbooks,* U.S. Bureau of Mines *Minerals Yearbooks.*

tional distribution of steel production. Figure 10.3 plots where steel has been produced in two eras of expansion and relative peace, 1880–1913 and 1953–87, without focusing on international trade. Steelmaking is spread more evenly over the globe than it was a century ago. Before World War I, as Figure 10.3 shows, four fifths of the world's steel was made in just three countries: the United States, the United Kingdom, and Germany. Now the top three producers—the Soviet Union, Japan, and the United States—make less than half the world's steel, and the trend is for this share to go on shrinking as smaller-share producers such as Korea and Brazil grow rapidly.

Why has steel production spread out so much? The answer seems to be a mixture of deliberate policy intervention, market forces, and aging institutions.

For one thing, there has been a *rise of government protection.* The steel industry has long been favored by special government aid, both because it used to be a symbol of modernity and because it has been viewed as key to national military strength. The form of government aid has depended on the size of the national market. For a small country, the practical way of encouraging the domestic steel industry is to subsidize its production and exports, rather than to protect its small home market against imports. For a large country, however, the home market is large enough to allow large-scale, low-cost production without exporting products. Large countries have therefore turned to import protection for the steel industry. The United States did that consistently before World War II, as we shall note again. So, of course, did the Soviet Union, which has traded relatively little but has made growth in steel production a central national goal. Brazil, too, has helped its steelmakers by protecting its large, growing market. Even Japan, now a relatively free-trading steel exporter, favored steelmakers that had substantial import protection in the 1950s and early 1960s. The result: steelmaking has spread around the world in part because large protected markets have been a rising share of the whole world market.

On the other hand, the spread of steelmaking around the globe apparently *has not been due to product-cycle effects.*

Recall from Chapter 5 that the product-cycle theory of trade patterns says a product will migrate from the technologically leading country out toward the least developed periphery once its technology becomes more static and standardized. Examples were textiles, leather goods, and tire manufacture. Steel might seem to fit the product-cycle pattern, since steel production is diffusing, with the Third World taking a rising share.

But the steel industry does not satisfy the premise of the product-cycle model: its technology has not stagnated into a more standardized and transferable form. As far as we can tell from U.S. data, technological advances such as the basic oxygen furnace, continuous casting, and increasing automation have kept steel-industry productivity advancing as fast in the postwar decades as it did earlier. The rate of productivity growth in steel may also have been as fast as the productivity growth rate for the whole economy. Steel is not a stagnating industry whose technology can be embodied in standard equipment that any country's labor force could operate. Its spread must have other explanations, such as the government protection already noted.

Apart from the general diffusion of steelmaking, the position of leading nation has changed hands. Just who is the leader depends on whether we are interested in the leader in production or the leader in exports. The *production* leadership has passed from the United States to the Soviet Union due to the firm Soviet commitment to expanding heavy industry. More challenging is the task of explaining why *export* leadership changed.

Before World War I, the leading exporters of steel were Britain and Germany, but not the United States. In fact, the United States was a heavy net importer of steel until the turn of the century. Unlike Japan and other countries since the 1950s, the U.S. steel industry before world War I became the top producer basically by gaining control of its giant home market for steel. Yet, the United States did become a net steel exporter just before World War I, joining Germany in crowding the British out of third-country markets.

The two world wars, by disrupting production in Europe, Russia, and Japan, left the United States as the dominant producer and even the top net exporter (in absolute tons) by the 1950s. It was in the late 1950s that America's comparative advantage in steel started to fade. So did the comparative advantage of steelmakers in Britain and other West European countries. Japan took over as the comparative-advantage country, the one with the highest net steel exports. Japan remains in that leading position, even though the rise of Korean, Brazilian, and other new competition is eroding its trade surplus in steel products.

Why should leadership have changed hands the way it did? Why did the American and the German steel industry rise at the expense of British leadership before World War I, only to become a depressed industry later on? Why should Japan have become the leading steel exporter and the leading producer outside of the Soviet Union? Why should Japan now feel the heat of export competition from Korea and Brazil? This set of questions is the focus of the next two sections. Once the reasons for losing leadership are better understood, we can turn to the debate over steel trade policies.

Relative-Price Accounting

We need a way of measuring which nation has a cost advantage and what shares of its advantage stemmed from differences in input prices versus differences in productivity performance. Figure 10.4 summarizes the method to be used here. Let us first compare a product's prices in two countries, a and b. The two prices (P_a and P_b) can differ as long as there are barriers to trade, such as transportation costs or tariffs. Their difference, or the departure of P_a/P_b from unity, is the net result of differences in average costs (C_a versus C_b) and differences in price markups ($m_a = P_a/C_a$ versus $m_b = P_b/C_b$). The markups can differ from each other because of differences in monopoly power or just because our measurements of costs happen to be incomplete.

Average costs can differ, in turn, because producers face different prices for inputs, such as raw materials or labor, and because producers differ in their productivity, that is, their ratios of output to inputs. In symbols,

$$C_a = W_a \cdot I_a \quad \text{and} \quad C_b = W_b \cdot I_b$$

so that:

$$(C_a/C_b) = (W_a I_a/W_b I_b)$$

FIGURE 10.4   Accounting for International Price Differences

Compare prices of the same product in two settings. Let one setting be a (e.g., for America) and the other b (e.g., for Japan).*

A. *Product Prices Depend on Markups and Average Costs*

$$P_a = C_a \cdot m_a \quad \text{and} \quad P_b = C_b \cdot m_b$$

where the Cs are the average unit costs of production and the ms are markup (price/cost) ratios.

B. *Average Costs Depend on Input Prices and Physical Input-Output Ratios*

$$C_a = W_a \cdot I_a \quad \text{and} \quad C_b = W_b \cdot I_b$$

where the Ws are average input prices (W for "wage" rate of the average input) and the Is are physical input/output ratios.[†]

C. *Relative Product Prices Therefore Depend on Relative Input Prices, Productivity, and Markups*

$$(P_a/P_b) = (W_a/W_b) \; times \; (I_a/I_b) \; times \; (m_a/m_b),$$

or (relative price in a) = (relative input price in a)

  times (relative productivity of b's producers)
  times (relative markup in a).

This is the formula used in Figure 10.5.

---

* The producer prices in settings a and b (or P_a and P_b) can differ due to transport costs and other trade barriers between the two settings.
† Each W or each I is a weighted average of input prices or input-output ratios averaged across all inputs. W_a, for example, is a weighted average of the prices of all raw materials, fuels, electricity, different kinds of labor, capital, and land, where the weights are the input-output ratios from some setting used as a base for comparison. Correspondingly, I_a is a weighted average in the ratios of each input per unit of output—e.g., labor hours per ton of output, barrels of fuel oil per ton of output, etc.—where the weights are the input prices from some setting used as a base for comparison.

---

where the Ws are average prices of all inputs, and the Is are the real ratios of inputs to output in each country. So price differences are the result of:

a. Differences in input prices,
b. Differences in productivity, and
c. Differences in markups.

or in terms of ratios:

$$(P_a/P_b) = (W_a/W_b) \cdot (I_a/I_b) \cdot (m_a/m_b)$$

Each of these three sources of price differences, each departure of a ratio from unity, suggests a particular set of possible causes. Differences in factor input prices suggest factors that are beyond the control of producers. Differences in productivity suggest that producers in one country have a more efficient way of producing than producers in the other. And differences in price markup suggest differences in monopoly power (or differential errors in measuring costs).

The Accounting Results, 1956–1976

The American steel industry that emerged as a world leader just before World War I was still the dominant national steel industry in the first decade after World War II. Yet, as mentioned earlier, a long slide began with the second half of the 1950s. By 1976–77, imports had carved a durable toehold in the American steel market, plants were being closed, and Japanese steelmakers in particular were being praised as models of efficiency for America to follow. The decline of the U.S. steel industry's competitive edge thus roughly paralleled the decline of American supremacy in automobile manufacture.

Why was the decline so serious and so prolonged? We have an abundance of good clues, thanks to economic research that reached high tide when Washington began to protect the steel industry in earnest around 1977.

The most efficient device for sorting out the main causes of the U.S. competitive decline in steel is the relative-price accounting just introduced. Figure 10.5 accounts for differences in the steel prices of the United States, a declining market leader, and Japan, the new market leader. The estimates presented here compare 1956, a year in which the United States still enjoyed a commanding lead in productivity and price cutting, with 1976, a year in which American steelmakers were in full retreat from Japanese competition.

Leadership changed hands partly because the challenger's supply of iron ore and coal was getting cheaper faster. What is odd, however, is that the challenger benefiting from a new advantage in access to raw materials is *Japan,* a country famous for being deprived of domestic raw materials. The usual image of a resource-starved Japan did fit the data for 1956 well enough. As the first number in Figure 10.5 shows, Japanese steelmakers had to pay 73 percent more than America for iron ore and 125 percent more for coal in 1956. Yet, by 1976, Japan was getting iron ore 43 percent *cheaper* than U.S. steel firms (the figure of 0.57 for 1976). By the 1970s, Australia and Brazil had become rich new suppliers of iron ore. The shipping costs of getting these ores to Japan were less than the costs of reaching the steel heartland of America's Midwest. Furthermore, the top Japanese steel firms had wisely secured long-run supply contracts with Australia on favorable terms. The dramatic reversal in relative ore costs and in coal costs is thus a story of uncommon Japanese good fortune with an imported raw material.[4] By itself, the iron-ore advantage of Japan would account

---

[4] Again, one can wonder whether the lower price of iron ore for Japan is to be treated as something beyond the control of firms in the leading country, or whether U.S. firms passed up chances to profit from trading in the same Australian and Brazilian iron ore.

FIGURE 10.5 Accounting for Steel Price Ratios, Japan/United States, 1956 and 1976

	1956	1976
1. Japanese input prices/U.S. input prices (parts of $W_J/W_{U.S.}$):		
Iron ore	1.73	0.57
Coking coal	2.25	0.96
Noncoking coal	2.37	*
Fuel oil	0.98	1.03
Natural gas	*	*
Electric power	0.72	1.08
Scrap	1.37	1.18
Labor	0.12	0.43
Capital	(n.a.)	(n.a.)
2. Index of all Japanese input prices relative to all U.S. input prices $(W_J/W_{U.S.})$		
using U.S. input quantities as weights	0.43	0.63
using Japan's input quantities as weights	0.84	0.66
3. Productivity of Japanese producers relative to the productivity of U.S. producers $(I_{U.S.}/I_J)$		
using U.S. input prices as weights	0.41	1.17
using Japan's input prices as weights	0.81	1.13
4. Japanese average costs relative to U.S. average costs $(C_J/C_{U.S.}) = (W_J I_J/W_{U.S.} I_{U.S.})$	1.05	0.56
5. Japanese markup ratio (and unmeasured inputs) relative to U.S. markup ratio $(m_J/m_{U.S.})$	1.14	1.30
6. Japanese steel prices relative to U.S. steel prices $(P_J/P_{U.S.})$	1.20	0.73

* No price ratio is shown for this input because it was widely used in only one of the two countries, according to David G. Tarr in Duke et al. (1977). Its cost in that one country does affect the total (all-input) calculations, however.

Rows 2–4 were derived as follows:

Row 2. $W_J/W_{U.S.}$ *either* $\Sigma_{is}(w_{iJ}I_{iU.S.}/w_{iU.S.}I_{iU.S.})$ using U.S. input weights, or $\Sigma_{is}(w_{iJ}I_{iJ}/w_{iU.S.}I_{iJ})$ using Japanese input weights, where the is are the inputs (i = iron ore, . . . , labor).

Row 3. The ratio of Japanese to American productivity (steel per unit of input), or $I_{U.S.}/I_J$, is *either* $\Sigma_{is}(I_{iU.S.}w_{iU.S.}/I_{iJ}w_{iU.S.})$ using U.S. input prices as weights *or* $\Sigma_{is}(I_{iU.S.}w_{iJ}/I_{iJ}w_{iJ})$ using Japanese input prices as weights.

Row 4. The same cost ratio, $C_J C_{U.S.} = (W_J I_J/W_{U.S.} I_{U.S.})$, can be derived from rows 2 and 3 in either of two ways. One can divide the $W_J/W_{U.S.}$ index that uses U.S. input weights by the $I_{U.S.}/I_J$ productivity ratio that uses Japanese input prices, or one can divide the $W_J/W_{U.S.}$ index that uses Japanese input wiehgts by the $I_{U.S.}/I_J$ productivity ratio that uses U.S. input prices.

The cost of the eight inputs accounted for 85.3 percent of the U.S. steel price in 1956 and for 97.1 percent of the U.S. steel price in 1976.

It may seem odd that Japan's productivity advantage in 1976 looks greater when evaluated at U.S. input prices than at Japanese input prices. Ordinarily, this would not be the case, since a country usually makes heavier use of the inputs that are cheaper in that country, making its productivity performance look better under its own conditions. Yet in the mid-1970s Japan's steelmaking techniques were more laborsaving than those of America, so that Japan's relative productivity looked better when its laborsaving was evaluated at the higher American wage rates.

Source: Richard M. Duke et al. (1977), Tables 3.2, 3.3.

for about 15 percent of the observed difference in average steelmaking costs in the two countries in 1976.

Wage rates for labor differed even more radically between Japan and the United States. Japan's average steelmaking wage rate was only 12 percent of the U.S. rate in 1956 and still only 43 percent of it in 1976. Cheaper labor was crucial to Japan's ability to compete at all in steel markets in 1956. Twenty years later, it was still important, accounting for perhaps half, or a little more than half, of the Japanese steelmakers' cost advantage over the United States.[5] Yet cheap labor does not help explain the *rise* of Japanese competitiveness, since the wage gap narrowed while the cost gap shifted in favor of Japanese firms.

Wage rates can differ either because competitive labor markets face different supply and demand conditions, or because unions or other forces create more artificial labor scarcity in one country than in another. Both competitive forces and union power were at work in the market for steelworkers between 1956 and 1976. The higher wage of U.S. steelworkers was partly, but only partly, due to the market power of the United Steel Workers (USW). As of 1976, at the height of its power and membership, the USW had secured average wage rates that might have been 13 percent higher than those in less unionized industries employing similarly skilled workers. Turning this 1.13 ratio upside down, the workers in similar sectors were getting 0.88 times the wage rate of the USW. This is a wide gap, but not as wide as that implied by the 0.43 ratio of Japanese to U.S. steel wages in 1976. Even with perfectly competitive labor markets and no United Steel Workers, Japanese wage rates would have been only 49 percent (= 0.43/0.88) of American wage rates in 1976, because all labor, unionized or not, is scarcer relative to other inputs in America than in Japan. Conclusion: while the high wage rates of U.S. steelworkers account for a little over half the cost advantage of Japanese steelmaking firms, only about a fifth [= (1 − 0.88)/ (1 − 0.43)] of this labor cost advantage, or a little over a tenth of the

---

[5] While you might have sensed that labor costs were this important by studying the numbers in Figure 10.5, they do not directly show you the "perhaps half, or a little more than half" of Japan's cost advantage that was due to labor costs. To see this you need the following information, which had to be omitted from Figure 10.5 to save space:

Japanese steelmakers cost advantage due to lower wage rates = (U.S. wage rate minus Japanese wage rate) *times* Labor-hours per ton of steel

= ($12.14 per hour − $5.25 per hour) *times either* 11.82 (in United States) *or* 10.04 (in Japan)

= *either* $81.44 a ton *or* $69.18 a ton

= *either* 63% or 53% of the Japanese cost advantage of $129.54 a ton in 1976, depending on which country's labor-hours per ton one uses.

overall Japanese cost advantage, was due to the ability of the United Steel Workers to extract above-market wage rates.[6]

Combining all inputs, it turns out that Japan had a large input-price advantage over the United States, regardless of whether input prices are weighted by Japanese or by U.S. inputs per ton of steel (see row 2 in Figure 10.5).

Yet, unit costs depend on productivity as well as on input prices, and the productivity differences between the two countries have been changing dramatically. In 1956, Japanese steelmakers were getting less steel output from each unit of input than the leading American firms. Just how much less depends on which input-price conditions one uses to compare the two productivity performances. Under Japanese conditions, with labor cheap and ore and coal expensive, Japanese firms' performance fell only 19 percent short of that by U.S. firms (the 0.81 ratio in row 3). This figure is more relevant than the 59 percent gap (the 0.41 ratio), which judges Japanese firms too harshly for using labor-intensive techniques that look wasteful when appraised at American wage rates and other input prices. But Japanese performance *was* apparently below the American standard, a judgment that the Japanese firms themselves shared in the 1950s.

By 1976, the productivity contrast was reversed. Now, the Japanese industry was 13–17 percent more productive in converting inputs into steel (the 1.13 and 1.17 in row 3). Japan appears to have found ways of using less labor and other inputs in making a given amount of steel. The productivity lead established by Japan in 1976 appears to have continued ever since. Thus, Japan emerged from a productivity deficit to a lead of about 15 percent, much as Germany and America before World War I advanced from a productivity deficit around the 1850s to take a 15 percent lead just before World War I.

The switch to higher Japanese productivity in the 1970s raises anew the question of whether the early leader, this time the U.S. steel industry, made avoidable mistakes. The spotlight of blame should probably be shared by steel-firm management and the United Steel Workers. For their part, the USW won a number of concessions on work rules, promotions, hirings, and firings that may have retarded productivity at the same time the USW was winning the above-market wage rates discussed above. We cannot tell, however, how much of the retardation in American productivity growth relative to that of Japan's steel industry was due to lackluster labor performance. One cannot determine labor's performance, or labor's effects on industry performance, without more detailed studies than have been conducted so far. Merely measuring what is usually called "labor productivity"—

---

[6] However, getting higher wage rates is not the only way in which a powerful union can raise labor costs. It can also reduce labor productivity through restrictions on work efficiency. Also, the figure of 13 percent as a USW markup may be too conservative. The Labor Department found a 19 percent USW markup for 1983 (Webbink, 1985).

output per labor hour—doesn't do the job, since it doesn't say whether low productivity was labor's fault (e.g., working too slowly) or management's fault (e.g., underinvestment in capital for the workers to use) or both or neither. To make progress toward allocating blame for the 13–17 percent productivity shortfall, we must turn to more measurable effects, leaving labor's work performance buried in the residual unexplained category.

There are signs that steel-industry management, especially in the large U.S. steel firms, passed up chances to keep the U.S. steel industry as productive as its competitors in Japan and Europe.[7] U.S. steel managers missed profitable opportunities to install the basic oxygen furnace in the 1950s and 1960s, and opportunities to convert to continuous casting from the 1960s on. They may also have missed chances for profitable automation in the 1970s and 1980s.

One must be careful, of course, in criticizing an established firm (or industry) for not investing in a new technique or type of equipment. The established firm may be perfectly rational in not replacing existing old-style facilities with something new. It is often true that the unit *variable* cost of using an old-style facility in good condition is less than the unit total cost of building and operating a new one. In this case the firm is rational in using the old facility while it lasts, even if the new one costs less than the old the old one would have cost if it were built from scratch. Much of the old-style U.S. steelmaking capital in the 1950s and 1960s was efficient, given that it was already built and still serviceable. Furthermore, it can be very costly to fit a new facility, say a basic oxygen furnace, into a plant that is already arranged on different lines. It has been estimated that it might cost 27 percent less to build a whole new steel mill in Japan, or 12 percent less in Europe, than in the United States, partly because of the old structures already in place in the United States (Crandall, 1981, chapter 4; Duke et al., 1977, chapter 7).

Yet the U.S. steel industry did seem to pass up investments that would have been profitable. Even in the early 1960s, more than five years after virtually all experts had concurred that no old-style, open-hearth furnaces should be built, the larger U.S. firms were building new ones on the old open-hearth lines instead of building the more economical basic oxygen furnaces that were a higher share of gross investment in Japan and elsewhere than in the United States (see Adams and Dirlam, 1966). The U.S. steel industry may also have been slower than necessary to channel its gross

---

[7] The argument that follows disagrees with the conclusions of the Federal Trade Commission study (Duke et al., 1976), while using the FTC's data and taking the side of earlier studies criticized by the FTC. There is not space here to list the ways in which I am unpersuaded by the FTC conclusions absolving steel-industry management from blame for the industry's increasing cost disadvantage. Suffice it to say that the FTC report did not explore the overall productivity implications of its data, and presented arguments that overstated the vigor of the U.S. steel industry in pursuing the most efficient techniques.

IT HAPPENED BEFORE: HOW PRE-WAR BRITAIN LOST LEADERSHIP IN STEEL

Japan's overtaking the United States as a producer and exporter of steel had a close parallel in earlier history. Between 1880 and 1913, both Germany and the United States surpassed Britain in steel output. How did they do it? What role did government play? Did British policy or British steelmakers make mistakes?

Part of the rise of German and American steel was clearly beyond Britain's control. British steelmakers were shut out of the faster-growing markets of Central Europe and the United States by protectionist tariffs imposed by Germany, the United States and other governments. Peter Temin (1966) has pointed out that even if British steelmakers had reduced the cost of their steel to zero, some foreign tariffs would probably have been raised high enough to keep British goods out, and Britain's share of world output would still have declined. To this extent, a relative decline was beyond Britain's control.

The relative-accounting framework of Figure 10.4 allows us to say more. We can judge the vigor of the British steel industry, and the cost constraints it faced. As it turns out, the situation in 1906–1913 was similar to the contrast between Japan and the United States in 1976.

According to a relative-price accounting estimated by Robert Allen (1979), America and Germany were blessed with cheaper supplies of two key raw material inputs, iron ore and fuel. American firms paid only 87 percent as much for ore and 65 percent as much for fuel as British firms, while German firms paid only 69 percent as much for ore and 88 percent as much for fuel. The credit or blame for this lay with geography and geology, not with managers

steel investment away from primary rolling mills into continuous casting mills in the 1960s and early 1970s. By 1985, it still lagged in the adoption of continuous casting, which had risen to only 44 percent of U.S. mill capacity but 55–91 percent of capacity in Korea, Japan, and the EC.

In these cases of specific investment choices—when to install basic oxygen furnaces or when to install continuous-casting mills—the evidence against the U.S. firms' investment decisions is not clearcut. But there is enough circumstantial evidence to buttress Figure 10.5's finding that *something* seems to have gone wrong with the industry's performance.

The 13–17 percent difference in measured productivity is too great to be

CONTINUED

of firms in any country. As for wage rates, German firms had access to the cheapest labor, at 83 percent of the British wage, but American firms had to pay 70 percent higher wage rates than British firms, just because of the general scarcity of manual labor in America.

Taking all measurable input prices into account explains a 17 percent cost advantage for German firms over British, but implies no advantage for American firms.

British firms had a 15 percent lower total factor productivity (output/input) than their American or German counterparts. The literature points to a few likely mistakes by British management, though it is hard to allocate blame between management or labor. The 15 percent productivity gap, interestingly enough, is just like the one between Japanese and American productivity as of 1976.

By 1906–1913 German firms should have been the lowest-cost producers in the world. What kept them from taking over the British and other markets was their decision to charge a slight monopoly markup on exports (and an even higher monopoly markup in their protected home markets).

The prewar and postwar episodes were thus similar: the rising challenger had some raw-material price advantages and achieved about 15 percent better productivity. The raw-material advantage may have been beyond the control of the British steelmakers being overtaken, but the productivity gap was not.

canceled by either higher capital productivity in America or the advantages of America's having old plants in place. The share of annual capital costs in U.S. steel prices in 1968 was only 18 percent at most, making differences in capital productivity and capital input prices unimportant. Studies suggest, in any case, no clear difference in output/capital ratios between the United States and Japan.

Thus far we have two cases, one prewar (see box) and one postwar, in which the leading national steel industry dropped from pace-setting productivity to a productivity deficit somewhere near 15 percent. The steel experience thus promotes the fear that something about the comfort of early leadership exposes a firm, industry, or nation to competitive sluggishness. Economists are still far from resolving whether this is the general case, or why it occurs when it does. Are strong entrenched unions to blame? Is management to blame, either in its attitude toward innovation or in its acquiescence to union demands? Such questions remain open, underlined by the productivity results we have examined.

Meanwhile, we must turn to a relative-cost issue not addressed in Figure 10.5. What about government-imposed costs, such as special regulatory burdens and taxes? Could it be that the U.S. steel industry was hobbled by heavy costs imposed by government, while the Japanese and other steel industries got subsidies from their governments? This charge is often advanced by the steel industry itself, and deserves study.

A study for the FTC on the competitive position of the U.S. steel industry went to some length to quantify the effects of different government policies on steelmaking costs (Duke et al., 1977). Three results of that study set boundaries on the possible role of government as a special competitive handicap to the U.S. steel industry as of about 1976.

1. Government-mandated costs for *pollution control* were actually lower in the United States than in Japan, especially in the period 1972–76. A later government study also found steel-industry pollution control costs higher in Japan (U.S. Congress, Office of Technology Assessment, 1980). In the early 1980s, pollution control costs were only slightly higher in the United States than in Japan (Eichengreen, 1988, p. 332).
2. Special government *subsidies* for the steel industry were trivial in Japan (and zero in the United States). They gave Japanese firms a cost advantage of only about 46 cents a ton, or less than a quarter of a percent of total cost.
3. *Price controls* imposed by the U.S. government did hurt steel industry profits significantly in one brief episode. During the Nixon price controls of 1971–74, during a steel boom, the industry was forced to take significantly lower profits. The price controls can be viewed as a cost-raising factor in the sense that they cut the supply of profits (inside funds) for reinvestment in the industry during that three-year period.

As far as the first two quantified cost factors go, government was not a net handicap to the U.S. steel industry in its struggle against Japanese competition (though pollution control costs may have exceeded those borne by other competitors, such as Brazilian steelmakers). Only the hard-to-quantify costs of the 1971–74 price control episode linger as a way in which government may be responsible for the competitive decline of the U.S. steel industry. These costs are not likely to have been a dominant factor, however. Government intervention is apparently not the reason why U.S. steel is in trouble.

To summarize the accounting results, let us ask what explains the fact that Japanese firms made steel about 44 percent cheaper ($= 1.00 - 0.56$) in 1976. Of this overall cost gap, our explanations break down as follows:

About 15 percent of the cost gap was due to cheaper ore for Japanese firms;

About 50 percent due to lower wage rates in Japan, of which ⅓ (or 10 percent of the total cost gap) seems due to the wage-raising power of the United Steel Workers in the United States;

About 30 percent due to higher total factor productivity in Japan than in the United States;[8] and

About 5 percent due to all other factors (net).

The American steel industry (managers plus workers) could be blamed for the wage premium (10 percent of the cost gap), the productivity gap (30 percent), and possibly the ore cost gap (15 percent, on the argument that U.S. firms could have been as aggressive in getting new ore supplies as Japanese firms were). The contribution of government intervention appears to have been negligible.[9]

The U.S. Steel Policy Response

The U.S. steel industry responded to the surge of steel imports by investing heavily in politics. Their lobbying in Washington paid off in partial government protection against imports.

U.S. steel protection went through three waves, involving different import barriers in the spirit of Chapter 8. All of the waves led to the same result: the United States forced its foreign steel suppliers into "Voluntary Export Restraints" (or VERs, or VRAs for voluntary restraint agreements, or OMAs for orderly marketing arrangements). Recall from Chapter 8 and Appendix F that these involve having foreign exporters administer their own quota system limiting sales to a particular importing country (e.g., the United States). In the first of the three waves, the U.S. government got foreign suppliers to agree to VERs by directly demanding the VERs. Then VERs

---

[8] The 30 percent figure is the share of the cost reduction due to higher productivity in Japan ($1/1.15 = 87\%$, or 13% below the U.S. cost) in the total observed cost advantage of Japan ($1 - 0.56 = 44\%$), or 13%/44%, or about 30%.

[9] The only major help of the government of Japan to Japanese steelmakers came before the successful export drive. From the 1930s to the late 1960s, Japan protected its steel industry against imports. One could argue that this was a case of wise infant-industry protection, which was wisely removed after the industry had become a significant exporter. The infant-industry argument has some hurdles to overcome, however. It must explain why infant-industry protection was needed for more than 30 years before the industry could meet outside competition, and it must show that infant-industry protection to Japanese steel didn't have an equally negative effect on the infant industries (e.g., automobiles) that used steel as an input.

became redundant by 1972 because the value of the dollar dropped in foreign-exchange markets, making foreign steel expensive, at the same time that U.S. price controls kept down the cost of domestic steel. In the second wave, from 1974 to 1982, the United States got new VERs indirectly, by campaigning for something else. Invoking an escape clause in the Trade Act of 1974, U.S. steel firms petitioned for relief on the grounds that they and their workers suffered "serious material injury" from import competition. U.S. officials ruled in favor of their complaints in several cases. The new policy regime allowed the government to set up a new "trigger price mechanism." As soon as the price of imported steel fell below a reference price decreed by the Department of Commerce, the low price was considered to be proof that the foreign suppliers were guilty of "dumping" (in the sense of Chapter 8), so that an import tariff could be slapped on quickly, without waiting for legislation from Congress. Foreign suppliers responded to the new threat by policing their own export cartels, with each firm charging a high price on limited exports to the United States. In other words, they came up with new VERs. In the third wave, since 1982, U.S. steel firms made it a habit to charge foreign competitiors with dumping and foreign governments with subsidizing steel exports. The result was VERs again: rather than fight each case, the more established foreign suppliers preferred to raise their prices and restrict their exports to the U.S. market.

The effects of Voluntary Export Restraints on the United States are more negative than even import quotas, for reasons mentioned in Chapter 8 and Appendix F. Instead of collecting either tariffs or quota-license auction revenues, the government lets the foreign suppliers pocket the full markup of prices in the U.S. over world prices. David Tarr (1989) of the U.S. Federal Trade Commission has estimated that VERs cost the United States $906 million a year in the mid-1980s. True, the arrangements were good for the U.S. steel industry. They saved about 20,700 extra steel jobs, for example. On the other hand, making steel more expensive costs other jobs, so that the net national job gain was on the order of only 4,300 jobs. At a cost of $906 million, even after including the gains to steel workers, that's a net national loss of over $210,000 per U.S. job saved (though if you cared only about steel jobs and nobody else's jobs, you could say the net national cost was only $906 m./20,700 = $43,768 per steel job saved).

Most of the national cost of VER's would have been avoided if the United States had used import quotas or tariffs instead. Tarr's study estimates that of the $906 million net national loss from steel VERs, $777 million could be recaptured by replacing the VERs with government-auctioned quotas, capturing the price markup that is now given to foreign suppliers.

So why do the governments of United States, Canada and the EC prefer the most costly way of getting the same protection for their steel (and other) industries? The answer lies in international political economy. One "benefit" of voluntary export restraints is that the importing-country government keeps the illusion of not imposing import barriers, and it is therefore technically not violating GATT rules. Another is that the voluntary arrangements give price markups to the exporting firms, most of them in East Asia. In the usual case, these firms gain more on the price markup than they lose on the extra sales they have to sacrifice. Their net gains can be substantial, even though they are eventually eroded by the entry of new exporters who were not party to the agreements. So, the political deal struck with VERs converts foreign suppliers from enemies to friends of domestic protectionists—all at the expense of consumers.

Meanwhile, the U.S. steel industry has continued to shrink, because its protection is only partial. By the 1990s, the industry has retreated to defensible high ground. It now makes fair profits in high-quality specialty steels, and largely with electric-arc furnaces in mini-mills. The specialty steels and the electric-arc processes are characterized by greater flexibility. They serve smaller markets that rise and fall rapidly, calling for quicker attention to market changes.

Japan's Decline

The 1980s initiated a new era of relative decline by a world leader in steelmaking. Japan, the leading exporter and second only to the Soviet Union as a producer, has seen its share of world steel production drop from 16 percent in the 1970s to 13.5 percent by 1987. While all observers expect Japan's decline to continue, none fault the Japanese firms for the decline. The main reason for the decline is simply that more and more nations are rising to the best technological standard in steelmaking, and often this is done with the help of government subsidies. Korea, in particular, is capturing steel markets from Japan with the best-practice mills of its giant state-controlled steel firm, the Pohang Iron and Steel Corporation.

In fact, a clear lesson about steel is to avoid it in long-run planning. If a nation is not yet saddled with a huge commitment to steel, the nation can avoid considerable losses by resolving to import its steel. Steel production is heavily subsidized the world over, especially in socialist countries, Korea, the Third World, and the European Community. Chapter 8's analysis of export subsidies in a highly competitive industry still applies: importing countries can afford to welcome cheap foreign steel.

OTHER CASES

Automobiles

Global leadership in producing and selling passenger cars went through the same kind of change as in steel, for roughly the same reasons. Japan overtook the United States, high American wage rates were a factor, entrepre-

FIGURE 10.6   Leading Countries' Shares of World Passenger Car Output, 1958–1987

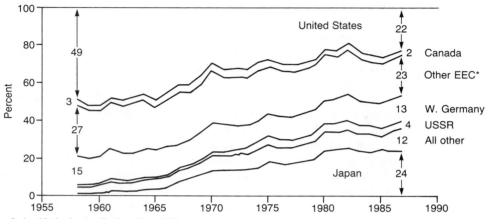

*France, Italy, Netherlands, Spain, United Kingdom.

Sources: United Nations, *Yearbook of Industrial Statistics,* Motor Vehicle Manufacturers Association, *World Motor Vehicle Data.*

neurial failure was a factor, and government support to Japanese firms played little role. The auto outcome by the start of the 1990s resembled the outcome for steel, except that the U.S. auto industry kept a larger market share, and became less American, than the U.S. steel industry.

In the late 1950s, the United States produced nearly half the world's cars, as shown in Figure 10.6. The most noticeable import invasion into the U.S. auto market was the arrival of Volkswagen "bugs" from Germany. Japanese autos were still inferior and received infant-industry protection against imports of American and European cars. Japanese firms had a long-run plan, however, and the North American market was the primary target. Starting at the lowest-price end of the spectrum of passenger cars, Toyota and Nissan (Datsun) led the advance into American markets in the late 1960s and early 1970s. The number of defects per car, initially high, became impressively low by the mid-1970s, allowing Japanese firms to follow the earlier Volkswagen strategy of building a reputation for low maintenance as well as low purchase price, before grooming an image of luxury or engine-power.

The import invasion of the American auto market peaked in 1980–82. Japanese cars rose to about 22 percent of the U.S. market, a share that was maintained across the 1980s. U.S. imports from all countries rose from 12 percent in 1973 to 27 percent in 1980, and they also held steady across the 1980s. Japan's export success is the main reason why it displaced the United States in total number of cars produced, as shown in Figure 10.6. As a share of world output, as in export penetration, Japan's advance stabilized across the 1980s, neither retreating nor advancing overall. The trends would look much the same even if we could adjust the passenger-car counts for differences in the average quality of different countries' cars. Cars from Japan had lower average quality than American or European makes up to the late 1970s, but thereafter Japanese firms shifted their export and production mixtures toward higher-price cars with more features.

Why was the American automobile industry in such a crisis by 1980? Government aid to automakers in Japan can be only part of the story. True, high import barriers protected Japan's automakers when they were getting established in the 1950s and 1960s. These were removed as soon as export success was established. The protection by itself could only have allowed Japanese firms to approach, not to surpass, advantages held by American automakers. By securing the home market, the protection gave Toyota, Nissan, and others a secure profit base and good credit ratings for financing export expansion. Yet their financial base could hardly have been as secure as that of America's Big Three (General Motors, Ford, and Chrysler). Had the American firms remained at the cost-cutting frontier, Japanese firms could not have carved out 22 percent of the U.S. auto market.

North American firms lost out to import competition in part because of a growing wage-markup premium earned by members of the United Auto Workers (UAW). The automobile industry stood out, even more than the steel industry, in the wage-hiking power of its labor union. As far back as 1963, the average U.S. auto worker received a wage that was 57 percent above that of the average worker in all manufacturing. That premium was probably too high to be explained as a reward for higher skill or for doing an unpleasant job, given that it was higher in the United States and Canada than in other industrial countries. More tellingly, the U.S. auto wage premium advanced across the 1960s and 1970s, even as the industry suffered increasing import competition. By 1980, the auto wage markup over the all-manufacturing average peaked at 124 percent, that is, more than double the overall average wage in manufacturing, before falling back in the 1980s. Economists agree that noncompetitive U.S. wage rates must have played a major role in the auto import invasion.

In addition, American automaking productivity fell behind that of Japan across the 1970s. Econometric estimates suggest that total factor productivity (outputs/inputs, after adjusting for the quality of both) in U.S. auto production had fallen significantly below that of Japan by 1980.[10] Simpler indicators suggest the same. By 1980, the average American car cost about $2,000 more than the comparable Japanese model sold in the United States. Also

---

[10] The estimates are those of Fuss and Waverman (1985, 1986), though our interpretations of their results differ. Fuss and Waverman chalk up most of the productivity shortfall of the American firms around 1980 to insufficient utilization of capacity, as if it were a demand-side force independent of any auto-industry failure. I consider it a prime symptom of the American auto industry's own failure to cut costs and raise quality at that time.

in 1980, the average American new car had more defects: 6.7 per new Ford car, 7.4 per new General Motors car, and 8.1 per new Chrysler car, versus 2.0 per car imported from Japan.

Blame for the shortfall in productivity and product quality must apparently be shared by both the United Auto Workers and by management, with greater blame probably falling on the management side. Regarding this the evidence is only indirect and suggestive, but abundant. Managers of the Big Three firms have admitted to earlier strategic errors (or have accused their predecessors of those errors). They admit that they underestimated the need for greater fuel efficiency, especially after the first oil crisis of 1973–74. They admit that they also underestimated the ability of foreign firms to advance from their initial beachhead in low-priced minimal cars into sports-car and luxury-car lines once a reputation for quality had been established. There is also consensus on some of the key organizational defects in the American auto industry, defects pointed out by Japan's success. The American firms undervalued dialogue and teamwork between divisions and job specialties. They relied, and still rely, on serial functional separation, in which each stage works in relative isolation and "throws it over the wall" to the next stage when its task seems done. By contrast, in the major Japanese firms, the designers, product engineers, process engineers, and line workers interact more simultaneously on each stage of design and production.

An important indirect clue to the blame for the poor productivity around 1980 is the course of subsequent events in the American auto industry. Across the 1980s, the industry made several adjustments that help us decide how much blame to put on American workers, their union pay packages, and American management. If the main culprit had been a drop in the inherent quality of American workers across the 1970s, a main response of the 1980s would have been a mass shutdown of U.S. plants, to be replaced by foreign plants with the same management. Production in the United States would have dropped as a share of world production, while U.S. *firms'* production would have held steady, helped by a rapid expansion in their operations outside the United States. That was not the dominant trend (despite some powerful imagery in Michael Moore's film "Roger and Me"). In the 1980s, new plants opened up in the United States almost as fast as other plants closed, with relatively little exodus of U.S. firms to other countries.

The key trends in the auto industry of the 1980s were changes in ownership, management and the type of pay contract, not an emigration of jobs and output. Within the United States, the net shutdown of plants by the American Big Three was offset by the opening of eight new U.S. auto and truck plants under Japanese ownership (one, in Fremont, California, was a joint venture between Toyota and General Motors). A similar replacement of local firms with Japanese-owned and Japanese-managed firms occurred in Europe. With the change in ownership came changes in production techniques and in pay contracts. On the pay front, the high UAW pay packages were replaced with initially lower wage rates, mostly but not exclusively in non-UAW work forces.

The 1980s saw an improvement in the cost and quality performance of American-made cars, both in strictly American firms and in the new Japanese-run "transplants." By 1989, prices on cars produced by the Big Three ran only $500–600 over the prices of comparable Japanese models, versus the gap of $2,000 back in 1980. Also, by 1989 the rates of defects per car on Ford, GM, and Chrysler products had dropped to only 1.5, 1.7, and 1.8, respectively, not far above the average of 1.2 for Japanese brands. The Japanese "transplant" units in America achieved nearly the same low rate of defects as units in Japan.

At the height of the import invasion, the U.S. government responded by protecting its automakers. The temporary bailout loans to Chrysler in 1978 seem to have helped move that company back from the brink of extinction to greater efficiency, a better result than is usual with government bailouts. In 1981, Washington compelled the government and automakers of Japan to cooperate with Voluntary Export Restraints, which remained in effect (first formally and then informally) throughout the 1980s. How badly or how well the protection worked is still uncertain. If we take the usual static welfare analysis, the VERs were worse for the United States than either free trade or import quotas. David Tarr (1989) has calculated that the VERs cost the United States $5,900 million a year in the mid-1980s. He also calculated that the United States could have gained $6,200 million a year by replacing VERs with equivalent import quotas but capturing the price markup that VERs gave to Japanese firms.[11] The net national loss, and the U.S. auto industry's gain, would have been greater if Japan's automakers had not shifted the quality of their exports in response to the VER policy. As Feenstra (1984) has shown, the Japanese firms, faced with a limit on the number of cars they could export, shifted to exporting higher-price cars (e.g., sports cars) to the United States, spreading smaller price effects and welfare losses between the markets for different kinds of cars. So far, it still looks as though the VERs were a bad policy for the United States. Yet they may not have been so bad relative to free trade at the height of the import invasion. The creditworthiness of the retreating U.S. firms may have received an important boost from the temporary protection, helping them finance the improvements that yielded higher auto quality and lower costs by the late 1980s. The VERs also helped convince more Japanese auto firms to open plants in the United States in order to get

---

[11] The United States gains more by keeping its own import quotas than by returning to free trade because it has some monopsony power as the world's largest importer of automobiles. A good diagram for picturing the choice between VERs, free trade, and quotas is Figure F.3 in Appendix F. In terms of that figure, Tarr's estimate of $5,900 million refers to areas $b + c + d$, while his estimate of $6,200 million refers to areas $c + e$.

around import barriers. Raising the supply of Japanese capital and management to the United States must have offset, and may have reversed, the costs of automobile protectionism for the United States.

Three Electronics Sectors

Another crucial arena of changing leadership is the whole range of electronics industries, from consumer sight and sound electronics (radios, tapes, compact discs, televisions, video recorders, video games, etc.) to the highest-technology computer industries. In this section we note some apparent lessons emerging from the rise of Japan relative to the United States in three particular electronic sectors. In two of them, Japanese giant firms have vanquished American competition almost completely, with strong help from the government of Japan. In a third, Japan has not yet overtaken American leadership, despite the same kind of help from the government of Japan.

Television.   The change of international leadership was especially stark in the market for television sets. In the 1950s, U.S. firms controlled almost all the American market, and they did export products to some extent. By the late 1980s, only Zenith continued to produce television sets within the United States (along with Sony, one of Japan's giants). The rest of U.S. firms' production had migrated abroad, but still could not match the market share of the Japanese firms even in North America.

The rapid displacement of U.S. firms by imports, mostly from Japan, seems to have been less the fault of American firms than of government policy on both sides. Although there are signs that the American consumer-electronic firms made organization mistakes like those of U.S. auto firms, the signs are not strong. Nor did workers in consumer electronics plants get an inflated noncompetitive wage rate. Rather, the main explanation is that one government encouraged the industry while another obstructed it.

Japan's Ministry of International Trade and Industry (MITI) made television sets and related consumer-electronic goods a top target for export expansion. As with steel and autos, consumer electronics were protected against imports. The government also permitted domestic cartel-like collusion among the seven electronic giants: Hitachi, Matsushita (Panasonic), Mitsubishi, Sanyo, Sharp, Sony, and Toshiba. Japan's labyrinthine distribution system also systematically excluded American electronic goods. Dividing the protected domestic market among themselves, the seven firms attracted enormous private and government investments and launched their export drive.

American government policy slightly hindered American firms in the new international competition. The American tradition of stern antitrust policies kept large American firms from launching drives that would have brought a large share of the U.S. television market under the control of one or two efficient U.S. giants. Since American firms were kept smaller and less secure, the race to finance research and development and expanded production was won in Japan. Instead of buying political support for outright import protection, the U.S. firms stood on higher ground, maintaining that only unfair Japanese trade practices needed to be stopped. They pressed antidumping and antitrust cases against Japan, with only minor success in the television sector. In the end, they sold off U.S. plants to Japanese buyers and set up production abroad.

Semiconductors.   Equally ruinous was the effect of new foreign competition on the U.S. firms producing semiconductor devices, a key intermediate good for the entire electronic sector. Similar to most electronic products, the pioneering inventions were American, as was the early stage of product development, centered in Silicon Valley. At its peak around 1977, the American semiconductor industry served 95 percent of the U.S. market, half the European market, and 57 percent of the entire world market. Significantly, it served only a quarter of the Japanese market, where again formidable barriers blocked imports. By 1987, the United States had become a net importer of semiconductors, and a quarter of its demand was supplied by Japan. The American share of world production had dropped from 60 percent to 40 percent, Europe's share had dropped from 15 percent to 10 percent, and Japan's share had risen from 28 percent to 50 percent.

The two leading nations have very different semiconductor industries. The American industry consists of myriad small venture-capital innovating firms, whereas in Japan semiconductors are but one product in the operations of giant conglomerates like Fujitsu, Hitachi, NEC, and Toshiba. It is not surprising that the atomistic American firms have their advantage in the small business of pioneering invention, while the Japanese industry controls all the rest of the product's development and sales. The question to ask is: Why don't American giants like AT&T or IBM, heavy users of semiconductors, stand as equal rivals with their counterparts in Japan? Again, as with televisions, U.S. antitrust policy seems to have cancelled the hunt for large market shares. An antitrust settlement forced AT&T to license out its patented semiconductors in the 1950s, and the threat of antitrust suits would plague any pursuit of a dominant market share by either AT&T or IBM. Accordingly, large U.S. firms left the semiconductor industry to the small venture capitalists, who could not compete with Japan's giants in the long run.

The Computer Industries.   Ever since the 1950s, the government of Japan has targeted the entire computer sector—core hardware, peripherals, and software—as a key sector for national development. MITI and other government agencies have gone out of their way to keep IBM from playing a major role in Japan, and they have subsidized product lines suitable for export. For their part, private companies like Fujitsu, Hitachi, and NEC have taken a characteristically long view, investing more in research and development than even IBM.

To date, however, their export success has been more mixed than in the cases of television and semiconductors. They have achieved greatest success in peripheral equipment, a less research-intensive, more engineering-intensive sector. They have had the least success in software, a sector where the product is varied, changeable, and often dependent on a command of the local idiom. In the software subsector, indigenous cottage industries still flourish, though research and development by large Japanese firms may yet win out. In the core computer hardware sectors, the competition between Japan and the United States is still balanced and unresolved. Government policy gives Japan an advantage, as in other electronic lines. The U.S. government does not support its computer industry the way MITI supports Japanese firms. True, defense contracts once gave IBM and other American firms a decided edge. But these contracts have dropped off, and the U.S. Justice Department spent ten years and millions of dollars prosecuting IBM for monopolistic behavior. Although the case against IBM was dropped in 1982, IBM agreed to stop certain kinds of behavior that could have secured its national and world dominance. All in all, the advantages of the United States in software and related technology have kept the core hardware sector competitive with Japan, despite the difference in government willingness to help.

STRATEGIC POLICIES FOR TRADE LEADERSHIP

Two sources of change in trade leadership have been illustrated by the cases of steel, autos, and electronics. One is private failure in the country that lost leadership, such failures as managerial complacency or abuse of union power. The other is a difference in government policy, in which the challenging country's government provides more support for an industry than the government of the country that loses leadership. In sector after sector, the government of Japan encouraged industrialists to export and protected them against imports. Such Japanese policies are considered "unfair trade" by Americans concerned about the trade imbalance between the two countries.

Fair or not, does a policy of targeting and subsidizing a sector really work? Does a **strategic trade policy,** a government campaign to develop export advantage and cut import competition in targeted sectors, really raise national welfare? Presumably, it backfires if foreign governments retaliate with their own barriers against trade with this country. But suppose they do not retaliate, just as the United States has seldom retaliated against Japan.

If we were to rely on the perfect-competition analysis of Chapters 6 through 9, we would conclude that government intervention is inappropriate unless it is based on some special consideration such as externalities. In the case of a subsidy on exports, we saw in Chapter 8 that it was bad for the country imposing it. Yet the oligopolistic nature of the successful Japanese export industries leaves us a clue: perhaps we should drop the standard assumption of perfect competition and see if there is a strong case for strategic trade policies under imperfect competition.

How It Could Work

The rhetoric of strategic trade policies suggests that there are monopoly rents awaiting the nation that wrests an export market from its rivals. Some models of imperfect competition give this result, whereas others do not. The model of monopolistic competition in Chapter 5, for example, did not give this result. When the nation's monopolistically competitive firms reached out to a new export market, only consumers ended up gaining in the long run. On the other hand, Chapter 8's model of dumping did imply that the foreign market could bring extra monopoly rents. In the scholarly literature of the 1980s, controversy rages over the idea that large rents await capture by the nation whose firms move first, or move with most government help. Led by James Brander and Barbara Spencer, scholars have developed models of successful ''profit shifting.'' The models are inspired mainly by the renewed popularity of game-theoretic models of oligopoly, but they have also drawn inspiration from the real-world example of export targeting, especially by Japan and Korea. The chances for profit shifting are thought to be especially great in high-technology products.

To capture the spirit and the real-world possibilities of gains from aggressive pursuit of monopoly rents in export markets, let us consider a hypothetical case that may resemble a real-world situation around 1996. Japan, Europe, and North America are in a race to develop high-definition television (HDTV), upgrading the world's 750 million sets with movie-quality picture and compact-disc-quality sound. There is a strong chance of a struggle between Japan and Europe for the huge North American market. Supplying North America could create 100,000 jobs; supplying the world could create 350,000 jobs. Whichever national group wins the North American market can get its design written into the specifications for TV manufacture, excluding rivals for a long time to come. As of 1990, American suppliers are barely in the running. Zenith, Kodak, and smaller firms are trying to develop key components. The U.S. Federal Communications Commission helped out in 1988, by ruling that future HDTVs must be compatible with all existing makes of TV sets, prohibiting a design by, say, the colluding Japanese firms that would force all manufacturers of sets for the U.S. market to buy Japanese technology and parts. Yet in 1989, the White House cut off all federal support for research and development of HDTV, preferring to leave that to the private marketplace. Product development by American firms lags far behind the government-backed research of Japan's colluding conglomerates and the European Community team of firms, led by N. V.

Philips of Holland, Robert Bosch of Germany, and Thomson S. A. of France. To portray the situation that might develop when HDTV is perfected around 1996, let us imagine that the American firms are forced out of the race, and Japan and Europe (the EC) are in a head-to-head struggle for the large North American market.

FIGURE 10.7   Fighting for an Export-Market Monopoly, with and without Government Subsidies: Japan and the EC Face the North American Market for HDTVs

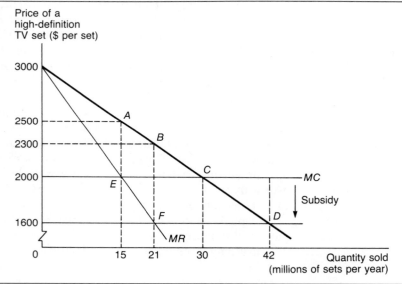

Situation:	Exporting Firm(s)	Government	American Consumers	World
Standoff (no exporters to this market)	0	0	0	0
Private leadership (no subsidy, just a monopoly at *A*)	7,500*	0	3,750	11,250*
Subsidized leadership (one subsidy, monopoly at *B*)	14,700*	−8,400	7,350	13,650*
Private shoot-out (no subsidy, firms compete at *C*)	0*	0	15,000	15,000*
Subsidized shoot-out (both governments subsidize, firms compete at *D*)	0*	−16,800	29,400	12,650*

Gains (in millions of dollars/year)

* Minus fixed costs.

Figure 10.7 shows the main possible outcomes of the struggle for large monopoly rents on HDTV exports to North America. As is usual with duopolistic (two-seller) competition, the outcome depends on who strikes first, who has outside help, and how the second rival responds. We can get useful conclusions from a look at the range of possibilities shown in Figure 10.7:

1. *A standoff.* It is risky to invest in capturing a new foreign market, especially if a powerful foreign rival might win the market in the end, leaving you with a loss on your investment. Both sides could decide that the risk is too great, and refrain from developing any exports for the North American market. That is unlikely in the case of high-definition television, but it might happen in other cases. If the investment opportunity is passed up, nobody gains or loses from it.

2. *Private leadership at Point A.* Suppose that one team of large private firms, say Japan's team of electronic giants, strikes first and captures the entire North American market, with Europe clearly afraid to challenge them. The team from Japan will enjoy monopoly power in the North American market. Figure 10.7 shows the monopolist's profit-maximizing situation in the usual way (as is also done in Chapters 8 and 11). The monopolistic group of firms maximizes profits by charging more and selling less than a perfectly competitive industry. Instead of selling at Point *C,* it charges a high enough price so that its sales and output are only at 15 million sets a year, where profit is maximized because marginal revenue equals marginal cost at Point *E.* The profit-maximizing price is $2,500 a set, up at Point *A.* On those 15 million sets sold in North America, Japan's firms get pure profits equal to 15 million sets times ($2,500 − 2,000), or $7,500 million a year (minus some fixed costs of getting started in North America). Consumers also gain $3,750 million in consumer surplus (to the northwest of Point *A*) from the availability of HDTVs, leaving a clear world gain.

The monopoly gains at Point *A* (or pure profits, or rents) might go to Europe instead of to Japan. Which rival wins the race depends on which has lower costs or which acts more decisively. To bring out the possible role of policy, let us assume that the private costs are exactly the same in either Japan or Europe. Both countries have the same marginal cost of $2,000 per set, and the same fixed costs of getting started in North America.

3. *Subsidized leadership at Point B.* If the monopoly gains from the North American market beckon equally to either rival, the race to get them could be decided by a government subsidy to one rival. Suppose that the European Community makes the decisive move, with a permanent subsidy of $400 on every set sold in North America.[12] Suppose that the subsidy

---

[12] If the subsidy were really just on exports, it would violate the GATT, and Canada and the United States might levy antisubsidy duties. Let us imagine a $400 subsidy on every set produced in the EC, whether or not it is sold in North America.

convinces Japan that they cannot compete against Europe in the North American market. The team of European firms wins handsomely, capturing a subsidy from their governments as well as the monopoly on HDTV in North America. For the European firms, the marginal cost is now $2,000 minus the $400 subsidy, or only $1,600. Their profit-maximizing response will again be to equate marginal revenue and marginal cost, now at Point *F*. The profit-maximizing price in American markets is $2,300, as shown at Point *B* on the demand curve. On each of the 21 million sets a year, the European firms gain $2,300 minus $1,600, for a total profit of $14,700 million (minus fixed costs). European taxpayers lose the subsidy paid to the firms, but Europe as a whole clearly gains in this case. So does the world as a whole.

4. *A private shoot-out at Point C.* Just letting the free market work without subsidies can bring gains, but it can also have its problems if there are only a few possible suppliers (in this case, there are only two). Point C shows one way that the gains and problems might work out. The gains go to the consumers, who get to buy 30 million sets a year at a price of only $2,000 a set. The firms in Japan and Europe do not gain. Because they compete with each other, each must accept a price no higher than marginal cost. Both lose the fixed costs of entering the (North American) market. One side or both sides might eventually go broke. So if a nation's firms are going to pursue a lucrative export market elsewhere, it helps to strike first and show potential rivals that they cannot win by entering the same market later.

5. *A subsidized shoot-out at Point D.* If both the government of Japan and the European Community simultaneously subsidized their HDTV sectors to make a run at the North American market, they would both pay dearly, yet the world as a whole would gain. Such a rivalry would bring keen price-cutting competition. Japanese and European firms would find that their effective marginal costs were only $1,600, and would cut their price down to that level in open competition. This is the best bargain of all from the standpoint of American consumers, who gain consumer surplus all the way down to Point *D*. The outcome is therefore good for the world, because the shoot-out solves an old problem of artificially restricted supply.[13]

Thus the export-monopoly case says that a country can gain by striking first, and that having governments subsidize production of an exportable good makes the world as a whole better off. Similar results came from Chapter 5's treatment of an exportable good with external economies (Figure 5.3) and a good subject to monopolistic competition (Figure 5.4). In those cases, too, consumers clearly gained from a subsidy or any other event

---

[13] The exporting countries lose their subsidies plus fixed costs. If they could somehow have colluded, they might have reaped net gains as a joint monopolist. Operating at Point *B*, they might have split a single dose of fixed costs and subsidies, while also splitting profits from the joint monopoly.

triggering the industry's expansion, whether or not the firms themselves gained. Again, we have the result that an export-promoting nudge, from either policy or luck, can generate large gains from trade and propel a national industry into world leadership. All three cases—export monopoly, external economies, and monopolistic competition—lie in the world of "second best" where, as stressed in Chapter 7, having a distortion in the market can make policy intervention look reasonable.

How Often Does Strategic Trade Policy Work Well?

The three cases for export promotion look somewhat realistic: export monopoly, external economies, and monopolistic competition all seem to have real-world examples, especially where technological advance is rapid. How many other cases give the same result, and how often are they met in the real world?

The theory of oligopoly (competition among the few) offers little here because it offers too much. Economists have found an infinite menu of possible results, whose policy recommendations flip-flop with changes in technical assumptions that seem equally unrealistic. Consider the basic case of an export subsidy, which seemed to work well in the three cases just mentioned. If we had oligopoly in an export market, theorists have shown that an export subsidy can be optimal if there is competition in which each of the rivals sets its quantity rather than its price—but an export *tax* can be optimal if each of the rivals sets its price rather than its quantity (Brander and Spencer 1981, Eaton and Grossman 1986, Cheng 1988). Imagine trying to tell legislators that exports should be either taxed or subsidized, depending on what kind of oligopoly we have, and nobody can say what kind we have. How about a production subsidy to get a national start in a high-tech industry? It works well under some technical assumptions about oligopolistic competition (Brander and Spencer 1985), but under slightly different assumptions it fails and production should even be taxed (Eaton and Grossman 1986, Cheng 1988). You can get anything you want in theory's restaurant, especially when the theory of oligopoly is being served. So far, a large literature on oligopolistic international competition lacks a reliable policy conclusion (Stegemann 1989).

Would actual experience give a clearer guide? Are there abundant cases in which the road to trade leadership was clearly paved with government aid to strategically chosen industries? There are indeed, though the record must be handled with care. Here are a few cautious conclusions about experience with strategic trade policies:

1. *In high-technology sectors, success has often had to be national, suggesting a role for government.* In industries pushing back the technological frontier, there seem to be strong external economies (as in Chapter 5) or strong enough chances of developing monopoly power in export markets (as in Figure 10.7). In such cases, government help makes some sense. It need not take the form of a simple output subsidy like that in Figure 10.7. More typically, successful help seems to take two other forms: cheap credit for long-term expansion, and a relaxation of antitrust policies.

2. *The main cases of successful government promotion of world-leading exports relate to postwar Japan and Korea.* Developing world leadership in export lines is an art that has eluded most governments. Japan and Korea seem to have gained a large export success with government advanced targeting of key industries, cheap government loans and protection of a profitable home market as a springboard to worldwide exporting. The correlation between government encouragement and export success is impressive in these two countries.

3. *The overall correlation between government support and export success is weak, however.* Some countries, like Taiwan, have succeeded in developing vigorous exports in manufacturing, and sometimes high-technology, sectors without government direction. Others have poured growing aid into industries that never grow up or become competitive exporters, as in the sad case of Australian government protection of its automobile industry. In fact, industries slated for special development by their governments, instead of by the marketplace, have a low global success rate. It takes considerable finesse, or luck, for a government to find just the right industry for developing a dynamic comparative advantage.

DOES THE EARLY LEADER HAVE A DISADVANTAGE?

It might seem that catching-up countries have all the advantages, and that early leaders find it harder to retain their dynamism, forcing them to fall behind. This is false. There may be social or political reasons *inviting* the leaders to fall behind, but there is no economic logic *forcing* them to fall behind.

There are only two ways in which the early leader has a disadvantage, and both problems erase themselves as rivals catch up to the leader. One is that firms in the catching-up country can hire cheaper labor, gaining a competitive edge. Yet the cheap-labor argument cannot explain any change in international leadership. Leadership means a higher level of income per capita, which is almost perfectly correlated with high wage rates because human skills are the key to both wage rates and overall income per capita. The closer a catcher-up (e.g., Japan) approaches the leader (e.g., the United States), the smaller the gap in wage rates. Second, the catching-up country can borrow or buy the latest technology at a low cost, without having to develop it first. True as this may be, it is also self-erasing. The closer the catcher-up approaches the technological frontier, the less it can borrow cheaply, and the more it must invest in its own research and development.

All of the cases in which international trade leadership has changed at the top show a large role for avoidable mistakes. Historically, the most important mistakes by leaders have been these:

1. Underinvestment in education and training, allowing another country to surpass the leader's early advantage in human skills. Before World War I, Britain underinvested in education, especially in technological education. Between the mid-1960s and the early 1980s, the United States allowed the quality of its primary and secondary schooling to dip, costing students over a year of learning by age 18. While we can theorize that such failures were the result of complacency bred by world leadership itself, the complacency was still avoidable, and it was not dictated by any tight economic logic.

2. As in the steel and auto cases, leadership has often changed hands in part because of managerial failures and union power in the early-leader country. Again, complacency may have been bred by early leadership. That is, both management and unions may have been lulled to sleep by their early monopoly advantages. Yet complacency in unions and management, like complacency in educational policy, is avoidable.

3. Economic leaders have also been military leaders. Military leadership has bred arms races, in which both sides lose resources even if peace is maintained. Countries wasting less of their national product on arms races can invest more in developing their civilian economies. Thus, the United States gained by being outside the arms race between European nations before 1940 (except for the two years of U.S. involvement in World War I). Similarly, Japan has gained since World War II by spending only about one percent of GNP on military defense, versus over six percent in the United States. Had the leaders avoided the arms race (e.g., through negotiation) they could have invested more in economic competitiveness.

SUMMARY

The most meaningful way to define international leadership is in terms of average national living standards. The closest proxy to this is GNP per capita. On this measure, the United States and Canada retain leadership, aside from small oil-rich nations. Japan's more rapid growth across the 1980s suggests a catch-up to the United States by the mid-1990s. Defining leadership in terms of using the latest technology, or being a net exporter of high-technology products, is less logical.

The catching-up of Asian industrial countries to North American levels of living standards seems correlated with their emphasis on manufacturing, raising the question of whether or how manufacturing might be a leading sector raising the entire national growth rate.

A study of how international leadership changed hands in selected manufacturing sectors turns up some basic explanations, most of them not relating to the role of government. In the steel industry, relative-price accounting shows that Japan caught the United States by 1976 largely because of differences in wage rates, differences in the industry's productivity, and differences in the cost of raw materials, in that order of importance. Extraordinary union power explains part of the high labor cost of American steel. The slight inferiority in U.S. steelmaking productivity was an avoidable industry fault, blame for which is shared by management and the union in uncertain proportions. Government policies in Japan and the United States played almost no role in Japan's overtaking America in steel.

Among other industries, the automobile industry most closely resembles steel's experience. Again, extraordinarily high union wages were a factor. So was apparent productivity failure, peaking around 1980. Management of the main American auto firms admitted to a series of mistakes in the 1960s and 1970s, and estimates bear them out. The role of government again seems secondary, though it helped in two settings. The government of Japan did protect its auto industry in the 1950s and early 1960s, and the U.S. government did protect its auto industry noticeably from 1978 to about 1985.

The electronics sector, here represented by television, semiconductors, and computer products, give a clearer signal that government help was crucial. Japan's government targeted electronics for rapid export growth, underwrote research and development, and protected the home market against imports. The government of the United States, on the other hand, discouraged the formation of large competitive U.S. conglomerates on antitrust grounds.

The experience with electronics raises a question for economic theory: under what realistic conditions can government play a crucial role in developing a national industry that will be a leader in world markets? The conditions under which this seems clearest are the case of competing for an export monopoly (Figure 10.7), cases where external economies are present, and cases of monopolistic competition. There is no clear pattern under oligopoly. Under perfect competition and no externalities, we revert to the conclusions of Chapters 6–8, which generally favor free trade.

There is no economic logic forcing economic leaders to fall behind any rival. There are only two advantages to being the catching-up country instead of the early leader, and both advantages are self-eliminating. Firms in the catching-up country can take advantage of cheap labor, but catching up means that the labor stops being cheaper. They can also borrow the latest technology at low cost, but that only brings them closer to the technological frontier, where they must turn to costly research instead of cheap borrowing. Initial leadership may invite failures, but they are all avoidable. In the British and American past, the main kinds of economic failures related to leadership have been educational policy failures, managerial complacency, union power, and wasteful arms races.

SUGGESTED READINGS

A theoretical case for export promotion in the spirit of Figure 10.7 is given by James Brander and Barbara Spencer (1985). Our understanding of the issue of strategic trade policy is aptly summarized in Paul R. Krugman (1986) and Klaus Stegemann (1989).

The literature on real-world trade competition is enormous, growing, and often readable. If your library uses the Library of Congress system, you can find an abundance of relevant material in the range from HF1411 to HF1414. For a balanced view of the practice of strategic industrial policy in Japan, see Chalmers Johnson (1982), Kozo Yamamura (1986), and Clyde Perkowitz, *Trading Places: How We Allowed Japan to Take the Lead* (Basic Books, 1988). An enthusiastic survey of similar policies in Korea is Alice Amsden (1989). On the "sad and sorry story" of Australia's targeting of the auto industry, see Robert Gregory (1988). A survey of many countries' industrial policies is Mutoh et al. (1986).

A superb survey of America's competitive position in manufactures is *Made in America* by the MIT Commission on Industrial Productivity (Dertouzos, Lester, and Solow 1989), which deals out warnings and advice. On the other hand, Robert Z. Lawrence (1984) rejects many popular fears about America's competitive ability. Two other surveys of the basic trends are Morici (1988b) and Porter (1990). Sophisticated studies of competitive currents in the auto and semiconductor sectors are presented in Robert C. Feenstra (1988). The policy debate is well portrayed in Hufbauer (1989), a task force report with conflicting opinions.

QUESTIONS FOR REVIEW

1. Of the industry studies in this chapter (steel, autos, electronics), which gave the best case for government strategic trade policies?

2. *a.* Describe how you would measure an industry's productivity performance (or failure) relative to the same industry in another country.

b. If the measure shows productivity failure, who is to blame for the failure?

3. Of the industry studies in this chapter, which yielded a verdict of productivity failure by the American industry?

4. *a.* How could an export subsidy benefit both the exporting country and the world as a whole? Explain.

b. Reconcile your answer to 4a with Chapter 8's analysis of the Korean steel export subsidy, which was supposedly bad for Korea and for the world. What explains the difference?

11

▼

OPEC and Other International Cartels

•

History records many attempts at international **cartels,** or international agreements to restrict selling competition.

The greatest seizure of monopoly power in world history was the price-raising triumph of the Organization of Petroleum Exporting Countries (OPEC)[1] in 1973–74 and again in 1979–80. One task of this chapter must therefore be to explain what OPEC had going for it that other cartels lacked. The other task, however, is to explain how economists know that cartels are destined to lose power sooner or later. Basic economic analysis points to pressures that tend to make cartel power erode. As we shall see, recent experience with OPEC has confirmed the correctness of this analysis. We take up the two tasks in order, first explaining the rise and power of OPEC, then explaining why OPEC must weaken. A final section will extend what we have learned to a quick look at the prospects facing cartels in products other than oil.

OPEC VICTORIES

A chain of events in late 1973 revolutionized the world oil economy. In a few months' time, the 13 members of the Organization of Petroleum Exporting Countries (OPEC) effectively quadrupled the dollar price of crude oil, from

---

[1] OPEC was created by a treaty among five countries—Iran, Iraq, Kuwait, Saudi Arabia, and Venezuela—in Baghdad in September 1960. Since that time, the following countries have joined: Qatar, January 1961; Indonesia, June 1962; Libya, June 1962; Abu Dhabi, November 1967; Algeria, July 1969; Nigeria, July 1971; Ecuador, 1973; Gabon, associate member by 1973, full member in 1975.

$2.59 to $11.65 a barrel. Oil-exporting countries became rich, though still "underdeveloped" in some cases, almost overnight. The industrial oil-consuming countries sank into their deepest depression since the 1930s. The economic miracles of superfast growth in oil-hungry Japan and Brazil slowed down, perhaps permanently.

OPEC had already been building its collective strength earlier in the 1970s, after having little apparent power for the first decade after its formation in 1960. First in 1971 and again in 1972 OPEC had demanded and won both higher official oil prices and a greater share of oil profits and ownership at the expense of the major international oil companies. The rise in OPEC's power was greatly accelerated when the Arab-Israeli Yom Kippur War broke out in early October 1973. The war stiffened the resolve of the Arab oil-exporting countries, whose representatives were then in Vienna arguing over oil prices with the major private international oil companies. The Arab negotiating team became excited at the early news of Arab military successes and began passing around newspaper photographs of huge U.S. shipments of arms to Israel. The team's new firmness matched that of the oil companies, and negotiations ceased. Then, at a historic meeting in Kuwait on October 16, six key Persian Gulf oil countries decided that henceforth oil prices would be set by each country without consulting the major oil companies.

Meanwhile, oil buyers were beginning to panic. The Arab boycott against selling oil to the United States or other countries suspected of being pro-Israeli added to already existing fears that oil would become very scarce. The fears soon fulfilled themselves. Iran tested the market by auctioning off crude oil in early December 1973. Several smaller oil companies bid $16–$18 a barrel for oil that cost less than a dollar a barrel to produce and that had earlier sold for $5 or less. There were also reports that Libyan and Nigerian crude oil was fetching as much as $20 a barrel. With such solid evidence of buyer panic, OPEC imposed a price of $11.65 a barrel at its Tehran meeting of December 22–23, 1973. This price remained, even after the Arab oil embargo was lifted in early 1974.

Figure 11.1 shows 1974's near tripling of the "real" price of oil (what the price of a barrel of oil could buy in terms of manufactured exports from industrial nations). This was the most successful artificial price hike of all time, far eclipsing any shrewd monopoly move by John D. Rockefeller in his Standard Oil heyday. Figure 11.1 also shows the sequel, a plateau of OPEC prosperity, a further jump, and finally growing signs of weakness. From 1974 to 1978 the real price of oil dipped by about a sixth, but stayed much higher than it had been at any time before 1973. Next came the second wave of OPEC price hikes, the second "oil shock," in 1979–80. Led by the Iranian Revolution and growing panic among oil buyers, the oil price more than doubled. In the early 1980s it even crept up further, for an accidental reason: oil was priced in dollars, and the dollar rose more than 50 percent in value relative to other currencies. This made it easier

FIGURE 11.1   OPEC Oil Prices and Production, 1961–1989

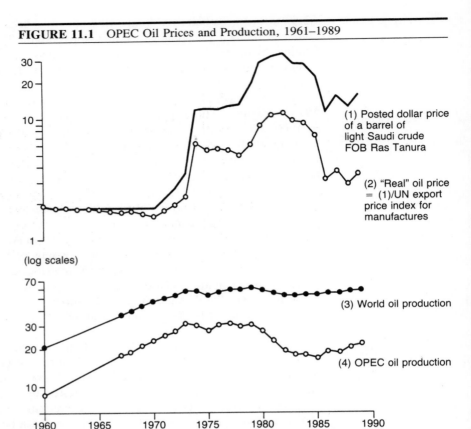

(1) Posted dollar price of a barrel of light Saudi crude FOB Ras Tanura

(2) "Real" oil price = (1)/UN export price index for manufactures

(log scales)

(3) World oil production

(4) OPEC oil production

Sources: UN, IMF, U.S. *Monthly Energy Review:* Gilbert Jenkins, *Oil Economist's Handbook* (London: Applied Science, 1977).

for each barrel of OPEC oil, along with each dollar, to be exchanged for manufactures priced in European currencies or the Japanese yen.

In the mid-1980s, however, OPEC weakened. Even though OPEC's own production dropped in 1985, the real price of oil also dropped suddenly in 1985, from 4–5 times the old (pre-1973) real price in 1980–84 to only 1.84 times the old price for 1985–89, as shown in Figure 11.1. Still, the whole episode since 1973 left us with that 84 percent increase in the real price of oil between 1973 and the late 1980s, even before Iraq invaded Kuwait.

Here, then, were two dramatic cartel victories, a subsequent retreat, and a large net rise overall. The victories, the retreat, and the net overall rise all need careful explanation.

REASONS FOR THE RISE OF OPEC

The first "oil shock" in 1973–74 climaxed a more gradual convergence of forces that tipped the balance of power in favor of oil-exporting countries. The three most important forces were:

1. The changing world demand-supply situation for oil.
2. The rising determination of oil-rich Arab nations to use oil as a weapon against Israel.
3. A new dependence of Israel's guardian, the United States, on oil imports.

World demand for crude oil had grown rapidly by 1973. World energy consumption had been growing a bit faster than 5 percent a year between 1950 and 1972. Oil's share of world energy consumption rose from 29 percent to 46 percent over the same period, so that oil use itself grew at about 7.5 percent a year, a rate well above the growth rate of world output of all products.

The *world* supply of crude oil grew at least as fast as world demand. World "proved" reserves represented about 34 years' oil consumption as of the end of 1972. This ratio of reserves to annual consumption had been maintained, with some fluctuations, ever since the mid-1950s, despite the rapid growth of oil consumption. Postwar oil price trends also failed to show any tendency for world oil supply to lag behind demand. Between 1950 and 1970, the ratio of the price of crude oil to the prices of manufactures that OPEC nations bought from the leading industrial nations dropped slightly, giving no hint of imminent scarcity. Nor were the costs of oil extraction rising much. Throughout the early 1970s, the production cost of a barrel of Persian Gulf crude was still only about 10 cents (plus that part of the oil companies' 50-cent profit representing average fixed costs), while the Persian Gulf nations raised their take from \$1.62 to \$7.01 a barrel (Figure 11.1). The 1973–74 oil price jumps were man-made, and not the result of exhaustion of the earth's available oil reserves.

Yet world demand was growing far faster than *non*-OPEC supplies. Postwar oil discoveries have been very unevenly distributed among countries. The invisible hand of Allah has given OPEC most of the world's oil. The share of OPEC countries in world crude oil production rose from about 20 percent in 1938 to over 40 percent when OPEC was founded in 1960, and to over 50 percent by 1972. Furthermore, OPEC's share of proved reserves—roughly, its share of future production—is over two thirds, as shown in Figure 11.2. Ample oil reserves are still being discovered the world over, but they happen to be concentrated increasingly in the Middle East, forcing importing nations into greater dependence on OPEC nations.

Meanwhile, the steady deepening of Arab-Israeli hostilities began to affect the oil-rich Arab countries. In the early 1970s, Saudi Arabia informed the

FIGURE 11.2   Proved Oil Reserves, Late 1978 (billions of barrels)

	OPEC		Non-OPEC	
	Country	*Billions of Barrels*	*Country*	*Billions of Barrels*
North America			United States	29.50
			Mexico	14.00
			Canada	6.00
South America	Venezuela	18.20	Argentina	2.50
	Ecuador	1.64	Colombia	0.96
			Brazil	0.88
			Peru	0.73
			Trinidad and Tobago	0.65
			Other	0.81
Western Europe			Britain	19.00
			Norway	6.00
			Other	1.86
Africa	Libya	25.00	Tunisia	2.60
	Nigeria	18.70	Egypt	2.45
	Algeria	6.60	Angola-Cabinda	1.16
	Gabon	2.05	Other	0.64
Middle East	Saudi Arabia	150.00	Syria	2.15
	Kuwait	67.00	Turkey	0.37
	Iran	62.00	Other	0.03
	Iraq	34.50		
	Abu Dhabi	31.00		
	Other emirates	12.92		
	Neutral zone	6.20		
Other Asia and Pacific	Indonesia	10.00	India	3.00
			Australia	2.00
			Malaysia	2.50
			Other	2.25
Socialist bloc		75.00	USSR*	75.00
			China	20.00
			Romania	1.09
			Other	1.91
Total OPEC		445.81		
Total World		645.86		

* USSR figures include all "proved" reserves, all "probable" reserves, and some "possible" reserves.

Source: *New York Times*, November 19, 1978, citing *Oil and Gas Journal*.

United States that the spread of Arab radicalism would pose an increasing threat to both governments if the United States did not pressure Israel to withdraw from the territories occupied by Israel after the Six-Day War, in 1967. The defection of Saudi Arabia from traditional ties to the United States was a crucial step toward the oil price showdown.

And by the early 1970s, the United States was for the first time becoming vulnerable to pressure from oil-exporting countries. In the United States, as elsewhere, the demand for oil had consistently grown faster than either total energy consumption or gross national product. This rapid growth pushed a new generation of "independent" U.S. oil companies to seek new foreign sources of crude oil. Oil-exporting countries found that they could now circumvent the eight international "majors,"[2] which had held sway over oil production, prices, and exploration in the OPEC countries.

The rising U.S. oil demand increasingly spilled over into imports, aided by several developments in the late 1960s and 1970s. The rise of U.S. concern over environmental quality not only accelerated the demand for oil, which polluted less than coal, but also held back the expansion of domestic energy supply. Nuclear power plants, oil and gas leasing, oil pumping in the Santa Barbara Channel, and the Alaskan pipeline were all held up by (valid) objections that they would cause environmental damage. Discoveries of oil and gas reserves in the United States were tapering off. Thus, the United States, which had been largely immune to oil threats in earlier Middle East crises, found itself importing a third of its oil consumption, part of it from Arab countries, by 1973.

These were the main reasons why the OPEC countries were able to observe a scramble among buyers to pay higher prices for oil in 1973.

CLASSIC MONOPOLY AS AN EXTREME MODEL FOR CARTELS

How bad could it get? That is, if a group of nations or firms were to form a cartel, as OPEC did, what is the greatest amount of gain they could reap at the expense of their buyers and world efficiency? Clearly, if all of the cartel members could agree on simply maximizing their collective gain, they would behave as though they were a perfectly unified profit-maximizing monopolist. They would find the price level which would maximize the gap between their total export sales revenues and their total costs of producing exports. When cutting output back to the level of demand yielded by their optimal price, they would take care to shut down the most costly production

---

[2] Exxon, Mobil, Gulf, Texaco, Standard of California, all U.S.-based; British Petroleum, based in the United Kingdom before British Petroleum's merger with Standard of Ohio in the early 1970s; Royal Dutch/Shell, based in the United Kingdom and the Netherlands; and Compagnie Francaise des Petroles, based in France.

FIGURE 11.3   A Cartel as a Profit-Maximizing Monopoly

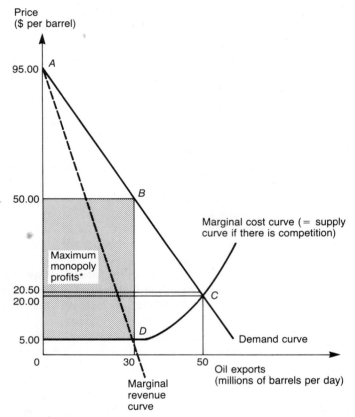

* Including some fixed costs.

If a cartel were so tightly disciplined as to be a pure monopoly, it would maximize profits according to the familiar monopoly model. It would not keep prices so low and output so high as to behave like a competitive industry, out at Point *C*. Why not? Because the slightest price increase, starting at Point *C*, would give them net gains. Instead the cartel would set price as high, with demand and output as low, as shown at Point *B*. At this level of output (30 million barrels a day), profit is maximized because the marginal revenue gained from a bit more output-raising and price-cutting just balances the marginal cost of the extra output.

units (e.g., oil wells) and keep in operation only those with the lowest operating costs.

Figure 11.3 portrays a monopoly or cartel that has managed to extract maximum profits from its buyers. To understand what price and output yields that highest level of profits, and what limits those profits, one must first understand that the optimal price lies above the price that perfect competition would yield, yet below the price that would discourage all sales.

If perfect competition reigned in the world oil market, the marginal cost curve in Figure 11.3 would also be the supply curve for oil exports. Competitive equilibrium would be at Point C, where the marginal cost of raising oil exports has risen to meet $20, the amount that extra oil is worth to buyers (as shown by the demand curve). Point C is not the optimal point for the set of producers. If they were to agree to raise prices a tiny bit, say to $20.50 a barrel, they would surely gain. Demand would be cut only very slightly, costing sellers little business. At the same time, they would get a costless 50-cent markup on all of the nearly 50 million barrels that they would continue to sell. The markup on the 50 million barrels would easily outweigh the profits lost on the small amount of lost sales, making a slight positive price increase and export reduction better than competitive pricing.

Yet, the negative slope of the demand curve for the cartel's product limits how high its members could push their common price. This point is clear enough if we just consider the extreme case of a prohibitive price markup. If the cartel were foolish enough to push the price to $95 a barrel in Figure 11.3, it would lose all of its export business, as shown at Point A. The handsome markup to $95 could be worthless, since nobody would be paying it to the cartel. Thus, the cartel's best price must be well below the prohibitive price, and the more elastic the demand curve for the cartel's product, the lower the best price for the cartel must be.

The cartel members could find their most profitable price through trial and error, trying out several prices in between the competitive and prohibitive limits to see what price seemed to maximize profits. The basic model of monopoly shows that the highest possible profits are those corresponding to the level of sales at which the marginal revenue curve intersects the marginal cost curve. These maximum profits would be reaped at Point B in Figure 11.3, with a price set at $50 a barrel, yielding 30 million barrels of export sales a day and monopoly profits of ($50 − $5) × 30 million barrels = $1,350 million a day. If the cartel had not been formed, competition would have limited the profits of its members to the area below the $20 price line and above the marginal cost curve (minus some fixed costs not shown in the diagram). (If an exact number were put on this competitive-profit area as drawn in Figure 11.3, it would come to a little over $600 million a day, well below the cartel's maximum of $1,350 million a day.) Given the demand curve and the marginal cost curve, the profits reshaped by pushing price and quantity to Point B is the best the cartel can do.

The cartel that is optimal for its members is not optimal for the world, of course. The extra profits for the cartel above the $20 price line are just a redistribution of income from buying countries to the cartel, with no net gain for the world. Furthermore, the cartel causes net world losses by curtailing oil exports that would have been worth more to buyers around the world than those exports would have cost the cartel members themselves. The world net loss from the cartel is represented in Figure 11.3 by the area *BCD* (which would equal a little over $450 million a day as drawn in Figure 11.3). This area shows that what the cartel is costing the world as a whole is the gaps between what buyers would have willingly paid for the extra 20 million barrels a day, as shown by the height of the demand curve, and the height of the marginal cost curve between 30 million barrels and 50 million barrels.

THE THEORETICAL LIMITS TO CARTEL POWER

The theory of cartel policy can identify several constraints on cartel success, and by international politics it can pose some additional practical constraints. Let us look first at the limits to cartel market power in the extreme case in which the cartel members succeed in behaving just like the unified monopoly in Figure 11.3. We then note some additional theoretical reasons for expecting cartel success to fade away with time. In the following section, we compare these theoretical hunches with actual OPEC experience.

The Optimal Markup for a Pure Monopoly

The basic theory of monopoly stresses that the elasticity of demand limits the power of any monopoly. More specifically, the formula for the optimal monopoly markup is (as explained in Appendix E):

$$t^* = \frac{\text{Optimal price} - \text{Marginal cost}}{\text{Price}} = \frac{1}{|d_c|},$$

where d_c is the elasticity of demand for the cartel's sales (here, the elasticity of export demand, if the cartel members do not charge the same high price within their own countries). This formula applies equally to pure private domestic monopolies and to international cartels behaving like monopolies. It shows that the more (less) elastic the demand for the cartel's sales over the relevant range of prices, the lower (higher) is the optimal monopoly markup. In the extreme case, in which the cartel faces an infinite elasticity of demand at a given world price, the optimal markup is zero, and the cartel might as well be dissolved.

The elasticity of demand facing the cartel (d_c) depends on three other parameters:

1. The elasticity of world demand for the product (d).
2. The elasticity of competing noncartel supply of the product (s_0).
3. The cartel's share of the world market (c).

The importance of each factor is easy to see. A highly elastic world demand for the product (a highly negative d) means that buyers find it easy to find other ways of spending their money if the price of the product rises much, so that the cartel has very limited power to raise profits by raising prices. A cartel's chances for continued high profits also depend on the elasticity of supply from other countries (s_0) in the obvious direction: the harder it is for other countries to step up their competing output and sales when the cartel posts its high prices, the better are cartel's chances of success. That is, a low s_0 enhances cartel power in the world market. Finally, the higher the cartel's current share of world sales (c), the better the cartel's prospects.

The dependence of the cartel's success on these three factors can be summarized in a single convenient formula. As shown in the middle of Appendix E, the demand elasticity facing the cartel is related by definition to the other three parameters:

$$d_c = \frac{d - s_0(1 - c)}{c},$$

and the optimal cartel markup rate, as a fraction of price, is

$$t^* = \frac{c}{|d - s_0(1 - c)|}.$$

To see how the formula works, consider two examples. The first is a case in which cartel members control half of world exports when their cartel is set up $(c = \frac{1}{2})$, and face a world elasticity of export demand of only -2 $(d = -2)$ and an equal positive elasticity of competing supply $(s_0 = 2)$. In this case, the formula implies that the optimal cartel markup can be as high as one sixth of price, so that marginal costs are only five sixths of price. Alternatively, consider a cartel that commands only a quarter of world export sales $(c = \frac{1}{4})$, and faces a world demand for exports of the product of -6 and a supply elasticity from other countries of 8 $(d = -6, s_0 = 8)$. Then the formula implies that the optimal markup is only $\frac{1}{48}$, or just above 2 percent of price. Even this small markup could bring handsome gains to selling countries if costs were already a high share of revenue without the cartel, but buying countries would not experience a large percentage price increase.

Why Cartels Erode with Time

Even when perfect solidarity makes a cartel able to act like the maximal monopoly, theory points out that the forces summarized in the formula above work increasingly against the cartel over time. When the cartel is first set up, it may well enjoy low elasticities and a high market share. Yet, its very success in raising price is likely to set three countervailing trends in motion.

Sagging Demand. First, the higher price will make buying countries look for new ways to avoid importing the cartel's product. They search for new domestic supplies of the product and will seek substitutes for it. The price would make private parties search for new supplies, even if there were no government policy of fostering reductions in imports of the newly cartelized product. If the search has any success at all, the imports of the buying countries will drop increasingly for any given cartel price, making these countries' long-run demand curve for imports of the product more elastic than their short-run demand curve. The elasticity d will become more negative with time.

New Competing Supply. Second, the initial cartel success will accelerate the search for exportable supplies in noncartel countries. If the cartel product is an agricultural crop, such as sugar or coffee, the cartel's price hike will cause farmers in other countries to shift increasing amounts of land, labor, and funds from other crops into sugar or coffee. If the cartel product is a depletable mineral resource, such as oil or copper, noncartel countries will respond to the higher price by redoubling their explorations in search of new reserves, as countries the world over have done in the wake of OPEC's victory. Again, if the noncartel countries have any luck at all, their competing supply will become increasingly elastic with time, and s_0 will rise.

Declining Market Share. Finally, the cartel's world market share (c) will surely fall after the cartel's initial price hike. To raise its price without piling up ever-rising unsold inventories, the cartel must cut its output and sales. Since nonmembers will be straining to raise their output and sales, the cartel's share of the market must drop even if all of its members cooperate solidly. Thus, c will fall while the absolute values of the key elasticities d and s_0 rise, undercutting the cartel's optimal markup and its profits on three fronts at once.

Theory and experience add another reason why the cartel's market share drops: cartel members may defect, or "cheat," by behaving competitively. The cartel will, if it can, prevent this by having some overseeing government pass laws forbidding competition. Yet defection cannot be thus prevented when there is no overseeing government, as with cartels among sovereign nations, or when the government will not condone cartel-enforcing laws on behalf of the private firms in the cartel. Without government checks on competition, cartel members with small individual market shares will indeed feel strong incentive to behave competitively. To see why, suppose that you were a small member of the successful oil export cartel shown back in Figure 11.3 and that when the cartel was set up, your exports were only 1 percent of the cartel total. Yet, let us say, you have enough oil reserves to go on pumping and selling 3 percent of the total cartel exports for as long in the future as you need to plan. Raising your output above the 1 percent share might cost you only, say, a dollar a barrel at the margin.

Yet buyers are willing to pay $10 for each barrel you sell, since the larger cartel members are faithfully holding down their output. Why not attract the extra buyers to you by shaving your price just a little bit below $50, say to $48.50? Why not do so in grand style, until you are competitively selling the 3 percent of the cartel's market that you can afford to sell without depleting your reserves too fast? If the other cartel members have any economic or military clubs over you or could finance the overthrow of your government, you should compete clandestinely by disguising your export volumes and prices somehow. But if they wield no such clubs, you can compete openly, while justifying your behavior as necessary to develop your nation's economy. You can do so in the knowledge that you are still so small a share of the cartel that your individual actions will not cause the cartel price to drop much, if at all. Theory says that if a large share of cartel output consists of the outputs of individually small members, their incentive to act competitively undermines the whole cartel. The individually large members can keep the cartel effective to some extent by drastically cutting their own outputs to offset the extra sales from competitors. Their aggregate size determines how long they can hold out.

The usual theory of cartels thus points to several reasons for believing that cartel profit margins and profits will erode with time, that is, if no new members with large individual shares of the world market join the existing cartel.[3] Yet, the theory does *not* say that cartels are unprofitable or harmless. On the contrary, it underscores the profitability of cartel formation to cartel members. Even a cartel that eventually erodes can bring vast fortunes to its members. What the theory does do is offer a listing of four key indicators to watch when judging the prospects for an existing or potential cartel: the demand elasticity for the product, the competing-supply elasticity, the members' initial market share, and the share of the cartel held by defection-prone small members.

INTERNATIONAL OIL EXPERIENCE SINCE 1973

How does experience since the 1973 OPEC victory compare with the basic theory of cartels? The events of these early years of OPEC power confirm several of our theoretical hunches but enrich our understanding of international cartels by contradicting others. The clearest lessons so far are described below.

---

[3] These same reasons also subtly imply that a cartel would be wise to charge a lower markup, *even at the start,* than the markup implied by short-run elasticities and the formula given above. The higher the initial markup, the faster the erosion of the cartel's market share and the lower the optimal markup that cartel can charge later on. Charging the optimal markup at each point in time is a more delicate art than the simple static formula implies.

OPEC Is Not a Classic-Monopoly Cartel

In the classic script for a cartel, the group sets a unified optimally exploiting price structure and works out formal rules about how much each member should produce and sell. This pact slowly erodes as members defect and outside demand gets more elastic. But OPEC has not followed the script. Its members have never been able to agree on who should cut back their output by how much. Populous countries with big development plans, such as Iran and Iraq, have tried to get the oil-rich countries like Saudi Arabia to do the output cutting while they have pumped near capacity at the highest sustainable prices. The Saudis have not agreed. At the same time OPEC has lost its pricing unity, as individual members have increasingly returned to autonomous price announcements. All this disunity has led to defections and competition.

OPEC Power Is Being Undermined

Speaking to students at the University of Petroleum and Minerals in Saudi Arabia at the start of 1981, the Saudi oil minister Sheikh Zaki Yamani warned that the cartel's huge price increases would damage future demand for its oil:

> If we force the West to invest heavily in finding alternative sources of energy, they will. This would take no more than seven years and would result in reducing [the West's] dependence on oil as a source of energy to a point that will jeopardize Saudi Arabia's interests. (As quoted in *The Wall Street Journal*, April 13, 1981, p. 21.)

Events since the early 1980s followed his warning.

The gradual rise in demand elasticity (d_c) can be seen in the behavior of output since the second great price hike (see Figure 11.1). Across the early 1980s, OPEC output has dropped radically. This is *not* because the cartel decided to cut its output to hold prices up. Indeed, the member nations were slow to reach an agreement for limiting output, and that one agreement in the early 1980s was violated by several members as soon as it was signed. Rather, the output drops have come from the demand side: given the high price of OPEC oil and the increasing availability of non-OPEC oil (from Britain, Mexico, the Soviet Union, and other suppliers), importing nations simply have not wanted so much OPEC oil as before. Accordingly, OPEC's share of world production (one measure of the share c in the theory above) dropped from 55.5 percent in 1973 to 30 percent in 1985.

OPEC members are also cheating, as theory would predict. Virtually every member nation has done so in the 1980s. Some, like Nigeria, are openly offering price discounts. Others, like Libya, Iran, or Saudi Arabia, are more clandestine, hiding the lower price of oil in complex barter deals involving technology and other services in exchange for oil.

If OPEC is being steadily undermined in accordance with the basic economic theory of cartels, why hasn't it fallen apart faster? Why was there so little real-price drop and no output drop after the first oil shock? Why was the real price of oil in 1989 still 84 percent higher than it was in 1970? This is the remaining question about OPEC, now that we understand both its rise before 1973 and its ultimate weakness.

OPEC Got Help from Special Forces

One special force helping OPEC after the first oil shock was:

1. *U.S. oil import subsidies [!] in effect between 1974 and 1981.* When the Arab oil embargo and OPEC price hikes first hit in the winter of 1973–74, President Nixon declared "Operation Independence," and U.S. officials pledged to reverse the rise of U.S. oil imports swiftly. They enacted policies that had exactly the opposite effect, policies in helping to set the stage for the second great exercise of OPEC power in 1979.

This irony sprang from the best of government intentions, as if Washington were acting out a morality play written by Milton Friedman. When the oil crisis first hit, the public, already numbed by rising inflation, suspected oil-company gouging. Washington responded by freezing the price of domestic oil. With the world price soaring above the controlled U.S. price, international oil firms responded in January and February of 1974 by shipping less oil to the United States and more to countries paying the world price, exacerbating the U.S. shortages. Washington saw the problem and changed the rules several times. By mid-1974 a complex *"entitlements"* program was evolving to deal with the dilemma posed by expensive imported oil and cheap controlled domestic oil. The entitlements program tried to eliminate price inequities by forcing firms to buy an entitlement to each barrel of the low-priced domestic oil. To earn each barrel of entitlement, a firm had to show documents from the purchase of another barrel at the high world price. The upshot was that by importing oil a firm got a valuable salable ticket to buy cheap domestic oil. The price of foreign oil thus seemed cheaper to the buyer than the true world price being paid by the nation as a whole. Meanwhile, domestic oil seemed just as expensive to U.S. buyers (who needed to come up with the import tickets to buy it legally), but none of the extra price margin was gained by the well owners, who saw less incentive to pump domestic oil. This policy explains part of the continued growth of U.S. dependence on imported oil. (The oil price controls and entitlements were finally repealed by President Reagan in February 1981.)

2. *Conservation-mindedness has helped limit OPEC output.* The fact that oil is a depletable, nonrenewable resource has been one reason why OPEC members have not tried to sell more aggressively. At times members have accepted reduced export orders without cutting prices because they have reasoned that what is not sold now can be sold later at a respectable price. This remains to be seen, but at least oil kept in the ground is not lost to the nation, unlike manufactured goods or crops, for which the chance to produce this year never returns. Willingness to conserve oil reserves is thus a force limiting cartel output, even without a formal output-cutting agreement.

3. *Panic buying was crucial to the two OPEC successes.* The two great price jumps were made possible largely by panic in the oil-importing countries. The OPEC decision to raise the price of oil abruptly late in 1973 came amid clear signs of frantic bidding in oil auctions, as mentioned above. Panic was again crucial at the start of 1979. The interruption of Iranian oil supplies during that country's revolution late in 1978 sparked fears of a new major oil shortage. OPEC responded to the new seller's market across 1979 by throwing away freshly signed agreements for modest price increases and doubled prices instead.

If the panic among buyers were just a temporary foolishness, it could not sustain permanent shifts in the balance of economic power. Once it was clear to buyers that the sky was not falling, the excessive inventories of oil had to be sold at much lower prices, weakening OPEC's power almost as much as the panic had strengthened it. Yet the fears behind the waves of panic are partly justified for the long run as well as for the short. As oil companies realize, 1973–74 dramatized a new vulnerability that is not likely to go away for a long time. Many of the key oil-exporting countries are unstable. Oil wealth is raining upon countries strained by tensions between rapid modernization and traditional values. These internal tensions, plus border disputes, mass migrations, and perennial Arab-Israeli clashes, make the Middle East particularly explosive. To use oil is to be vulnerable to sabotage, palace coups, and revolution in the exporting countries. In this climate both private companies and national governments see greater need for holding large oil inventories and show jitters that are likely to last for some time. Even if OPEC were to break up soon, sheer uncertainty about oil supplies would keep the relative price of oil above what it was before 1973.

America Is Still the Key

Just as the United States played a key role in helping OPEC grab power, so too it continues to buoy up a larger and larger share of world oil demand. Between 1973 and 1989 the share of the United States in the OECD (industrial) countries' oil consumption rose from 44 percent to 47 percent, far higher than any other nation's share. The share of the world's production consumed in the United States also stayed high, dropping slightly from 31 percent to

29 percent over the same 16 years. America's dependence on net oil imports rose from 35 percent to 44 percent of U.S. oil consumption. America's shares of world oil remain so large for two reasons: America generates a large share of the world's income, and gasoline remains only half as expensive in the United States as it is in Europe and Japan, today as in 1973. OPEC's ability to hold up the world price of oil depends in large part on America's cheap energy policy.

CARTELS FOR OTHER PRIMARY PRODUCTS

The success of OPEC has inspired countries exporting primary products other than oil to rejuvenate the previously unsuccessful idea of forming international cartels for their primary-product export staples. In the wake of the OPEC victory even speculators in buying countries seemed to expect new cartels for primaries. Between late 1973 and the spring of 1974 the world prices on all sorts of primary products jumped faster than did the worldwide inflation of industrial product prices. For most of these primary products the bubble burst within months, and prices were soon as low as before 1973, despite general inflation. Yet, in the meantime, hard talks about forming cartels went on around the world, with some temporary results.

Cartel gains were temporarily posted in two other minerals besides oil. One is phosphate rock, in rapidly growing demand for use in fertilizers and detergents; the other is bauxite. Led by Morocco (which controls one third of world exports) and Tunisia, the main phosphate exporters converted a low price elasticity of demand into a 400 percent price rise between mid-1972 and the end of 1974. In March 1974, the International Bauxite Association (IBA) was formed (Australia, Guinea, Guyana, Jamaica, Sierra Leone, Surinam, and Yugoslavia). Both cartels made gains in the 1970s, but then faded.

Among crops, the food grains sector has the best economic basis for international cartelization. Canada, the United States, and Australia together account for a large share of world food grains exports, and world demand is notoriously inelastic. Such a three-country grain cartel could be effective, despite the elasticity with which some other countries could become competing suppliers. The main constraints on grain cartelization, however, are political. Extracting monopoly rents on food grains in a partially starving world wins few friends. And the major exporters are not united: in a recent test of the solidarity of grain exporters, the U.S. attempt to cut off grain shipments to the Soviet Union after the Afghanistan invasion in 1980 gained only slight cooperation from Canada and Australia and none from Argentina.

Cartelization would seem to provide poor prospects for other agricultural crops. Some crops have the advantage of being concentrated into a small number of countries that already have regional ties: natural rubber, dominated by Malaysia, Indonesia, Thailand, and Sri Lanka; tea, by India and Sri

Lanka; coffee, by Brazil and Colombia; and bananas, by Central American countries and Ecuador. Yet some of these crops, especially bananas, face a highly elastic world demand, and all of them face a very high elasticity of competing supply, since land in many countries can be shifted from other crops into newly cartelized crops. Agricultural crops are not very likely candidates for long-lived international cartels.

The overall verdict is that all international cartels other than OPEC have died after only temporary impact on prices. Of 72 commodity agreements signed between World Wars I and II, only two survived past 1945 (Suslow 1988). Of the few dozen inspired by the commodity scarcity of the 1970s, only five lived as late as 1985: cocoa, coffee, rubber, sugar, and tin. Both the coffee and cocoa agreements had collapsed by 1989, and all five had to give up and become passive at times when market forces complicated their attempts to control prices. To be sure, other cartels will always be formed in the future. But it appears that only OPEC (and illegal drug cartels) have the right mixture of inelastic curves and concentrated production within cartel countries.

SUMMARY

A **cartel** is an agreement among independent units to control production and to get better prices. The term usually refers to agreements among sellers to raise price, as opposed to buyer cartels.

The most successful exercise of cartel power in history, the victory of OPEC in late 1973, resulted from several simultaneous developments. World demand for oil had grown rapidly, world supply growth was concentrated in OPEC countries, and the Arab-Israeli conflict broke out anew in a context of new U.S. dependence on oil imports.

If international cartels are able to act like unified monopolists, they can reap large gains at the expense of buying countries and world efficiency. Their ability to do so is proportional to the inelasticity of world demand for their exports. This dependence of buying countries on a cartel's exports can, in turn, be linked to four factors: the elasticity of world demand for the cartel's product, the elasticity of competing supply, the cartel's share of the world market, and the share of cartel sales, consisting of sales by small cartel members, who are likely to feel a strong incentive to behave competitively despite their cartel membership. A formula given above links the optimal cartel price markup over marginal cost to the first three of these four factors.

The experience of OPEC and other attempts at primary-product cartels can be interpreted with the help of the monopoly model of cartel success and failure. The case of OPEC shows all the expected signs of cartel erosion, as the textbook model would have predicted. Yet OPEC is no ordinary cartel. It survives without internal agreement over who should restrict output or even over pricing. OPEC has been helped by special forces: U.S. policies that raised U.S. dependence on oil imports between 1974 and 1981; willingness of many members to accept declining orders and leave some extra oil in the ground; and, above all, waves of panic buying. OPEC's success has been emulated by countries exporting phosphate rock and bauxite, but very few other primary products entering world trade are likely to be cartelized with lasting success.

SUGGESTED READINGS

The best narrative of the events leading to the 1973–74 OPEC victory, and of the roles played by several countries and the major oil companies, is to be found in Raymond Vernon (1976). For two opposing views of the proximate causes of the 1973–74 oil crisis, see Jahangir Amuzegar (1973) and Morris Adelman (1974).

The standard theory of cartels along the lines of the group monopoly model is surveyed in George J. Stigler (1964) and Frederick M. Scherer (1971). For an application of the standard theory to the international cartelization of copper, bauxite, coffee, and bananas, see Carl Van Duyne (1975).

Institutional details on commodity cartel schemes are helpfully cataloged by Fiona Gordon-Ashworth (1984). Valerie Suslow (1988) analyzes why some cartels died faster than others before World War II. The World Bank's *World Development Report 1986,* pp. 133–73, gives a bleak appraisal of recent agricultural cartels.

QUESTIONS FOR REVIEW

1. The United States, China, India, Brazil, and Turkey have formed an international association known as Tobacco's Altruistic Raisers, to set the world price of tobacco at the most profitable level. TAR covers 60 percent of world exports. The price elasticity of world demand for tobacco is −0.6, and the price elasticity of competing supply from non-TAR countries is 0.75. For as long as these elasticities persist,

a. What is the price elasticity of demand for TAR's tobacco exports?

b. What is the profit-maximizing rate of cartel markup?

2. What is the optimal cartel markup if the price elasticity of demand for the cartel's exports is below one in absolute value (e.g., if it is −½)? How do we interpret an optimal markup in this situation? Could this elasticity hold at all prices? How or why not?

3. You are the head of state of a large thoroughly industrialized country faced with powerful cartels in oil and coffee. What national policies would you adopt to deal with the cartel power? What international agreements would you seek? Should you do nothing and let market forces take care of the cartel?

▼

12

Trade Policies and Developing Countries

•

WIDENING GROWTH GAPS IN THE THIRD WORLD

The economic race that receives the most media attention is the race for leadership between Japan, North America, and Europe. The attention is not surprising, given that these areas represent 70 percent of world product and an even greater share of the supply of media services. Yet Japan's growth-rate advantage over the other leading countries is less dramatic than the differences in the growth fortunes of different parts of the less developed Third World. Ever since 1950, the fastest growth rates in the world have been experienced by less developed countries. So have the most serious economic declines.

Figure 12.1 summarizes the best available measures of growth rates in real gross domestic product (GDP) per person for broad regions. Since the 1950s the market economies with initially low incomes have not been catching up to the high-income industrial countries. On the contrary, their average product per person has grown more slowly than in the industrial market economies. As a result, their share of world product has dropped, even though their share of world population has risen.

The initially middle-income countries that were not major oil exporters fared better than the low-income countries until the 1980s. Their advantage was particularly great in the 1970s, when they borrowed heavily to finance an investment boom. The 1970s were the heyday of the ''NICs'' (newly industrializing countries) on two continents: Brazil and Mexico in Latin America, and the East Asian ''Four Tigers'' (South Korea, Taiwan, Hong Kong, and Singapore).

In the 1980s, however, world poverty has taken on an ominous geographic pattern. The debt crisis hit in 1982 and lingers into the 1990s (see Chapter

24). Up through 1987 it brought stagnation and absolute decline to much of Latin America and the Caribbean. Africa south of the Sahara also has been getting absolutely poorer, dropping to the bottom of the international income ranks, as these World Bank estimates on product per capita suggest:

Group of Market Economies	*Growth Rate in Real GDP per Capita per Year, 1980–1987*	*Level of GDP per Capita, 1987*[1]
Industrialized market economies	2.0%	$14,430
Rapid growth:		
Hong Kong	4.2	8,070
Singapore	4.3	7,940
Korea	7.2	2,690
Mainland China (1980–1985 only)	8.6	290
Absolute decline:		
Latin America and the Caribbean	−1.1	1,790
Africa south of the Sahara	−2.2	330

While whole continents of poor got absolutely poorer, the East Asian NICs continued their rapid growth, threatening to polarize the Third World into a newly prosperous East Asia and impoverished stagnation elsewhere.

The middle-income oil-exporting nations, in the third column of Figure 12.1 (p. 254), have been on an economic roller coaster in the postwar era. Across the 1950s and 1960s they expanded rapidly, helped by major oil discoveries. Across the 1970s their output per person grew only 0.6 percent a year, yet they became rich overnight thanks to the oil price jumps chronicled in Chapter 11.[2] In the 1980s, their output per person absolutely declined, and their real purchasing power declined even faster, as the price of oil dropped. Like Africa and Latin America, the oil-rich Middle East has faced the prospect of falling further behind East Asia and isolated other fast-growth NICs.

The greatest inequalities of growth rates are thus within the ranks of the "developing countries," some of which have not been developing.

---

[1] The values of per-capita product given here are the readily available World Bank figures converted to U.S. dollars at the 1987 average exchange rate. These are less satisfactory than the estimates based on separate price measurements in separate countries, as in the University of Pennsylvania's International Comparisons Project, whose estimates were used in Figure 12.1. The World Bank estimates overstate the relative poverty of low-income countries.

[2] Their lightning-fast rise to riches does not show up in the growth rates of Figure 12.1 because the GDP figures used there are not adjusted for changes in the terms of trade. The GDP figures, instead, imply that a barrel of oil in 1969 is the same as a barrel of oil in 1981, ignoring the implications of the OPEC price jumps for a country's material well-being.

FIGURE 12.1   The Growth of Per-Capita GDP and Changes in Shares of World Product, Main Regions, 1950–1987

A. *Growth Rates in Gross Domestic Product (GDP) per Capita (percent per year):*

	Market Economies				Centrally Planned Economies	World
	Low-Income	Middle-Income Nonoil	Middle-Income Oil Nations	Industrial Nations		
1950–1960	2.2	2.4	2.7	3.0	4.1	2.8
1960–1970	0.8	3.2	5.0	3.8	3.4	3.0
1970–1980	1.6	3.6	0.6	2.4	3.2	2.2
1980–1987	1.4	0.7	−1.9	2.0	4.8*†	2.2

B. *Shares of Real World Product (percent):*

1950	8.6	10.9	2.3	56.0	22.2	100.0
1960	8.2	11.1	2.5	52.9	25.3	100.0
1970	6.9	12.0	3.3	52.1	25.7	100.0
1980	6.9	14.8	3.2	47.6	27.5	100.0
1987	7.0	14.1	2.2	44.6	32.1	100.0

C. *Shares of World Population, 1980:*

1980	29.7	18.6	2.4	16.9	32.4	100.0

* Dominated by China's per-capita growth rate of 8.6 percent a year. For the eight other centrally-planned economies the rate was 1.8 percent a year.
† Rates for 1980–1985 only.
Sources: Summers, Kravis, and Heston (1984) for 1950–1980. Summers and Heston (1988) for centrally planned economies 1980–1985. World Bank, *World Development Report 1989*, pp. 164–69, 214–15, for noncentrally planned economies, 1980–1987. The figures are, of course, rough approximations, especially for the centrally planned economies and the lowest-income countries. Figures for different countries' GDP for 1950–1980 have been converted into dollars at "international prices" using a detailed comparison of prices of goods and services, included nontraded ones, rather than merely converting national values at official exchange rates. The 1987 real shares of world product are based on slightly different measures from those for 1950–1980.

WHICH TRADE PATH FOR DEVELOPING COUNTRIES?

The severity of the international income gaps in the 1950s and 1960s, and the new international voice gained by the appearance of so many newly independent nations, led to a collective Third World program for a global attack on economic underdevelopment. The new collective movement acquired an institutional base, a named debate, and a program for restructuring trade. The institutional base was **UNCTAD**, the United Nations Conference on Trade and Development, set up in 1964 and still operating from headquarters in Geneva. The debate came to be known as the **North-South dialogue,** a very rough description of the geography of the division between richer and poorer nations (as long as Australia and New Zealand are included in the "North"). The dialogue, stirred by a series of global UNCTAD conferences, led to a Third World call for a **New International Economic Order** (NIEO), centered on three negotiated trade policies:

1. Global agreements to raise the prices of primary products exported by developing nations,
2. Global cooperation to stabilize those same prices, and
3. Opening industrial-country markets for manufactures exported by the developing countries.

There was good political logic behind the new focus on trade policies as a mechanism for redistributing income toward developing countries. Direct foreign aid, the most obvious way of attacking the task of redistribution, was clearly waning by the 1960s, as reductions in the U.S. commitment to foreign aid were only partly offset by rising contributions from other high-income countries. Direct aid has an additional drawback for the recipient: it is a conspicuous budget item. Every year the donor countries must vote to give again, a procedure that leaves foreign aid an easy prey to budget-cutting backlash. The developing countries, like farmers and powerful industrial lobbies within the high-income democracies, have come to prefer that their aid come in the more durable and less conspicuous form of price-propping or tariff-discriminating laws and agreements.

Across the 1980s the global-conference collectivity of the North-South dialogue gave way to separate trade strategies for separate nations. One possible reason for the return to national debates from global ones was the increasing disparity of national interests, and that disparity of growth rates among the "developing" countries.

Yet the trade policy choices remained the same. Each country, with or without a global agreement, must choose among three paths to comparative advantage:

1. Rely on primary-product exports? Many developing countries have comparative advantages in exporting primary products (agriculture, forestry, fisheries, minerals, crude petroleum and gas, other raw materials). One option is to let these products be exported with a minimum of government intervention. The NIEO clearly argued against this, calling for trade restrictions that would raise, as well as stabilize, primary-product prices.

2. Develop manufacturing industries producing for protected home markets? This strategy, called import-substituting industrialization (**ISI**), has prevailed in separate national policies throughout the Third World, even though it was not a part of the NIEO program.

3. Develop manufacturing industries producing for export to the already industrialized countries? The NIEO program called on the industrialized countries to open the doors for such exports.

The choice, in other words, is between primary-product exports and two paths to industrialization, one antitrade and one protrade. Which path is better? Before reviewing the options at length, let us note a simple clue from the data, and a false inference that many draw from that clue. The clue is that the developing countries that have succeeded in achieving fast growth lately have generally been industrializing in the process. Even the name for fast-growing Third World countries offers a clue: NICs, or newly industrializing countries. A partial correlation between fast growth and the shift toward manufacturing was already noted in Chapter 10 (Figure 10.2). Is industrialization simply the better way to develop any Third World country? Should governments tax and discourage production of primary products, and should they favor manufacturing with either import protection or export subsidies?

The best answer is quite different, as we shall see. The postwar Third World is a vast laboratory of experiments in widely differing trade policies. The results suggest that having government try to manipulate final-product prices with restrictions and subsidies is not the key to success, regardless of whether primaries or manufactures are favored. The usual debate has made the mistake of thinking that the choice is between using *product-market interventions* (taxes, subsidies, etc. on the products themselves) to encourage one sector or the other. It turns out that such intervention has generally been overdone, regardless of the sector. Rather, government's comparative advantage, to borrow a trade term, is really in *social investments in productive infrastructure:* in human health and education, transportation and communications. While social investments in infrastructure need not favor either primary products or manufactures, it will turn out that if the development effort is successful, the country will industrialize anyway, because improving health, knowledge, transportation, and communications tilts productivity and demand toward manufactures (and services). There is still room for specific trade policies, but they must be chosen with care and finesse.

For a fuller review of the subtleties of trade strategy for developing countries, let us turn to the three strategies in the order in which they were introduced: reliance on primary product exports, import-substituting industrialization, and promotion of industrial exports.

THE PRIMARY-PRODUCT PATH

Long-Run Price Trends for Primary Products

In the 1950s Raul Prebisch and other leaders in forming UNCTAD's program argued that developing countries are hurt by a downward trend (and also an instability) in primary-product prices. International markets, ran the argument, distributed income unfairly, trapping the exporters of primary products into worsening trends in their terms of trade (the price of their exports divided by the price of their imports, or P_x/P_m). And since the less developed countries were net exporters of primary products, the alleged downward trend in their earning power was seen as a force widening the income gap between the world's rich and the world's poor. To help out primary-product exporters, especially those in the Third World, one of three things was called for: either (a) raise primary-product prices through some kind of international agreement, or (b) encourage developing countries to shift their resources out of primary production, or (c) give primary-product exporters direct foreign aid to offset the downward trend in their terms of trade.

Does the fear of falling prices sound reasonable? Economists have studied the issue for over a century. It is clear that there are at least two major forces depressing, and at least two forces raising, the trend in the prices of primaries relative to manufactures. The relative price of primary products is depressed by:

1. *Engel's Law.* In the long run, per-capita incomes rise. As they rise, the world's demand shifts towards luxuries, or goods for which the income elasticity of demand (percent rise in quantity demanded/percent rise in income causing the change in demand) is greater than one. At the same time, the world's demand shifts away from staples, or goods for which the income elasticity of demand is less than one. The 19th-century German economist Ernst Engel (not Friedrich Engel*s*) discovered what has become known as **Engel's Law:** the income elasticity of demand for food is less than one (i.e., food is a staple). Engel's Law (already noted briefly in Chapter 5) is the most durable law in economics that does not follow from definitions or axioms. It means trouble for food producers in a prospering world. If the world's supply ability went up at the exact same rate for all products, the relative price of foods would go on dropping, because Engel's Law says that demand would keep shifting (relatively) away from food toward luxuries.

2. *Synthetic substitutes.* Another force depressing the relative prices of primary products is the development of new man-made substitutes for these natural materials. The more technology advances, the more we are likely to discover ways to replace crops, minerals, and other raw materials that were needed in centuries past. The most dramatic case is the development of synthetic rubber around the time of World War I, which ruined the incomes of rubber producers in Brazil, Malaya, and other countries. Another case is the development of synthetic fibers, which have lowered the demand for cotton and wool.

On the other hand, two basic forces tend to raise the relative prices of primary products:

3. *Nature's limits.* Primary products use land, water, mineral deposits, and other nonrenewable resources. As population and incomes expand, the natural inputs become increasingly scarce, other things being equal. Nature's scarcity eventually raises the relative price of primary products, which use natural resources more intensively than do manufactures.

4. *Generally slower productivity growth in the primary sector.* Over most historical experience, productivity has advanced more slowly in agriculture, mining, and other primary sectors than in manufacturing. This lack of speed translates into a slower relative advance of supply curves in primary-product markets than in manufacturing markets, and therefore a rising relative price of primaries (or a falling relative price of manufactures), other things being equal. One reason for this tendency is, again, the greater relevance of nature's limits in primary production. Another reason is the tendency for cost-cutting breakthroughs in knowledge to be more important in manufacturing than in primaries (though exceptions to this rule are increasingly frequent in the age of biotechnology).

So, we have two tendencies that depress the terms of trade for primary producers, and we have two that raise them. How does the tug-of-war work out in the long run? Figure 12.2 summarizes 20th-century experience.

Obviously, it depends on when you look at the data and how far back into history you look. Studying Figure 12.2, we can understand why the fear of falling relative primary prices was greatest in the 1930s, the 1950s (when Prebisch's argument achieved popularity), and the 1980s. There were periods of falling or depressed primary prices. On the other hand, little was written about falling primary prices just before World War I, the historical heyday of high prices for farm products and other raw materials. (Little wonder that the farm lobby likes to measure the terms of trade for agriculture against the "parity" norm of 1910–1914.) Nor was there much discussion of depressed prices during World War II, or during the Korean War of 1950–53, or during the OPEC-led speculative boom in primary product prices around 1973–74. During such times, many writers revived the old Malthusian arguments about the limits to planet Earth.

To stand back from the volatile swings in the terms of trade, let us look over as long a period as possible. For Figure 12.2, it is convenient to scan the period 1900–1986, though following some price series back to 1870 would tell a similar story. The overall change is clear: by 1986, relative primary-product prices were about half of what they were in 1900. The trend has indeed been downward. Somehow, Engel's Law and the technological biases toward replacing primary products have outrun nature's limits and the relative slowness of productivity growth in primary sectors. (Or, if you want it in shorthand, Prebisch outran Malthus.) Cutting the relative price in half over 87 years means a downward trend of 0.8 percent a year. Although that is not a rapid trend, it helps argue in favor of shifting resources into industry *if* we expect the same trend to continue.

Some commodities have declined in price more seriously than others. The price of rubber snapped downward between 1910 and 1920 and has

---

FIGURE 12.2   The Terms of Trade for Primary Products, 1900–1986

(P_x/P_m) = dollar-price index for primary-product exports/dollar
price index for exports of manufactures

A. Overall indexes

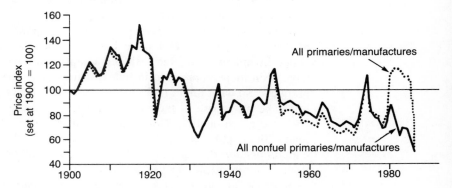

B. Three subgroups of primary commodities

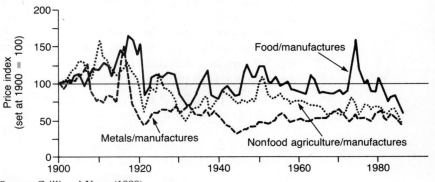

Source: Grilli and Yang (1988).

---

never really bounced back since, with an overall downward trend of 6 percent a year. Significant price declines have also been the rule for cocoa, sugar, copper, tin, wheat, and rice, as shown in the left-hand columns of Figure 12.3. Only wool and coffee showed significantly upward trends between 1900 and 1982, and the price of coffee has weakened since 1982. Even fuels like oil and coal have lacked a net upward price trend over the 20th century to date, despite the resounding price flare-ups of 1973–74, 1979–80, and 1990.

While the net downward trend in primary prices stands as a tentative conclusion, there are three downward-trend biases in the available measures, measures like those presented in Figures 12.2 and 12.3.

1. *The fall in transport costs.* The available data tend to be gathered at markets in the industrial countries. Yet technological improvements in transportation have been great enough to reduce the share of transport costs in those final prices in London or New York or Tokyo. That has left more and more of the final price back in the hands of the primary-product exporters. Quantifying this known change would tilt the trend in the prices received by producers toward a flatter, less downward, trend.

2. *Faster unmeasured quality change in manufactures.* Often, we have to deal with long runs of price data on products that have been getting better in unknown degree. Hidden quality improvements are thought to have been more impressive in manufactures (and services) than in primary products. So what might look like a rise in the relative price of manufactures might be just a rise in their relative quality, with no trend in the terms of trade for given quality. This data problem is potentially serious, given that many 20th-century data have, for example, followed the prices of machinery exports *per ton* of exports, as if a ton of today's computers were the same thing as a ton of old electric motors.

3. *Price cuts on new products are often unmeasured.* When a new product appears, its price typically drops rapidly before stabilizing. Officials gathering price data have a hard time incorporating the price data on the new products into their overall price indexes until the product has aged and its price has already dropped a great deal. Since new products are much more important in the manufacturing sector than in the primary sector, such measurement lags hide much of the relative drop in the prices of manufactures, overstating the relative rise of primary-product prices.

When all is said and done, the relative price of primary products *may* have declined as much as 0.8 percent a year between 1900 and 1986, or there could have been no trend. It is unlikely that the three measurement biases have been so strong that the true trend was upward (i.e., in favor of primaries). There is a weak case for worrying about being a producer of agricultural or extractive products on price-trend grounds.

International Agreements to Raise the Prices of Primaries

Inspired by OPEC's resounding success in the 1970s and early 1980s, part of the call for a New International Economic Order has been for international manipulation of the prices of primary products, to raise them as well as to stabilize them. The purpose of raising primary-product prices is, of course, to redistribute incomes from industrial to primary-product exporting countries.[3] To get the higher prices, the main exporting countries of each

---

[3] One frequent defense of the goal of raising primary-product prices is that economic forces in the past have conspired to lower the relative prices received by exporters of these goods. As this chapter shows, the verdict on long-run trends in these relative prices is unclear. Still, one can insist on price manipulation as a way of redistributing income *whatever* the past and likely future price trends in the absence of manipulation.

primary product must agree, perhaps with outside help, to restrict their competition and export less. If they achieve this goal by forming a sellers-only cartel, the analysis of Chapter 11 applies fully. The UNCTAD-based discussions sought at times to involve the buying countries, such as the United States and Canada, in the case of tropical crops like cane sugar or coffee, in the regulation of an international cartel.

The leading industrial countries have shown little enthusiasm for participating in such price-propping. This is hardly a surprise. As we saw in Chapter 11, the essence of a cartel is that it reduces world income by causing more damage to buyers than the gains it brings to sellers. This might seem justified if one feels that it is worth, say, $2.50 in damage to buying countries to bring each dollar of benefit to the selling countries. Buying countries resist this redistributive welfare yardstick. They are reluctant to help pay

FIGURE 12.3 Long-Run Trends and Instability in the Terms of Trade for Primary Products in World Markets, 1900–1982

(As in Figure 12.2, the terms of trade are indices of P_x/P_m, or the ratio of the world dollar price of primary-product exports to the dollar price of U.S. exports of manufactures.)

Commodity	Real-Price Trend (percent per year; downward = −)	Is the Trend Statistically Significant?	Real-Price Instability (average percentage departure from trend)
Cereals	−0.6	yes	18
Beverages	0.5	no	32
Food	−0.3	yes	14
Nonfood primaries	−1.7	yes	26
All agriculture	−0.8	no	17
Individual products:			
Wheat	−0.7	yes	20
Maize (corn)	0.8	no	21
Rice	−0.6	yes	24
Coffee	1.0	yes	39
Cocoa	−4.6	yes	40
Tea	1.2	no	25
Sugar	−3.2	yes	43
Cotton	1.3	no	21
Wool	2.2	yes	19
Rubber	−6.0	yes	51
Copper	−2.7	yes	25
Tin	−1.3	yes	20
Lead	0.1	no	20
Zinc	−0.9	no	25

Note: Statistical significance here means significance at the 5 percent confidence level.

The measure of price instability is, more precisely, the standard error of the trend estimate as a percentage of the grand mean of the observations.

Source: Scandizzo and Diakosawas (1987, pp. 37–38, 71).

to keep up primary-product prices—unless the producers are their own citizens. Primary-product exporters wanting to emulate OPEC will have to work out deals on their own, without the blessings of buying countries, and Chapter 11 has already noted how bleak the prospects are for such seller cartels.

Given that international cartel arrangements tend to break down, a developing nation could still tax its own primary-product exports for the sake of economic development. In principle, the strategy could work well. A tax on exports of Nigerian oil, or Ghanaian cocoa, or Philippine coconuts or copper from Zaire could generate revenues for building schools, hospitals, and roads. Or the export-tax revenues could replace some other tax, reinforcing market incentives within the country. It is an excellent idea, as long as there are external benefits to the newly encouraged activities. Unfortunately, the political economy of the Third World seems to divert the export-tax revenues away from the most productive uses (as we hinted in Chapter 7 when discussing the similar infant-government argument for import tariffs). So it has been with the four examples just imagined. Nigeria's oil revenues are lost in a swollen government bureaucracy. For two decades Ghana's cocoa marketing board used its heavy taxation of cocoa farmers to support luxury imports by officials. The Marcos government distributed the coconut tax revenues among a handful of Marcos's friends and relatives. And Mobutu has kept much of Zaire's revenues from copper and other exports to himself. The potential merits of taxing exports of a primary product are so abused in practice that having no policy would be better.

Price Instability for Primary Products

A recurrent complaint about primary-product prices is that they are very unstable on world markets, complicating planning and sending shock waves through the economies that depend on primary-product exports. The complaint is based on a correct premise: primary products do fluctuate more in their nominal (currency) price than do the prices of manufactures or services. Their greater volatility has been a fact of life for at least two centuries.

Price instability has been more dramatic for some primary commodities than for others. As shown in Figure 12.3 above, the primary commodities showing the worst price instability are tropical products such as rubber, cocoa, and coffee and sugar (a semitropical product). Instability has been less serious in such temperate-zone products as food grains.

Commodity Price Stabilization: The Idea

If primary products are subject to particular price instability, isn't it a good idea to have some international organization stabilize them? UNCTAD and its offshoot international conferences have given more discussion to the idea of stabilizing primary-product prices than to schemes for raising them. The extra attention seems warranted, since there are conditions under which a price-stabilizing plan could benefit the world as a whole, and not just sellers at the greater expense of buyers.

To understand how a price stabilization plan could bring welfare gains, we must first clear away some of the intellectual baggage that usually goes with it. The case for stabilizing prices does not need (1) any proof that price fluctuations for the commodity in question are larger than for other commodities (though we have seen that this seems true) or (2) any proof that price fluctuations mean severe earnings fluctuations.

It is good that the second proof is not needed because it is often untrue. Many primary products seem to be subject to gyrating prices, but the price fluctuations do not mean that earnings from these products are unstable. This link depends on what shocks are causing the instability of price. If prices are responding mainly to supply-side shocks, earnings could fail to respond or could move in the opposite directions. For example, harvest failures like the Brazilian coffee frost of the mid-1970s will tend to raise prices but not earnings since smaller quantities are being sold. Similarly, bumper crops could cause prices to plummet yet still raise earnings if the quantities increased by a greater percentage than the prices decreased. Only in the case of demand-side shocks, more characteristic of minerals than of crops, is it clear that prices and earnings should be correlated. But, as we said, a well-run price stabilization scheme could be a good thing in principle as long as there are any price fluctuations at all.

Officially stabilizing the prices of a commodity requires that some oversee-ing body, formed by one or more governments, stand ready to buy and sell the commodity in large amounts. In one way or another a *buffer stock* of the commodity must be maintained. When the price rises to the ceiling that the officials consider the highest acceptable price, they must be ready to sell as much of the commodity as necessary to match the current excess demand at that high price. Only in this way can the officials keep the price from going higher. When market conditions threaten to push the price of the commodity lower than the level wanted by the officials, they must be prepared to buy the commodity in amounts sufficient to absorb the excess supply. Maintaining the funds and the commodity stocks necessary to stabilize in this way obviously entails certain costs. The commodity must be stored at an expense for space, labor, insurance, and so forth. Both the commodity and money must stand at readiness at a cost in interest forgone. If the overseeing body is international, there is the further problem of negotiating which governments will bear which shares of the total costs of the buffer stock scheme.

The key task in stabilizing price with a buffer stock is that of correctly guessing what the long-run trend price will be, and mustering sufficient resources to keep the price near that trend. If the contracting parties fail to foresee just how steep the upward trend in the commodity's price will be, they are likely to run out of stocks sooner or later. Once they have run out, the price will rise further than it would have if they had let it rise gently earlier by selling out of their stocks at a slow rate. If they have failed to foresee downward trends in the price, they will find themselves stuck with increasing stocks of a good whose market value will fall faster than they had anticipated. As soon as the contracting parties give up and sell off their stocks to cut official losses, the price will drop faster than if they had let it sag more gently by buying stocks at a slower rate. In either case of trend misjudgment, the final result is that the buffer stock authorities have made the price a bit less stable and have lost some money themselves by guessing wrong. Given the limits on the amounts the officials want to devote to the task of stabilizing prices, it would be better, both for smoothing the price trend and for avoiding financial losses, if they guessed correctly and spread their purchases or sales evenly over the periods in which market pressures pushed the price away from trend.

If the authorities could really keep the price right on its long-run trend in the face of fluctuations in private demand and supply, who would benefit from their actions? Would selling countries benefit more than buying countries? Would the world experience any net gain or loss? It turns out that the world is likely to experience a net gain from price stabilization, though the division of this gain between selling and buying countries is an elusive matter that is pursued at greater length in Appendix G.

1. *How the world could gain.* To see the likely net gain to the world, let us assume that the authorities can maintain a buffer stock of tin at low cost and can correctly guess that the long-run trend in the price of tin is the same as that for other goods in general, so that there is no net trend in the real price of tin. In all years with extraordinarily high demand for tin relative to its supply, the officials sell off tin from their stocks. In years of relatively flagging demand, they buy up tin. If they have correctly guessed the trends, as we assume, they can keep the same average stock indefinitely by selling off the same amount in high-demand years as they buy up in low-demand years. By successfully stabilizing prices, the officials are bringing the world the same net gains that any merchant or arbitrageur brings by improving the connections between buyers who value a good highly and sellers who can produce it at low cost. What the officials are doing is transporting tin across time in a way that evens out prices between times. They are, in effect, taking tin from the time periods in which private parties give it a low value and selling it in the time periods in which it is assigned a high value. The gaps between the peak-period net demand curves and the trough-period net supply curves (minus the costs of maintaining the buffer stock) are a measure of what the world as a whole gains by having the officials buy cheap and sell dear so as to stabilize prices. This net gain exists even if one ignores any special arguments about the subjective gains obtained from being able to plan on stable prices.

2. *Do sellers gain?* Whether selling countries (or buying countries) gain from price stabilization is less clear than one might presume from the fact that price-stabilizing schemes have usually been justified as beneficial to the interests of sellers.[4] To see why the sellers may not be the ones to gain, consider the case of tin where price fluctuations usually come from the *demand side* of the world market and where supply is a bit upward-sloping. If there were no price stabilization, the tin price on the markets in London and New York would be higher in some years than in others. It is also the case that stabilizing the price tends to stabilize the year-to-year export gains reaped by the exporting countries (Bolivia, Malaysia, and Thailand). But this stability has a cost. By stabilizing the price to exporters, the international officials have kept the producers from taking advantage of the higher prices in peak-demand periods by making larger sales at those times. The international officials have in effect helped out the buying countries by keeping them from having to buy their peak-period volumes at higher prices. The net effect on the overall gains for the exporting countries can end up negative, even though the scheme does stabilize their gains across periods.

3. *The overall pattern.* The complexity of the effects of price stabilization on the two sides of the world market is shown in Appendix G. The general pattern is that:

1. The world as a whole would gain from a price stabilization scheme if it worked ideally.
2. In markets where instability is due to *demand-side* fluctuations (e.g., the metals), stabilizing price tends to make importing countries bear a greater share of the overall risk, though it should bring them long-run average gains at the expense of exporters.
3. In markets dominated by *supply-side* instability (e.g., coffee), stabilizing price tends to make exporting countries bear a greater share of the overall risk, though it should bring them long-run gains at the expense of importers.

Commodity Price Stabilization: Problems in Practice

Actual experience with international price stabilization strongly underlines the essential problem stressed above: how to forecast the long-run trend

---

[4] Sellers' interest in international price-stabilizing agreements may be sustained by a subtle consideration mentioned briefly in the next section. They may see an agreement as a step toward a *price-support scheme* or even a cartel. This is sound. The mere establishment of the official buffer stock is a net increase in world demand for their product. And within the new agreement they may be able to lobby for above-market support prices that bring them gains at the expense of official capital losses on excessive stocks, losses that are divided among selling and buying countries together.

(equilibrium) prices that the stabilizing officials can maintain without exhausting or overaccumulating buffer stocks. Here, as always, forecasting is no easy task.

We can appreciate how hard it is to make the best-laid stabilization plans work correctly by reflecting on a simple question that deserves a sober answer before any governments embark on any international commodity programs: Why not leave price stabilization to private commodity markets? It is tempting to answer immediately that that is already being done and that the markets look too volatile. But price gyrations may just be the result of shocks (harvest failures, strikes, wars, recessions, etc.) that nobody, public or private, could predict with reliability. To strengthen this suspicion, recall that in our example of successful official stabilization, the officials succeeded by buying cheap and selling dear in the right amounts. They made a net profit by correctly guessing the long-run trends in prices. Yet, this is what informed professional private speculators try to do even without official intervention. As we shall see in Part Three, defenders of the private marketplace have indeed argued that profitable private speculation is, on balance, a stabilizer of price. With so much informed greed in the world, why commit tax money to setting up an official speculation fund (the buffer stock)?

The case for gambling on an official price stabilization scheme must therefore rest on the belief that groups of governments are better informed and equipped to gamble correctly than individual private speculators. This is possible. Governments can have better information on their own confidential market-relevant intentions. The United States, for example, has some idea about its own confidential plans for its military reserves of tin, copper, and other minerals. On the other hand, international negotiations to set up and maintain commodity agreements have revealed great conflicts of national self-interest: conflicts serious enough to raise doubts about the competence of intergovernmental groups in managing commodity markets. Exporting and importing countries tend to prefer to run different kinds of risks. Exporting countries press for higher officially maintained prices and greater accumulation of buffer stocks with tax funds, arguing that the equilibrium price trend will be strongly upward. They would rather run the risk of having the whole group accumulate excess stocks that may prove worth less than the price paid (to them). Importing countries argue that the price trends are more toward weakness, and that the group had better keep prices and stocks low in the anticipation of the inevitable low future prices. It takes a great leap of faith to believe that this tug-of-war will add to price stability.

In fact, repeated experiences with international agreements trying to stabilize the prices of cocoa, coffee, sugar, tea, tin, and other primary products have consistently broken down. This experience was already reviewed in Chapter 11. There it wore the disguise of a history of cartels. It is virtually the same history, however: the attempts to raise primary-product prices and the attempts to stabilize them overlapped. They failed at both fronts.

As things now stand, the idea of official price stabilization is plausible in principle but unworkable in past practice. We return to the same proposal in Part Three, where it takes the form of trying to keep exchange rates fixed in international currency markets.

ISI: IMPORT-SUBSTITUTING INDUSTRIALIZATION

The final trade policy option considered here is not a collective action among nations, but a unilateral step that an individual developing country may take with or without new agreements between North and South.

It is natural to think that industrialization is the surer way to overall economic improvements. Most high-income countries are industrial countries, the obvious main exceptions being the rich oil-exporting countries. To develop, officials from many countries have argued, they must cut their reliance on exporting primary products and must adopt government policies allowing industry to grow at the expense of the agricultural and mining sectors. Can this emphasis on industrialization be justified, and, if so, should it be carried out by restricting imports of manufactures?

The Great Depression caused many more countries to turn toward import substituting industrialization (ISI). Across the 1930s world price ratios turned severely against most primary-product-exporting countries. Although this decline in the terms of trade did not prove that primary exporters were suffering more than industrial countries, it was common to suspect that this was so. Several primary-product-exporting countries, among them Argentina and Australia, launched industrialization at the expense of industrial imports in the 1930s.

The ISI strategy gained additional prestige among newly independent nations in the 1950s and 1960s. This approach soon prevailed in most developing countries whose barriers against manufactured imports came to match those of the most protectionist prewar industrializers. Though many countries switched toward more protrade and export-oriented policies between the mid-1960s and mid-1970s, ISI remains a widespread policy among developing countries.

ISI at Its Best

To see the state of knowledge about the merits and drawbacks of ISI, let us begin by noting the three main arguments in its favor. If ISI could be fine-tuned to make the most of these arguments, it would be a fine policy indeed.

1. There can be large economic and social *side benefits from industrialization*. These side benefits were reviewed in Chapter 7: gains in technological knowledge and worker skills transcending the individual firm, new attitudes more conducive to growth, national pride, and perhaps self-sufficiency. As we saw in Chapter 7, the economist can imagine other tools more suitable to each of these tasks than import barriers. But in an imperfect world these better options may not be at hand, and protection for an infant modern-manufacturing sector could bring gains.

2. For a large country in particular, replacing imports can bring *better terms-of-trade effects* than expansion of export industries. Here we return to a theme sounded first in the discussion of "immiserizing growth" in Chapter 4 and again during Chapter 7's discussion of the nationally optimal tariff. The country's own actions could affect the prices of its exports and imports on world markets. Expanding exports might lead to some decline in export prices, as illustrated with the extreme case of export growth that is absolutely immiserizing. To this danger we can add a point just noted in the previous section: successful development of new export lines can be sabotaged by protectionist backlash in the main importing countries, as has happened to Asian manufactures in the markets of North America and Europe. By contrast, replacing imports with domestic production will, if it has any effect at all on the price of the continuing imports, tend to lower these prices (excluding the tariff or other import charge) and offer the nation a better bargain.

This terms-of-trade argument works best for very large developing countries such as Brazil. It is for these that the chances of affecting the terms of trade are the greatest. Large countries also face greater danger of importing-country protectionist backlash when pushing new export lines. And large countries can manufacture in plants large enough to take advantage of economies of scale, even without exporting.

3. Replacing imports of manufactures is a way of using cheap and *convenient market information*. A developing country may lack the expertise to judge just which of the thousands of heterogeneous industrial goods it could best market abroad. But central planners (and private industrialists) have an easy way to find which modern manufactures would sell in their own markets. They need only look at the import figures. Here is a handy menu of goods with proven markets. If the problems of cost and product quality can be conquered by new domestic producers, there is a clear basis for a protected industry (though protection still brings the costs described in Chapter 7). Here again, large countries are more likely to have markets large enough to support efficient-scale production.

Experience with ISI

History and recent economic studies offer four kinds of evidence on the merits of ISI and autarky. Casual historical evidence suggests a slightly charitable view, while three more detailed tests support a negative view of ISI.

In support of ISI, it can be said that today's leading industrial countries protected their industry against import competition earlier, when their growth was first accelerating. The United States, for example, practiced ISI from the Civil War until the end of World War II, when most American firms no longer needed protection against imports. Japan in the 1950s launched its drive for leadership in steel, automobiles, and electronics with heavy government protection against imports. As soon as each industry was able to compete securely in export markets, Japan removed its redundant protection against imports into Japan. Laura Tyson has recently argued that Japan's experience supports policies like ISI, with a set of rhetorical questions:

> What would Japan's trade in automobiles look like today if the Japanese domestic market had not been closed to foreign auto imports in the 1960s, when at the very least Fiat, if not General Motors, had a competitive product to offer Japanese consumers? Would the Japanese semiconductor industry have its technological and competitive edge today if not for the closure of the Japanese market to low-cost, high-quality 16k DRAMs produced by U.S. firms in the 1970s? And would Japan be at the cutting edge in fiber optics today if [Nippon Telephone and Telegraph] had not orchestrated closure of the Japanese market to Corning Glass to encourage the development of a domestic production . . . capability? (Tyson cited in Feenstra (1989b, p. 177))

It is possible to read such history in either of two ways. Critics of ISI could note that growth accelerated mainly *after* the protection against imports. But in its defense, we could note that the path to domination of worldwide markets was not inconsistent with, and might have been paved by, early "infant-industry" protection. More tests are needed.

The first kind of test casting serious doubt on the merits of ISI is the estimation of its static welfare costs, using the methods introduced in Chapter 6. A series of studies quantified the welfare effects of a host of Third World trade barriers in the 1960s and early 1970s, many of which were designed to promote industrialization (Balassa, 1971; Bhagwati and Krueger, 1973–76). The barriers imposed significant costs on Argentina, Chile, Colombia, Egypt, Ghana, India, Israel, Mexico, Pakistan, the Philippines, South Korea, Taiwan, and Turkey. Only in Malaysia did the import barriers bring a slight gain, because of a favorable terms-of-trade effect.

There is a rebuttal to this argument however. The standard calculations of welfare costs of trade barriers are vulnerable to the charge of assuming, not proving, that ISI is bad. Such calculations assume that all the relevant effects are captured by measures of consumer and producer surplus, without allowing protection any chance to lower cost curves as it is imagined to do in the infant-industry case. It would be fair to demand firmer proof.

A second kind of test compares the growth rate that a country experienced in a period of ISI with its rate of growth in a period of export promotion. Figure 12.4 makes such comparisons for 41 countries grouped according to the quality of their trade policies, first during the faster worldwide growth of 1963–1973 and then during the crises of 1973–1985. In both periods,

FIGURE 12.4   Trade Policy Orientation and Growth Results, 41 Developing
Countries, 1963–1985

Trade Policy Orientation	Average Annual Growth in Real GNP Per Capita	
	1963–1973	*1973–1985*
Strongly outward	6.9%	5.9%
Moderately outward	4.9	1.6
Moderately inward	4.0	1.7
Strongly inward	1.6	−0.1

"Outward" means that the government has low trade barriers and some export subsidies. "Inward" means reliance on trade barriers. The three strongly outward economies in both periods were Hong Kong, Korea, and Singapore. In 1963–1973 the 16 strongly inward (antitrade) regimes in the sample were Argentina, Bangladesh, Burundi, Chile, Dominican Republic, Ethiopia, Ghana, India, Pakistan, Peru, Sri Lanka, Sudan, Tanzania, Turkey, Uruguay, and Zambia. For 1973–1985 the 14 strongly inward countries were the previous 16 plus Bolivia, Madagascar, and Nigeria, but minus Chile, Pakistan, Sri Lanka, Turkey, and Uruguay.

Source: World Bank, *World Development Report 1987,* pp. 83–86, and data from the *1986* volume.

the three countries with strongly outward-oriented trade policies (Hong Kong, Korea, and Singapore) grew fastest, and the many countries with strongly inward orientation grew slowest.[5] Did their growth rates differ *because* their trade policies differed? The comparisons can only suggest; therefore they fall far short of proof.

The third test casting doubt on ISI is provided by a World Bank investigation of policies in 31 countries in the 1970s. The Bank's researchers developed rough indexes of the degree of price distortion in the policies of a developing country. For most goods and services, the term *price distortion* means departures from world prices, the sort of distortion that ISI would create. The distortion index can therefore be used as a proxy for ISI, even though it also reflects the Bank's measurements of distortions in labor and capital markets.

Correlating the World Bank measure of price distortions with rates of growth, it is possible to comment on the likely effect of price-distorting policies like ISI on economic growth. Fortunately, the sample of 31 countries is such that the degree of price distortion is uncorrelated with many other potentially relevant variables, such as the initial income level, geographic

---

[5] In practice, the two kinds of policy were applied in very different dosages. What the World Bank calls "strongly outward" orientation should be thought of not as policies of aggressive subsidies to trade, but as policies closer to free trade than the opposite "strongly inward" policies. For example, the government of "outward-oriented" Korea paid less in export subsidies than it collected in import tariffs from 1965 on, and removed most of both the subsidies and the tariffs by the mid-1980s. The text can thus talk of the outward-oriented policies as something closer to free trade and *laissez faire.*

FIGURE 12.5   Government Price Distortions of the 1970s and Growth Results for 1973–1983, in 31 Developing Countries

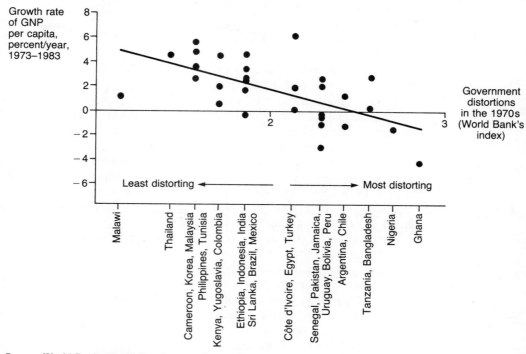

Source: World Bank, *World Development Report 1985.*

location of the country, and oil-exporting versus oil-importing status. Comparing growth rates with the degree of price-distorting (roughly, ISI) policies is thus a fair way of gathering hints about the role of such policies, holding at least some other variables constant.

Figure 12.5 shows the results.[6] Countries are arranged according to the World Bank's judgment of the degree to which their prices were artificially distorted in the 1970s.

As a rough tendency, growth in GDP per person was slower in countries whose government policies distorted prices more. Growth in the period 1973–83 was very negatively correlated with price-distorting policies in

---

[6] For an alternative presentation confined to the years 1970–80, see Chapter 6 of the World Bank *World Development Report, 1983* (Washington: World Bank, 1983). The World Bank arranged its results in a way that showed a stronger correlation of price distortions with GDP growth. Their results are extended to 1973–83 here, to give a better sense of the lagged effects of price distortions and to show that the pattern is not sensitive to slight changes in the testing period.

the 1970s. The results suggest, though they only suggest, some interesting international contrasts. Is it really true that South Korea grew much faster than Pakistan because the Korean government distorted price less? Did Kenya outgrow more interventionist Tanzania for the same reason? Certainly, the extreme cases are impressive: Korea's export orientation is an undeniable economic success, while Ghana's economy sank into overregulated ruin by 1983.

Care must be taken in interpreting the results. The price-distortion variable explains less than half the observed variation in growth rates, as is evident in the deviations of the dots from the solid regression line in Figure 12.5. Some outliers did not conform well to the alleged pattern. Price-liberal Malawi, in particular, grew much too slowly to fit a story of growth based solely on the degree of commitment to free trade.

Yet, there is a general pattern: policy distortions in the 1970s help explain why some countries grew more slowly than comparable countries in the period 1973–1983. The contrast has left its impression on policy-makers and scholars alike: ISI, like central planning in general, has lost much of the respect it enjoyed in the 1960s and earlier.

How can we reconcile the negative economic effect of price-distorting policies like ISI in the 1970s and 1980s with the success of postwar Japan's protected infant industries? The best answer seems to be that infant-industry protection was not key to Japan's success. Infant-industry protection in postwar Japan only gave a helping nudge to industries and firms that were destined to become world leaders in any case. Even though in Chapter 10 we took care to note the ways in which strategic trade planning could have helped Japan's industrial development, it is also clear that slower-working social investments were more important in the long run. Japan accumulated private capital, social infrastructure capital, and human skills faster than any other country in the postwar world. These basic investments were likely to make her an industrial power, even without infant-industry protection. More to the point, the general absence of such investments in Third World countries makes it very difficult for them to emulate Japan's success, with or without ISI. Most attempts in that direction ended up being wasteful protection of inefficient industries and government bureaucracies. Without the background of rapid accumulation, skills, and the work ethic, just protecting domestic industries against foreign competition does not put a developing country on the road to becoming another Japan. More often, the ISI route is the road to Albania.

EXPORTS OF MANUFACTURES TO INDUSTRIAL COUNTRIES

In the 1980s, developing countries have turned increasingly toward the third path, emphasizing new exports of manufactured goods to the industrialized countries. As Figure 12.6 shows, the switch from primary-product

FIGURE 12.6   The Changing Mix of Exports from Developing Countries, 1963–1987

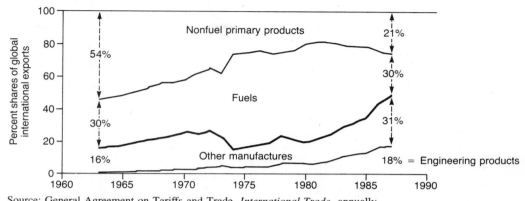

Source: General Agreement on Tariffs and Trade, *International Trade,* annually.

exports to manufactured exports began in the 1960s or earlier, but gained momentum in the 1980s. Disillusionment with both primary-product cartels and ISI was probably a factor in the new push.

Is it wise for a developing nation to plan on being able to raise its exports of manufactures to the already-industrialized countries? Should Mexico, Egypt, and India follow the example of Korea, making strategic plans to become major exporters of manufactures? Would the same thing happen without planning, as in the market-directed development of Hong Kong and Taiwan?

For their part, the industrialized countries have not made the task easy. They have, in fact, discriminated against exports of manufactures from developing countries. Nontariff import barriers apply to a greater percentage of goods from developing countries than to goods from other industrial countries, as Figure 12.7 shows. Only Japan has refrained from discriminating against developing countries in her nontariff barriers. Finland and Norway discriminate the most, followed by the European Community and the United States. As for tariffs, the rates are in principle nondiscriminatory. The tariff rates differ, however, by type of product. In general, the highest tariff rates among manufactures are those on textiles, apparel and footwear—the kind of manufactures in which developing countries have their broadest comparative advantage.

The Third World is thus justified in charging the industrial nations with hypocrisy. The industrial nations have not practiced the policies of free trade and comparative advantage that they have urged on developing countries. Furthermore, the departures of practice from preaching have been greatest on manufactures exported from developing countries. Tensions will

FIGURE 12.7   Discrimination against Developing Countries' Exports of Manufactures by Nontariff Barriers in Industrial Countries, 1983

Importing Country	Percent Shares of Industrial Countries' Imports Subject to Nontariff Barriers on Imports from		
	Developing Countries	Industrial Countries	World
Australia	26	24	25
Austria	3	2	2
EC (ten nations)	23	16	18
Finland	26	7	9
Japan	5	5	5
Norway	19	2	3
Switzerland	18	16	16
United States	18	11	12
All industrial countries	21	13	15

Source: Kym Anderson and Ross Garnaut (1987, p. 10), citing a 1985 study by Norgues, Olechowski, and Winters.

continue over this issue. For newcomers to world manufacturing markets, such as the People's Republic of China, the issue is particularly sensitive because the quotas or Voluntary Export Restraint agreements tend to ration the limited business to older exporters, such as Japan, shutting newcomers out.

Despite some discrimination against their exports, newly industrializing countries have been able to break into world markets for their exports of manufactures. One reason is the product life cycle described in Chapter 5. Developing countries have been able to become exporters in standardized manufacturing lines where technological progress has cooled down, such as textiles, tires, and simple electrical applicances. Another reason is that the barriers against imports of their manufactured goods are not all that solid. Especially in the case of America's Voluntary Export Restraints, a newcomer from the Third World can gain market access. By opening up new manufactured-export lines in the American market, the newly industrializing country can reap gains in either of two ways. If it decides to join into the next round of renegotiating VER allotments, it shares in the price markup (cartel profits) and gains even though it must agree to restrict its export volume. If it refuses to join, it can keep expanding its sales effort and benefit from the higher price of the VER participants' competing products. Of course, aggressive export expansion does not work if the importing countries turn to outright import quotas. But as long as they have a political preference for VERs over explicit import barriers, a developing country can gain valuable new export markets, despite the protectionism of the industrial countries.

SUMMARY

The gaps in living standards are widening within the Third World. Rapid growth continues with a small group of **Newly Industrializing Countries (NICs)**, mostly in East Asia (lead by Hong Kong, Korea, Singapore, and Taiwan). Yet for two whole continents, Latin America (including the Caribbean) and Africa south of the Sahara, average income fell from 1980 to 1987.

Developing countries must decide what trade policies to adopt toward primary-product exports, industrial imports, and industrial exports. In the primary sector, they must choose between letting comparative advantage be dictated by market forces, trying to raise prices in the classic cartel fashion, or trying to stabilize commodity prices with the help of other nations. The United Nations Conference in Trade and Development (UNCTAD) has campaigned since the 1960s for a **New International Economic Order (NIEO)**, built on international agreements to raise and stabilize primary-product prices, and to open doors for exports of manufactured goods from developing countries. The lack of progress on such global cooperation leaves it to individual developing countries to choose among the same trade policies toward primary products and manufactures.

Many developing countries have tried **commodity price stabilization** schemes, both separately and in cooperation with other countries. The case for stabilizing primary-product prices is more complicated than it might at first appear. It is true that nominal-price instability on world markets is worse for primary products than for manufactures or services. Yet, it does not follow that export price fluctuations have done more damage to primary exporters. The effects on their incomes depend critically on what caused the market fluctuations (productivity shifts versus demand shifts, etc.). The welfare economics of price stabilization is also tricky. It is easy to argue that the world as a whole gains from truly successful price stabilization that somehow manages to keep price at its long-run equilibrium trend. But how these world gains are distributed between buying and selling countries is a complicated matter, depending mainly on whether the source of the instability is on the demand side or the supply side of the world market.

A strategy open to developing countries is that of **import-substituting industrialization (ISI)**. It could raise national skill levels, bring terms-of-trade gains, and allow planners to economize on market information (since they can just take industrial imports themselves as a measure of demand that could be captured with the help of protection). Detailed studies of ISI and related policies, however, have given ammunition to critics of ISI. A study of 41 nations shows that income growth is negatively correlated with antitrade policies like ISI. Another study of 31 countries shows that growth is negatively correlated with government price interference in general (not just ISI). So far, the best available evidence supports the fears about ISI raised by static welfare calculations like those in Chapter 6, though the evidence is still not conclusive.

The other road to industrialization is to concentrate on developing exports of manufactured goods. This has been a slowly prevailing trend since the 1960s, though ISI remains more widely practiced among developing countries than export-oriented policies. Relying on exports of manufactures has its risks, however. Developing nations have rightly complained about import barriers against their new manufactures on the part of the more developed countries. Such barriers have indeed been higher than the barriers on manufactures traded between developed countries, and have risen since the late 1960s. If developing countries are to remain sanguine about the wisdom of relying on new manufacturing exports, they will need to see a new willingness of developed countries to shift their own resources out of these sectors, perhaps with the help of the sort of adjustment assistance discussed in Chapter 8, instead of erecting new barriers against imports.

SUGGESTED READINGS

For a recent survey of the literature on trade policy options for developing countries, start with Krueger (1984).

The best overview of the vast literature on long-run trends in the relative prices of primary products are Scandizzo and Diakosawas (1987) and Grilli and Yang (1988).

On the "new international economic order," see Bhagwati (1977), Behrman (1979), and Cline (1979). On the theory and practice of commodity agreements, see the sources cited in Appendix G plus Behrman (1979).

Detailed studies of industrial protection and the ISI strategy are found and cited in the studies by Balassa (1971), Bhagwati and Krueger (1973–76), Krueger (1983), and the World Bank's *World Development Report* (1983, 1986, 1987).

The implications of the pattern of protection in North America and Europe for developing countries seeking to export manufactures are explored at length by Cline (1984).

QUESTIONS FOR REVIEW

1. Is it true that the terms of trade shift against primary producers in the long run? Is it true that they face more unstable prices for their products than for manufactures?

2. Compare the likely effects of successful price-stabilization schemes on exporters of these two products: copper (subject to swings in buyers' import demands) and wheat (subject to swings in harvest yield).

3. Drawing on material from this chapter and earlier chapters, weigh the pros and cons of restricting and taxing exports of primary products. How could it raise national income? What are the drawbacks of such a policy for a developing country?

4. List the main pros and cons of taking the import-replacing road to industrialization versus concentrating government aid and private energies on developing new comparative advantages in manufacturing exports.

5. (An alternative to Question 4.) Under what conditions would ISI have the greatest chance of being better than any alternative development strategy? What other policies should accompany it?

▼

The Political Economy
of Trade and Agriculture

•

Understanding the causes and consequences of trade policies requires a mixture of political and economic insights. It also requires separate treatment of policies toward agriculture, since they are very different both in their motivation and in their effects on trade. This chapter rounds out our pursuit of such understanding in Parts One and Two. There are four main topics to cover, as represented by the following schematic boxes:

	The Political and Economic Causes of Our Trade Policies	Economic Consequences of Our Trade Policies
All Trade Policies	This chapter. ⇓	Chapters 2–12.
Policies toward Agriculture and Agricultural Trade	This chapter. ⇒	This chapter.

The main task, that of measuring and judging the economic consequences of all trade policies has been addressed in the chapters above. Here we take the L-shaped journey through the three remaining tasks.

WHAT EXPLAINS OUR TRADE BARRIERS IN GENERAL?

Several broad facts about real-world trade barriers demand an explanation:

• Why are they generally higher than the welfare analysis of Chapters 6–8 would warrant?

- Why are they higher for consumer goods than for raw materials and intermediate goods?
- Why, in international trade negotiations, does each nation act as if lowering its own import barriers is a *concession* to foreigners, when doing so benefits that same nation?
- Why are trade barriers raised more in depressions than in booms and inflations?
- How do we explain the longer-run historical trends in import protection?

Economists and political scientists tend to agree on at least some of the answers to these questions, even though they have only begun to think about the longer-run trends. There is a growing literature on the "political economy of trade barriers," which explains the lobbying incentives that individuals and pressure groups use in the political system and the self-interested behavior of political representatives who seek to maximize their influence and their chances for staying in office.

A Simplified View of Trade Lobbying

A quick partial answer to the set of basic questions about real-world trade barriers rests on a very simplified look at how an individual views the political process. To capture key points quickly, suppose that political participation on an issue like a fight over protective tariffs is just a yes-or-no proposition: either you do participate or you don't. Let us ignore degrees of participation, such as large or small campaign contributions. One person, one and only one vote.

Your decision whether to participate in the fight over the tariff issue depends on four key factors:

1. The **inefficiency,** or not national loss from the tariff—the worse it gets, other things being equal, the greater the forces against the tariff;
2. **Group size:** the size of the group sharing your interests—the greater the group, other things being equal, the more poorly it mobilizes to fight for those shared interests;
3. How much **sympathy** your group gets from others, including some who would not benefit if your side won; and
4. How much **representation** you have in the government under current institutions.

To show how the first two forces, inefficiency and group size, influence whether or not we get a protectionist tariff, think of the costs and benefits of fighting over a bill to protect the textile industry for one year. For the average person whose income depends on protecting the textile industry, the "profit" from a successful fight for textile protection is:

The average protectionist's net political gain = $\pi_p = (B_p/N_p) - C_p$.

Here B_p = the producer surplus gain from securing government protection, or the same thing as area a in diagrams like Figure 6.1 in Chapter 6. N_p is the number of persons (voters) to be protected, so that dividing B_p by N_p gives the producer surplus for the typical protectionist. But each active protectionist bears a cost C_p of fighting for the year of protection for textiles. Each must spend time, energy, and maybe money on this issue instead of doing other things (or fighting other political fights). So the net gain per person is only π_p. Let us assume for now that each individual believes her or his own vote to be crucial in determining the political outcome.

The rest of society typically loses more from protection than the protectionists gain. This is the general rule to which Chapter 7 catalogued some exceptions. To look at their stake in the political fight, let us define the rest of society as "consumers" of textiles.[1] They too can gain from winning the political fight over a textile tariff. Consumers' gain B_c takes the form of avoiding the loss from the tariff. Yet they too, like the protectionist opposition, must share the gains and bear individual costs:

The average consumer's
net political gain from
defending free trade $= \pi_c = (B_c/N_c) - C_c.$

Each term is defined as it was for the typical protectionist above.

Under some circumstances, inefficient trade barriers would be rejected, and we would have a world closer to free trade than what we observe. For example, if we had simple majority rule and voting was costless, the only measures that would pass would be ones benefitting a majority. Most trade barriers, however, protect only a minority, even when many of them are combined into a single piece of legislation. That would not happen under simple majority rule, because the decisive median voter would vote against the trade barrier. So, we observe that the actual trade policy outcomes depart from what simple majority-rule democracy would give us.

Another example of conditions under which inefficient trade barriers would not arise: if politics were equally costly in the two opposing camps (so that $C_p = C_c$) and they were of the same size $(N_p = N_c)$, efficiency and free trade would rule. The mere fact that the tariff brought a net national "deadweight" loss, equal to $B_c - B_p$ should doom the idea. Those opposed to the tariff would be willing to spend up to the greater stake B_c to prevent the tariff, while the protectionists would not rationally spend more than the smaller stake B_p. While almost anything is possible in the political

---

[1] More precisely, the rest of society here consists of textile consumers plus the government. The government tariff revenue is assumed to be paid back to the consumers in "lump-sum" payments not proportional to consumption of textiles. Then, in terms of the areas in Figure 6.1 back in Chapter 6, the "consumers" lose areas $a + b + d$ from the tariff, but not area c, which is just redistributed among them.

marketplace, the greater the net inefficiency of the tariff $(B_c - B_p)$, the less the chance that it will become law. For all its clumsiness, the political system may weed out more protectionist proposals, which have greater net deadweight costs. While the influence of efficiency looks like an important truth, we still observe many inefficient trade barriers. Why?

The most important explanation for trade barriers that bring the nation a net loss relates to group size. Protectionists often, though not always, derive strength from being a smaller group. The simple benefit-cost equations show us one reason why. The smaller the group, the greater the average gain per member (other things being equal). Protectionists, while only a minority of those who are affected, can have a greater average stake in the trade fight than their opponents, even if the measure brings a net national loss. (In symbols, with $N_p < N_c$, we can have $B_p/N_p > B_c/N_c$, even though $B_p < B_c$). The difference in benefits per person can be crucial because being politically active has costs. If consumers' benefits from defeating the protectionist measure are small per person because their group is large, they may decide it is not worth it to fight against protectionism. (That is, they may see that $B_c/N_c < C_c$.)

Protectionists often win partly because their self-interest is *concentrated* into a small number of persons. The simple benefit-cost algebra shows one source of small groups' power in political competition, namely, the fact that splitting gains among fewer members keeps individuals motivated to participate. Another, possibly more important, source of that power is the fact that the **free rider problem** afflicts the large-group opposition more seriously than it afflicts the small group. The free rider problem arises whenever the benefits of a group effort fall on everyone in a large group regardless of how much they spend as individuals (in time, effort, voting rights, or money). Each individual knows that her or his contribution to the group effort is not likely to be crucial. Therefore, each selfishly rational individual tries to get a free ride, letting the others advance the common cause. The individual's benefits from the common cause do depend on the group's victory or defeat, but that does not depend much on the individual's own effort.

The free rider's selfish calculation can be expressed in terms of our benefit-cost algebra. Suppose that the individual consumer knows that there is only a 0.003 chance that her or his contribution will be crucial in fighting off protectionism. Then, the individual's benefit of joining the fight is only 0.00003 times B_c/N_c, not all of B_c/N_c. The lower payoff (0.00003 B_c/N_c) could easily fall below the cost of participating, so that the individual decides to remain passive and "free ride" on the group's effort. With many individuals feeling the same way, the large group's aggregate stake (B_c) is underdefended, and the protectionists win, even though their stake (B_p) is lower.

Conquering the free rider problem is what political action groups—or "special interests," if you wish—are all about. To some extent, it is possible to conquer the problem by forming an organization that taxes all members for the common political cause and tries as much as possible to exclude others who will not contribute. Thus, we see effective political lobbying by labor unions, by the National Rifle Association, by the Sierra Club, by trade associations representing industries, and by others. Even political parties themselves are attempts to overcome the free riding problem when common goals are shared by large numbers.

Government officials and political candidates are well aware of the greater power of interests that are more effectively concentrated into small groups or organizations that have effectively solved the free rider problem in larger groups. They know that such a group is a one-issue lobby, giving or taking money and votes in response to the officials' or candidates' stands on the one issue that is key to the group's income. The less organized masses of, say, consumers have many issues to pay attention to, and they will not vote for or against a candidate on the basis of this one issue. Even if each auto consumer knows that protecting the auto industry against imports will cost him 0.14 percent of income in the form of higher car prices, there are so many other battles to fight in life that consumers fail to mobilize against auto-industry protectionism.

Applications to Other Trade Policy Patterns

Another general symptom of the importance of group size and concentration into effective lobbying units is the **tariff escalation** pattern. Economists have found that effective and nominal tariff rates rise with the stage of production. That is, they are typically higher on final consumer goods than on intermediate goods and raw materials sold to producing firms.[2] The explanation would seem to be that consumers of final product are a peculiarly weak lobby, being many people not well organized into dues-collecting lobbying associations. Consumer groups face massive free rider problems in trying to get the diffuse consumer population to fight for its interests in policy battles. They fight only weakly against the suppliers of final products, whose cause is championed by influential large firms and trade associations. When it comes to fights over protecting sellers of intermediate goods, the story can be quite different. The buyers of intermediate goods are themselves firms and can organize lobbying efforts as easily as their suppliers can. The outcome of a struggle over tariffs on intermediate goods is thus less likely to favor protection.

The same bias in favor of producer interests over final-consumer interests

---

[2] See also Appendix D. The tariff escalation pattern does not apply to agricultural products, however. Farmers get at least as much effective protection as the wholesalers and retailers to whom they sell.

shows up in international negotiations to liberalize trade, such as the eight postwar rounds of GATT negotiations. There are curious explicit guidelines as to what constitutes a fair balance of concessions by the different nations at the bargaining table. A "concession" is any agreement to cut one's own import duties, thereby letting in more imports. Each country is pressured to allow as much import expansion as the export expansion it gets from other countries' import liberalizations. It is odd to see import liberalization treated as a sacrifice by the importing nation. After all, cutting your own import tariffs should usually bring net national gains, not losses, according to Chapters 6–8. The concession-balancing rule can only be interpreted as further evidence of the power of producer groups over consumer groups. The negotiators view their own import tariff cuts as concessions simply because they had to answer politically to import-competing producer groups but not to masses of poorly organized consumers.

So far we have applied two of the four working parts of our very simple framework for explaining patterns in trade barriers. We have applied the parts relating to (1) inefficiency and (2) group size, but have not yet shown the relevance of (3) sympathy and (4) unequal representation. Each of these leaves its own mark on trade policy.

Interest groups are often victorious because they gain the sympathy of others, that is, of people who will not directly gain if policy helps the interest group. Political sympathy often surges when a group suffers a big income loss all at once, especially in a general depression. The sympathy can spring from either of two sources. One is simply compassion for those suffering large income losses. Political sentiments often yield to pleas for protection when a surge of import competition wipes out incomes, just as we provide generous relief for victims of natural disasters. The other source shows up more when a great depression hits the whole economy. In a depression more people are at risk of having their incomes cut. More of them identify with the less fortunate, thinking "that could be me." One policy response is to help those damaged by import competition, whose pleas are heard above the mild complaints of many consumers who would suffer small individual losses from import barriers. Thus, both a surge in import competition and a general depression raise sympathy for protectionism.

Unequal representation also shapes trade policy outcomes. People working in some industries have inordinate political representation in the executive and legislative branches of government, while those in other industries have no representatives. Even in full democracies, voters are unequally represented because some regions have extra power. An example is the United States Senate, which gives the same two senators to each state, regardless of population. Even when every voter has a representative, it can help to have the voters in your industry spread over several states or districts so that a large number of elected officials hears your cry for protection, as opposed to an industry that is concentrated in one state or district, with fewer elected representatives.

Trends in Protection Economywide

Another task of any simplified framework for understanding the political economy of trade is to account for long-run trends in the degree of protection against imports. Here we find a sharp difference between what has happened economywide and what has happened in the agricultural sector. Let us look at the ambiguous trends in overall protection, before taking a look at agricultural policies in the next section.

We know the trends in many nations' tariffs on manufactured goods across this century (Figure 13.1), plus the trends in a few countries' overall average tariff rates since the early 19th century (Figures 13.2 and 13.3). The most dramatic change was America's conversion to relatively free trade in the 1940s, after being outstandingly protectionist from the Civil War through the Great Depression. One reason for the three quarters of a century of American protectionism was the inability of a key exporting region, the South, to lobby effectively for free trade from the Civil War on. Northern industrial protectionists generally prevailed.

In the United States and the United Kingdom, though not so much in Canada, tariff rates rose in depressions and fell during booms and inflations. The classic example: in 1930, in an effort to combat the effects of the Great Depression, the U.S. Congress passed the Smoot-Hawley tariff (it

---

FIGURE 13.1   Average Tariff Rates on Imports of Manufactures, Selected Industrial Countries, 1902–1970

	1902	*1913*	*1925*	*1970*
United States	73	18	13	7
Canada	17	26	23	6
Japan	10	20	13	12
Australia	6	16	27	23
New Zealand	9	na	na	23
Belgium	13	9	15	
France	34	20	21	
Germany	25	13	20	EEC = 8
Italy	27	18	22	
Netherlands	3	4	6	
Denmark	18	14	10	na
Norway	12	na	na	11
Sweden	23	20	16	7
Switzerland	7	9	14	3

Note: Tariff duties as a percent of all imports of manufactures.
Source: Anderson and Garnaut (1987, p. 7), citing the League of Nations and GATT.

FIGURE 13.2 Average Import Duties, United States, 1821–1987

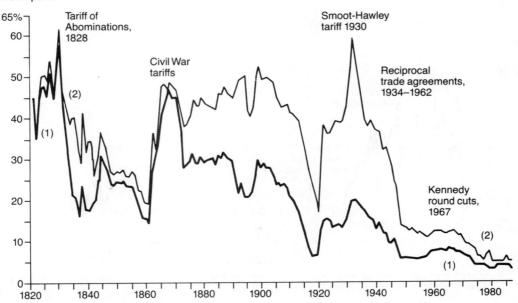

(1) = Duties as a percentage of all net imports.

(2) = Duties as a percentage of dutiable imports only.

did not work). In part, protectionism was correlated with depressions because of the sympathy pattern noted earlier. In part, it was an automatic response to price changes: many tariffs are specified in fixed amounts of money per physical unit, so that a drop (rise) in prices would make the tariff automatically rise (fall) as a percentage of the price of the product. Sometime between 1925 and 1970, according to Figure 13.1, tariffs came down not only in the United States, but also in Canada, Australia, Sweden, Switzerland, and four EC countries. The reduction was due partly to the hegemony of the United States, which was a strong exporter and could afford a free trade stance.

In general, Figures 13.1 through 13.3 suggest the higher a nation's income per capita, the lower its tariff rate. Certainly the industrialized countries as a whole have lower tariff rates than the developing nations. What is true of tariff rates is still true, but less true, of overall import protection. In the

FIGURE 13.3 Average Import Duties, United Kingdom, 1796–1966, and Canada, 1867–1984*

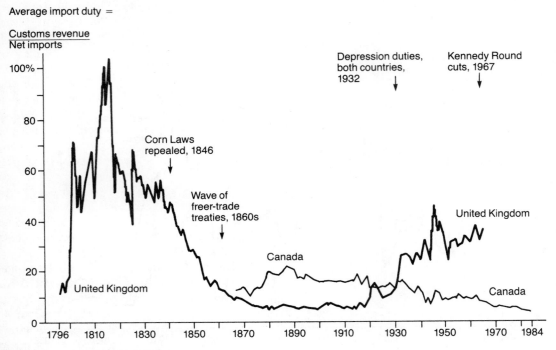

Average import duty =

Customs revenue
Net imports

* Duties as a percentage of all imports.

Sources and notes for Figure 13.2 and Figure 13.3: United States: U.S. Bureau of the Census, *Historical Statistics of the United States: Colonial Times to 1970*. (Washington, D.C.: Government Printing Office) series U193, U211, U212 and Y353: and idem, *Statistical Abstract of the United States, 1975*. (Washington, D.C.: Government Printing Office, 1975 and 1988), tables 1370 and 1378.

United Kingdom: B. R. Mitchell, *British Historical Statistics*. (Cambridge: Cambridge University Press, 1988), and Great Britain, Central Statistical office, *Annual Abstract of Statistics* recent years.

Canada: M. C. Urquhart and K. A. H. Buckley, *Historical Statistics of Canada* (Toronto: Macmillan, 1965 and 1983). Canada, Statistics Canada, *Canada Yearbook* (Ottawa: Information Canada, various years).

For the United Kingdom and Canada, some of the ratios compare fiscal-year customs revenues with calendar-year imports.

1970s and 1980s most industrialized countries shifted toward nontariff barriers, as we saw in Chapters 8 and 12. Proper measures of protection, if available, would probably show that the trend toward freer trade was impressive between 1925 and 1970, but then stopped and was reversed slightly. The long-run trend, at any rate, has been toward lower import barriers for the economy as a whole.

THE PROTECTION AND TAXATION OF AGRICULTURE

Agriculture is another matter. Where the farm population is directly involved, government intervention has become a highly developed art form, with major effects on international trade.

In today's high income countries, government protection and subsidization of agriculture has been carried to such extremes that the laws of nature have been turned upside down. We naturally expect that food grains, for example, will be exported by the countries with the best climates and soils for growing grain. Yet, since the early 1980s *Saudi Arabia* has grown more wheat than that country can consume, forcing it to subsidize wheat exports! Why? The government has placed such a high priority on being able to see wheat fields in the desert around Riyadh that it has not only blocked wheat imports but has heaped subsidies (and expensive water) on home-grown wheat, leading to a surplus for export.[3] Wheat is also exported by other countries with unfavorable climates and soils, including Great Britain and France. And crowded industrial Japan has been a net exporter of rice. Presumably, with enough government intervention bananas could be grown in Antarctica and exported to Ecuador.

As extremely as agriculture is protected in some settings, it is taxed and exploited in others, primarily in the Third World. Take the case of cocoa in Ghana around 1980. Ghanaian cocoa farmers had to sell their crops to the government's cocoa marketing board, which gave them only about 40 percent of the world price at which the board sold the same cocoa beans. In addition to pocketing the other 60 percent, the government put up import barriers that made industrial imports (e.g., clothing, fuel) artificially expensive for farmers to buy. Under such policies, Ghanaian agriculture had reached a ruinous state by the early 1980s, but it has had some recovery since then. Similarly, heavy taxation of exportable crops, especially beverages (cocoa, coffee, tea) and cotton, is common throughout the Third World.

Global Patterns in Agricultural Policy

In fact, economists have found that extremes like these are part of two policy patterns that show up both in history and in today's global comparisons.

---

[3] In 1983, for example, the Saudi government spent $1.3 billion buying desert-grown domestic wheat that could have been imported for $225 million. Responding to American charges that this was crazy, Saudi farmer Abdulrahman al-Khorayef replied "The United States [government] spends something like $40 billion for farmers not to grow crops and we spend just $1 billion. We're paying that price not just for wheat. We are getting technology and experience and the basic structure for our future food supply. I don't think we are crazy. I think they are crazy."

While there are exceptions, and there are difficulties of getting precise measurements, two general patterns stand out:

- *The developmental pattern:* Low-income countries generally burden farm producers with taxes and poor terms of trade, whereas high-income countries generally subsidize and protect their agriculture.
- *The antitrade bias:* In all countries, policies tend to tax producers of exportable agricultural products while protecting producers of importables against import competition.

To discover these patterns, economists needed measurements of the effects of government policy on agricultural incomes. There is a trade-off in measures of policy impact, a trade-off between availability and accuracy. The most available measure is the **nominal protection coefficient (NPC):**

$$\text{NPC} = P_{prod}/P_{world} = \text{the ratio of the price received by domestic producers}$$
to the world price of the same product at the nation's border. NPC > 1 means producers are protected by government, while NPC $<$ 1 means they are effectively taxed.

The nominal protection coefficient is sometimes calculated with an adjustment for the effect of disequilibrium exchange rates on the world price as expressed in domestic currency. The main limitation of the NPC is that it cannot take account of government policies that affect farmers' incomes without affecting domestic agricultural prices. For example, if a government paid its farmers generous income subsidies but let free trade dictate domestic prices, NPC would equal one, wrongly implying no government help at all. Another limitation is that it does not take account of what the government is doing to the prices of things farmers buy. The NPC fails to reflect government protection of industry raised the prices of farm inputs and the consumer goods farm families buy. Yet because the NPC requires only the measurement of two prices, it is readily available. And because it is available, we use it.

A slightly better measure, already introduced in Chapter 6 and Appendix D, is the **effective rate of protection (e.r.p.):**

$$\text{e.r.p.} = \frac{P_{prod} - P_{world} - (\text{input cost markup due to government policies})}{P_{world}}$$

or

$$\text{e.r.p.} = \text{NPC} - 1 - (\text{input cost markups as a share of } P_{world})$$

Relative to the NPC, the e.r.p. has the virtue of taking account of the effects of government policy on the prices of farm inputs. It can thus capture subsidies to fertilizer use, where they exist, or government protection of industries supplying farm inputs. Its two most serious omissions are (1) government subsidies or taxes that do not affect price and (2) government effects on farm families' cost of living.

A third, more comprehensive, measure of policy impacts on agricultural incomes is being developed by economists connected with the U.S. Department of Agriculture and the Organization for Economic Cooperation and Development. Subsidies and taxes are expressed as shares of farmers' original incomes, and combined with the percentage income effects of price-affecting policies. In rough schematic summary, this **producer subsidy equivalent (PSE)** can be described as:

$$\text{PSE} = \frac{(P_{prod} - P_{world}) + (\text{gov't subsidies minus input price markups})}{P_{world}}$$

or

$$\text{PSE} = \text{e.r.p.} + (\text{gov't subsidies}/P_{world})$$
$$= \text{NPC} - 1 + (\text{gov't subsidies minus input price markups})/P_{world}$$

The PSE measure has the advantage of its greater comprehensiveness in capturing effects of government policy on agricultural incomes. Even it, though, omits important effects. In practice, it quantifies only some of the government's influences on the prices of farm inputs. Specifically, it quantifies the influences of farm policies, not all policies. Government's protection of industry often raises agricultural costs in ways missed by the PSE's focus on policies aimed directly at agricultural producers. And the PSE, like all the other measures, misses effects of government on farm households' cost of living. No measure has yet reached the goal of quantifying all the effects of government on agricultural incomes. When PSE measures are refined for many countries, they will be the best available measures. For the present, only the cruder NPCs offer broad international coverage.

How agricultural policy evolves over the course of economic development, and how it is biased against trade, can be shown with NPC estimates for several dozen countries around 1980.[4] Figure 13.4 graphs NPCs separately for importable and exportable goods, with trend (regression) lines showing how NPCs for the average importable and the average exportable tend to advance with GNP per capita. Both tend to rise, showing the developmental pattern. In Figure 13.4, the rise is not steady, but occurs mainly as a jump toward protection, or away from taxation, as a country first joins the ranks of the developed industrial countries. History does not necessarily show the same jump. Aside from a temporary jump in agricultural protection and subsidies in the Great Depression of the 1930s, the drift toward protected agriculture was more gradual in the modern history of Japan, North America, and Western Europe than in the global snapshot shown for 1980 in Figure

---

[4] The year 1980 happened to be one of relatively low protection for producers of agricultural products in the high-income industrial countries. Heavier protection and subsidies followed in the mid- and late 1980s.

FIGURE 13.4   The Net Protection or Taxation of Agricultural Producers, 249 Cases in 39 Countries, circa 1980

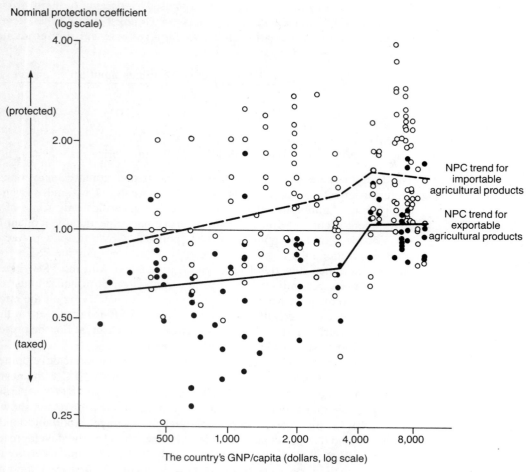

Sources: Binswanger and Scandizzo (1983), Anderson and Hayami (1986).

13.4. It is important to remember that in all cases, the drift was more pronounced than nominal protection coefficients can show. While the NPCs were rising over the course of economic development, the protection of industry was falling. Thus, governments shifted both toward raising agricultural incomes and toward removing policies that raised the farm cost of living and the cost of inputs into farming.

The antitrade bias is evident in the separation of the two trend lines in Figure 13.4. In the Third World, producers of exportables are clearly burdened, mainly through export barriers denying them the world price for their product. Examples include NPCs between 0.32 and 0.74 for African beverage crops, cotton, and groundnuts, 0.39 for Thai rubber, and 0.64 for Argentine wheat. Third World producers of importable agricultural products are treated more ambiguously. Some are protected: NPC = 1.13 for Kenyan wheat, 1.30 for Kenyan rice, and 1.50 for Turkish rice. Others are forced to accept a below-world price (typically as part of a program to subsidize consumers, as in the case of Egyptian wheat, for which NPC = 0.76). Among industrial countries, farmers producing for export are given only slight net help from government. This is one reason why the average NPC is close to one for the naturally agricultural-exporting nations of North America and Australasia. By contrast, importable farm products are heavily protected, especially sugar and dairy products, but also beef and grains in the case of the EC and Japan.

Tentative Explanations for the Agricultural Policy Patterns

> *I don't want to hear about agriculture from anybody but you.* . . .
> *Come to think of it, I don't want to hear about it from you either.*
>
> President Kennedy to his top agricultural policy advisor.

Why do governments intervene in the agricultural sector with policies so different from those applied to other sectors? Why do they drift from taxing agriculture to protecting it, while drifting in the opposite direction for industrial sectors? Why are they harder on farmers producing for export than on those competing against imports? Here is a set of puzzles on the active research frontier of political economy. The answers surely depend on history and on political institutions. Yet, more can and should be said. The patterns summarized in Figure 13.4 emerge from dozens of countries, some of them democracies and some of them dictatorships. The earlier histories of the leading countries suggest the same patterns. It seems unlikely that a global tendency is just the accidental result of unique events and institutions in separate countries. Broad patterns call for broad explanations. But which ones?

The developmental pattern seems to result from two changes, both of them illuminated by our simplified model of trade policy:

1. The shrinkage of the agricultural sector raises its lobbying efficiency and the sympathy of the nonagricultural population.
2. The agricultural lobby is increasingly mobilized by its rising sensitivity to price movements, movements which government could control.

Over the course of economic development, agriculture shrinks faster as a share of the labor force and GNP than does any other sector. While no sector would welcome decline for its own sake, a drop in the population earning a living from agriculture has the political advantage of solving some of the problem of organizing a large and diverse group. The more the fortunes of agriculture, good and bad, accrue to fewer farmers and landlords with higher individual stakes, the more effectively they band together to lobby for government support. In addition, the more agriculture declines as a "way of life," the more the nonagricultural population reveres it and feels sympathy for the cause of protecting that way of life. It is odd that people who reject the farm life willingly pay to revere it, but that sentiment is common in industrialized countries, and it seems to have been fed by the sheer magnitude of agriculture's decline.

As the national economy develops, agricultural household incomes become more sensitive to market prices. The clearest reason for this is the fact that the share of their incomes derived from trading with markets goes up. In early settings, say in 17th-century England, farm families consumed up to half their own production. A 10 percent drop in the price of all farm products would lower the farm sector's real income by only 5 percent. In the United States in 1910, the share marketed off the farm had risen to 78 percent, and today it is over 90 percent. So today the same 10 percent drop in all farm product prices would cut farm real income by 9 percent (90 percent of the 10 percent price drop). Although there may be other forces raising farmers' income sensitivity to prices, this one clear force, the rise in farm families' exposure to market prices, suffices to make the point that rising sensitivity to price was one source of increasing farmer agitation.

As for the antitrade bias in agricultural policy, the most likely suspect is the government's own desire to raise revenues. Both taxing exports (to the disadvantage of domestic farmers) and taxing imports (to their advantage) are ways to raise revenue for the government. Even when governments use quotas instead of taxes and somehow fail to collect revenues on the price markup, their trade restrictions at least avoid the budgetary drain of outright subsidy payments. The positive revenue side of antitrade policies thus recommends them to government officials. The government sector is usually an effective lobby, being situated where political bargaining takes place. It makes a strong ally for powerful private groups.

For example, some observers describe the high protective barriers against sugar imports into the United States as a problem-free policy of farm income support. Problem-free, because the sugar duties protect domestic farmers *and* bring government revenue. American consumers and foreign sugar growers, of course, lose even more than farmers and government gain, but consumers and foreigners are politically weak.

Similarly, taxing agricultural exporters such as Thai rice farmers or Ghanaian cocoa farmers forges a powerful private-public alliance. Private urban interests, say in Bangkok or Accra, approve of using export revenues from agricultural products to pay for investments in modernizing the urban-industrial sector. For government officials the export tax revenues spell budgetary relief.

THE EFFECTS OF DEVELOPED COUNTRIES' AGRICULTURAL POLICIES

Just how the usual policies affect trade and welfare is an involved story, because the policies themselves are varied. Some encourage trade, some discourage it. The effects on consumption and production are equally varied. Only the direction of effects on national or world welfare is consistent, though the identities of the gainers and losers vary. Let's reapply the tools of earlier chapters to analyze the main kinds of agricultural policies, starting with the various forms of farm income support in the more developed economies.

Farm Price Supports

The United States, Japan, and the EC all try to straddle the price fence by offering farmers higher prices than those prevailing in the outside world market. The methods of supporting producer prices vary greatly. The basic results, however, can all be established with two manageable examples.

The basic economics of price supports for *an exportable product* can be shown with the stylized portrayal of U.S. price supports for wheat in Figure 13.5. Price supports are intended to effect a redistribution of income from nonfarmers to farmers. The government buys all output, in this case output of wheat, at a price that exceeds the market price by enough to satisfy society's desire to raise the incomes of farmers. In Figure 13.5 the government has purchased the entire crop *(FD)* at $6 a bushel. The government's next problem is to decide what to do with the government-held wheat. If it were destroyed, the full amount ($6.00 × *FD*) would be lost, and there would be a public outcry about wasting food that somebody needs. To some extent the government tries to give the surplus to needy citizens in a way that keeps it from spilling back onto the market. This is done, with partial success, through food stamps and other aid-in-kind programs. But there are limits to how much surplus can be disposed of in this way without the recipients' reselling some of it back onto the market, undercutting the intention of keeping prices high.

Government thus turns to the export market and sells the surplus abroad at the lower world price.[5] In Figure 13.5, it is selling *ED* of surplus wheat

---

[5] In practice, surplus-exporting governments also offer export subsidies to foreign buyers, to compete for business that saves them some surplus-storage costs.

FIGURE 13.5   Price Supports for an Exportable Crop: the Case of U.S. Wheat

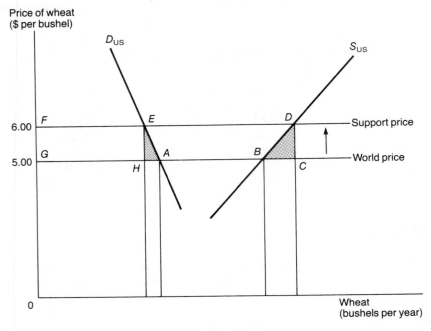

Effects of $1.00 Price Support

On prices and quantities:

Assume no change in world price. Domestic buyers must pay $1 more, buy less.

Domestic producers get $1 more, and produce more. Government pays the high support price for the surplus *ED*, and cuts its losses by exporting the surplus at the world price.

On welfare:

U.S. consumers lose area *AEFG*.

U.S. producers gain area *BDFG*.

U.S. government pays $6 times *ED*, resells at $5 times *ED*, to foreign buyers. It therefore loses $1 times *ED*, or area *CDEH*.

Total effect: United States as a whole loses the shaded triangles *BCD* and *AEH*.

abroad at $5 a bushel. Buying at $6 and selling at $5 means a loss, of course, but losing a dollar a bushel is the best that officials can do to minimize the taxpayers' loss. The government must also enforce import barriers on wheat, to keep people from bringing $5 wheat into the country to be sold at $6 a bushel. So, U.S. consumers continue to pay $6 a bushel for wheat.

The welfare effects are predictable. As consumers of expensive wheat and as taxpayers paying to lose a dollar on every bushel of government-purchased wheat, nonfarmers lose twice over while farmers gain, as intended. The nation as a whole loses because (1) consumers are unnecessarily discouraged from buying wheat products (the nation loses triangle *AEH*) and (2) wheat is grown and delivered at a marginal cost of $6 when its world-price value is only $5 (the nation loses triangle *BCD*). As time passes, the social loss *BCD* will grow, because the supply curve will become more elastic. Elastic supply plagues all price-support programs: farmers respond to the better price with greater and greater supplies, raising the budgetary cost and social loss.

As Figure 13.5 is drawn, the world price is assumed to be fixed, even though more exports are being dumped on the international wheat market. For a small exporter, the diagram's assumption is valid. For a larger exporter, like the United States or Canada, however, dumping more surplus grain into the world market is likely to push down the world price of wheat. Pushing down the world price means a further social loss for the United States not shown in Figure 13.5. It also means a bargain for countries importing wheat at the world price. Governments with wheat price-support programs find themselves scrambling to export and minimize their growing budgetary and social costs, while the main beneficiaries of lower world prices (and some export subsidies) are such wheat-importing areas as the Soviet Union, Egypt, the OPEC countries, west Africa, and industrial east Asia.

Similar, but more dramatic, effects have occurred in recent experience with what could be called *switch-over* goods—goods that countries convert from importables to exportables by offering very generous subsidies to domestic producers. Wheat itself is a switch-over good in the case of the EC: as mentioned at the start of this chapter, its traditional importance as an import has been replaced since the 1970s by EC wheat exports.

An outstanding case of a switch-over good is that of butter (and other dairy products) in the EC.[6] The effects are similar to those of the U.S. wheat support program, but with a little more complexity because of the switch from excess domestic demand to excess supply. Figure 13.6 sketches how the EC support for butter prices has worked.

---

[6] Butter policy is only one part of the EC's "Common Agricultural Policy" (CAP). The CAP covers a broad range of agricultural products, and involves these main policy dimensions:

1. A straightforward customs union for some agricultural products, like the EC.
2. Price-support programs for dairy products, sugar, poultry, other meats, wheat, and wine, like the butter program illustrated in Figure 13.6.
3. A controversial and potentially unstable formula for distributing the net tax burdens of the CAP across member nations.

FIGURE 13.6   Price Supports for Butter in the Common Market

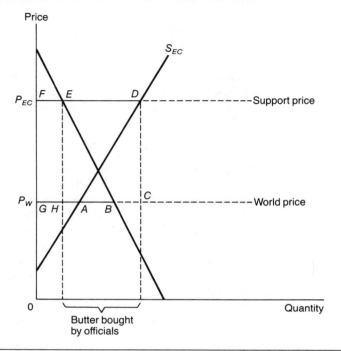

Official EC price supports for butter have been generous enough to move the region beyond self-sufficiency into the net exporting range. Officials buy up surplus butter *(ED)* at the high price P_{EC}, and resell it outside the EC so that it cannot be available to EC buyers. The welfare effects:

EC butter consumers lose area *BEFG*.
EC butter producers gain area *ADFG*.
EC taxpayers lose *CDEH* on the resale of butter.
 Total effect:
EC as a whole loses the overlapping triangles *ACD* and *BEH*.

If exporting the surplus lowers the world price (not shown here) the EC loses more and foreign buyers gain.

With free trade and no supports, Western European dairy farmers would compete with butter imported from New Zealand and elsewhere at the low world price *PW*. Imports would equal *AB*. To give farmers the higher price *PEC*, the member governments pool tax funds to buy up the surplus butter represented by *ED*. The support price has been so far above the world price (sometimes twice it, sometimes four times it) that farmers have raised their butter production enormously, converting the EC into a heavy net exporter of butter, as shown here.

The welfare effects of EC butter supports resemble those of U.S. wheat supports. EC dairy farmers have prospered, gaining extra producer surplus (area *ADFG* in Figure 13.6). EC butter consumers have paid a large part of the bill in lost bargains (area *BEFG*). Taxpayers lose (area *CDEH*) when butter bought at the high EC price is exported at the low world price.

Again, as with wheat, foreign customers stand to gain a great deal from the special bargain in butter. Now that the EC has become the world's largest butter exporter, their venting of surpluses is likely to bid down the world price. This brings gains to butter importers, the largest of which is the Soviet Union, while forcing the EC taxpayers to take an even bigger loss.

Because it is international, the EC's farm-support system has an extra problem beyond those that plague the support programs of the United States or Canada. Which countries will pay the taxes (to cover the lost *CDEH*)? A large part of the heavy tax burden is raised through duties on agricultural imports from outside the EC. Part is proportioned to sales of all products through a uniform value-added tax. The tax burden does *not* end up being nicely proportional to farmers' benefits from country to country. France, with about a quarter of EC output, is the main net gainer from the farm-support programs, which give its farmers more than it pays in extra taxes and higher farm-product prices to consumers. Britain has often been the biggest loser, since it has only a tiny farm population and must pay the EC duty on its continuing heavy imports of non-EC food. This sort of international redistribution has generated frictions beyond those felt in the usual intranational agricultural policy debates.[7]

---

[7] A final complication of EC farm supports relates to changes in exchange rates. It is a technical point, and only secondary to the purposes of this chapter. But it has posed a policy nightmare for the EC and deserves the following summary: Since the late 1960s, exchange rates between currencies have fluctuated widely in response to differences in national rates of inflation and to such shocks as the OPEC oil price hikes. If EC governments had simply let the same changes affect farm products along with other products, there would be nothing more to say here. But they did not. Instead, nervous governments tried to shield agricultural prices in their countries from the changes in overall exchange rates. By luck, the nightmare of having price unity dissolved and new tax burdens raised by the whim of exchange rates has recently abated because EC exchange rates have moved nearly in unison. But the technical problem of exchange rates and the Common Agricultural Policy remains unsolved.

Agricultural Import Barriers

The other main type of agricultural policy intervention in the developed countries is import restriction, through tariffs and quotas.[8] The policies in question are of the familiar types introduced back in Chapters 6–8. Here we need only a brief description of their qualitative effects on trade and welfare.

The developed countries tend to rely on ordinary import barriers most heavily in the agricultural products they import largely from the developing countries of the Third World. A classic case is sugar for which heavy duties must be paid to get it into the United States, Japan, or the EC. Sugar protection became increasingly tight during the 1970s and early 1980s. Some exporting countries were shut out more than others. Australia, Brazil, Jamaica, and Mauritius were excluded and forced to sell their sugar at the low world market price, while former colonies and current proteges (e.g., Philippines sugar to the United States, Cuban sugar to Soviet Union) retained generous quota allotments on favorable terms.

An advanced nation that relies more heavily on import barriers and less heavily on direct farm-support payments is Japan. Japan protects its farmers

---

[8] Less needs to be said about another developed-country agricultural policy, namely, acreage and output restriction, as in the U.S. acreage-retirement program, in which farmers are paid by the taxpayers (through the federal government) to avoid planting certain crops on acreage that they had used to grow these crops in previous years.

The welfare effects of such a system are not hard to figure out. For the world as a whole, the acreage-retirement system, or any other system that artificially cuts output, brings a net loss. If the world produces less, it has less to consume. For the single nation, it is conceivable that paying farmers not to plant some crop could bring net gains. That could happen if the country is a large exporter of a product with inelastic world demand. It is conceivable that the United States, as a giant exporter of wheat and soybeans, could get foreigners to pay implicitly for part of its acreage-retirement program by having the cut in U.S. export supply raise the world price. That a large exporting country could gain from an output-cutting government program may seem odd, but it is really just another application of Chapter 7's optimal tariff argument (here seen from the export side). It is also the reverse of the immiserizing-growth argument of Chapter 4: if the country is a large exporter and can be immiserized by expanding its export supply, it can gain by cutting that export supply. It is at least conceivable that these gains could outweigh the cost of the acreage-retirement program.

Still, the acreage-retirement program and other devices for cutting output pose enough problems to make the output-cutting approach relatively unpopular. Aside from harming the world as a whole, cutting acreage and output is inconsistent with other farm policies. The output and trade effects of the acreage restriction are counteracted by the supply encouragement of any price supports. Furthermore, the same governments that restrict acreage adopt other policies, such as payments for agricultural research or local laws to keep urbanization from encroaching on farm land, that are clearly designed to raise farm output. Is the idea to raise or to lower output? If it is to lower output but make farms more efficient so that they use up less and less labor and other inputs, what of the goal of keeping a large share of the labor force on family farms? It is also hard to reconcile paying farmers not to plant with the desire to provide food relief to famine victims.

A Japanese superman wards off an invasion of his American counterpart, in the form of insidiously cheap beef, fruit, and rice. Should he?

against imports of beef, rice, sugar, and wheat. It also keeps tight limits on imports of fresh fruit. The foreign countries most aggrieved by these barriers are the United States (beef, fruit, rice), Thailand (rice), and the sugar exporters.

The United States has protested indignantly that Japan's import barriers are inconsistent with its expectations of freedom of export to the United States. They *are* inconsistent, and they bring clear welfare losses of the sort measured in Chapters 6–8. It should be noted, however, that if Japan were to reform and remove its import barriers, it would be able to compete *more* effectively as an exporter to the United States. Extra imports into Japan would lower the value of the yen and cause Japan to specialize even more in exporting autos, steel, and electronic products to the United States and other countries. It is unlikely, however, that Japan would substantially remove its agricultural import barriers. The ruling Liberal Democratic Party, faced with declining electoral pluralities, has been more and more dependent on the small but vehement farm voter lobby.

THE EFFECTS OF AGRICULTURAL POLICIES IN DEVELOPING COUNTRIES

The developing countries have an equally varied arsenal of agricultural policies that affect international trade. As we saw in Figure 13.4, they tend to tax the agricultural sector yet do not do so consistently. They also tend to discourage foreign agricultural trade, though again with exceptions. Agricultural policy tends to include miscellaneous, and sometimes inconsistent, elements of protection and taxation. Here we focus on two examples that typify the main policy lines. Each discourages trade, but in a way that also makes both producer and consumer prices depart from world prices.

Taxing Exportables: The Case of Egyptian Cotton

The governments of developing countries are often empowered to intervene in all marketplaces, sometimes in the name of rational central planning, sometimes in the name of pushing industrialization, and sometimes just to get tax revenues for general public expenditure programs. In Egypt, for example, the government regulates most prices and rations a wide range of goods. Cotton is one good which Egypt taxes heavily: cotton farmers get only about 44 percent of the world price for their crop. Cotton farming also fits the description common to many taxed sectors in the Third World: export-oriented, rural, and labor-intensive.

Figure 13.7 traces the effect of Egyptian cotton controls in two stages: first, a simplified view of cotton controls as a pure production tax imposed by a government monopoly, and, second, a view closer to Egyptian reality.

A pure production tax on an exportable product would have effects like those shown in the upper half of Figure 13.7. The state cotton marketing monopoly lowers the price that private Egyptian cotton farmers receive, from P_{world} down to P_{prod}. Cotton production is reduced as farmers shift some resources to other pursuits or to leisure. The state, receiving the cotton crop at the set price P_{prod}, resells it at the world price, making a profit (areas $a + b + c$). Domestic textile mills and consumers of cotton textiles are unaffected because it is assumed that the government will sell cotton to the mills at the same world price the mills would have paid anyway. Therefore, all of the drop in farmers' output becomes a drop in exports of cotton. If Egyptian exports were a large share of the world market, the cotton controls might raise the world price of cotton. But Egypt probably

FIGURE 13.7 Taxing Producers of an Exportable: The Case of Egyptian Cotton

A. If the government just imposed a uniform tax, by buying all cotton at the controlled producer price P_{prod} and reselling it at the world price:

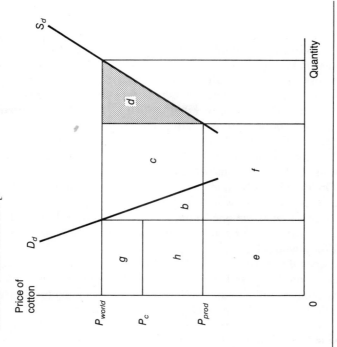

Effects in This Case:

On prices and quantities:
Officials decree a lower domestic producer price. Less cotton would be grown and exported, but domestic consumption would stay the same.

On welfare:
Consumers are unaffected.
Producers lose $a + b + c + d$.
Government buys all cotton for $e + f$ and resells it for $e + f + a + b + c$, gaining $a + b + c$.
Total effect: Nation as a whole loses d.

B. More accurately, the government gives the same low controlled price to producers, but resells a rationed part of the output to domestic textile mills at P_c:

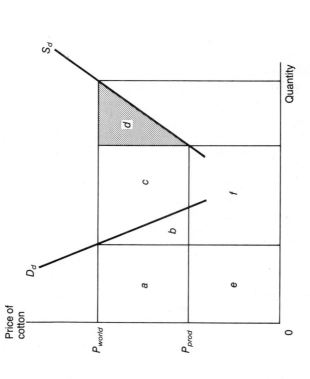

Effects in This Case:

On prices and quantities:
Again, a lower producer price is decreed. Now, in addition, domestic mills are sold cotton at P_c. All quantities stay the same as above.

On welfare:
Egyptian mills gain g.
Egyptian growers lose $g + h + b + c + d$.
Egyptian government gains $h + b + c$.
Total effect: Egypt as a whole loses d.

does not loom large enough on the world market to have much effect on the world price.

Egyptian practice is actually more complex than Figure 13.7A. The extra complexity of greatest importance here is that the government rations cotton among textile mills. As shown in Figure 13.7B, mills are allowed to buy an amount of cotton approximating what they would want to buy at the world price. They are sold cotton, however, at a concessionary price P_c, which is below the world price. Thus, the government, for its own reasons, gives some of the tax it makes from cotton farmers as a transfer to textile mills. On domestically sold cotton, the government gets only the profit represented by area h, while textile enterprises get area g thanks to the lower price of their rationed cotton. Yet, the price break offered to the mills cannot affect their total cotton purchases, which are rationed in the amount they would have bought anyway.

What does this regime do for Egyptian welfare? In terms of our standard analysis of producer and consumer gains, it brings a net national loss, equal to area d. This is the welfare loss from not exporting extra cotton that would have cost Egypt less than it would have been paid for the cotton on the world market. What other redeeming features does such a system have to offset this loss? None is immediately evident. There is no clear social gain in redistributing income from cotton farmers to the government and textile mills. Nor is the infant-government argument applicable to a government sector that has long been large, now spending a quarter of the national product, without counting transfer payments. Yet, as we have seen earlier in this chapter, the tendency to tax production of exportable agricultural products is prevalent among developing countries.

Policies toward Agricultural Imports

Developing countries have groped for uneasy compromises regarding their agricultural imports, most of which are staple foods. On the one hand they would like to have them be cheaply available for mass consumption. Yet, the instinct to tax imports and protect producers is also strong. What often emerges is a policy pattern that subsidizes consumption of staple importable foods but might give producers a price either above or below the world price.

One such case is the controlled market for Egyptian wheat, where the government gives consumers a generous wheat subsidy, taxes producers slightly, and accepts some U.S. food aid. Let's look at two different views of this market, starting from an oversimplified view of the effects of the consumer subsidy alone and proceeding to a more complicated picture by adding the producer subsidy.[9]

---

[9] In what follows I abstract from two complications of the Egyptian market that are discussed elsewhere (McCalla and Josling, 1985, Chapter 8). One is that Egypt imports a significant

Egypt's wheat policy is dominated by the desire to make flour cheap for Egypt's retail shops and consumers. The government uses taxpayers' money to buy wheat at a higher price and resells it at a lower price, as shown in Figure 13.8A. In this way its policy resembles the U.S. government's wheat surplus disposal program (see Figure 13.5). One difference is that although the U.S. government bought wheat from domestic farmers and resold to other countries, the Egyptian government buys from both domestic and foreign wheat suppliers and resells within Egypt. Figure 13.8A shows the effects of this consumption subsidy, assuming temporarily that the government does not intervene in any other way. The government of Egypt, as the decreed intermediary between buyers and sellers of wheat, stands ready to meet the total domestic demand for wheat at the subsidized price P_c. This involves more imports (M_1) than the country would have imported without the subsidy (M_0). The government gets the wheat it needs by paying foreign and domestic suppliers the world price P_W (see Figure 13.8). It gives up taxpayer money to cover the loss from buying high and selling low (the loss equal to area $a + b + c + d$). Consumers get a break on the cost of living, gaining area $a + b + c$ in extra consumers' surplus. Egypt's wheat farmers remain unaffected as long as the government pays them the world price.

But the government does not actually pay wheat farmers the world price. Instead, they must deliver grain to the government at the controlled price P_P.[10] At this price they are not inclined to plant and sell as much as they would at the higher world price. They cut back production, and the extra wheat demand must be met by expanding imports further (importing M_2 instead of M_1).

What does Egypt get from the combination of controls it applies to the wheat market? The conventional analysis, summarized in Figure 13.8B, points to two kinds of social loss: importing at the world price some grain that could have been produced for less (yielding the net loss of area g) and consuming extra wheat that is worth less to the consumer than the world price at which the country purchased it (area d). What redeeming

---

share of its wheat from the United States under the generous terms of U.S. Public Law 480 (PL480). PL480 allows Egypt to pay for these special imports at a price that is below the subsidized consumer price P_c in Figure 13.8. Implicitly, Figure 13.8 shows a demand curve D_d that has already subtracted out (been shifted to the left by) the imports of wheat under PL480.

The other complication suppressed here is the interaction of production incentives and of consumption incentives in different products all subject to government intervention. One might want to ask how intervention in one market complicates the effects of intervention in related markets. For example, how does the tax on production of cotton (Figure 13.7) affect farmers' decisions about, and costs of, raising wheat (in Figure 13.8)? These complications should be addressed in a detailed study, but are set aside here.

[10] Wheat cannot be exported at the world price without government approval. Also, the government will buy wheat from farmers at the price P_P only up to certain assigned quota amounts. Additional wheat must be sold on the domestic market at the lower price P_c.

FIGURE 13.8 Controlling an Importable-Good Market: The Case of Egyptian Wheat

A. A consumption subsidy alone:

B. The consumption subsidy plus a smaller producer tax:

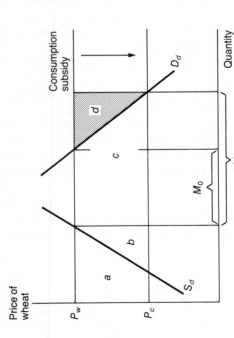

Effects in this case:

Relative to free trade at the world price, the government subsidy lowers the consumer price P_c. Consumers buy more, buying extra wheat imports

Consumers gain $a + b + c$

Government loses $a + b + c + d$

Total effect: Nation as a whole loses d

Effects in this case:

Things look the same to consumers. But producers are now forced to accept a price P_P below the world price. They produce less, channeling more demand into imports. Relative to free trade at the world price:

Consumers gain $a + b + c = e + f + g + b + c$

Producers now lose $f + g$

Government still pays consumption subsidy, but collects area f from producers, so it pays only $e + b + c + d + g$

Total effect: Nation as a whole loses $d + g$

features offset these losses? Again, there is no obvious answer. One might argue that a developing country should indeed redistribute income from taxpayers toward consumers of staple food, who tend to be poor. But this egalitarian thrust is seriously blunted by the incidence of Egypt's taxation. Much of Egypt's tax revenue comes from taxes borne by farmers who grow wheat (Figure 13.8), cotton (Figure 13.7), or other crops. Given that past land reform has already raised the share of land owned by the tillers, it seems that the agricultural tax base consists largely of people of ordinary or low income. Taxing these people to subsidize food does not bring a strongly egalitarian redistribution.

The Food Security Issue

Governments need some sort of policy toward food supply in order to minimize the threat of malnutrition and famine during times of poor harvests. Some try to encourage domestic food supply with barriers against food imports. Food security concerns are also voiced in some industrial countries, especially Japan and Switzerland, two nations scarred by memories of shortages during World War II.

What are the pros and cons of different ways of trying to assure the best possible food supply? Should countries strive for self-sufficiency, meaning no net food imports? Do they do so in practice? It turns out that raising domestic food supplies up to self-sufficiency is not the revealed preference of most governments, even among those paying lip service to that ideal. Third World governments tax domestic food producers more often than not, and industrial-country governments subsidize domestic producers to degrees that do not fit the self-sufficiency goal. It turns out that the goal of food security does not really call for import protection in the first place.

In actual practice, few developing countries protect their domestic food suppliers, despite the intellectual popularity of the self-sufficiency goal. Food production, like domestic agriculture in general, tends more often to be taxed and discouraged. Drawing on the results of studies that produced the estimates of nominal protection coefficients (NPCs) in Figure 13.4, we can put several developing countries into three categories relating to the price signals that government policy sends out to farmers and peasants about growing staple food grains like wheat, rice, and maize:

Protect Domestic Growers (NPC > 1.2)		*Neutral or Mixed Incentives (0.8 < NPC < 1.2)*		*Tax Domestic Growers (NPC < 0.8)*	
Kenya	Korea	Colombia	Mexico	Argentina	Bangladesh
Malawi	Nigeria	Côte d'Ivoire	Sudan	Brazil	Cameroon
		Tunisia	Turkey	Egypt	Ghana
		Yemen		India	Pakistan
				Philippines	Portugal
				Senegal	Tanzania
				Yugoslavia	Zambia

Thus, out of 25 cases of individual food crops for which NPCs were measured around 1980, only the four on the left received genuine protection from government. Seven others were nearly neutral, and governments strongly taxed food producers in fourteen cases.

Among the industrialized countries, food security also fails to explain the degree and pattern of agricultural protection we observe. Take the case of rice in Japan, supposedly the focus of food-security fears exacerbated by World War II. Since 1968, the government of Japan has been disposing of surplus rice beyond what the nation wants to stockpile for emergency reserves. Japan has even become a net *exporter* of rice since 1977. In addition, the government has been paying farmers to take land *out* of rice production since 1969, especially in 1971–1973, around 1980, and again since 1987. Sometimes the intent has been to encourage shifts to other food crops, but sometimes the subsidy allows shifts to nonfood crops and to fallow. Nor is Japanese rice the only case of a glaring departure from food-security goals. Canada, the United States, and the EC also subsidize acreage reductions and exports on food crops. EC dairy products, as we have seen, were converted from importables to exportables by generous producer subsidies. While food-security rhetoric continues, it is cheap. The types and levels of farm subsidies among the high-income countries reveal that farm income support, not food security, is the driving motive.

There are good economic reasons to doubt that import protection is the right road to food security. Food security does not call for protecting growers. What it calls for is maximizing crisis supply at the lowest cost. The right form of food insurance depends on the type of crisis that is most likely. The four main possibilities are:

1. Temporary bad harvests,
2. Prolonged bad harvests (e.g., Sahelian drought),
3. Temporary siege or embargo by a hostile power, and
4. Prolonged siege or embargo by a hostile power.

The first two cases are ones in which growing food yields low returns. Whatever causes the bad harvests is also likely to make subsidies to growers look particularly unpromising relative to the obvious option of stockpiling food at noncrisis prices. While the biblical advice of Joseph to the pharoah is as valuable as ever, protection against imports does little to offset bad harvests. If the concern is hostile interruption of food supplies from other countries, the prescription depends on the likely length of the interruption. If the interruption is not likely to extend beyond the next full crop season or animal-breeding cycle (as in case 1), what the nation must have ready is a stockpile of food, not a stockpile of farmers. Protecting farmers during noncrisis is a food-security policy only for the contingency of a prolonged interruption of import supply (case 4). This case seems least likely for the high-income countries that are doing the protecting. It also requires a strained argument about supply dynamics, claiming that only years of noncrisis subsidy can build up a food-growing capacity to be mobilized in the crisis, and years of stockpile management cannot do the job. While the economics of food-supply insurance says that protecting growers against imports could be better than doing nothing in some cases, it is almost never the best food security policy.

THE EVOLVING EFFECTS OF AGRICULTURAL POLICIES

The analysis above can be used to shape conjectures about how agricultural policies and their effects on trade and welfare are likely to evolve. The key word here is "conjectures": economic forecasts are always subject to wide margins of error, and those that follow are not as solidly based as many other forecasts.

The first guideline in any forecast of agricultural policies is to avoid predicting any rapid changes. Inertia rules supreme. In developed countries, the farm lobby retains power far beyond its share of the population and has had little trouble outmaneuvering its critics. In developing countries, existing policies (import duties, producer taxes, etc.) are built into the government budgetary structure. If things change, the wisest prediction is that they will do so at a slow average pace. Crises and showdowns are likely to be few and far between.

Yet, things are likely to change, for better and worse. First, examination of how the social costs of agricultural policies vary from country to country suggests how these costs might change over time. Figure 13.9 presents some reasons for suspecting that the net social damage from agricultural policies might drop over time. Note first that the costs as a share of agricultural product (the middle columns) drop as one moves from developing countries up to the most developed, suggesting that the percentages of price distortion are smaller for the most advanced countries than they are for developing countries. As more and more countries develop, the costs as a share of agricultural product may gradually decline as developing countries move away from taxing agriculture so heavily.

Next, recall that agriculture's share of the national economy also declines as a country develops, partly because of Engel's Law. Thus, any given percentage of agricultural product represents a lower and lower percentage of overall GNP. Even if government price distortions remained more serious for agriculture than for other products, the cost as a share of GNP will go on declining as countries develop and move away from agriculture.

On the other hand, the development of today's Third World countries may have trade effects that exacerbate the costs of the agricultural policies of the most advanced countries. As more and more countries develop, they are likely to shift from taxing agricultural production to protecting it against import competition, as observed in both the international cross-section and the course of history in North America and Japan. This gradual policy

FIGURE 13.9   Social Welfare Losses from Selected Agricultural Policies, Nine Countries in the Mid-1970s

| | Social Losses (e.g., the inefficiency triangles in Figures 13.5–13.8) | | |
| | Percent of Overall GNP | Percent of Agricultural GNP | Share of Agriculture in GNP |
Country	Low–High	Low–High	(percent)
France	0.05– 0.16	1.0– 3.2	5
Germany	0.06– 0.19	2.0– 6.3	3
United Kingdom	0.01– 0.04	0.3– 1.3	3
Japan	0.43– 0.80	8.6–16.0	5
Yugoslavia	0.34– 1.03	2.1– 6.4	16
Argentina	0.48– 1.46	3.7–11.2	13
Egypt	3.52–10.58	12.6–37.8	28
Pakistan	1.01– 3.04	3.1– 9.2	33
Thailand	0.21– 0.62	0.8– 2.3	27

Source: Bale and Lutz (1981, table 4).

shift will release more production onto the open world market, through decontrol of exportable production, through the rise of price-support programs, and through new barriers to imports. The terms of trade may shift against certain agricultural products, especially the staple grains, for which Engel's Law, rising incomes, and slowing world population growth could combine to depress prices even without such a policy drift. The lower the world market price of staple grains, the lower the price that developed-country governments can get for their dumped grain surpluses and the more burdensome the support programs become to taxpayers.

There is no way of predicting whether developed-country policy will crack under the growing fiscal burden. The past trend may continue: the supported-product sector may be able to win increasingly generous support as a tiny share of a prosperous economy. Yet, there may come a point, with rising program costs and a dwindling farm population, when the farm lobby simply becomes too small to retain its political clout. If that happens, developed-country farm supports could be dismantled in North America and Europe. A showdown over support payments is most likely in the EC, where separate nations are involved, making the burdened groups (e.g., Britain) more impatient with perennial transfers to others (e.g., French farmers). A showdown seems less likely in Japan, whose agriculture is more import-competing, leaving it the option of protecting it without causing a net revenue drain for the government. As long as Japan can resist American pressure for agricultural-import reform, and as long as the Liberal Democratic Party is not swept out of office, Japanese farmers will continue to be protected.

SUMMARY

Three tasks are undertaken in this chapter: a partial explanation of some economywide patterns in trade barriers, a partial explanation of patterns in agricultural policy, and comments on the effects of agricultural policies on trade and welfare.

The political economy of trade barriers explains them (partially) in terms of an individual's costs and benefits from participating in a political fight over trade policy. The individual's decision about a trade policy depends on four main factors: (1) the inefficiency, or national loss, it brings; (2) the size of the group the individual would ally with; (3) how much sympathy the group gets from others, who would not directly benefit from its proposed trade policy; and (4) how much representation the group is given by electoral and governmental institutions. A campaign for, say, import protection is hurt by greater inefficiency (deadweight loss) from the protection. It is helped by having the benefits of protection concentrated into a small group. This is because the free rider problem is more easily solved in a small group, and because greater benefits per person heighten individual commitments to the cause. The same protectionist campaign is helped in recent reverses for the group to generate sympathy among the rest of the population. Finally, it is advantageous to have your economic group spread among as many electoral districts as is consistent with your group's being well represented in each. Considerations such as these, especially the group-size argument, also help to explain other patterns, such as the tariff escalation pattern.

The long-run trend in overall import barriers might be downward, that is, toward freer trade.

The long-run trend in agricultural policy, however, is very different. The **developmental pattern** of agricultural policy is that as a nation becomes more developed, its policy switches from heavily taxing agriculture to heavily subsidizing it. There is also an **antitrade pattern**: governments tend to tax exportable-good agriculture and to subsidize (protect) importable-good agriculture. The two patterns together mean that the greatest departures of agricultural policy from laissez-faire and free trade are the taxing of exportable-good agriculture in the Third World and the protection of importable-good agriculture in industrialized countries.

The agricultural policy patterns have yet to be explained systematically. Two partial explanations for the developmental pattern are that (1) the shrinkage of the agricultural sector raises its lobbying efficiency and the sympathy of the nonagricultural population and (2) the agricultural lobby is increasingly mobilized by its rising sensitivity to price movements, movements which government could control. A partial explanation for the antitrade pattern is that it serves the government's own demand for extra revenue. Taxing trade can generate revenues, either when imports are taxed (protecting domestic farmers), or when exports are taxed (hurting domestic farmers). In such cases officials can ally, either explicitly or implicitly, with private interests in favor of restricting trade.

Developed countries practice a wide variety of farm support policies. Their only common denominators are that they (1) raise farm incomes, (2) harm consumers of agricultural products, and (3) involve significant net social costs. Some encourage extra output, while others cut it. Some cost the government revenue, and some raise revenue. Most tend to raise the agricultural trade balance, though one (acreage restrictions) worsens it.

Developing countries in the Third World also have varied agricultural policies. They tend to tax agriculture and foreign trade, and they especially tax the two together (exportable agricultural products). Typically, policy is complicated by the desire to keep both producer prices and consumer prices separate from each other and from international trade. The Egyptian cotton and wheat programs illustrate the effects of some typical policies on trade and welfare.

The goal of providing food security against future harvest failures or hostilities is not well served either by existing policies in developing countries or by the protectionist goal of enforced self-sufficiency. In the spirit of Chapter 7's specificity rule, the key element in assuring food security is stockpiling for emergencies. Yet, this is given little attention in official policies, relative to the elaborate controls erected to tax agriculture. The opposite pricing policy of protecting domestic agriculture also offers little security in emergencies. It is inferior to stockpiling imported food supplies in the face of threats of harvest failure or short-term hostilities. Only in the case of hostilities that would last more years than a nation's storage capacity (but fewer years than it takes to shift people and resources back into a previously unprotected agriculture) would protection against imported food be the preferred policy tool. This is a relatively unlikely case.

SUGGESTED READINGS

Two pioneering theories of political behavior and lobbying biases are Anthony Downs (1957) and Mancur Olson (1965). Downs deals with tariff examples at some length. Albert Breton (1974) offers similar theories with applications to Canada. Magee, Brock, and Young (1989) take us on an imaginative and sometimes technical tour of political-economic models that might describe the shaping of trade policy.

The vast empirical literature testing many hypotheses about trade-policy pressure groups includes:

On Canadian protection: Caves (1976), Helleiner (1977), Saunders (1980), and Cline (1984);

On U.S. protection: Cheh (1974), Pincus (1975), Ray (1981), Lavergne (1983), Baldwin and Krueger (1984), Cline (1984), and Ray and Marvel (1984);

On other countries: Baldwin (1984), Cline (1984, Appendix C), and Ray and Marvel (1984).

Comparative international perspective on agricultural policies is offered by Bale and Lutz (1981), the World Bank's *World Development Report* for 1982 and 1986, Anderson and Hayami (1986), Tyers and Anderson (forthcoming), Lindert (forthcoming), and Krueger, Schiff and Valdés (forthcoming).

Excellent economic analyses of the effects of agricultural policies on international trade are McCalla and Josling (1985) and Gardner (1988).

Guides to the complexities of the EC's Common Agricultural Policy are Bowler (1985) and Moyer and Josling (1990, Chs. 2–4, 9). A shorter overview is Peterson and Lyons (1989).

QUESTIONS FOR REVIEW

1. What are the main reasons for the political success of trade barriers that bring net national losses?

2. What is the "free rider problem," and how does it affect trade policy?

3. Define and explain the tariff "escalation" pattern.

4. What are the major international exports and imports of your home district or province or state? (Local banks, chambers of commerce, and governments often publish brochures on this subject.) Where do your elected representatives stand on national trade policy issues?

5. What is the nominal protection coefficient (NPC)? What does it measure, and what dimension of agricultural policy does it omit?

6. Do the agricultural price and tax policies of the Brazilian government give better income support to coffee farmers or to growers of maize? Why? Which would one expect Jamaican policy to favor—the incomes of maize growers or those of sugar growers?

7. Suppost that Nigeria wants to give wheat and rice farmers higher prices than the world prices, yet wants to make wheat and rice cost domestic millers of flour less than the world price, to keep down the cost of living to consumers.

a. Describe a policy or set of policies that could do this.

b. [More difficult.] Try diagramming a grain market subject to such a policy or policies and determining its (their) welfare costs.

Understanding Foreign Exchange

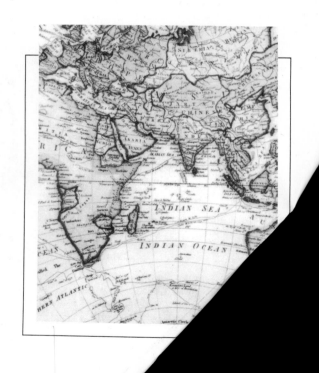

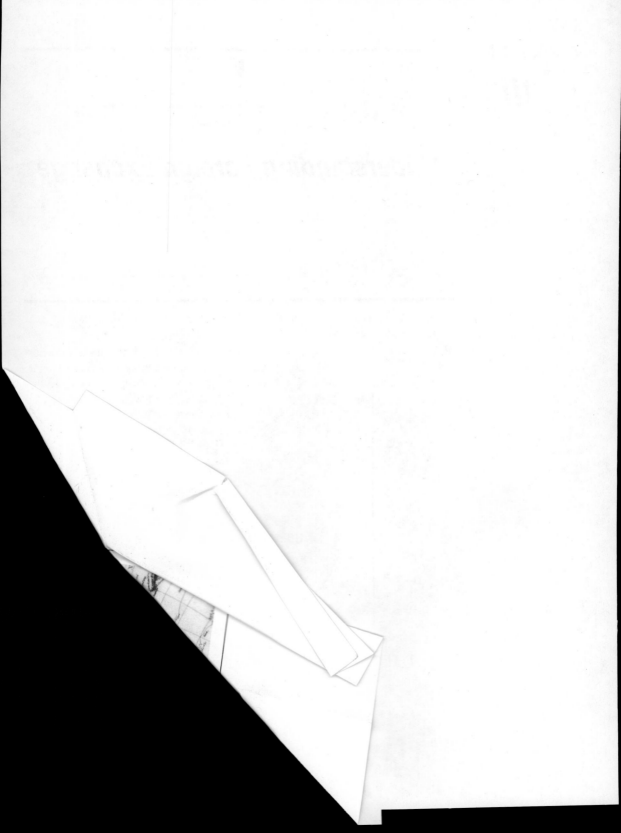

▼

Payments among Nations

•

The bridge that links all the separate parts of international economics is the **balance of payments,** the set of accounts recording all flows of value between a nation's residents and the rest of the world. Until one is familiar with the balance of payments, it is hard to see what the U.S. government's borrowing abroad has to do with the decision to buy a Sharp hand calculator in a department store, how repaying that foreign debt relates to our sales of aircraft, or how trade events like the purchase of the calculator or the sale of the aircraft could affect the nation's money supply and interest rates. Understanding the balance of payments is also key to understanding how people trade one country's money for that of another country. Even the international flow of humans shows up in the balance of payments, when the migrants make purchases or send money back home. Fortunately, for all the diverse traffic over that bridge, its design is easy to understand. We now cross it to widen our view from trade alone to all the exchanges of values between nations and between currencies, with their many links to macroeconomic concerns like growth, inflation, and unemployment.

TWO SIDES TO ANY INTERNATIONAL EXCHANGE

Any exchange between a country and the rest of the world involves two flows of value to be recorded in the balance-of-payments accounts. From that country's point of view each exchange, each transaction, involves two opposite flows of equal value:

A **credit** (+) is a flow for which the country is paid. Exports are an example.

A **debit** (−) is a flow for which the country must pay. Imports are an example.

Any exchange automatically enters the balance of payments accounts twice, as a credit (+) and as a debit (−) of the same value. This is just an international application of the fundamental accounting principle of double-entry bookkeeping, which is taught in the first week of any accounting course.

To build a set of accounts showing useful summary information, accountants distinguish between different categories of flows and put the two flows for each transaction into two of the different categories. The main kinds of flows in the balance-of-payments accounts are:

Merchandise trade flows (flows of goods).

Service flows.

Unilateral transfers (gifts).

Private capital (asset) flows.

Official asset flows.

To show how international transactions affect these five useful categories, let us imagine a set of just five illustrative transactions between the United States and the rest of the world in a short time period.

First, suppose that the United States government sells $29 billion worth of wheat to the Soviet Union from its surplus stockpiles, being paid with $29 billion in gold by the Soviet government. There is an outflow of $29 billion worth of wheat, an export of merchandise, for which the United States must be paid. The offsetting inflow is the payment itself, in this case $29 billion in gold to the U.S. government. The wheat-for-gold transaction creates these two bookkeeping entries (in billions of dollars):

	Credit (+) ($ billion)	Debit (−) ($ billion)
Merchandise exports (wheat)	$29	
Increase in official assets (gold)		$29

Note that the payment of gold is a debit item, an inflow of value. It qualifies as a debit because it is something for which the United States must give up something else, namely wheat.[1]

Consider a second international transaction also involving merchandise trade: Northern Illinois Gas, a U.S. utility company, buys $34 billion in

---

[1] In every case, the credit and debit entries have the opposite signs in the accounts of the other country. In the Soviet Union's balance of payments, this transaction entails a credit of $29 billion for gold exports and a debit of $29 for wheat imports.

Note that gold is viewed as an official asset, but wheat is not, even though it might have been held by government officials. The term *official assets* here refers more strictly to official money-like assets, an attribute possessed by gold but not wheat.

natural gas from a Canadian firm. Suppose that it pays for the natural gas by writing a check on its deposits in a New York bank. Two accounting entries are made regarding the U.S. accounts:

	Credit (+) ($ billion)	Debit (−) $ billion)
Merchandise imports (natural gas)		$34
Private capital inflow (bank's deposit liability to a foreign resident)	$34	

The debit entry probably seems easier and more natural than the credit entry in this case. It is clear that importing natural gas is an inflow of something valuable, for which the United States must pay. But why should the payment be recorded as a "private capital inflow"? Because the writing of the check placed a bank liability (obligation to pay) into the hands of foreign residents. Before the purchase, the bank owed that bank deposit to Northern Illinois Gas, a resident of the United States. That was a purely domestic matter, not involving the balance of international payments. Once the gas is paid for, however, the New York bank owes an obligation—the right to redeem the checking deposit for cash—to a resident of Canada. This means that the New York bank is borrowing (incurring a new obligation to repay in the future) from Canada. When you borrow, you gain the right to be paid now. In this key respect, borrowing is like an export of goods. It entitles you to be paid now. It is a credit item.

The rule regarding capital flows is this:

Capital inflows are credits (+). They take the form of either an increase in a nation's liabilities to foreign residents or a decrease in assets held in other countries. Each of these is a flow for which the nation must be given payment right now, so each is a credit entry.

Capital outflows are debits (−). They take the form of either an increase in a nation's assets in other countries or a decrease in its liabilities to other countries. Each of these is a flow for which the nation must give up payment right now, so each is a debit entry.

Capital outflows arise in some of the examples to which we now turn.

Next, imagine that Brazilian soccer fans spend $16 billion as tourists in the United States during a soccer tournament in 1994, paying for their hotels, meals, and transportation through New York bank deposits. The two flows are entered in the U.S. accounts as:

	Credits (+) ($ billion)	Debits (−) ($ billion)
Service exports (travel)	$16	
Private capital outflow (reduction in bank's obligations to foreign residents)		$16

Again, one entry fits intuition more easily than the other, even though both are correctly recorded here. It is easy to see that the sales of tourist services to Brazilians are a U.S. export, a value given up, for which the United States must be paid. And if that is clearly a credit item, it makes sense that the other entry must be a debit item. But why would it be labeled a "private capital outflow"? The answer is because reducing your liability to foreigners is like buying a claim on them, the usual sense of the phrase *capital outflow*. It is a use for which you must pay right now, just like any form of lending. Both reducing your liabilities and lending (buying somebody else's IOUs) are debits.

Our fourth transaction offers a further look at the financial side of the accounts. Suppose that the United States Treasury pays $25 billion in interest on its past borrowing from Japanese investors, paying with checks on a New York bank. The two accounting entries are:

	Credit (+) ($ billion)	Debit (−) ($ billion)
Service import (interest paid for use of money)		$25
Private capital inflow (increase in bank's obligations to foreign residents)	$25	

The payment of interest represents a payment for a service, the service of using somebody else's money for a period of time. Therefore, the U.S. government is importing such lending services from Japan. It must pay for these services, so they are a debit. The means of payment is a credit. Why is this credit counted as a "private capital inflow"? The private New York bank on whom the U.S. government wrote the check now has a new liability to residents of Japan. It is borrowing anew from foreigners. The bank uses the borrowing from foreigners to cancel an equal checking-account obligation to the U.S. government, which has less claim on the private bank now that it has written checks. Such entries occur all the time, and this example is worth reviewing.

So far, we can see that every transaction has two equal sides. If we add up all the credits as pluses and all the debits as minuses, the net result is zero. That is, the total credits must always equal the total debits. That is correct. To see just how correct it is, though, let us turn to a case that might look like a violation of this accounting balance.

Our fifth hypothetical transaction involves giving away money. Suppose that the United States government simply gives $8 billion in foreign aid to the government of Egypt, in the form of wheat from the U.S. government stockpiles. This case differs from the sale of wheat to the Soviet Union (above) because Egypt is not paying, with gold or checks or anything else. The correct way to record the credit and debit flows is as follows:

	Credit (+) ($ billion)	Debit (−) ($ billion)
Merchandise export (wheat)	$8	
Unilateral transfer to Egypt		$8

The $8 billion credit is straightforward, since this is just another merchandise export, for which the United States must be paid. The accountants get around the fact that the United States was *not* paid by Egypt by inventing a debit item for the unilateral transfer (gift) to Egypt. They invent the fiction that the United States received $8 billion in good will—or gratitude—from Egypt for its gift of wheat. That good will is something received, a debit, for which the United States pays in wheat. In this way, even a one-way flow is transformed by accounting fiction into a two-way flow, preserving the overall balance of double-entry bookkeeping.

PUTTING THE ACCOUNTS TOGETHER

To arrange the credit and debit flows from separate transactions into a useful summary set of accounts, group them according to the five types of flows. Figure 14.1 does this for our simplified set of five transactions. In this set of transactions, the United States was a slight net exporter of merchandise (selling $37 billion of wheat and importing $34 billion of natural gas). It was a net importer of services, since its import of lending services from Japan (its interest payment of $25 billion to Japan) exceeded its sales of travel services to the Brazilian soccer fans. For all goods and services together, the United States was a net importer by $6 billion, which is a deficit in the **goods and services balance** of $6 billion. These had to be paid for somehow. In addition, the nation gave away $8 billion in unilateral transfers to Egypt, so there were $14 billion that had to be paid for somehow.

The net flow of currently used goods, services, and gifts is the **current account** surplus. If this is truly a positive surplus, the nation earns that much in extra assets or reduced liabilities in its dealings with other countries. If it is negative, that is a current account deficit, for which it must pay by giving up assets of increasing its liabilities. In the simple case of Figure 14.1, the United States has a current-account deficit of $14 billion. It paid for this by incurring greater debts to foreigners. In this case, its extra debts took the form of extra private-bank deposit liabilities to foreigners, worth $43 billion, minus a buildup of $29 billion in official gold reserves acquired from the Soviet Union, or net new liabilities of $14 billion covering the $14 billion deficit for goods, services, and gifts.⌉

The simple view of Figure 14.1 shows us a skeletal balance of payments with the main categories in clear view: goods flows, service flows, gifts, private capital flows, and official asset flows. Now that we understand the

FIGURE 14.1   A Simple Balance-of-Payments Account for the United States, Resulting from Only Five Transactions ($ billions)

Flows and Balances	Credits (+)	Debits (−)	Credits Minus Debits = Net Surplus (+) or Deficit (−)
Merchandise trade flows $(29 + 8 =) 37		$34	$ 3
Service flows	16	25	−9
Unilateral transfers (gifts)		8	−8
Private capital flows (25 + 34 =) 59		16	43
Official asset flows		29	−29
Grand balance of credits minus debits:			0

Five Key Balances	
Merchandise trade (goods) balance	3
Goods and services balance	−6
Current account balance (goods, services, gifts)	−14
Net private capital inflows	43
Overall balance (current account + private capital flows)	29

main categories, let us take a closer look at the varieties of entries that actually go into those categories. Figure 14.2 gives some extra detail, using the actual balance-of-payments accounts of the United States for 1988.

At the top of the accounts, there is little detail to add. Merchandise exports and imports are easy to understand. The only wrinkle is that some of them go unrecorded, due to smuggling, or negligence, or national secrecy (such as the hiding of some military sales and gifts from the United States balance of payments). Basically, though, merchandise exports and imports are straightforward. The net balance of merchandise trade (Line 26), or the "trade balance," is widely cited in the news media because it is measured promptly from customs data each month. There is no other good reason, however, for publicizing a balance of trade in goods without services.

Services take a miscellany of forms. In the simple examples above, we only considered interest payments and travel services. There are others. There are other kinds of payments for investment services besides interest, such as dividends and repatriated business profits. Nations also pay each other royalties and fees, such as managerial fees for hired management services. And to travel services like tourism we should add insurance services and transportation services, such as the hiring of a foreign shipping company to transport automobiles or oil across the ocean.

Unilateral transfers also take a variety of forms. There are official government grants in aid to foreigners, as in the simple example of a U.S. grant of wheat to Egypt. Private individuals also make unilateral transfers. Histori-

FIGURE 14.2   The Balance of Payments Account of the United States, 1988 ($ billions)

	Credit (+)	*Debit (−)*
1. **Exports of goods and services**	**$530**	
2. Merchandise exports	319	
3. Service exports (travel, investment income, etc.)	211	
4. **Imports of goods and services**		**$−641**
5. Merchandise imports		−446
6. Service imports (travel, investment income, etc.)		−195
7. **Unilateral transfers, net**		**−14**
8. U.S. government transfers to foreigners		−12
9. Private remittances by U.S. residents		−2
10. **U.S. assets abroad, net (increase/capital outflow = −)**		**−82**
11. U.S. official reserve assets, net flow		−3
12. U.S. government assets abroad, other	3	
13. U.S. private assets, net flow		−82
14. Direct investments abroad		−18
15. Foreign securities held in U.S.		−8
16. Nonbank claims on foreigners		−2
17. Bank claims on foreigners		−54
18. **Foreign assets in the U.S., net (increase/capital inflow = +)**	**219**	
19. Foreign official assets in the U.S., net flow	39	
20. Foreign private assets in the U.S., net flow	180	
21. Direct investments in the U.S.	58	
22. U.S. Treasury securities, other securities	46	
23. Foreign liabilities of private U.S. nonbanks	7	
24. Foreign liabilities of private U.S. banks	69	
24. **Statistical discrepancy**		**−12**
25. Net balance of credits − debits	0	

Five Key Balances

26. Merchandise trade balance (exports − imports: Line 1 and Line 5)	−127
27. Goods and services balance (Lines 3, 6, and 26)	−111
28. Current account balance (net foreign investment: Lines 7 and 27)	−125
29. Net private capital flows and stat. discrepancy (excl. reserves)*	89
30. Overall balance (current account + private capital)†	−36

* Lines 12, 13, 20, and 24. † Lines 28 and 29, or Lines 11 and 19.
Source: U.S. Bureau of Economic Analysis, *Survey of Current Business,* December 1989, p. 28.

cally, the largest kind of private transfer is international migrants' remittances of money and goods back to their families in the home country. Another kind of private aid is charitable giving, such as international famine relief. Some of the varieties of private capital flows call for special comment,

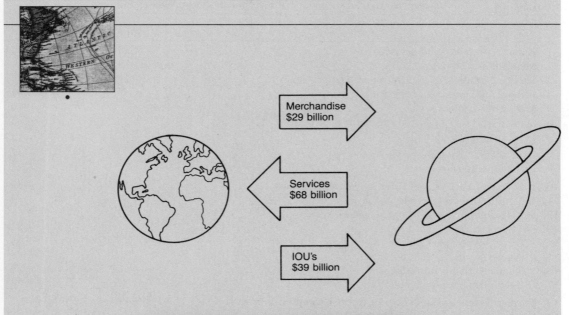

PLANET EARTH'S BALANCE OF PAYMENTS

Planet Earth has been trading heavily with the rest of the galaxy for years. Throughout the 1980s, and perhaps earlier, we have been exporting billions of dollars of goods into space. We have been importing even bigger amounts of services and good will, especially lending services, from space. To cover our current-account deficit, we have been sending out ever greater IOU's, or promises to repay somebody out there in space. In 1987, for example, we exported $29 billion in goods, imported $68 billion in services and good will, and sent out $39 billion in promises to repay. How long can this continue?

You may feel that something is wrong with the basic facts here. Yet, these flows are consistent with all the world's official balance-of-payments statistics. If you add up the trade balances and current-account balances of every country

here and in Part V. **Direct investments** are defined as any flow of lending to, or purchases of ownership in, a foreign enterprise that is largely owned by residents of the investing country. Chapter 25 offers a more detailed definition. Foreign investments that are not direct are often called "portfolio" investments, indicating that the investor's home country does not own a

CONTINUED

in 1987, you find that $29 billion of merchandise imports and $39 billion of current-account surplus are unaccounted for, implying that a net outflow of $68 billion in services and good will are also unaccounted for. How could that happen? We cannot rule out the possibility that the missing flows went to the rest of the galaxy, as suggested. A more likely explanation, however, is that there are systematic patterns of misreporting international flows right here on Earth. The $29 billion of lost imports are probably imports that went unreported because of smuggling or other incentives to underreport. (Drug traffic is probably not the reason why, since drug trade is unreported on *both* the export and the import sides.) The $68 billion in lost service exports is probably income on foreign investments, hidden to avoid taxes and regulation. Most of the $39 billion in missing current-account surpluses (capital exports) probably represents unreported "capital flight," the secret sending of wealth to foreign countries, away from the supervision of one's home government. Separate estimates suggest that unreported capital flight is particularly severe from developing nations, especially in Latin America. The underreporting of payments in Eastern Europe does not explain the world imbalances, since Eastern Europe is believed to have too little volume of trade and asset exchange to account for the billions mentioned here. Most likely, the creatures from space are government-evading citizens of all countries, especially in Latin America.

How serious are errors of this magnitude? The world's missing net current-account surplus was about two percent of the value of world exports of goods and services across the 1980s. By itself, that is an acceptable rate of error. However, it is just a *net* error, the result of offsetting errors in both directions.

Sources: IMF, *International Finance Statistics Yearbook 1988* and IMF, *World Economic Outlook 1989.*

large share of the enterprise being invested in, but is just buying minority shares and loans as part of a diversified portfolio. The official U.S. parlance cited in Figure 14.2 now avoids the term *portfolio,* referring instead to securities, claims, and liabilities not falling under the direct investment heading. In general, the securities are long-term bonds and stocks, and most of the claims and liabilities are short term (that is, maturing in less than a year).[2]

The distinction between private capital flows and official capital flows is not quite the same as the distinction between private and government. The term *official* in Lines 11 and 19 refers to assets held by *monetary*-type officials, not all government. Other government assets are included in the private category. The purpose of that distinction is to focus on the monetary task of regulating currency values, to which we return in discussing the overall surplus or deficit.

At the bottom of the accounts comes the suspicious item statistical discrepancy. If the flows on the two sides of every transaction are correctly recorded, there should not be any statistical discrepancy at all. Line 24 in Figure 14.2 should be zero. In fact, it is a debit of $12 billion, meaning that the credit items for the United States are more fully measured than its debit items. The accountants add the statistical discrepancy to make the accounts balance and to warn us that something was missed. In fact, the statistical discrepancy may understate what was missed. It is the net result of errors on both the credit and debit sides. In truth, more than $12 billion of debits were missed, but some were offset by failure to count all the credits.

How do the measurement errors arise? Which items have be most seriously undermeasured in the United States accounts? It is hard to know just by looking at one nation's accounts. We get good clues, however, by adding up all the balance of payments accounts in the world. These should balance, but do not. For the world as a whole, there is a tendency to underreport merchandise imports, service exports (especially investment incomes), and capital exports. (See the box on "Planet Earth's Balance of Payments.") The main difficulty is probably that many people succeed in hiding their imports, their foreign investment incomes, and their capital flight from their own government officials.

THE MACRO MEANING OF THE CURRENT ACCOUNT BALANCE

The current account balance has a special second meaning, one relating it to many macroeconomic concerns. Its first meaning is the one already introduced: the net surplus on goods, services, and gifts. When all these flows for current uses have been netted out, what is left is the increase in all

---

[2] Note that each asset or liability category is defined as an increase in that asset or liability. Decreases in one or the other will have the opposite sign. Thus, for example, Mexican repayment of principal on a U.S. bank loan would reduce the bank claims of the United States, bringing a credit entry (a capital inflow) on Line 24 of Figure 14.2. Another example: U.S. repayment of principal on a Treasury bond held by investors in Japan would bring a debit entry (a capital outflow) on Line 22.

U.S. foreign assets minus U.S. foreign liabilities.[3] The reason is straightforward. The only (nonhuman) things being exchanged between nations are goods, services, gifts and assets. If all credits must equal all debits, then the net surplus on goods, services, and gifts—that is, the current account surplus—must equal **net foreign investment,** the net accumulation of foreign assets minus foreign liabilities.

The fact that the current account surplus equals net foreign investment links it to savings, investment, and national income. A nation that has net foreign investment (I_f, the current account surplus, > 0) is a nation that is investing part of its national saving (S) abroad instead of in domestic capital formation (I_d). So, the value of *national saving equals domestic investment plus foreign investment: $S = I_d + I_f$.*

The net foreign investment, or $I_f = S - I_d$, also equals something else. It is the amount by which all national income or product (Y) exceeds what the nation is spending for all purposes including domestic capital formation. These total expenditures (E) are expenditures for private consumption of home plus foreign goods and services (C), plus government purchases of goods and services (G), plus private investment purchases of capital goods $(I_d$ again). You can see the link between this total national expenditure and national product by remembering a national-product identity from introductory courses:

National product = All purchases of our national product, or
$$Y = C + I_d + G + X - M.$$

This implies that national product (Y) differs from national expenditure $(E = C + I_d + G)$ by the amount of the current account balance, or the difference between exports and imports of goods and services (including gifts), or $X - M$:

$$Y - E = X - M$$

---

[3] Here the text follows the usual convention of talking as though *assets* were something different from *goods* or *services*. This is a convenient shorthand. Strictly speaking, though, the distinction between items for current account and items for capital account is something different. The goods and services in the current account are flows that take place between nations only in the present time period (year or quarter year). It is in this sense that goods and service belong in a current account. But the assets in the capital account could also be flows of goods, and they could represent direct claims on future international flows of services. They appear in the capital account because they directly create an international claim.

Here are two tough cases near the border of the accounting distinction between current and capital account: (1) Arab purchases of hotels in Canada are a capital inflow for Canada, not an export of merchandise, even though a hotel can be thought of as "goods." The reason: the Arab investors are acquiring a long-term asset that will yield a stream of income payments from Canada. (2) Chinese purchases of oil-drilling equipment from the Soviet Union are just an export of "goods" or merchandise from the Soviet Union and a merchandise import by China, even though the equipment can be called a capital good. The transfer does not belong in the capital account because it does not give rise to a direct international claim to future payment (let's say China paid in cash).

So the current account surplus in the balance of payments turns out to equal four different things:

Current account surplus	$X - M$
= Net foreign investment	$= I_f$
= National saving not invested at home	$= S - I_d$
= Difference between national product and national expenditure	$= Y - E$

These identities help us see what must be changed if the current account on the balance of payments is to be changed. They also help us to understand what forces might be causing changes in the balance of payments. To understand some uses for the current account surplus, let us look at how it has behaved recently, as a share of gross national product, in the four countries in Figure 14.3.

The first panel in Figure 14.3 shows that the United States has evolved from an exporter and lender after World War II to a borrower that is still receiving interest and profits from earlier investments. Up through the 1960s, the United States had a positive current account balance, matched or exceeded by its positive trade balance. The United States was a net exporter and lender largely because Europe and Japan, still recovering from World War II, badly needed American goods and loans (and foreign aid under the Marshall Plan). During the 1970s and up through 1982, a new pattern began to emerge. The United States became a net importer of merchandise, but still kept its current account in balance, thanks largely to interest and profit earnings on previous foreign investments. After 1982, the United States shifted into dramatic trade and current account deficits, becoming the world's largest borrower. The underlying reason: led by new federal government deficits, the United States cut its rate of national saving (S/Y) much faster than its domestic investment (I_d/Y) and therefore borrowed heavily from Japan and other countries (negative I_f/Y = negative X = M/Y). In fact, between 1982 and 1985, the United States switched from being the world's largest net creditor to being its largest net debtor. The chronic trade deficits and borrowing then lessened slightly as a share of GNP.

Canadian experience fits a classic pattern of a borrowing country with good growth potential. Most of the time Canada has borrowed capital from other countries (especially from the United States), as shown by Canada's current account deficits for most years. Canada has helped pay for its borrowings out of the proceeds from growth itself, using much of its trade surplus to pay foreign investors for their earlier investments. The payment of interest and profits on past borrowings shows up as a widening gap between the trade surplus and the current account balance in Figure 14.3.

Japan's trade and current account balances have been rising as a share of its economy since the 1950s. Its controversial trade surplus, representing that invasion of Japanese goods into markets the world over, has been only partly offset by a deficit in services and gifts. Thus, its net foreign

FIGURE 14.3   Current Account Balances and Trade Balances, United States, Canada, Japan, and Mexico, 1960–1988

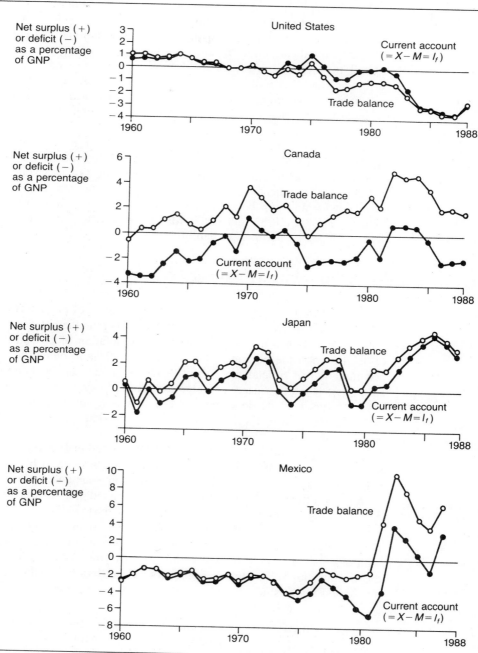

investment ($I_f = X - M > 0$) became a large positive share of GNP. By the mid-1980s, Japanese foreign investment, including heavy lending to the United States, became the dominant force in international finance. Behind this drift toward net foreign lending, interrupted only by the two oil crises, lay a widening gap between Japan's outstanding national savings and her domestic capital formation (again, $I_f = S - I_d$).

Until the debt crisis of 1982, Mexico was a consistent borrower. Its current account was in deficit (negative I_f), and net outpayments of interest and dividends to foreign creditors showed up as a widening gap between the trade balance and the current account balance. Figure 14.3 shows part of the tremendous shock Mexico felt when its debt crisis hit in 1982. Its trade balance jumped to more than 10 percent of GNP in 1983, not because exports grew (they did not) but because it had to cut out two thirds of its imports in the belt tightening necessary to meet most of its swollen interest and principal payments to foreign creditors. The interest payments show up as a widening gap between the trade balance and the current account balance. Between 1983 and 1987, Mexico was actually a net creditor, in that it reduced its net foreign liabilities.

THE MACRO MEANING OF THE OVERALL BALANCE

The overall balance, near the bottom of the balance of payments accounts, measures the sum of the current-account surplus plus the net private capital inflows. If it is in surplus, it equals an accumulation of official net assets (a debit item at the bottom of the accounts). If it is in deficit, it equals an accumulation of official net liabilities (a credit item at the bottom of the accounts). It is often used as a clue to a nation's monetary condition. The kind of clue depends on whether the nation is trying to maintain a fixed exchange rate or is just trying to keep a floating exchange rate within reasonable bounds.

If the nation's officials are trying to keep a fixed exchange rate between their currency and other currencies, the overall balance is like a weather watch. It warns about the buildup of claims on your country in the hands of foreign officials. Those officials are presumed not to want to go on accumulating claims against you, and they may try to exchange these claims for reserve assets, bringing your currency under attack. In such a world, it is useful to have a measure that compares changes in your reserve assets with changes in foreign official claims against you. A typical definition of the overall surplus or deficit is the **official settlements balance** used by the United States since the late 1960s:

$$\begin{matrix} \text{Official} & \text{Net increase in} & \text{Net decrease in liquid} \\ \text{settlements} = & \text{official U.S.} & + \text{ U.S. liabilities to} \\ \text{surplus} & \text{reserves} & \text{foreign officials,} \end{matrix}$$

or,

$$\begin{array}{lll}\text{Official} & \text{Net decrease in} & \text{Net increase in liquid} \\ \text{settlements} = & \text{official U.S.} & + \text{U.S. liabilities to} \\ \text{deficit} & \text{reserves} & \text{foreign officials.} \end{array}$$

Here the emphasis is on liquid, or money-like, foreign claims. The idea is that such claims can be unloaded quickly, posing a threat to a nation's currency during a speculative crisis. It is not clear that we should focus only on official reserves or on those foreign claims held by officials. Private liquid claims are also relevant during a speculative crisis.[4]

If a nation lets the exchange rate fluctuate, as most exchange rates have done since 1971, there is less urgency, though still a need, for a weather forecast from the balance of payments accounts. The overall balance could be used to indicate what is happening to the demand and supply of a currency, an indirect clue to whether there is danger of wide swings in the exchange rates set in world currency markets. If foreign residents do not prefer to hold dollars as faithfully as American residents, then a buildup of dollars in foreign hands might foreshadow a decline in the market value of the dollar.

One good use of having a measure of overall balance is that it reminds us that the flows of goods, services, gifts and private capital on top of the accounts are inseparable from the flows of money at the bottom. In fact, we should be careful to avoid the common trap of assuming that causation flows from the top down. It may flow from the bottom up. The flows of official reserves and liabilities, those money flows at the bottom of the accounts, are not necessarily the *result* of trade, services, gifts, and private lending. They could as easily be the *cause*. Here we can use **the monetary approach to the balance of payments,** which argues that a payments deficit can be the result of increased foreign demand for the nation's money for use as a reserve. Take an example from Line 19 of Table 14.3. In 1988, the $39 billion of buildup in foreign official holdings of assets in the United States (such as bank deposits in New York or holdings of U.S. government bonds) might have been the result of a greater foreign official desire to hold onto dollars. If foreign officials really wanted to hold extra dollars, they would get them somehow (e.g., by borrowing from the United States

---

[4] Largely for this reason, there is debate over whether the official settlements balance is the right way to measure the overall balance. One alternative measure of overall balance is the *liquidity balance,* whereby a surplus equals the increase in official reserves minus the increase in liquid liabilities to *all* foreign residents, not just foreign officials. Another is the *basic balance,* whereby a surplus equals the increase in holdings of foreign liquid assets by all residents of your country minus the net increase in liquid liabilities to all foreigners. The choice comes down to what you think is a measure of the kinds of claims held by people who are most likely to get rid of them during a crisis. There really is no best measure of this.

or from sales of goods to the United States). It would be wrong to look at their buildup of dollar balances as a sign that the dollar is in trouble. It could be the exact opposite. In fact, the dollar's market value was steady in 1988. Thus, the monetary approach to the balance of payments says that an overall payments deficit (surplus) may be a way of meeting extra demand (lower demand) for the nation's currency relative to other currencies. In other words, beware how you read causation into the balance-of-payments account. The exchange of reserves and other money-type assets at the bottom of the account could be a cause, instead of a result, of the flows listed higher up in the account.

We shall return to the monetary approach to the balance of payments in another guise in Chapter 16. In that chapter, it takes the form of a theory of exchange rates based on supply and demand for national moneys.

THE INTERNATIONAL INVESTMENT POSITION

Complementing the balance of payments accounts is a balance sheet called the **international investment position,** a statement of the stocks of a nation's international assets and foreign liabilities at a point in time, usually the end of a year. The international investment position is closely related to the current account balance. In fact, the current account balance is the change in the nation's net foreign assets during a time period. The link between the two kinds of accounts also relates to a subtle but common semantic distinction. We say that a nation is a *lender* or a *borrower* depending on whether its current account is in surplus or negative over a time period. We say that a nation is a *creditor* or *debtor* depending on whether its net foreign assets are positive or negative. The first refers to flows over time, and the second to stocks at a point in time.

Within the 20th century, the United States has come full circle in its international investment position. As shown in Figure 14.4, the nation was a net debtor before World War I, borrowing both on long-term and on short-term accounts. World War I suddenly transformed the United States into the world's leading creditor, a role this country played very reluctantly for the first 20 years. Over most of the postwar period, the United States was increasingly a creditor in nominal dollar terms, though not as a share of GNP, reaching a peak nominal creditor position by the end of 1982. The creditor position built up over 60 years was erased and reversed within the next 3 years. By early 1985, the United States was already a net debtor, and the nominal indebtedness kept rising into the 1990s. Figure 14.4 dramatizes the change with the stark contrast in the net positions at the end of 1982 and the end of 1988. The United States used to lend on long term and borrow on short term, acting as a world banker making a large net interest income off the fact that it lent at higher interest (and dividend and profit) rates than it borrowed. That has all changed. By 1988, the United

FIGURE 14.4 International Investment Position for the United States at the End of Selected Years, 1897–1988 ($ billions)

	1897	1914	1930	1946	1960	1982	1988
U.S. investments abroad	**0.7**	**3.5**	**17.2**	**18.7**	**66.2**	**824.8**	**1253.7**
Private	0.7	3.5	17.2	13.5	49.3	716.2	1120.4
Long-term	0.7	3.5	15.2	12.3	44.5	283.1	483.7
Direct*	0.6	2.6	8.0	7.2	31.9	207.8	326.9
Portfolio[†]	0.1	0.9	7.2	5.1	12.7	75.3	156.8
Short-terms[§]	–	–	2.0	1.3	4.8	433.1	636.7
U.S. government	0.0	–	–	5.2	16.9	74.6	85.5
Long-term	0.0	–	–	5.0	14.0	72.9	84.9
Short-term	0.0	–	–	0.2	2.9	1.7	0.6
U.S. official reserve assets[‡]	0.6	1.5	4.3	20.7	19.4	34.0	47.8
Foreign investments in the United States	**3.4**	**7.2**	**8.4**	**15.9**	**40.9**	**688.1**	**1786.2**
Long-term	3.1	6.7	5.7	7.0	19.2	376.1	819.1
Direct	–	1.3	1.4	2.5	6.9	124.7	328.9
Portfolio	–	5.4	4.3	4.5	11.6	251.4	749.5
Short-term[§]	0.3	0.5	2.7	8.9	21.6	312.0	967.1
U.S. net creditor position (excluding reserves)	**–2.7**	**–3.7**	**8.8**	**2.8**	**25.3**	**55.3**	**–580.3**
Net long-term	–2.4	–3.2	9.5	10.3	39.3	–53.3	–250.5
Net short-term[§]	–0.3	–0.5	–0.7	–0.7	–14.0	108.6	–329.8

* *Direct investment* refers to any international investment in a foreign enterprise owned in large part by the investor's home country.
[†] *Portfolio investment* is all other long-term investment. For 1983 and 1988 this is the "securities" category, with the "claims" categories counted as short-term.
[‡] U.S. official reserve assets consist of gold and foreign exchange reserves plus IMF credit tranches and special drawing rights.
[§] Includes government securities. After 1983, also includes some private long-term loans.

Sources: U.S. Bureau of the Census, *Historical Statistics of the United States: Colonial Times to 1970* (Washington, D.C.: Government Printing Office, 1976); and U.S. Bureau of Economic Analysis, *Survey of Current Business*, June 1989.

States was a debtor for the long term and the short term. Even direct foreign investment, long an American specialty, is now nearly balanced in the U.S. accounts.[5]

SUMMARY

Basic definitions abound in this chapter. Terms introduced here appear constantly in the news media, and they will reappear throughout the rest of the book. Definitely review any of them that is not familiar at first sight.

A country's **balance of payments** is a systematic account of all the exchanges of value between residents of that country and the rest of the world during a given time period. Two flows occur in any exchange, or transaction, according to double-entry bookkeeping:

A **credit (+)** is a flow for which the country is paid.

A **debit (−)** is a flow for which the country must pay.

Flows from international transactions are grouped into five flow categories. Each category contains flows of more detailed types whose definitions also should be learned. The five flow categories, with some important subcategories, are:

1. **Merchandise trade** flows (i.e., goods flows);
2. **Service flows,** including payments for investment services (earnings of interest, dividends, profits), fees and royalties, transportation and insurance and travel services;
3. **Unilateral transfers,** including government foreign-aid grants and private gifts and remittances;
4. **Private capital flows,** including direct foreign investments, portfolio investments in securities, changes in bank deposits, changes in other financial claims, and statistical discrepancy;
5. **Official asset flows,** including changes in official gold and foreign exchange assets, in Special Drawing Rights (SDRs) with the IMF, and in official liabilities to foreigners.

To highlight what is happening to wealth and reserves and currency markets, flow categories are summed into five special net balances, each defined so that a surplus is positive and a deficit is negative:

---

[5] The data in Figure 14.4 imply that the United States was already a slight net recipient of more foreign direct investment than it invested in enterprises abroad, as of the end of 1988. Yet, the official figures undervalue U.S. direct investments abroad more than they undervalue foreign direct investments in the United States. The United States probably still had a slight net asset position in direct investments at the end of the 1980s.

1. The **merchandise trade balance** equals the net credits minus debits, or net exports, on merchandise flows. This is the usual meaning of the term *trade balance.*
2. The **goods and services balance** equals the net exports of both goods and services. Though less publicized, it is a more meaningful definition of a trade balance.
3. The **current account balance** equals the net credit minus debits on the flows of goods, services, and unilateral transfers. It also equals the change in the nation's foreign assets minus foreign liabilities, also known as **net foreign investment.**
4. The net **private capital inflows** equals net credits minus debits involving changes in private national residents' foreign assets and liabilities. This balance is in surplus if the nation is a net private *borrower, or capital importer,* not if it is a net creditor piling up more foreign assets than liabilities.
5. The **overall balance** equals the sum of the current-account surplus plus the net private capital inflows. If it is in surplus, it is counterbalanced by an accumulation of official net assets (a debit item at the bottom of the accounts). If it is in deficit, it is counterbalanced by an accumulation of official net liabilities (a credit item at the bottom of the accounts).

   The current account balance has special macroeconomic meaning. As net foreign investments, of I_f, it equals the part of national saving (S) that is not used in domestic capital formation (I_d). That is, it fits into the basic identity that saving equals investment: $S = I_d + I_f$. A nation that is running a current-account deficit, like the United States since 1976, is a nation that is saving less than its domestic capital formation, so that the current-account deficit represents its net foreign borrowing. Viewed another way, a net current-account deficit represents intertemporal trade, with the nation importing more goods and services (and gratitude for any gifts) for current use and promising to repay with net exports or goods and services (and gratitude for any gifts) in the future. Japan, by contrast, has run massive current-account surpluses, accumulating claims to future goods and services (and gratitude).

   The overall balance also has special macroeconomic meaning, though its actual definition cannot quite match the concept it is supposed to represent. One idea is that an overall surplus shows the nation has a net demand for holding foreign money, while the rest of the world willingly supplies that money in exchange for other things. The overall balance is thus viewed as a measure of temporary disequilibrium in the foreign-exchange markets we explore in the rest of Part III. In practice, though, the different measures of overall balance (official settlements balance, liquidity balance) can only be indirect clues to the state of net money demand.

   A nation's **international investment position** shows its stocks of international assets and liabilities at a moment of time. These stocks are changed each year by the flows of private and official assets measured in the balance of payments. Within three years in the mid-1980s, the United States switched from being the world's largest net creditor to being its largest net debtor.

SUGGESTED READINGS

The balance-of-payments accounts of most nations are summarized in the IMF's *International Financial Statistics* and also in its *Balance of Payments Yearbook*. More detailed accounts for the United States appear regularly in the *Survey of Current Business*, while those for Canada are in the *Canada Yearbook*.

QUESTIONS FOR REVIEW

1. Which of the following transactions would contribute to a U.S. current account surplus on the balance of payments?

a. Boeing barters a $100 million plane to Yugoslavia in exchange for $100 million worth of hotel services on the Yugoslav coast.

b The United States borrows $100 million long term from Saudi Arabia to buy $100 million of Saudi oil this year.

c. The United States sells a $100 million jet to Turkey for $100 million in bank deposits.

d. The U.S. government makes a gift of $100 million to the government of Greece, in the form of New York bank deposits, to pay for injuries caused by Turkish jet attacks.

e. The U.S. government sells $100 million in long-term bonds to Germany, getting bank deposits in Germany and promising to repay in five years.

2. Which of the above transactions contributed to a U.S. deficit in the overall (official settlements) balance?

Answers: 1. *c.*
2. *d.*

3. Using the line numbers in Figure 14.3, decide which lines should contain the credit and debit items for each of the following transactions from the point of view of the United States:

a. In 1990 Pepsico signed an agreement with the Soviet Union bartering Pepsico's managerial services and trademarks in making Pepsi Cola in the Soviet Union for an equivalent dollar value of Stolichnaya vodka and Soviet merchant ships.

b. Manufacturers Hanover of New York lends the government of Brazil $184 million in a new loan, so that Brazil simultaneously pays Manufacturers Hanover $184 million in interest on an old loan.

c. The City of Kobe, Japan, pays Americans $3 billion in Kobe city bonds (IOUs) to buy the Dallas Cowboys football franchise (i.e., Kobe acquires all future paper title to profits from the Cowboys and their name.)
d. U.S. tourists pay $280, with a check written on a Vermont bank, to stay in Toronto's SkyDome Hotel, overlooking the Blue Jays baseball stadium.

Answers: For each case, the line numbers in Figure 14.2 for the credit and debit entries are: *a.* credit Line 3, debit Line 5. *b.* credit Line 3, debit Line 17. *c.* credit Line 21, debit Line 16. *d.* credit Line 6, debit Line 24.

4. What is the current account balance of a nation with a government budget deficit of $128 billion, private savings of $806 billion, and domestic capital formation of $777 billion?

(Answer: $I_f = S - I_d = 806 - 128 - 777 =$ a deficit of $99 billion.)

▼

The Foreign Exchange Market

•

In foreign exchange, as in international dialogue, somebody has to translate. People in different countries are used to different currencies as well as different languages. The translator between different currencies is the exchange rate, the price of one country's money in units of another country's money. You can go only so far using just one currency. If an American wants to buy something from a foreign resident, the foreign resident will typically want to have the payment translated into her or his home currency. They are less willing to keep dollars than the American, just as they are less willing to speak only English.

What determines the exchange rate, or the pressures on it, is the subject of the rest of Part III. This chapter introduces the real-world institutions of currency trading. It also begins to build a theory of exchange rates, starting with the role of forces that show up in the balance of payments entries of Chapter 14.

Much of the study of exchange rates is like a trip to another planet. It is a strange land, far removed from the economics of an ordinary household. It is populated by strange creatures—hedgers, arbitrageurs, the Gnomes of Zurich, the Snake in the Tunnel, the gliding band, the crawling peg, and the dirty float. It is an area in which it is unsafe to rely on ordinary household intuition. In fact, it is an area in which you cannot apply ordinary micro- or macroeconomic theory without major modifications.

Yet the student of exchange rates is helped by the presence of two familiar forces: profit maximization and competition. The familiar assumption that individuals act as though they are out to maximize the real value of their net incomes (profits) appears to be at least as valid in international financial behavior as in other realms of economics. To be sure, people act as though they are maximizing a subtle concept of profit, one that takes account of a wide variety of economic and political risks. Yet, the parties engaged in international finance do seem to react to changing conditions in the way that a profit-maximizer would.

It also happens that competition prevails in most international financial markets, despite a folklore full of tales about how groups of wealthy speculators manage to corner those markets. There is competition in the markets for foreign exchange and in the international lending markets. Thus, for these markets, we can use the familiar demand and supply analysis of competitive markets. Here again, it is important to make one disclaimer: it is definitely not the case that all markets in the international arena are competitive. Monopoly and oligopoly are evident in most of the direct investment activity we shall discuss in Part V, as well as in the cartels already discussed in Chapter 11. Ordinary demand and supply curves would not do justice to the facts in these areas. Yet, in the financial markets that play a large role in the material of Parts III and IV, competitive conditions do hold, even more so than in most markets usually thought of as competitive. Accordingly, this chapter and the next return to a familiar market land: demand and supply.

THE BASICS OF CURRENCY TRADING

Foreign exchange is the act of trading different nations' moneys[1] The moneys take the same forms as money within a country. The greater part of the money assets traded in foreign exchange markets are demand deposits in major banks traded between the banks themselves. A minority consists of coins and currency of the ordinary pocket variety.

Each nation's money has a price in terms of each other nation's money.[2] This is the **exchange rate.** In today's increasingly international world, more and more newspapers keep daily track of the exchange rates with quotations like those shown in Figure 15.1. Notice that each price is stated in two ways: first as a U.S. dollar price of the other currency and next as the price of the U.S. dollar in units of the other currency. The pairs of prices are just reciprocals of each other: saying that the British pound sterling costs 1.6700 U.S. dollars is the same as saying the U.S. dollar is worth 59.88 British pence, or £0.5988 (1.6700 = 1/0.5988), and so forth. Each

---

[1] The term *foreign exchange* also refers to holdings of foreign currencies as well as the act of trading one currency for another.

[2] Exchange rates are one kind of price that a national money has. Another is its ability to buy goods and services immediately. The second kind of price, the usual "value of the dollar," is just the reciprocal of the money cost of buying a bundle of goods and services. A third kind of price of money is the cost of just renting it, and having access to it, for a given period of time. This is (roughly) the rate of interest that borrowers pay for the use of money, and it is analogous to other rental prices such as the price of renting an apartment or a rental car.

FIGURE 15.1   Exchange Rate Quotations

EXCHANGE RATES

Tuesday, May 8, 1990

The New York foreign exchange selling rates below apply to trading among banks in amounts of $1 million and more, as quoted at 3 p.m. Eastern time by Bankers Trust Co. Retail transactions provide fewer units of foreign currency per dollar.

Country	U.S. $ equiv. Tues.	U.S. $ equiv. Mon.	Currency per U.S. $ Tues.	Currency per U.S. $ Mon.
Argentina (Austral) ...	.0002075	.0002075	4820.21	4820.21
Australia (Dollar)	.7570	.7565	1.3210	1.3219
Austria (Schilling)	.08576	.08587	11.66	11.64
Bahrain (Dinar)	2.6525	2.6525	.3770	.3770
Belgium (Franc)				
Commercial rate	.02923	.02928	34.21	34.16
Brazil (Cruzeiro)	.01984	.01974	50.40	50.67
Britain (Pound)	1.6700	1.6695	.5988	.5990
30-Day Forward	1.6604	1.6598	.6023	.6025
90-Day Forward	1.6430	1.6426	.6086	.6088
180-Day Forward	1.6180	1.6186	.6180	.6178
Canada (Dollar)	.8598	.8602	1.1630	1.1625
30-Day Forward	.8561	.8565	1.1681	1.1675
90-Day Forward	.8495	.8500	1.1771	1.1765
180-Day Forward	.8410	.8414	1.1890	1.1885
Chile (Official rate) ...	.003441	.003441	290.62	290.62
China (Renmimbi)	.211820	.211820	4.7210	4.7210
Colombia (Peso)	.002083	.002083	480.00	480.00
Denmark (Krone)	.1589	.1590	6.2940	6.2900
Ecuador (Sucre)				
Floating rate	.001241	.001241	805.50	805.50
Finland (Markka)	.25510	.25478	3.9200	3.9250
France (Franc)	.17963	.17989	5.5670	5.5590
30-Day Forward	.17944	.17969	5.5730	5.5650
90-Day Forward	.17910	.17937	5.5835	5.5750
180-Day Forward	.17862	.17892	5.5985	5.5890
Greece (Drachma)	.006127	.006150	163.20	162.60
Hong Kong (Dollar) ..	.12834	.12833	7.7920	7.7925
India (Rupee)	.05787	.05787	17.28	17.28
Indonesia (Rupiah) ...	.0005501	.0005501	1818.02	1818.02
Ireland (Punt)	1.6190	1.6225	.6177	.6163
Israel (Shekel)	.4973	.4973	2.0110	2.0110
Italy (Lira)	.0008227	.0008237	1215.51	1214.00
Japan (Yen)	.006341	.006323	157.70	158.15
30-Day Forward	.006348	.006330	157.53	157.97
90-Day Forward	.006361	.006342	157.22	157.67
180-Day Forward	.006383	.006363	156.67	157.15
Jordan (Dinar)	1.5076	1.5076	.6633	.6633
Kuwait (Dinar)	3.4371	3.4371	.2909	.2909
Lebanon (Pound)	.001653	.001653	605.00	605.00
Malaysia (Ringgit) ...	.3701	.3695	2.7020	2.7063
Malta (Lira)	3.0166	3.0166	.3315	.3315
Mexico (Peso)				
Floating rate	.0003574	.0003574	2798.00	2798.00
Netherland (Guilder) .	.5369	.5373	1.8625	1.8610
New Zealand (Dollar)	.5750	.5735	1.7391	1.7437
Norway (Krone)	.1553	.1552	6.4375	6.4450
Pakistan (Rupee)	.0460	.0460	21.75	21.75
Peru (Inti)	.00003501	.00003501	28565.72	28565.72
Philippines (Peso)	.04525	.04525	22.10	22.10
Portugal (Escudo)	.006798	.006798	147.11	147.11
Saudi Arabia (Riyal) ..	.26667	.26667	3.7500	3.7500
Singapore (Dollar)	.5355	.5338	1.8675	1.8735
South Africa (Rand)				
Commercial rate	.3785	.3778	2.6420	2.6469
Financial rate	.2442	.2451	4.0950	4.0800
South Korea (Won) ...	.0014332	.0014332	697.73	697.73
Spain (Peseta)	.009634	.009648	103.80	103.65
Sweden (Krona)	.1655	.1655	6.0435	6.0415
Switzerland (Franc) ..	.6986	.6986	1.4315	1.4315
30-Day Forward	.6980	.6981	1.4327	1.4325
90-Day Forward	.6975	.6974	1.4337	1.4338
180-Day Forward	.6973	.6971	1.4341	1.4345
Taiwan (Dollar)	.038022	.038183	26.30	26.19
Thailand (Baht)	.03864	.03864	25.88	25.88
Turkey (Lira)	.0003995	.0003995	2503.00	2503.00
United Arab (Dirham)	.2723	.2723	3.6730	3.6730
Uruguay (New Peso)				
Financial	.001014	.001014	986.00	986.00
Venezuela (Bolivar)				
Floating rate	.02235	.02235	44.75	44.75
W. Germany (Mark) ..	.6037	.6039	1.6565	1.6560
30-Day Forward	.6038	.6040	1.6561	1.6555
90-Day Forward	.6041	.6043	1.6553	1.6549
180-Day Forward	.6043	.6044	1.6548	1.6545
— — —				
SDR	1.31491	1.31412	.76051	.76097
ECU	1.23700	1.23301	....	....

Special Drawing Rights (SDR) are based on exchange rates for the U.S., West German, British, French and Japanese currencies. Source: International Monetary Fund.

European Currency Unit (ECU) is based on a basket of community currencies. Source: European Community Commission.

exchange rate can thus be read in either of two directions. This is done simply because both sides of the price are money, unlike regular prices of goods and services where only one of the things being traded is money (as in $1.15 per gallon of gasoline). To avoid unnecessary confusion **the rest of the book will refer to the exchange rate as the price of the foreign currency.** When the home currency is the dollar, the exchange rates will be dollar prices of other currencies, like $1.6700 per pound, $0.6037 per German Mark, and other figures in the left-hand columns of Figure 15.1.

As explained at the top of the foreign-exchange table, the rates generally quoted refer to trading among banks. This is where the main marketplace for foreign currencies can be found: on telephone lines and radio signals between banks. Aside from some specialized futures-oriented "pit" markets like the International Money Market in Chicago, the foreign exchange market is not a single gathering place where traders shout buy and sell orders at each other. Rather, the market takes the form shown in the photograph in Figure 15.2. Skilled traders work at desks in their separate banks dealing with each other by computer and by phone. The computer terminals show current exchange-rate ranges on all major currencies for delivery at various dates. Every major bank around the world posts the exchange-rate ranges at which it is probably willing to trade currencies with other banks. Any bank shopping for the best rate, on behalf of itself or a customer, first consults the ranges quoted on the computers (as on the screens shown in Figure 15.2). Finding a likely prospect, the buyer bank deals with the other bank directly by phone to get a firmer price bid. Within about a minute, as a rule, any haggling is settled and a transaction is made by verbal agreement. If necessary, documents consummating the trade are mailed later. To repeat, what the banks are trading are demand deposits denominated in different currencies.

Foreign exchange trading in this interbank market is not for the little guy. Notice that the quoted rates in Figure 15.1 are for amounts of $1 million or more. In fact, traders often save time on the phone by referring to each million dollars as a "dollar." With millions being swapped each minute, extremely fine margins of price profit or loss can loom large. For example, a trader who spends a minute shopping and secures 10 million pounds at $1.6699 per pound, instead of accepting a ready offer at $1.6700 has brought his or her bank an extra $1,000 within that minute. That's a wage rate of $60,000 an hour. Correspondingly, anyone who reacts a bit too slowly or too excitedly to a given news release transmitted over the wire services (e.g., announcement of rapid growth in the Canadian money supply, rumors of a coup in Libya, or a wildcat steel strike in Italy) can lose money at an even faster rate. On the average, these professionals make more than they lose, enough to justify their rates of pay. But foreign exchange trading is a lively and tense job. That department of a large bank is usually run as a tight ship with no room for "passengers" who do not make a good rate of return from quick dealings at fine margins.

FIGURE 15.2 Foreign Exchange Traders in the Interbank Market

Courtesy of The Bank of America.

At the Bank of America in San Francisco, foreign exchange traders deal with other banks' traders by phone. The computer terminal at the center produces displays of all other banks' current price-offer ranges and can also be used for special calculations. A trading room of this scale swaps about $5 billion in foreign exchange daily. New technology is now removing one kind of equipment visible here: paper. Recently developed electronic touch-pads, like those used by cashiers in fast-food restaurants, instantly record all dimensions of a transaction without any note-taking by the trader herself (himself). All records are printed out elsewhere by computer.

Today's streamlined foreign exchange markets are truly worldwide. From Monday through Friday the market is open around the clock. It follows the sun around the globe with the help of communications satellites. German marks, for example, can be traded between Europe and New York when the sun is over the Atlantic, between New York and San Francisco as the sun crosses America, between San Francisco and East Asia as the sun crosses the Pacific, and between East Asia and Europe as the sun returns to Europe. The volumes traded are enormous. As of April 1989, the world's currencies markets were trading over $500 billion dollars *a day,* versus a daily turnover of only $125–150 billion for U.S. government securities and only $6.2 billion on the New York Stock Exchange. Yet, the number of persons employed in this industry is only a few thousand for the world as a whole (see the box on ''Foreign Exchange Traders: A Breed Apart.'').

PRIVATE USES OF THE SPOT FOREIGN EXCHANGE MARKET

People and firms want to trade currencies for various reasons. Some are engaged in exchanges of goods and services and want to get or give up currencies that are of more interest to the other parties they are dealing with. For such persons the foreign-exchange market provides clearing services, helping each party to end up holding the kind of currency it prefers. The same market also helps others, often the same people, "hedge" by getting rid of any net asset or liability commitment to a particular currency. It also lets others "speculate," owning or owing a currency and thus gambling on the future of its price. Let us look more closely at each of these three overlapping uses.

Clearing

The foreign exchange market provides clearing services to many kinds of businesses and individuals. Ordinary tourists usually meet this marketplace in some airport, such as Juarez Airport in Mexico City or Heathrow in London, at the exchange counter with the signboard announcing the current rates. Less familiar to most is the larger flow of billions each year in transactions involving international trade in goods. At the center of the market process determining the value of any nation's currency is the set of currency transactions established by that nation's exports and imports of goods and services.

A nation's exports of goods and services cause foreign currencies to be sold in order to buy that nation's currency. If the United States sells $100 million worth of aircraft to a foreign buyer, it is likely, though not necessary, that somebody will end up trying to sell foreign currencies to get $100 million. Let us say, as in most of the examples that follow, that the foreign country, here buying the aircraft, is the United Kingdom. If the British government or a private British firm pays by writing a check in pounds sterling, the U.S. firm receiving the sterling check must either be content to hold onto sterling bank balances or try to sell the sterling for dollars. Alternatively, if the U.S. firm will accept payment only in dollars, then it is the British buyer or his or her representative who must go searching for an opportunity to sell sterling to get the dollars on which the U.S. exporter insists. Either way, U.S. *exports of goods and services will create a supply of foreign currency* and a demand for U.S. dollars to the extent that foreign buyers have their own currencies to offer and U.S. exporters prefer to end up holding U.S. dollars and not some other currency. Only if U.S. exporters are happy to hold onto pounds (or the United Kingdom importers somehow have large reserves of dollars to spend) can U.S. exports keep from generating a supply of pounds and a demand for dollars.

FOREIGN EXCHANGE TRADERS: A BREED APART

Our world is a difficult place in which to find expert advice. Those whose opinions I value will not volunteer it; those who volunteer it I find of no value.

Bertrand Russell

Everybody speculates in one way or another, but only a few thousand professionals make foreign exchange speculation their living. As of 1983, the core of the profession consisted of traders in major banks in the following centers:

	Number of Banks with Foreign Exchange Depts.	Number of Traders
North America		
New York	96	667
Toronto	12	88
Chicago	14	84
San Francisco	8	52
Los Angeles	8	38
Western Europe		
London	227	1,645
Luxembourg	68	356
Paris	64	378
Zurich	30	199
Frankfurt	47	300
Milan	35	212
Brussels	29	186
Asia and the Middle East		
Tokyo	27	150
Singapore	49	234
Hong Kong	54	246
Bahrain	26	106

Source: Mayer, Duesenberry, and Aliber (1984, p. 503).

London continues to lead, in trade volume as well as in personnel, even though the British pound's share of foreign exchange (9 percent in 1986) is below the shares of the dollar (49 percent), the yen (17 percent), or the Deutsche-

CONTINUED

mark (14 percent). In April 1989, London traded $187 billion a day in foreign exchange (after the figures are adjusted to eliminate double-counting), versus daily volumes of $129 billion for the United States and $115 billion for Japan. Japan's share of currency trading is rising, however, as a natural byproduct of its growing share of world wealth.

There are good reasons why there are so few foreign exchange traders. One is the capital-intensity of this particular business: it takes a lot of money but only a few decision makers. The other is the nature of the work itself.

Trading millions of dollars of foreign exchange per minute is a harrowing job, in the same category with being an air traffic controller or a bomb defuser. A trader should be somebody who loves pressure and can take losses. Many who try it soon develop a taste for other kinds of work. Once an economics student visiting a foreign exchange trading room in a major bank asked a trader, "How long do people last at this job?" The enthusiastic answer: "Yes, it is an excellent job for young people."

Yet, for all the job turnover, many thrive on this particular kind of risk. Who are these people? What credentials did they bring to this business, and what can they teach us? Here are two who have cast their lot with foreign exchange trading with differing results.

Richard Dennis, Prince of the Pit

Richard Dennis of Chicago would seem to have found the secret to foreign exchange trading. His rise illustrates the elusiveness of the formula for success in this career. Some traders enter their jobs with MBAs from the top schools, whereas others walk in with unskilled jobs and no visible training. Richard Dennis was in the latter group. After high school he dabbled in philosophy courses but left college to work for a trading firm as a runner. At age 21 he borrowed $1,600 from his parents to buy a "seat" in the "pit"—a trading position on the commodity and foreign-exchange floor of the Chicago Board of Trade. By age 34, he had amassed hundreds of millions of dollars and had joined the *Forbes* list of the 400 wealthiest individuals in America.

Rugged individualism is clearly part of his formula. His three basic rules of market analysis: figure out the market yourself, try not to be influenced by

---

CONTINUED

---

news, try not to be influenced by others' opinions. He further stresses the importance of being able to take losses. Have the strength to go home, after a day of losing millions, happy about having done the right thing even if it happened to lose: "The biggest strength I've had in trading . . . is [that] at some level I could stand to fail." On his reckoning, a successful strategy loses most of the time, but wins enough on a few key days to come out way ahead. That sounds like a formula for success—or failure. It is only slightly more informative than "buy low, sell high" or "the trend is your friend."

What kind of person would Dennis prefer to hire as a new trader?

> Well, people who have high math aptitude, super achievers in their [college test] scores, people with some interest in computers or market methods or who worked in systematizing things. . . . [T]he majority of people we wound up hiring had some interest in games. They were chess players or backgammon players.

Dennis hired and trained 20 young traders, who averaged a 103 percent rate of return over four years before he stopped the training program. Over the same years, Dennis did poorly on his own trades, sustaining a personal loss of $20 million in 1988. He felt, though, that his training program had proved something: "Trading is not a mystical, ineffable art. It's an empirical, readily understandable science. . . . Trading can be taught." He has not published any guides or formulas, however. Nor have his trainees.

At age 39, with his fortune down to $200 million, Dennis quit trading and went into politics as a "liberal libertarian." He gives to certain liberal foundations, backs liberal candidates, and wants a new tax on the rich to reduce the federal deficit. His op-ed articles and public radio broadcasts espouse free-market economics but back the welfare state and defend civil liberties against social conservatives.

Mr. X: No Mariachi Music, Please

Some traders lose, of course. Consider the case of a Mr. X (real name withheld), who trusted the Mexican government and bet against the marketplace back in 1976.

Mr. X, a 59-year-old New York financial consultant, had been doing well speculating in the Mexican peso. Over two years, he had netted $750,000 on peso speculation, in addition to his ordinary business income. Then, in August of 1976, the market became jittery about signs of excessive inflationary spending by the Mexican government on the eve of the upcoming election.

CONTINUED

Most reasoned there was a danger that the peso would become too abundant and sink in value. They began to sell pesos, depressing the peso's value in the (unpegged) forward market. The Mexican government scoffed at such rumors, running full-page ads proclaiming Mexico's good health and its pledge to continue its policy of keeping the peso pegged to the dollar, as it had been for over 20 years.

Mr. X believed them. He promised to buy $7.2 million in pesos at the forward rate of 8 cents a peso (or 90 million pesos) for delivery in September of 1976. Of this, only $0.7 million was to be his own money. The rest was pledged by five brokerage houses, including Merrill Lynch and E. F. Hutton, who respected his previous financial track record. As long as the spot peso turned out to be worth more than 8 cents in September, he and his brokers would make money.

On August 31, the Mexican government announced it was forced to let the peso float after all. Within a week, the peso had dropped to 5 cents, making his September pesos worth $4.5 million—once he had bought them for the stipulated $7.2 million. As soon as the brokers saw this loss of $2.7 million looming, they seized as many of his assets as they could. But they could only seize $0.9 million, leaving a further loss of $1.8 million to fight over. Mr. X was summoned to an angry meeting with the brokerage houses.

What the meeting showed was, as one brokerage official sourly noted, "if you are going to lose in the market, you want to lose big." Mr. X's losses were so great that he could not possibly repay soon. If the brokers took him to court, he would be bankrupt. He calmly proposed that they should lend him more money for a while so that he could try his hand at some new ventures. That is, they should pay themselves back with their own money. When tempers cooled, the compromise was that he would get a five-year moratorium on his debts. Translation: he was allowed to default on part of his obligations. In this respect, his 1976 behavior was to be matched by the Mexican government itself six years later. In the great debt crisis of 1982, as discussed in Chapter 24, Mexico declared it was unable to repay all its debts to industrial-country banks and eventually forced them to take partial losses on their loans to Mexico.

What lesson did Mr. X learn? "As soon as I get liquidity again, I'm going back into the market and make it all back. This is the day of the trader."

Sources: *The Wall Street Journal,* January 6, 1977; *InterMarket,* 1984; *Chicago Tribune* August 30, 1988; *The Wall Street Journal,* August 30, 1988; *Chicago Life* XXVI, 1989; *Reason* March 1989. I am indebted to Jennifer L. O'Reilly for most of these sources.

Importing goods and services correspondingly tends to cause the home currency to be sold in order to buy foreign currency. If the United States imports, say, a million dollars of British automobiles, then somebody is likely to want to sell a million dollars to get pounds. If the U.S. importer is allowed to pay in dollars, the British exporter of the automobiles faces the task of selling the million dollars to get pounds if he wants to end up holding his home currency. If the British exporter insists on being paid in pounds, it is the U.S. importer of the autos that must take a million dollars to the foreign exchange market in search of pounds. Either way, U.S. *imports of goods and services will create a demand for foreign currency* and a supply of the home currency to the extent that U.S. importers have dollars to offer and foreign exporters prefer to end up holding their own currencies. Only if foreign exporters are happy to hold onto dollars (or the U.S. importers somehow have large reserves of foreign currencies to spend) can U.S. imports keep from generating a supply of dollars and a demand for foreign currency.

The traders entering the foreign exchange market in order to exchange currencies seldom transact directly with each other. Rather, each trader deals with a bank, usually in his or her own country. The large banks accustomed to foreign exchange dealings then buy and sell currencies both among themselves and with specialized foreign exchange brokers. Thus, the U.S. firm selling aircraft exports in exchange for payment in pounds would take the British importer's promise to repay and sell it to a U.S. bank, which sells this IOU in sterling to another bank wanting to buy sterling with dollars. The dollars received by the U.S. bank compensate it for the dollars it paid to the U.S. aircraft exporter (along with small fees pocketed by the bank for helping the exporter get rid of his sterling). In financial jargon, one could reexpress this pair of transactions as follows: The U.S. aircraft exporter "draws a bill on London" and "discounts" it with a U.S. bank, which "rediscounts" it, "repatriating" its proceeds through the foreign exchange market.

Although foreign trade transactions loom large in the foreign-exchange market, they are not the only kind of transactions generating demand and supply for currencies. People can demand British pounds even without wanting to buy British goods and services. They may simply want to hold their assets in sterling, either to make an expected high rate of return or to hold sterling balances ready in case they should later want to buy British goods or services. People in the United States and Canada often also demand foreign currency in order to be able to send remittances and cash gifts to relatives in Italy or Mexico or some other country from which they emigrated.

Hedging

The fact that exchange rates can change makes people take different views of foreign currencies. Some people do not want to have to gamble on what exchange rates will hold in the future, and they want to keep their assets in their home currency alone. Others, thinking they have a good idea of what will happen to exchange rates, would be quite willing to gamble by holding a foreign currency, one different from the currency in which they will ultimately buy consumer goods and services. These two attitudes have been personified into the concepts of hedgers and speculators, as though individual persons were always one or the other, even though the same person can choose to behave like a hedger in some cases and like a speculator in others.

Hedging against an asset, here a currency, is the act of making sure that you have neither a net asset nor a net liability position in that asset.

We usually think of hedgers in international dealings as persons who have a home currency and insist on having an exact balance between their liabilities and assets in foreign currencies. In financial jargon, hedging means avoiding both kinds of "open" positions in a foreign currency—both "long" positions, or holding net assets in the foreign currency, and "short" positions, or owing more of the foreign currency than one holds. An American who has hedged a position in German marks has assured that the future of the exchange rate between dollars and marks will not affect his or her net worth. Hedging is a perfectly normal kind of behavior, especially for people for whom international financial dealings are a sideline. Simply avoiding any net commitments in a foreign currency saves on the time and trouble of keeping abreast of fast-changing international currency conditions.

The foreign exchange market provides a useful service to hedgers by allowing hedgers of all nationalities to get rid of net asset or net liability positions in currencies they don't want to own or owe. Suppose, for example, that you are managing the financial assets of an American rock group and that the group has just received £100,000 in checking deposits in London as a result of selling recordings in Britain. The group wants to hold onto the extra money in some form for a while, say for three months. But doing so exposes the group to an exchange-rate risk. The value of each pound sterling, which is now (say) $1.67/£, may drop or rise over the next three months, affecting the value in dollars that the group ends up with when selling the pounds in the future. Let us suppose that the group does not want to take on this risk and headache and that it wants to ensure itself right now of a fixed number of dollars. It can use the foreign-exchange market, selling its £100,000 for $167,000, and then investing those dollars at interest in the United States. Whether or not the group ends up making more money by getting out of sterling now is of limited relevance because the group had decided that it does not want to have the value of its wealth depend on the future of the exchange rate between sterling and the dollar.

The foreign-exchange market provides the same kind of hedging opportunity to people in all sorts of other situations involving foreign currencies. An American who will have to *pay* £100,000 three months from now need not wait that long to buy sterling at a future and uncertain exchange rate. This person can hedge against this sterling liability by buying sterling now and holding enough money in Britain to be able to repay the £100,000 after three months. Similarly, somebody in Britain with dollar assets to get rid of can sell them at today's exchange rate and thus end any uncertainty about the money's worth in terms of pounds sterling. British residents with dollar debts to discharge in the near future can similarly buy dollars with pounds now and eliminate any uncertainty about how many pounds it will cost them to pay off their dollar debts. The same foreign exchange market that produces changing exchange rates gives hedgers a way to avoid gambling on the future of exchange rates.

Speculation

The opposite of hedging is **speculation,** the act of taking a net asset position ("long" position) or a net liability position ("short" position) in some asset class, here a foreign currency.

Speculating means committing oneself to an uncertain future value of one's net worth in terms of home currency. Most of these commitments are based on conscious, though vague, expectations about the future price of the foreign currency.

A rich imagery surrounds the term *speculator*. Speculators are usually portrayed as a class apart from the rest of humanity. These Gnomes of Zurich, in the frequent newspaper imagery, are viewed as being greedy— unlike you or me, of course. They are also viewed as exceptionally jittery and as adding an element of subversive chaos to the economic system. They come out only in the middle of storms: we don't hear about them unless the economy is veering out of control, and then it is their fault. Although speculation has indeed played such a sinister role in the past, it is an open empirical question whether it does so frequently. More to the present point, we must recognize that the only concrete way of defining speculation is the broad way just offered. Anybody is a speculator who is willing to take a net position in a foreign currency, whatever his or her motives or expectations about the future of the exchange rate.[3]

The foreign exchange market provides the same bridge between currencies for speculators as for hedgers, since there is no credentials check that can sort out the two groups in the marketplace. The American rock group holding

---

[3] By contrast, most practitioners would use definitions more laden with judgments about speculators' motives, as in the following passage from author Holbrook Working: "In ordinary usage and in much economic discussion the word *speculation* refers to buying and selling (or, more accurately, holding) property purely for the sake of gain from price change, and not merely as an incident to the normal conduct of a producing or merchandising business or of investment." Chicago Board of Trade, *Selected Writings of Holbrook Working* (Chicago: Board of Trade, 1977, p. 253). A drawback of this common usage is that there is no way of measuring how much net owning or owing of an asset is done "purely for the sake of gain from price change." Furthermore, knowing that the party in question gains a certain percentage of its income from "producing," "merchandising," and "investment" sheds no

£100,000 in London has the option of speculating in sterling. It need not sell its sterling now but can hold onto it in Britain for three months, earning interest and waiting to see how many dollars its pounds, including interest, are worth after three months.

Whether a person willing to speculate in a foreign currency does so depends on home and foreign interest rates and also on that person's expectations about the future movement in the exchange rate. Suppose that the 90-day (three-month) interest rate is 4 percent in Britain and 3 percent in the United States. The group holding £100,000 could invest it in Britain at 4 percent and have £104,000 after the 90 days or it could sell the £100,000 in the foreign exchange market at the exchange rate of $1.67/£ and invest this $167,000 at 3 percent, ending up with $167,000 × 1.03 = $172,010.

Whether it is more profitable to end up with £104,000 or $172,010 clearly depends on what the exchange rate will turn out to be after 90 days. If the group feels certain that the pound sterling will not change in value over the 90 days, it will see merit in the idea of holding onto the sterling and earning 4 percent, bringing home £104,000 × $1.67/£ = $173,680, which is about 1 percent better than having held the money in the United States and ending up with only $172,010. If sterling is expected to rise in value over the 90 days, this is all the more reason to hold the money in sterling. But if the value of sterling is expected to fall by more than 1 percent, then it is not a good idea to hold it. For example, if sterling were to drop 16 percent in value and be worth only $1.40 a pound after 90 days, the group would lose considerably by holding it. Keeping the money in sterling would yield only £104,000 × $1.40/£ = $145,600 instead of the $172,010 that could be safely earned by selling pounds for dollars right away and earning 3 percent interest in the United States.

So the profitability of speculating in a foreign currency depends on whether or not one expects the value of that currency to drop by as great a percentage as its interest rate exceeds the domestic interest rate. The existence of a foreign-exchange market does not guarantee that speculation will be profitable. It only makes speculation feasible for those willing to take the chance.

FORWARD EXCHANGE RATES

There are many bridges between any two major currencies. In this chapter we focus on the largest foreign-exchange market, the spot market, or market

---

light on the motives for holding a particular asset. Our definition, by contrast, is easily measurable.

Semantic confusion about speculation is often deliberately fostered by persons aware of the term's pejorative connotation. Banks and other international investors often claim that *they* invest while *others* speculate, implying that the latter action is more risky and foolhardy. We see the distinction but not the difference, unless the party claiming not to be speculating can show balance sheets revealing no net positions in any of the assets in question.

for delivery on the spot (within two working days). Yet, people often find it more convenient to sign contracts for future exchange.[4] The rates of exchange negotiated now for later delivery are called *forward* exchange rates. The following examples are from Figure 15.1:

	British Pound	*Japanese Yen*	*West German Mark (DM)*
Spot rate	$1.6700	0.6341 cent	$0.6037
30-day forward rate	$1.6604	0.6348 cent	$0.6038
90-day forward rate	$1.6430	0.6361 cent	$0.6041
180-day forward rate	$1.6180	0.6383 cent	$0.6043

Each rate refers to purchase or sale contracts to be sealed now but with delivery at the future date specified. Somebody agreeing to sell 90-day sterling in May must be prepared to deliver it at the agreed price of $1.6430 at a particular date in August. That person need not own any sterling at all until August, but the rate at which he gives it up in August is already fixed as of May. *Do not confuse the forward rate with the future spot rate,* the spot rate that ends up prevailing on the August date. The forward rate could be above, below, or equal to the spot price of sterling come August. In this respect, a forward exchange rate is like a commodity futures price or an advance hotel reservation.

Why the various rates for the same currency can differ, and what determines them, will be explored at length in Appendix H. Here we need only note that any of the major functions of a foreign exchange market—clearing, hedging, or speculation—can be performed with a forward exchange as well as with a regular spot exchange.

Hedging can be accomplished with the forward market as easily as with the spot market. The American rock group in our example above does not

---

[4] In addition to the spot and forward markets, an *options market* in foreign exchange has become increasingly important since it was introduced in the United States in the early 1980s. You can buy or sell currency options either to hedge or to speculate. What is distinctive about an option is that you are protected against price movements in only one direction, and you have the option not to transact at all.

Buying an option on, say, the Japanese yen means buying the right, but not the obligation, to buy yen later from somebody at a particular price. If the yen turns out to have spot value lower than your option price (or strike price), then don't use your yen option—just buy yen cheaper in the spot market instead. But if the yen turns out to be worth more than your option price, use the option. You can demand that the party that sold you the option deliver at the stipulated option price. You have cheap yen, which you could resell at the now-higher spot price. The option to buy yen is especially valuable to (1) a hedger wanting to avoid the risk of paying a high yen price, but who doesn't care much whether the yen price ends up much lower or (2) a speculator who thinks there is a good chance that the yen will rise above the option price. In either case, the option buyer must pay a fee to the seller, who takes on a risk by giving the buyer an option. For more on currency options, see Giddy (1988) and Levich (1988).

have to choose between exchange risk and selling their £100,000 in sterling at the spot rate of $1.67/£. Another option is to leave the £100,000 in Britain while at the same time fixing the price at which they can sell off all their sterling later. They could, for example, invest their sterling for 90 days at the 4 percent interest rate used above but sell the $1.04 \times £100,000 = £104,000$ immediately in the 90-day forward market at, say, the rate of $1.6430/£ given in Figure 15.1. If this transaction takes place in May, the group knows in May that they will have exactly $170,872 (= 104,000 \times 1.6430) in August regardless of what happens to exchange rates between now and then. Now the 90-day forward rate of $1.6430 may strike the group as a good price or a bad one, depending on the rate at which they can sell sterling in the spot market. The point remains, however, that they can ensure against any uncertainty about exchange rates by dealing in the forward market.

The forward market also gives an extra option to speculators. If a speculator thinks he or she has a fairly good idea of what will happen to the spot exchange rate in the future, it is easy to bet on the basis of that idea using the forward market. It is so easy, in fact, that the speculator can even bet with money he or she does not have in hand.

To illustrate this point, suppose that you are convinced that the pound sterling, worth $1.67 in May, will take a dive and be worth only $1.20 in August. Perhaps you see a coming political and economic crisis in Britain that others do not see. You can make an enormous gain by using the forward market. Contact a foreign exchange trader and agree to sell £10 million at the going 90-day forward rate of $1.6430. If the trader believes in your ability to honor your forward commitment in August, you do not even need to put up any money now in May. Just sign the forward contract. How will you be able to come up with £10 million in August? Given your knowledge of a coming crisis, there is nothing to worry about. Relax. Take a three-month vacation in Hawaii. From time to time, stroll off the beach long enough to glance at the newspaper and note that the pound is sinking, just as you knew it would. Two days before the contract date in August, reap your rewards painlessly: show a bank that you have a forward contract from some poor trader committing him to give you $16.43 million for your £10 million in two days' time. Since the pound has sunk to about $1.20 in the spot market, the banker is happy to accept your contract as collateral and lend you $12 million. Giving the banker a tiny payment for two days' use of the $12 million to buy £10 million, which you immediately exchange for the guaranteed $16.43 million, netting $4.43 million for a few minutes' effort and a lot of foresight. If you are smarter than the others in the marketplace, you can get rich using the convenient forward exchange market.

Your speculation may turn out differently, however. Suppose you were wrong. Suppose that Britain's prospects brighten greatly between May and August. Suppose that when August comes around, the spot value of the pound has risen to $2.00. Now you must come up with $20 million to get the £10 million you agreed to sell in exchange for only $16.43 million. It does not take much arithmetic to see what this means for your personal wealth. It is time to reevaluate your lifestyle.

As this example shows, forward-market speculators make their gains or losses from the difference between the forward rate and the later spot rate. Since there are two sides to every contract, the forward rate will settle at the level where just as much money is committed to the belief that the spot rate will end up below it as is committed to the opposite belief. The forward rate thus equals an average expected value of the future of the spot rate (Appendix H elaborates). If you want to see what informed opinion thought the pound would be worth in 90 days' time, just look up the 90-day forward rate. It is the average expectation of the future spot value, just as the "point spread" in football betting is the number of points by which the average bettor expects the stronger team to win.

FORWARD VERSUS SPOT EXCHANGE RATES

If hedgers and speculators can choose between using the spot market and using the forward market, why should the spot and forward exchange rates differ?

The answer is that the spot and forward rates should differ by about as much as interest rates differ in the two countries' currencies. To see why, return to the options facing the rock group above. Their £100,000 can be converted into future dollars in either of two ways. First, they can sell the pounds in the spot market and invest them in America, getting $172,010 (= 100,000 × 1.67 × 1.03) after 90 days. Second, they can earn interest in Britain and sell the resulting £104,000 in the forward exchange market. Since many people face such options, the forward exchange rate will tend to be whatever makes the two ways of moving between currencies look equally profitable. If, as in the examples above, the interest rate is 1 percent higher in Britain, then the forward rate should *not* equal the spot rate. If it did, everybody would do their lending in Britain rather than in the United States. Those wanting to end up with dollars would sell pounds in the forward market after lending in Britain, rather than in the spot market. Such a stampede would force the exchange rates (or the interest rates) to change. To equalize the two opportunities open to each investor, the forward rate on sterling should be 1 percent lower than the spot rate to offset the fact that interest rates are 1 percent higher in Britain.

Such reasoning, spelled out at more length in Appendix H, leads to the following result:

Interest parity: the forward exchange value of a currency will tend to exceed its spot value by as much (in percent) as its interest rates are lower than foreign interest rates.

Here is an explanation for the differences between spot and forward rates. A country with 1 percent higher interest rates will tend to have a 1 percent "forward discount" (shortfall of the forward rate below the spot rate) on its currency. In fact, Britain's pound sterling did have a forward discount in Figure 15.1.[5] In the same figure, France and Canada also had forward rates below their spot rates because their interest rates were above U.S. interest rates. By contrast, the forward Japanese yen, German mark, and Swiss franc were at a premium (above the corresponding spot rates) because interest rates tended to be lower in these countries. The relationship of the spot and forward rates is thus dictated by the international interest-rate gap. As long as this gap stays the same, the spot and forward rates will keep differing by the same percentage, and whatever moves the spot rate up and down will do the same to the forward rate.

For a firmer understanding of how the interest parity condition comes about and how it can be used, let us go back through the previous example, this time using algebra that handles all cases, not the numbers of just one case (again, see Appendix H for a longer explanation). You can convert today's pounds into a known amount of dollars 90 days from now in either of two ways:

- You can convert present pounds into future dollars by selling them at the spot exchange rate (r_s, measured as dollars per pound) and investing those dollars at the American interest rate i_a. In this case:

$$\text{future dollar value per present pound} = r_s \cdot (1 + i_a)$$

Or:

- You can convert present pounds into future dollars by investing the pounds in Britain at the interest rate i_b and selling the later earnings right now at the forward exchange rate r_f, again measured in dollars per pound. In this case:

$$\text{future dollar value per present pound} = (1 + i_b) \cdot r_f$$

If you can get from present pounds to future dollars in either of two ways, you will surely take the more profitable way. But everybody else will figure out the same thing. Since investors have choices, the exchange rates and interest rates will adjust so that the two future dollar values are equal. That is,

$$r_s \cdot (1 + i_a) = (1 + i_b) \cdot r_f, \text{ or } r_f/r_s = (1 + i_a)/(1 + i_b)$$

This can be called the interest parity condition. First, though, let us convert it into a more memorable form, with a little algebraic substitution:

---

[5] In fact the 90-day forward discount on the pound sterling in Figure 15.1 was about 1.6 percent, rather than the simple 1 percent. On the same date the 90-day difference between British and American interest rates was also about 1.6 percent.

$$\frac{r_f - r_s}{r_s} = \frac{i_a - i_b}{1 + i_b}$$

This equation gives the **formula for interest parity.** In other words, the

| **Forward rate premium**
on the British pound
(as a share of the spot rate) | *equals* | **the difference between American**
and British interest rates
(as a share of $1 + i_b$) |

Use this to see how changes in interest rates will relate to the forward premium. A rise in American interest rates by one percent is likely to raise the premium of the forward price of the pound over its spot price by one percent. A rise in British interest rates would have the opposite effect. One event that could cause both a rise in American interest rates and a rise in the forward premium on the pound is a rise in expectations of inflation in the United States. That would raise American interest rates because lenders would demand a higher interest rate to compensate them for expected inflation. It would also logically raise the forward premium on the pound: fearing more inflation in the United States, investors would expect the dollar to sink between now (spot price) and then (affecting today's forward price).

DEMAND AND SUPPLY FOR A CURRENCY

To understand what makes a country's currency rise and fall in value, you should proceed through the same steps used to analyze any competitive market: first, portray the interaction of demand and supply as determinants of the equilibrium price and quantity and then explore what other forces lie behind the demand and supply curves. The first step is taken in this chapter and the second step in the next.

The supply and demand for foreign exchange determine the exchange rate, within certain constraints imposed by the nature of the foreign exchange system under which the country operates. Anybody wanting to make any of the international transactions discussed in Chapter 14—exporters, importers, banks, brokers, and so forth—will want to trade in a competitive foreign exchange market.

The simplest system is the **floating exchange-rate system** without intervention by governments or central bankers. The major countries have been on something close to this system since 1971. The spot (or forward) price of foreign currency is determined by the interaction of demand and supply for that currency, which are in turn determined by a host of factors discussed at more length in the next chapter. The market clears itself through the price mechanism.

The two parts of Figure 15.3 show how such a system could yield equilibrium exchange rates for the pound sterling and the German mark at the E points. The vertical supply curve in each case is the entire stock of national

FIGURE 15.3 The Spot Exchange Market, with and without Official Intervention

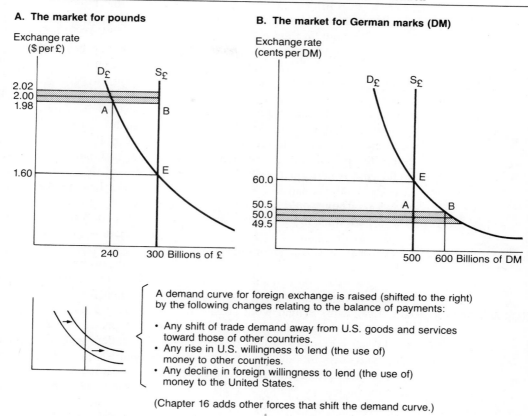

A. The market for pounds

B. The market for German marks (DM)

A demand curve for foreign exchange is raised (shifted to the right) by the following changes relating to the balance of payments:

• Any shift of trade demand away from U.S. goods and services toward those of other countries.
• Any rise in U.S. willingness to lend (the use of) money to other countries.
• Any decline in foreign willingness to lend (the use of) money to the United States.

(Chapter 16 adds other forces that shift the demand curve.)

money.[6] In our increasingly international world, it is important to think of all of a nation's money as part of the relevant supply, not just some part held by active currency traders. The vertical supply curve implies that the amount of a nation's money in existence is not affected by the exchange rate, a somewhat reasonable assumption.

_____

[6] It is useful to equate the supply of pounds or DM or any other currency with the money supply as usually defined, that is, the sum of circulating currency plus demand deposits held in banks by nonbank depositors. This definition helps keep our attention on monetary policy as a central force behind exchange rates. Strictly speaking, the supply of, say, pounds should refer to the stock of all promises to repay in pounds, whether these promises are money or not (examples of nonmoney promises to repay pounds: British treasury bonds, private companies' debts in sterling.)

What makes the demand curve slope downward? That is, why should a lower (higher) price of a currency generally mean that more (less) of it is demanded? To see the likelihood of the downward slope, imagine that the supply of pounds in Figure 15.3A has just shifted from £250 billion up to £300 billion. The initial exchange rate of $1.98 cannot be sustained. People do not want to hold just any amount of money in pounds sterling at the exchange rate of $1.98. Having the supply suddenly expand up to £300 billion means there are more pounds to be lent and spent. The price of the pound, or the exchange rate, will start dropping. Yet it is not likely to drop all the way to zero. As the pound declines below $1.98, people will discover more uses for it. One use would be to buy wool sweaters in Britain. Before the pound sinks, a sweater selling for £50 in London looks like it would cost American tourists $99 (= 50 × 1.98). If the pound suddenly sinks to $1.60, the same £50 wool sweater would cost the American tourists only $80. They would start buying more. To pay for the extra sweaters, they would want more pounds sterling, to be paid to British merchants. As long as the level of business remains higher, there is more demand for a stock of pounds to conduct that business.

The case of British wool sweaters is just one illustration of the forces that might make the demand curve for a currency slope downward. There are usually many such quick responses of trade to a change in the exchange rate. Even with British wool sweaters, the response does not depend on American tourists alone. In fact, if the pound is sinking in value relative to all other currencies, a host of alert buyers and sellers will notice. When the pound sinks in value, more French and Belgian shoppers tend to cross the Channel (e.g., by hovercraft) searching for new bargains in such British clothing outlets as Marks and Spencer. At the same time, fewer British shoppers cross the Channel to shop in Belgium or France, where the franc prices now look higher when translated into pounds. The same effects show up for other commodities: a sinking pound means more bicycles bought from British companies and less bought from Schwinn or Nishiki. A sinking pound means more British customers will settle for a British car and forgo the Fiat or Honda, and so forth. In every case, there is more reason to buy British and therefore more reason for a perpetual demand for pounds as a currency to facilitate such transactions.

As long as a lower exchange rate raises the quantity demanded, the foreign-exchange market should be stable. The pound and mark markets in Figure 15.3 are drawn this way, with the demand curves crossing the vertical supply curves in the right way for stable equilibriums at the E points. This comforting case of stable exchange rates need not always hold. In Chapter 18, we shall see different ways in which the curves could cross the wrong way and cause exchange markets to become unstable.

To explain what makes the floating exchange rate rise or fall, we need to know the forces that shift the supply and demand curves in Figure 15.3. The supply curve, again, is identified with foreign countries' money supplies. The demand curve is shifted by a variety of changes in the economy, changes discussed in the next chapter. Here we can note, however, that some of the demand-side forces relate to the balance of payments categories of Chapter 14. Anything that shifts wealth into the hands of persons residing outside the United States is likely raise demand for non-U.S. currency and lower demand for the dollar because people tend to hold the currency of their residence. Examples are noted at the bottom of Figure 15.3. Shifts in trade demand away from the United States would put money into the hands of non-U.S. residents, who have less incentive to hold the dollar. Their extra attempts to sell the dollars and buy foreign currency can be graphed as an upward (rightward) shift of the demand for foreign exchange. Similarly, a rise in U.S. residents' willingness to lend money to foreign borrowers puts money temporarily in the hands of people who have less incentive to keep holding dollars than did the U.S. residents who lent the money. The same effect is produced by a decline in foreign willingness to lend money to residents of the United States.

The same diagrams can be used to introduce the other main foreign-exchange institution, the **fixed exchange-rate system.** Here, officials strive to keep the exchange rate virtually fixed even if the rate they choose departs from the current equilibrium rate. Figure 15.3 shows how officials could keep the exchange rate essentially fixed. Their usual procedure under such a system is to declare a "band" of exchange rates within which the rate is allowed to vary. If the exchange rate hits the top or bottom of the band, the officials must intervene. In Figure 15.3A, sterling has weakened so that its equilibrium rate of $1.60/£ is well below the officially declared "par value" of $2.00. Officials have announced that they will support the pound at 1 percent below par, or about $1.98, and the dollar at 1 percent above par, or about $2.02. In Figure 15.3A, they are forced to make good on this pledge by holding 50 billion pounds instead of dollars, filling the gap *AB*. Only in this way can they bring the total demand for pounds, private plus official, up to the 300 billion of sterling money in existence. If their purchases of pounds with dollars fall short, total demand cannot meet the supply and the price must fall below the official support point of $1.98. Needless to say, officials wanting to defend the fixed exchange rate may not have sufficient reserves of dollars to keep the price fixed indefinitely, a point to which we shall return several times.

Another case of official intervention in defense of a fixed exchange rate is shown in Figure 15.3B. Officials of some government or central bank, perhaps in Germany itself, have declared that the par value of the German mark shall be 50 cents in U.S. currency, and that the support points are 50.5 cents and 49.5 cents. As the demand and supply curves are drawn, they must intervene in the foreign exchange market and sell off 150 billion DM to meet the strong demand at 50.5 cents. If the government officials do not have enough DM reserves, or if they cannot tolerate buying enough dollars to plug the gap *AB* and keep the exchange rate down at 50.5 cents, they will have to give up and let the price rise.

The fixed-rate system has taken several forms. Before World War I, it was often maintained by the workings of the **gold standard.** When a currency fell in value, as sterling has fallen to $1.98 in Figure 15.3A, it fell in terms of other currencies with fixed official values in terms of gold. Even without official intervention, the gap *AB* tended to become gold exports from Britain. More and more individuals turned their sterling paper currency in for gold at the Bank of England at the official price and took it to the United States, where gold was being officially exchanged at par for money that now looked more valuable. Conversely, under the gold standard a gap like *AB* in Figure 15.3B would tend to become an inflow of gold into Germany. Under a true gold standard, officials let gaps eliminate themselves by draining gold (and other forms of international reserves) from deficit countries and sending it to surplus countries. Gold flows shift the demand and supply curves until they intersect at the fixed exchange rate, as we shall see in Chapter 17.

Changes in exchange rates are given various names depending on the kind of exchange-rate regime prevailing. Under the floating-rate system a fall in the market equilibrium price of a currency is called a **depreciation** of that currency; a rise is an **appreciation.** We refer to a discrete official reduction in the otherwise fixed par value of a currency as a **devaluation; revaluation** is the antonym, describing a discrete raising of the official par. Devaluations and revaluations are the main ways of changing exchange rates in a nearly fixed-rate system, a system where the rate is usually, but not always, fixed. The main historical example of this variation on fixed rates was the adjustable-peg or Bretton Woods system prevailing between 1944 and 1971, a system discussed in Chapter 17.

SUMMARY

A **foreign exchange** transaction is a trade of one national money for another at a negotiated exchange rate. The spot foreign exchange market, the market for immediate delivery, allows people either to hedge or to speculate. **Hedging** is the act of equating your assets and liabilities in a foreign currency, so as to be immune to risk resulting from future changes in the value of the foreign currency. **Speculating** means taking a net asset position (a "long" position) or a net liability position (a "short" position) in a foreign currency, thereby gambling on its future exchange value. You can either hedge or speculate in the spot market for foreign exchange.

The **forward market** for foreign exchange serves the same private uses as the spot market. You can buy or sell a currency for future delivery at a price fixed now, instead of buying or selling spot (for immediate delivery). The choice depends on the forward rate, the spot rate, and interest rates in each country. You can *either* hedge or speculate in *either* the forward market or the spot market. The fact that either forward or spot markets can be used leads to the:

Interest parity conditions, that is, the forward exchange value of a currency will tend to exceed its spot value by the same percentage as its interest rates are lower than foreign interest rates.

One other key condition emerges from the ease of using the forward market as a way of betting on the future spot value of a currency: the forward rate equals the average expected value of the future spot rate.

In either a spot or a forward market, the exchange rate is determined by supply and demand in ways affected by exchange-rate institutions. Under the freely flexible exchange-rate system, without government intervention, changes in price clear the market. Under the fixed-rate system, officials buy and sell a currency so as to keep its exchange rate within an officially stipulated band. When the currency's value lies at the bottom of its official band, officials must buy it by selling other currencies or gold. When the currency's value presses against the top of its official price range, officials must sell it in exchange for gold or other currencies.

SUGGESTED READINGS

Three good alternative textbook views of the foreign exchange market are Yeager (1976, Chapter 2); Grubel (1981, Chapters 11 and 12); and Mayer, Duesenberry, and Aliber (1984, Chapters 27 and 28). For an update on innovations in foreign-exchange institutions, and international financial innovations in general, see Levich (1988) and Stern and Chew (1988).

QUESTIONS FOR REVIEW

1. This chapter introduces a number of terms worth reviewing. Be sure you are able to define each of the following:

a. Hedging.

b. Speculation.

c. "Long" and "short" positions.

d. Forward rate (versus expected future spot rate).

e. Par value.

f. Devaluation and revaluation.

g. Depreciation and appreciation.

2. Are you hedging or speculating if you agree to sell a thousand pounds forward and have no other assets or liabilities in sterling?

3. Describe two ways in which a Canadian, who knows he will receive £10,000 in London 90 days from now can convert his funds into Canadian dollars payable 90 days from now. What determines which of these two routes is the cheaper way to move his money?

Answers:

2. Speculating, since you are "short" in sterling.

3. He can just wait 90 days for the sterling and sell it for Canadian dollars at whatever spot exchange rate prevails 90 days from now, or he can borrow against the £10,000 in Britain, sell the proceeds of the loan for Canadian dollars in the spot market, and invest the dollars in Canada for 90 days. Which route is better depends on the difference between the British and Canadian rates of interest. If the British rate at which he borrows is lower, he should follow the second course unless he expects the value of sterling to rise.

▼

What Determines Exchange Rates?

•

Thinking in terms of supply and demand is a necessary first step toward understanding exchange rates. The next step is the one that has to be taken in any market analysis: finding out what underlying forces cause supply and demand to change.

We need to know what forces have caused the wide shifts in exchange rates observed since the start of widespread "floating" back in 1971. Figure 16.1 reminds us just how wide these shifts have been. Between 1971 and the end of 1973, most currencies rose in value relative to the dollar, the average rise being about 20 percent. The dollar gained only slightly in value between 1973 and 1976. From 1977 through 1980, the dollar sank—that is, other currencies rose again by an average of 13 percent. Then, during the first half of the 1980s, nearly all observers were stunned as the dollar rallied. By the time it peaked in February 1985, the dollar had gained about 53 percent relative to other currencies since 1980, ending up about 22 percent stronger than it had been in 1971. The dollar then fell almost 40 percent in three years, before rising from April 1988 into the 1990s.

Within these broad movements in the value of the dollar in terms of all other currencies, there were striking contrasts in the behavior of individual currencies. Figure 16.1A shows how far Japan's yen, the Swiss franc, and the German mark rose against the dollar. The yen and Swiss franc actually doubled in dollar value over the 1970s and 1980s. In contrast, other leading currencies—notably the pound, the lira, and the Canadian dollar—went through a net decline, as shown in Figure 16.1B. Still other currencies, such as the Israeli shekel or the Argentine peso, dropped so far in value that they could not be graphed in Figure 16.1.

Why such swings in the position of the dollar, and why the wide differences in the net movements of individual currencies? We need to know because exchange-rate movements set off many macroeconomic effects, some of

FIGURE 16.1   Selected Exchange Rates, 1970–1989 (monthly)

A. Swiss franc, West German DM, Japanese Yen and U.S. dollar

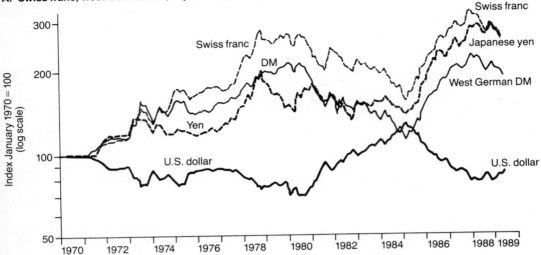

B. Canadian dollar, French franc, pound sterling and Italian lira

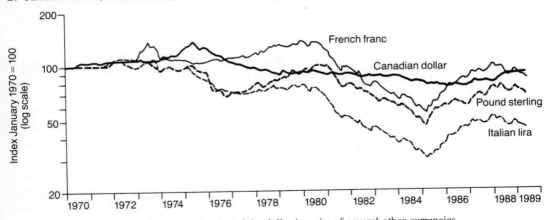

For U.S. dollar, a trade-weighted average price of the dollar in units of several other currencies.

For all other currencies, the dollar price of that currency (e.g., $/£).
So, for any currency: ↑ = it rises in value (appreciates)
↓ = it declines in value (depreciates).

Sources: IMF, *International Financial Statistics* and U.S. Federal Reserve Board.

them negative. This chapter presents what economists believe, what they think they know, and what they admit they do not know, about this challenging scientific puzzle.

Most of what economists believe can be summarized by the broad **"asset market" approach to exchange rates,** which explains exchange rates in terms of the demands and supplies of assets denominated (priced) in different currencies. Surveying the asset market approach, and supplementing it with a few borrowed ideas that seem to fit the data, will lead us to the following summary of the main determinants of exchange rates:

The exchange rate r, the price of foreign currency in units of ours, is raised by the following changes in "fundamentals":

- A rise in our money supply relative to foreign money supply (M/M_f).
- A rise in foreign real national product relative to ours (y_f/y).
- A rise in our rate of expected price inflation (π) relative to expected foreign inflation (π_f).
- A rise in the foreign real interest rate $(i_f - \pi_f)$ relative to our real interest rate $(i - \pi)$.
- A decline in our trade balance (TB) due to a shift in demand toward foreign goods.

Be prepared for an intermediate result. Scholars and professional traders do agree on some of the "fundamentals" that drive exchange-rate movements,[1] but they all readily admit that their understanding and their ability to forecast are limited.

THE ROLE OF MONEY SUPPLIES

As long as nations have their own currencies, trying to analyze exchange rates or international payments without looking at national money markets is like playing *Hamlet* without the Prince of Denmark. A change in exchange rates is, after all, a change in a price ratio between national moneys. And, as stressed in Chapter 15, the supply of the asset called "foreign exchange" really includes the entire money supply of a nation, not just the working bank balances of a few foreign exchange specialists.[2]

---

[1] The forces examined here are central not only to an understanding of what causes floating rates to change, but also to an understanding of the pressures on a system of fixed rates. Whatever would make a floating currency sink would also make a fixed exchange rate harder to defend. The material that follows thus has more uses than simply this chapter's search for determinants of the exchange rate. It will also apply to the analysis of the balance of payments under a fixed-rate system or a managed floating rate.

[2] The definition of the relevant supply of a currency can be even broader than the national money supply. Proponents of the "portfolio balance" branch of the modern asset-market theory argue for including, or even concentrating on, interest-paying government debt in the definition of currency supply. The merits of focusing on government debt are still being

Relative money supplies obviously affect exchange rates. On the international front as on the domestic, a currency is less valuable the more of it there is to circulate. Extreme cases of hyperinflation dramatize this fundamental point. The trillionfold increase in the German money supply in 1922–23 was the key proximate cause of the trillionfold increase in the price of foreign exchange and of everything else in Germany at that time. Hyperinflation of the money supplies is also the key to understanding why the currencies of Israel and several Latin American countries lost almost all their value in recent times.

TRANSACTIONS DEMAND FOR MONEY: NATIONAL MONEY AS TICKETS TO GNP

Turning to the demand side of overall money markets, we first recall that money is used as a medium of exchange. A certain stock should be on hand to cover an uncertain value of transactions that may arise requiring the exchange of money for goods and services. This transaction demand varies with the annual turnover of transactions requiring money, a turnover that is fairly well proxied by the level of national product (GNP).

The same idea holds whether or not the national economy is open to world trade. The currencies people choose to hold for possible future transactions are those of the countries in which they expect to spend. Anybody wanting to buy U.S. national product will want to have U.S. dollars on hand for transactions, whether they live in the United States or in another country, simply because sellers of U.S. national product generally prefer to be paid in dollars. The demand for U.S. dollars is a demand for tickets granting the right to purchase some U.S. GNP. This demand should be proportional to U.S. national product, regardless of where the dollar demanders live.[3] The same should hold for any other country's currency.

The link between national product and the demand for the nation's money is central to the quantity theory of demand for money. The **quantity theory equation** says that in any country the money supply is equated with the demand for money, which is directly proportional to the value of gross national product. In separate equations for the home country and the rest of the world, the quantity theory equation becomes a pair:

$$M = k \times P \times y$$

---

debated. For an excellent review and tests of the different branches of the modern asset theory, see Frankel (1983).

[3] The "portfolio balance" branch of the modern asset-market theory takes a different tack here. It ties the demand for a currency not to that country's national product, but to the wealth of its residents. In practice, however, this should not make much difference because national product and national wealth are closely correlated.

and

$$M_f = k_f \times P_f \times y_f$$

where M and M_f are the home and foreign money supplies (measured in dollars and pounds, respectively), the Ps are the home and foreign price levels, the ys are the real (constant-price) national products, and the ks are behavioral ratios defined by each equation. Sometimes quantity theorists assume the ks are actually constant numbers, sometimes not (the facts say that any k varies). For the present long-run analysis, we follow the common presumption that the Ms are dictated by monetary policy alone and the ys are governed by such supply-side forces as productivity improvement or harvest failure.

The quantity-theory equations can be used to determine the ratio of prices between countries:

$$(P/P_f) = (M/M_f)\,(k_f/k)\,(y_f/y)$$

This does not yet tell us what determines the exchange rate between countries. The next step is a famous hypothesis that links relative prices (P/P_f) to the exchange rate (r).

PURCHASING-POWER PARITY (PPP)

The Hypothesis

In the long run, there is a predictable relationship between price levels and exchange rates, one built by the fact that goods and services can be bought in one country or another.

Goods that are substitutes for each other in international trade should have similar price movements in all countries when measured in the same currency. This should hold, at least, for a run long enough for market equilibrium to be restored after major shocks. The belief that international trade irons out differences in the price trends of traded goods has led to the **purchasing-power-parity hypothesis** linking national currency prices to exchange rates:

$$P = r \times P_f$$

or

$$r = P/P_f$$

Here the exchange rate r is again the price of the foreign currency (say, the pound) in dollars, and the price levels P and P_f are price levels in the home country (say, the United States) and the rest of the world, respectively, each denominated in its own currency.

Something like the purchasing-power-parity theory has existed throughout the modern history of international economics. The theory keeps resurfacing whenever exchange rates have come unfixed by wars or other events. Sometimes the hypothesis is used as a way of describing how a nation's general price level must change to reestablish some desired exchange rate, given the level and trend in foreign prices. At other times it is used to guess at what the equilibrium exchange rate will be, given recent trends in prices within and outside the country. Both of these interpretations crept into the British ''bullionist-antibullionist'' debate during and after the Napoleonic Wars, when the issue was why Britain had been driven by the wars to dislodge the pound sterling from its fixed exchange rates and gold backing, and what could be done about it. The purchasing-power-parity hypothesis came into its own in the 1920s, when Gustav Cassel and others directed it at the issue of how much European countries would have to change either their official exchange rates or their domestic price levels, given that World War I had driven the exchange rates off their prewar par values and had brought varying percentages of price inflation to different countries. With the restoration of the fixed exchange rate during the early postwar era, the purchasing-power-parity hypothesis again faded from prominence, ostensibly because its defects had been demonstrated, but mainly because the issue it raised seemed less compelling as long as exchange rates were expected to stay fixed. After the resumption of widespread floating of exchange rates in 1971, the hypothesis was revived once again.

Evidence on PPP

The purchasing-power-parity hypothesis has received mild, though mixed, empirical support. Using movements in P/P_f to predict the exchange rate r leads to small errors in some settings and large errors in others.

PPP predicts well at the level of one heavily traded commodity, either at a point in time or for changes over time. Suppose that No. 2 soft red Chicago wheat costs $4 a bushel in Chicago. Its dollar price in London should not be much greater, given the cheapness of transporting wheat from Chicago to London. To simplify the example, let us say that it costs nothing to transport the wheat. It seems reasonable, then, that the dollar price of the same wheat in London should be $4 a bushel. If it were not, it would pay someone to trade wheat between Chicago and London to profit from the price gap. Now if some major disruption temporarily forced the price of wheat in London up to $4.80, yet free trade were still possible, one would certainly expect that the two prices would soon be bid back into equality, presumably somewhere between $4 and $4.80 for both countries. In the case of wheat, which is a standardized commodity with a well-established market, one would expect the two prices to be brought into line within a week. For a highly-traded good like wheat, something called "the law of one price" is a fair approximation. The **law of one price** says that a single commodity will have the same price anywhere, once the prices at different places are expressed in the same currency. Thus, in the wheat example, if the exchange rate is $1.60 per pound and wheat costs $4.80 a bushel in Chicago, the law of one price predicts that the London price of wheat will be £3.00, so that wheat costs $4.80 a bushel (= 3.00 × 1.60) in London as well as in Chicago.

PPP predicts only moderately well at the level of all traded goods, either at a point in time or for changes over time. If P_T is a domestic price index for the whole bundle of our nation's exports and imports, and $P_{T,f}$ is a foreign-currency price index for the same bundle in other countries, it will turn out that $P_T/P_{T,f}$ is only a fair predictor of the exchange rate r. Once we get up to the level of several goods, we get into technical difficulties of comparing index numbers. We also confront a wide range of commodities, some of which have significant transport costs and official trade barriers, so that their prices differ between countries.

PPP predicts least well at the level of all goods in the economy. The kind of price level that relates most closely to national money supplies and national incomes is the overall "GNP price deflator," the price index for the whole bundle of all goods and services that make up gross national product. This is the concept we need for the P and the P_f of our theory. Unfortunately, this broad price concept includes many prices that fail to equalize between countries. As the box on "Price Gaps and International Income Comparisons" makes clear, price levels that the PPP theory assumes equal can be in a 3:1 ratio to each other. In fact, there is a clear pattern to the international failure of PPP to hold for GNP price deflators. The "worst" behaved prices are those for nontraded commodities, such as housing, haircuts, and other local services. The prices of nontraded commodities differ more radically between lower income and higher income countries than the purchasing-power-parity theory would predict, as the box also explains.

At any level of aggregation, *PPP predicts better over the long run than in the short run.* It takes time for market equilibrium to return after any given shock. The longer the number of years over which we examine prices and exchange rates, the closer we come to the PPP condition $r = P/P_f$. We shall document this finding in some tests below.

For all its limitations, the purchasing-power-parity theory has its social uses. It was a rough guide, but only a rough one, to the mistake made by Britain in returning to the prewar gold parity for the pound sterling in 1925 despite greater price inflation in Britain than in Britain's trading partners. The hypothesis has generally survived tests covering the 1940s. It also has an important message to offer countries such as Switzerland and Germany, which are seeking to keep domestic prices stable when the rest of the world is inflating. If prices elsewhere are rising 10 percent a year, in the long

PRICE GAPS AND INTERNATIONAL INCOME COMPARISONS

There is tremendous social importance to international comparisons of average income levels. To judge how fast Japan is overtaking the United States, we compare Japanese and U.S. gross national products per capita. To judge which nations are most "in need" of United Nations aid, World Bank loans, and other help, officials again compare their incomes per capita. All such comparisons are dangerous as well as unavoidable. The comparisons are likely to contain a host of large errors.

One of the worst pitfalls comes in converting from one national currency to another. It turns out that the exchange rate is a poor way to convert, precisely because the purchasing-power-parity theory is least reliable when applied to all the goods and services that make up GNP. To see how exchange rates can mislead, consider what happened to the comparison of Japan and the United States between 1984 and late 1986. As of 1984, according to the World Bank, Japan's GNP per person was only 69 percent of that of the United States, despite the press coverage of Japan's superior efficiency in many industries. In October 1986, a cover story in the London *Economist* trumpeted the news that Japan now had an average income that was 12 percent *higher* than that of the United States. Yet data on the real growth rates of the two countries differed very little between 1984 and 1986. How could Japan jump from being so far behind to being ahead in just two years without growing much faster?

The exchange rate was at fault. In 1984, the dollar was nearing its peak value in terms of yen. By October 1986, the dollar had fallen so far that it took about 33 percent fewer yen to buy a dollar than in 1984 (though the dollar rose again after 1988). So the *Economist* was calculating Japan's GNP in dollars per capita at a very different exchange rate from that used by the World Bank for 1984. The result was a mirage. No great change in the ratio of Japanese to American incomes had really occurred in those two years. The exchange rate oscillates wildly in response to asset market news and, to a lesser extent, in response to the prices of the most heavily traded goods.

If the exchange rate is unreliable, what should we use for comparing values of GNP per capita between countries? The principle is clear: we want to take the national products per capita expressed separately in two currencies and divide each by the overall price of the same bundle of goods and services. That way, we are comparing how many units of the same bundle of goods

CONTINUED

and services the average resident of each nation could buy. But it is difficult to get data on the separate prices of a wide-ranging bundle of goods and services for every country.

That is where the United Nations International Comparisons Project (ICP) came in. A team of economists at the University of Pennsylvania, led by Alan Heston, Irving Kravis, and Robert Summers, did the hard work of measuring the costs of items in separate countries, with financial backing by the United Nations (and also by the World Bank and the U.S. National Science Foundation). Today the ICP group has assembled useful annual data on the price structures and income levels of over 130 countries since the 1950s. What they have found, in effect, are the true levels of P and P_f for deflating the current-price national product figures. They confirm what was widely feared: the exchange rate r is often far from the ratio P/P_f that PPP says it should equal.

The table below shows the typical pattern in departures from PPP and the importance of replacing exchange-rate conversions of GNP per capita with the better comparisons based on the domestic price levels P and P_f. The data are from the year 1985:

Country	Each Country's GDP per Capita Relative to U.S. = 100,		Domestic Price Level (this country/U.S.) as a Percent of the Level Predicted by PPP
	Using the Exchange Rate	Using True Domestic Prices	
United States	100.0	100.0	100.0
Canada	83.9	90.6	92.6
Switzerland	89.4	83.5	107.1
West Germany	63.9	79.9	80.0
France	57.5	77.8	74.0
Sweden	74.5	75.5	98.8
Japan	67.2	69.6	96.6
United Kingdom	49.2	67.7	72.7
Italy	39.1	57.5	68.0
Mexico	14.0	29.5	47.4
Brazil	10.8	24.8	43.6
Korea	12.3	23.3	53.0

CONTINUED

| Country | Each Country's GDP per Capita Relative to U.S. = 100, | | Domestic Price Level (this country/U.S.) as a Percent of the Level Predicted by PPP |
	Using the Exchange Rate	Using True Domestic Prices	
Peru	5.4	15.9	34.0
Philippines	3.7	10.7	35.0
Bangladesh	1.1	5.1	22.1
Kenya	1.8	4.5	39.7
Ghana	2.1	2.6	81.6

Source: Summers and Heston (1988).

If purchasing-power parity really held, then every number in the right-hand column would have been 100. The departures from that PPP norm are great enough to reshuffle some of the international rankings, making the better (ICP) measurements of the center column differ substantially from the exchange-rate based measures on the left. In general, the usual comparisons, the ones using exchange rates, overstate the real income gaps between rich and poor nations, as illustrated with the figures given here. Another pattern shows up more clearly in other years than in the high-dollar 1985: the price distortion ratio in the right-hand column is often above unity for Japan and many West European nations, so that their ICP-measured real average income is not as high relative to that of the United States and Canada as the exchange-rate figures often imply.

   Why should lower income countries seem to have prices so much lower, relative to U.S. prices, than PPP predicts? Almost all of the departures come from the wide international gaps in the prices of nontraded goods like housing and other services. The gaps in the prices of these services seem to be widened by two forces. One is the tendency of the price of a fixed factor of production—most important, land—to be highly sensitive to the income of the country's residents. So, a country with twice as high an income would have more than twice as high a cost for space, making the space-intensive nontraded goods cost much more. A related explanation is that as a country develops, its productivity in making traded goods rises much faster than its productivity in making nontraded goods and services. Therefore, the latter can differ widely between poor and rich nations, while the former stay closer to parity.

run, these countries can keep their domestic prices stable only by accepting a rise of about 10 percent a year in the exchange values of their currencies in terms of inflating currencies. They could resist this rise only with painfully elaborate exchange controls. In pointing out this conflict between domestic price stabilization and exchange-rate stabilization, the purchasing-power-parity theory is performing a valuable service.

MONEY AND PPP COMBINED

Combining the purchasing-power-parity equation with the quantity-theory equations for the home country and the rest of the world yields a prediction of exchange rates based on money supplies and national products:

$$r = P/P_f = (M/M_f) \cdot (k_f/k) \cdot (y_f/y)$$

The exchange rate between one foreign currency (say, the British pound) and other currencies (here represented by the dollar, the home currency in our examples) can now be related to just the Ms, the ks, and the ys. The price ratio (P/P_f) can now be set aside as just an intermediate variable determined, in the long run, by the Ms, ks, and ys.

The equation predicts that a foreign nation (say, Britain) will have a rising currency (r up) if it has some combination of slower money-supply growth (M/M_f up), faster growth in real output (y_f/y up), or a rise in the ratio k_f/k. Conversely, a nation with fast money growth and a stagnant real economy is likely to have a depreciating currency. Over spans of several years this seems to fit the facts.

Going one step further, we can use the same equation to quantify the percentage effects of changes in money supplies or national products on the exchange rate. The equation implies that some key elasticities are equal to one. That is, if the ratio (k_f/k) stays the same, then:

r rises by 1 percent f or each 1 percent rise in the dollar money supply *(M)*,

> or each 1 percent drop in the pound money supply *(M_f)*, or each 1 percent drop in dollar-area real GNP *(y)*, or each 1 percent rise in British GNP *(y_f)*.

As we will note again, statistical studies suggest that these unit elasticities of exchange-rate response are realistic. The exchange-rate elasticities imply something else that seems reasonable, too: an exchange rate will be unaffected by balanced growth. If money supplies grow at the same rate in all countries, leaving M/M_f unchanged, or if national products grow at the same rate, leaving y_f/y unchanged, there should be no change in the exchange rate.

FIGURE 16.2   Shifts in Money Supplies Affect the Exchange Rate

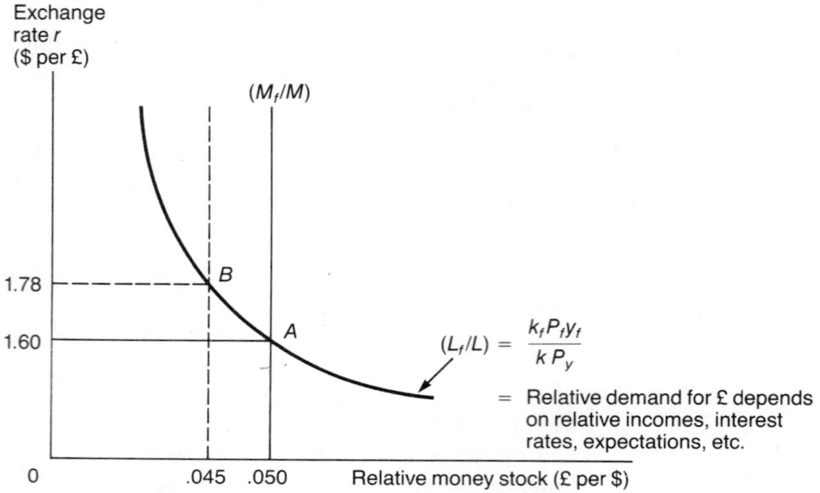

Reminder: since the £ is called "foreign exchange" here, the subscript $_f$ refers to Britain as the "foreign" country, with the other (home) country being the rest of the world, whose currency is the dollar.

The Impact of Money Supplies on an Exchange Rate

Let us take a closer look at these results with the help of Figures 16.2 and 16.3. Figure 16.2 explores the likely effects of shifts in money supplies. To show the role of *relative* money supply more clearly, the supply curve is now the ratio of Britain's money supply to that of the rest of the world, or M_f/M, where the rest of the world is called the dollar country or "home" country in order to talk about the pound as "foreign exchange." Thus, the initial stock at Point A is the fraction .050 rather than an absolute value like the British money stock of £300 billion imagined back in Figure 15.3A. At Point A, the demand for holding sterling balances relative to holdings of dollars (L_f/L) exactly matches the relative supply of pounds to dollars (M_f/M), making $1.60 the equilibrium value of the pound.

If the supply of pounds was cut by 10 percent, each pound would become more scarce and more valuable. The cut might be achieved by much tighter British monetary policy. This contractionary policy would restrict the reserves of the British banking system, forcing British banks to tighten credit and the outstanding stock of sterling bank deposits, which represent most of the British money supply. The tighter credit would make it harder to borrow and spend, cutting back on aggregate demand, output, jobs, and prices in Britain. With the passage of time, the fall in output and jobs should dwindle, and the reduction in prices should reach 10 percent. Both immediately and later, the pound should rise in value because each pound is more expensive to rent (at the higher British interest rate) or to purchase (with goods whose money price is dropping). The 10 percent cut in Britain's money supply should eventually lead to a 10 percent higher exchange-rate value of the pound, or $1.78 at Point B. This 10 percent rise is what the quantity theory equations above would predict.[4]

The same shift from A to B in Figure 16.2 should result from a 10 percent rise in the dollar money supply. If central bankers in the United States and other countries pegged to the dollar let their money supplies rise another 10 percent, the extra dollar money available should end up inflating dollar prices by about 10 percent. For a time, the higher dollar prices would cause international demands for goods and services to shift in favor of buying the sterling-priced goods, which are temporarily cheaper. Eventually, purchasing-power parity should be restored by a 10 percent rise in the exchange rate, r. One other result predicted above follows as a corollary: if the equations above are correct, a balanced 10 percent rise in all money supplies, both pounds and dollars, should have no effect on the exchange rate. Starting from Point A, we should stay at A in this case.

The Effect of Real Income on an Exchange Rate

The same kind of reasoning can be used to explore how changes in real income should affect an exchange rate. Figure 16.3 portrays the effect predicted by the combination of the quantity-theory equation and PPP. Let us first follow this reasoning on its own terms and then add a word of caution.

Suppose that Britain's real income shifts up to a growth path 10 percent above the path Britain would otherwise have followed. This might happen if vast new oil reserves were discovered in Britain or offshore. The extra sales of Britain's oil would call forth a new demand for holding pounds as a currency to facilitate purchases of British oil. If the extra oil results in a 10 percent rise in British national income, the quantity theory predicts a 10 percent higher transactions demand for the pound. Starting at Point A, the 10 percent income rise should push the demand for pounds out from 0.050 to 0.055 of the stock of dollars at Point B. But this extra demand cannot be met because Britain's money stock is still only 0.050 as large as the dollar stock. Result: the general clamor to get pounds, by borrowing them or by selling Britain goods to get them, will lead to a rise in the

---

[4] If you are still not sure why the equation should predict exactly a 10 percent exchange-rate rise in response to a 10 percent cut in money supply, you may have good reason: this result has only been imagined and not yet supported by any evidence. When we turn to the evidence later in this chapter, we will again find that the hypothesized result looks about right for the long run, but is much less reliable as a prediction of responses within a year or less, when the ks may move in response to the same cut in money supply.

FIGURE 16.3   Shifts in Money Demand Affect the Exchange Rate

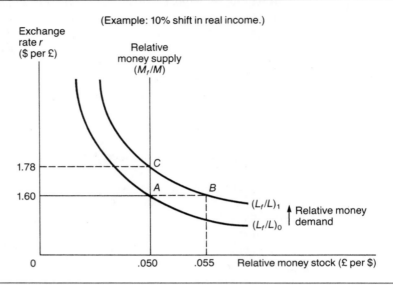

value of the pound, from $1.60 up to $1.78 at Point B. The rise is again portrayed as equaling about 10 percent because that is what the equations above predict (for given *k*s). Again, we have two corollaries that can be seen from the equations or from Figure 16.3: a 10 percent decline in dollar-area real income should also raise *r* by about 10 percent, and a balanced 10-percent rise in incomes in both Britain and the rest of the world should leave the exchange rate the same.

A caution must be added to this tidy result, however. You can be misled by memorizing a single "effect of income" on the exchange rate. Income is not an independent force that can simply move by itself. What causes it to change has a great effect on an exchange rate. In the British oil-discovery example above, real income was being raised for a *supply-side* reason—Britain's extra ability to supply oil. It is easy to believe that this would strengthen the pound, either by using the quantity-theory equation or by thinking about the extra oil exports as something other countries would need pounds to pay for. But suppose that Britain's real income is raised by the Keynesian effects of extra government spending or some other aggre-gate-*demand* shift in Britain. This real-income increase might or might not strengthen the pound. If its main effect is to make Britons buy more imports, then there would be reason to believe that the extra aggregate demand would actually lower the value of the pound.

This ambiguity is nothing new. Judging the "effect of income" on the exchange rate is analogous to the familiar problem of judging the "effect of income'' on the price level within a country. It all depends on what is causing the income shift itself. If income is raised by an extra ability to supply, then the exchange value of the country's currency *(r)* rises just as the domestic purchasing power of money (Britain's $1/P_f$) would rise; conversely, if income is raised by extra domestic demand, then the exchange value of the country's currency *(r)* falls, just as the domestic purchasing power of money $(1/P_f)$ would.

Since the effects of aggregate demand shifts tend to dominate in the short run, while supply shifts dominate in the long run, the quantity theory and Figure 16.3 yield the longer run result, the case in which higher income means a higher value of the same country's currency. We follow such reasoning for the rest of this chapter.

OTHER DETERMINANTS OF AN EXCHANGE RATE

More forces on the demand side of money markets can play a major role in determining exchange rates. Lurking behind the money-demand ratio (L_f/L), along with incomes, are a number of forces that can cause movements in the ks, those monetary coefficients we have been ignoring so far. Let us look at three forces: the crucial role of price expectations, the conspicuous but tricky influence of interest rates, and the possible role of the trade balance.

Expected Future Inflation

Nobody wants to hold an asset that is likely to shrink in purchasing power. A currency will shrink in purchasing power if prices of goods and services rise in that country, that currency. Investors will be less willing to hold a currency, for any given exchange rate, if they expect price inflation in that country. The role of price expectations can be represented in our equations by making k depend on π, our expected rate of price inflation, and making k_f depend on π_f, the foreign rate of inflation. Other things equal, the price of foreign exchange r will be raised by greater π and lower π_f, that is by greater fear of inflation in the United States and lower fear of inflation abroad. The same kind of shift can be represented in Figure 16.3 as a rise in the demand curve for pounds. At some point we will want to know, of course, what forces lie behind the inflationary expectations π and π_f. The answer is simply that the forces expected to raise the price level in the future are the same ones that govern the price level today. That is, π depends positively on the expected future growth of our money supply *(M)*, negatively on expected growth in our real income *(y)*, and on the forces expected to change k in the future. A similar list applies to expectations of inflation abroad.

Interest Rate Differentials

Foreign-exchange markets do seem sensitive to movements in interest rates. Jumps of exchange rates often seem to follow changes in $(i - i_f)$, the differential between home (i) and foreign (i_f) interest rates. The response often looks prompt, so much so that press coverage of day-to-day rises or drops in an exchange rate typically point first to interest rates as a cause.

It is easy to see how interest differentials could matter. If our interest rate (i) jumps 1 percent while the foreign rate (i_f) remains constant, investors can see an extra reason for wanting to buy dollars in the spot market. Part of the gains from holding a currency for a while and gambling on its future value consists of the interest earned on the deposits, bills, or bonds held in that currency. So for any given expected rate of change in the spot price of the dollar, a rise in U.S. interest rates makes it more attractive to buy and hold dollars, thus bidding up the spot value of the dollar. It looks simple: interest rates up in dollars, more reason to get dollars and lend them at interest.

Things are not always so simple, though. The role of interest rates, like the role of real income, depends on what is causing them to move. When we read that interest rates are going up in a country, we think first of tighter money (i.e., a restriction of the supply of money in that country) and the interest rate we have in mind is the *real interest rate* $i - \pi$. That is, we are thinking of a rise in the nominal interest rate i relative to the expected rate of inflation π. If that is the true cause of the higher interest rates, then the usual intuition is correct: higher U.S. interest rates, for example, reflect a tighter U.S. money supply and should raise the value of the dollar in foreign exchange markets. Similarly, a rise in the foreign real interest rate $(i_f - \pi_f)$ should make investors shift some of their currency demand toward the foreign currency, raising the exchange rate r.

But be careful when reading that "interest rates" are going up in one country more than in other countries. What if the reason why U.S. interest rates are rising is because people now expect faster U.S. price inflation or because the U.S. government is headed for bigger deficits? If these trends are the source of the higher U.S. interest rates, there is reason to doubt the future strength of the dollar. An extreme case can help drive home the same point: interest rates are sky-high in the hyperinflating economies, such as Israeli and Latin America, but investors know better than to be attracted to these high nominal rates. They know that inflation is also high in those currencies, and they are unlikely to react to a rise in interest rates by investing more.

The role of differences in nominal interest rates thus depends on what is causing them. They are not as sure a guide to exchange-rate prediction as the money-supply variable. For this reason, our list of fundamental influences on exchange rates should not include the nominal interest rates i and i_f, but the more reliable four variables π, π_f, $(i - \pi)$, and $(i_f - \pi_f)$. The exchange rate *r* should be raised by higher values of the first and fourth, and by lower values of the other two.

The Trade Balance or Current-Account Balance

Foreign exchange markets seem to react sensitively to news of official figures about two balance-of-payments measures examined in Chapter 14. One measure is the trade balance, a nation's net surplus of exports of goods over imports of goods. The other measure is the current-account balance, a nation's surplus of exports over imports of both goods and services and net gifts between nations. There is good logic in the market's reaction to such news. For example, a deficit in either the trade balance or (especially) the current-account balance is a sign that the nation is giving up more money than it earns abroad. Such an imbalance must be sending its currency to foreigners, who typically want it less and are likely to try to unload it soon. Or, in terms of our discussion of national money as a ticket to GNP, the trade and current-account deficits could be viewed as signals that somebody somewhere has shifted toward buying foreign-currency-priced goods and services and thus wants to hold (as well as spend) more in the foreign currency. The market seems to accept this judgment since it often finds a currency less valuable in the wake of official news of larger deficits.[5]

These, then, are the main forces that seem to lie behind movements in exchange rates between currencies. The chapters that follow will take a closer look at some of them to help us judge how workable the different policies toward foreign exchange will be.

HOW WELL CAN WE PREDICT EXCHANGE RATES?

Any theory needs to prove its value by making accurate predictions. The whole purpose of having theories is to explain tendencies in the real world, and prediction is the best test of explanation. International experience since the switch to fluctuating exchange rates in 1971 has provided some illuminating tests. The news is not all good. Let us first confront the bad news about our ability, *anyone's* ability, to predict exchange rates up to 12 months ahead. Then we will explore the mixture of bad and good news about our ability to forecast exchange rates more than a year ahead.

---

[5] There are counterexamples, though. Suppose that a nation's deficits simply reflect a desire by foreigners to hold more of its currency for international business, selling the nation more goods and services in the process. In this case, the deficit should be accompanied by a rise in the nation's currency, not a decline. Something like this may have happened during the rise of the dollar in the early 1980s.

A Formal Test of Short-Run Forecasts

A systematic test of the power of exchange-rate predictions requires some statistical work. Meese and Rogoff (1983) have set up a tough direct test in three stages. First, they formulated a model that captures what most economists believe is behind exchange-rate movements. In this "structural" model, the k s from the equations above are allowed to depend on home and foreign interest rates (i, i_f), expected inflation rates at home (π) and abroad (π_f), and the home country's trade balance (TB). The equation for predicting the price of the foreign currency (r) thus becomes:

$$r = (M/M_f) \cdot (y_f/y) \cdot K(i - i_f, \pi - \pi_f, TB)$$

where K is the old ratio k_f/k. This general equation captures economists' main predictions about exchange rates:

The price of a foreign currency, r, should be raised by:

- A rise in the home country's money supply (M).[*]
- A *drop* in the foreign country's money supply (M_f).[*]
- A rise in the foreign country's real income (y_f).[*]
- A *drop* in the home country's real income (y).[*]
- A rise in the foreign country's interest rate (i_f).
- A *drop* in the home country's interest rate (i).
- A rise in the home country's expected inflation rate (π).
- A *drop* in the foreign country's expected inflation rate (π_f).
- Or a *drop* in the home country's trade balance (TB).

---

[*] Reminder: these effects are believed to have an elasticity of 1, with the exchange-rate response just equaling the same percentage as any one percentage change in a money supply or income. (Hint: review these.)

The second step toward a direct test is to fit this model statistically to some data. Meese and Rogoff fit a logarithmic form of the equation above, including the whole past history of each explanatory variable as well as its current value, to monthly data for several currencies between March 1973 and November 1976. The variables listed above generally showed the correct directions and correct amounts of influence. So far, the results are not so bad for the beliefs that are shared by most economists studying exchange rates.

Next comes the tough part. The third step taken by Meese and Rogoff is one that any predictive model should have to pass: how well does it predict beyond the sample years for which it was statistically fitted? Does it predict better than cruder and simpler forecasting devices? They made the model, as fitted to the period March 1973 to November 1976, show its stuff by forecasting monthly exchange rates for December 1976 to June 1981.

FIGURE 16.4   Average Short-Run Forecast Errors for Competing Exchange-Rate Predictors, December 1976–June 1981 (approximate percentage root-mean-square forecast errors)

Predicted Exchange Rate	Predicted How Far Ahead?	*Forecast Errors Made by These Competing Predictors*			
		Economists' "Structural" Model (see text)	Just the Forward Rate	Just the Current Spot Rate	Several Months' History of the Spot Rate
$/mark	1 month	5.4%	3.2%	3.7%	3.5%
	6 months	11.8	9.0	8.7	12.4
	12 months	15.1	12.6	13.0	22.5
$/yen	1 month	7.8	3.7	3.7	4.5
	6 months	18.9	11.9	11.6	22.0
	12 months	23.0	19.0	18.3	52.2
$/pound	1 month	5.6	2.7	2.6	2.8
	6 months	13.0	7.2	6.5	7.3
	12 months	21.3	11.6	10.0	13.4
Trade-weighted dollar	1 month	4.1	n.a.	2.0	2.7
	6 months	8.9	n.a.	6.1	6.8
	12 months	11.0	14.2	8.7	11.1

n.a. = not available.

Source: Meese and Rogoff (1983, Table 1). The authors also perform extra tests, including tests of narrower models that are special cases of the structural model above. There are, of course, still other economists' models of the exchange rate not reported here, but the present structural model fairly represents their predictive performance.

Figure 16.4 shows the results, in the form of the average percentage errors of each competing predictor. The three kinds of competitors in the race are (1) the economist's model just presented; (2) the opinion of foreign-exchange traders themselves, represented by the forward exchange rate, and (3) a naive model that just thinks the spot exchange rate will go on being what it was recently.

The *structural model* introduced above has the virtue of making explicit what forces economists think the exchange rate should depend on. Yet its predictive power is modest, according to the first column of Figure 16.4. Its average errors in forecasting the West German mark, the yen, or the pound sterling are 5 to 8 percent when predicting only a month ahead of the available information (on money supplies, etc.) and rise to 15 to 23 percent for forecasts 12 months ahead of the available information (e.g., forecasting for November 1977 on the basis of data on November 1976 and earlier). Given the chance to forecast the exchange rate of the dollar against a trade-weighted average of other currencies, the model achieves smaller errors, basically because its errors on each individual rate (£/$, Y/$, etc.) tend to cancel out.

The *forward rate* alone actually predicts better than the economists' structural model. This means, for example, that in November 1976, a better forecast of the November 1977 spot value of the mark would have been just the November 1976 12-month forward rate on the mark. Why should this work better than the available information on how exchange rates related to money supplies, incomes, interest rates, and so on for November 1976 and earlier? The answer can be found in Chapter 15. The forward rate is the *market's* best forecast. It represents all the information, intuitions, and emotions possessed by professional traders. Whatever predictive value the structural model has is already available to those professional traders who keep up on the econometric literature and have their staff researchers try out a host of models. It is not surprising that the forward rate set by their expectations could outperform a structural model carrying only part of the available information.

Even the market's forward-rate forecast is far from perfect. The second column in Figure 16.4 reports that the market is wrong about next month's mark by an average of 3.2 percent and wrong about next year's mark by an average of 12.6 percent, with comparable errors about the yen and pound.

Are these errors large or small? It depends on what you want to compare them to. They are large errors relative to perfect foresight. If you made a Faustian bargain to sell your soul for a lifetime of perfect foreign-exchange foresight, and managed to keep your secret, you could make 3.2 percent a month on forward marks. That's an average return of 46 percent a year (or an even better return if you gambled with borrowed money). Clearly, there is financial value in the information the market does not now have. But perfect foresight is an unrealistic norm. At the other extreme, you could cheerfully describe the market forecasts as "the best available unbiased forecasts." That is correct. They still make the kinds of errors shown in Figure 16.4, however.

If we chose to compare the foreign exchange markets with other kinds of markets, we would again get an intermediate result. Jacob Frenkel (1981) has compared the unpredicted part of movements in commodity prices, exchange rates, and stock markets to see which market-forecast errors look largest. Foreign exchange surprises turn out to be greater than those in commodity-price bundles but not as "bad," as volatile, as the unpredicted movements in stock markets. Two possible stabilizers in foreign exchange markets not shared by stock markets are: (1) the possible equilibrating role of trade-balance responses to changes in exchange rates and (2) possibly successful stabilization of exchange rates by officials under the "managed float." We return to these issues in Chapter 18. The track record in predicting exchange rates, here again, is only partially successful. The glass can be said to be half empty or half full.

We turn next to the naive model that our structural model and the market's opinion should be able to beat. Unfortunately, the naive model, using only the current spot rate to predict the future, does as well as the structural model and the market experts! The *spot rate* alone performs about as well as the forward rate. Actually, that setback should have been expected. As we noted in Chapter 15 and Appendix H, the spot and forward rate often run together, differing from each other only by the international difference in interest rates. They embody similar market information. So the spot rate, like the forward rate, is not so naive a forecaster as we might infer from its being just a single number instead of a basketful of data.

The poorer performance of the *history of the spot rate* may seem paradoxical. It predicts the future from the best statistically fitted linear combination of earlier exchange rates, where the fit was made to the earlier sample data (March 1973 to November 1976, in this case). How could statistical predictions based on a whole series of recent rates be worse than those using just the latest rate in the series? Isn't more information better? No, not necessarily, when we are predicting the future beyond the statistical sample. The reason: the world may change. In this case, the underlying pattern relating exchange rates to earlier exchange rates may have changed after November 1976. If it did, just predicting a few months ahead from the latest rate can be better than locking ourselves into trusting an obsolete historical pattern. Judging from the two right-hand columns in Figure 16.4, this must have been the case.

The Meese-Rogoff results are not simply an artifact of the particular time period and currencies they studied. Other researchers have found the same results, despite differences in the time period and currencies covered and differences in the form of the equation tested (Frankel, 1984; Somanath, 1986; Boughton, 1987; Meese, 1990). Only one careful study of the dollar-mark rate for 1974–1981 seemed to beat the naive spot-rate forecasts with forecasts from an economic model (Woo 1985), but that result has not been replicated in other periods. It looks as though our typical economic models and our market experts do not forecast exchange rates over the next month, half year, or year any better than the naive belief that the exchange rate will stay the same.

Longer Run Forecasts

If our models and the market experts are no better than a naive model at forecasting up to a year ahead, perhaps they can do better if given the task of forecasting several years ahead. That is a reasonable expectation, given that the pressure to return to purchasing-power parity exerts itself only quite slowly. To see if our models work well in the long run, we need a long run of actual experience in which exchange rates were free to fluctuate. The best laboratory is one still being built: the flexible-rate era since 1971. Starting from 1973, when the shock of unpegging exchange rates had already brought some adjustment, we can study the ability of two very simple models to look as far as 10 years ahead, for different time spans starting as early as 1973 and ending as late as 1988. One simple model just uses PPP again: use changes in P/P_f to predict changes in the exchange rate *r*. Another is to use changes in the money supplies and real incomes that were supposed to have unit-elastic influences on the exchange rate, using the expression $M \cdot y_f / M_f \cdot y$ to predict *r*. We will give our hypotheses a little help by letting them use the *contemporaneous* values of *P*s, *M*s and *y*s to predict *r*s (e.g., using the 1988 values of them to predict *r* in 1988, instead of using values from back at the start of each several-year period). That amounts to saying, "If we could perfectly forecast prices and money supplies and incomes, how well could we forecast exchange rates?"

Figure 16.5 summarizes the long-distance race pitting two of this chapter's models against a crude spot-rate prediction. Each model predicts changes in exchange rates over time periods ranging from 1 year to 10 years in length. The different predictions starting as early as 1973 and ending as late as 1988 are averaged.[6] The three cases selected here represent the industrial economy whose currency rose the most (Japan), the largest economy, and the industrial economy whose currency fell the most (Italy) among the countries represented in Figure 16.1 above.

To understand the stories told by Figure 16.5, let us begin with the case that casts our models in the least favorable light, the case of the U.S. dollar in the middle of Figure 16.5. In this case, our two predictors—the PPP predictor and the one using money supplies and incomes—fail to make errors below those of a crude model. The crude model is crude indeed: it predicts that the spot exchange rate will stay the same, for 1 year, for 2 years, and so on up to a 10-year horizon. Yet the dollar diagram shows that for forecasts up through 7 years in length, the PPP prediction is no better than guessing that the exchange rate would stay the same, and the predictor based on changes in money supplies and incomes actually does worse than the crude spot-rate forecast. Only as we get into the 8–10 year range do our models look better than just using the latest spot rate to forecast years into the future. This is sobering. Straining to find good news in the

---

[6] The forecasts span overlapping time periods within 1973–1988. The errors made in 1-year predictions are averages of predictions of 1974 exchange-rate changes from 1973, 1975 from 1974, and so forth, up to 1988 from 1987. The 10-year predictions are averages of predictions of changes for 1973–1983, 1974–1984, and so forth up to 1978–1988. Similar averages are calculated for time spans between 1 year and 10 years. By the time we reach 10-year forecasts, the sample of experiences since 1973 gets thin (only six overlapping cases), and random noise makes longer range predictions unadvisable.

The average percentage error is, more specifically, the percentage-change equivalent of the root mean square error, or 100 times (exp (square root (average (square of (natural log of (actual − predicted *r*)))))) − 1).

The "other nine countries" are derived from 10-country averages, followed by removal of the single country mentioned. The 10 countries, and the 1973 GNP weights used to average *r*s, *P*s, *M*s and *y*s, are United States (weight of .5174), Canada (.0432), Japan (.1042), United Kingdom (.0648), West Germany (.0989), France (.0804), Italy (.0491), Netherlands (.0167), Belgium (.0137), and Switzerland (.0115). The data are from IMF, *International Financial Statistics*.

FIGURE 16.5   Average Long-Run Forecast Errors for Competing Exchange-Rate Predictors, Years 1973–1988 (approximate percentage root-mean-square forecast errors)

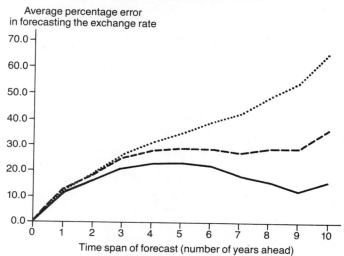

The yen versus an average of nine other currencies

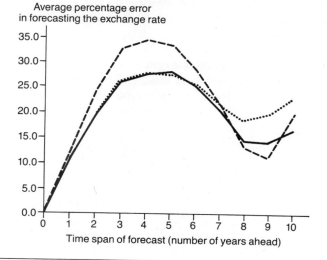

The U.S. dollar versus an average of nine other currencies

FIGURE 16.5   (concluded)

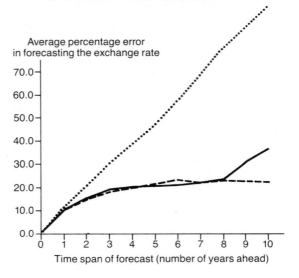

The Italian lira versus an average of nine other currencies

Average percentage error
in forecasting the exchange rate

Time span of forecast (number of years ahead)

Average errors in forecasts based on:

—— PPP (using changes in P/P$_f$ to predict changes in r).

——- Money supplies and income (using My$_f$/M$_f$y to predict r).

········ Just the earlier spot rate.

dollar (middle) diagram of Figure 16.5, one could point out that the errors of our models at least decline as we lengthen the forecast period beyond 5 years. But that improvement would also show up if we extended the naive spot-rate forecast into the future, just because in the long run the yearly positive and negative errors of even the naive forecast would tend to cancel out.

There are more agreeable results in the yen and lira diagrams, however. In both these cases the naive spot-rate prediction gets worse and worse the further into the future it predicts. Our preferred predictions, based on PPP and on Ms and ys, show less hump for the yen and lira than for the dollar, staying below the 30-percent rate of average error until forecasts are projected 9 or 10 years ahead. By using PPP and the asset-market explanations, we get a much better understanding of what moved the yen and lira exchange rates than if we had just predicted that the spot rate would stay near its earlier value.

The reason why the naive spot-rate forecast was easier to beat in the yen and lira cases than in the dollar case is straightforward. The yen and lira were currencies whose value kept changing in the same direction. As you can see from a glance back at Figure 16.1, the yen rose relative to all other major currencies between 1973 and 1988. The lira sank. So, using an earlier spot rate to predict a later spot rate makes a bigger and bigger error the further into the future one looks. Our preferred models, by contrast, contain valuable information that reduces error: as long as we can accurately predict the course of prices, money, and incomes, we can easily outpredict a model that doesn't see the trends in these variables. The value of the dollar, by contrast, oscillated without a net trend. In this case, the spot-rate forecast has its errors kept down, just because the earlier and later values of the dollar stayed in the same broad neighborhood.

So our models add more explanatory power, the stronger the trend in the exchange rate. Their relative power is clearest in explaining what happens to the exchange rate during a hyperinflation. Take the case of Argentine hyperinflation between 1983 and 1989. The exchange rate (price of the U.S. dollar in Argentina) went from an index of 100 to 8,975,000 in those years. Prices rose from 100 to 3,475,309. The money supply rose from 100 to about 500,000, whereas real GNP stagnated, changing from 100 to only 103 in six years. The rates of depreciation and of price inflation were highly variable. In such a situation, our PPP or asset-market models still commit large *absolute* percentage errors in predicting the exchange rate. But their errors look small in *relative* terms: they are much better than just using the earlier spot rate, or even the whole volatile history of the spot rate, to predict future exchange rates. A sceptic could say that our predictors looked better only because we borrowed the *later* values of prices, money supplies, and incomes to generate those predictions. This is a valid way to question just how much "predicting" our models do. Yet they at least *explain* longer run trends in exchange rates, showing us the fundamentals that govern the long run. And we can return to the safe statement that *if* we develop good predictors of the money supply and incomes, or of just prices, we have fair predictors of long-run movements in exchange rates.

With these perspectives, we can return to the major-currency experience shown in Figure 16.1 and see where our models help and where they do not. They help most over the whole long sweep of the flexible-exchange-rate era since 1971, rather than as explainers of shorter run swings. Over the whole era, we know part of the reason why the Japanese yen rose: Japan's stronger real economic growth (growth in y), combined with the fact that her money supply did not grow much faster than the average, kept inflation down in Japan, and raised the international value of the yen. The Swiss franc rose because Switzerland kept tight control over its money supply. The lira sank because Italy's money supply rose faster than average. Despite its failure to improve our short-run forecasting, our basic framework does help explain the long run, just as it helps explain what happens to the exchange rate in even a short-run hyperinflation.

SUMMARY

This chapter has surveyed the modern asset-market approach to the determination of exchange rates.

Since the foreign exchange market is one where money is traded for money, any explanation of exchange rates should start with the supplies and demands for national moneys. The transactions demand for a national money can be expressed as kPy, or a behavioral coefficient (k) times the price level (P) times the level of real national product (y). The equilibrium $M = kPy$ matches this demand against the national money supply (M), which is regulated by the central bank's monetary policy. A similar equilibrium holds in any foreign country: $M_f = k_f P_f y_f$.

The separate money-market equilibriums can be converted into a theory of the exchange rate with the help of the purchasing-power-parity (PPP) theory. PPP predicts that international competition will tend to equalize the home and foreign prices of any traded good or service, so that $P = rP_f$ overall, where r is again the price of the foreign currency (e.g., £) in units of domestic currency (e.g., $). The PPP theory works tolerably well for periods of, say, a decade or more under normal rates of price change. Its prediction errors are more serious for the short run. From 1973 through 1983, for example, PPP comes close to explaining the overall slight net rise in the dollar but fails to explain the large drop in the dollar in the late 1970s and the larger rebound in the earlier 1980s.

Combining the basic monetary equilibriums with PPP yields an equation for predicting the exchange rate (r) for the currency of a foreign country (f): $r = (M/M_f) \cdot (y_f/y) \cdot (k_f/k)$. Ignoring changes in the ks, we can use this equation to predict the exchange rate given data on money supplies and real incomes. Such a prediction will help explain exchange-rate movements but will leave most exchange-rate changes unexplained. The theory can be sharpened by recognizing that the ks probably depend on home and foreign interest rates (i,i_f), inflationary expectations at home and in the foreign country (π, π_f), and the home country's trade balance (TB). In summary, most economists' models of the exchange rate predict that the price of the foreign country's currency, or r, is raised by:

A rise in (M/M_f).

A rise in (y_f/y).

A rise in $(i_f - i)$.

A rise in $(\pi - \pi_f)$.

Or a decline in TB.

The elasticities of impact of (M/M_f) and (y_f/y) on r should each be approximately equal to 1.

Tests find this asset-market theory of exchange rates only moderately successful. Again, success is more evident in the explanation of longer run trends, where the roles of money supplies and real incomes have their best chance to show. As a one-month, six-month, or one-year forecaster of the spot exchange rate, neither the prevailing theory nor the opinions of professional foreign exchange traders, whose forecasts are embodied in the forward exchange rate, can predict better than a naive theory predicting that the spot rate will stay the same. Yet for predicting exchange rates several years ahead, or for explaining what happens to the exchange rate in a hyperinflation, it helps to know about PPP and to know the likely trends in money supplies and incomes.

SUGGESTED READINGS

Different versions of the modern asset-market approach to exchange-rate determination are surveyed and tested in Allen and Kenen (1980), Dornbusch (1980), Frenkel (1981), and Frankel (1983); the latter three are available in Bhandari and Putnam (1983). Further tests and perspectives can be found in Frenkel and Johnson (1978), Frenkel (1985), Hooper and Morton (1982), and Schafer and Loopesko (1983), as well as Meese and Rogoff (1983), Frankel (1984), Woo (1985), Somanath (1986), Boughton (1987), and Meese (1990), quoted above. An excellent synthesis of the whole subject is Levich (1984).

The purchasing-power-parity (PPP) theory has been subjected to a wide range of tests. A fair sampling includes: Yeager (1958), Balassa (1964), Officer (1976), Isard (1977), Krugman (1978), McKinnon (1979, chapter 6), Kravis and Lipsey (1978), Dornbusch (1980), and the spirited counter-defense of PPP by McCloskey in Bordo and Schwartz (1984).

QUESTIONS FOR REVIEW

1. As a foreign exchange trader, how would you react to the following news items as they come over the news service ticker tapes:

a. Mexico's oil reserves prove much smaller than touted earlier.

b. Social Credit Party wins national elections in Canada and promises generous expansion of money supply and credit.

c. The United States imposes stiff barriers against auto imports.

d. New process generates cheap solar energy using Canadian nickel.

(Answers: *a.* sell pesos; *b.* sell Canadian dollars; *c.* buy U.S. dollars and sell yen; *d.* buy Canadian dollars *if* the nickel export prospects outweigh Canadian losses of natural gas and oil exports from the new process.)

2. Suppose that Brazil wants to stabilize the cost of foreign exchange (cruzeiros/dollar) in a world in which dollar prices are generally rising at 5 percent per year. What rate of inflation of domestic cruzeiro prices must it come down to, and what rate of money supply growth would yield this rate, if the quantity theory of money holds with constant k and Brazilian output is growing at 6 percent per annum?

Answer: Inflation must drop to 5 percent, and the money supply growth must be held to 11 percent per year.

3. How should a rise in Brazil's national income affect the dollar value of its currency, the cruzeiro? Explain carefully.

4. How should a rise in French interest rates affect the dollar value of the franc? Explain carefully.

5. Why might the forward exchange rate for a currency be a better predictor of its future spot rate than information on present and past values of money supplies, incomes, interest rates, price expectations, and trade balances?

6. Why did the yen rise in dollar value over the period of flexible exchange rates since 1971? Why did the Swiss franc rise? Why did the Italian lira sink?

CHAPTER

17

▼

Modern Foreign-Exchange Policies

•

Chapters 14 through 16 have introduced the basic analysis of how currencies are exchanged and what seems to determine the exchange rate. It is time to begin exploring the main policy issue of international macroeconomics: how should a nation manage its foreign exchange, that is, its transactions with the rest of the world? The issue lends itself to general guidelines gradually developed over several chapters but not to a simple optimization routine. We cannot simply define a social welfare function and find the foreign-exchange regime maximizing that welfare. Social welfare has many dimensions, and foreign-exchange policy affects many of them. We must advance through several stages:

1. This chapter lays out the five policy options facing a single country, narrows the choices a bit, and explores some lessons of history about the remaining choices.
2. Chapter 18 addresses some difficult questions about possible exchange-market instability under pegged- and floating-rate policies.
3. Chapters 19–21 describe how aggregate demand is to be managed in a national economy within a larger world economy, and they also describe how this task of domestic demand control is complicated by the choice of exchange-rate policies.
4. Chapter 22 pulls together a long-range view of how world money institutions are evolving, and the pros and cons of fixed versus floating exchange rates are explained.

FIVE POLICY OPTIONS FOR ONE COUNTRY

To survey the options open to a country pursuing macroeconomic stability, we begin with five basic ways of dealing with a foreign-exchange problem, that is, either a balance-of-payments problem or a shock to the foreign-exchange market. To introduce the choices more easily, let us look at each choice as a way of responding to payments *deficits* or *depreciation* in the nation's currency. You can reverse each stated choice to deal with the case of inconveniently large payments surpluses or currency appreciation.

The five choices, with a few variants, are:

1. Just **financing** the overall payments deficit, without adjusting the exchange rate or the condition of the national economy.
    1*a*. **Temporary financing:** if the imbalance is temporary, the nation can simply draw down its reserves for a time, keep the reserve loss from affecting the national money supply, and wait to replenish reserves when the overall balance shifts back to surplus.
    1*b*. **Key-currency "deficits without tears":** if our economy is based on a key-currency country, we have some more freedom to let deficits continue without "correction."
2. **Exchange controls:** at the other extreme, the national government can tightly control all transactions between the nation's residents and the rest of the world. Specifically, it can ration the ability of its residents to acquire foreign exchange for spending abroad, keeping the official exchange rate (or rates) fixed.
3. **Floating exchange rates:** the nation can allow the exchange market to take care of the exchange rate by letting the value of its currency drop until exchange-market equilibrium is restored.
4. **Permanently fixed rates:** officials can adjust the whole national economy to fit the exchange rate. If deficits persist and foreigners do not want to hold more of our money, let our reserve losses drain the national money supply, deflate our economy, lower our prices and our incomes until supply and demand for foreign exchange are again equal at the same fixed exchange rate. (This has been referred to as "taking classical medicine" for a payments imbalance.)
5. **Exchange-rate compromises:** the nation can try a mixture of options 3 and 4, letting the exchange rate handle some adjustment tasks but not others.
    5*a*. **The adjustable-peg** or **Bretton Woods system** (as practiced between 1944 and 1971): the nation can defend a fixed rate with option 4 as long as small doses of domestic adjustment will suffice to defend the fixed exchange rate, or it can devalue its currency and peg it at a new official exchange rate if defending the old fixed rate requires too much domestic adjustment.
    5*b*. **Managed floats:** officials can try to change the exchange rate gradually until a new equilibrium is reached. During the movement to a new equilibrium, they can devalue the national currency at a preannounced steady rate per day (the gliding band), or in larger steps at a preannounced frequency (the crawling peg), or at their unan-

nounced day-to-day discretion (the dirty float). Meanwhile, they must somehow adjust the domestic economy or find financing to make exchange-market manipulation possible.

This chapter narrows down the range of choice by describing the limits to the first two options. It also summarizes some lessons learned from a century of experience with the remaining three options. Later chapters will extend this historical view with deeper analysis of the issues of world financial stability and macroeconomic stability.

FINANCING TEMPORARY DISEQUILIBRIUMS (OPTION 1a)

The first option, that of financing imbalances while keeping the exchange rate fixed, is convenient and attractive for as long as it is possible. A nation running a payments deficit would be delighted to have the chance to go on financing it forever by just relaxing and having the rest of the world accept evergrowing amounts of its money liabilities (bank deposits). This is handy for the deficit country, which need not even pay interest on its accumulating money liabilities. What is more, in a world of rising commodity prices, the rest of the world is accepting this country's obligations and earning a negative real rate of return by having less purchasing power when it comes time to spend the same amount of currency reserves later on.

The reserve-accumulating surplus countries quickly lose patience with this form of implicit charity, especially if the deficit country is not in the favored position of a key-currency country (to be discussed shortly). Before too long, private parties in the surplus country will turn in the deposits in the deficit country, earned through trade and international capital transactions, to their central banks for conversion into domestic money. The central banks of the surplus countries will, in turn, demand that the monetary authorities of the deficit countries honor their domestic banks' liabilities by giving up foreign exchange or gold. After this continues for a while, the deficit country will be in danger of running out of internationally acceptable reserves. Even if the International Monetary Fund or some other international agency helps deficit countries finance their deficits, the ability of the international agency to extend this financial aid depends on how much reserve assets the surplus countries are willing to let the agency lend out. Thus, financing cannot cover a permanent deficit in the balance of payments, and true adjustment of payments must take place.

There is one set of circumstances, however, under which payments imbalances can be properly financed forever. This is the case in which the imbalances are clearly *temporary,* meaning that officials can finance a succession of deficits and surpluses indefinitely without being compelled to run out of reserves or to accumulate large amounts of unwanted reserves. In this case, one can argue that financing temporary deficits and surpluses is better than letting the exchange rate float around, as in option 3 above. This point is

FIGURE 17.1 A Successful Financing of Temporary Deficits and Surpluses at a Stable Exchange Rate

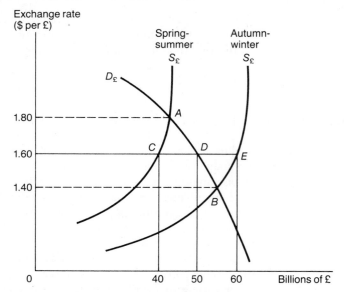

Autumn and winter: officials buy DE = £50 billion in foreign exchange.
Spring and summer: officials sell CD = £50 billion in foreign exchange.

Figure 17.1 is an adaptation of the demand-supply presentation of the market for sterling in Chapters 14 and 15. Instead of comparing total demand for sterling with the British money supply, Figure 17.1 compares U.S. demand with net foreign supply (i.e., with British money supply minus non-U.S. demand for sterling). The resulting diagram better fits the task of talking about demand and supply from the U.S. point of view, though it is equivalent to the diagrams focusing on the whole British money supply.

quite important for the debate over exchange-rate regimes, and it deserves an illustration.

Figure 17.1 gives an example of perfectly successful and socially desirable financing of temporary surpluses and deficits with a fixed exchange rate.[1] Here the home country is the dollar country. We have imagined that the temporary fluctuations in the balance of payments and the foreign-exchange market arise from something predictable, such as a seasonal pattern in foreign exchange receipts, with the dollar country exporting more and earning more foreign exchange (£) during the autumn-winter harvest season than during

---

[1] Those who have read Appendix G will recognize here another application of its treatment of the welfare economics of commodity price stabilization. The analogy is valid and requires only that we substitute a foreign currency for the commodity whose price was being stabilized.

the nonharvest spring-summer season. To help the example along, let us assume that it is costly for producers of the export crop to refrain from selling it during the harvest season and that something also prevents private speculators from stepping in and performing the equilibrating function being assigned to officials here. If the officials did not finance the temporary imbalances, the exchange rate would drop to $1.40 at Point B in the harvest season, when the nation had a lot of exports to sell, and it would rise to $1.80 in the off-season. In this instance there is a certain economic loss, since it would be better if the people who wanted foreign exchange to keep up imports during the off-season did not have to pay $1.80 for foreign exchange that is readily available for only $1.40 during the harvest season. The officials can recapture this economic gain by stabilizing the price at $1.60. Their stabilization is made possible because they have somehow picked the correct price, $1.60, the one at which they can sell exactly as much foreign exchange during one season as they buy during the other, exactly breaking even while stabilizing the price.

The official financing of spring-summer deficits with autumn-winter foreign exchange reserves brings a net social gain to the world. This gain arises from the fact that the officials gave a net supply of foreign exchange at $1.60 to people who would have been willing to pay $1.80 a pound during the spring-summer season, while also buying up at $1.60 the same amount of foreign exchange from people who would have been willing to sell it at $1.40. The net gain is measured as the sum of areas *ACD* and *BDE* (or about $1 billion a year). In this case, financing was successful and superior to letting the exchange rate find its own equilibrium in each season (see also Appendix G).

In order for the financing of temporary disequilibriums to be the correct policy option for dealing with the balance-of-payments and exchange markets, some stringent conditions must be met. First, it must be the case that private potential speculators do not see, or cannot take advantage of, the opportunity to buy foreign exchange in the fall and winter, invest it for a few months, and then sell it in the spring and summer. If private parties could do this, their own actions would bring the exchange rate close to $1.60 throughout the year, and there would be no need for official financing. (We return to the possibility of stabilizing private speculation in Chapter 18.)

It is crucial that the officials correctly predict the future demand and supply for foreign exchange at all likely exchange rates and that they also predict what would be an equilibrium path for the exchange rate in the absence of their intervention. If they do not forecast correctly, their attempt to finance a deficit or a surplus at a fixed exchange rate can be very costly because it involves them in unwanted net accumulation or depletion of their foreign-exchange reserves.

To see some of the economic costs of trying to finance a "temporary" disequilibrium that turns out to be a *fundamental* disequilibrium, consider the attempt of Her Majesty's Government and the Bank of England to

---

FIGURE 17.2 An Unsuccessful Temporary Financing of a Fundamental Disequilibrium

---

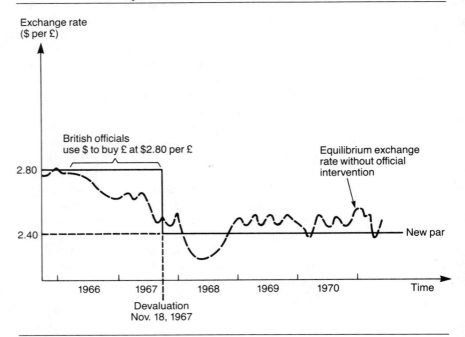

prop up the sagging pound sterling at a value of $2.80 before they had to give up and devalue to $2.40 on November 18, 1967. The situation before and after that date is sketched in Figure 17.2. Throughout the period 1964–67, the official exchange rate of $2.80 was higher than the rate would have been without official intervention. If this had been only a temporary disequilibrium, as the officials dearly hoped, it would have soon been followed by a surge of demand for the pound, making the implicit equilibrium exchange rate rise above $2.80 and allowing the officials to switch from financing a deficit to financing a surplus by adding to their dollar holdings. The disequilibrium was not temporary. British officials found themselves buying up increasing amounts of pounds at the higher price of $2.80, partly with dollars borrowed from the International Monetary Fund (IMF) and the Federal Reserve. When their reserves and their credit lines were exhausted, they had to give up and devalue to $2.40. As a result, they created a sudden shock to the international financial system. They also lost billions of pounds of taxpayers' money. The losses stemmed from their having tried to buy pounds that were dear, only to end up having to sell them cheap to recover the dollars they had sold earlier. They had to regain dollar reserves and repay the IMF and the Federal Reserve the borrowed dollars, by giving up pounds now worth only $2.40 each, versus the $2.80 paid for them by British officials. Buying dear and selling cheap is not the formula for profits.

The same misfortune has befallen officials whose currencies are bound to rise in value despite their vigorous attempts to hold down their values. For example, the Japanese governments did not want the dollar value of the yen to rise in August 1971, even though President Nixon had openly invited speculation in favor of the yen by calling for its revaluation (rise in dollar value). Hoping to ride out a temporary surplus situation in order to keep Japan's export and import-competing goods competitive (to the advantage of powerful trading groups but to the disadvantage of Japanese consuming groups), Japanese officials bought up billions of dollars during a few months as a way of financing the "temporary" surplus. Dollars threatened to become the sole asset of the Bank of Japan if the trend continued. The Japanese officials soon gave up and let the dollar value of the yen jump by more than 30 percent. This involved the Japanese officials in the same kind of currency losses as the British officials had sustained in 1967. The difference was that the Japanese officials were stuck holding *foreign* currency that was worth less than they had paid for it (the depreciating dollars), whereas the British ended up holding less valuable domestic currency.

These experiences do not prove that it is futile to try to keep exchange rates fixed: They prove that when the existing official exchange rate is becoming a disequilibrium exchange rate for the long run, trying to ride out the storm with financing alone is costly. Something more must be added. Fundamental disequilibrium calls for true adjustment, not merely financing.

It is not easy for officials to judge what constitutes fundamental disequilibrium, any more than it is easy for them to forecast gross national product for the next five years. This problem has existed throughout the postwar attempt to allow countries to change their exchange rates only when disequilibrium is fundamental. The Articles of Agreement of the IMF, signed at Bretton Woods, New Hampshire in 1944, permitted exchange-rate adjustment within limitations. These percentage limitations could be exceeded only in the case of fundamental disequilibrium. Yet, nowhere in the Articles of Agreement is fundamental disequilibrium defined, nor have the deliberations of the IMF directors, for over 30 years, produced any further enlightenment on this issue. We are left with the knowledge that a fundamental disequilibrium is one that is too great and/or too enduring to be financed but without a clear way of identifying one until after it has happened.

RESERVE-CENTER FINANCING (OPTION 1*b*)

The opportunity to have the rest of the world gladly accept your bank deposits and hold them is more available to reserve-center countries such as the United States or Japan than to other countries. If the national currency is a key currency in international transactions, even in transactions that do not involve this nation, then the growth of the world economy is likely to lead to growth in the demand for this currency as a means of international payment. Throughout the postwar period, at least until the early 1970s, foreign demand for dollar bank balances grew.

The growth of foreign demand for the dollar as a key currency allowed the United States to run what the French economist Jacques Rueff called *deficits without tears*. Surplus-country critics, particularly in France, charged that the United States was helping itself to a "free lunch" by having the rest of the world hold the dollar bank deposits supplied by U.S. payments deficits. Since the rest of the world was willing to hold increasing amounts of its money liabilities, the United States could go on buying more foreign goods and services and firms than it earned through its own sales. The deficits without tears charge was correct to the extent that it described the effects of the deficits on the United States. Despite official hand-wringing, the United States refrained from the kind of severe adjustment, such as deflation of the entire U.S. economy, that would have been necessary to eliminate the deficits in a context of fixed-exchange rates without exchange controls. The United States was thus given extraordinary leeway to "finance" its deficits. In contrast, the rest of the world did get something for its holding of dollar balances; it got the implicit services of the most widely recognized and accepted international money. By the 1970s, because its private demands were essentially satiated, the United States could only accumulate dollar liabilities to foreign governments, such as Japan, that were still trying to prop up the dollar to keep their currencies down and their goods competitive. The time had come when the United States, like other countries before it, had to contemplate options for adjustment and abandon the financing of deficits with growing money liabilities.

EXCHANGE CONTROLS (OPTION 2)

Among the options for true adjustment when financing is no longer possible, one can be indicated as socially inferior to the others. Oddly enough, it is widely practiced.

Many countries have responded to persistent disequilibriums in their external payments by defending the fixed exchange rate with elaborate government controls restricting the ability of their residents to buy foreign goods or services, to travel abroad, or to lend abroad.

Exchange controls are closely analogous to quantitative restrictions (quotas) on imports, already analyzed in Chapter 8. In fact, the analogy with import quotas fits very well, so well that the welfare economics of exchange controls is simply the welfare economics of import quotas expanded to cover imports of IOUs (lending abroad) and tourist services as well as imports of ordinary commodities. In Chapter 8 and Appendix F, we argue that the import quota

FIGURE 17.3 The Best of the Worst: Welfare Losses from Well-Managed Exchange Controls

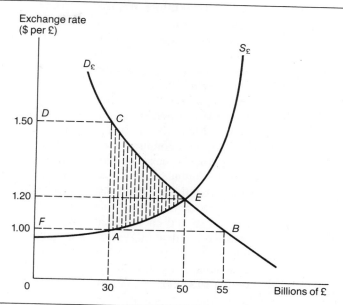

is at least as bad as an import tariff on a one-dollar, one-vote welfare basis. So it is with exchange controls as well: they are at least as damaging as a uniform tax on all foreign transactions, and probably they are much worse.

To show the economic case against exchange controls, it is useful to start with an oversimplified view of exchange controls that is almost certain to underestimate the social losses coming from real-world controls. Figure 17.3 sketches the effects of a system of binding exchange controls that is about as well managed and benign as one can imagine. Figure 17.3 imagines that the U.S. government has become committed to maintaining a fixed exchange rate that officially values foreign currencies less, and the dollar more, than would a free-market equilibrium rate. This official rate is $1.00 for the pound sterling, with similar subequilibrium rates for other foreign currencies. The exchange-control laws require exporters to turn over all their claims on foreigners (which we shall equate with claims in foreign currencies) to the U.S. government. The U.S. government, in turn, gives them $1.00 in domestic bank deposits for each pound sterling they have earned by selling abroad. At this exchange rate, exporters are earning, and releasing to authorities, only £30 billion. This figure is well below the £55 billion that residents of the United States would want to buy in order to purchase foreign goods, services, and assets. If the U.S. government feels committed to the $1.00 rate, yet is not willing to contract the whole U.S. economy enough to make the demand and supply for foreign exchange match at $1.00, then it must ration the right to buy foreign exchange.

Let us imagine that the U.S. officials ration foreign exchange in an efficient but seldom-tried way. Every two months they announce that it is time for another public auction-by-mail. On January 21, they announce that anyone wanting sterling (or any other foreign currency) for the March–April period must send in bids by February 15. A family that plans to be in England in April might send in a form pledging its willingness to pay up to $3 per pound for 700 pounds to spend in England and its willingness to pay $2.50 per pound for 1,000 pounds. An importer of automobiles would also submit a schedule of amounts of foreign currencies he wished to buy at each exchange rate in order to buy cars abroad. Receiving all these bids, the government's computers would rank them by the prices willingly pledged, and the totals pledged would be added up at each price, thus revealing the demand curve $D_£$ in Figure 17.3. Estimating that it could allocate £30 billion over a year, or £5 billion for March–April, the government would announce on February 20 that the price of $1.50 per pound was the price that made demand match the available £30 billion per year. The family who wanted to be in England for April would thus be able to get £1,000 by taking a check for $1,500 = £1,000 × $1.50 to the local post office, along with the officially signed pledge form it had submitted before February 15. Thus, all who were willing to pay $1.50 or more for each pound would receive the pounds they applied for, at the price of only $1.50 a pound, even if they had agreed to pay more. Anyone who did not submit bids with prices as high as $1.50 would be denied the right to buy abroad during March or April.

This system would give the government a large amount of revenues earned from the exchange-control auctions. Collecting $1.50/£ × £30 billion = $45 billion while paying exporters only $1.00/£ × £30 billion = $30 billion, the government would make a net profit of $15 billion, minus its administrative costs. This government profit could be returned to the general public either as a cut in other kinds of taxes or as extra government spending. Area *AFDC* in Figure 17.3 represents these auction profits taken from importers but returned to the rest of society, and it does not constitute a net gain or loss for society as a whole.

The foreign currency auction just described does impose a welfare loss on society as a whole, however. This loss is measured by the area *ACE*. To see why, remember the interpretation of demand and supply curves as marginal benefit and cost curves. When the exchange controls are in effect and only £30 billion is available, some mutually profitable bargains are being prohibited. At Point *C*, the demand curve is telling us that somebody would be willing to pay up to $1.50 for an extra pound. At Point *A*, the supply curve is telling us that somebody else, either a U.S. exporter or his customers, would be willing to give up an extra pound per year for as little as $1.00. Yet, the exchange controls prevent these two groups from getting together to split the $0.50 of net gain in a marketplace for pounds. Thus the vertical distance $AC = \$0.50$ shows the social loss from not being able to trade freely another pound. Similarly, each extra vertical gap between the demand curve and the supply curve out to Point E also adds to the measure of something lost because the exchange controls hamper private transactions. All these net losses add up to area ACE (or something like £5 billion).

Actual exchange-control regimes are likely to entail higher social costs than this hypothetical one. In practice, governments do not hold public foreign currency auctions. They allocate the right to buy foreign currency at the low official rate according to more complicated rules. To get the right to buy foreign currency, we must go through involved application procedures to show that the purpose of the foreign purchase qualifies it for a favored-treatment category. Importing inputs for factories that would otherwise have to remain idle and underutilized is one purpose that often qualifies for priority access to foreign exchange, over less crucial inputs, or imports of luxury consumer goods, or acquisition of private foreign bank deposits. Using exchange controls as a way of rationing according to some sort of officially appraised social merit can have its positive effects, of course. But the clearest difference between actual exchange controls and our hypothetical one is that the actual controls incur much greater administrative costs to enforce the controls, private resource costs in trying to evade them or comply with them, and social-psychological costs of the inevitable perceived injustices created by the controls or their evasion.

The costs of actual exchange controls are generally great enough to raise anew the question of what good purpose they were intended to serve. Because controls are one alternative to floating exchange rates, one might imagine that they reduce economic uncertainty by holding fixed the external value of the national currency. Yet, they are unlikely to help reduce uncertainty if they leave individual firms and households in doubt as to whether or not they will be allowed to obtain foreign exchange at any price. Controls are likely to appeal mainly to government officials as a device for increasing their discretionary power over the allocation of resources. Controls, undeniably, have this effect. A charitable interpretation is that the extra power makes it easier for government officials to achieve social goals through comprehensive planning. A less charitable interpretation, consistent with the facts, is that officials see in exchange controls an opportunity for personal power and its lucrative exercise. In general, the costs of exchange controls seem so great that we shall drop this alternative from the list of policy options for true adjustment and focus on the three-way choice among floating rates, fixed rates with classical medicine, and variations on the adjustable-pegged exchange rate.

TWO DOWN, THREE TO GO

Two of the five main options for adjusting a nation's foreign exchange have been dealt with. They are now put aside. The option of simply financing deficits and surpluses with changes in reserves and money liabilities at a fixed-exchange rate (option 1) is set aside, not because it is flawed, but because its use has clear limits. A nation can absorb deficits with reserve losses and with the issuance of new money only as long as the rest of the world lets it. The use of exchange controls (option 2) clearly entails serious inefficiencies.

Our journey through the remaining three main options—firmly fixed rates, floating rates, and the compromises—will proceed in stages. The rest of this chapter surveys historical experience with these three systems and reports some lessons learned from that experience. The lessons are based on a combination of theory and experience, rather than on experience alone. Later chapters will add some of the theory behind lessons reported here. Chapter 18 explains the theoretical issues relating to possible instability of the foreign-exchange market itself. Part Four will begin wtih an analysis of how the problem of stabilizing the domestic economy (national product, jobs and prices, rather than the foreign exchange market as such) is affected by the choice of a policy for regulating foreign exchange, and it will conclude with a summary of the whole foreign-exchange policy issue.

INTERNATIONAL CURRENCY EXPERIENCE

Much can be learned from the history of relations between national currencies since the establishment of a nearly worldwide gold standard over a century ago. This historical experience sheds light on truly fixed rates, on floating rates, and on the adjustable-peg system.

The Gold Standard Era, 1870–1914 (one version of Option 4)

Ever since 1914, the prewar gold standard has been the object of considerable nostalgia. Both the interwar period and the postwar period saw concerted international efforts to reestablish fixed-exchange rate systems whose desirability was viewed as proven by the experience of the gold standard. Among scholars, too, the "success" of the gold standard has been widely accepted and research has focused on *why*, not whether, it worked so well.

The international gold standard emerged by 1870 with the help of historical accidents centering on Britain. Britain tied the pound sterling ever more closely to gold than to silver from the late 17th century on, in part because Britain's official gold-silver value ratio was more favorable to gold than were the ratios of other countries, causing arbitrageurs to ship gold *to* Britain and silver *from* Britain. The link between the pound sterling and gold proved crucial. Britain's rise to primacy in industrialization and world trade in the 19th century enhanced the prestige of the metal tied to the currency of this leading country. Also, Britain had the further advantage of not being invaded in wars, which further strengthened its image as the model of financial security and prudence. The prestige of gold was raised further by another lucky accident: the waves of gold discoveries both in the middle of the 19th century (California, Australia) and at the end of this century (South Africa, the Klondike) were small enough not to make gold too suddenly abundant to be a standard for international value. The silver mining expansion of the 1870s and 1880s, by contrast, yielded too much silver, causing its value to plummet. Through such accidents, the gold standard, in which each national currency was fixed in gold content, remained intact from about 1870 until World War I.

In retrospect, it is clear that the success of the gold standard is explained, in part, by the tranquility of the prewar era. The world economy simply was not subjected to shocks as severe as World Wars I and II, the Great Depression of the 1930s, and the OPEC oil price shocks of 1973–74 and 1979–80. *The gold standard looked successful, in part, because it was not put to a severe worldwide test.*

The pre-1914 tranquility even allowed some countries to have favorable experiences with flexible exchange rates. Several countries abandoned fixed-exchange rates and gold convertibility in short-run crises. Britain itself did so during the Napoleonic Wars. Faced with heavy wartime financial needs, Britain suspended convertibility of the pound sterling into gold and let the pound drop by as much as 30 percent in value by 1813, restoring official gold convertibility after the wars. Other countries repeated the same experience, as shown for selected countries in Figure 17.4. During the U.S. Civil War, the North found itself unable to maintain the gold value of the paper dollar, given the tremendous need to print dollars to finance the war effort. The newly issued greenback dollars had dropped in value by more than 60 percent as of 1864, before beginning a long, slow climb back to gold parity in 1879. Heavy short-run financial needs also drove other countries off gold parity. War was the proximate culprit in the cases of Russia, Austria-Hungary, and Italy.

The prewar experience with flexible exchange rates reveals some patterns borne out by most of 20th-century experience as well. Most countries that abandoned fixed exchange rates did so in a context of growing payments deficits and reserve outflows. Note that in Figure 17.4 the end of fixed-exchange rates was accompanied by a drop in the value of the national currency. This drop shows indirectly that the fixed-rate gold standard imposed strain mostly on countries which were in payments deficit situations, not on countries in surplus. Indeed, countries in surplus found it easy to continue accumulating reserves with a fixed exchange rate.

In general, the prewar experiences with flexible exchange rates did not

FIGURE 17.4 Selected Exchange Rates, 1860–1913

Value of this currency
in gold $ (U.S. or Canadian)
(ratio scale)

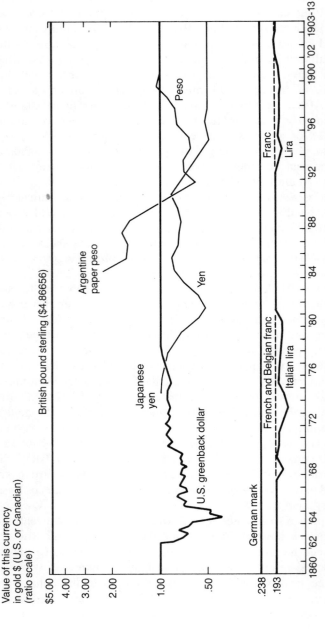

The data are annual averages of market exchange rates, except for the rates on the greenback dollar from 1862 through 1872, which are monthly averages for every third month. The Argentine paper peso rates are the John H. Williams gold premiums cited in Alec G. Ford, *The Gold Standard, 1880–1914: Great Britain and Argentina* (Oxford: Clarendon, 1962), p. 139. The Italian series is from Istituto Centrale di Statistica, *Sommario di Statistiche Storiche Italiane, 1861–1955* (Rome, 1958), p. 166. The gold value of the paper Japanese yen was calculated using the midrange New York dollar value of the metal-backed yen (Bank of Japan, Statistics Department, *Hundred Year Statistics of the Japanese Economy* [Tokyo, 1966], p. 318) and the average price of silver in paper yen for the period 1877–86 (Henry Rosovsky, "Japan's Transition to Modern Economic Growth, 1868–1885," in *Industrialization in Two Systems*, ed. Henry Rosovsky [New York: Wiley, 1966], pp. 129 and 136. The U.S. greenback dollar series is the W. C. Mitchell series cited in Don C. Barrett, *The Greenback and Resumption of Space Payments, 1862–1879* (Cambridge, Mass.: Harvard University Press, 1931), pp. 96–98. The virtually fixed rates are available in the *Economist* for prewar years.

reveal any tendency toward destabilizing speculation. For the most part, the exchange-rate fluctuations were within the range that would be experienced by Canada and other countries during the postwar era, and they did not represent wide departures from the exchange rate one would have predicted, given the movements in price indexes. Two possible exceptions related to the U.S. greenback dollar and the Russian ruble. In 1864, the greenback dollar jumped 49 percent between April and July, even though the wholesale price index rose less than 15 percent, suggesting that speculation greatly accelerated the drop in the greenback, which then promptly rebounded. Similarly, in 1888, political rumors caused a dive in the thinly marketed Russian ruble. With the exception of these two possible cases of destabilizing speculation, it appears that flexible rates were quite stable in the prewar setting, given the political events that forced governments to try them out.

The method of payments adjustment under the prevailing fixed exchange rates puzzled Frank Taussig and his Harvard students after World War I. They found that international gold flows seemed to eliminate themselves very quickly, too quickly for their possible effects on national money supplies to change incomes, prices, and the balance of payments. The puzzle was heightened by the postwar finding of Arthur I. Bloomfield that central banks had done little to adjust their national economies to their exchange rates before 1914. Far from taking classical medicine, prewar central banks, similar to their successors in the interwar period, offset ("sterilized") external reserve flows in the majority of cases, shielding their national money supplies from the balance of payments. What, then, actually kept the prewar balance of payments in line?

First, it must be noted that most countries were able to run payments surpluses before 1914, raising their holdings of gold and foreign exchange. This removed the cost of adjustment to fixed-exchange rates because surplus countries were under little pressure to adjust. Widespread surpluses were made possible by, aside from the slow accumulation of newly mined gold in official vaults, the willingness and ability of Britain—and Germany to a lesser extent—to let the rest of the world hold growing amounts of its ready liabilities. Between 1900 and 1913, for example, Britain ran payments deficits that were at least as large in relation to official (Bank of England) gold reserves as the deficits that caused so much hand-wringing in the United States in the 1960s. In fact, it would have been impossible for Britain to honor even one third of its liquid liabilities to foreigners in 1913 by paying out official gold reserves. The gold standard was thus helped along considerably by the ability of the key-currency country to give the rest of the world liquid IOUs whose buildup nobody minded—or even measured.

There were times, of course, in which Britain was called upon to halt outflows of gold reserves which were more conspicuous than the unknown rise in its liquid liabilities. The Bank of England showed an impressive ability to halt gold outflows within a few months, faster than it could have if it had needed to contract the whole British economy to improve the balance of payments. It appears that monetary tightening by the Bank of England was capable of calling in large volumes of short-term capital from abroad, even when central banks in other countries raised their interest rates by the same percentage. This command over short-term capital seems to have been linked to London's being the reserve center for the world's money markets. As the main short-term international lender (as well as borrower), London could contract the whole world's money supply in the short run if and when the Bank of England ordered private banks in London to do so. In this way, the prewar gold standard combined overall surplus for most countries with short-run defensive strength on the part of the main deficit country.

The prewar gold standard seemed to succeed for one other reason: *"success" was leniently defined* in those days. Central banks were responsible only for fixing the external value of the currency. Public opinion did not hold central bankers (or government officials) responsible for fighting unemployment or stabilizing prices as much as after World War I. This easy assignment shielded officials from the demand-policy dilemma discussed in Chapter 19.

Interwar Instability

If the gold standard era before 1914 has been viewed as the classic example of international monetary soundness, the interwar period has played the part of a nightmare that postwar officials have been determined to avoid repeating. Payments balances and exchange rates gyrated chaotically in response to two great shocks, World War I and the Great Depression. Figure 17.5 plots the exchange-rate history of the interwar period. The chaos was concentrated into two periods, the first few years after World War I (1919–23) and the currency crisis in the depths of the Great Depression (1931–34).

After World War I the European countries had to struggle with a legacy of inflation and political instability. Their currencies had become inconvertible during the war because their rates of inflation were much higher than that experienced in the United States, the new financial leader. In this setting, Britain made the fateful decision to return to its prewar gold parity, achieving this rate by April 25. Although the decision has been defended as a moral obligation and as a sound attempt to restore international confidence as well as Britain's role at the center of a reviving world economy, the hindsight consensus is that bringing the pound back up to $4.86656 was a serious mistake. It appears to have caused considerable unemployment and stagnation in traded-goods industries, as theory would predict.

France, Italy, and some other European countries chose a more inflationary route for complicated political reasons. A succession of French revolving-

FIGURE 17.5   Selected Exchange Rates, 1913, 1919–1938

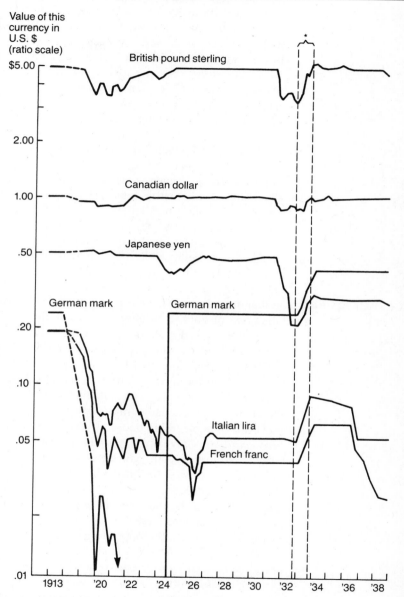

* March 1933–February 1934: the United States raises the price of gold from $20.67 per ounce to $35 per ounce.
Source: Monthly averages from U.S. Federal Reserve Board, Board of Governors, *Banking and Monetary Statistics* (Washington, D.C., 1943).

door governments was unable to cut government spending or raise taxes to shut off large budgetary deficits that had to be financed largely by printing new money. Something similar happened in Italy, both before and immediately after the 1922 coup d'etat that brought Mussolini to power. The ultimate in inflation, however, was experienced by Germany, where the money supply, prices, and cost of foreign exchange all rose more than a trillionfold in 1922–23. Money became totally worthless, and by late 1923, not even a wheelbarrowful of paper money could buy a week's groceries. The mark had to be reissued in a new series equal to the prewar dollar value, with old marks forever unredeemable.

The early 1930s brought another breakdown of international currency relations. The financial community, already stunned by the early postwar chaos and the Wall Street collapse, became justifiably jittery about bank deposits and currencies as the depression spread. The failure of the reputable Creditanstalt in Austria caused a run on German banks and on the mark because Germany had lent heavily to Austria. The panic soon led to an attack on the pound sterling, which had been perennially weak and was now compromised by Britain's making heavy loans to the collapsing Germans. On September 19, 1931, Britain abandoned the gold standard it had championed, letting the pound sink to its equilibrium market value. Between early 1933 and early 1934, the United States followed suit and let the dollar drop in gold value as President Roosevelt and his advisers manipulated the price of gold in an attempt to create jobs.

What lessons does the interwar experience hold for postwar policymakers? During World War II, expert opinion seemed to be that the interwar experience called for a compromise between fixed and flexible exchange rates, with emphasis on the former. The Bretton Woods agreement of 1944 set up the International Monetary Fund and laid down a set of rules calling for countries to change their exchange rates only when fundamental disequilibrium made this unavoidable. This decision was paralled by Ragnar Nurkse's book on *International Currency Experience,* written for the League of Nations in 1944. Nurkse argued, with some qualifying disclaimers, that the interwar experience showed the instability of flexible exchange rates. Figure 17.5 adds some evidence to his premise: exchange rates did indeed move more sharply during the interwar era than at any other time before the 1970s.

Yet, subsequent studies have shown that a closer look at the interwar experience reveals the opposite lesson: *the interwar experience showed the futility of trying to keep exchange rates fixed in the face of severe shocks and the necessity of turning to flexible rates to cushion some of the international shocks.* At the same time, these studies have shown that even during the unstable interwar era, speculation tended to be stabilizing—it was domestic monetary and fiscal policy that was destabilizing.

This revisionist conclusion began to emerge from studies of Britain's fluctuating rates between 1919 and 1925. Both Leland Yeager and S. C. Tsiang found that the pound sterling fluctuated in ways that are easily explained by the effects of differential inflation on the trade balance. Relative to the exchange-rate movements that would be predicted by the purchasing-power-parity theory of the equilibrium exchange rate (see Chapter 16), the actual movements stayed close to the long-run trend. The cases in which Figure 17.5 shows rapid drops in currency values were cases in which the runaway expansion of the national money supply made this inevitable under any exchange-rate regime. This was true of France up until 1926; it was even more true, of course, of the German hyperinflation.

Closer looks at the currency instability of the early 1930s suggest the same conclusion. The pound sterling, the yen, and other currencies dropped rapidly in 1931–32 due to the gaping disequilibrium built into the fixed-exchange-rate system by the depression (and, for Japan, by the invasion of Manchuria). Once the fixed rates were abandoned, flexible rates merely recorded, rather than worsened, the varying health of national economies.

The Bretton Woods Era, 1944–1971 (Option 5*a*)

The great compromise of 1944. Meeting at the Bretton Woods resort in New Hampshire, the monetary leaders of the Allied powers had an opportunity to design a better system. Everyone agreed that the system needed reform. The United States dominated the Bretton Woods conference, just as it dominated the world economy and the world's gold reserves in 1944. America wanted something like fixed exchange rates. Indeed, all leaders sought to get close to the virtuous fixed-exchange-rate case sketched in Figure 17.1 above. If only there were enough reserves to tide countries over temporary disequilibria, and if only countries followed policies that made all disequilibria temporary, then we could capture those welfare gains from successful stabilization.

Two expert economists, John Maynard Keynes of Britain and Harry Dexter White of the United States, came up with workable plans to give the world a new central bank that would allow deficit countries enough reserves to ride out their temporary deficits. White's plan also called for international pressure on national governments to change their macroeconomic policies to serve the goal of balanced international payments. The grand design, in other words, was to combine our Options 1*a* and 4 (temporary financing and fully fixed exchange rates).

In the end, however, the United States, Britain, and other governments had difficulty accepting the grand design. The Americans balked at putting billions of dollars at the disposal of other governments and at having to inflate the American economy just because it had a balance-of-payments surplus (as was then expected). Seeing the limits to what the Americans were prepared to give raised the fears of Britain and others about how they could adjust to their likely balance-of-payments deficits. In exchange,

FIGURE 17.6   Selected Exchange Rates, 1950–early 1981

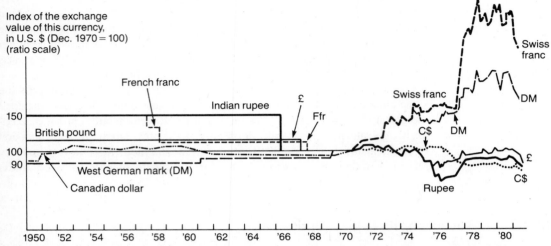

Sources: Year-end figures, 1950–69, and end-of-month figures, 1970–March 1981, from International Monetary Fund, *International Financial Statistics,* various issues.

they insisted on the right to resort to devaluations and exchange controls when deficits threatened to persist.

The resulting compromise is what we have come to call the **Bretton Woods system.** Its central feature is the **adjustable peg** (Option 5*a*), which calls for a fixed exchange rate and temporary financing out of international reserves until a country's balance of payments is seen to be in "fundamental disequilibrium." A country in that condition will then change its "fixed" exchange rate to a new official par value that looks sustainable. The international reserves are augmented by the International Monetary Fund (IMF). The IMF was set up with contributions of gold and foreign exchange from member governments. It grants all member countries the right to draw on the global reserves to finance temporary deficits. The IMF, in other words, is something like the global central bank that Keynes and White tried to design in their two different ways. Its resources and prerogatives, however, are more limited than Keynes and White envisioned. Also limited is the international community's ability to bend nations' macroeconomic policies in order to keep their international payments in line.

For the first postwar generation the Bretton Woods compromise institutions looked successful. Countries grew rapidly and unemployment stayed low. Most exchange rates stayed fixed for long time periods, as shown in Figure 17.6.

The strong economic growth probably contributed more to the look of success for monetary institutions than they contributed to the strong growth.

The good growth climate was consistent with flexible exchange rates, too, to judge from the Canadian experience of 1950–62. As shown in Figure 17.6, the annual average exchange rates between Canada and the United States showed little movement. By itself this does not prove that the Canadian experience was one in which speculation was stabilizing and flexible rates worked well. However, detailed studies of Canada's floating rate have borne out this inference. Statistical regressions have suggested that if the exchange rate on the Canadian dollar had any effect on capital movements, this effect was in the stabilizing direction; that is, a lower value of the Canadian dollar tended to cause greater net capital inflows into Canada, as though speculators expected the Canadian dollar to rise more when it was at low levels. Other studies have confirmed that the fluctuations in the exchange value of the Canadian dollar were no greater than one would have predicted by following movements in the relative U.S. and Canadian prices of traded goods. Given a stable economic environment, the Canadian flexible rate, like the fixed rates of the prewar gold standard, lived up to the claims of its advocates.

The one-way speculative gamble. The postwar experience with adjustable pegged rates recorded only rare changes in exchange rates among major currencies, as Figure 17.6 suggests. Yet the adjustable-peg system revealed a new pattern in private speculation, one that caused a great deal of official consternation. As the world economy grew, so did the volume of internationally mobile private funds. The new system of pegged-but-adjustable exchange rates spurred private speculators to attack currencies that were "in trouble." The adjustable-peg system gave private speculators an excellent one-way gamble. It was always clear from the context whether a currency was in danger of being devalued or revalued. In the case of a devaluation-suspect currency, such as the pound sterling, the astute private speculator knew that the currency could not rise significantly in value. She thus had little to lose by selling the currency short in the forward market. If the currency did not drop in value, she had lost nothing but her forward transactions fees and a slight gap between the forward rate and the spot rate, but if she was right and the currency was devalued, it might be devalued by a large percentage over a single weekend, bringing her a handsome return. In this situation, private speculators would gang up on a currency that was moving into a crisis phase. As one foreign-exchange specialist in a leading U.S. bank put it, "in those days we could make money just by following the crowd."

This pattern of speculation under the adjustable-peg system meant serious difficulties for any government or central bank that was trying to cure a payments disequilibrium without adjusting the peg. A classic illustration of these difficulties was the attempt of Harold Wilson's Labor government to keep the pound worth $2.80 between 1964 and November 1967. When Wilson took office, he found that Britain's trade and payments balances were even worse than previous official figures had admitted. His government used numerous devices to make the pound worth $2.80: tighter exchange controls; soaring interest rates; selective tax hikes; promises to cut government spending; and massive loans from the IMF, the United States, and other governments. Speculators who, in increasing number, doubted Britain's ability to shore up the pound were castigated by the Chancellor of the Exchequer as "Gnomes of Zurich." Yet, in the end, all of the belt-tightening and all of the support loans worked no better than had the attempt to make the pound worth $4.86656 from 1925 to 1931. On November 18, 1967, Britain devalued the pound by 14.3 percent, to $2.40. The gnomes had won handsomely. Those who had been selling sterling forward at prices like $2.67 just before the devaluation were able to buy the same sterling at about $2.40, pocketing the 27 cents difference. The British government and its taxpayers lost the same margin, by committing themselves to pay $2.67 for sterling that they had to concede was worth only $2.40 after November 18.

The existence of the one-way speculative gamble seems to make the adjustable peg of the Bretton Woods system look less sustainable than either purely fixed rates or purely flexible rates. If speculators believe that the government is willing to turn the entire economy inside out to defend the exchange rate, then they will not attack the exchange rate. Britain could have made speculators believe in $2.80 in the mid-1960s if it had shown its determination to slash the money supply and contract British incomes and jobs until $2.80 was truly an equilibrium rate. But as the speculators realized, few postwar governments are prepared to pay such national costs in the name of truly fixed exchange rates. Alternatively, the speculators might have been more cautious in betting against sterling if the exchange rate had been a floating equilibrium rate. With the float, speculators face a two-way gamble: the exchange rate could be higher or lower than they expect it to be, since the current spot rate is an equilibrium rate and not an artificial official disequilibrium rate.

Although the speculative attacks on an adjustable-pegged rate are certainly unsettling to officials, it is not clear that they should be called *destabilizing*. If the official defenses of the currency are primarily just ways of postponing an inevitable devaluation and not ways of raising the equilibrium value of the currency, then it could be said that the speculative attack is stabilizing, in the sense that it hastens the transition to a new equilibrium rate. Whether it performs this stabilizing function is highly uncertain, however: officials may be induced to overreact to the speculative attack and to overdevalue the pegged rate, necessitating another parity change later.

The dollar crisis. The postwar growth of the international economy led to a crisis involving the key currency of the system, the U.S. dollar. As the economy grew, and as Europe and Japan gained in competitive ability relative to that of U.S. firms, the U.S. payments position shifted into large overall deficits (as defined in Chapter 14). In part, those deficits represented the fact that a growing international economy wanted more dollar bank deposits in foreign hands to meet the monetary needs of international transactions. After a time, however, the deficits became a source of official concern in Europe and Japan. More and more dollars ended up in official hands. Something like this had happened in 1914, when other countries accumulated growing official reserves of sterling. In the postwar setting, however, few governments felt that they could be as relaxed about the gold backing of the U.S. dollar as the rest of the world had felt about the link between gold and Britain's sterling before 1914. U.S. gold reserves dwindled as France led the march to Fort Knox (actually, the basement of the New York Federal Reserve Bank), demanding gold for dollar claims. It became questionable whether the U.S. dollar was worth as much gold as the official gold price ($35 an ounce) implied.

In this situation, the United States clearly had the option of contracting the U.S. economy until foreigners were constrained to supply gold to the United States to pay for U.S. exports. Other alternatives were tight exchange controls and devaluing the dollar in terms of gold. Exchange controls were tried to a limited extent (in the form of the Interest Equalization Tax on lending abroad, the "Voluntary" Foreign Credit Restraint Program, and the like), but these controls ran counter to the official U.S. stance of encouraging free mobility of capital between countries. Devaluation of the dollar in terms of gold would have marked up the dollar value of U.S. gold reserves but would not have stemmed the payments deficits and would have brought politically distasteful windfall gains to the Soviet Union and South Africa (the two major gold exporters).

Faced with these choices under the existing international rules, the United States opted for changing the rules. On March 17, 1968, a seven-country meeting hastily called by the United States announced the "two-tier" gold price system. The private price of gold in London, Zurich, and other markets was now free to fluctuate in response to supply and demand. The official price for transactions among the seven agreeing governments would still be $35 an ounce. As it turned out, the seven governments soon stopped dealing officially in gold at all at the $35 price. The gold-dollar price link had been severed, probably forever. Gold rose in value, no longer held down by official gold sales.

Though gold had been demonetized (or, if you prefer, the dollar had been stripped of its international gold value), the U.S. overall payments deficits continued and had to be financed by increasing sales of U.S. foreign-exchange reserves. Eventually, the United States would have to adjust, either by taking classical medicine, or by imposing exchange controls, or by changing the international monetary rules and allowing the dollar to float in foreign-exchange markets. Again, the United States chose to change the rules, on April 15, 1971.

Floating Rates after 1971 (Options 3 and 5*b*)

After President Nixon set the dollar afloat in 1971, exchange rates went through some moderately wide swings, as graphed in Figures 16.1 and

17.6. More countries decided to float in the 1970s than had during the depression of the 1930s, when a few countries experienced wide exchange-rate swings while others resorted to exchange controls.

Despite the near universality of the float after 1971, one of the most noteworthy features of this recent experience has been the extent of official resistance to floating. In the 1970s, the government of Japan tried to hold down the dollar value of the yen, apparently in order to give Japanese sellers of traded goods an extra competitive edge in international markets. In the process, official Japanese institutions have bought tremendous volumes of U.S. dollars that have nonetheless declined somewhat in yen value. The Japanese determination to resist the rise of the yen is a leading example of what has been called the "dirty float," a floating exchange rate involving considerable official intervention in one direction.

Governments of the European Economic Community strove to prevent movements in exchange rates among their currencies, setting up "the snake" within "the tunnel" in December 1971. They agreed on maximum ranges of movement for the most appreciated versus the most depreciated member currency (the tunnel), and on maximum bands within which pairwise exchange rates could oscillate (the snake). This gesture at European unity, however, was short-lived. Britain, Italy, and France soon allowed their currencies to drop well below the tunnel, leaving little more than a fixed set of rates between the West German mark and the Benelux currencies.

The official desire for fixed rates has remained strong, but fixed rates are hard to maintain, given the large international flows of private funds and the absence of strong U.S. support for fixed rates. Once the link to gold had been severed, the United States switched to advocacy of floating rates, and often (e.g., the early 1970s and 1980–1983) followed a policy of "benign neglect" toward exchange rates, declining to intervene in exchange markets. By 1985, when the dollar had soared to peak rates, the U.S. government participated in an international accord to stabilize exchange rates somewhat. But, as we have seen, exchange rates still oscillate widely.

The idea of official intervention in foreign-exchange markets suffers from a further weakness that will be discussed in the next chapter. Official attempts to replace a pure float with a "managed float" have proved financially costly. Intervention brought central banks exchange losses like those they had suffered during crises under the adjustable peg of the Bretton Woods era. Speculators again spotted desperate attempts by officials to maintain unrealistic exchange rates and used the one-way gamble to make private profits at the expense of officials.

Economists are still debating whether the post-1971 experience shows the stability or the instability of floating exchange rates. Critics of the float start at the obvious point: exchange rates have fluctuated "a lot," "more than anybody expected." Defenders of the float can argue for demonstrated stability of the floating-rate system by pointing to several facts about the 1970s and early 1980s. The initial movements of 1971–73 can be viewed as indications of how badly the previous fixed rates had departed from equilibrium rates, just as the sharp drops in several currencies in 1931–33 partly reflected how far out of line the earlier official parities had become. The decade after 1971 also saw two OPEC oil-price jumps, which stirred up inflation in different unpredictable amounts in different countries. It is not clear that the observed exchange-rate movements caused any more problems than the attempt to keep rates fixed would have brought in the face of the same shocks. Still, an advocate of more fixed rates need not be impressed by the performance of the float, especially if he or she thinks (plausibly) that the float itself contributed to inflation and instability by freeing national officials from the "price discipline" of fixed exchange rates (an issue to which we return in Chapter 22).

SUMMARY

Nations are repeatedly faced with foreign exchange problems. Under fixed exchange rates, they face deficits or surpluses in the overall balance of payments. Under floating rates, they face pressures on exchange rates. An individual nation can choose among five main kinds of institutions for adjusting to foreign-exchange problems:

1. **Financing** deficits or surpluses with changes in reserves and in money liabilities to other countries is one approach.
    a. **Temporary financing** can bring world welfare gains, but it requires good predictions of future equilibrium exchange rates.
    b. **Key-currency "deficits without tears"** give the key-currency country a windfall in extra resources in exchange for the world's use of its liabilities as international money. This "free lunch" is limited by the world's willingness to accept more of the key currency as extra money worth holding.
2. **Exchange controls** with a fixed official exchange rate are perhaps the most widely used single foreign-exchange regime and probably the worst.
3. The nation can let **floating exchange rates** be determined in free foreign-exchange markets without official intervention.
4. **Permanently fixed exchange rates** can work as long as the nation is willing to adjust its level of prices, output, and employment in any way necessary to preserve the fixed exchange rate.
5. The nation can try **exchange-rate compromises.**
    a. It can mix generally fixed exchange rates with occasional large devaluations or revaluations, according to the **adjustable-peg** or **Bretton Woods system,** as practiced between 1944 and 1971.
    b. It can try a **managed float,** changing exchange rates gradually, along with interim macroeconomic adjustments to the domestic economy. Variations are the crawling peg, the gliding band, and the dirty float.

The option of controlling financial payments imbalances by letting reserves fall and rise can be defended as long as the imbalances are temporary and self-reversing. In this case, it is not hard to show that the world experiences a welfare gain from stabilizing the exchange rates and letting official reserves vary. This approach assumes that private speculators cannot perform the same stabilizing function and that officials correctly foresee the sustainable long run for the exchange rate. If these assumptions do not hold, the case for financing deficits and surpluses with a fixed exchange rate breaks down.

The option of exchange controls is likely to involve large social costs, even when that option is exercised with perfect hypothetical efficiency. In addition to the ordinary static welfare losses from prevented transactions, exchange controls are likely to involve large administrative costs and resource waste in the process of trying to evade the controls or of applying for foreign-exchange licenses. These costs make exchange controls an apparently inferior alternative to the three remaining options: floating rates, fixed rates, and such compromises as the adjustable-pegged rate.

The success or failure of different exchange-rate regimes has depended historically on the severity of the shocks with which those systems have had to cope. The fixed-rate gold standard seemed extremely successful before 1914, largely because the world economy itself was more stable than in the period that followed. Many countries were able to keep their exchange rates fixed because they were lucky enough to be running surpluses at established exchange rates without having to generate those surpluses with any contractionary macroeconomic policies. The main deficit-running country, Britain, could control international reserve flows in the short run by controlling credit in London, but it was never called upon to defend sterling against sustained attack. During the stable prewar era, even fluctuating-exchange-rate regimes showed stability (with two brief possible exceptions).

The interwar economy was chaotic enough to put any currency regime to a severe test. Fixed rates broke down, and governments that believed in fixed rates were forced into fluctuating exchange rates. Studies of the interwar period showed that in cases of relative macroeconomic stability flexible rates showed signs of stabilizing speculation. Those signs were less evident in economies whose money supplies had "run away" or whose previous fixed exchange rates were far from equilibrium.

Postwar experience has shown some difficulties with the adjustable-peg system set up in Bretton Woods in 1944. Under this system, private speculators are given a strong incentive to attack reserve-losing currencies and force large devaluations. The role of the dollar as a reserve currency also became increasingly strained in the Bretton Woods era. Growing private foreign demand for dollars gave way to increasingly unwanted official accumulations that led to conversions of dollars into gold. Ultimately, the United States was forced to bear large adjustment costs or to change the rules. The United States opted for new rules, breaking the gold-dollar link in 1968 and floating the dollar in 1971.

SUGGESTED READINGS

On exchange controls, see Krueger (1974) and the empirical series edited for the National Bureau of Economic Research by Bhagwati and Krueger (1973–76).

Two pioneering studies of the stability of fluctuating exchange rates in the interwar period are Tsiang (1959) and Aliber (1962).

The best detailed survey of international currency experience up to the mid-1970s can be found in several chapters of Yeager (1976). The prewar gold standard is analyzed in more depth by Bloomfield (1959), Lindert (1969), and Gallarotti (1989). A masterly survey of the interwar experience is Eichengreen (in press). For more detail on the Bretton Woods era, see Solomon (1977).

The dollar crisis under the Bretton Woods system was predicted and diagnosed in Robert Triffin's classic (1960) and by Jacques Rueff (translation, 1977).

For the wave of reaction doubting that floating rates worked well in the 1970s, see Artus and Young (1979), McKinnon (1981), McCulloch (1983), and Williamson (1983).

QUESTIONS FOR REVIEW

1. Under what conditions can officials successfully support a fixed exchange rate and prevent otherwise wide swings around that rate without capital losses or exchange controls?

2. What are deficits without tears, and what kinds of countries have them?

3. Review the international currency experience of each of these four periods:

a. The gold standard, 1870–1914.

b. The interwar period.

c. The Bretton Woods era, 1944–71.

d. The flexible-rate era since 1971 (including the discussion in Chapter 16 on exchange-rate movements in the early 1980s).

For each period, identify:

(1) The main shocks to the international currency system.

(2) The evidence as to whether speculation seemed to stabilize or destabilize exchange rates.

(3) The role of the key-currency country in the success or breakdown of the currency system.

▼

The Threat of Unstable Exchange Rates

•

*The trouble with speculation is
it's also speculative.*

Fritz Machlup

How great is the danger that foreign exchange markets will be unstable? And under what policies will the danger be greatest? If the market is unstable—that is, if ordinary shocks cause wide and self-feeding swings in exchange rates—serious damage could result. Intuition suggests that wide swings in any price will complicate business planning, especially when the swings are hard to forecast. Static welfare analysis agrees: as we have seen in Chapter 17 and Appendix G, official stabilization of a market price can in principle bring welfare gains that would be lost in an uncontrolled market.

This chapter explores six key parts of the unstable-market issue:

1. The danger of **destabilizing speculation,** which exacerbates swings in flexible exchange rates.
2. The danger of private speculators' **attacks on a pegged or managed rate.**
3. **The danger of an unstable trade-balance response** or current-account response to changes in an exchange rate.
4. The role of **unstable policies** in making exchange rates less stable.
5. How a change in fundamentals can cause **exchange-rate overshooting** by rational investors.
6. How costly it is to buy **private insurance against exchange-rate risks.**

These six concerns will loom large in Part Four's overall judgments about foreign exchange institutions.

DESTABILIZING SPECULATION

Many officials and scholars have argued that speculators can behave in a very destabilizing way when exchange rates are flexible, disrupting foreign exchange markets by making swings in the exchange rate wider than they would be otherwise. The wider swings, in turn, are said to damage confidence in exchange rates and to give traders and investors a heightened fear of exchange-rate risk. Such destabilizing speculation is seen as an argument against both floating exchange rates and the adjustable-pegged-rate system, since if officials showed that they were fully committed to absolutely fixed rates, speculators would not second-guess them and would themselves believe that rates will be stable.

The debate over destabilizing speculation can be summarized with the help of a diagram like Figure 18.1. It is imagined that speculative behavior, here defined as taking long or short currency positions in response to expected movements in the exchange rate, affects the extent to which the actual exchange rate deviates from its long-run trend. In Figure 18.1A, speculation smooths out the fluctuations in the exchange rate. There the trend line represents a steady trend in the exchange rate caused by a steady drift in the basic determining factors stressed in Chapter 17 (money supplies, national products, interest rates, etc.). The "without speculation" curve imagines that one of the underlying factors also behaves cyclically, generating a sine-curve departure from the trend, in order to portray swings that speculators might interpret in different ways. The "with speculation" curve in Figure 18.1A shows the exchange-rate results of stabilizing speculation, speculation that sells more of the currency when its price is above trend but buys more of it when its price is below trend.[1] In this case speculators' actions have exactly the kind of stabilizing effect that officials are often told to achieve.

In Figure 18.1B, by contrast, speculators' expectations tend to magnify swings in the exchange rate. Such an undesirable outcome could result if,

---

[1] The curves of Figure 18.1 could be generated by any of a variety of exchange-rate equations. Here is one type that could lie behind the trend, the "without speculation" curve, and the "with speculation" curve. Let the trend exchange rate at time t be ρ_t = the sort of expression discussed in Chapter 16 (one depending on such fundamentals as money supplies, national products, interest rates, etc.). Let the "without speculation" curve reflect this plus a sine disturbance: $r_t = \rho_t + a \cdot \sin(t)$, under the assumption that speculators blankly expect each current exchange rate to continue, as in the naive spot-rate (random walk) model mentioned in Chapter 16. Let the "with speculation" curve reflect the same forces plus speculators' beliefs, which depend on the latest departure of the exchange rate from its trend (say, on the day before, or day $t - 1$): $r = \rho_t + a \cdot \sin(t) + s(r_{t-1}/\rho_{t-1})$, where s is the coefficient of speculators' response to departures from trend. For the stabilizing speculation in Figure 18.1A, $s < 0$, whereas $s > 0$ for the destabilizing speculation in Figure 18.1B. If foreign-exchange traders all believed in the same fundamental forces, we would probably have stabilizing speculation ($s < 0$). But if they react just to the latest exchange-rate movements, we could have destabilization.

FIGURE 18.1   Hypothetical Cases of Stabilizing and Destabilizing Speculation in the Foreign Exchange Market

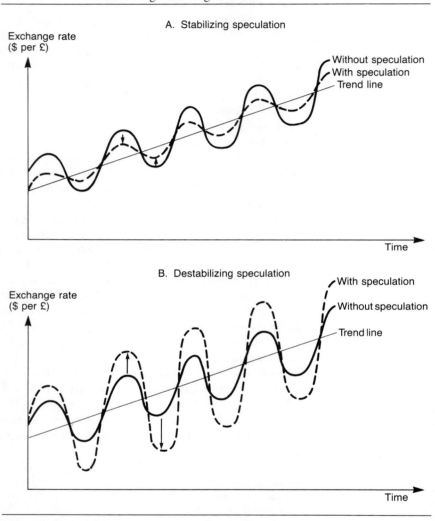

A. Stabilizing speculation

Exchange rate
($ per £)

Without speculation
With speculation
Trend line

Time

B. Destabilizing speculation

With speculation

Exchange rate
($ per £)

Without speculation

Trend line

Time

for example, net speculative purchases of the foreign currency were in fixed positive proportion to the deviations of the nonspeculative equilibrium rate from the long-run trend. In this case, speculators seem to expect rises in the exchange rate when its level is high, and they seem to expect drops when its level is low. They may be using "bandwagon" reasoning, figuring that what goes up (down) is likely to go up (down) further (or, as one market saying goes, "the trend is your friend"). They buy high and sell low, making the foreign-exchange market less stable and more risky.

How likely is destabilizing speculation? In 1953, Milton Friedman set off a debate with a simple and powerful point:

> *Stabilizing speculation makes money, destabilizing speculation loses money. Corollary: destabilizing behavior is driven out of the market.*

In Figure 18.1A, the stabilizers are making profits because they buy low and sell high across each cycle of exchange-rate movements. The destabilizing speculators of Figure 18.1B, however, are clearly losing money by buying at higher prices than those at which they sell. Friedman's argument is the same even if the pattern is more jagged and irregular than the smooth cycles shown here. As long as stabilizing means buying low and selling high and destabilizing the opposite, Darwinian "survival of the fittest" will drive out destabilizing behavior (and anybody who insists on practicing it). Friedman's argument prompted a search for hypothetical cases in which destabilizing speculation was profitable. William Baumol offered some apparent hypothetical examples, but others questioned whether the destabilizers really made money in Baumol's examples. They are, in any case, restrictive and unlikely examples. Friedman's point seems sustained: destabilizing speculation is unprofitable.

Notice, however, that Friedman's point does not rule out destabilizing speculation on a large scale. Even if destabilizing speculators do lose money, as he argued, they might still bring chaos to the markets in which they take their losses. To see how little the debate over speculators' profits educates our guesses about their possibly destabilizing nature, imagine a debate in 1927 over the possibility of destabilizing speculation in stocks on Wall Street. A theorist might have argued, as Friedman did later, that destabilizing speculation would be unprofitable and, therefore, self-eliminating and might have concluded that speculation would keep stock prices near the long-run trend dictated by the long-run growth of real corporate profits. Others might have countered with hypothetical mathematical cases of destabilizing but profitable speculation. None of these contributions, however, could have resolved the key empirical question of whether speculation stands a good chance of being destabilizing in such unregulated markets. That question had to be answered by a study of actual experience. Such a study would have turned up many cases in which sharp changes in price expectations destabilized markets for stocks, real estate, and other assets. And subsequent events bore out the possibility. Speculators between 1927 and mid-1929 took their own willingness to pay higher share prices as a sign that the stock market would go even higher, and then they reversed their opinions and ruined themselves in the aggregate in the Great Crash. These destabilizing speculators lost money, of course, but that didn't prevent disaster.

Most experts view the baffling peak of the dollar during the 1984–1985 period as a destabilizing speculative bubble.[2] There is good circumstantial evidence that foreign exchange traders followed bubble-prone rules. After 1981, foreign-exchange traders despaired of being able to predict exchange rates with fundamentals like those featured in Chapter 16. They switched to using "technical" or "chartist" models, based in direct gazing at short-run patterns in exchange-rate movements instead of long-run fundamental trends. Their new models often seemed to be based on extrapolating the very latest brief trend. That looks like destabilizing behavior of the sort separating the two curves in Figure 18.1B. Such behavior probably magnified the unsustainable rise of the dollar to its peak in February 1985.

So far, we get an intermediate result about destabilizing private speculation. Friedman may be correct in saying that its unprofitability makes it less common. But it *does* happen, even in foreign-exchange markets.

SPECULATIVE ATTACKS ON A PEGGED OR MANAGED RATE

The danger of destabilizing speculation is a drawback of any system that is likely to allow it. The only institution immune to this possibility is one with rigidly fixed exchange rates, with policy makers willing to defend them, even if it means unemployment or inflation or both. The danger affects all variants on flexible exchange rates or exchange controls.

Is the danger of destabilizing speculation greater under a pure float or under the compromise systems, such as the adjustable-peg or managed floats? More and more evidence points to a clear result: *the danger is actually greater under the compromise systems than under a pure float.* This may contradict intuition. We might think that the destabilizing bulls and bears will do more damage in the unsupervised china shop, the pure floating-

---

[2] Definitions of a speculative "bubble" vary. The common denominator is that investors expect the latest asset price movement to continue and behave in a way that magnifies departures from values dictated by long-run fundamentals. For a readable review of where we stand on the issue of speculative bubbles, see the symposium on bubbles in the Spring 1990 issue of the *Journal of Economic Perspectives.*

For warnings of likely overvaluation of the dollar, see Frankel (1985a, 1985b). Similarly, according to the eighth edition of this text, which was written at the start of 1985, "The 53 percent rise in the value of the dollar [from 1980 to the start of 1985] can be viewed as a reversible oscillation around an understandable long-run trend. . . . Up to 1983, it could have been called a return to the long-run trend set by basic real and monetary trends. But the rise continued into early 1985, and there is still the question of why such swings around a long-run trend should occur at all." (pp. 360, 362.)

rate system. But experience has revealed that the most frequent kind of destabilizing speculation is a kind peculiar to officially managed systems. In fact, the destabilizers are the officials themselves.

To understand how pegs or floats managed by central bankers seeking to stabilize could be even more unstable than pure floats, first recall the recent history of unsuccessful official attempts to defend exchange rates. In Chapter 17 we noted the **one-way speculative gamble** that private speculators could take when a pegged or managed currency was under attack. One example was the futile British attempt to prop up the pound sterling before officials were forced to devalue it in November 1967. Another was the futile attempt of the Bank of Japan to keep the yen from rising between 1971 and 1973. In both cases, the officials lost billions in taxpayers' money by trying to defend exchange rates that were no longer equilibrium rates. Private speculators were able to exploit the officials' commitment to unrealistic rates and make money by "following the crowd" and overwhelming officials' ability to defend the old rate. Such cases of official defeat cast the money-losing officials in the role of destabilizing speculators who tried to bet on the continuation of a disequilibrium rate.

How often do managed exchange rates yield this unsettling result, with officials getting themselves committed to unrealistic rates and losing money in the end? The facts are not highly publicized because any official exchange losses are cosmetically hidden in the official financial statements. Yet Dean Taylor (1982) has followed official sales and purchases of foreign exchange in several countries and compared them with subsequent movements of exchange rates to get a rough measure of official profits and losses on exchange-market intervention.

Figure 18.2 gives the official track record for "managed float" experiments in nine countries since 1970. It appears that officials in these nine countries lost money overall. Their unpublicized losses were generally greater, and sometimes significantly greater, than they would have had if they had intervened in a purely random way (or if they had not intervened at all). The British (unpublicized) foreign-exchange loss was greater than the highly publicized losses on the nationalized British steel corporation over a comparable period.

The evidence seems to show that officials let themselves be trapped into playing the role of losing destabilizers more than they played the role of profitable stabilizers. Why? There is no obvious reason, either political or economic. Yet somehow their commitment to stable exchange rates has become strongest when it should be abandoned (i.e., when the rates being defended were most clearly unsustainable). Meanwhile, private speculators gained profits at the expense of these officials. Reapplying Friedman's guideline that destabilizing speculation is unprofitable thus suggests that officials have added an extra *instability* to *managed* floating rates.

FIGURE 18.2   Net Profits and Losses from Official Foreign Exchange Trading under the "Managed Float"

Country	Period Beginning	Period Ending	Profit (+) or Loss (−) ($ millions)	Probability of an Equal or Greater Loss from Purely Random Trading
Canada	June 1970	December 1979	−82	0.42
France	April 1973	December 1979	1,035*	n.a.
			−2,003[+]	n.a.
Germany	April 1973	December 1979	−3,423	0.24
Italy	March 1973	December 1979	−3,724	0.0001
Japan	March 1973	December 1979	−331[++]	0.44
Spain	Feb. 1974	December 1979	−1,367	0.0003
Switzerland	Feb. 1973	December 1979	−1,209	0.39
United Kingdom	July 1972	December 1979	−2,147	0.029
United States	April 1973	January 1980	−2,351	n.a.
United States	January 1988	December 1988	−1,000	n.a.

n.a. = not available.
Official figures did not permit the calculation of losses or gains on foreign currency reserves held at the start of each period, but only those "realized" on foreign currencies purchased or sold.
* In this case, the French official gains are calculated in dollars.
[+] In this case, the French official losses are calculated in marks.
[++] Note that the heavy official Japanese losses of the last-ditch attempt to defend the adjustable-pegged exchange rate before March 1973 are excluded from this "managed float" period.

Sources: Taylor (1982, Table 1) and *The Wall Street Journal,* October 4, 1989.

HOW WELL DOES THE TRADE BALANCE RESPOND TO THE EXCHANGE RATE?

If there is a source of stability or instability peculiar to foreign-exchange markets, it must lie in trade responses to exchange-rate changes.[3] Speculators will have reason to believe that the exchange markets are stable if a rise in the cost of foreign exchange makes traders have a greater excess supply of it. If this condition holds, then a devaluation of a currency will be followed by the news that the devaluing country's trade balance is improving.

---

[3] There are two main reasons for this assertion. First, the channeling of trade-flow transactions through an asset market, in which money assets are traded for each other, has no direct analogue in domestic asset markets, making it dangerous to infer exchange-rate stability or instability from the way domestic markets behave (despite our cautionary glance at the stock market crash of 1929). Second, trade-flow behavior seems more likely to bring cumulative changes in exchange rates than do international capital movements. The latter have a built-in element of self-reversal, since each flow brings a later reverse flow as interest and principal are repaid.

Such news would help convince speculators to bet on a rise in the value of that currency. Conversely, if the trade balance reacts to a devaluation by worsening, yielding an even greater excess supply of the nation's currency (i.e., an even greater demand for foreign exchange), the speculators would have stronger reason to panic and rush to abandon the currency, accelerating its decline in the process. If we are to believe that an exchange market is likely to be stable, then we should be able to argue that devaluing improves the trade balance and the current account balance, so that it can shift net wealth toward the home country (raise I_f, the current account balance), which will have greater demand for the home currency.

It Isn't Obvious

It is not obvious whether devaluation will improve the net balance of trade in goods and services (and gifts). We will need more information. To see what information, consider the likely directions of change in a nation's trade prices and quantities when its currency (here, the dollar) drops in value:

TB (our current account balance, measured in £/year)	$= P_x^£$	$\cdot$	X	$-$	$P_m^£$	$\cdot$	M
	£ Price of Exports $\downarrow$		*Quantity of Exports* $\uparrow$		*£ Price of Imports* $\downarrow$		*Quantity of Imports* $\downarrow$
Effects of a devaluation of the dollar	= No change or *down*	$\cdot$	No change or *up*	$-$	No change or *down*	$\cdot$	No change or *down*

As indicated in shorthand here, a dollar devaluation is likely to lower the pound price of exports if it has any net effect on this price. This is because U.S. exporters are to some extent willing to accept lower pound prices because the dollar prices still look higher. If there is any effect of this price twist on export quantities, the change would be upward, as foreign buyers take advantage of any lower pound prices of U.S. exports to buy more from the United States. It is already clear that the net effect of devaluation on export value is of uncertain sign, since pound prices probably drop and quantities exported probably rise. On the import side, any changes in either pound price or quantity are likely to be downward. The devaluation is likely to make dollar prices of imports look a bit higher, causing a drop in import quantities as buyers shift toward U.S. substitutes for imports. If this drop in demand has any effect on the pound price of imports, that effect is likely to be negative. The sterling value of imports thus clearly drops, but if this value is to be subtracted from an export value that could rise or fall, it is still not clear whether the net trade balance rises or falls. We need to know more about the underlying elasticities of demand and supply in both the export and import markets.

How the Response Could Be Unstable

A drop in the value of the dollar (i.e., a rise in r, the price of foreign exchange) actually could worsen the trade balance, shifting even more currency into foreign hands and weakening the likely overall demand for the dollar. It would do so in the case of *perfectly inelastic demand* curves for exports and imports. Suppose that buyers' habits are rigidly fixed, so that they will not change the amounts they buy from any nation's suppliers despite changes in price. Examples might be the dependence of a nontobacco-producing country on tobacco imports, or a similar addiction to tea or coffee or petroleum for fuels. In such cases of perfectly inelastic demand, devaluation of the country's currency backfires completely. Given the perfect inelasticity of import demand, no signals are sent to foreign suppliers by devaluing the dollar. Buyers go on buying the same amount of imports at the same pound price, paying a higher dollar price without cutting back their imports. No change in the foreign exchange value of imports results. On the export side, the devaluation leads suppliers to end up with the same competitive dollar price as before, but this price equals fewer pounds. U.S. exporters get fewer pounds for each bushel of wheat they export, yet foreigners do not respond to the lower price by buying any more wheat than they would otherwise. Thus, the United States merely ends up earning less foreign exchange, and the deficiency of foreign-exchange earnings becomes even more severe as a result of the ill-advised devaluation.

In the case of perfectly inelastic demand curves for exports and imports, the changes in the TB (or current account) equation are as follows:

$$TB^£ = P_x^£ \cdot X - P_m^£ \cdot M$$
$$down = (down \cdot no\ change) - (no\ change \cdot no\ change)$$

A numerical illustration of this case is given in Figure 18.3A. There devaluing the dollar merely lowered the value of foreign exchange the United States earned on exports, from 80 ($= 1.00 \times 80$) to 60 ($= 0.75 \times 80$), worsening the trade balance.

It might seem that this perverse, or unstable, result hinged on something special about the export market. This is not the case, however. It only looks as though the change is confined to the export side because we are looking at the equation expressed in sterling. If we had looked at the *TB* equation in dollar prices, the deterioration would still have appeared:

$$TB^\$ = P_x^\$ \cdot X - P_m^\$ \cdot M$$
$$down = (no\ change \cdot no\ change) - (up \cdot no\ change)$$

Why the Response Is Probably Stable

In all likelihood, however, a drop in the value of the home currency improves the trade balance (and, along with it, the current account balance), especially

---

FIGURE 18.3   Devaluation Affects the Trade Balance

A. How devaluation could worsen the trade balance

Exchange Rate	$P^{\pounds}_x$		X	$-$	$P^{\pounds}_m$		M	$=$	$TB^{\pounds}$
Before dollar devaluation: $1.60/£	1.00	·	80	$-$	1.00	·	120	$=$	-40
After dollar devaluation: $2.00/£	0.75	·	80	$-$	1.00	·	120	$=$	-60

The key to this case: demand curves were inelastic, so that the volumes of exports and imports did not change. Devaluing our currency just lowered the value of foreign exchange we earned on exports, worsening the trade deficit.

B. The small-country case

Exchange Rate	$P^{\pounds}_x$		X	$-$	$P^{\pounds}_m$		M	$=$	$TB^{\pounds}$
Before dollar devaluation: $1.60/£	1.00	·	80	$-$	1.00	·	120	$=$	-40
After dollar devaluation: $2.00/£	1.00	·	105	$-$	1.00	·	100	$=$	$+5$

The small-country case illustrates the ability of high demand elasticities to guarantee that devaluation improves the trade balance. The essence of the small country case is that foreign curves are infinitely elastic, so that the world (£) prices are not affected by our country's actions. On the export side, the infinite elasticity of foreign demand means that our own supply elasticity dictates what happens to the volume of exports (X). We probably export more, raising our earnings of foreign exchange. On the import side, the infinite elasticity of foreign supply means that our demand elasticity dictates what happens to volume (M). We probably import less, cutting our demand for foreign exchange.

Appendix I generalizes from such special cases, showing how greater demand elasticities raise the ability of devaluation to improve the trade balance.

---

in the long run.[4] The reason, basically, is that export and import demand elasticities end up being high, and, as Appendix I proves, this is enough to ensure the stable response.

One quick way to see why the case of perfectly inelastic demands does not prevail is to note its strange policy implications. It implies, first, that we make it harder for ourselves to buy foreign goods with each unit of exports (i.e., $P^{\pounds}_x/P^{\pounds}_m$ drops), yet this impoverishing effect fails to get us to cut our spending on imports. The result looks even stranger upside down: it implies that a country could succeed in cutting its trade deficit and at the same time buy imports more cheaply (in terms of the export good) by cleverly *revaluing* its currency (for example, raising the purchasing power of the dollar from $1.60/£ to $1.00/£). If that were a common occurrence,

---

[4] Note that this section speaks about both the trade balance and the current-account balance as if they moved together. For present purposes, they do. The popular meaning of the term *trade balance* refers to exports minus imports of goods alone, as in Chapter 14. We use the same shorthand here, but are mainly interested in the similar effects of exchange rates on the whole current-account balance—goods, services, and gifts. Later, in Part IV, we will speak of the trade balance as a shorthand for the whole current-account balance.

FIGURE 18.4   The J Curve: How the Trade Balance Probably Responds to a Drop in the Value of the Home Currency

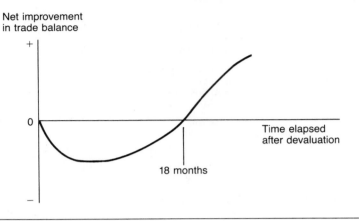

governments would have discovered it long ago, and they would have solved their trade deficits by happily raising the values of their currencies.

Over the long run, all elasticities tend to be higher, and each nation tends to face elastic curves from the outside world, both the foreign demand curve for its exports and the foreign supply curve for its imports. In the extreme *small-country case,* the home country faces infinitely elastic curves. Foreign-currency (£) prices are fixed, and the current account balance (or here, the "trade balance" *TB*) is affected by a drop in our currency as follows:

$$TB^£ = (P_x^£ \cdot X) - (P_m^£ \cdot M)$$
$$Up = (no\ change \cdot up) - (no\ change \cdot down)$$

We know that if the real volume of exports *(X)* changes, it will rise, because the same pound price of exports means more dollars per unit for sellers. They will respond to the new incentive with extra production and export sales. Similarly, we know that any change in the real volume of imports *(M)* will be a drop because the same pound price for imports leaves the dollar-country consumers with a higher dollar price. In the small-country case, both sides of the current account move in the right direction: export revenues rise and import payments decline. Figure 18.3B provides a numerical illustration that underlines the contrast with the pessimistic case of Figure 18.3A.

The crucial role of elasticities, illustrated in the two halves of Figure 18.3, also emerges from the technical formulas of Appendix I.

The fact that the elasticities of response to a given change (here, the devaluation or depreciation of the dollar) rise over time brings a second key result: *devaluation is more likely to improve the trade balance, the longer the span of elapsed time.* The trade balance (and the current-account balance) may dip for several months after a devaluation or depreciation of the home currency, but this should switch to a net improvement and remain improved for some time thereafter. Figure 18.4 gives a schematic diagram of what economists think is a typical response of the trade or current account balance to a drop in the home currency. The typical curve is called a **J curve** because of its shape over the first couple of years of response to devaluation. In the long run, all countries look "small," in the sense of facing prices set in a larger outside world. The drop in the dollar is likely to improve the later balance long enough to offset any possible early deterioration. As long as speculators sense as much, they should have no reason to expect a dropping currency to drop further because of a feedback through the trade (or current account) balance.

THE ROLE OF UNSTABLE POLICIES

Thus far we have looked at ways in which markets can stabilize in the sense of guiding the exchange rate back to its long-run equilibrium path. Speculators profited by pushing the exchange rate back toward its equilibrium trend in Figure 18.1A, driving out destabilizers who failed to bet on the true equilibrium trend. In the case of adjustable-pegged rates or managed floats, speculators played the same constructive role again, this time defeating officials whose sales and purchases of foreign exchange were wrongly aimed at keeping an exchange rate that was no longer a true equilibrium rate. Our look at trade-balance responses was similar: again, there was a basis for believing that the trade balance would eventually improve in response to a drop in the home currency, bringing the exchange rate itself back to a stable equilibrium. In each case, market forces brought us back toward the long-run equilibrium trend.

But what if there is no equilibrium trend? What if the underlying forces at work are themselves unstable? It is hard to see how foreign-exchange institutions could restore a steady equilibrium that does not exist. Three simple points are in order here.

First, the main source of instability that markets must cope with is macroeconomic policy, particularly monetary policy. Chapter 15 emphasized the central role of monetary policy in the determination of exchange rates. Historically, cases where exchange rates have run wild have usually been cases in which national money supplies have run wild. The extreme cases are the famous hyperinflations (e.g., in Germany and East European countries right after World Wars I and II, or in Latin American countries throughout this century). This is not to say that the private marketplace never generates its own instability. There are too many past examples of speculative bubbles unrelated to changes in government policy—Wall Street in 1929 and in 1987 serves as the best example. But unstable monetary policy is usually near the center of the storm (as it was even in the aftermath of the Wall Street crash of 1929). A stabilizing monetary policy is an integral part of the task of stabilizing foreign-exchange markets.

Second, if the policy environment is unstable, *any* foreign-exchange institution will probably fail to keep order. Floating exchange rates will gyrate. Managing floats will break down, leading to official losses and sudden delayed changes in exchange rates. And a truly fixed exchange-rate system will send macroeconomic shocks back and forth among countries, in a way examined more closely in Part IV.

Finally, in such an unstable policy environment, floating rates may well overreact to perceived changes in policy trends, causing undesirable swings and reversals in exchange rates. If policy signals change rapidly, rumors will abound and markets will swing back and forth. In fact, even if speculators react rationally to any policy change, the dynamics of the foreign-exchange market can be such that exchange rates will adjust to news by swinging beyond the ultimate equilibrium rate, reversing themselves later. We turn next to such a case, that of rational overshooting.

The central point about the role of policy is clear: stable and predictable policy trends are a necessary, and probably sufficient, condition for stable foreign-exchange markets.

EXCHANGE-RATE OVERSHOOTING

The subtle relationship between markets and policies produces oddities. One oddity in the area of foreign exchange is the case in which speculators react *rationally* to news of a change in policy by driving the exchange rate *past* what they know to be its ultimate equilibrium rate and then back to that rate later on.

Figure 18.5 shows how exchange rates could overshoot their new equilibrium, even if all speculators correctly judge the future equilibrium rate. Suppose that the domestic money supply unexpectedly jumps 10 percent at time t_0, then resumes the rate of growth speculators had already been expecting. Speculators understand that this permanent increase of 10 percent more money stock should eventually raise the price of foreign exchange by 10 percent, because the demand for a currency is unit-elastic with respect to money supplies in the long run, as argued in Chapter 16. In the very long run, both the domestic price level (P) and the price of foreign exchange (the exchange rate r) should be 10 percent higher.

But two realistic side effects of the increase in the domestic money supply intervene and make the exchange rate take a strange path to its ultimate 10 percent increase:

1. Prices are somewhat sticky in the short run so that considerable time must pass for purchasing power parity (see Chapter 16) to raise domestic prices by 10 percent relative to foreign prices.

FIGURE 18.5   A Case of Exchange-Rate Overshooting

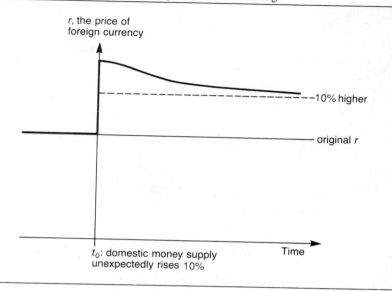

2. Because prices are sticky at first, the increase in money supply drives down the domestic interest rate, both real and nominal.

With the domestic interest rate (i) lower, investors will shift their lending abroad. But some other adjustments are in order. A lower domestic interest rate and the same foreign interest rate (i_f) cannot coexist with the same ratio of the forward rate (r_f) to the spot rate (r_s) as before. The decline in (i) now violates the interest parity condition of Chapter 15 and Appendix H, making $(1 + i) < (r_f/r_s) \cdot (1 + i_f)$.

With arbitrage money flowing out of the home country, something has to give to restore interest parity. If the foreign interest rate is fixed by foreign financial conditions, then (r_f/r_s) must fall so that $(1 + i) = (r_f/r_s)(1 + i_f)$. But if correct speculation makes the forward rate (r_f) approach the ultimate 10 percent increase, the spot rate (r_s) must have jumped by *more* than 10 percent to keep interest parity. Speculators must have the prospect of seeing the domestic currency appreciate later to stem their outflow in search of higher foreign interest rates. This can only happen if the action of arbitrageurs has bid the spot price of foreign exchange beyond its ultimate level.

So, once the news of the extra 10 percent money supply is out, speculators will bid up the spot price of foreign exchange by more than 10 percent (Dornbusch, 1976). One test by Jeffrey Frankel (1979) has suggested that perhaps the announcement of a surprise 10 percent increase in domestic

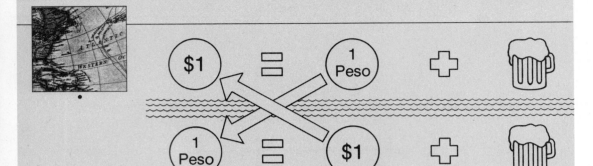

HIGH FINANCE, OR THE INTERNATIONAL BEER-DRINKING PUZZLE

At several points in Part III we have touched briefly on the issue of the welfare aspects of disequilibrium exchange rates. Here is a puzzle, and a real-life counterpart, to ponder on that subject.

In a certain town lying on the border between Mexico and the United States, a peculiar currency situation exists. In Mexico, a U.S. dollar is worth only 90 centavos of Mexican money, whereas in the United States the value of a Mexican peso (= 100 centavos) is only 90 cents of U.S. money.

One day, a cowhand strolls into a Mexican cantina and orders a 10-centavo beer. He pays for it with a Mexican peso, receiving in exchange a U.S. dollar, worth 90 centavos in Mexico. After drinking his beer, he strolls over the border to a saloon in the United States and orders a 10-cent beer. He pays for this with the just-received dollar, receiving a Mexican peso (worth 90 U.S. cents in the United States) in exchange. He keeps on repeating the process, drinking beer happily all day. He ends up just as rich as he started—with a peso.

The question: Who really paid for the beer?

(In addition to explaining who really paid for the beer, discuss the foreign-exchange aspects of this situation. What conditions are necessary for such a situation to persist for a long time, and what might bring it to a stop? What are the effects of this situation on the domestic economies of the United States and Mexico?)*

The beer-drinking puzzle may strike you as unrealistic. Not so. It happens all the time. The puzzle is but one illustration of the real-world phenomenon of arbitrage profit, the gains accruing to persons taking riskless advantage of

---

* The source of this puzzle is E. Krasner and J. Newman, *Mathematics and the Imagination* (1940), p. 162. Sorry, they didn't include the answer, and I leave that to you.

CONTINUED

price inconsistencies. A large part of the high incomes earned by professional traders comes from their ability to engage in arbitrage. (The rest comes as a reward for their speculation.)

For a real-life example of the same street-level arbitrage between currencies, consider the case of Wendy and Jim of Portland, Oregon, in 1982. They noticed different prices in Portland for the Canadian quarter. Most merchants were willing to accept Canadian quarters as worth 25 U.S. cents. You could also mix Canadian quarters into rolls of U.S. quarters and, again, get 25 U.S. cents for each. But Wendy and Jim were able to get Canadian quarters for much less than 25 U.S. cents. For one thing, the Canadian dollar had fallen from the old parity with the U.S. dollar to being worth only 80 U.S. cents, making the Canadian quarter available at 20 U.S. cents. Some banks would even sell Wendy and Jim Canadian quarters in bulk for as little as 16 cents each, just to save the expense of shipping them back to Canada.

So Wendy and Jim engaged in arbitrage. They would get large amounts of Canadian quarters from Portland banks at 16 to 20 U.S. cents each and spend them on whatever they wanted in Portland stores (or mix them into rolls of U.S. quarters at 25 cents each). They make up to $25 an hour that way, though usually somewhat less.

How long could their arbitrage last? For quite a long time if the Canadian dollar stays well below the U.S. dollar in value and if nobody else horns in on their business. They are not worried, reasoning that other people in Portland are too busy to make a living this way. Wendy and Jim find the pay better than their alternatives. Wendy was fired from her university job for teaching in the nude, and they have made little profit on their unpublished novels and musical compositions or their trade in rare records.

Who really pays for their profit on Canadian quarters? "That's what we were trying to figure out," says Wendy. "Nobody is, but somebody must be."[†]

[†] The source in this case is Lisa E. Vickery, "Free Money! Some Folks Snatching $25 an Hour Right Out of Thin Air," *The Wall Street Journal*, August 18, 1982, p. 24.

money supply would trigger a jump of the spot rate by 12.3 percent, before it began retreating back to just a 10 percent increase.

Here, then, is a case of rational speculation that overshoots its long-run target. Is such rational speculation and overshooting a sign of destabilizing private speculation? No, it's just a sign of volatile reactions to a policy surprise, the increase in the money supply. The extent of exchange-rate overshooting depends on the extent of monetary policy surprises.

PRIVATE SHELTER AGAINST EXCHANGE RISKS

Another argument introduced into the exchange-rate debate by advocates of fixed rates is one stressing the role of risk in international trade and investment. People are generally risk-averse. We prefer less risk to more, as is evidenced by the fact that the insurance business is much bigger than the gambling business, even in places where gambling is perfectly legal. It has been traditionally argued that flexible exchange rates increase risk. With the exchange rate free to change, traders and investors will feel less certain about its future. Fearing its changes, they will tend to be discouraged somewhat from socially profitable investments in developing foreign trade or production abroad. World product will be reduced. Hedging against exchange-rate risk by buying forward cover involves resource costs (work done by foreign-exchange dealers). The fixed-rate system, it is argued, gives people rates they can count on and saves them worry and hedging costs.

This argument works against flexible-exchange rates only in a much narrower range of cases than its proponents tend to think. It can hold if a nation's external payments are in a state of fundamental equilibrium, so that departures from that state are temporary and self-reversing. In such a case, it makes good sense to keep the exchange rate fixed at its sustainable equilibrium level. Doing so cuts the risk of short-run fluctuations without introducing social costs. The same conclusion in favor of smoothing out temporary disequilibriums was advanced in Chapter 17, although risk was not introduced there. On the other hand, if the disequilibriums are clearly temporary, one might expect private speculators to perceive this trend and to iron out the temporary swings, even with a freely floating exchange rate.

As soon as one broadens one's view of the relevant risks, the risk argument ceases to damage the case for floating-exchange rates. The risk that people care most directly about is the overall risk of fluctuations in their real incomes, not just price or exchange-rate uncertainty. With this broader perspective in mind, let us compare the kinds of risks brought by each major exchange-rate institution.

Fixed exchange rates bring macroeconomic risks. A system of truly fixed rates imposes adjustment costs on individual countries. Deficit countries sometimes put up with unemployment and deflation in order to adjust their entire economies to the exchange rate. Surplus countries, if they adjust, are burdened with unwanted inflation in the name of fixed rates.[5] For individuals and firms these adjustment costs can be viewed as a part of the risk cost imposed by a fixed-rate system that may in the near future call on a country to sacrifice its internal balance to defend the exchange rate. The adjustment costs of taking classical medicine may seem inordinately great in a country which, like the United States, devotes only a small share of its economic activity to international trade and investment. The risk of having your government unexpectedly deflate or inflate the economy to maintain a fixed exchange rate in the face of outside shocks may seem costlier than the risk of changes in the exchange rate.[6]

The adjustable-peg system has its own set of risks for the private investor or trade. It cuts the risk of nationwide deflation or inflation associated with a fully fixed rate by letting occasional devaluations and revaluations do some of the adjusting. But these occasional devaluations and revaluations pose a new threat. Investors or traders now perceive that over a single weekend (a common time for official exchange-rate changes) they could lose or gain a very large percentage on any currency holdings. Fortunately, this kind of risk comes only when general opinion perceives that a currency is "in trouble," but when it comes, it can strike traders and investors as a large risk indeed.

Freely floating rates bring a different structure of risk. As compared with truly fixed rates, they allow generally greater stability of income in the face of foreign-trade shocks, but less stability in the face of internal shocks, as explained next in Chapter 20. As compared with the adjustable-pegged-rate system, they face traders and investors with the likelihood of more frequent but smaller rate changes.

An important difference between the risks of a truly fixed-rate system and the exchange risks of the float or adjustable peg is that the latter can be insured against. Traders or investors who want to avoid exchange-rate risk can hedge and buy forward cover for time periods of up to a year or so, to ensure that their assets and liabilities are in the currencies they want. It has been argued that this kind of cover is *(a)* expensive and *(b)* more in demand with changing than with fixed exchange rates. Argument *(b)* is correct, but *(a)* is definitely not. The resource cost of forward cover as an

---

[5] This argument implies pessimism about Chapter 20's policy formulas for achieving both internal and external balance with fixed exchange rates. Clearly, if both goals can be achieved easily, the fixed-rate system need not bring unwanted deflation or inflation. Yet, as will be argued in Chapter 20, there are many reasons to doubt the practical feasibility of rectifying both payments imbalance and internal imbalance with just monetary and fiscal policies, and without changing the exchange rate.

[6] It is assumed here that flexible rates do not make government policy less stable, even though they might make it somewhat more inflationary (i.e., they might weaken price discipline).

insurance service is trivial. The forward exchange market occupies the time of only a few thousand specialists at most.

What is the private cost of exchanging currencies to protect oneself against exchange-rate risk? It is *not,* as some have thought, the percentage of difference between the forward and spot exchange rates. Somebody wanting to get rid of pounds to end up holding dollars might view a 1.3 percent "forward discount" on the pound (forward rate 1.3 percent below spot rate) as a cost. That idea would be incorrect. The person could just as easily avoid the risk of holding pounds by selling at the higher spot rate. And the same forces that would make the pound 1.3 percent cheaper in the forward market (e.g., fear of inflation in Britain) would make interest rates 1.3 percent higher in Britain because lenders would hold out for better interest rates on the sagging pound. In other words, the interest parity condition of Chapter 14 and Appendix H would assure that the investor seeking to avoid pounds could do so equally well through either the spot or the forward market, with no obvious cost at all.

If the resource cost of hedging is negligible, then another traditional argument must also be wrong. It would be incorrect to argue that exchange-rate risk discourages foreign trade, if everyone can buy cheap insurance against that risk in the foreign-exchange market. Indeed, an important study by Hooper and Kohlhagen (1978) found no significant negative effect of exchange-rate fluctuations on the real volume of foreign trade between leading countries. Hooper and Kohlhagen did find that exchange fluctuations seemed to have increased price levels, at least in the short run, but so far their finding of no effects on real trade volumes stands as the more important result, pending future tests. It appears that the ease of acquiring private insurance against exchange-rate risk under flexible rates makes the macroeconomic risks (induced unemployment and inflation) of fixed rates look more serious. We return to these macroeconomic risks in Part IV.

SUMMARY

The analysis of this chapter combines with the historical experience surveyed in Chapter 17 to sharpen our judgment of some debates over the possible instability of foreign exchange markets.

1. *Destabilizing speculation,* or speculative behavior that makes exchange rates fluctuate more widely, can bring social costs. Friedman has countered this fear with a skillfull defense of floating exchange rates. Friedman argues that since destabilizing speculation is unprofitable, destabilizers will eventually be driven out of the market, and the market will soon be left to those who promote stability. Friedman is correct in his assumption that destabilizing speculators should have a higher "death rate" than stabilizing speculators, provided the underlying equilibrium-rate trend is stable. But we have no real assurances that the "birth rate" of new destabilizing beliefs will be desirably low. There could always be a supply of born-again destabilizers for future crises. So far, the best examples of mass destabilizing and foolishness on the part of investors do not relate to the foreign exchange market, but we cannot conclude that it is immune to such behavior.

2. *Private attacks on a pegged or managed exchange rate* seem to have been more destabilizing than attacks on a purely floating rate. An analytical reason for this is the speculative one-way gamble facing private speculators when an officially defended exchange rate is in trouble. The speculators gang up on the beleaguered officials and force them to yield and change exchange rates, bringing profits to the private speculative attackers and losses to the taxpayers who pay for the official currency trading. During the managed floats of the 1970s, officials were definitely net losers, suggesting that their attempts to hold disequilibrium rates are a main source of destabilizing speculation under managed or pegged rates.

3. *The response of the "trade balance" or current-account balance to exchange-rate changes* is probably in the stabilizing direction (toward surplus in response to home-currency devaluation or depreciation). The higher the price elasticities of demand for exports and imports, the more stable the result is likely to be. There is the J-curve possibility that the trade balance will worsen right after a drop in the domestic currency, but eventually the decline will result in a net improvement.

4. *Unstable policies* can play a critical role in the functioning of exchange-rate regimes. When overall macroeconomic policies are unstable, no foreign exchange institution can be expected to produce stability by itself. Unstable monetary policy can produce curious results in a floating exchange rate.

5. An unexpected jump in money supply can cause *exchange-rate overshooting*, making the value of that country's currency drop further than the percentage of money-supply increases and to retreat to the same percentage change later. The overshooting is actually rational on the part of private speculators. It is caused by the combination of the unpredictable policy shock, by the interest parity, and by the fact that asset markets respond faster than prices in commodity markets.

6. The *private cost of exchange-rate insurance* is negligible when compared with uninsurable risks like unemployment. Individuals who seek to avoid foreign-exchange risks can do so at little or no cost (unless there are official exchange controls). One study has confirmed that there is no clear negative effect of exchange-rate fluctuations on the volume of foreign trade.

SUGGESTED READINGS

On the issue of destabilizing speculation, see Friedman's classic argument (1953) and Stern (1973, Chapter 3).

Dean Taylor's (1982) estimation of official foreign-exchange losses is more readable than most journal articles written for other economists, and his exercise could be repeated for other times and currencies.

The original, relatively technical, statement of the case of rational exchange-rate overshooting in response to a money-supply shock is in Dornbusch (1976).

For a survey of the literature searching for an influence of exchange-rate variability on trade volumes, see Braga and Mendez (1988). Important contributions to that literature include Hooper and Kohlhagen (1978) and a careful follow-up study by Cushman (1983). Using similar data sets and somewhat similar models, Hooper-Kohlhagen and Cushman reach somewhat different conclusions.

QUESTIONS FOR REVIEW

1. How likely is destabilizing speculation? Has it happened before? In what markets?

2. How can a prospective exporter protect himself against fluctuations in a floating rate? How would you measure the social cost of this protection?

3. Suppose that people are very fixed in their habits. They buy the same physical volumes of imports no matter what. If this is true of both U.S. importers and foreign importers, will a 10 percent depreciation of the dollar (say, from $1.60 to $1.76 a pound) improve the U.S. trade balance?

4. Suppose that sellers keep each U.S. export price at a fixed number of dollars and that sellers keep the prices of U.S. imports fixed in pounds (and in other foreign currencies). Will a 10-percent depreciation of the dollar improve the U.S. trade balance?

5. Will the depreciation of the dollar in Question 4 improve or worsen the U.S. terms of trade (P_x/P_m)?

6. Criticize this view: "Sure, officials generally lose taxpayers' money in exchange losses trying to stabilize exchange rates, but it's worth it. Society benefits from the more stable exchange rates."

Answers:

3. No, it will worsen it.

4. It depends on how elastic are the demands for imports. You should be able to construct numerical examples illustrating the possible improvement or worsening of the trade balance, using the trade-balance equation of this chapter. (If you read Appendix I, relate this case of fixed seller's prices to the Marshall-Lerner condition and the general stability formula.)

5. The terms will worsen by 10 percent.

6. The quote shows inconsistent reasoning. If officials are losing money, then they are *not* stabilizing the exchange rate, despite their good intentions. Their foreign-exchange losses are strong evidence that they are failing to bring society the hypothetical stabilization gains illustrated in Chapter 17.

Macro Policies for
Open Economies

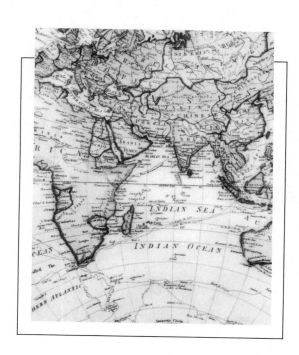

▼

Income and Foreign Exchange

•

The analysis of Part III brought us part of the way toward a judgment of what kinds of policies toward foreign exchange would best serve a nation's needs. Chapters 17 and 18 in particular spelled out the kinds of situations in which exchange between nations would be most—or least—stable and efficient as a marketplace unto itself.

In Part IV, our focus shifts to the other kind of stability issue previewed when the basic policy choices were laid out at the start of Chapter 17. This and the next two chapters address the problem of *macroeconomic* stability—the task of managing national output, jobs, and prices in the face of changing world conditions. This task is tricky business, because of the many ways in which the national economy and the world economy interact. Yet some valuable policy rules can be established. Once these rules have been laid out in Chapters 19–21, Chapter 22 can provide a series of lessons about where the international macroeconomic system is headed and how well different exchange-rate institutions work.

This chapter erects one of several building blocks on which policy judgments about international macroeconomics must rest, by sketching how national income interacts with foreign trade and how it is affected by changes in the exchange rate. Its analysis will become part of the larger macroeconomic model used in Chapters 20 and 21.

SETTING PRICES ASIDE

Ever since the onset of the Keynesian revolution in the 1930s, one of the main difficulties in macroeconomics has been the forming of a satisfactory framework for predicting both changes in real incomes and changes in prices. A general consensus has formed, despite some lingering skirmishes, about the monetary and other forces that lie behind the aggregate demand side of the economy, raising and lowering both real incomes and price levels in tandem. But we lack a satisfactory supply side for standard macroeconomic models, which would allow us to determine income and price levels separately. Three solutions have been tried, each satisfactory for some purposes, but not for others:

1. One can make the extreme Keynesian assumption that prices do not matter to the internal processes of the economy, so that income and spending might just as well be measured in real (deflated) terms.
2. One can assume a Keynesian upward-sloping supply curve, relating real income and the price level, so that the effects of any upward shift in aggregate demand for what the nation produces are split between an increase in real income and a price increase.
3. One can assume a vertical supply curve, fixing real income (national product) at either ''full employment'' or at ''the natural rate of unemployment,'' from which it can be expanded only by supply improvements (productivity gains, population growth, capital accumulation, land improvement, and supply-raising institutional changes).

   Much of the analysis of this chapter was first developed within the context of the first assumption, the extreme Keynesian, which sets aside prices as either fixed or irrelevant and concentrates on processes relating real spending to real income. We shall follow that path for this chapter. If the Keynesian analysis of income and international adjustment were useful only under this assumption, we would find it embarrassing in today's inflation-ridden world and would be inclined to omit much of what follows. Fortunately, the same predictions follow, though with more price movement and less output movement, under assumptions 2 and 3, and not just under assumption 1.

   In what follows, the level of national income, or Y, will be measured in current prices (not adjusted for inflation). In settings where unemployment is so great that one suspects that aggregate demand affects real income strongly and prices weakly, this analysis is to be used with the understanding that Y could stand for real national income as affected by demand-side forces. In settings of full employment and inflation, Y can be read as a measure of the price level of a real national income that cannot be changed by demand shifts. And in settings where both incomes and prices seem to be affected by demand changes, changes in Y are to be interpreted as changes in both real incomes and prices in response to demand changes. It is in this sense that we push prices to one side here—they can still be changed and are still relevant to international trade, but we shall consider their changes to be just a by-product of changes in income stemming from changes in demand.

TRADE DEPENDS ON INCOME

According to a host of empirical estimates for many countries, the volume of a nation's imports depends positively on the level of real national product. This positive relationship seems to have two explanations. One is that imports are often used as inputs into the production of the goods and services that constitute national product or, roughly speaking, national income. The other explanation is that imports respond to the total real spending, or "absorption," in our economy. The more we spend on all goods and services, the more we tend to spend on the part of them that we buy from abroad. Although a nation's expenditures on goods and services are not the same thing as its national income from producing goods and services, the close statistical correlation between income and expenditure has allowed statistical studies to gloss over this distinction when estimating import functions.

The most important parameter of the dependence of imports on income is the **marginal propensity to import,** which is the ratio of a change in import volumes to the change in real (constant-price) national income causing the import change. By linking extra income to extra imports, the marginal propensity to import shows the extent to which extra prosperity spills over into imports, worsening the balance of trade, rather than adding to the domestic-multiplier process by becoming a further new demand for domestic goods and services. The marginal propensity to import, in other words, is a "leakage" from the expenditure stream.

The dependence of *exports* on national income is more complex. It depends primarily on whether any changes in national income are the result of domestic-demand changes, domestic-supply changes, or changes in foreign demand for our exports. If domestic national income is raised by a surge in domestic aggregate demand that triggers an expansion of output and/or prices throughout the economy, there is a good chance that the increase in national income will be accompanied by a drop in export volumes, as domestic buyers bid away resources that otherwise might have been exported. Although such a negative dependence of export volumes on national-income-as-determined-by-domestic-demand is plausible, the evidence for it is somewhat sparse, and most Keynesian models of an open economy assume that export volumes are independent of national income.

Two other outside forces can make export volumes seem to vary positively with national income. One is a supply-side expansion, or any cost cutting, whether due to productivity improvements, price-cutting institutional changes, or any other supply-side shift. If national income is being expanded under such influences, this expansion will be accompanied by a rise in exports because the price reductions give the country a greater competitive advantage. Alternatively, the country could be experiencing a surge in foreign demand for its exports, allowing both exports and national income to expand.

We shall consider just such a linkage when discussing foreign income repercussions below. The usual Keynesian starting point, however, is to assume that the demand for exports is exogenous.

INCOME DEPENDS ON AGGREGATE DEMAND

The existence of exports and the dependence of imports on the level of national income add a slight complication to the Keynesian model of national income determination that is traditional in introductory courses in macroeconomics. The equilibrium level of national income is still the level matched by the level of spending on the nation's product that is desired for that level of national income. But now the aggregate demand for our national product is no longer the same thing as our national expenditures, as was the case in the simple closed-economy model of introductory courses. Recall from Chapter 14 that:

$$Y = E + X - M \tag{19.1}$$

or

$$\text{National product} = \text{National expenditures (or ``absorption'')} + \text{Exports} - \text{Imports}$$

In Chapter 14 these magnitudes referred to values in current prices. They can also double for real values (in constant prices) if each represents a domestic currency measure deflated by the same overall price index.

This equation can be interpreted either as an identity relating actual observed magnitudes or as an equilibrium condition relating desired magnitudes that depend on real income. Let us follow the latter interpretation here. Let the equation above be read as the following kind of equilibrium condition:

$$Y = \text{Aggregate demand for our national product} = E(Y) + X - M(Y) \tag{19.2}$$

Our desired expenditures depend on our national income, among many other things. This is most clearly true of our expenditures for consumption purposes. And since consumption depends on income, or $C = C(Y)$, so does total expenditure, which is the sum of consumption, domestic capital formation, or investment, and government purchases of goods and services $(E(Y) = C(Y) + I_d + G)$. Figure 19.1A illustrates the equilibrium level of national income, showing the matching between national income and aggregate demand at Point A. At levels of national income below 100, the aggregate demand would exceed the level of production, as shown by the fact that the AD curve is above the 45-degree line to the left of A. At any such lower levels of income, the combination of home and foreign demand for what this nation is producing would be so great as to deplete the inventories

FIGURE 19.1   Equilibrium National Income in an Open Economy, Shown in
Two Equivalent Ways

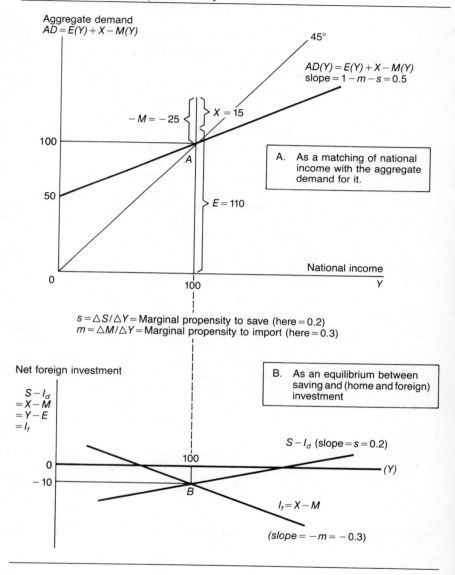

Aggregate demand
$AD = E(Y) + X - M(Y)$

45°

$AD(Y) = E(Y) + X - M(Y)$
slope $= 1 - m - s = 0.5$

$-M = -25$ { } $X = 15$

100

A

50

$E = 110$

National income

0

100

Y

$s = \Delta S / \Delta Y =$ Marginal propensity to save (here $= 0.2$)
$m = \Delta M / \Delta Y =$ Marginal propensity to import (here $= 0.3$)

Net foreign investment

B.   As an equilibrium between
saving and (home and foreign)
investment

$S - I_d$
$= X - M$
$= Y - E$
$= I_f$

A.   As a matching of national
income with the aggregate
demand for it.

$S - I_d$ (slope $= s = 0.2$)

0

100

-10

B

$I_f = X - M$

(slope $= -m = -0.3$)

(Y)

of goods held by firms, and the firms would have to respond by raising
production and creating more jobs and incomes, moving the economy up
toward *A*. Similarly, levels of income above 100 would yield insufficient
demand, accumulating inventories, and cutbacks in production and jobs
until the economy returned to equilibrium at point *A*.

Figure 19.1A does not give a complete picture of how the nation's foreign trade and investment relate to the process of achieving the equilibrium national income. To underline the role of the foreign sector, it is convenient to convert the equilibrium condition into a different form. This can be done with an algebraic step like one taken in Chapter 14, when we were discussing the current account of the balance of payments. The equilibrium condition given in Equation 19.2 becomes an equilibrium between saving and investment once we have subtracted private and government expenditures for current use $(C + G)$ from both sides:

$$Y = AD = E + X - M$$
$$(Y - C - G) = (E - C - G) + (X - M)$$

or

$$S = I_d + I_f \qquad\qquad (19.3)$$

In other words, saving, which is the nation's net accumulation of assets, must match its domestic investment in new real assets (buildings, equipment, inventories) plus its net foreign investment, or its net buildup of claims on the rest of the world. In Chapter 14, this was an identity between actual saving and investment. Here, it is interpreted as a condition that is necessary for an equilibrium level of national income, since both desired saving and desired imports (and, therefore, desired net foreign investment) depend on national income.

Figure 19.1B expresses this saving-investment equilibrium in a way highlighting the current account balance $(X - M$, or $I_f)$. As drawn here, Figure 19.1B shows a country having a current account deficit with more imports than exports of goods and services. This could serve as a schematic view of Canada's usual past situation since Canada typically has a net import balance on current account, financed partly by net capital inflows. In the past, the United States has usually had its version of Point B lying above the horizontal axis, representing a net export surplus and a positive net foreign investment. Recently, however, the U.S. position has reversed. The net-borrower status shown by Point B was characteristic of both the United States and Canada in the late 1980s (as shown in Figure 19.1).

THE SPENDING MULTIPLIER IN A SMALL, OPEN ECONOMY

When national spending rises in an economy having enough unemployment to fit the Keynesian model, this extra spending sets off a multiplier process of expansion of national income, whether or not the country is involved in international trade. Yet, the way in which the country is involved in trade does affect the size of the national income multiplier. Suppose that the government raises its purchases of goods and services by 10 and holds them at this higher level. The extra 10 means an extra 10 income for whoever sells the extra goods and services to the government. The extent to which this initial income gain gets transmitted into further income gains depends on how the first gainers allocate their extra income. Let us assume, as we already have in Figure 19.1, that out of each extra dollar of income, people within this nation tend to save 20 cents (part of which is "saved" by the government as taxes on their extra income) and tend to spend the remaining 80 cents (30 cents of it on imports of foreign goods and services). In Keynesian jargon, we would say that s, the marginal propensity to save (including the marginal tax rate) is 0.2; that the marginal propensity to consume domestic product $(1 - s - m)$ is 0.5; and that the marginal propensity to import (m) is 0.3.

The first round of generating extra income produces an extra two in saving, an extra three in imports, and an extra five in spending on domestic goods and services. Of these, only the five in domestic spending will be returned to the national economy as a further demand stimulus. Both the two saved and the three spent on imports represent "leakages" from the domestic-expenditure stream. Whatever their indirect effects, they do not directly create new jobs or income in the national economy. (Extra imports could feed demand back into our own economy by raising foreign incomes and stimulating their demand for our exports. But we do not consider this possibility until the next section, and we will assume for the present that this is a small country in the sense that foreigners spend almost none of their extra income on our goods.) In the second round of income and expenditures, only five will be passed on and divided up into further domestic spending (2.5), saving (1), and imports (1.5). And for each succeeding round of expenditures, as for these first two, the share of extra income that becomes further expenditures is $(1 - m - s)$, or $(1 - 0.3 - 0.2) = 0.5$.

This multiplier process carries its own multiplier formula, as was the case in the simpler closed-economy models of introductory macroeconomics. The formula is easily derived from the fact that the final change in income equals the initial rise in government spending plus the extra demand for this nation's product that was stimulated by the rise in income itself:

$$\Delta Y = \Delta G + (1 - m - s)\Delta Y \qquad (19.4)$$

so that:

$$\Delta Y(1 - 1 + m + s) = \Delta G \qquad (19.5)$$

and

$$\text{The \textbf{spending multiplier in} \textbf{a small, open economy}} = \frac{\Delta Y}{\Delta G} = \frac{1}{(m + s)} \qquad (19.6)$$

Thus, in our example, the rise in government spending by 10 billion ultimately leads to twice as great an expansion of national income, since the multiplier equals $1/(0.3 + 0.2) = 2$. The value of this multiplier is the same, of

FIGURE 19.2 The Effect of a Rise in Government Spending of Foreign Trade and National Income

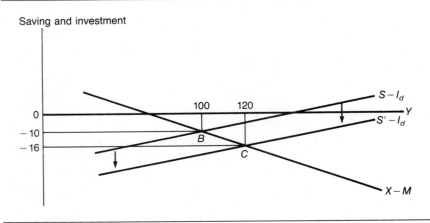

course, whether the initial extra domestic spending was made by the government or resulted from a surge in consumption or a rise in private investment spending. Note also that the value of the multiplier is smaller in an open economy than the multiplier in a closed economy. Had m been zero, the multiplier would have been $1/s = 5$.

The results of the multiplier expansion in response to a rise in domestic spending can be reexpressed in a diagram like Figure 19.2. Here, the initial rise in government spending is portrayed by a downward shift of the $S - I_d$ curve. It can be portrayed this way because a rise in government spending by 10 is a change in government saving by -10 since government saving is the difference between government tax revenue and government spending. The rise in government spending by 10 produces the same final rise in national income by 20 here as in the discussion above. Note further that the multiplier of two works its effects not only on the final rise in income, but also on the final rise in imports. Imports rose by three, thanks to the first round of new expenditures, but rose by twice as much, or $[m/(m + s)] \cdot \Delta G = 6$ over all rounds of new expenditures, the amount of trade-balance worsening shown in Figure 19.2.

FOREIGN INCOME REPERCUSSIONS

In describing the marginal propensity to import as a leakage, we have argued as though whatever is spent on imports is permanently lost as a component of aggregate demand for our national product. This assumption works well enough for a small country whose trade is negligible as an average or

FIGURE 19.3   Foreign Trade and Income Repercussions Starting from a Rise in Our Spending

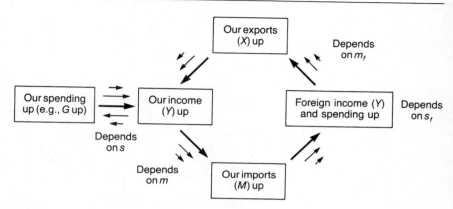

Reminder: these effects take different forms in different settings. In the Keynesian setting of this chapter, they are real-income and real-import responses to rises in real spending. In a full-employment setting, they could be transmissions of price inflation.

marginal share of world income. However, when a nation looms larger in the economies of its trading partners, this assumption underestimates the multiplier. When the nation's extra spending leads to extra imports, these imports raise foreign incomes and create foreign jobs. This is true, of course, for either a small country or a large country. However, if a country is large, the expansion of foreign incomes encourages foreign purchases of the country's exports in amounts dictated by the foreign marginal propensities to import from that country. The extra demand for exports raises the country's income further, thus raising the value of the multiplier response to the initial domestic spending.

Figure 19.3 illustrates the process of foreign repercussions. An initial rise in our government purchases of goods and services, on the left, creates extra income in our national economy. Some fraction (s) of the extra income will be saved, some will be spent on domestic national product, and some will be spent on imports. The fraction (m) spent on imports will create an equal amount of income for foreign sellers. They, in turn, will save a fraction of this additional income (s_f), spend some in their own countries, and import a fraction (m_f) from us. We divide that extra export income into saving, domestic purchases, and imports, and the cycle continues. Each round passes along a smaller stimulus, until the multiplier process comes to rest with a finite overall expansion.

The foreign income repercussions can easily be incorporated into the multiplier formula. To see how, one should recognize that the income-determination model now has a separate equilibrium condition for the rest of the world as well as for this country. In equations, the saving-investment equilibriums for this country and the rest of the world are:

$$S(Y) - I_d = X(Y_f) - M(Y) \qquad (19.7)$$

and

$$S_f(Y_f) - I_{d,f} = M(Y) - X(Y_f) \qquad (19.8)$$

where the f subscripts refer to the rest of the world, and imports and exports are consistently defined as seen from our country and $I_{d,f}$ refers to the foreign country's domestic capital formation. To derive the multiplier formula, it is necessary to let our spending rise by the amount A in Equation 19.7 and to differentiate the two equations with respect to national and rest-of-world incomes, solving for the effects on incomes. Using the intervening steps given in footnote 1 we arrive at the result:

The **spending multiplier** **with foreign income** **repercussions** $= \dfrac{\Delta Y}{A} = \dfrac{1 + (m_f/s_f)}{s + m + (m_f s/s_f)} \qquad (19.9)$

This formula reduces to the simpler multiplier formula of Equation (19.6) when the rest of the world does not raise its purchases of our exports in response to higher incomes (i.e., when $m_f = 0$). The effect of recognizing foreign repercussions is to raise the value of the spending multiplier, in

---

[1] The two equations expressing income changes as functions of the shift in expenditures A are:

$$s\Delta Y - A = m_f \Delta Y_f - m\Delta Y$$

and

$$s_f \Delta Y_f = m\Delta Y - m_f \Delta Y_f.$$

Solving these for $\Delta Y/A$ yields the formula in Equation (19.9).

The multiplier is slightly different in the case where demand for our product is raised by an *international shift in demand* from foreign goods and services to our own. In this case, the stimulus to our economy is partly offset by the fact that the shift in demand depresses demand for foreign goods and services, canceling some of the stimulus to our exports.

To derive the multiplier effect on our income in this case of demand shift (Z), let Z disturb the two economies by shifting up net exports in this country and shifting them down for the rest of the world:

Δ our
equilibrium: $s\Delta Y = m_f \Delta Y_f - m\Delta Y + Z$, and
Δ their
equilibrium: $s_f \Delta Y_f = m\,\Delta Y - m_f \Delta Y_f/Z.$

Solving these for the multiplier $\Delta Y/Z$ yields the formula of Equation (19.12):

$$\Delta Y/Z = 1/\,(s + m + (m_f s/s_f))$$

which is less than the multiplier $\Delta Y/A$ above because foreign income is initially reduced by the demand shift.

this formula as well as in common sense. To return to the example above, in which the nation had a marginal propensity to save of $s = 0.2$ and a marginal propensity to import of $m = 0.3$, adding the same values for the rest of the world ($s_f = 0.2$ and $m_f = 0.3$) would raise the value of the spending multiplier from its previous level of 2 to 3.125.

The existence of such foreign-income repercussions helps account for the parallelism in business cycles that has been observed among the major industrial economies. Throughout the 20th century, when America has sneezed, Europe and Japan have caught cold, and nowadays this is vice versa. Such a tendency was already evident in the business cycles in Europe and the United States in the mid-19th century, though the correlation between the European cycles and the U.S. cycles was far from perfect. The Great Depression of the 1930s also reverberated back and forth among countries, as each country's slump caused a cut in imports (helped by the beggar-thy-neighbor import barriers that were partly a response to the slump itself) and thereby cut foreign exports and incomes. Correspondingly, the outbreak of the Korean War brought economic boom to West Germany, Italy, and Japan, as surging U.S. war spending raised their exports and incomes, leading to a further partial increase in their purchases from the United States. The same interdependence of incomes persists today, so that any drop in U.S. imports, whether due to a U.S. slump or to new U.S. barriers against imports, would end up cutting U.S. exports somewhat through the foreign-income repercussions.

Economists have gone to some trouble to estimate the spending multipliers in major industrial countries that are subject to foreign income repercussions. They came up with the plausible patterns shown in Figure 19.4. The multipliers tell the tales one would expect of such international multipliers, even though they are expressed in elasticity form (*percent* change/*percent* change), instead of the usual multiplier form (absolute change/absolute change). To follow the numbers across the top row, Figure 19.4 says that U.S. national income would be raised 1.47 percent if aggregate demand rose by 1 percent in the United States alone, or by 0.05 percent if demand rose 1 percent in Germany alone, 0.04 percent if demand rose by 1 percent in Japan alone, and so forth. Or following the numbers down the Canada column, the estimates say that a 1 percent rise in Canadian spending would raise U.S. national income by 0.06 percent, German national income by 0.03 percent, and so forth.

Two basic patterns emerge from the estimates given in Figure 19.4. First, there is the role of *national size*. The bigger the country, the more its spending affects other countries. Thus, the effect of U.S. spending in any one other country, or on all the countries of the Organization for Economic Cooperation and Development (OECD), tends to be greater than the effect of any other foreign country's spending. For example, Germany is more affected by spending shifts in the United States (0.23 percent) than it is by those in Japan or Canada (0.05 or 0.03). Similarly, the income of the

FIGURE 19.4   Spending Multipliers with Foreign Income Repercussions:
Industrial Countries of the OECD in the 1970s

On National Income in	The Effects of a 1 Percent Rise of Spending in				
	United States	Germany	Japan	Canada	All OECD Countries
United States	<u>1.47</u>	0.05	0.04	0.06	1.81
Germany	0.23	<u>1.25</u>	0.05	0.03	2.38
Japan	0.25	0.60	<u>1.26</u>	0.03	1.84
Canada	0.68	0.60	0.06	<u>1.27</u>	2.32
All OECD	0.74	0.23	0.21	0.10	<u>2.04</u>

* Each figure gives the percent rise in the national income of the country whose row is named on the left that is caused by a 1 percent rise in the spending of the country whose column is named along the top of the table.

Source: Organization for Economic Cooperation and Development, "The OECD International Linkage Model," OECD Occasional Paper, Paris, January 1979.

whole set of OECD member nations is more affected by a 1 percent spending swing in the United States (0.74) than by spending shifts in any one other country. The other pattern relates to the *openness* of the economy, which is usually measured by the share of either exports or imports in its GNP. Knowing that other industrial countries tend to be more open to trade than the United States, where *m* is lower, we are not surprised that the foreign multipliers in most rows are highest in the U.S. spending column.

Another useful kind of multiplier also uses the idea of foreign-income repercussions. Often we are interested in the income repercussions from an *international-demand shift*. Buyers could shift their demand from the products of one country to the products of another, in response to tariffs or devaluation or just unexplained shifts in tastes. When that happens, both the domestic and the foreign markets are upset at once. If Z is the amount of demand shifted from foreign products to our products, then it shows up as a shift in both equilibrium equations:

$$S(Y) - I_d = X\,(Y_f) - M(Y) + Z \qquad (19.10)$$

and

$$S_f\,(Y_f) - I_{d,f} = M(Y) - X(Y_f) - Z \qquad (19.11)$$

Taking differences in Equations 19.10 and 19.11, as in footnote 1, yields a useful formula for:

$$\textbf{The international demand shift multiplier} = \frac{\Delta Y}{\Delta Z} = \frac{1}{s + m + (m_f s / s_f)} \qquad (19.12)$$

The quickest thing to grasp about the formula for the international demand-shift multiplier is the slight difference between it and the spending multiplier in Equation 19.9. The demand-shift multiplier has to be smaller, because it lacks the extra positive term (m_f/s_f) in the numerator. It makes sense that a shift in demand from one country to another should not expand incomes as much as a rise in demand at the expense of desired savings. The international demand shift lowers demand for product somewhere (in this case, the rest of the world), while a pure rise in spending does not.

HOW AGGREGATE DEMAND AND SUPPLY CAN AFFECT THE TRADE BALANCE

We have seen that a rise in domestic-aggregate demand can, by raising our national income, raise our imports. To the extent that this worsens the trade balance, it is a force that will contribute (in the chapters that follow) to either a bigger balance-of-payments deficit or to a drop in the exchange value of our home currency. But one cannot simply say that whatever raises our national income worsens our balance of trade. We must take a more careful look at three realistic cases:

1. *If our income is raised by increases in domestic spending,* then the trade balance will *probably*[2] *"worsen"* (i.e., shift toward net imports). This is just a corollary of the multiplier process sketched in connection with Figure 19.3. We make use of this in the next two chapters, when analyzing the performance of both the fixed exchange rates implied here and various floating-rate regimes.

2. *If our income is raised by an international demand shift* from foreign to home-country goods and services (e.g., due to a change in tastes, or a devaluation of the home currency, or a lowering of foreign import barriers), the home country's trade balance will *clearly improve.*

3. *If our income is raised by improvements in our aggregate supply* of goods and services, our trade balance will *probably improve.* The analysis of this case is not easily handled within the Keynesian framework that dominates this chapter, since that framework lets changes in income be dictated by aggregate demand. Yet the importance of aggregate supply is easy to see, even without going to the trouble of drawing demand and supply curves as functions of price. Suppose that our aggregate supply is

---

[2] A rise in domestic spending could actually improve the trade balance. Suppose that the foreign marginal propensity to import from us is larger than our marginal propensity to import from them. Each round of increase in imports by us could trigger not only immediate foreign purchases of our exports, but further export increases as well, in response to the foreign multiplier process. Under some possible parameter values, this could assure the perverse result: our spending increase would actually raise our trade balance.

raised by technological improvements (or bumper-crop harvests, or peaceful settlements of labor strikes) that are evenly distributed across the exportable, import-competing, and nontraded sectors. Our extra ability to supply and compete will win more export markets as well as home markets away from foreign suppliers. This will raise net exports, as long as the trade-balance stability conditions of Chapter 18 and Appendix I hold.[3]

HOW DEVALUATION CAN AFFECT NATIONAL INCOME

Another set of links relating to national income helps us interpret certain recurring news items and also helps us to build the analytical structure used in the next two chapters.

Does devaluing our currency raise or lower our national income? At first it might seem obvious that devaluation raises it. After all, devaluing tends to raise the real volume of exports and to reduce the real volume of imports, thus providing extra income and jobs to our exportable and import-competing sectors. This was the result predicted for international demand shifts in the preceding section.

Yet, the effect of devaluation on national income is not quite this clear-cut, for three reasons:

1. Devaluation might not even improve the trade balance itself. The stability conditions of Chapter 18 and Appendix I must hold. They usually do, but not always.

2. Devaluation might worsen the international terms of trade (P/P_m), making our country pay more in real exports for each unit of imports purchased. If the terms of trade worsen, then our nation's real purchasing power, a more relevant measure of well-being than just our ability to purchase what we ourselves produce,[4] could be reduced by a devaluation. Sensing this reduction in real purchasing power, households might cut back on spend-

---

[3] Yes, it is necessary to add this last qualifying clause. Improved domestic supply can do more to the trade balance than simply raise the physical volume of exports and cut the physical volume of imports. It can also change prices. In an extreme case of very inelastic demand for our exports, it is conceivable that their price would drop far enough to make the innovation worsen the trade balance. This seems unlikely, however.

[4] There is a difference between our real national income $(y = Y/P)$ and the more welfare-relevant measure, the real purchasing power of our national income (or y_p), because a trading country buys a different bundle of goods from the bundle it produces. The real purchasing power of national income is:

y_p = (Nominal value of national product)/(Prices of the home and foreign goods we buy)
    = Y (or P_y)/$(1 - a)P + aP_m$

where a is the share of our national expenditures spent on imports, $(1 - a)$ is the share spent on home purchases of exportable goods and services, P is the price index for the ing, adding to the problems caused by devaluation. Yet, notice the limit to this danger: *devaluation can lower national income only if it worsens the terms of trade.* A sufficient condition for a rise in national income is that the devaluation leaves the terms of trade the same or better. In the small-country case, the terms of trade (P/P_m) are likely to end up where they started.

So far, our macroeconomic reasoning might suggest that any devaluation is good for the devaluing country, except when it temporarily worsens the terms of trade. But another, more important, proviso must be added. We must worry about the long-run foreign exchange losses that the nation would suffer if its devaluation worsened, instead of cured, an imbalance in the overall balance of payments. As Chapters 17 and 18 have stressed, official maintenance of disequilibrium exchange rates means foreign exchange losses. The third complication is therefore the most serious:

3. Devaluation succeeds only as long as it moves the balance of payments toward equilibrium. As long as the devaluation is serving to remove a deficit, it is helping. It gets the country out of the capital losses that would be felt if the central bank or the treasury used up its gold and foreign-exchange reserves to hold up an artificial value of the nation's currency, only to realize when its reserves ran out that they were worth more of the national currency than it sold them for before they ran out.

If the nation overplays the devaluation idea, or takes official steps that overdepreciate the home currency in a free foreign-exchange market, it is asking for a new kind of trouble. The resulting balance-of-payments surpluses would force its central bank or treasury to pile up foreign exchange reserves that in the long run would not be worth as much as their present artificial price. The possibility of official losses from buying up too much foreign currency at a disequilibrium price means that devaluation's chances of improving national income are good only as long as the devaluation is correcting a payments deficit.

So, we have the following sufficient conditions for favorable effects of devaluation on national well-being:

> *A devaluation or depreciation improves the nation's well-being if (1) it does not worsen the trade balance, (2) it does not worsen the terms of trade, and (3) it cuts the net gain or loss in official reserves.*

---

whole bundle of goods and services our economy produces, and P_m is the price index for imports. The denominator is a price index using weights based on what we buy, not what we produce. Its use of expenditure-share weights (a and $1 - a$) makes it more analogous to a cost-of-living index than to a "GNP deflator."

Clearly, whatever lowers our terms of trade (P/P_m) could lower our real purchasing power (y_p), even without lowering our real national income (y). Because devaluation could conceivably have this effect, it could lower our real national well-being.

FIGURE 19.5   Devaluation and the Trade Balance with Changes in Income

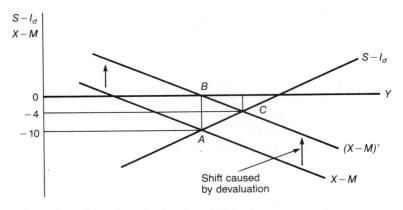

The trade balance still improves, but less than at first.

Notice that if devaluation succeeds in initially improving the trade balance and national income, it ends up improving the trade balance less than it did initially. Figure 19.5 illustrates this by showing the multiplier effect of a successful devaluation on national income. At first, the trade balance improves from *A* up to *B*, an improvement of 10 per year. But this shifting of aggregate demand toward our national product sets up a multiplier process through which national income expands until we reach the new equilibrium at Point *C*. The income expansion brings with it some extra imports, now that the nation can afford to buy more, leaving the trade-balance improvement smaller than the initial 10 per year.

SUMMARY

The fact that imports depend on income levels alters the income effects of shifts in aggregate demand. The higher a nation's marginal propensity to import (the share of extra income going into extra imports), the more any rise in aggregate demand spills over into a worsening trade balance. This leakage into imports, like the leakage into saving, cuts down the value of the multiplier and dampens the effect of extra spending on the final change in national income. It also means that any boom or slump in one nation's aggregate demand has repercussions on foreign incomes. If the rest of the world has a significant marginal propensity to import from this nation, then swings in the business cycle are likely to be internationally contagious and cumulative, a conjecture easily supported by the experience of the 1930s.

The roles played by the different marginal propensities to save and import can be reviewed by comparing this chapter's three kinds of multipliers with the conventional closed-economy spending multiplier:

Spending multiplier in a closed economy $= \Delta Y / \Delta G = 1/s$

The **spending multiplier in a small, open economy** $= \dfrac{\Delta Y}{\Delta G} = \dfrac{1}{(m + s)}$ (19.6)

The **spending multiplier with foreign income repercussions** $= \dfrac{\Delta Y}{A} = \dfrac{1 + (m_f/s_f)}{s + m + (m_f s/s_f)}$ (19.9)

The **international demand shift multiplier** $= \dfrac{\Delta Y}{\Delta Z} = \dfrac{1}{s + m + (m_f s/s_f)}$ (19.12)

Note that of the three open-economy multipliers introduced in this chapter, the one with the largest value will always be Equation 19.9's spending multiplier with foreign income repercussions. The one with the smallest value will be the international demand-shift multiplier in Equation 19.12.

The forces that change national income might or might not "worsen" our balance of trade (i.e., shift it toward deficit). The result depends on which of three kinds of forces are at work: (1) a rise in domestic spending will probably worsen the balance of trade; (2) an international shift in demand toward our product (e.g., due to shifts in tastes, our devaluing, or changes in trade policy) will definitely improve our trade balance; and (3) a rise in our aggregate supply, that is, in our ability to cut costs and to compete, will probably improve our balance of trade.

Devaluation can raise or lower national income, depending on three key conditions. The first is whether devaluation improves the trade balance. It is likely to do so. Second, it can raise national income as long as it does not worsen the terms of trade. Third, and most important, it must not move the overall balance of payments further away from equilibrium. If it does, it will bring exchange losses of the sort described in Chapter 18.

SUGGESTED READINGS

Algebraic treatments of foreign-trade repercussions are given in Vanek (1962, Chapters 6–9) and Robert M. Stern (1973, Chapter 7). Empirical estimates of dynamic income-and-trade repercussions, using complex "linkage models," are summarized in Heliwell and Padmore (1984).

QUESTIONS FOR REVIEW

1. By how much will an extra $1 billion of government spending raise national income in a Keynesian underemployed economy having a marginal propensity to import of 0.2 and a marginal propensity to save of 0.1? Ignore foreign repercussions.

2. Extend the analysis of Question 1 by calculating the net effect of the extra $1 billion in government spending on this country's imports.

3. If the home and foreign marginal propensities to import and to save are $m = 0.3$, $m_f = 0.2$, $s = 0.2$, and $s_f = 0.1$, by how much would a $1 billion drop in our government spending cut our national income?

4. Using the same parameter values as in Question 3, calculate how much our national income would drop if $1 billion of world demand were shifted from our products to foreign products. (Bonus question: by how much would the same shift raise *foreign* national income?)

5. What are the key conditions ensuring that devaluation of the national currency will improve the nation's real purchasing power?

Answers:

1. By $1/(m + s) = 1/(0.1 + 0.2) = 3.33 billion.

2. Imports will rise by the final change in y times m, or 3.33 (0.2) = $0.67 billion.

3. Using the formula in Equation 19.9 yields a rise in y of $3.33 billion.

4. Using the formula in Equation 19.12 yields a drop of $1.11 billion in U.S. national income (and a rise of foreign income of $2.22 billion, derived by switching the roles of the home and foreign countries).

▼

Internal and External Balance with Fixed Exchange Rates

•

If a nation wants to keep its exchange rate fixed, it will have to juggle two policy problems at once. One is the problem of **external balance:** keeping the balance of payments in line so that the exchange rate can stay fixed. The other is the problem of **internal balance:** controlling aggregate demand so as to approximate full employment without inflation.[1] This chapter sketches a modified-Keynesian view of an economy open to international trade and finance in order to frame the macropolicy choices facing a nation on fixed exchange rates.

The juggling act is a challenge. Internal balance and external balance are often hard to reconcile. A government that pursues external balance alone, tidying up its balance of payments while letting inflation or unemployment get out of hand at home, may be thrown out of office. On the other hand, controlling aggregate demand alone, with fiscal or monetary policies, may widen a deficit or surplus in the balance of payments, jeopardizing any promise to keep the exchange rate fixed.

A more subtle mixture of policies is needed. One way of managing both internal and external balance with fixed exchange rates is to assign to monetary policy the task of reacting to the state of the balance of payments, while assigning fiscal policy to the domestic task of controlling aggregate demand.

---

[1] Controlling aggregate supply would also help, of course. If there are effective steps that raise national productivity, cut prices, raise output, and increase the number of jobs at the same time, they should be taken. Many people have argued that government can improve supply with tax and spending cuts, or subsidies to research, or policies to match jobs and workers more smoothly. Yet, all supply-side policies remain controversial and, most important, slow-acting. Their benefits show up only after many years of gradual response to any new incentives. For the shorter run, the problem of internal stabilization is still primarily a problem of controlling aggregate demand through fiscal and monetary policy.

FIGURE 20.1   An Overview of the Macromodel of an Open Economy with Fixed Exchange Rates

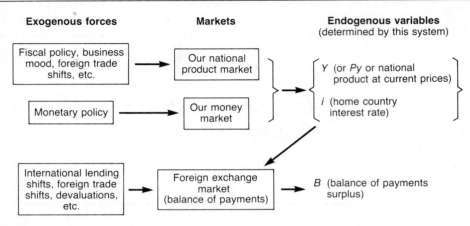

Note that *B*, the balance-of-payments surplus, does not affect the other variables. In the jargon of this and the next chapter, the diagram assumes that *B* is "sterilized." If it is not, and it can affect the money supply, draw an arrow from *B* to the money market.

Under some extreme conditions of international capital mobility (and fixed exchange rates), monetary policy becomes so chained to the balance of payments that it loses all control over the money market. These are some of the policy results developed here.

THREE MARKETS

Keeping aggregate demand and the balance of payments in line together requires finding the right mixture of policies that affect three markets simultaneously. Figure 20.1 sketches the basic problem. On the left side are the basic causes of short-run macroeconomic change, grouped by the markets on which they have their main influences. Here we concentrate on monetary policy and fiscal policy, our two main ways of controlling the domestic economy. When the full chain of influence is traced through, either policy simultaneously affects income *(Y)* and the balance of payments *(B)* and, to a less extent, interest rates *(i)*. There is no obvious way to make either monetary policy or fiscal policy affect only *Y* or only *B*. To pursue this point, let us look at each of the three key markets in turn, using both words and diagrams.

The National Product Market

How successful the economy is at avoiding inflation and unemployment depends on aggregate demand and supply. As in Chapter 19, we assume a passive supply curve and focus on what determines aggregate demand. The aggregate demand for the goods and services our country produces depends above all on our nominal income (Y),[2] as it did in Chapter 19. Demand also depends, though, on the interest rate (i). The higher the interest rate,[3] the less attractive it is to spend with money that either is borrowed at that interest rate or could have been lent out at that interest rate. Demand also depends on the exchange rate (r), because the higher that price of foreign currency, the cheaper and more competitive our goods and services look, raising our current-account balance, also known as our net foreign investment (or I_f). Finally, demand depends directly on fiscal policy or any other shifter of aggregate demand listed in the upper left-hand box of Figure 20.1. The national product market is in equilibrium when aggregate demand, which now depends on interest rates (i), income (Y), and such shifts as those of fiscal policy, is equal to the level of national product (Y again).

It is useful to reexpress the equilibrium between aggregate demand and supply as an equilibrium between desired saving and desired investment, just as in Chapter 19. In a summary equation, the national product market is in equilibrium when:

$$\overset{+,-}{I_d(Y,\ i)} + \overset{-,+}{I_f(Y,\ r)} = \overset{+,+}{S(Y,\ i)} \tag{20.1}$$

Here the signs above the equation state the most likely direction of each influence in parentheses on the value of domestic investment (I_d), the current account balance (I_f), or national saving (S).

To arm ourselves for an attack on the basic policy dilemma of internal and external balance, let us also use another diagram of equilibrium in the national product market. Figure 20.2 draws the "IS curve" from "ISLM analysis" in intermediate macroeconomic theory courses, representing the investment-savings equilibrium of Equation (20.1). The **IS curve** shows

---

[2] This is, again, a Keynesian simplification. More accurately, aggregate real spending demand depends positively on real income (y) and negatively on prices (P). Saying that it depends on nominal income $(Y = Py)$ requires some extra assumption, such as an assumption that prices are fixed. We also ignore foreign income repercussions here, although they would not change any of the conclusions that follow.

[3] More simplification here: let us talk as though any changes in the nominal interest rate were also changes in the real interest rate, even though any change in the expected rate of inflation would complicate things. We also set aside foreign interest rates until later in this chapter.

FIGURE 20.2   The IS Curve: Equilibria in the National Product Market

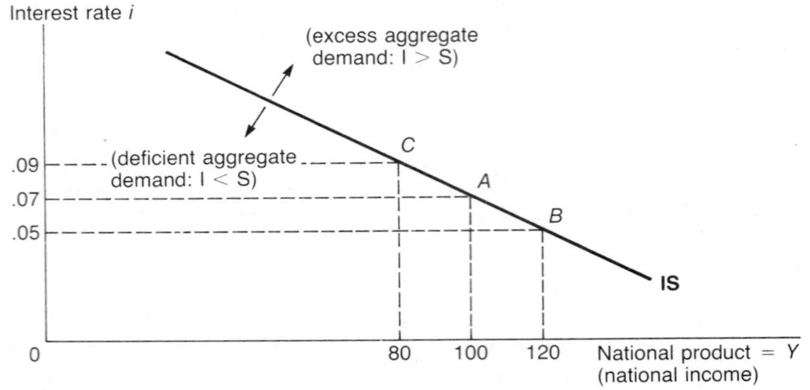

all combinations of income levels and interest rates for which the national product market is in equilibrium. So, every point on the curve is an equilibrium, unlike most points of a demand curve or a supply curve.

To see why the IS curve slopes downward, let us start with one equilibrium point on it and then ask where other equilibria could lie. Let us start at point *A*, where national income equals 100 and the interest rate is 0.07 (seven percent a year). We are given that this combination brings equilibrium in the national product market. That is, given the exchange rate *(r)* and other conditions, having $Y = 100$ and $i = 0.07$ makes investment $I_d + I_f$ match savings *S*. How could equilibrium in the product market be maintained if the interest rate were lower, say only 0.05? The lower interest rate would make the nation build more real capital or consume more (save less). That higher level of aggregate demand can be sustained only at a higher level of national product. According to the IS curve, the higher level of national product matching aggregate demand for that low interest rate is $Y = 120$, as represented at Point *B*. Similarly, if Point *A* is one equilibrium, then others with higher interest rates must lie at lower income levels, as at Point *C*. So, the IS curve must slope downward: the higher the interest rate, the lower the level of national product that is consistent with it. Points that are not on the IS curve find the national product market out of equilibrium.

The Money Market

The next market in which macroeconomic forces interact is that for the money of each nation. As usual, there is a balancing of supply and demand.

The supply side of the market for owning units of a nation's money is, roughly, the conventional "money supply," or the set of central-bank policies, institutions, and bank behavioral patterns governing the availability of bank checking deposits and currency in circulation. Monetary policy, featured on the left-hand side in Figure 20.1, is the top influence on money supply.

The demand for holding money depends positively on the level of economic activity or roughly on the level of gross national product *(Y)*. The more national product there is each year, the greater the amount of money balances that firms and households will want to keep on hand to cover uncertain amounts of spending needs. This is the same "transactions demand" for money we looked at in Chapter 16. The demand for holding money depends *negatively* on the general level of interest rates *(i)*. A negative correlation exists because the interest rate is a reward for holding your wealth in an interest-earning form instead of holding it in money, which pays little or no interest to its holder. A higher interest rate tempts people to hold interest-earning bonds rather than money. That is, it lowers the demand for holding money. So, the equilibrium between money supply and money demand can be summarized in the equation:

$$\overset{+\quad-}{\text{Money Supply} = M = L(Y,\ i)} = \text{Money Demand} \qquad (20.2)$$

Here again, the plus and minus signs serve to remind us of the direction of influence of Y and i.

The money-market equilibrium can be reexpressed with the "LM curve" of Figure 20.3. The **LM curve** shows all combinations of income levels and interest rates for which the money market is in equilibrium.

To see why the LM curve slopes upward, begin with the equilibrium at Point *A* and think of where the other equilibria could lie. If the interest rate were higher, say at 0.09, people would hold less money in order to earn the higher interest rate by holding bonds instead. To have the money market in equilibrium at that higher interest rate, people would have to have some other reason to hold the same amount of money as at Point *A*. They would be willing to hold the extra money only if the level of national income were higher, raising their transactions demand for holding money. That happens to just the right extent at Point *B*, another equilibrium. In contrast, going in the other direction, we can ask how people would be content to hold the same money supply as at Point *A* if the interest they gave up by holding money were suddenly lower than at Point *A*. By itself, the lower interest rate on bonds would mean a greater demand for cash because cash is convenient. People would be willing to refrain from holding extra cash only if some other change reduced the demand. One such change is lower national product, meaning lower transactions demand for cash. Point *C* is a point at which the lower interest rate and lower income leave the demand for money the same as at Point *A*. The LM curve is, again, the set of all such points where the demand for money *(L)* equals the supply of money *(M)*.

FIGURE 20.3   The LM Curve: Equilibria in the Money Market

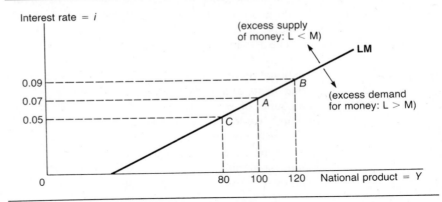

So far, we have two markets whose equilibria depend on how national product *(Y)* and interest rates *(i)* respond to shifts in the exogenous forces listed on the left-hand side of Figure 20.1. For any given state of fiscal policy, business mood, foreign-trade demand, and monetary policy, these two markets simultaneously determine the level of national product and the interest rate. (Appendix J spells out this process in equations that lead to explicit algebraic statements of the points of this and the next chapter.)

The Foreign-Exchange Market (or Balance of Payments)

The third market is the one where the availability of foreign currency is balanced against the demand for it. This market can be called either the "foreign exchange market," if we want to keep the exchange rate in mind, or "the balance of payments," if we are talking only of a fixed-exchange-rate world in which the overall balance of payments surplus *(B)* reflects the net private trading between our currency and foreign currency. We take the latter view in this chapter. We will think of the overall payments surplus, *B*, as a net inflow of money from abroad and a deficit *(B < 0)* as an outflow of money.

What affects *B*, the balance-of-payments surplus, when exchange rates are fixed? The influences on *B* can be divided into trade-flow effects and financial-flow effects. The trade balance, or the current account balance, depends negatively on our national product and positively on the exchange rate (still in $/£).[4] It can also be shifted by exogenous (independent) shifts

---

[4] Reminder: the trade balance responds positively to a higher exchange rate (i.e., to devaluation of our currency) *if* the trade-balance stability condition of Chapter 18 and Appendix I is met. That seems likely.

in world trade demand, such as a shift toward buying domestic, instead of foreign, cars.

The financial side of the balance of payments depends mainly on interest rates (both at home and abroad), as shown by the arrow from *i* to the foreign exchange market in Figure 20.1 above. A higher interest rate in our country will attract capital from abroad, provided the higher interest rate is viewed as a higher *real* interest rate, and not just as a nominal interest rate raised by the specter of faster inflation.

The easy intuition that a higher interest rate in our economy will attract lending from abroad and give us a balance-of-payments surplus (a money inflow) is valid but only in the short run (say, for a year or less after the interest rate rises). Over the longer run, this effect stops and is even reversed for at least two reasons:

1. A higher interest rate attracts a lot of lending inflow from abroad at first, as investors adjust the shares of their stock of wealth held in loans in our country. Soon, though, the inflow will dwindle because wealth stocks have already been adjusted.
2. If a higher interest rate in our country succeeds in attracting funds from abroad and raising *B* in the short run, it must have the opposite effect later on, for the simple reason that all loans must be repaid. If a higher interest rate gives us borrowed money now, we must repay with interest later. We cannot talk of using higher interest rates to attract capital (lending) to this country without reflecting on the fact that those higher interest rates would have to be paid back out, along with the borrowed principal.[5]

---

[5] The balance-of-payments cost of attracting the extra capital from abroad could be even greater than the interest rate alone might suggest. To see how, let us suppose that the home country (a) is a net debtor country and (b) is large enough to be able to raise its own interest rate even though it is part of a larger world lending market. Let us imagine Canada is in this position.

Suppose that a rise in Canada's interest rate from 9 percent to 12 percent succeeds in raising foreign loans to Canada from $500 billion to $600 billion. What interest will Canada pay out each year on the extra $100 billion of money (a temporarily higher *B*)? The annual interest bill on the new $100 billion itself comes to $12 billion a year. But, in addition, to continue to hold the original loans of $500 billion within the country—i.e., to "roll over" these loans as they come up for renewal or repayment—Canadian borrowers would have to pay an extra $15 billion [= $500 billion × (.12 − .09)]. The total extra interest outflow each year is thus the $12 billion plus the extra $15 billion, or payments of $27 billion just to hold onto an extra $100 billion in borrowed money. That's an effective interest rate of 27 percent, not just 12 percent. This is an expensive way to attract international "hot money."

Of course, if the home country were a large net *creditor* country, both before and after the worldwide hike in interest rates, it would actually gain net interest income from the interest hike, making the marginal cost of attracting loans from abroad lower than the interest itself. Japan is in this situation. But for a debtor country like Canada or the United States, the cost of attracting loans with higher interest rates is at least as high as the interest rate itself.

For these reasons, the notion that a higher interest rate in our country can "improve" the balance of payments is valid only in the short run. We can use the short-run reasoning if the policy problem before us is how to raise *B* right now in some immediate crisis. The rest of this chapter and the next will follow this usual short-run focus, but only with the warning that in the longer run a higher interest rate has an ambiguous effect on the overall balance of payments.

We can reexpress the dependence of the foreign-exchange market on income, interest rates, and the exchange rate in two other ways. One is with an equation. When the exchange rate is fixed, the overall balance-of-payments surplus *(B)* equals the current account balance *(I_f)* plus the net inflows of private capital *(F)*:

$$\overset{-}{B = I_f(Y)} + \overset{+}{F(i)} \text{ with a fixed exchange rate} \tag{20.3}$$

or

$$\overset{-,+}{B = I_f(Y, r)} + \overset{-}{F(i)} = 0 \text{ with a flexible exchange rate}$$

Raising our national product lowers the current-account surplus (or raises the deficit) because it gives us more demand for imports of foreign goods and services. Raising our interest rate, on the other hand, attracts an inflow of capital from abroad, raising our overall balance-of-payments surplus if the exchange rate is fixed. If the exchange rate is flexible, the foreign-exchange market finds an equilibrium with no surplus or deficit (i.e., with *B* = 0). It does so by moving toward the equilibrium exchange rate as described in Chapters 15 and 16. The higher the price of foreign currency *(r)*, the better our current-account balance (if the trade balance responds in the stable way discussed in Chapter 18).

To link the balance of payments with *i* and *Y* under fixed exchange rates, we can also use the FE curve of Figure 20.4. The **FE curve** shows the set of all interest-and-income combinations in our country that allow equilibrium in our foreign-exchange market.

The FE curve, like the LM curve, slopes upward. To see why, begin again with an equilibrium at Point *A*. Let us say it is the same Point *A* as in the last two diagrams, though that need not be true with a fixed exchange rate. If Point *A* finds our international payments in overall balance, how could they still be in balance if the interest rate were higher, say at 11 percent? That higher interest rate would attract a greater inflow of capital, bringing a balance-of-payment surplus unless something else was also changed. With the higher interest rate, *B* could still be zero (no surplus, no deficit) if income were higher. A higher income would induce us to spend more on everything, including imports. The extra imports would shift the balance of payments toward a deficit. In just the right amounts, extra income and a higher interest rate could cancel each other's effect on

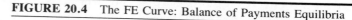

FIGURE 20.4   The FE Curve: Balance of Payments Equilibria

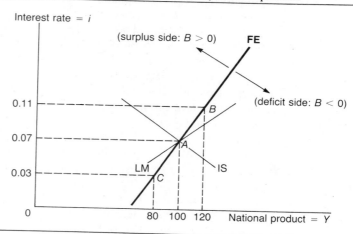

the balance of payments, leaving $B = 0$. That happens at Point B. Correspondingly, some combinations of lower interest rates and lower incomes could also keep our payments in balance, as at Point C.

Bringing the three markets together, we get a determination of the level of national product (Y), the interest rate (i), and the overall balance of payments (B). The economy will gravitate toward a simultaneous equilibrium in the national product market (on the IS curve) and the money market (the LM). With Y and i thus determined, we also know the state of the balance of payments (B). This section has given the same reason about three markets in three alternative forms: the causal-arrow sketch of Figure 20.1, the listing of Equations 20.1–20.3, and the use of IS-LM-FE diagrams (Figures 20.2–20.4). We can now use the three-market model to understand what happens when conditions shift.

FROM MONETARY AND FISCAL POLICY TO THE BALANCE OF PAYMENTS

Our three-market view of the open economy allows us to trace the effects of our country's monetary and fiscal policies on its balance of payments, effects that reveal a challenging policy problem.

The effects of *monetary policy* on the balance of payments are clear-cut: expanding the money supply worsens the balance of payments, especially at first. If the central bank offers private domestic banks extra lendable reserves (e.g., by buying extra government bonds in the open market), the banks will typically respond by making more loans to earn more. In the process, their competition to lend more is likely to bid down interest rates. As sketched at the top of Figure 20.5, the lowering of interest rates has two effects on the balance of payments. The newly borrowed funds are used to engage in extra spending—on new houses, new plants and equipment, and new consumer durable goods. The extra spending leads to a multiplied expansion of spending and national income, probably accompanied by rising prices. The rise in incomes and prices, in turn, raises imports and worsens the trade balance. Meanwhile, the decline in interest rates causes some holders of financial assets to seek out higher interest rates abroad. Their switch from lending here to lending abroad takes the form of selling bank deposits in this country in order to acquire interest-earning assets in other countries and probably in other currencies. Later, of course, the lending abroad will be repaid with interest, bringing a positive feedback to the balance of payments. But the negative effect on the trade balance will continue. Thus, an expansion of the money supply unambiguously worsens the overall payments balance in the short run. Conversely, a contraction of the national money supply unambiguously improves the overall balance.

The logic of this clear monetary result is underlined by the IS-LM-FE diagram in the lower half of Figure 20.5. Starting from Point A's equilibrium in both the national product market (on the IS curve) and the money market (on the LM curve), expanding the money supply creates an excess supply of money available for lending. There is downward pressure on the interest rate, making people more willing to hold the extra money instead of interest-earning bonds. The spending financed by the new loans sets off a multiplied expansion of national product. The greater national product evokes more transactions demand for holding money. Thus, the extra money supply induces a demand to hold it, by lowering interest rates and by raising national product. The rising demand for money finally overtakes the extra supply at Point D in Figure 20.5, where both the national product market and the money market are back in equilibrium. The balance of payments, meanwhile, has clearly fallen into the deficit range below and to the right of the FE curve.

Fiscal policy affects the balance of payments both through an income effect and through an interest-rate effect. Let us follow the case of an expansionary fiscal policy, say a rise in government purchases of goods and services. The extra government purchases are likely to expand spending throughout our economy, raising our national product *(Y)*. The extra desire to spend will spill over into extra import demand, "worsening" our trade balance and our overall balance-of-payments surplus *(B)*. So far, it seems clear that expansionary fiscal policy lowers *B*.

But the short-run interest-rate effect works in the opposite direction. The extra government purchases mean bigger government budget deficits (or, we could say, reduced budget surpluses, although government budget surpluses are so rare that they belong on the endangered species list). The government will be borrowing more money and driving up interest rates. The extra borrowing and higher interest rates should attract some lending from abroad, raising *B* while these inflows last. So, it is possible that an

FIGURE 20.5   Expanding the Money Supply Worsens the Balance of Payments

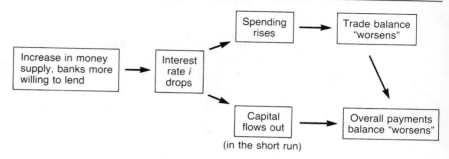

For the case of a monetary contraction, reverse all changes. In terminology introduced later in this chapter, *B* is assumed to be "sterilized," so that it does not have a feedback effect on our money supply.

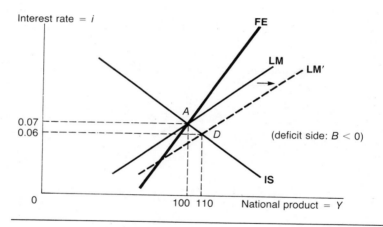

expansionary fiscal policy will actually improve the balance of payments. In the longer run, though, the lending attracted with higher interest rates must be repaid with interest, canceling the international reserves gained from the initial inflow of borrowed money.

Our conclusions about the effect of fiscal policy on the balance of payments are summarized at the top of Figure 20.6. Expansionary fiscal policy affects the balance of payments through two channels—an income effect and an interest-rate effect. The net result is probably a worsening of the balance, though there would be a short-run improvement if enough lending were attracted by our higher interest rates.

The lower part of Figure 20.6 shows the more likely of the two possible changes in the balance of payments from easier fiscal policy. Fiscal expansion shifts the IS curve to the right, meaning that either income or the interest

FIGURE 20.6   How Expansionary Fiscal Policy Affects Our Balance of Payments with Fixed Exchange Rates

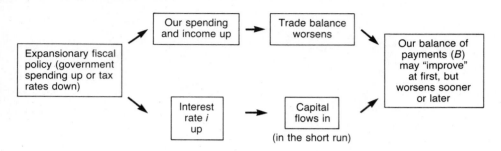

For the case of fiscal contraction, reverse all changes. Again, *B* is assumed to be sterilized, so that it does not have a feedback effect on our money supply.

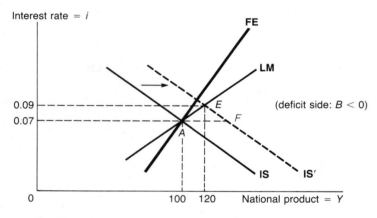

(In the case shown here, expansionary fiscal policy worsens the balance of payments.)

rate (or both) must rise. If something kept interest rates the same, income would go up a lot, by the amount AF.[6] More likely, the extra pressure to have cash to support a higher national product would bid up the interest

---

[6] The shift *AF* is not just the extra government spending, but the maximum rise in national income implied by the Keynesian multiplier formula for an open economy. In the small-country case discussed in Chapter 19, the rightward shift would equal $\Delta G/(s + m)$, where ΔG is the initial change in government spending, *s* is the nation's marginal propensity to save, and *m* is the nation's marginal propensity to import. It makes sense that the rightward shift should represent this extreme Keynesian expansion because the extreme Keynesian multiplier analysis was based on the assumption that interest rates did not change, as in the movement from *A* to *F*.

rate. A rise in the interest rate drives the demand for money down to equ the available money stock as the economy returns to a new equilibrium Point *E*. During the journey from the old equilibrium at Point *A* to t new one at Point *E*, two opposite things happened to the balance of paymen The higher income pushed us toward the deficit side, but the higher intere rates pushed us toward the surplus side. As the lower part of Figure 20 is drawn, the move to deficit prevails. This is because the FE curve drawn steeper than the LM curve. If the FE curve had been flatter, wi the balance of payments relatively more responsive to interest rates as oppos to income, fiscal expansion would have moved us to the surplus side.

THE BASIC DEMAND-POLICY DILEMMA

The effects of monetary and fiscal policy on the balance of payments a thus quite similar. With either policy, expanding the economy will resu in a negative income effect on the balance of payments in the short rur The two policies differ mainly in their effects on interest rates, which a bid up by expansionary fiscal policy but bid down by expansionary monetar policy. As just noted, this difference imparts only a temporary differenc in balance-of-payments effects: if one attracts foreign funds and the othe repels them, sooner or later these international lending flows will be repai with interest. The more durable effect of either policy on the balance o payments is the income-related effect they have in common.

If we temporarily set aside the interest rate effects of monetary and fisca policies and focus just on their power over spending and income, we discove a basic dilemma of macroeconomic policy: *it is often impossible to improv both the level of domestic demand and the balance of payments using jus aggregate-demand policies.* The reason for the dilemma is that we hav two goals (internal and external balance) and essentially only one tool aggregate-demand policy (in its fiscal and monetary variants).

Under fixed exchange rates, the dilemma of having to choose whicl goal to pursue plagues some but not all countries. Figure 20.7 catalogs the four possible departures from the blissful state of having both internal anc external balance. The dilemma has historically been felt most acutely by countries in the lower left-hand cell, where aggregate demand is too low and the balance of payments is in deficit. This was the tragedy facing Britain after it tried to rejoin the gold standard in 1925 and was forced back off it in 1931. This was also the problem facing the Kennedy and Johnson administrations between 1961 and 1965. In both cases, it was evident that curing unemployment called for raising aggregate demand (with expansionary fiscal or monetary policies). Yet, this meant worsening the balances of trade and payments. The dilemma remained unresolved: interwar Britain was driven off the gold standard and into depression, and the United States was cured of its unemployment of the early 1960s only after the

FIGURE 20.7 Aggregate Demand Policies for Internal and External Balance

	State of domestic economy	
State of balance of payments	High unemployment	Rapid inflation
Surplus (B > 0)	Expand aggregate demand	??
Deficit (B < 0)	??	Cut aggregate demand

In some situations policies to change aggregate demand can serve both internal and external goals, but in some cases (marked "??" here) they cannot. To deal with high unemployment and a payments surplus, policymakers should clearly expand aggregate demand (upper-left case). To deal with inflation at full employment and a payments deficit, they should clearly cut aggregate demand (lower-right case). But with the other two combinations of imbalances, there is no clear prescription for aggregate-demand policy.

introduction of inflation caused by U.S. participation in the Vietnam War.

The opposite dilemma faces governments worried about excessive inflation while running payments surpluses, as shown by the upper right-hand cell in Figure 20.7. This is the sort of position frequently faced by West Germany, Switzerland, and Japan, which were fully employed surplus countries during the postwar years of fixed exchange rates. Again, the conflict is inescapable: the threat of inflation calls for restraint on aggregate demand, while the surpluses will be exacerbated by the same demand restraint.

A country's policy makers could get lucky, of course. They might face the more solvable problems represented by the upper-left and lower-right cells in Figure 20.7. Faced with certain mixtures of initial payment surplus and unemployment, for example, policy makers could win applause by expanding aggregate demand. Faced with certain mixtures of initial payments deficits and rapid inflation, they could do the right thing by cutting back on aggregate demand. But even in the upper-left and lower-right cells, solutions may prove elusive. A country with deficits and inflation (lower-right cell), for example, might start out contracting aggregate demand to serve two goals at once, only to find that one goal gets met before the other, exposing the country to a new dilemma. Inflation might give way to moderate unemployment before the payments deficits are eliminated, posing again the dilemma of the lower-left cell. Only in lucky special cases would both the inflation and the deficits be solved by one and the same dosage of demand restriction.

To get out of the basic aggregate-demand dilemma, a country must either give up on one of the two goals or add more policy tools. Specifically, a country can choose to:

a. Abandon the goal of fixing the exchange rate, letting foreign exchange markets find the equilibrium rate (we explore this possibility again in the next chapter).
b. Abandon the goal of controlling domestic demand (and output jobs, and prices), letting the domestic money supply be whatever the balance of payments requires.
c. Come up with more policy tools.

Giving up is unpopular, and the natural tendency is to search for more tools.

The most logical candidate for curing an aggregate-demand dilemma is manipulation of aggregate supply. Why not come up with policies that create more national income and jobs by improving our productivity and aggregate supply? Such policies would also improve our ability to compete in international trade and give us balance-of-payments surpluses. It sounds too good to be true. And it is. Policy makers have no free-lunch way of improving aggregate supply. That comes only through sources of growth that respond sluggishly, if at all, to government manipulation, such as the advance of human skills and technology.

A SHORT-RUN SOLUTION: MONETARY-FISCAL MIX

There is, however, a way to buy time and serve both the internal and external goals for a while using conventional demand-side policies while staying on fixed exchange rates. Looking more closely at the basic demand-policy dilemma, Robert Mundell and J. Marcus Fleming noticed that monetary and fiscal policy, those two main arms of demand management, have different relative impacts on internal and external balance. The difference means that we do have two policy weapons after all.

The key difference between the impacts of fiscal and monetary policies is that easier monetary policy tends to lower interest rates and easier fiscal policy tends to raise them, as noted in connection with Figures 20.5 and 20.6. To see how this makes any combination of Y and B possible in principle, imagine a simultaneous shift to tighter monetary and easier fiscal policy, in amounts that just kept aggregate demand unchanged. This combination would raise interest rates greatly, and lending would be restricted by the cut in money supply and the government's additional borrowing. This illustrates a larger point: for any given change in aggregate demand (here, no change at all), any level of interest rates can be achieved with some monetary-fiscal mix. And since interest rates affect the balance of payments,

FIGURE 20.8   How Monetary and Fiscal Policy Could Combine to Cure Both Unemployment and a Balance-of-Payments Deficit

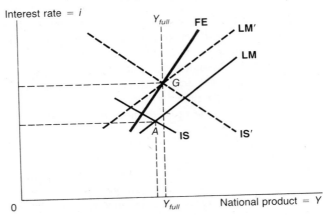

At the starting Point *A*, national income is below the full employment level Y_{full} and the balance of payments is in deficit. To reach full employment and payments balance at Point *G*, combine the right amounts of tight monetary policy and easy fiscal policy.

any payments surplus or deficit can be eliminated with any given change in aggregate demand.[7]

More generally, *monetary and fiscal can be mixed so as to achieve any combination of aggregate demand and overall payments balance.* Figure 20.8 illustrates the opportunities for solving one of the four policy challenges posed in Figure 20.7, namely, the case of excessive unemployment and payments deficits, starting at Point *A*. Shifting only one policy would not work, as we have seen, but shifting both can work. In this case, it is best to shift to tighter, (more contractionary) monetary policy to attract foreign capital with higher interest rates, and to easier (more expansionary) fiscal policy in pursuit of full employment. In the right amounts, the monetary tightening and fiscal easing can bring us exactly to full employment and payments balance. In Figure 20.8, this is achieved by shifting IS to IS' and LM to LM'.

This sort of escape from Point *A's* unemployment and deficits is precisely the policy prescription offered by Mundell, Fleming, and others. It is a politically convenient prescription since it tells the elected government and the central bankers to follow their instincts: elected officials, with upcoming

---

[7] This we assume to be the general case. It is possible, though, that expansionary policy, by raising interest rates, could attract so much capital from abroad in the short run that it would improve the balance of payments even though it would raise aggregate demand and imports.

elections in mind, often seek a justification for expanding the economy, whereas the central bank (e.g., the U.S. Federal Reserve) is typically more concerned with the balance of payments and maintaining stable prices, as befits policy makers recruited largely from the banking (creditor) community.[8]

A similar recipe can be used to get from any starting point to full employment and payments balance. Figure 20.9 catalogs the kinds of fiscal-monetary mixtures that do the trick. The principle is clear: as long as there are as many different policies as target variables, as in the present case of two policies and two targets, there is a solution. (Appendix J derives the policy solution that applies to all cases.)

THE ASSIGNMENT RULE

The pattern of policy prescriptions reveals a useful guideline for assigning policy tasks to fiscal and monetary policy. This is Robert Mundell's **assignment rule:** assign to fiscal policy the task of stabilizing the domestic economy only, and assign to monetary policy the task of stabilizing the balance of payments only. We can see from Figure 20.9 that such marching orders would guide the two arms of policy toward full employment and payments balance. Studying the different cases in Figure 20.9, you will find that the assignment rule generally steers each policy in the right direction. There are exceptions, as Figure 20.9 notes, but even in these cases it is likely that following the assignment rule does nothing worse than make the economy follow a less direct route to the goal of internal and external balance.

The assignment rule is handy. It allows each arm of policy to concentrate on a single task, relieving the need for perfect coordination between fiscal and monetary officials. It also directs each arm to work on the target it tends to care about more, since the balance of payments (and exchange-rate stability) have traditionally been of more concern to central bankers than to elected officials.

The rule might or might not work in practice. We have already mentioned problems with the interest-rate twist that is supposed to guarantee the existence of a solution. Furthermore, if either branch of policy lags in getting signals from the economy and responding to them, the result could be unstable oscillations that are even worse than having no policy at all.

---

[8] The prospect of mixing tight money with fiscal ease starting from Point *A* raised the specter of an exaggerated rise in interest rates, as increased government borrowing and the tightening of the money supply combined to squeeze out private borrowers. It is reasonable to fear that such a jump in interest rates would hold back productive private investment. Something of the sort happened in the early 1980s, when the combination of the Federal Reserve's restraint on money growth and the Reagan administration's tax cuts and deficits seems to have held back capital formation.

FIGURE 20.9 Monetary-Fiscal Recipes for Internal and External Balance

| | | Initial state of the domestic economy | |
		High unemployment	Rapid inflation
Initial state of the balance of payments	Surplus	Easier monetary policy, easier fiscal	Easier monetary, tighter fiscal
	Deficit	Tighter monetary, easier fiscal	Tighter monetary, tighter fiscal

These recipes conform to the **assignment rule**: assign monetary the task of balancing the country's international payments, and assign fiscal policy the task of bringing the domestic economy to full employment without excessive inflation. There are exceptional cases, however, when the assignment rule fails to follow the most direct route to the goal. In the diagram below, the assignment rule is wrong for monetary policy at points like *B* and *F,* and it is wrong for fiscal policy at points like *D* and *I.*

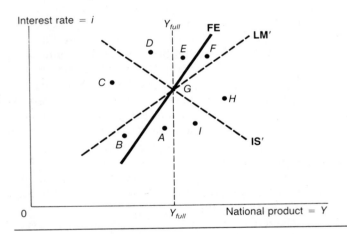

FROM THE BALANCE OF PAYMENTS BACK TO THE MONEY SUPPLY

So far, our look at the task of reconciling internal and external balance has assumed that policy makers have complete control over their own policy instruments (i.e., the money supply and the government budget). The assumption is valid either for the short run or for a large country whose policy makers can affect the whole world economy and not just their own national economy. But there are limits to the independence of a nation's monetary policy under fixed exchange rates. The rest of this chapter will attempt to explain and explore how difficult it can be to follow a national monetary policy when the nation is tied to a world money system by fixed exchange rates. We will find that:

> under fixed exchange rates, the overall balance of payments *(B)* can affect the nation's money supply. The smaller the nation, or the longer the response-time lag to its monetary policies, the harder it is to keep control of the national money supply.

We begin by exploring how the balance of payments can affect the nation's money supply under different monetary institutions, and then we see what it would take for a central bank to keep its money supply from being influenced by the balance of payments.

When Reserves Equal Money (Metallic Standard)

In times long past, money was the same thing as the international reserve asset. Gold (and silver) circulated freely as domestic money and as international money. The equivalence of domestic and international money was particularly close before the emergence of fractional-reserve domestic banking in the 18th century. Banks stayed close to the cloakroom function of issuing banknotes that could be fully redeemed in gold whenever the depositor wished to turn them in. Even in the 20th century, something similar held for many colonial economies before their independence. The colonizing country's currency circulated in the colony as its money supply; the currency was raised or lowered in amounts depending on the colony's payments surplus or deficit.

When reserves and money are the same thing, and they are the same asset domestically as internationally, there is a simple identity tying the national money supply to the balance of payments:

$$B = \Delta R = \Delta M$$

where B is (as above) the balance-of-payments surplus, ΔR is the change in national reserves, and ΔM is the change in the national money supply. The rate of growth of the nation's money supply depends only on the balance of payments:

$$(\Delta M/M) = (B/M).$$

So it was in the mercantilist era from the 16th century into the 18th, with many writers fixing their gaze on the problem of attracting gold from abroad, partly in order to provide more money supply for growing national economies.

With Domestic Fractional-Reserve Banking

Today most countries' monetary institutions are more complex. The money supply is no longer confined to an amount equaling the nation's monetary reserves, either domestic reserve assets or international reserve assets. Gold has long since been retired from private monetary circulation, even though it is still an industrial and consumer good of rising value. A nation's international reserve assets are held largely by its central monetary authorities (central bank and treasury) and by its private banks, as part, but only part, of the backing for the nation's money supply. Most of modern money consists of demand deposits in banks backed up by only fractional reserves held by the banking system.

To simplify without changing any key results, we shall view the monetary officials and the private banks they oversee as one consolidated banking sector. We shall also assume that all foreign currency is held by this banking sector, that all money liabilities to foreigners are owed by it, and that the national money consists solely of bank demand deposits. We shall ignore currency in circulation. Under these assumptions, the national money supply (M) consists of the reserves held by the banking system (R) plus the domestic assets of the banking system (D) corresponding to the rest of its demand deposit liabilities.

When reserves and money are not the same thing.

$$M = R + D$$

and since $B = \Delta R$,

$$\Delta M = B + \Delta D$$

so that the rate of growth of the money supply depends not only on the balance of payments but also on domestic credit:

$$\Delta M/M = (B + \Delta D)/M$$

Looking at money-supply growth in this way allows us to see three ways in which domestic monetary policy can react to the balance of payments:

1. Central banks sometimes passively accept the balance-of-payments surplus or deficit as a net effect on the money supply (with $\Delta D = 0$ so that $\Delta M = B$).
2. Sometimes they "sterilize" part or all of the surplus or deficit, offsetting some or all of its effect on the money supply (with ΔD between $- B$ and zero, so that $\Delta M/B < 1$).
3. Sometimes they play by the fixed-exchange rate "rules of the game" and reinforce the effects of the balance of payments on the money supply in order to restore payments equilibrium faster (with ΔD having the same sign as B, so that $(\Delta M/B) > 1$).

The first choice, passively accepting B as an influence on the money supply, means that D stays the same and the payments surplus or deficit affects the money supply just as directly as if there were no difference between reserves and money. If the money supply is initially $800 billion, a payments surplus of $80 billion per year would raise the money supply by 10 percent a year. The other two choices have occurred more often, and these need more discussion.

Sterilization

Under modern banking institutions, the banking system can offset, or "sterilize," some or all of the payments imbalance, keeping it from having any effect on the domestic money supply. Sterilization can be achieved either by the central bank or by private banks. The central bank can do it by responding to any payments surplus (deficit) by cutting (raising) the ability of private banks to lend, using such instruments as open-market operations, changing the discount rate, or changing reserve requirements. Private banks could do it, if they somehow wanted to, by changing their lending to domestic borrowers in response to changes in the balance of payments. In the extreme case of complete sterilization, the entire payments imbalance could be offset, keeping the domestic money supply on a growth path unrelated to the balance of payments. For example, a surplus of $80 billion per year could be kept from inflating the money supply if the banking system were to cut its domestic credit by $80 billion (i.e., $\Delta M = 0$ if $\Delta D = -B = -\$80$ billion). Correspondingly, a payments deficit could be completely sterilized if the banking system raised its domestic lending by the amount of the payments deficit each year. Thus, *a payments surplus or deficit affects the money supply only if the banking system does not completely sterilize the payments imbalance.*

There are limits to the ability of a banking system to shield its national money stock from the balance of payments. If the country keeps running deficits ($B < 0$), the banking system will soon run out of reserves (R down to zero). If it runs out of reserves, the country would either have to give up on the fixed exchange rate, impose exchange controls, or resign itself to cutting the money supply after all in order to stop the net outflow of money. In contrast, if the country runs surpluses ($B > 0$), it will eventually run into a different problem. Its reserves (such as deposits in foreign banks) will become as high as the total money supply, and further surpluses will raise the money supply.[9]

---

[9] That is, sterilizing a payments surplus could drive D down to zero, while R rises to equal M. For sterilization to continue at that point, D would have to become negative. In other words, the banking system would have to borrow from, rather than lend to, the rest of the domestic economy. This role reversal has never happened and, presumably, would meet with resistance.

Thus, the balance of payments is likely to influence the money supply sooner or later. How long sterilization can postpone this influence depends on the relative sizes of B and R. Deficits could be sterilized for a long time if reserves were large or if the deficits were small or temporary.[10] Surpluses could be sustained for a long time if reserves were expandable or if the surpluses were small or temporary.

The Fixed Exchange Rate "Rules of the Game"

If their goal were to eliminate payments imbalances speedily, central bankers would prefer the opposite of sterilization. They would read a payments deficit as a sign that the domestic money needed to be cut in order to cut domestic spending and imports. A surplus, correspondingly, would call for inflating the domestic money supply to stimulate spending and imports. So, if central bankers were truly committed to defending fixed exchange rates by quickly eliminating any payments imbalance, they would make their domestic lending (D) change in the same direction as the payments imbalance (B), so that $(\Delta M/B) > 1$.

This staunch defense of fixed exchange rates has been called "the rules of the game," "the rules of the gold-standard game" or "taking classical medicine," one of the main institutional choices introduced in Chapter 17. It was once thought to have been a code of behavior that central bankers lived by under the gold standard before World War I. Yet, as we have seen in Chapter 17, a study by Arthur Bloomfield has shown that even then central banks did not stick to this rule, violating it with partial sterilization (so that $(\Delta M/B < 1)$ more often than not. If followed, however, the rules of the game would amount to sacrificing the goal of stabilizing the domestic economy through monetary policy for the sake of speedier elimination of payments surpluses and deficits.

PERFECT CAPITAL MOBILITY

Sterilizing payments deficits and surpluses becomes nearly impossible, and the rules of the game become almost mandatory, under conditions that economists describe as *perfect capital mobility:*

Perfect capital mobility means that a practically unlimited amount of lending shifts between countries, in response to the slightest change in one country's interest rates.

---

[10] Deficits could be ignored for an especially long time by a key-currency country whose extra money liabilities are willingly held by foreigners, leaving its reserves untouched, as we noted in Chapter 17.

If international lending is highly sensitive to slight temporary interest-rate changes, then it practically dictates each country's money supply. Why? When international lenders shift their lending toward a country in pursuit of its slightly raised interest rates, what they are lending is money itself, usually checking deposits. A nearly unlimited surge of borrowing from abroad gives the country with the slightly raised interest rate a new availability of money that is more than the central bank can restrain. Conversely, a nearly unlimited outflow of lending in pursuit of slightly higher interest rates abroad can quickly drain away all of a nation's international reserves (gold, foreign exchange reserves, etc.). Sterilization of the money supply is impossible under such conditions. The balance of payments rules the money supply. (Sterilization also proves impossible in the face of perfect capital mobility in the algebra of the open-economy macromodel in Appendix J).

This could happen, at least to countries that are too small to manipulate the entire world money supply. Indeed, the very success of a system of fixed exchange rates makes perfect capital mobility very likely. If investors are convinced that exchange rates will remain fixed, they will be very willing to move back and forth between currencies in response to the difference in interest rates. For any small country the supply of credit is a world supply, and the supply of money is also a world supply. As a result, interest rates move together in much the same way throughout the world in response to conditions outside the small country, giving substance to the Canadian complaint that "Canadian interest rates are made in Washington." There is evidence that interest-rate correlation between countries grew stronger during prolonged periods of fixed exchange rates.

Perfect capital mobility can rob monetary policy of its ability to influence the domestic economy. During periods when exchange rates stayed fixed for many years, central bankers found it hard to tighten (or loosen) credit. When they tried to cut the home-currency money supply, thus raising interest rates, borrowers found willing lenders from other countries and other currencies, and they found enough lenders to keep the interest rate from rising at all. In terms of the money supply, this meant that the supply available to borrowers in any country or any currency did not even change when central bankers tried to change it.

For fiscal policy, perfect capital mobility actually means enhanced control over the domestic economy. Expansionary fiscal policies do not raise interest rates because the extra government borrowing is met by a large influx of lending from abroad. Thus, the borrowing does not tend to crowd out private borrowers with higher interest rates, allowing fiscal policy its fullest multiplier effects on the economy. In other words, with perfect capital mobility and interest rates fixed outside the country, fiscal expansion cannot be guilty of crowding out private investment from lending markets. This extra potency of fiscal policy under fixed exchange rates and perfect capital mobility may be a poor substitute for the loss of monetary control since governmental handling of spending and taxes is notoriously crude and subject to the vagaries of politics. Yet, this is apparently a fact of life for small countries under truly fixed exchange rates.[11]

The policy implications of perfect capital mobility can be reexpressed with the IS-LM-FE perspective of Figure 20.10. Here the LM and FE curves are perfectly flat because of perfect capital mobility between nations (or between currencies). FE is flat because the tiniest change in interest rates, either in this country or in the rest of the world, would trigger a practically infinite flow of capital between countries. So, if international payments were balanced at Point A, there is no home-country interest rate above seven percent that could avoid a massive balance of payments surplus. Correspondingly, there is no interest rate below seven percent that could avoid a massive outflow of capital and payments deficit. Therefore the FE curve must be flat at seven percent.

Why must the LM curve also be flat? Because a flood of international capital swamps any other influence on the nation's money supply. The inward rush of capital caused by a tiny increase in the home country's interest rate would cause an explosive expansion of the domestic money supply, as lenders made fresh bank deposits (money) available to residents of the home country. Likewise, the outrush of capital caused by a tiny drop in the home country's interest rate would drain the country of all its money supply. So, only the interest rate of seven percent, dictated by financial conditions in the world as a whole, is consistent with equilibrium in the home country's money market. Therefore, the entire LM curve must lie along the seven-percent line.

Under the conditions of Figure 20.10, it is useless to try changing the home country's money supply. If the central bank tries to expand domestic credit, this action only shifts the LM curve horizontally to the right (i.e., it does not shift it at all). Any extra domestic credit, with a slight momentary drop in the interest rate, causes an equal outflow of capital in search of seven percent interest. Starting from Point A, the economy ends up at point A again.

By contrast, fiscal policy takes on its greatest power under these conditions. Raising government spending or cutting tax rates causes the usual rightward shift of the IS curve. As soon as the extra government deficit raises the home country's interest rate even slightly, there is a rush of capital inflow, as international lenders seek the slightly higher interest rate in this country. The inflow raises the money supply until the interest rate is bid back down

---

[11] With perfect capital mobility, as with the other cases discussed in this chapter, we must again add those two caveats about interest rates: (a) it is not clear that cutting the money supply would tend to raise interest rates momentarily, and thus it may not attract capital at all and (b) any attracted capital must be paid for later with reflows of interest and principal back to the foreign creditors.

FIGURE 20.10 With Perfect Capital Mobility, Monetary Policy Is Impotent but Fiscal Policy Is Strong

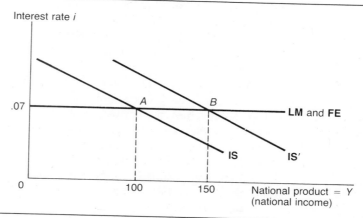

to seven percent. So, a rightward shift of the IS curve has a large effect on national product and no effect on the interest rate.[12]

The likelihood of increasingly perfect capital mobility under fixed exchange rates means that the number of conventional policy instruments for controlling aggregate demand drops back again from two to one: fiscal policy alone. The basic demand-policy dilemma thus reappears in the form it took back in Figure 20.7. In countries that suffer heavy unemployment and payments deficits, and in countries that suffer rapid inflation and surpluses, there is no easy resolution of this dilemma with fixed exchange rates.

SUMMARY

Stabilizing an open macroeconomy with fixed exchange rates is not easy. If a country has only one policy for controlling aggregate demand, it would have to be very lucky for the level of aggregate demand that is best for the domestic economy to turn out to be the one that keeps external payments in line.

One way out of the dilemma was proposed by Robert Mundell and J. Marcus Fleming. They noted that expansionary monetary policy is more

---

[12] In fact, fiscal policy's impact on national product fits the Keynesian multiplier formula of Chapter 19. For example, suppose that the home country in Figure 20.10 were a small, open economy, with a marginal propensity to save of 0.2 and a marginal propensity to import of 0.3. This would make the multiplier equal to 2, according to Chapter 19. In this case, the rightward shift of $\Delta Y = 50$ from Point A to Point B in Figure 20.10 could be achieved by $\Delta G = 25$.

likely to lower interest rates than is fiscal policy and, thus, more likely to cause capital outflows. This means that monetary policy has a comparative advantage in affecting the external balance, whereas fiscal policy has a comparative advantage in affecting the domestic economy. One can thus devise a monetary-fiscal mix to deal with any pairing of imbalances in the external accounts and the domestic economy, as shown in Figures 20.8 and 20.9.

When policy makers cannot confidently estimate the positions of the curves, they can still follow a simpler **assignment rule** with fair chances of at least approaching the desired combination of internal and external balance. When policies are adjusted smoothly and take quick effect, internal and external balance can be reached by assigning the internal task to fiscal policy and the external task to monetary policy. This assignment rule can yield unstable results if policy changes discontinuously or if there is a long lag between implementation and desired effect.

The short-run solutions just mentioned (the monetary-fiscal mix and the assignment rule) assume that the country's monetary officials can **sterilize** the balance of payments (i.e., keep it from affecting the domestic money supply). They are less likely to have such power in the long run than in the short and less likely to have it in small countries than in large ones with a high ratio of reserves to likely payments imbalances. When officials cannot sterilize, the money supply is no longer an instrument of policy control, and keeping exchange rates fixed may mean giving up some monetary sovereignty and playing by the fixed-exchange-rate **rules of the game.**

In the extreme, conditions of **perfect capital mobility** between countries can effectively fix the nation's interest rate and take control of the money supply away from the central bank (under fixed exchange rates). Something like this situation occurred when world financial markets were integrated increasingly under fixed exchange rates, first before World War I and again during the 1960s. In the case of perfect capital mobility and fixed exchange rates, an expansion of the domestic money supply causes an amount of money to migrate into foreign hands, leaving the level of national income unaffected. Expansionary fiscal policy, by contrast, has great impact in this setting because it triggers an inflow of money.

The theorizing that has produced these conclusions rests on some shaky assumptions. In particular, it is based on a very short-run analysis that ignores such delayed effects as changes in price expectations, international interest payments on induced capital flows, and capital accumulation itself. Yet the theory is useful as a rough guide for the short run.

SUGGESTED READINGS

Some of Robert Mundell's pioneering articles on internal and external balance and the implications of international capital mobility are reprinted in his

International Economics (1968, Chapters 16 and 18). The same pathbreaking analysis was simultaneously developed by J. Marcus Fleming (1962).

The basic macromodel of this chapter, the next chapter, and Appendix J is presented in Parkin (1984, Chapter 42) and in Rivera-Batiz and Rivera-Batiz (1985, Chapter 7).

QUESTIONS FOR REVIEW

1. *(a)* Describe the mixture of fiscal and monetary policies that can simultaneously cure rapid inflation and a balance-of-payments deficit (e.g., at Point *H* in Figure 20.9). *(b)* Devise a cure for rapid inflation combined with balance-of-payments surplus (e.g., at Point *E* in Figure 20.9). *(c)* Devise a cure for insufficient aggregate demand and a balance-of-payments surplus (e.g., at Point *C*).

2. What is the assignment rule? What are its advantages and possible drawbacks?

3. If a central bank acts in such a way as to convert a payments deficit of $100 billion a year into a money supply decline of $75 billion a year, is it sterilizing the deficit, playing by the rules of the fixed-exchange-rate game, or doing neither? Explain.

4. What does perfect capital mobility mean for the effectiveness of monetary and fiscal policies under fixed exchange rates?

CHAPTER
21

▼

Floating Exchange Rates and Internal Balance

•

An obvious way to reconcile the goals of internal and external balance is to let the exchange rate take care of external balance and to direct macroeconomic policies toward the problem of internal balance alone. Some preliminary support for this idea came in Chapter 18 and in Appendix I in the form of evidence that floating exchange rates probably do respond in self-equilibrating ways.

What would be wrong with giving ourselves only one problem (internal balance) to worry about instead of two problems (internal and external balance)? The danger to be faced here is that letting the floating exchange rate handle external balance might make it *harder* to keep our internal balance in a changing world. To judge this danger, the present chapter explores how the economy responds to different kinds of macroeconomic shocks under floating versus fixed exchange rates. Whichever exchange-rate institution makes aggregate demand less sensitive to a given kind of shock eases the task of stabilizing an economy beset by such shocks.

To compare fixed and floating rates, we can use the same model used in Chapter 20, but with some changes designed to handle the case of floating exchange rates. Figure 21.1 summarizes the version of the model used for the floating-rate case. Again, there are three markets—a national product market, a national money market, and a foreign-exchange market. Again, there are three endogenous variables. But the switch to a floating-rate system has replaced B, the balance-of-payments surplus, with a new endogenous variable, the exchange rate r. The exchange rate brings the foreign-exchange market into equilibrium, as was the case in most of Part Three, by affecting people's choices about whether to buy goods and services abroad or at

FIGURE 21.1   An Overview of the Macromodel of an Open Economy with Floating
Exchange Rates

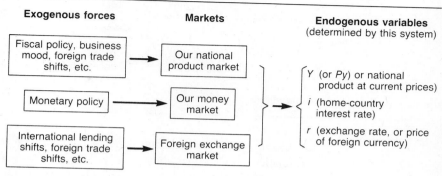

Note that all three endogenous variables—*Y, i,* and *r*—are now determined simultaneously
by all three markets, in contrast to the derivative role of the foreign exchange market in
Figure 20.1.

home. Therefore, it also has a feedback effect on demand for our national
product.[1]

MONETARY POLICY WITH FLOATING RATES

With floating or flexible exchange rates, monetary policy exerts a strong
influence over national income. To see how, let us consider the case of a
deliberate expansion of the domestic money supply.

An expansion of the money supply makes it easier to borrow our national
currency, cutting the interest rate and raising spending. As we saw in Chapter
20, both the rise in spending and the drop in the interest rate should worsen
the balance of payments in the short run. If the exchange rate were held
fixed and the balance of payments were not allowed to affect the money
supply, then there would be nothing to add to the reasoning advanced in
Chapter 20. (If the payments deficit were not sterilized and were allowed
to pull down the money supply as money left the country, then the economy
would return to its starting point with no net changes.) In the case of flexible

---

[1] Because the exchange rate, like the interest rate and the level of national product, has
effects on different markets, we now have a truly simultaneous market system. Our simultaneous
market system is unlike that in Figure 20.1, where the payments surplus *(B)* and the foreign-
exchange market played a derivative role, being affected by *Y* and *i* but not affecting them
as long as sterilization continued.

FIGURE 21.2   Short-Run Effects of Monetary Expansion under Floating Exchange Rates

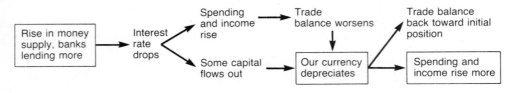

For the case of monetary contraction, reverse all changes.

exchange rates, however, the deficit cannot last. With demand for foreign currencies now greater than supply, our national currency depreciates in value (foreign currencies rise in value) as noted in Figure 21.2. Depreciation of our currency makes it easier for domestic firms to compete with foreign firms. Such competition is likely to improve our trade balance, bringing it back to its initial position. (That is, we assume the Marshall-Lerner stability conditions of Chapter 18 and Appendix I hold here.) The new competitive edge for domestic firms raises aggregate spending for what this country produces. Such an extra aggregate demand due to depreciation augments the rise due to the extra money supply, expanding the economy even more, as stated in Figure 21.2.

Thus, monetary policy has greater unit effect over national income under flexible exchange rates than under fixed exchange rates (especially if central bankers do not sterilize under the fixed exchange rates). This conclusion holds, whatever the degree of international capital mobility. Even if capital were mobile between currencies, the effect of monetary policy would still be greater with flexible exchange rates. Expanding the money supply would still cause a depreciation, and this would further expand aggregate demand. Whether or not perfect capital mobility holds the interest rate fixed, it does not frustrate monetary policy's attempts to control national income, as it does with fixed rates.

FISCAL POLICY WITH FLOATING EXCHANGE RATES

How fiscal policy works with flexible exchange rates is a little more complicated. Fiscal policy can affect the exchange rates in either direction as shown in Figure 21.3. Aggregate spending and national income will be raised by higher government spending and/or lower tax rates. This will tend to raise imports, worsen the trade balance, and weaken the domestic currency. Meanwhile, the fiscal expansion will bid up interest rates as the government borrows more, as we saw in Chapter 20. Higher domestic interest rates will attract capital from abroad, at least temporarily. So, there are two opposing tendencies, an aggregate-demand rise that weakens the domestic

FIGURE 21.3   Short-Run Effects of Fiscal Expansion under Floating Exchange Rates

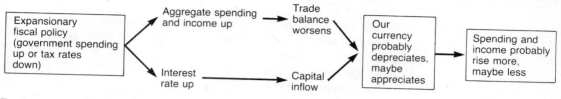

For the case of fiscal contraction, reverse all changes.

currency and a capital inflow that strengthens it for a while. Which tendency will prevail? There is no firm answer, but it appears more likely that the aggregate-demand effect would be stronger and longer-lasting since the capital-inflow effect is offset by later outflows of interest and principal repayments on the attracted capital. The result: fiscal policy probably causes the currency to depreciate and, thus, probably gives an extra trade-based stimulus to domestic production.

Figure 21.4 summarizes what we have gained from studying Figures 21.2 and 21.3, by ranking the alternative exchange-rate systems according to the power of domestic policy over national income. As we saw from Figure 21.2, monetary policy is unambiguously more powerful under flexible exchange rates than under fixed rates. Figure 21.4 says that the same tends to be true for fiscal policy, with a proviso: flexible exchange rates enhance the power of fiscal policy *if* fiscal expansion worsens the balance of payments, as seems likely.

FIGURE 21.4   Ranking Exchange-Rate Systems by the Unit Impacts of Monetary and Fiscal Policies on National Income

Monetary Policy Is:	*When Exchange Rates Are:*
1. Most effective	1. Flexible (floating).
2. Somewhat effective	2. Fixed, with sterilization.
3. Least effective	3. Fixed, with no sterilization.

Fiscal Policy Is:	*When Exchange Rates Are:**
1. Most effective	1. Flexible.*
2. Somewhat effective	2. Fixed, with sterilization.*
3. Least effective	3. Fixed, with no sterilization.*

* *If* expansionary fiscal policy tended to cause payments surpluses and/or appreciation of the national currency, then these rankings should be exactly reversed: fiscal policy would be most effective with fixed exchange rates and no sterilization (as in the case of perfectly mobile capital in Chapter 20) and least effective in the case of flexible exchange rates.

IS NATIONAL INCOME MORE STABLE WITH FIXED OR WITH FLEXIBLE EXCHANGE RATES?

If monetary and fiscal policies could smoothly stabilize the domestic economy, then the question posed in this section would seem to have been answered by the discussion just completed. If, as just argued, monetary policy and fiscal policy are likely to be more effective under flexible exchange rates, then it might seem clear that flexible rates allow officials to keep the economy more stable.

Yet monetary and fiscal policies work very imperfectly. Often, they end up destabilizing the economy, either out of ignorance or for political purposes.[2] Even when officials have the best information and intentions, it is hard for them to know how great or how prompt an effect a given policy action will have. Lacking this knowledge, they have difficulty in deciding just what policy actions they should take at any given moment. A current recession, for example, either might or might not call for stimulative action. If the authorities expected the recession to reverse itself in the near future, they would not want to provide a stimulus to the economy that would start to raise aggregate demand only after a long lag, since the stimulus could then end up just heating up an inflation and making the economy less stable. Such are the knotty practical considerations of stabilization policy.

Given the difficulties of stabilization policy, it would help a lot if institutions could be designed in such a way as to make stabilization more automatic and less dependent on officials' fallible discretion. One such design would be a progressive tax structure that builds ''automatic stabilizers'' into aggregate demand by automatically siphoning off a large share of any extra income into extra taxes. International economists have been debating whether fixed or flexible exchange rates would be more likely to play the role of automatic stabilizer. Which exchange-rate regime would tend to cushion the economy from outside shocks, thereby lessening the size of the disequilibriums with which that policy has to contend? The answer turns out to hinge critically on the kinds of shocks to which the economy is most liable.

Export Demand Shocks

A common source of major shocks to many economies is the variability of foreign demand for exports. This variability is particularly acute for countries specializing in exporting a narrow range of products, the demand for which is highly sensitive to the business cycle in importing countries. This instability

---

[2] A good example of destabilizing out of ignorance: the Revenue Act of 1932, which raised tax rates as the economy dropped toward its severest depression ever. A good example of destabilizing for political purposes: the inflationary fiscal and monetary policy of the Nixon administration and the Federal Reserve (chaired by Nixon associate Arthur Burns) before the election of 1972.

of export demand has plagued exporters of metals, such as Chile (copper), Malaysia (tin), and, to a lesser extent, Canada. Although these countries could react to unpredictable shifts in export demand with offsetting macroeconomic policies stabilizing aggregate demand, the fact that discretionary stabilization policies are hard to design means, again, that it would help very much to have an exchange-rate system that obviated the necessity of correct discretionary policies.

Flexible exchange rates seem to perform better in the face of shifts in export demand. To see why, suppose that foreign demand for Malaysian tin drops off sharply. There is no exchange-rate policy that can shield Malaysia from income losses when this happens, but some policies cushion the shock better than others. An intermediate degree of income loss occurs in the simplest case in which Malaysia rides out the slump with a fixed exchange rate and monetary sterilization. In this case, the export sector suffers a loss of incomes and jobs in the usual Keynesian way and the multiplier process transmits this income loss through the economy. If Malaysia does not sterilize the new payments deficit, the loss of export revenues and the accompanying outflow of money will reduce the money supply, causing still further contraction of the economy. Clinging to the fixed exchange rate when sterilization is not practiced (or unfeasible) yields the worst outcome, the largest drop in income in the wake of a drop in export demand.

Flexible exchange rates offer an automatic partial cushioning against export demand shocks. When export revenues drop, the national currency starts to depreciate. This depreciation will generate some new demand for national product (assuming the stability conditions of Chapter 18 and Appendix I). Exporters will find that foreign demand for their product is buoyed up by the fact that their prices denominated in the depreciated home currency now look cheaper to foreign buyers. Import-competing industries will also tend to win a larger share of domestic markets now that the competing foreign goods look more expensive. These effects of the exchange-rate depreciation do not erase the effect of initial loss of export incomes, which is still being transmitted through the economy, but they do help to offset that effect with demand stimuli, helping to stabilize the economy automatically. Flexible exchange rates also make it easier to shield the domestic money supply from an external money drain by bringing the net international flow of money back to equilibrium after any shock (the case of unanticipated rises in export demand is symmetrical to the case of demand drop discussed here, with the threst being excessive inflation rather than excessive unemployment and real income loss).

Import Supply Shocks

The interaction of national income with exchange-rate regimes in the face of import supply shocks is more complicated. The results depend critically on the initial effects of the shock on (a) national purchasing power and on

(b) the total value of imports. Yet, we can get a clear result if we confine ourselves to the most likely and most dangerous kind of import supply shock: a sudden cutback in foreign supply that (a) lowers national purchasing power and (b) initially raises the total value of imports. This would happen if foreign cartels, or wars, or blockades, or strikes, or harvest failures deprived us of supplies of crucial imports, imports that take a large share of our national spending and those for which our import demand is very inelastic. Examples of supply shocks for crucial imports are oil shocks, like those of 1973–74, 1979–80, and 1990, or a worldwide harvest shortfall in staple foods that some countries must import heavily.

If import supplies of, say, oil are suddenly curtailed, our national purchasing power will be lower and our import bills higher (since our demand curve is price inelastic). With fixed exchange rates and sterilization, the loss of purchasing power will spread through the economy, cutting national income in a multiplier fashion. If the central bank cannot or will not sterilize the effects of the extra payments deficit on the money supply, then the money supply will also shrink and the oil-fired recession will worsen. On the other hand, flexible exchange rates would soften the blow. As soon as the deficits began, the national currency would depreciate, giving a temporary competitive advantage to domestic firms over foreign ones. Some imports would be replaced and some exports encouraged, causing a partial rebound in the national currency. These import replacements and export stimuli would cushion the economy against some of the recession and unemployment coming from the initial oil shock (note, though, that they would add to the price-inflation side of the oil shock).[3]

International Capital-Flow Shocks

Another external shock to which economies are subject is the unpredictable shifting of internationally mobile funds in response to such events as rumors about political changes or new restrictions on international asset holding. This kind of shock threatens to upset the domestic economy by causing a surge or plummeting of the money supply. A sudden capital inflow threatens to raise the money supply that can be lent, driving down interest rates and expanding spending, with inflation as a possible end result. A sudden capital outflow, conversely, threatens to drain off part of the money supply that would trigger a recession.

To determine which exchange-rate system offers the most stability in the face of such capital-flow shocks, let us take the case of sudden capital

---

[3] There are still other complications to the case of an import-supply shock. The sketch just given presumes that the crucial imports are priced in some foreign currency, perhaps that of an exporting country. In the case of oil, there is the complication that oil tends to be priced in U.S. dollars, so that a jump in the international price of oil may raise the demand for the U.S. dollar as a reserve currency, possibly causing the dollar to *ap*preciate. We set this case aside here and in the listings in Figure 21.5.

flight from the country. It is easy to see that the stablest exchange-rate system in this situation is that of a fixed exchange rate with sterilization of all payments imbalances. If the authorities can keep the capital outflow, with its transfer of money into the hands of foreign borrowers, from affecting the domestic money supply, the shock will have no effect on the domestic economy. The central bank will simply make up the loss of some money into foreign hands by lending more money to domestic residents. On the other hand, if the money outflow cannot be offset, the resulting contraction of the money supply will cut national income.

Flexible exchange rates yield an intermediate outcome in the face of capital-flow shocks. They clearly cushion the economy relative to the case of fixed exchange rates without sterilization, which allows the capital outflow to bring an equal reduction in the money supply available to domestic residents. In the case of flexible rates, the capital outflow is allowed to depreciate the nation's currency in the foreign-exchange markets. This depreciation makes it easier for the nation's producers to compete with foreign producers, improving the trade balance. Such a stimulative effect is not possible with fixed exchange rates in the absence of sterilization. With flexible exchange rates, however, the net effect of the capital-flow shock on income depends on what happens to the money supply. With flexible rates, it should be easy for the central bank to offset the initial effect of the capital outflow on the money supply by an expansion of its domestic lending. If the central bank does sterilize the money outflow in this way, then the effect of the capital outflow is the stimulative effect just described, and the capital outflow actually adds an expansionary shock to the economy.

In the case of an economy that is subject to erratic capital movements, we get a variety of outcomes. Clearly the most stable exchange-rate policy, if it is possible, is to maintain a fixed exchange rate with sterilization. In this case, the capital flows have no effect on aggregate demand. The least stable case is likely to be that of fixed exchange rates without sterilization, in which capital outflows bring an equal contraction of the money supply. In between, and less certain, is the case of flexible exchange rates. In this case, the capital outflows could range between being less contractionary than fixed rates without sterilization and being somewhat stimulative.

Internal Shocks

Instability in national income can also be caused by erratic movements in domestic spending demand and monetary demand.[4] The disruption caused

---

[4] Note that the case of domestic aggregate-supply shocks is being ignored here (as in almost all of the literature on the macroeconomics of exchange-rate policy). Aggregate-supply shocks, such as labor strikes and harvest failures, make national production drop while prices rise. Letting such shocks depreciate the currency and cause a stimulus to demand for exports and import-competing goods and services would help offset the cut in real national income but would add to inflation. The choice between exchange-rate systems would then depend on society's relative preferences about output stability and price stability.

FIGURE 21.5   Rankings of Exchange-Rate Systems by the Unit Impacts of Various Exogenous Shocks on National Income

	Rankings		
	(1) Most Disruptive— Least Stable	*(2)*	*(3)* Least Disruptive— Most Stable
External shocks:			
Export demand shocks	Fixed, no sterilization	Fixed, sterilization	*Flexible*
Import supply shocks*	Fixed, no sterilization	Fixed, sterilization	*Flexible*
International capital-flow shocks	Fixed, no sterilization	*Flexible*	Fixed, sterilization
Internal shocks:			
Domestic spending shocks†	*Flexible*	Fixed, sterilization	Fixed, no sterilization
Domestic monetary shocks†	*Flexible*	Fixed, sterilization	Fixed, no sterilization

Illustration: For "Export demand shocks," the table says that such shocks are most disruptive to national income under fixed exchange rates without sterilization of payments imbalances and least disruptive (that is, the economy reacts most stably) under flexible exchange rates.
* See text above for qualifications.
† Compare to results in Figure 21.4.

by such shocks again depends on the exchange-rate system. We have already dealt with the implications of these shocks when we discussed the effect of monetary and fiscal policies under flexible exchange rates. We found that monetary policy was more powerful with flexible exchange rates. It follows that erratic shifts in money demand, such as runs on banks or scrambles to unload money when inflation is feared, will be more powerful (i.e., more disruptive) under flexible exchange rates. The analysis of fiscal policy also carries over as an analysis of the disruptiveness of any domestic spending shocks. Under the plausible assumption that expansions in domestic spending end up worsening the balance of payments, domestic-spending shocks seem more disruptive under flexible exchange rates for reasons described when we discussed fiscal policy.

Figure 21.5 is a report card on the stability of national income in the face of exogenous shocks under different exchange-rate systems. Studying this table, one can see a rough general pattern:

> As a rule, it is easier to stabilize the economy with flexible exchange rates if the shocks are external, but easier to stabilize with fixed exchange rates if the shocks are internal.

Flexible exchange rates offer some cushioning against foreign shifts but tend to magnify the disruption from shifts of domestic origin.

Whether a country that is worried about macroeconomic stabilization should choose fixed or flexible rates thus depends above all on the kinds of shocks it expects to experience in the future. Flexible rates would seem to recommend themselves to a country which must export metals such as copper or tin to industrial economies whose demands depend on the business cycle. To the extent that Canada, for example, fits such a description, it has at least a macroeconomic reason for preferring flexible exchange rates (which it chose in the period from 1950 to 1962 and which it has chosen again since 1971).

On the other hand, countries subject to highly unstable domestic spending demand might be better off with fixed exchange rates. If, for example, fiscal policy is unstable because of recurrent attempts to buy election votes with spending binges that are reversed after the election, then the central bank (if it retains policy independence) should consider choosing fixed exchange rates on the grounds that flexible rates would magnify the instability bred by erratic fiscal policy.

SUMMARY

The effects of monetary and fiscal policy under flexible exchange rates are complex, but clear patterns can be found. Monetary policy affects national income more strongly with flexible exchange rates than with fixed rates. Fiscal policy can have the same effect under the plausible assumption that expansionary fiscal policy worsens the balance of payments.

The debate over whether it is easier to keep national income stable with fixed or with flexible exchange rates can be partly resolved with a rough rule: it is usually easier to stabilize with flexible rates if the economy is subject to external shocks, such as fluctuations in export demand or capital flows, and it is usually easier to stabilize with fixed rates in the face of internal shocks. This rule emerges from Figure 21.5's more careful cataloging of some important cases.

It should be remembered that these conclusions rest on the assumptions listed in Chapter 20.

In reviewing this chapter, you may find it helpful to note and follow the procedure we used in handling each case. Start by thinking about the simplest policy regime: fixed exchange rates with sterilization, in which you can ignore changes in the exchange rate and the money supply. Then go on to comparing the other two regimes (flexible rates, and fixed rates without money-supply sterilization) with the simplest one.

QUESTIONS FOR REVIEW

1. You will definitely want to review what it is about a floating exchange rate that makes each of these shocks have a different effect on national income than the effect of the same shock under fixed exchange rates:

(a) A drop in foreign demand for our exports;

(b) Sudden "capital flight" from our country, with international investors deciding to lend to other countries instead of to us;

(c) A mistaken overexpansion of our own money supply;

(d) A sudden drop in domestic capital formation (e.g., a drop in home building).

2. *(a)* Describe the effects of a sudden rise in domestic liquidity demand (a shift from wanting to hold domestic bonds to wanting to hold domestic money) on our national income under flexible exchange rates. (Hint: a rise in demand for money is like a cut in money supply.) *(b)* Is this change in income greater than or less than under fixed exchange rates?

3. *(a)* Describe the effects of a sudden surge in foreign money supplies on our national income under flexible exchange rates. *(b)* Is this change in income greater than or less than under fixed exchange rates? (To answer, you may want to convert the foreign money-supply change into separate effects on demand for our exports and international capital flows.)

▼

The World Money Climate and the Ultimate Exchange-Rate Choices

•

Parts III and IV have thus far concentrated on the affairs of a single nation within a larger world economy. The first half of this chapter shifts from the parts to the whole, the overall world monetary climate experienced by all nations. The second half returns to the policy choices for single nations within this overall climate.

The world monetary climate has been changing in a way parallel to the evolution of national money. Gold, silver, and other commodity standards survived for many centuries but were then phased out in favor of the more convenient use of national paper currencies. Both for nations and for the world this historical transition from metal to paper came in two overlapping phases: first metallic money was removed from ordinary circulation and turned over to officials, and then even the officials gave their paper currency less and less metallic backing. Finally, within the postwar era, conventional currency and bank deposits were replaced more and more with devices that allowed individuals to rely less on holding regular money and more on access to large unregulated markets where money can be rented. In the international sphere, these large private markets are the wholesale markets for Eurocurrencies, which are in some ways analogous to the rise in credit cards and business credit lines within the more developed nations. Let us trace this remarkable change from metallic money to fluid international markets for hiring any major currency and explore what it can mean for the world money supply and inflation.

HOW SHOULD A WORLD MONEY SUPPLY BEHAVE?

Aside from its many effects on individual nations, a world money system should be judged by three global criteria:

1. It should provide a money or moneys that are accepted the world over, to facilitate world trade.
2. It should make the world money supply grow at an optimal rate.
3. The benefits of creating that money should be spread fairly across countries.

The first global criterion has proved easy to meet. Modern history has produced many internationally accepted assets, some of them commodities, some of them leading currencies, and some of them special international credit lines.

The second criterion, that of optimal world money growth, implies some way of quantifying just how fast world money should grow. This is not easy, but we can start with a rule borrowed from domestic macroeconomics. As applied to international money, the *stable money growth rule* prescribes that:

The world's money supply should grow at a steady and predictable rate. Its rate of growth should be consistent with stable prices.

Keeping the growth rate of world money stable is viewed as one way to stabilize the growth of world output. To find what steady growth rate would keep prices fixed, let's recall the basic quantity-theory equation from Chapter 16:

$$M = KPY$$

where M is now the world money supply measured in units of a currency that dominates international payments. P is the average world price level measured in the same leading currency, Y is real-world product, and K is a coefficient depending on financial innovations (such as the development of credit cards and new kinds of checking accounts) and on rates of return that govern the incentive to hold money (such rates of return as interest rates and stock yields). To focus on growth rates, use lowercase letters to represent percentage growth rates per year. Then the percentage growth rate for the world money stock (m) is easily related to the other growth rates:

$$m = k + p + y$$

Keeping world prices stable means keeping $p = 0$. The equation shows that this would be possible if $m = k + y$. That is, to prevent world inflation and deflation, world money should be designed so that it grows at a rate equal to the long-run growth rate of world output (y) plus a rate of drift, k, in the incentive to hold money for given growth of world product. One rough way of judging any world money system is to ask whether it makes the world money supply grow at the rate $k + y$. In what follows, we shall look at how well different modern monetary systems have met this guideline.

The third criterion, fairness in the international distribution of the windfall gains from creating new world money, does not lend itself so easily to analysis. Fairness, like beauty, is in the eyes of the beholder. What looks fair to one country usually looks unfair to another. In the rest of this chapter, the windfall gains from money creation, or "seigniorage," will be noted without value judgment, allowing the reader to decide on their fairness.

YE OLDE COMMODITY STANDARD

Before the 19th century, a suspicious and fragmented world relied on real commodities as its money, its medium of exchange. The monetary function could be served by any commodity that was durable, transportable, easy to appraise, and unlikely to fall or rise suddenly in its aggregate supply. Many commodities were tried, though by the 19th century the world had settled on gold as the main international (and national) money, as we noted in Chapter 17. As long as gold was the ultimate world money, its supply and value were dictated by mining luck and by the level of world money demand, which, in turn, depended on world production of goods and services.

How was the world supply of commodity money shared among nations? In early modern times nations feared losing money to other countries so badly that they tried a variety of laws and schemes for exporting more nonmoney goods than they imported, in order to gain extra gold reserves from foreigners. In the aggregate, the obsession with importing gold (and silver) could not add up: the world as a whole could not gain more gold than was being mined each year. What could keep an individual nation from losing all its gold reserves to other countries?

Hume's Price-Specie-Flow Mechanism

It fell to the Scottish philosopher, historian, essayist, and economist David Hume in the mid-18th century to expose the illogic of the mercantilist obsession with grabbing a greater share of the world's gold. Hume showed that if any shift should create payments surpluses in some countries and deficits in others, these imbalances themselves would set in motion forces that would automatically stop the flow of specie (gold and silver money) itself. In shorthand, Hume's argument ran thus:

Payments surplus and gold inflow		Prices (and perhaps income) up		Trade balance worsens		Surplus and gold inflow cease
	⇨ *M* up ⇨		⇨		⇨	

The first link in the argument was noncontroversial in Hume's own day, because money and reserves and specie were all the same thing then.[1] The next step also seemed logical once he pointed it out. Like other observers since the 16th century or earlier, Hume felt that an increase in the supply of money would end up inflating price levels. This was a reasonable conclusion. He next argued that if our price levels were being bid up, our competitive position in international trade would be worsening. The higher prices of domestic products would make our exports less competitive in foreign markets and also would cause more of our buyers to prefer foreign goods, which have not risen in price. Hume therefore reached the policy conclusion that mercantilist attempts to generate larger trade and payments surpluses with import restrictions and export subsidies would backfire once the price-specie-flow mechanism sketched here transformed the surplus into higher prices and declining surpluses.

Hume envisioned the opposite adjustment process for countries that were initially thrown into deficit. They would lose specie reserves, contracting their money supply. This, in turn, would bid down their price levels and improve their ability to compete in international trade. The value of the trade balance would improve until payments equilibrium was again restored, ending the deficits that set the whole process in motion.[2]

The modern monetary theory of the balance of payments has added an extra layer of assurance to Hume's dictum: this theory considers any payments surplus or deficit its own direct cure because a surplus is simply a way of adjusting to a temporary excess demand for money and a deficit is simply a way of adjusting to a temporary excess supply of money. The flow of specie eliminates the imbalances promptly. The monetary theory of the balance of payments also notes that the movements in relative prices need never occur: with purchasing-power-parity holding in the long run (see Chapter 16), we should not expect to see prices rising faster in surplus countries than in deficit countries. Rather, prices should be smoothly correlated over time in all countries. There is fair evidence to support this view from the behavior of prices in the gold-standard era.

---

[1] In terms of Chapter 20's discussion of how the balance of payments can affect the money supply, Hume's assumption was that $B = \Delta R = \Delta M$; that is, that the balance of payments translates directly into changes in the money supply.

[2] It should be noted that the step in Hume's logic running from domestic prices to the trade balance requires a condition of underlying stability. A general rise (decline) in all domestic prices has the same effects on whether buyers decide to buy this country's products or foreign products as would a revaluation (devaluation) of this country's currency. Both changes would tend to make this country's goods and services look more (less) expensive to buyers relative to foreign prices. The condition that must hold for general price rises to worsen the balance of payments, and for general price declines to improve it, is the same condition of trade-balance stability discussed in Chapter 18 and derived in Appendix I. If—and only if—this condition is met, Hume's argument is valid for the institutional setting in which money and reserves are the same thing.

There is thus a reasonable basis for believing that a commodity standard like the gold standard has an automatic way of achieving the equilibrium distribution of reserves among nations. The other question to ask in deciding whether a commodity standard is workable is whether it lets the world money supply grow at the correct rate.

World Money Growth under a Commodity Standard

Would a commodity standard make the world's money supply grow at the correct rate dictated by institutional change and output growth? That is, in the equation introduced above, would $m = k + y$, so that prices could remain stable ($p = 0$)?

This stable-price outcome might seem to have a good chance if the commodity being used as money were a unit "basket" of all the goods and services produced in the world—the same proportions of pizza, shoes, steel rails, beauticians' services, living-space rental, and so on—as the world actually produces. Then the supply of this money basket would be likely to grow at the same rate as output (the rate y). But nobody has yet figured out how to make a portable money out of such a complete basket of goods and services. Instead, commodity currency has always been embodied in only a couple of very storable goods.

How well does gold serve as a substitute for an all-commodity standard? Does its supply grow about as fast as the supplies of other commodities, paving the way for stable prices? We can get an idea by looking at how prices have behaved and how the growth of the gold stock compared with the growth rate $(k + y)$, during past gold-standard periods.

Figure 22.1 compares overall price movements with movements in the currency price of gold in England over four centuries. (American data would tell a similar story about the last 200 years.) The gold-standard periods show up as long stretches of time when the price of gold stayed fixed, especially the century of peace and British domination between 1815 and 1914. In this century, when the international gold standard spread outward from London, price trends were sometimes steady and sometimes downward. They fell in Britain and other countries between the height of Napoleanic inflation and the early postwar era (say, up to 1819), then were impressively steady from 1819, when Britain resumed pegging the pound sterling to gold, to 1873. That half century of price stability suggests that the gold standard may have been doing a good job of equating the demand and supply of gold at stable prices. Over the next quarter century (1873–96), however, prices dropped by about a third, and they regained their earlier level by 1913. Here is a sign that there may have been imbalances between the growth of world money supply and world money demand. Perhaps gold, and the money it backed, was becoming too scarce in the era of

Figure 22.1 The Prices of Gold and Other Commodities in England, 1560–1981

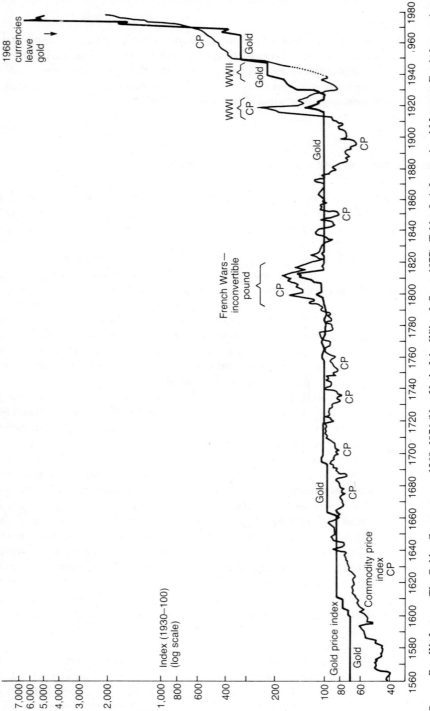

Source: Roy W. Jastram, *The Golden Constant . . . 1560–1976* (New York: John Wiley & Sons, 1977), Tables 2–4; International Monetary Fund, *International Financial Statistics*, recent issues. (The same series could be extended back to 1343, using Jastram's Table 4 and the Brown-Hopkins consumer price index in *Economica*, 1956.)

falling prices (1873–96) and too abundant in the inflationary period (1896–1913) at the end of the classic gold-standard era.

Comparing rough estimates of the growth in gold stock with the growth in real-world output *(y)* also hints at growing imbalances between gold supply and world money demand. On the demand side, world money demand was accelerating, as the following estimates suggest:

Period	y = Growth Rate of World Product	k = Growth Rate of Money-Demand Coefficient
1800–1850	1.0% a year	Positive
1850–1900	1.9% a year	Positive
1900–1950	2.0% a year	Positive
1950–1980	5.1% a year	Slightly negative

Yet the world's monetary gold supply was growing erratically. It was also growing more slowly, especially in the periods of falling prices (1800–20 and 1873–96):

Period	Growth Rate (g) of World Monetary Gold Stock
1800–1820	0.4% a year
1820–1850	0.7% a year
1850–1873	2.9% a year (mining booms in California, Australia)
1873–1896	1.7% a year
1896–1913	3.2% a year (mining booms in Klondike, Transvaal)
1913–1950	2.2% a year
1950–1980	1.8% a year

With such fluctuations in the stock of monetary gold, it is hard to argue that the gold standard assured a steady expansion of the world money base. And in the two periods of deflation, 1800–20 and 1873–96, slowness of growth in the gold stock probably contributed to worldwide price deflation. Certainly by 1950–80, the world economy was growing far too rapidly (at 5.1 percent a year) to have been served well by a world money supply whose growth was tied at all closely to *g,* that slow rate of growth (1.8 percent a year) in the monetary gold stock. In fact, the acceleration of modern growth has been accommodated in large part by the *abandonment* of the gold standard. Already in the 19th century, gold was leaving domestic circulation into bank vaults, where it served as a narrowing reserve base for the accelerating supply of paper money. In the 20th century, gold was also being phased out of its role as a means of international payments, as we shall see again in the next section. (A way was found, in other words, to keep *m* well above *g.*)

Another shortcoming of the gold standard, in the eyes of many, is the way in which it distributes *seigniorage,* or the gains from creating new

GOLD AS A PRIVATE ASSET

Now that the link between gold and currencies has been cut since 1968, and especially since 1971, we can see at least one lesson for anyone trying to bet on gold, whether these are officials trying to peg their currencies to it again or private individuals considering speculating on it, as private Americans have been allowed to do since 1975. The central lesson is that the gold market is for risk-lovers. Its prices have gyrated wildly in recent times. Under these conditions, any government trying to return to a fixed-gold parity had better not do it alone: having your national currency gyrate in its exchange rates according to the recent movements in Figure 22.1 is a formula for chaos. And now that governments do not dare peg their currencies to gold, the private speculator can no longer count on officials to prop up the price of gold if it should plummet.

Why has the price of gold jumped around so much in recent years? The best single answer is that the gold market is where frightened people go. It may seem strange that frightened people should at times rush into an asset that has so volatile a price, yet this can make sense during times of extreme danger. Suppose that you are independently wealthy and that you live in an unstable region of the world, such as the Middle East. How can you protect your nest egg? Remembering that gold is unproductive, you should of course consider productive domestic assets such as land, factories, or bonds. But such items could be seized or heavily taxed during the next coup or revolution. Financial and productive real assets held abroad might seem safer, but these

money.[3] Having nations fix their currencies to gold is likely to raise their official demand for gold to hold as reserves. To attract gold inflows for the larger official stockpiles, they will have to fix the price of gold high enough so that gold miners have incentive to mine the extra gold. One way or another, this will tend to happen over the centuries, making the

---

[3] Definition: **seigniorage** is an important technical term in monetary economics that means the profits from issuing money. The term comes from the right of the king or lord, or "seigneur," to issue money and represents the difference between the value of money in exchange and the cost of producing it.

CONTINUED

items have their own political risks of sudden taxation or seizure (as when the U.S. government suddenly froze the U.S. assets of Iran during the 1979–81 hostage crisis). Clandestine gold can often prove easier to transport without disclosure or taxation. This sort of frightened portfolio rationality seems to have been behind the occasional speculative explosions in the gold market, most notably the January 1980 peak in the early phases of the U.S.-Iran hostage crisis. But such behavior is inherently unpredictable: we cannot forecast political crises well, and one person's mystical haven for wealth is another's unproductive "barbarous relic." Lest investors needed any further warning about the risks of investing in gold, its price dropped more than 50 percent in the early 1980s, as new price stability and relative peace punctured many speculative fears about worldwide inflationary chaos.

Over decades and centuries of relative peace, we would expect gold to rise in price similar to, or maybe a bit faster than, other commodities. It is likely to have growing industrial and ornamental use, and productivity in gold mining has shown little tendency to rise rapidly. Such prospects mean that the long-run trend in gold's real price is not likely to be downward. At the same time, elasticity in gold-mining investments means that any tendency for gold's real price to rise should be held in check by a rise in inputs into gold mining. This likelihood of continued stability in gold's real price though refers only to the long run. For any practical short run, gold's value is anybody's guess.

mine owners the main beneficiaries of official interest in holding gold. Who are the mine owners? Today, people in South Africa mine about half the world's new gold; those in the Soviet Union, about 30 percent; Canada, 3.8 percent; the United States, 2.3 percent; and those in all other countries, 13.9 percent. The thought of giving windfall seigniorage gains to people in these countries seems to many observers a reason for opposing any renewed commitment to peg to gold.

What a defender of the gold standard could rightly argue, though, is that it brought less inflation than the adjustable-peg and floating rate systems that have prevailed since 1929. This is true. There was indeed less inflation under the gold standard. Even in periods of gold-mining boom (the influx of American gold in the 16th and early 17th centuries, the California-Australia gold rush of mid-19th century, and the Klondike–Transvaal gold rush at the turn of this century), world inflation was not as serious as it has become since the abandonment of the gold standard. In other words, abandoning the gold standard has done more than simply free the demand for money from gold's slow growth rate: it has also ushered in a period in which monetary officials let the money supply grow even faster than the real demand for it, bringing price inflation.[4] We will draw on this historical experience, arguing that there is more "price discipline," or official resistance to price inflation, under the gold standard and other fixed-exchange-rate systems than under flexible exchange rates.

FROM GOLD TO KEY CURRENCIES

Curiously enough, a successful gold standard, or any other commodity standard, would tend to eliminate itself—as the last 100 years have shown.

A gold standard is supposed to give everyone confidence that currencies are "as good as gold." Yet, if one has this confidence, then the obvious questions become: "Why bother holding gold? Why not hold cash and interest-earning bills in strong currencies?" Gold is more expensive to hold or to ship. We should therefore expect to see gold decline as a share of private and official reserves once people are convinced that major currencies will be interchangeable with gold.

This happened, as Figure 22.2 shows. The placid prewar gold standard saw a quiet rise in foreign-currency holdings as a share of total international reserves on the part of central banks and treasuries. This official shift paralleled the gradual private replacement of gold and other metals with paper money. During the Bretton Woods, or adjustable-peg, era after World War II, the fixed-exchange-rate system, again pegged more or less to gold, found officials drifting toward holding dollars and other foreign currencies rather than gold, as shown by the movement from 1950 to 1970 in Figure 22.2. The abandonment of fixed exchange rates and fixed prices for gold checked this trend in the 1970s. Yet, for as long as it lasted, the system of fixing all exchange rates to gold caused a drift toward holding paper reserves; that is, a phasing out of the gold standard itself.

The emerging system of holding key currencies allows the key-currency countries to gain some extra resources in a somewhat secret way. Back in Chapter 17, we noted that the United States after World War II was able

---

[4] The trends since abandonment of the gold standard can be restated in terms of the quantity-theory growth rates. The abandonment of the gold standard has let officials make the growth rate of the world's money supply (m) exceed the growth rate that would be consistent with stable prices ($k + y$, with $p = 0$). Because $m > k + y$, there was inflation: $p > 0$, in line with the growth rate equation $m = k + p + y$.

Figure 22.2   The Changing Composition of the World's Official International Reserves since 1880

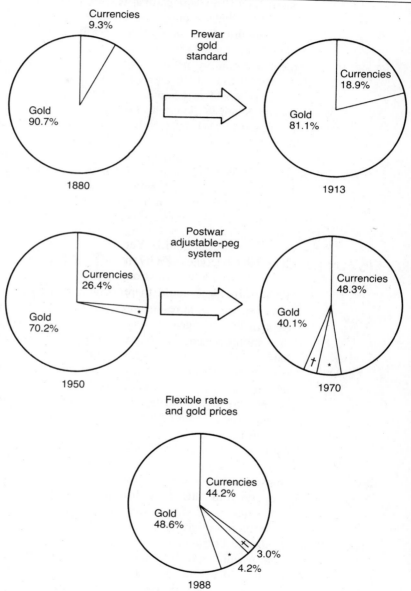

Prewar gold standard

1880
Currencies 9.3%
Gold 90.7%

1913
Currencies 18.9%
Gold 81.1%

Postwar adjustable-peg system

1950
Currencies 26.4%
Gold 70.2%
*

1970
Currencies 48.3%
Gold 40.1%
† *

Flexible rates and gold prices

1988
Currencies 44.2%
Gold 48.6%
* 4.2%
† 3.0%

* = IMF positions.

† = special drawing rights.

Source: Data are from Lindert (1962, Chapter 2), and International Monetary Fund, *Annual Reports,* various years.

to have its liquid dollar liabilities pile up in foreign hands without converting them into goods or services from the United States. This growth of unredeemed key-currency claims was referred to as the *deficit without tears,* in the French phrase quoted in Chapter 17. Under the key-currency system, the key-currency country gets to reap profits from producing international money costlessly. This is the problem, in the eyes of nonkey-currency countries: one country gets an implicit interest-free (or low-interest) loan from the rest of the world, a privilege other countries do not enjoy.

As we noted in Chapter 17, this problem of discriminatory seigniorage (or the deficit without tears) is real, or, rather, it *was* real before the 1970s. By that time, U.S. deficits had glutted world financial markets enough that foreign governments found themselves accepting and holding more dollars than they wanted. Since the abandonment of gold convertibility (March 1968) and of fixed exchange rates (August 1971), foreign residents have held extra dollars only when compensated with interest rates that are on a par with others in world financial markets. Now, the United States must pay as much interest as any other country for its foreign liabilities.

GROPING FOR OFFICIAL WORLD MONEY: THE IMF AND SDRs

To mitigate the seigniorage problem and to expand the total supply of official reserves, the major countries agreed at Bretton Woods, New Hampshire, back in 1944 to form the International Monetary Fund (IMF), an institution that still functions as something approaching a truly international central bank in Washington, D.C. (two blocks up from the White House). Membership in the IMF started with 30 nations when its doors opened in 1947; it now has expanded to more than 140 nations.

The IMF performs its central function by pooling member nations' contributed reserves and lending them out to deficit countries with international bills to meet. To become a member of the IMF, each nation must pay in a "quota," a contribution in dollars or some other internationally acceptable assets in an amount tied to that country's population, economic size, and importance in world trade. This quota contribution becomes the de facto property of the IMF, though voting rights within the IMF are also proportioned to the quotas. Countries that need extra international reserves to get through a payments crisis or a run on their currency can use a complex set of graduated borrowing rights that we shall refer to simply as the "IMF position," which can be thought of as a special line of credit. Permission to borrow up to half their previous quota contribution is nearly automatic. Countries can and do borrow more than 100 percent of their quota contribution, though the more they seek to dip into the IMF, the more pressure the IMF exerts on them to curb domestic spending, pay increases, and inflation.

At the IMF meetings in Rio de Janeiro in 1967, an agreement was reached to further internationalize the world's official reserves by creating new **special drawing rights** (or **SDRs**). SDRs are essentially permanent international official money. All members of the IMF are obligated to accept them in transactions with other governments and central banks. The new SDRs are money-type obligations of the IMF itself, handed out to member governments in proportion to their quota contributions. To keep the value of the SDR relatively steady in the present age of floating exchange rates, the IMF has controlled its issue and pegged its value to a "basket" (weighted average value) of several currencies. When using SDRs, a nation must pay interest to the IMF at a rate that is again a weighted average of several national rates.

The SDR embodies the hope of postwar officials for a truly international solution to the problem of controlling the world supply of international reserves. Yet, its use remains very limited. One central difficulty is that SDRs are ultimately usable only in transactions between governments and central banks. Private businesses and or citizens cannot get hold of them. And if they could, they would find little acceptance of SDRs at local shops. Figure 22.2 shows that even as a share of official reserves, SDRs, like the original IMF positions, remain very small.

THE RISE OF PRIVATE WORLD MONEY: EUROCURRENCIES

The postwar movement toward an official international reserve has been outstripped by innovations in private international financial markets. Today, we have a worldwide wholesale money market of enormous scope, one beyond the easy control of any government or the IMF. In this market, any government or large business can borrow or lend at interest any weekday, day or night. This is the large, complex, and sometimes mysterious Eurocurrency market that has sprung up since the late 1950s.

Definition

A **Eurocurrency** claim is a claim against a bank in a different currency from the currency of the country where the bank is located.

Eurocurrencies are almost money, though not money in the strictest demand-deposit or hand-currency varieties. Almost all Eurocurrencies are time deposits more akin to fairly accessible savings accounts than to outright checking accounts. To be used for making payments, a Eurocurrency balance is usually converted into an ordinary deposit with a bank located in the country of the currency unit (e.g., the United States, for a Eurodollar). Eurocurrencies thus belong in broader definitions of the world's money supply (like the M-2 definitions of a national money supply) but not in the narrowest definition (like M-1). They are also claims denominated in large amounts: the Eurocurrency market is a wholesale market used only by large banks, companies, and governments.

Euro*dollars* still account for over 60 percent of Eurocurrency deposits, although the share of nondollar Eurocurrencies is rising. Some Eurocurrencies are claims against banks in North America, Asia, and the Caribbean, despite the *Euro* prefix. For example, it is not abnormal today for, say, a Saudi bank to hold Euro*yen*, in Singapore or in the Bahamas. American and Japanese banks in particular owe almost half their Eurocurrency deposits in their "offshore" branches. Between 1981 and 1986, the dominant offshore banks were the U.S.-owned International Banking Facilities (IBF) in the Caribbean, Hong Kong, and Singapore. Since 1986, the IBF have been eclipsed by the surge of the Japan Offshore Market, through which Japanese banks owe foreign currency (and yen) deposits in branches outside Japan.

Reasons for the Rise of Eurocurrencies

Eurocurrencies in their modern form seem to have begun sometime in the late 1950s. They now dominate international lending and borrowing by banks. Their growth has been nourished by the desire to evade government, that is, to minimize financial disclosure, banking controls, and taxation.

1. *Secrecy.* An early innovator was the Soviet government, which in the late 1950s sought a convenient way to hold the U.S. dollars that often accumulated between its sales of gold and its purchases of wheat, equipment, and other goods priced in dollars. Soviet officials appear to have found dollars convenient yet sought to avoid holding large deposits in the United States, probably fearing disclosure (CIA, FBI) and possible future confiscation. They thus arranged with London and continental banks to keep deposits with them, deposits denominated in U.S. dollars, that is, Eurodollars, which the London and continental banks could match or not match with dollars held in New York, as they saw fit.

2. *Avoiding regulation.* Controls over U.S. banks by the Federal Reserve also fed the growth of the Eurodollar (and other Eurocurrency) markets. In particular, Regulation Q attached to the operation of the Federal Reserve Act empowered the Fed to keep a ceiling on the interest rates that U.S. commercial banks could offer their depositors on time and savings deposits. When the Fed tried to tighten credit in stages in the late 1960s, these ceilings became binding. At the same time, U.S. government controls on capital exports further hampered foreign lending by U.S. banks. Investors in the United States and other countries took increasing advantage of the opportunity to earn higher market rates of interest by shifting their dollar-denominated deposits to banks outside the United States. Frustrated by this loss of depositors, many U.S. banks accelerated their creation of new branches abroad so that they could conduct their own Eurocurrency lending and borrowing. Partly because of this flight from controls, the Eurocurrency markets are able to lend and borrow at finer interest-rate margins, offering depositors higher rates while still offering borrowers lower rates.

3. *Avoiding taxes.* Another reason for the rise of Eurocurrency business and for its ability to operate at smaller interest-rate differentials relates to taxation. By doing business in nonresident currencies, especially in the Caribbean and Asian tax havens, banks can have their interest earnings taxed very lightly or not at all. This competition from tax-haven governments is forcing the United States to relax some of its banking rules, offering less controls and lower taxes to bring home some of the runaway banking business.

The rise of the Eurocurrency markets has even benefited from some tacit approval and support of governments in the main Eurocurrency centers. Some central banks, both European and others, have taken to holding a portion of their dollar reserves in private European banks instead of investing them in U.S. Treasury bills or other claims on the United States.

How Eurocurrencies Are Created

To see better what is and what is not a Eurocurrency asset, let's imagine a set of transactions giving rise to a Eurodollar deposit, and then follow how such deposits could invite an expansion of the world's money supply.

Suppose that the Soviet Ministry of Foreign Trade sells oil to Japan and is paid with $100 million in dollar bank deposits in America. So far, as shown in the top panel of Figure 22.3, we have no Eurodollars, just an ordinary foreign-held bank deposit. But suppose the Soviet officials, keen on protecting their secrecy, want to keep any dollars outside the United States. They shift them to a Swiss bank, let us say Credit Suisse in Zurich, as illustrated in the bottom panel of Figure 22.3. The Soviet government writes a check on its balance in the Bank of America, which Credit Suisse accepts. The Soviets still have their $100 million in dollar deposits, only in a bank outside the United States. These, by definition, are Eurodollars, since they are dollar claims on a nonresident of the United States.

The creation of new Eurodollars sets up the potential for expanding the world money supply. Credit Suisse has new access to dollar deposits in America, and can use these as reserves for fractional banking. Furthermore, these deposits are not subject to official reserve requirements because Credit Suisse is not in the dollar country and Switzerland's own rules do not impose reserve requirements like those in America. They will lend out as much of the newly received deposits in the Bank of America as they deem prudent, given the need to hold onto some dollar deposits to meet a possible rush of depositors demanding conversion of their Credit Suisse dollar deposits into dollars in an American bank. Let us say Credit Suisse feels it can

FIGURE 22.3   The Birth of Some Eurodollars

Before: no Eurodollars

Original Depositor: *Soviet Foreign* *Trade Ministry*		*American Bank:* *Bank of* *America*	
Assets	Liabilities	Assets	Liabilities
$100 million in de- posits at Bank of America			$100 million de- posit liability to Soviet govern- ment

In this situation, right after the Soviets have just sold some of their oil to other countries in exchange for dollars, they temporarily hold actual dollars in an American bank.

Then, however, they shift them to the relative secrecy of Credit Suisse in Zurich, giving Credit Suisse the deposits in America:

After: Eurodollars are created

Soviet Foreign *Trade Ministry*		*Bank of* *America*	
$100 million time deposit in Credit Suisse			$100 million checking de- posit liability to Credit Suisse

Bank Creating Eurocurrency *Credit Suisse in Zurich*		
$100 million checking de- posit at Bank of America	$100 million time deposit held by Soviet govern- ment	◁ *Eurodollars*

Eurodollars are created for the technical reason that dollars are owed by a bank in a nondollar country.

afford to hold only six percent of its dollar deposit liabilities as reserves in the Bank of America. The other $94 million can be lent out at interest, and Figure 22.4 imagines that Credit Suisse lends it to IBM of South Africa, which is borrowing to expand its software-producing facilities in South Africa. The $94 million being lent takes the form of checking deposits in a bank. That bank could be either Credit Suisse itself or another bank. Suppose that IBM of South Africa wants to be lent checking deposits in

FIGURE 22.4 After Eurodollar Deposits Are Put to Work, More World Money Starts to Emerge

Soviet Foreign Trade Ministry		*Bank of America*	
$100 million time deposit in Credit Suisse			$6 million checking deposit liability to Credit Suisse
			$94 million checking deposit liability to IBM South Africa

⇦
Addition to world money supply

Credit Suisse of Zurich		*New Borrower: IBM of South Africa*	
$6 million checking deposit in Bank of America	$100 million time deposit held by Soviet government	$94 million checking deposit in Bank of America	$94 million debt to Credit Suisse
$94 million loan to IBM South Africa			

⇦
Same Eurodollars

After Credit Suisse has made a new loan of $94 million to IBM of South Africa and (let us say) IBM decides to transfer all of the $94 million to Bank of America to prepare for purchases. **$94 million of new money has been created.** The money supply is defined to include all deposit claims against banks by nonbank entities. The world now has $194 million of such money: the Soviet $100 million held against Credit Suisse in Zurich plus the $94 million held in Bank of America by IBM of South Africa. This is $94 million more than the original $100 million that the Soviet government momentarily held in the Bank of America in the upper panel of Figure 22.3.

the United States and receives $94 million in deposits at the Bank of America (in exchange for that IOU, the promise to repay with interest).

Figure 22.4 can be viewed as a snapshot freezing the action right after IBM of South Africa has acquired its newly borrowed deposits in the Bank of America. Some new money has been created, where money is defined as all deposit claims of nonbanks against banks. When we started, in the top panel of Figure 22.3, there was only $100 million in such money claims. Now, in Figure 22.4, there are $194 million, the $100 million still held by the Soviet Ministry of Foreign Trade plus $94 million held in the Bank of America by IBM. Thus money has been created.

The process of monetary expansion through the Eurodollar market could continue beyond the snapshot shown in Figure 22.4. Perhaps either IBM or the suppliers from whom it buys software-related goods would be content to hold some of the new deposits in Eurodollar form (e.g., back in the Credit Suisse). Once that happens, the non-U.S. banks would have extra freedom to continue lending more. The limits to the process depend on the rate of leakage of dollar reserves (dollar deposits in U.S. banks like Bank of America) out of the non-U.S. banks. These Eurobanks need to limit their lending according to the likelihood that lending would cost them reserves. But within these limits, they can create world money.

Parts of this tale should sound familiar. World money is being created through Eurocurrency banking in exactly the same way that a national money supply is expanded after the public deposits cash into the banking system. To underline the analogy, just go back through Figures 22.3 and 22.4 penciling in the following substitutions:

For	Write in
Soviet Ministry of Foreign Trade	Sohio (Standard Oil of Ohio)
Bank of America	First National Bank of Cleveland
Credit Suisse	First National Bank of Cincinnati
IBM of South Africa	Procter & Gamble

That is, the same story of bank expansion could have been told in terms of transactions in, say, Ohio. Whether the story takes place around the world or in Ohio, the outer limit to money-supply expansion is still dictated by the rate of leakage of reserves from the set of banks in question. True, we would not use the word *Eurocurrency* to mean a dollar deposit against an Ohio bank, but otherwise the process is the same.

Effects of the Eurocurrency Markets

Observers have been worried that the rise of Eurocurrency markets might overexpand the world money supply, adding to worldwide inflation.

Opinions differ on the Eurocurrency money multiplier, that is, the ratio of new international money to each extra unit of Eurocurrency deposits. Data on this issue are hard to come by and harder to interpret. Some scholars found a very high raw multiple of Eurodollar deposits to the apparent value of demand deposits held in the United States as backing for other countries' dollar liabilities. One study found a multiplier somewhere between 7 and 20. Most researchers, though, guess that the ratio is barely above unity, that is, for each extra Eurodollar a broad definition of world money supply is raised by only a little over a dollar. Econometric studies also suggest that there is little impact of the rise of Eurocurrencies on the aggregate growth rate of world money and prices.

One possible reason for the likelihood of a low Eurocurrency multiplier is that most Eurocurrency deposits are the result of bilateral swaps of claims between banks, a kind of transaction that does not add directly to the money supply in the hands of nonbank parties. For example, of the Eurocurrency liabilities of European banks, only about 13 percent were actually liabilities in the hands of nonbanks. With offsetting interbank claims so dominant, net Eurocurrency holdings by nonbanks must be a smaller multiple of the underlying dollar claims against the United States than some studies have implied.

Should Eurocurrency Banking Be Regulated? Can It?

With or without a significant money multiplier in the Eurocurrency market, central bankers worry that its existence can frustrate their attempts to control the supplies of their respective national moneys. Central bankers who want to tighten their money supplies, for example, worry that borrowers can simply borrow the same money, even the same currency, in the Eurocurrency markets, rendering their monetary tightening impotent. This is a legitimate fear for smaller countries whose private borrowers can use other currencies as easily as the domestic one. For countries that cannot affect world money-market conditions, the rise of Eurocurrencies weakens national monetary policies because it promotes the international capital mobility discussed previously in Chapter 20.

Yet, if the country in question has one of the key currencies in the Eurocurrency markets, its central bank seems to retain the same powers it would have had without those markets. By controlling the conventional money supply, it can control access to the domestic demand deposits that are the ultimate reserves of Eurobanking. The Federal Reserve, for example, can cut the U.S. conventional money supply knowing that this will raise the interest rate at which foreigners (e.g., London banks) will have to acquire extra U.S. deposits to back their Eurodollar liabilities. The Fed can control the world supply of dollars, not just the supply of dollars held in the United States. So, for key-currency countries, the rise of Eurocurrency markets does not pose any clear threat to the power of monetary policy. In fact, it offers an extra hidden reserve for officials in any country. They know they can borrow extra Eurocurrency reserves at the going interest rate. This simple fact means that conventional measures of a country's international reserves can be misleading. These days the supply of official reserves is not an amount held but a going price at which more reserves can be mustered from a lively and extensive international market.

THE CHOICES FOR A SINGLE COUNTRY

Within the world monetary climate, individual nations must cope. The rest of this chapter reviews and extends the exchange-rate policy lessons of Parts III and IV for single nations, using a logical order that should make it easier to judge which foreign exchange policies best fit which situations.

Recall the policy options introduced back in Chapter 17. As mentioned there, an individual nation can choose among these main kinds of institutions for adjusting to foreign exchange problems:

1. The nation can just *finance* temporary balance-of-payments deficits or surpluses with changes in reserves and in money liabilities to other countries, while keeping the exchange rate fixed.
2. The nation can enforce *exchange controls* with fixed official exchange rates.
3. The nation can let *floating exchange rates* be determined in free foreign-exchange markets without official intervention.
4. *Permanently fixed exchange rates* can work, as long as the nation is willing to adjust its level of prices, output, and employment in any way necessary to preserve the fixed exchange rate.
5. The nation can try *exchange-rate compromises:*
   a. It can mix usually fixed exchange rates with occasional large devaluations or revaluations, according to the adjustable-peg or Bretton Woods system, as practiced between 1944 and 1971.
   b. It can try a *managed float,* changing exchange rates gradually, along with interim macroeconomic adjustments to the domestic economy.

Recall that the menu of choice is actually narrower than this, however. First, the option of just *financing* deficits or surpluses can work only in narrow short-run situations. It requires that the current exchange rate happen to be the one sustainable forever, without any need to adjust the domestic economy to fit that rate. In a world of severe and unpredictable shocks, such good fortune is very unlikely. In all probability, the nation will soon either run out of reserves (in the case of continuing deficits) or run up unmanageable accumulations of foreign exchange reserves (in the case of continuing surpluses), as argued in Chapter 17. Sooner or later, the nation must choose one of the other options for adjusting to changing foreign exchange conditions.

Second, the option of *exchange controls* can be rejected. Chapter 17 imagined how the best possible exchange controls might work and found them inferior to floating exchange rates. When one recognizes the additional inequities and administrative costs of real-world exchange controls, they can be removed from the list of worthwhile options—even though they remain a common practice in Third World and socialist countries today.

Third, we can subordinate any discussion of the *adjustable-peg* or *Bretton Woods system* (Option 5a) to a discussion of the managed float (Option 5b). The former is, in fact, just a special case of the latter, one in which the ''floating'' exchange rate is ''managed'' in the sense of being fixed for long periods of time, but then abandoned in a large sudden change in the exchange rate. The adjustable peg is thus a crude version of a crawling peg or managed float. The comments on the adjustable peg system in Chapter

17 still apply, and they will be implicitly reapplied in the comments on managed floats later in this chapter.

So, the best choices facing a single nation reduce to these three:

- Purely *floating exchange rates* (Option 3 above).
- A *managed float* (Option 5*b*).
- Permanently fixed exchange rates, with the whole domestic economy being adjusted to keep the exchange rates sustainable (Option 4 above).

Let us weigh all the exchange-rate policy lessons of Parts III and IV, first by surveying the case for permanently fixed rates versus a pure float, then by surveying the case for a managed float versus a pure float, with a final section on the actual foreign exchange policies of the 1980s.

PERMANENTLY FIXED RATES VERSUS ANY FLOAT

It is now possible to draw together a list of ways in which permanently fixed exchange rates are better than, or worse than, any float. We begin with two arguments that usually favor fixed rates, and we move later to arguments less favorable to them.

Destabilizing Speculation

Any system invites trouble if it allows speculators' expectations about the future of the exchange rate to be unstable and to make the exchange rate more volatile. Chapter 18 gave Milton Friedman's argument that destabilizing speculation would be damaging to the destabilizing speculators themselves. It is also damaging to society as a whole. First, those speculators' losses are also society's losses, the same welfare losses from avoidable price movements shown in Chapter 17 (Figure 17.1) and Appendix G. Second, instability could cause financial panic and a real depression, as did the Wall Street boom and bust at the end of the 1920s.

Destabilizing speculation is more likely with floating rates than with permanently fixed rates. If officials are truly committed to keeping the exchange rate fixed come what may, speculators will have to believe in that fixity. Speculation will not be destabilizing. In contrast, in the case of a float officials do not signal any such commitment, and speculators could make exchange rates gyrate. This is not to say that they are likely to do so, but only that they are more likely to do so than if officials were absolutely chained to fixed exchange rates.

Price Discipline

One of the main arguments in favor of fixed exchange rates has been that letting rates float would weaken official price discipline and bring more inflation. The argument runs as follows:

1. The fixed-exchange-rate system puts more pressure on governments that have international payments deficits than on governments that have surpluses; it follows that allowing governments to switch to floating rates gives more new freedom to deficit countries than it gives to surplus countries.
2. Since "classical medicine" (or "the rules of the game") prescribes deflation for deficit countries and inflation for surplus countries, avoiding this medicine with floating rates permits policy to be more inflationary on the average.
3. This greater inflation with the float is bad because individual governments are biased toward excessive inflation if they are not disciplined by the need to defend a fixed exchange rate.

The first two parts to the price discipline argument seem roughly to fit the facts. The third requires a personal value judgment.

It does seem to be true that the fixed-exchange-rate system constrains deficit countries more than surplus countries. Deficit countries must face an obvious limit to their ability to sustain deficits: they will soon run out of reserves and creditworthiness. Surplus countries, by contrast, face only more distant and manageable inconveniences from perennial surpluses. After a while, constantly accumulating foreign exchange and gold reserves becomes inconvenient. The central bank or treasury must swallow these assets as private individuals turn them in for domestic currency. When the foreign reserve assets rise to some high level, it becomes technically impossible for the officials to keep further payments' surpluses from raising the money supply because the officials no longer have any ability to cut their domestic lending once it has hit zero. (Theoretically, the officials could go on becoming gross and net debtors to the domestic economy, issuing official nonmoney IOUs to sop up domestic money, but monetary institutions are seldom set up for such pursuits by central banks.) Yet, this constraint is quite distant. Countries can go on running surpluses for more years than they can go on running deficits that are the same percentage of initial reserves.

Experience seems to confirm this asymmetry. In the postwar period, it was possible for surplus countries, such as West Germany and Japan, to continue accumulating reserves for a considerable time without major inconvenience. It was harder for deficit countries, such as Britain, to hold out so long. The main exception of a deficit country being able to hold out is that of the United States. As we noted in Chapter 17, the United States was able to sustain deficits longer than were most countries because the reserve-currency status of the dollar made a growing world economy willing to accumulate dollars in large amounts for over a decade. The pre-1914 experience with fixed exchange rates looked much the same.

Given this asymmetry in the burdens of adjusting to a set of fixed exchange rates in a changing world, it follows that allowing countries to begin floating their currencies will on balance release more inflationary policies. This conclusion is supported by the observation that world inflation of money supplies and prices seemed to pick up a bit after the generalized float of August 1971, in the first 12 months, although this occurrence can have other explanations as well.

Whether or not flexible exchange rates lead to *too much* inflation is an open question. Somebody who cares very much about full employment and is not much bothered about price inflation might prefer flexible rates because they enhance the ability of deficit countries to avoid cutting jobs and income with deflationary policies. Somebody who fears inflation above all is more likely to favor fixed exchange rates for the same reason. The debate over fixed versus flexible exchange rates is thus partly a variant of the familiar debate over what mixture of unemployment and inflation is best. The price discipline argument thus makes some correct statements about how fixed-rate and flexible-rate systems differ in practice and adds a value judgment in favor of fixed rates and greater price stability, a judgment one may or may not share.

Types of Macroeconomic Shocks

The choice between fixed and flexible exchange rates should depend on which types of macroeconomic shocks will prevail, as explained in Chapter 21 (especially Figure 21.5).

Unforeseeable demand shocks from *within* the national economy will cause more trouble with a float than with fixed rates. To repeat the kind of reasoning used in Chapter 21, imagine a sudden depression in domestic demand. Under fixed exchange rates, it would cost us income and jobs to some extent. Its effects on the balance of payments would not worsen the domestic depression, and such effects might actually help offset it, if exchange rates are kept fixed. How? The depression would tend to improve our balance of payments because the reduced demand would cut our imports.[5] Gaining extra reserves from abroad might allow our banking system to expand the domestic money supply (in the case *without sterilization*, to use the terminology found in Chapter 21), helping to offset the depression. Even if it does

---

[5] As noted in Chapter 21, the drop in domestic demand would also affect the balance of payments through its effects on our interest rate. If demand was dropping because of a cut in the money supply, our interest rate would tend to rise, attracting capital and further improving the balance of payments in the short run, until it comes time to repay the borrowed capital with interest. If demand was dropping because of an independent cut in spending demand (e.g., a cut in government spending), then the opposite interest-rate effects would ensue. Here, as in Chapter 21, it is assumed that the balance-of-payments effects related to interest rates net out to something smaller than the simpler effect running from our aggregate demand through our demand for imports to the balance of payments. For this reason, the text here omits the interest-rate effect.

not, the depression is not magnified under fixed exchange rates. With floating rates, by contrast, the depression would become magnified through effects related to the exchange rate. Its tendency to improve the balance of payments would cause the value of our currency to rise. This rise in currency will make our goods and services look more expensive to anyone who might buy here or in other countries. We therefore lose even more business and more jobs, at least until the prices of home and foreign products return to the previous purchasing-power parity (as discussed in Chapter 15). Result: the depression is worse with floating rates. Score one for fixed rates.

On the other hand, if our economy is buffeted mainly by *foreign-trade* shocks, the contrast is reversed. Suppose that demand shifts away from our cars toward foreign cars, depressing the auto industry and, to some extent, the whole economy. With fixed exchange rates, this might be all. Or the depression could be made even worse: losing export business will worsen the balance of payments and cost us reserves; this could lower our money supply (if we don't sterilize the payments deficit), adding to the depression. With floating rates, though, the depression is offset to a large extent. The loss of export earnings would cause our currency to depreciate relative to other currencies. The depreciation, in turn, would make our products look cheaper relative to foreign products, shifting business toward our economy. Result: the depression is worse with fixed rates. Score one for the float.

The way in which the stability of our economy depends on where the shocks are coming from[6] leads to a pair of related arguments about how floating rates can be better.

The More Stable Is National Macroeconomic Policy, the Better Floating Rates Look

Domestic monetary and fiscal policies are prime sources of macroeconomic instability in most economies. Suppose that they were somehow made more stable and predictable. While other domestic shocks could still occur (e.g., housing booms and busts), the scales would now be tipped. Foreign trade shocks would loom larger as a source of instability for our economy. Since floating rates tend to provide better cushioning against foreign shocks than against domestic ones, they would look more advantageous when domestic shocks are less pronounced.

---

[6] The case of international capital-flow shocks is passed over here. As argued in Chapter 21, it gives an intermediate result: floating rates make such shocks more damaging than fixed rates with sterilization, but less damaging than fixed rates without sterilization.

The More We Insist on Autonomous National Policies, the More We Prefer Floating Rates

Whether or not our monetary and fiscal policies are really more stable, we may insist on running our own macroeconomy, for better or for worse.

A benign case is that of Switzerland since 1971: The Swiss, with relatively stable policies, have chosen to let the Swiss franc float up in value. The Swiss have viewed the float as a way of resisting the faster price inflation in the world around them. While others inflate their money supplies and prices, the Swiss have chosen the foreign-exchange institution that makes it easiest for them to avoid accelerating the growth of their own money supply. Had they chosen fixed exchange rates, while trying to hold down the growth of their money supply, they would have been forced to run balance-of-payments surpluses. These would have expanded their money supply, against the wishes of Swiss monetary officials. Letting the Swiss franc float gave them a way to reduce the inflow of money: the rise in the price of the franc made Swiss products look relatively expensive, cutting the payments surpluses, the inflow of money into Switzerland, and Swiss inflation.

Even in countries where policy is notoriously out of control, politics often dictates such autonomy. Being in control of one's own national economy is a goal in itself, even if it means subjecting the economy to home-grown instability.

The autonomy argument is perhaps the fundamental basis for the widespread use of floating exchange rates in a world that has been subject to great international shocks. In the last analysis, central banks and governments have been unwilling to sacrifice policy sovereignty to the vagaries of world demand and supply. As long as nations insist on national rather than international control over their money supplies and government budgets, they are likely to let exchange rates float.

The choice between truly fixed exchange rates and any kind of flexibility, then, depends on the factors just listed. Are truly fixed exchange rates better? There is no single answer. Instead, we have distilled a short list of factors that must be crucial in each nation's separate judgment of this issue. First, we have two arguments in favor of truly fixed rates—the fear of destabilizing speculation under flexible rates and the "price discipline" argument—that suggest possible benefits for the world as a whole. Then we have arguments saying that flexible rates might be better for certain kinds of nations—those whose domestic policies are very stable and those who insist on policy autonomy. The latter arguments, even though they offer gains only to the individual nations, may apply so strongly to those nations as to overrule the case for fixed rates. The result: truly fixed rates fit some countries better than others, and the choice depends on the factors listed above.

MANAGED FLOAT VERSUS PURE FLOAT

If a nation's economic policy makers insist on their policy autonomy, should they extend it further and manage the exchange rate itself by buying and selling foreign exchange? The idea of a managed float, in which movements in the exchange rate are smoothed out by official formula or official discretion, has gained favor since the onset of widespread floating, as we have seen in Chapter 17. Looking back over the conclusions of the previous chapters, what merits can we find in the idea of managing the float instead of leaving the exchange rate entirely to an unregulated market?

The Theoretical Case for Managing the Float

Even if a country has reasons to let exchange rates change, we can think of a theoretical reason for having the central bank manipulate the exchange rate by buying and selling foreign currency. As long as the central bank is letting the exchange rate follow its long-run equilibrium trend, why shouldn't the central bank buy and sell foreign exchange in such a way as to keep the rate right on that smooth long-run trend? Wouldn't that make the drift of the exchange rate smoother and more predictable? This is a familiar argument. It was applied back in Chapter 17 (Figure 17.1) and Appendix G. In those sections it was used as a theoretical argument for eliminating any movements in a trendless, fixed, exchange rate. Here, it can be reapplied as a case for removing movements around an upward or downward smooth trend. As a theory, it is appealing. Why not smooth out needless oscillations around a steady trend, making exchange rates more predictable and encouraging foreign trade?

Problems in Practice

Yet according to Chapters 17 and 18, there are reasons to question whether official intervention into foreign-exchange markets could smooth out oscillations effectively in practice.

First, it is not evident that the central bank has a clearer view of the long-run trend in an exchange rate than the private marketplace it is trying to outguess. If private speculators with billions at stake can be just as well informed about likely exchange-rate trends as monetary officials, why involve officials' talents in a task that is already taken care of as well as possible in the regular marketplace?

Second, both theory and experience suggest that officials may be *worse* than private speculators at making exchange-rate movements conform to long-run sustainable trends. As argued in Chapter 18, if officials guess wrong about the sustainable trend in an exchange rate, they could first cause the rate to depart from the long-run rate (by trying to smooth out the wrong trend) and then cause a speculative stampede against them. Whenever it begins to become clear that officials have guessed incorrectly about the sustainable trend, private speculators are given the ''one-way gamble'' described in Chapter 18: they cannot lose much money by betting that the officially supported exchange rate is wrong, and they could gain greatly if they force the officials to give up and let the rate readjust itself suddenly. The pursuit of such a one-way gamble gathers momentum and becomes self-fulfilling, forcing the officials to give up on the exchange-rate trend they had been trying to maintain. As shown in Chapter 18, the actual track record of officially managed floats has been poor since 1971. Officials have lost billions in foreign-exchange markets by betting less accurately than private investors about exchange-rate trends. Just letting the rates float would have avoided such losses and, by implication, some destabilizing behavior on the part of the officials themselves.

So far, having officials manage floating exchange rates has worked out worse than a pure float, contrary to some theories.

WHO FLOATS AND WHO DOESN'T?

With so many partial lessons at hand, it is natural to wonder whether actual policies toward exchange rates fit the international patterns the lessons imply. Looking at recent policies, do we find flexible exchange rates more popular among the kinds of nations for which theory most recommends flexibility? The answer is a qualified yes. Different countries' exchange-rate policies do differ in ways that make theoretical sense.

Figure 22.5 reveals some world patterns in exchange-rate policies as of early 1990.[7]

One pattern is that *floating exchange rates are more widespread among high-income market economies than in the Third World.* The United States, Canada, Japan, and Western Europe other than Scandinavia now have their exchange rates unpegged (aside from the European Monetary System, on which more below). Accordingly, statistical evidence from the 1970s has shown that exchange-rate flexibility varies directly with national income per capita (Holden, Holden, and Suss, 1979).

Why do so many Third World countries, especially in Africa or the Caribbean, peg their currencies to another individual currency, such as the dollar

---

[7] Bear in mind that the patterns have changed before, and will probably change in the future. Chapter 17's history of exchange-rate policies showed that the vast majority of countries having floating rates today held them fixed before 1971. In addition, some countries have switched regimes since 1971. Mexico, for example, kept its rate pegged to the U.S. dollar for over a generation, devalued in 1976, pegged to the dollar again, and began to float only in the crisis of 1982.

FIGURE 22.5 Types of Exchange-Rate Arrangements on March 31, 1990[1]

Currency Pegged to					Flexibility Limited in Terms of a Single Currency or Group of Currencies		More Flexible		
U.S. Dollar	French Franc	Other Currency	SDR	Other Composite[2]	Single Currency[3]	Cooperative Arrangements[4]	Adjusted According to a Set of Indicators	Other Managed Floating	Independently Floating
Afghanistan	Benin	Bhutan (Indian Rupee)	Burundi	Algeria	Bahrain	Belgium	Chile	China, P.R.	Argentina
Angola	Burkina Faso		Iran, I. R. of	Austria	Qatar	Denmark	Colombia	Costa Rica	Australia
Antigua and Barbuda	Cameroon	Kiribati (Australian Dollar)	Libya	Bangladesh	Saudi Arabia	France	Madagascar	Dominican Rep.	Bolivia
Bahamas, The	C. African Rep.		Myanmar	Botswana	United Arab Emirates	Germany	Portugal	Ecuador	Brazil
Barbados	Chad	Lesotho (South African Rand)	Rwanda	Cape Verde		Ireland		Egypt	Canada
Belize	Comoros		Seychelles	Cyprus		Italy		El Salvador	Gambia, The
Djibouti	Congo	Swaziland (South African Rand)	Zambia	Fiji		Luxembourg		Greece	Ghana
Dominica	Côte d'Ivoire			Finland		Netherlands		Guinea	Guatemala
Ethiopia	Equatorial Guinea	Tonga (Australian Dollar)		Hungary		Spain		Guinea-Bissau	Japan
Grenada	Gabon			Iceland				Honduras	Lebanon
Guyana	Mali			Israel				India	Maldives
Haiti	Niger			Jordan				Indonesia	New Zealand
Iraq	Senegal			Kenya				Korea	Nigeria
Jamaica	Togo			Kuwait				Lao P.D. Rep	Paraguay
Liberia				Malawi				Mauritania	Philippines
Nicaragua				Malaysia				Mexico	South Africa
Oman				Malta				Morocco	Switzerland
Panama				Mauritius				Pakistan	United Kingdom
Peru				Mozambique				Singapore	United States
St. Kitts and Nevis				Nepal				Sri Lanka	Uruguay
				Norway					

St. Lucia
St. Vincent
Sierra Leone
Sudan
Suriname

Syrian Arab Rep.
Trinidad and
  Tobago
Yemen Arab Rep.
Yemen, P.D. Rep.

Papua New
  Guinea
Poland
Romania
Sao Tome and
  Principe
Solomon Islands
Somalia
Sweden
Tanzania
Thailand
Uganda
Vanuatu
Western Samoa
Zimbabwe

Tunisia
Turkey
Viet Nam
Yugoslavia

Venezuela
Zaire

Number of nations in each group, March 31, 1990

30   14   5   7   34   4   9   4   23   22

Number of nations in each group, December 31, 1982

38   13   5   15   23   10   8   5   20   9

[1] Excluding the currency of Democratic Kampuchea, for which no current information is available. For members with dual or multiple exchange markets, the arrangement shown is that in the major market.
[2] Comprises currencies which are pegged to various "baskets" of currencies of the members' own choice, as distinct from the SDR basket.
[3] Exchange rates of all currencies have shown limited flexibility in terms of the U.S. dollar.
[4] Refers to the cooperative arrangement maintained under the European Monetary System.
[5] Includes exchange arrangements under which the exchange rate is adjusted at relatively frequent intervals, on the basis of indicators determined by the respective member countries.

Source: "International Monetary Fund," *International Financial Statistics*, June 1990.

or the French franc, instead of just floating? Some, as former colonies, retain currency ties to the previously colonizing country. Others find more tangible economic advantages in a pegged rate. Lacking established forward exchange markets, they must count on a firm bond to a major currency to ensure against exchange risk in trade between their countries.

Perhaps more important, the frequent pegging of Third World currencies may relate to a special relevance of the *price discipline* and destabilizing-speculation arguments. Inflationary policies are a clearer and more present danger in the Third World. Therefore, speculators seem especially quick, in Third World countries, to doubt the credibility of official commitments to keep prices stable. To prevent outbursts of destabilizing inflationary expectations, officials need a policy that credibly forces them to restrain inflation. Pegging the exchange rate to a major currency is thought to provide such desired coercion. Perhaps this is one motivation for the widespread use of pegged rates in small Third World countries.

In support of this price-discipline interpretation of fixed exchange rates in the Third World, notice that those few Third World countries who engage in independent floating (see the far right column of Figure 22.5) are countries who have failed to prevent hyperinflation of prices. Official resolve to prevent inflation is so questionable in most developing countries that we have a second pattern: *Third World countries divide sharply into two groups: a hyperinflating minority and a majority that use the fixed exchange rate as a tool of self-discipline.* To use an analogy, perhaps many Third World countries suspected of lacking price discipline adopt fixed rates much as some narcotics users seek out the coercion that will force them to quit. Regarding this analogy, Argentina and other hyperinflating countries on floating rates are cases where coercion was abandoned because they could not develop the political will to break the habit.

A third pattern relates to the trend in exchange-rate institutions over time: for whatever reason, *the global trend is still toward floating rates and away from fixed rates.* As the lower panel in Figure 22.5 shows, the number of currencies pegged to the U.S. dollar or to the Special Drawing Right declined across the 1980s. While one might expect some countries to peg their currencies to the yen, as part of the rising financial dominance of Japan, that had not happened as of 1990.

THE EUROPEAN MONETARY SYSTEM (EMS): A NEW TREND?

The European Community (EC) has set out to counter the gradual drift toward floating exchange rates. As part of their increasing unification, the countries of the EC agreed in March 1979 to set up a European Monetary System **(EMS),** within which exchange rates would be kept nearly fixed. At the same time, they called for a new currency and called for the eventual creation of a new European central bank. The currency is the European

FIGURE 22.6   Selected Exchange Rates within the European Monetary System, 1977–1989 (monthly)

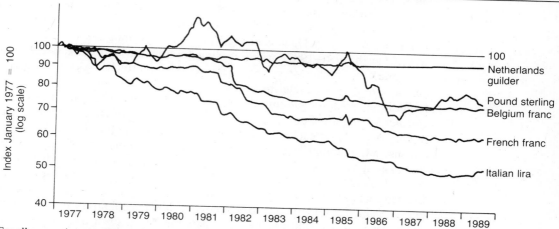

For all currencies, the German mark price of that currency (e.g., DM/£)
So, for any currency: ↑ = It rises in value (appreciates relative to the DM)
                       ↓ = It declines in value (depreciates).

Currency Unit or **ECU** (an acronym chosen in memory of the écu, an ancient French silver coin), which has a value tied to the average value of the EC national currencies. The central bank is the European Monetary Cooperation Fund (EMCF), a limited European analogue of the International Monetary Fund. The achievements of the new institutions are limited, but real.

Commitment to truly fixed exchange rates has been limited. The EMS agreements allowed EC member currencies to deviate 2.5 percent from the initial declared par values. Italy, more prone to inflation, was allowed to depreciate the lira by as much as 6 percent from the initial par. Meanwhile, Britain, Greece, and Portugal have refused to keep their currencies in line with other EC currencies (as noted in Figure 22.5). As a result, exchange rates between the national currencies of the EC have changed considerably. Figure 22.6 highlights this by plotting monthly exchange rates in terms of the deutsche mark (DM) since 1977. The DM/lira exchange rate fell almost 50 percent in the first decade of the EMS. The French and Belgian francs also drifted downward. Only the Dutch guilder kept close to its original value in terms of deutsche marks. The smoothness of the trends in the lira, franc, and guilder rates suggests some success in ironing out deviations from trend. Britain's refusal to go along with currency unification, however, is very evident in the behavior of the DM/pound exchange rate. A sceptic could say that the EMS is just a façade, and that there is no evidence that countries are willing to give up their monetary sovereignty to keep exchange rates fixed.

Yet, there are signs that member nations are becoming more willing to give up national monetary sovereignty (control of their own money supplies and price levels) to keep exchange rates fixed within the EC. The first sign came in 1981–1982, when President Mitterand of France decided to scale back his plans for government spending partly in order to keep up the value of the franc in terms of the deutsche mark and other EC currencies. In addition, some of the unification spirit of the Single European Act (see Chapter 9) and the German monetary union may well give new momentum to the EMS. Some experts have suggested that the high mobility of capital between EC countries after 1992 will make national monetary policy so weak that central bankers might as well acquiesce in fixing the exchange rates. This is not clear. Perfect capital mobility frustrates monetary policy under fixed exchange rates (Chapter 20), but not necessarily under floating exchange rates (Chapter 21). It remains to be seen how much unemployment or inflation EC governments would accept in the name of fixing exchange rates.

SUMMARY

The world has gradually moved from a pure commodity standard, the gold standard, to a complex system in which world paper money is created, rented, and held in large international markets. Figure 22.7 reviews some key features of the four characteristic international reserve assets. As can be seen, they differ both in their effects on the rate of world money-supply growth and in their distribution of the gains from seigniorage, or the gains from being the creator of new money units.

Before World War I, the gold standard was essentially workable and involved less inflation than its 20th-century paper-money descendants. It contained automatic mechanisms for eliminating net flows of gold between countries, though these mechanisms were actually more automatic than originally imagined by David Hume in his sketch of the price-specie-flow mechanism.

Yet, a successful gold standard tends to replace itself with paper standards. Success means that people come to believe that paper currencies are as good as the gold they are tied to, but this removes the incentive to hold gold itself, a more expensive and less remunerative way of storing wealth. Accordingly, paper reserves have risen faster than gold reserves from 1880 (or earlier) to the end of the era of fixed gold prices around 1970.

On its own, gold has shown a peculiar price history. It is not hard to explain why its real price has been more or less constant over periods of centuries or longer. Yet its short-run price can jump or crash at rates few investors can predict, apparently because of waves of fear that gold is the

FIGURE 22.7   Some Characteristics of Different World Moneys

Type of International Money Asset	If This Is the Main International Money Asset, World Money Supply Would Grow According to . . .	Who Gets the Resource Gains ("seigniorage") by Creating This International Money Asset?
Gold	Gold mining supply (unpredictable, and probably too slow).	Gold miners (South Africa, Soviet Union, etc.) get slight net gains.
Key currencies	Central-bank monetary policy (CBMP) and reserve country's balance of payments.	Banking systems of key-currency countries.
Eurocurrencies	Ditto, but with less central bank control.	Ditto, with extra gains for private international banks.
IMF special drawing rights (SDRs)	CBMP plus IMF decisions.	Ditto, plus those governments given the new drawing rights.

only haven in the event of total economic collapse or confiscation of private wealth.

The rise of key-currency reserves has brought seigniorage gains to the key-currency countries. To limit this seigniorage problem and to control the growth of reserves through an international body, the International Monetary Fund (IMF) was formed and given financial mechanisms for meting out reserves to countries in temporary need. Yet such international reserves remain a small share of world reserves today and are far less relevant than innovations in private international money markets.

The rise of Eurocurrencies has liberated international investors from direct national controls and some taxes, for better or for worse. **Eurocurrencies** are moneylike deposits in banks whose country of residence is not the country of the currency deposited. There has been considerable debate over the impact of Eurocurrency markets on the world money supply and inflation. The prevailing view is that the effect is not large, even though some expansion of world money supply must be implicit in any institution that so lubricates the wheels of short-term finance.

For a single nation, the following are the main advantages and disadvantages of an official commitment to permanently fixed exchange rates:

1. Destabilizing speculation is unlikely if officials are credibly committed to keeping rates fixed.

2. Fixed rates impose more "price discipline," giving the world as a whole less inflation (and perhaps less income and employment).
3. The net national gain or loss from pegging exchange rates depends on the types of shocks that dominate. Here again, as in Chapter 21, fixed rates look better if the dominant shocks come from domestic demand shifts, while flexible rates look better if they come from shifts in export demand.
4. As a corollary of 3 above, a country whose monetary and fiscal policies are stable and predictable is one for which flexible exchange rates look better. Removing policy instability as a source of domestic instability means that shocks will be more confined to the foreign-trade sector, and flexible exchange rates provide some insulation against such shocks.
5. Countries insisting on pursuing their own autonomous monetary and fiscal policies implicitly *prefer* to have their shocks come from within their own economies. They wish to be insulated against foreign shocks, while dealing independently with any instability within their economies. As a corollary of 3 above, such countries are better candidates for flexible rates.

The managed float, contrary to what many would expect, tends to look inferior to a pure float. It seems reasonable for officials to smooth out deviations around the long-run trend in an exchange rate by buying and selling foreign exchange at different times. Theory can second the idea: our analysis in Chapter 17 and Appendix G showed how official stabilization of exchange rates around the long-run trend can bring welfare gains. But there are problems with the idea in practice. It is not evident that officials have a better idea than the private market about where exchange rates are headed in the long run. In fact, there is evidence that their intervention in foreign exchange markets has been *destabilizing* since the early 1970s, causing them to lose some taxpayers' money and make exchange rates less stable than they would have been under a pure float.

There are rough international patterns in exchange-rate policies. Among market-oriented economies, those with higher incomes per capita use floating rates more than lower income countries, many of whom peg their currencies to the dollar or franc. This may be because lower income countries have no other way to ensure traders against exchange-rate risk and need to peg to a leading currency to convince speculators they will check inflation. Exceptions that seem to confirm the importance of this price-discipline argument in the Third World are countries whose politics have bred rapid inflation. Another pattern, not yet explained, is that the trend away from pegged rates toward floating rates continued across the 1980s, despite the spirited attempt of the European Community to build fixed exchange rates into the emerging European Monetary System.

No one policy is best for all countries.

SUGGESTED READINGS

On international monetary arrangements in general, see- the sources cited in Chapter 17 and in Ronald I. McKinnon [1979, Chapters 1, 2, 8–11 and Charles P. Kindleberger (1981)].

On Eurocurrencies, two quick readable guides are Milton Friedman (1971) and John R. Karlik (1977, also excerpted in Baldwin and Richardson, 1981). For more depth, see Niehans and Hewson (1976), McKinnon (1979, Chapter 9), and Grubel (1981, Chapter 15). On the extension of the same practices into Asia, see Kenneth Bernauer (1983).

For a fair overview of economists' judgments on exchange-rate policy, but with uneven quality of reasoning, see G. M. Meier (1982). The international pattern of actual exchange-rate policies in the 1970s is estimated statistically by Holden, Holden, and Suss (1979). For the related theoretical literature on who *should* float and who shouldn't, called the "optimal currency area" literature among economists, see McKinnon (1963) and Tower and Willett (1976). Canzoneri and Rogers (1990) extend the optimal currency area literature by suggesting an inflation tax hypothesis and applying it to the European Monetary System.

QUESTIONS FOR REVIEW

1. Return to the sketch of Hume's price-specie-flow mechanism for the surplus country. Would you conclude from Hume's model that price trends have to be the same in all countries (as the purchasing-power-parity hypothesis would predict for a fixed-exchange-rate system)? Explore this question under two different assumptions: (*a*) the initial surplus resulted from a drop in this country's aggregate demand, initially lowering its prices relative to those of the rest of the world; and (*b*) the initial surplus resulted because international demand shifted toward this country's goods and away from foreign goods, initially raising prices here and lowering them abroad.

2. Which of the following is a Eurocurrency claim?

a. A U.S.-dollar deposit by a London firm in a New York bank.

b. A sterling deposit by a London firm in a New York bank.

c. A U.S.-dollar deposit by a London firm in a London Bank.

d. A U.S.-dollar deposit by a New York firm in a London Bank.

e. A Canadian-dollar deposit by a London firm in a Toronto Bank.

f. A Swiss-franc deposit by a German firm in a Swiss bank.

(Answer: only *b, c,* and *d* are Eurocurrency deposits.)

3. Make sure you can describe both Eurocurrencies and the European Monetary System (EMS) and distinguish them from each other.

4. Reviewing the arguments in this chapter, put together a description of the kind of country that would be an excellent candidate for pegging its exchange rate to another currency.

5. Similarly, put together a profile of a hypothetical country that would be an excellent candidate for a pure floating rate regime.

6. Describe plausible conditions that would make a managed float work better than either a pure float or truly fixed exchange rates. (It isn't easy, but it is possible.)

PART

V

Factor Movements

CHAPTER
23

▼

The International Movement of Labor

•

THE HOT POTATO

Of all the flows that take place between nations, none is more sensitive than the flow of humans. The migrants themselves take great risks, and their arrival in the new country arouses deep fears in others, even in persons who have migrated themselves.

For the migrants themselves, the dangers are great but the average gain is high. A migrant risks disease or victimization by others, and may fail to find a better income in the country of destination. Many migrants return home unsuccessful and disillusioned. Yet, on the average, they experience great gains, as we might expect from so risky an activity. In some cases political and physical freedom itself is a large gain, as in the case of refugees from repressive regimes. In other cases, the economic gains stand out. Doctors, engineers, and other highly trained personnel from lower income countries such as India and Pakistan have multiplied their incomes severalfold by migrating to North America, Australasia, Britain, and the Persian Gulf. Mexican craftsmen and campesinos earn enough in Texas or California to retire early (if they wish) in comfortable Mexican homes and to support their children generously, Turkish ''guestworkers'' in West Germany also assure themselves a very comfortable living and a quantum jump up the income ranks. If this were not so, they would not choose to migrate, either temporarily or permanently.

Yet politicians worth their salt know that the migration issue is a hot potato they should avoid picking up. To get reelected, they try to speak on both sides of the issue and to direct more attention to other issues (unless they can ride the waves of hatred in a particularly anti-immigrant district). The landmark passage of the U.S. Immigration Reform and Control Act in 1986 is one of those exceptions that helps prove the rule. That act (earlier known as the Simpson-Mazzoli bill) had been in and out of Congress for more than a decade before it finally passed as a complicated compromise. Its long history testifies to the reluctance of politicians to confront the immigration issue. Why the reluctance?

Part of the answer lies in the objective costs to some people of having other people migrate. In the sending countries, having some people emigrate can wound national pride and bring economic losses to some who remain behind. Thus promoting emigration is not politically popular, even in countries like Mexico where the overall economic gains are unmistakable. In the receiving countries, ethnic prejudice, general xenophobia, and the direct economic stake of subgroups who fear competition from immigrants keep the issue especially sensitive. Wherever the concentration of immigrants swells suddenly, violent backlash threatens. Lightfooted politicians know better than to campaign on a slogan of free migration.

Behind these pressures lies the other explanation of why migration is such a hot potato: in any political arena, the migrating minority is "them," not "us." To migrate or request help in migrating is to lose voting rights. In a sending country, potential emigrants who speak up on behalf of their right to leave are signaling that they do not plan to be a part of that country's political future. The majority is unlikely to respond with best wishes and full freedom, especially if the issue of national pride surfaces. In the receiving country, the interests of possible future immigrants command few or no votes. Only lobbying by employers and church groups represents their cause. The gains they would make by migrating, as opposed to their future employers' gains, have almost no vote.

How do all these opposing forces balance out? What are the net economic gains to nations and the world, and how do they stack up against the less-economic side effects of migration?

HOW MIGRATION AFFECTS LABOR MARKETS

Let us tackle these complex issues in two stages. First, we squeeze as much as we can out of a thrice-squeezed orange, the familiar static welfare analysis already used extensively in Parts I and II. In this stage, repetition is a positive advantage, showing the power of the familiar framework in another setting. The second stage introduces social and economic dimensions of migration that do not lend themselves well to the usual analysis. Exploring the public-finance effects and social externalities of migration calls for more qualitative, less formalized analysis.

We begin with the standard effects of the migration on labor markets in the two countries. To simplify the analysis, we shall aggregate the whole world into two stylized countries, a low-income "South" and a high-income "North." Let us start with a situation in which no migration is allowed, as at the Points *A* in the two sides of Figure 23.1. In this initial situation

FIGURE 23.1 Labor-Market Effects of Migration

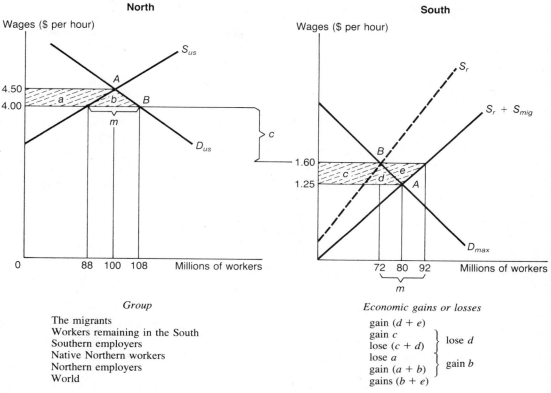

Group	Economic gains or losses	
The migrants	gain (*d* + *e*)	
Workers remaining in the South	gain *c*	lose *d*
Southern employers	lose (*c* + *d*)	
Native Northern workers	lose *a*	
Northern employers	gain (*a* + *b*)	gain *b*
World	gains (*b* + *e*)	

Note m = number of migrants = 20 million.

c = annuitized cost of migrating, both economic and psychological (being uprooted, etc.), which cancels $2.40 per hr. of extra pay.

(If part or all of the migration cost *c* were due to official restrictions on migration and not to the true economic and psychological costs of moving, then part or all of the value *c* × *m* should be added to the world gains from the migration that does occur.)

(By holding the labor demand curves fixed, we gloss over the slight shifts in them that would result from the migrants' own spending.)

Northern workers earn $4.50 an hour and Southern workers of comparable skill earn $1.25 an hour. (We can realistically ignore the theoretical possibility of factor-price equalization through trade alone, discussed in Chapter 4.)

If all official barriers to migration are removed, Southern workers can go north and compete for Northern jobs. If moving were costless and painless, they would do so in large numbers, until they had bid the Northern wage rate down, and the Southern wage rate up, enough to equate the two.

Yet moving is costly to the migrants, in economic and psychological terms. Migrants feel uprooted from friends and relatives. They feel uncertain about many dimensions of life in a strange country. They may have to endure hostility from others in their new country. All these things matter, so much so that we should imagine that wide wage rate gaps would persist even with complete legal freedom to move. Thus only a lesser number of persons, 20 million of them in Figure 23.1, find the wage gains from moving high enough to compensate them for the migration costs, here valued at $2.40 per hour of work in the North. The inflow of migrant labor thus bids the Northern wage rate down only to $4.00 at Point B, and the outflow of the same workers only raises Southern wage rates up to $1.60. The new equilibrium, at Points B, finds the number wanting to migrate just equal to the demand for extra labor in the North at $4.00 an hour.

Those who decide to migrate earn $4.00 an hour in the North, but it is worth only as much as $1.60 in the South because of the costs and drawbacks of working in the North. To measure their net gain, one should then take the area above the migrants' labor supply curve between the old and new wage rates $1.25 and $1.60, or areas d and e.[1]

It is not hard to identify the other groups of net gainers and losers in the two regions. Workers remaining in the South, whose labor supply curve is S_r, gain because the reduction in competition for jobs raises their wage rates from $1.25 to $1.60. We can quantify their gains with a standard producer-surplus measure, area c, in the same way used to quantify the gains to protected producers in Parts I and II above. Their employers lose profits by having to offer higher wage rates. The Southern employers' loss is area $(c + d)$. Employers in the North gain, of course, from the extra supply of labor. Having the Northern wage rate bid down from $4.50 to $4.00 brings them area $(a + b)$ in extra profits. Workers already in the North lose area a by having their wage rate bid down. (It is partly for this reason that Cesar Chavez of the United Farm Workers has spoken out against letting in large numbers of new Mexican farm workers.) So here, as in the analysis of trade barriers in Part II, some groups absolutely gain and others absolutely lose from the new international freedom.

The analysis in Figure 23.1 shows some clear and perhaps unexpected effects on the welfare of entire nations of nonmigrants. Let us turn first to the effects on the North, here defined so as to exclude the migrants even after they have arrived. As a nation these Northern "natives" unambiguously gain in standard economic terms: the gain to employers (and the general public buying their products) clearly outweighs the loss to workers: area

---

[1] The migrants' labor supply curve S_{mig} can be derived by subtracting the curve S_r from the combined curve $S_r + S_{mig}$. Note that their welfare gain would not equal the full product of ($1.60 - $1.25) times the 20 million unless their labor supply curve (S_{mig}) were perfectly vertical, meaning that the amount of time they would devote to work is independent of the wage rate. (Remember that their supply curve can be interpreted as a curve showing the marginal cost of their time.)

$(a + b)$ cannot be less than area a alone. The case for restricting immigration cannot lie in any net national economic loss, unless we can introduce large negative effects not yet shown in Figure 23.1. The sending country, defined as those who remain in the South after the migrants' departure, clearly loses: the employers' losses of $(c + d)$ cannot be less than workers' gain of c alone. So far it looks as though receiving countries and the migrants gain, while sending countries lose. The world as a whole gains, of course, because freedom to migrate sends people toward countries where they will make a greater net contribution to world production.

AVERAGE-INCOME PARADOXES OF MIGRATION

The gains for receiving countries and losses for sending countries pose what might be called average-income paradoxes. That is, they clash with some intuitions we might have about the effects of migration on that crude standard measure of welfare, national income per capita or "average income." Intuition might lead us to ask these two questions:

a. If the immigrants have a lower income than others in the new country, won't their arrival lower average income in this country? How can this be reconciled with the receiving-country gains shown in Figure 23.1?

b. If the same migrants had lower-than-average income in the sending country, won't their departure raise average income in that country? How can this be reconciled with the sending-country losses shown in Figure 23.1?

What is here imagined about average incomes is likely to be true—yet there is no contradiction. The logical consistency of the usual results is shown with a numerical example in Figure 23.2, an example based on the 1983 population and income levels of the United States and Mexico. Each country is divided into the same three groups featured in our discussion of the welfare effects in Figure 23.1: the migrants themselves, competing permanent-resident workers whose job markets the migrants affect, and a group consisting of employers and others benefiting from extra labor supply and population.

The example in Figure 23.2 starts from a realistic premise about the position of typical migrants: their income would be closer to the average in the sending country than in the receiving country. Numerous studies have found that international migrants are typically average or almost average in their earning power in the home country before they emigrate. They are usually not from the ranks of the poorest. The lowest income groups in the low-income countries lack the hope, the money, and the information to migrate internationally in large numbers. The international migrants tend to be venturesome individuals from more middling backgrounds. To underline

FIGURE 23.2 A Realistic Example of an Average-Income Paradox from Migration

Group	United States before Migration			Mexico before Migration		
	No. of Persons of Working Age (million)	Average Income	Total Income ($ million)	No. of Persons of Working Age (million)	Average Income	Total Income ($ million)
Competing permanent-resident workers	20 ×	8,000 =	160,000	19 ×	2,000 ×	38,000 =
Potential emigrants	— ×	— =	—	2 ×	2,000 =	4,000
Employers and others	137 ×	22,967 =	3,146,420	19 ×	6,686 =	127,040
Nation as a whole	157 ×	21,060 =	3,306,420	40 ×	4,226 =	169,040
	After Migration			After Migration		
Competing permanent-resident workers	19 ×	7,000 =	133,000	20 ×	2,200 =	44,000
Migrants*	2 ×	7,000 =	14,000	— ×	— =	—
Employers and others	138 ×	23,130 =	3,192,000	18 ×	6,558 =	118,040
Nation as a whole	159 ×	21,900 =	3,339,000	38 ×	4,264 =	162,040
Net change	+2	−60	+32,580	−2	+38	−5,000

*The costs of migration, psychological and other, have *not* been subtracted here, as they should be for judgments of overall well-being. This example also leaves the migrants' incomes in their pockets, not remitted to relatives and friends back in Mexico. The remittances are here viewed as income for the donor and not the recipient, taking account of the donor's satisfaction from being able to send the remittances but not of the value of remittances to the recipients.

Note the **paradox:** average income drops by $60 in the United States and rises by $38 in Mexico—yet total income rises for the United States and the world as a whole, while declining for Mexico! The key: the migrants are counted as Mexicans before they move but as residents of the United States after they move.

our paradoxes, however, let's assume the Mexican migrants in this example have initially below-average incomes in Mexico.

If 2 million adults of working age were to migrate from Mexico to the United States, the movement of their labor supply would probably have effects like those shown in Figure 23.2. The "net change" row at the bottom shows two average income paradoxes: the United States loses average income yet gains total income, whereas Mexico gains in average income yet loses total income. There's more: within the United States, there is a net gain for the 157 million permanent residents as well as for the migrants, but the U.S. average income declines; within Mexico there is a net income loss for all permanent residents, but Mexico's average income rises!

The key to all the paradoxes is that the migrants and their incomes are counted in the calculation of Mexico's average income before they migrate but counted in the calculation of U.S. average income afterwards. Let's look first at the receiving country, the United States. Migration had all the effects on separate Northern groups that we discussed in connection with Figure 23.1. Competing permanent-resident workers, especially unskilled workers, tend to lose income because of extra competition from immigrants. Although some authors have optimistically asserted that there is no such income loss for native U.S. workers because the immigrants take only jobs the natives refused to take, the most balanced judgment is that there is indeed some net job competition. Employers, landowners, and others tend to gain income from the arrival of the immigrants—from their labor, and from their demand for housing and other products. If they did not gain, we would have a hard time explaining why so many employers in California, Texas, and Florida spend a lot of dollars on lobbying against laws to cut immigration. Furthermore, both Figure 23.1 and Figure 23.2 realistically imagine that the gain to native employers and others outweighs the gain to competing workers, so that U.S. natives as a whole receive a slight gain from the immigrants' arrival. The migrants receive greater percentage gains. The seeming drop in U.S. average income is a mirage caused by inconsistently redefining the working-age population of the United States as excluding the migrants before they arrive but including them after. If we carefully define the United States either with the migrants both before and after or without them both before and after, then we come to the correct conclusion: average income rises for either definition of the United States, the receiving country.

The paradox for the sending country can be unraveled in the same way. If we carefully define Mexico as excluding the migrants both before and after they leave, Mexico loses average income. If we take the broader consistent definition of Mexico, one including the migrants both before and after they leave, then Mexico, as thus defined, gains.[2]

---

[2] For another interesting, but less realistic, average-income paradox, suppose that the migrants have above-average incomes in the sending countries but move to higher incomes that are

PUBLIC-FINANCE EFFECTS

Thus far our analysis has ignored the effects of migrants on taxes and public spending. Figure 23.1 implicitly assumed that everybody breaks even on the public-finance side effects of migration, both on the average and at all the relevant margins. Yet this dimension of the migration issue is rightly controversial and deserves a fuller treatment.

There are many possible effects. Migrants don't have to pay taxes in their countries of origin, but they face new taxes at their destination. These include income taxes, sales taxes, property taxes (either directly or through rents), social security payments, and liability to military draft. Migrants also switch from one set of public goods to another. They benefit from the new nation's national defense, police protection, natural scenery, and public schools, while giving up the same services in the old country. They also switch from old to new rights to such transfer payments as unemployment insurance, social security payments, and ordinary welfare payments. How are all these possible effects likely to net out?

For the migrants themselves, it is not clear whether the net gain on public goods minus taxes rises or falls with the move. By changing countries they may forfeit some accumulated entitlements, such as public pensions and social insurance, without being entitled to the same in the new country. On the other hand, migrants generally drift toward higher income countries, and public goods and services as a whole may be a better bargain there. The net public-finance effect for the migrants themselves is not clear. (Its unknown positive or negative value is buried within c, the perceived non-market cost of working in the new country.)

In the Sending Country

For the sending country, the loss of future tax contributions (and military service) from the emigrants is likely to outweigh the relief from having to share public goods and services with them. Many public-expenditure items are true "public goods" in the welfare-economics sense of being equally enjoyable to each party regardless of how many enjoy them. Having some

---

nonetheless below average in the receiving country. In this case, the usual careless way of defining income per capita (including the migrants wherever they show up) yields this sort of paradox: the migration lowers income per capita in both countries—yet raises it for the world as a whole! (Yes, that's correct, and such cases have arisen.)

Demographers will recognize the average-income paradoxes as the sort of compositional-shift paradox that abounds in demography. Readers of Part I of this book can discover a similar paradox there. When we analyzed the effects of the opening of trade on factor use in a two-sector economy, in Chapter 4 and Appendix C, we found that opening trade lowered the land/labor ratio in both sectors, yet kept the overall land/labor ratio unchanged (by shifting resources toward the land-intensive industry). See the section on "A factor ratio paradox" in Chapter 4.

leave does not greatly raise the others' enjoyment of such public goods as national defense or flood-control levees. The likelihood of a net fiscal drain from emigration is raised by the life-cycle patterns of public goods and migration. People tend to migrate in early adulthood. This means that emigrants tend to be concentrated in the age group that has just received some public schooling at taxpayer expense, yet the migrants will not be around to pay taxes from their adult earnings.

The sending country, then, may very well suffer a net public-finance loss from having people migrate.[3] One possible policy response is to block their escape or their transfer of assets abroad.

Jagdish Bhagwati and other economists have proposed a more defensible and workable policy response to emigration: a tax on outward-bound persons roughly equal to the net tax contribution society has made to them through public schools and the like. Specifically, Bhagwati has proposed a "brain-drain" tax on highly skilled emigrants. To the extent that the tax compensates the sending country for its public goods-inputs, it is a reasonable proposal.

In judging the sending country's stake in the emigration issue, one must note the flows of voluntary remittances sent back to relatives and friends in the home country. These are often very large, as Italian and Mexican experiences have shown. In fact, a country (defined as including the back-home family and friends) might reap a handsome rate of return from letting people leave.[4] Yet the economist is still likely to see the merits of a brain-drain tax on the outflow of human capital, letting the prospective migrants decide whether the remaining gains to themselves and their back-home family and friends are large enough to outweigh this justified compensation for public schooling and the like.

In the Receiving Country

It is common knowledge that immigrants are a fiscal burden, swelling welfare rolls, using public schools, and raising police costs more than they pay

---

[3] We can think up hypothetical counterexamples in which the sending country gets all of its chronically unemployed, its welfare recipients, and its felons to leave, relieving itself of a net fiscal burden through emigration. But actual migrations almost never take such a form. As mentioned earlier, emigrants tend to be from the more energetic and productive middle-income ranks that probably would be net taxpayers.

[4] Do migrants' remittances back to their home country represent a loss to the country they have moved to? The first instinct might be to say yes, it's a drain on the new country's balance of payments. But one must reflect further on the meaning of the remittances and just who is "the country." Migrants' remittances are a voluntary gift on their part, and do not represent a loss to the migrants themselves, any more than voluntarily giving to a charity makes one worse off. One could say the migrants are buying psychic satisfaction with their remittances to family and friends in the home country. And if importing this psychic satisfaction from the old country is not a clear welfare loss to them, it is not a welfare loss to their new country, because the payment is being made only by the migrants from money they earned.

back in taxes. But this common knowledge is probably wrong, to judge from the best recent information. Immigrants probably pay more in taxes than their arrival takes from other taxpayers.

To see why, reconsider the arguments just made about the financial stake of the sending country, inverting them for the receiving country. The life-cycle effect reappears: immigrants tend to arrive with an age distribution tilted toward *young adults,* who are entering the taxpaying prime of life, having received some schooling at foreign expense. They face these taxes even if they are low-paid workers in fields and factories, in the form of sales and excise taxes, payroll taxes and social security deductions, and property taxes that make housing more expensive. Young adult immigrants are also not extraordinarily heavy claimants on social welfare programs. They do not have extraordinarily high unemployment,[5] and they will not draw old-age benefits for many years.

To be sure, one could choose to focus on some particular groups of immigrants who are likely to pose net financial burdens. Political refugees fleeing countries with very different languages and economies often take a few years' help at public (or philanthropic) expense before assimilating. Yet others, such as highly skilled personnel already speaking the new country's language, are likely to be heavy net taxpayers.

Oddly enough, illegal aliens, such as the numerous Mexican illegals in the United States, are also on the net taxpaying side of the ledger. As illegals, they have very little access to public goods and services, yet they still pay payroll taxes, sales taxes, and so forth. On balance, immigrants taken as a whole are likely to bring a slight net benefit to other residents through public finances. This net benefit reinforces the receiving country's net gain shown in Figure 23.1 above (area *b*).

In the long run, after a couple of generations, the net fiscal impact of immigrants fades away, as their age distribution and their other characteristics converge to those of the long-native population.

EXTERNAL COSTS AND BENEFITS

Other possible effects of migration elude both the labor-market analysis and our rough fiscal accounting. Migration may generate external costs and benefits outside of the private and public-fiscal marketplaces. Three kinds of possible externalities merit mention here:

1. *Knowledge benefits.* People carry knowledge with them, and much of that knowledge has economic value, be it tricks of the trade, food recipes,

---

[5] Indeed, it would have been odd if the same immigrants who are suspected of taking jobs away from native residents were also prone to claim above-average amounts of unemployment relief, as some also suspect. It is hard to take others' jobs away while being unemployed, and many immigrants do neither (by taking jobs that natives decline to fill).

artistic talent, farming practices, or advanced technology. American examples include Samuel Slater, Andrew Carnegie, Albert Einstein, and many virtuosi of classical music. Often only part of the economic benefits of this knowledge accrues to the migrant and those he sells his services to. Part often spills over to others, especially others in the same country. Migration may thus transfer external benefits of knowledge from the sending to the receiving country.

2. *Congestion costs.* Immigration, like any other source of population growth, may bring external costs associated with crowding—extra noise, conflict, and crime. If so, then this is a partial offset to the gains of the receiving country and the losses of the sending country. This effect is probably small, however, if the migration flow is gradual.

3. *Social friction.* Immigrants are often greeted with bigotry and harassment, often even from native groups that would benefit from the immigration. Although the most appropriate form of social response to this kind of cost is to work on changing the prevailing attitudes themselves, policy makers must also weigh these frictions in the balance when judging how much immigration and what kind of immigration to allow. Indeed, the importance of this point might be easy to underestimate. Arguments of purported economic costs of immigration are façades for deep-seated bigotry. And long-lasting restrictions on the freedom to migrate, such as American discrimination against Asian immigrants at the turn of the century, the sweeping restrictions during the U.S. red scares of the early 1920s, and Britain's revocation of many Commonwealth passport privileges since the 1960s, have been motivated largely by simple dislike for the immigrating nationalities. In a flawed world policy makers must be prepared to consider immigration restrictions as one way to avoid social scars.

GRADUALISM AND SELECTIVITY

Thus far, only the arguments about congestion and social friction seem to weigh against liberal immigration policies. The objectives of these two arguments can be reduced greatly by the expedient of gradualism, that is, forcing gross immigration to be a low enough share of population each year to allow a peaceful transition. Within this constraint, there is a strong economic case for welcoming immigrants.

There is at least indirect support for the idea that admitting immigrants only gradually would go far to removing social frictions. The United States experienced its worst surge of anti-immigrant feeling in the early 1920s, when the immigration rate was jumping back up to the all-time historical peak rate it had reached just before World War I. The immigration rate was higher then, just before and after World War I, than it is today, even if we add reasonable estimates of the number of unrecorded illegal aliens. Even though some of the historical reasons for the anti-immigrant sentiment of that time (e.g., the Bolshevik Revolution) transcend economics, the high rate of immigration itself must have contributed to the fears and resentments of those Americans whose families migrated earlier.

Most receiving countries have come to see the merits of being selective in the kinds of immigrants they let in. They tend to twist immigration codes toward welcoming the highly skilled brain-drain migrants while shutting out most of the unskilled, who are more prone to unemployment and ghetto-related frictions. Far from welcoming "the wretched refuse of your teeming shore," the Statue of Liberty holds her lamp aloft for physicians, engineers, and computer scientists. Canada, Britain, Australia, and other high-income countries also select in favor of skilled groups. This makes excellent sense from a national standpoint, just as exclusive high-income zoning shields rich suburbs. But encouraging the brain drain imposes obvious costs on other countries, and shutting out the unskilled keeps more of the world's labor force locked into less-productive economies.

SUMMARY

The welfare analysis of migration flows is able to identify the main stakes involved and to quantify some of them. The main winners and losers from migration are the ones intuition would suggest: the migrants, their new employers, and workers who stay in the sending country all gain; competing workers in the new country and employers in the old country lose. Yet, the net effects on nations, defined as excluding the migrants themselves, may clash with intuition. The receiving country is a net gainer, not only through standard labor-market effects but also through public-budget effects. The sending country loses on both fronts. A case can be made for a brain-drain tax that compensates the sending country for its public investments in the emigrants.

SUGGESTED READINGS

The U.S. immigration policy dilemma in the wake of the Immigration Reform and Control Act of 1986 is aptly summarized by Chiswick (1988).

An optimistic view of the benefits of allowing immigration is that of Julian Simon (1989).

Clark Reynolds and Robert McCleery (1985, 1988) have forecast the impact of the 1986 U.S. immigration restrictions on the incomes of difference groups up to the year 2000. They predict that the restrictions would hurt U.S. high-wage workers, Mexican low-wage workers, U.S. capitalists, the excluded migrants, and the whole as a whole, even though the restrictions would help U.S. low-wage workers, Mexican high-wage workers and Mexican capitalists.

QUESTIONS FOR REVIEW

1. For each of the following observed changes in wage rates and migration flows from the low-wage South to the high-wage North, describe one shift in conditions which, by itself, could have caused all those changes:

a. A drop in Northern wage rates, a rise in Southern wage rates, and a fresh migration from South to North.

b. A drop in wage rates in both South and North, and a fresh migration from South to North.

c. A rise in wage rates in both South and North, and a fresh migration from South to North.

(Answers: *a.* a drop in the cost or difficulty of migration. *b.* population pressure in the South. *c.* A rise in labor demand in the North.)

2. Review the areas of gain and loss to different groups in Figure 23.1. Can you explain why the migrants gain only areas *d* and *e*? Why don't they each gain the full Southern wage markup ($1.60/$1.25)? Why don't they each gain ($4.00/$1.25)?

▼

International Lending and the World Debt Crisis

•

Capital, like labor, moves between countries. Yet international capital flows usually are not movements of productive machines or buildings.[1] Rather, they usually are flows of financial claims, flows between lenders and borrowers, or flows between owners and the enterprises they own. The lenders or owners give the borrowers or subsidiary-firm managers money to be used now, in exchange for IOUs or ownership shares entitling them to interest and dividends later. International capital flows are conventionally divided into privately held versus official claims, long-term versus short-term claims, and direct versus portfolio claims, as follows:

A. Private lending (or ownership purchases):
  1. Long-term (bonds, stocks, use of patents or copyrights).
    a. Direct investments (lending to, or purchasing ownership shares in, a foreign enterprise largely owned and controlled by the investor).
    b. Portfolio investments (lending to, or purchasing ownership shares in, a foreign enterprise not owned or controlled by the investor).
  2. Short-term (bills of credit, etc., maturing in a year or less—mostly portfolio investments).
B. Official lending (or ownership purchases—mostly portfolio, mostly lending, both long-term and short-term).

---

[1] Physical capital goods do flow between countries. Yet the term *international capital movement* has been reserved mainly for the financial flows of credit and ownership claims discussed here. When a company buys a machine, a capital good, this flow is typically treated as an ordinary trade flow, not a "capital flow." For more on the distinction between capital goods and "capital" in the international accounts, see footnote 3 in Chapter 14.

The subtleties of control that go with direct investments are explored in Chapter 25. Here we concentrate on protfolio investments, and especially on private lending.

International lending has been revolutionized. Until recently, the main lender was the United States, joined after 1973 by the newly rich oil exporters. The main borrowers, especially in the 1970s, were developing countries of the Third World. But since 1985, the United States has been the world's largest net borrower (as shown in Chapter 14), and the oil exporters are borrowing almost as much as they lend. The dominant lender in Japan. The type of lending has changed back to private loans to both government and private borrowers, away from the loans from governments and the direct investments in investor-controlled firms that prevailed between 1950 and 1973.

International lending is also in a state of severe crisis. A rush of lending to the Third World, from 1974 to 1982, ended abruptly in a crisis of confidence. Lenders scrambled to stop lending and get repaid. Dozens of national governments have failed to meet their agreed repayment schedules. The largest banks in the world face major losses on their international loans. The whole international financial structure, which had grown to become as large a share of economic life as it had been at any time since 1914, has been tottering. Why? How is international lending supposed to work, why have we had a world debt crisis, and how can such a crisis be solved?

To spot what is wrong with international lending today, we begin with a view of how competitive international lending *should* work.

GAINS AND LOSSES FROM WELL-BEHAVED INTERNATIONAL LENDING

If the world is stable and predictable, and if borrowers fully honor their commitment to repay, then international lending can be efficient from a world point of view, bringing gains to some that outweigh the losses to others. In such a world, the welfare effects of international lending are exactly parallel to the welfare effects of opening trade (Chapter 3) or those of allowing free labor migration (Chapter 23).

Figure 24.1 shows the normal effects of allowing free international lending and borrowing. The horizontal axis shows the invested capital and its ownership (or wealth, or net worth) of a two-country world, and the vertical axis shows percentage rates of return (say, a rate of interest) earned on wealth.

We begin with a situation in which international financial transactions are illegal. In this situation each country must match its financial wealth with its own stock of real capital. Figure 24.1 shows the consequences by dividing the world into two large countries, ''Japan'' having abundant financial wealth and less attractive domestic investment opportunities and an ''America'' in the image of Brazil, Canada, Mexico, and the United States,

having less wealth relative to its abundant opportunities for profitable investment (e.g., in its new technology, or its frontier areas rich in natural resources). If all lending must be domestic, Japan's lenders must accept low
rates of return because the supply of domestic real assets follows the declining
marginal-product-of-capital curve MPK_{Japan}. Competition thus forces lenders
in Japan to accept the low rate of return of 2 percent per annum (after
inflation, say) at Point R. Meanwhile, in America the scarcity of funds
prohibits any real capital formation to the left of Point S, since W_a is all
the wealth America has. Competition for borrowing the W_a of national
wealth bids the real rate of interest on lending up to 8 percent, at Point S.
The world's product, or the areas under the marginal-product-of-capital
curves, is just the shaded areas shown in Figure 24.1.

Now imagine that there have never been any barriers to international
finance. Wealthholders in Japan and borrowers in America have a strong
incentive to get together. Why should the one group lend at only 2 percent
and the other borrow at 8 percent if, as we assume here, the riskiness or
creditworthiness of the different borrowings are the same? Lenders in Japan
would choose to do part of their lending in America, the higher return
country. Over time, their lending to America would allow more capital to
accumulate in America, with less capital accumulating in Japan. The international lending leads, of course, to a different equilibrium in which the rate
of return is somewhere between 2 percent and 8 percent. Let us say that it
ends up at 5 percent, at point T. In this situation the wealth of Japan
exceeds its stock of domestic real assets by the same amount $(W_j - K_j)$
that America has borrowed to cover its extra real assets $(K_a - W_a)$.

With international financial freedom, world product is maximized. It equals
everything under either marginal product curve, or all the shaded areas
plus RST. This is a clear gain of RST (or areas a through f) over the
situation in which international lending was prohibited. The reason for the
gain is simply that freedom allows the individual wealthholders the chance
to seek the highest return the world over, and in this section we assume
they use that freedom wisely.

The world's gains from free lending are split between the two countries.
Japan's national product is the whole area under its MPK_{Japan} curve down
to point R *plus* the area $(a + b + c)$, which is gained by the chance to
lend wealth abroad at 5 percent instead of accepting less profitable domestic
investments from Point T down to Point R. Similarly, America has gained
area $(d + e + f)$, because it has expanded its productive real capital out
to point T (from the right), paying foreign lenders the rectangle $(a + b +
c + g)$ for the funds borrowed at 5 percent.

Within each country, there are gainers and losers from the new freedom.
Clearly, Japanese lenders gain from lending at 5 percent instead of at 2
percent. That harms Japanese borrowers, though, because competition from
foreign borrowers forces them to pay the same higher rate on all new borrowings. In America, borrowers have gained from being able to borrow at 5
percent instead of at 8 percent. Yet American lenders might be nostalgic

FIGURE 24.1   Gains and Losses from Well-Behaved International Lending

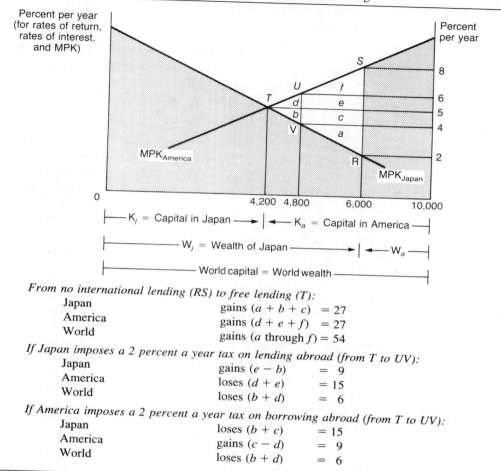

From no international lending (RS) to free lending (T):
Japan	gains $(a + b + c)$	$= 27$
America	gains $(d + e + f)$	$= 27$
World	gains $(a$ through $f)$	$= 54$

If Japan imposes a 2 percent a year tax on lending abroad (from T to UV):
Japan	gains $(e - b)$	$= 9$
America	loses $(d + e)$	$= 15$
World	loses $(b + d)$	$= 6$

If America imposes a 2 percent a year tax on borrowing abroad (from T to UV):
Japan	loses $(b + c)$	$= 15$
America	gains $(c - d)$	$= 9$
World	loses $(b + d)$	$= 6$

for the old days of financial isolation, when borrowers still had to pay them 8 percent. Note that the pattern of gains and losses is identical to the one established in the analysis of trade and of migration: international freedom benefits the world as a whole and the groups for whom the freedom means opportunity, while it harms the groups for whom the freedom means tougher competition.

TAXES ON INTERNATIONAL LENDING

We have thus compared free international lending with no international lending and have found the orthodox result: freedom raises world product and national products. We should also note, though, that another standard result carries over for trade analysis: the nationally optimal tax. *If* a country looms large enough to have power over the international market rate of return, it can exploit this market power to its own advantage, at the expense of other countries and the world as a whole.

In Figure 24.1 Japan can be said to have market power. By restricting its supply of foreign lending, it could force foreign borrowers to pay higher rates (moving northeast from Point *T* toward Point *S*). Let us say that Japan exploits this with a tax like the U.S. interest equalization tax of 1963. Let Japan impose a tax of 2 percent a year on the value of assets held abroad by residents of Japan. This will bid up the rate foreign borrowers have to pay and bid down the rate domestic lenders can get after taxes. Equilibrium will be restored when the gap between the foreign and domestic rates is just the 2 percent tax. This is shown by the gap *UV* in Figure 24.1. Japan has apparently made a net gain on its taxation of foreign lending. It has forced America to pay 6 percent instead of 5 percent on all continuing debt. This markup, area *e,* is large enough to outweigh its loss of some previously profitable lending abroad (triangle *b*). Setting such a tax at just the right level (which might or might not be the one shown here) gives Japan a nationally optimal tax on foreign lending.

Two can play at that game, of course. Figure 24.1 shows that America also has market power, since by restricting its borrowing it could force Japan's lenders to accept lower rates of return (moving southeast from Point *T* toward Point *R*). What if it was America that imposed the 2 percent tax on the same international assets? Then all the results would work out the same as for the tax by Japan—except that the American government pockets the tax revenue (areas *c* and *e*). America, in this case, gains area (*c* minus *d*) at the expense of Japan and the world as a whole. (If both countries try to impose taxes on the same international lending, the international economy will probably degenerate toward financial autarky—that is, back toward Points *R S,* with everybody losing.)

The analysis of a tax on international lending and borrowing assumes that the tax cannot be evaded. In practice, it often is. Lenders and borrowers can invent ways of hiding their dealings. They did so when evading the ban on usury in the Middle Ages, and they have done so in defiance of exchange controls and tax laws in recent times. The most common device is *transfer pricing,* which will be discussed at more length in Chapter 25. Lenders and borrowers often trade goods and services at the same time they are agreeing on loans. If they want to pretend that no loan is being made, they can disguise it with an off-market price for some goods or services. For example, they could sign agreements in which the borrower sells the lender some goods for cash now and the lender sells the borrower some goods for cash later. It can be done so that the lender underpays for some goods now and/or the borrower overpays for some goods later. In this way the rigged prices "transfer" the extra interest payment from borrower to lender. The borrower gets the temporary use of money, the lender gets repaid with interest, and the governments collect no international-lending tax. Such evasion, like any other kind of smuggling, brings the world closer to the free-trade point (*T* in Figure 24.1). Here again, as in the analysis of trade barriers, smugglers emerge as near-heroes by bringing the international economy back toward an efficient market position.

THE WORLD DEBT CRISIS: HOW BAD IS IT?

The generally benign results of well-behaved international lending have not shown up since the mid-1970s because lending has not been well-behaved.

Lenders have shown questionable judgment. Debtors have threatened not to repay, and some have in fact not repaid on time. The risks were enormous at first, and remained serious at the end of the decade. In 1982, the "exposure" of nine top U.S.-based banks to shaky foreign loans was twice the entire value of their own paid-in capital. In fact, even their lending to three countries alone (Argentina, Brazil, and Mexico) exceeded their paid-in capital. Even by 1990, the value of loans outstanding to problem debtor countries still exceeded the net worth of those nine top U.S. banks, even though they had already written off part of the loans as losses.

The problem is also very serious for the debtors. They borrowed in the 1970s at high nominal interest rates reflecting the widespread fear of dollar-price inflation. Then, around 1982, came a new era of tighter monetary policies, led by the U.S. Federal Reserve's decision to stop inflation even if it cost extra jobs for several years (which it did). Suddenly, the high nominal interest rates turned into high real interest rates, real rates that hit borrowers harder than any time since the Great Slump of 1929–32.

Is this "world debt crisis" an accident of recent history, or are there more basic defects in international lending that lead to such crises? Let's explore this issue both up close and from afar. First, we examine some interpretations of the timing of the world debt crisis. Then, we draw back and look at a more basic problem that afflicts all international lending to governments sooner or later.

THE SURGE IN INTERNATIONAL LENDING, 1974–1982

Figure 24.2 chronicles the revival in private international lending to Third World countries that occurred between the first oil price shock (1973–74) and the climax in world debt crisis in 1982. Such large shares of world wealth had not been lent at interest internationally since the 1920s, in part because massive defaults in the 1930s had frightened away international lenders up through the 1960s. Why the revival after 1974, when the world economy had just been numbed by a quadrupling of oil prices? Experts have four main explanations for this timing.

FIGURE 24.2   Developing Countries' Borrowings from and Payments to Private Creditors, 1973–1982

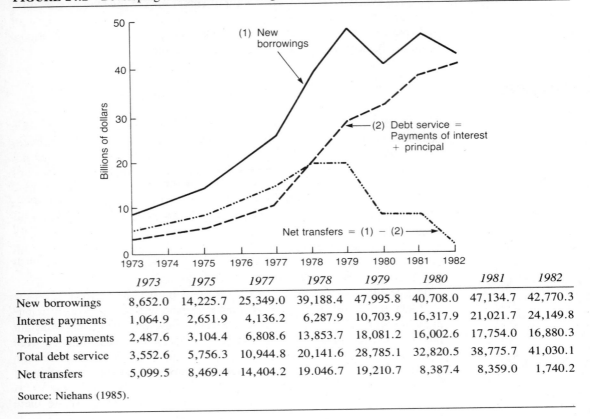

	1973	1975	1977	1978	1979	1980	1981	1982
New borrowings	8,652.0	14,225.7	25,349.0	39,188.4	47,995.8	40,708.0	47,134.7	42,770.3
Interest payments	1,064.9	2,651.9	4,136.2	6,287.9	10,703.9	16,317.9	21,021.7	24,149.8
Principal payments	2,487.6	3,104.4	6,808.6	13,853.7	18,081.2	16,002.6	17,754.0	16,880.3
Total debt service	3,552.6	5,756.3	10,944.8	20,141.6	28,785.1	32,820.5	38,775.7	41,030.1
Net transfers	5,099.5	8,469.4	14,404.2	19.046.7	19,210.7	8,387.4	8,359.0	1,740.2

Source: Niehans (1985).

The Surge in Private Bank Reserves after 1973. To some extent, the oil price hikes that depressed the world economy oddly raised the supply of investable funds. In the immediate wake of the price hikes of 1973–74 and 1979–80, large shares of world income were redistributed toward rich oil-exporting nations with a high short-run propensity to save out of extra income. It took a few years for the high-income countries of the Arabian Peninsula to come up with enough spending projects to turn massive new savings into budget deficits. While their savings were still piling up, they tended to lend in liquid form, holding more bonds, bills, and bank deposits in the United States and other established financial centers. The major international private banks thereby gained large amounts of new reserves to back aggressive lending.

The supply of bank reserves was further enhanced by the inflationary monetary policies of the industrial countries. When the oil price shocks made central bankers confront the tough choice between massive unemployment (if they kept private bank reserves from accelerating) and accelerating inflation (if they let reserves accelerate), they opted more for the latter.

Thus the ball got rolling. By itself, however, the search for ways of "recycling," or reinvesting, the new "petro-dollars" and the accommodating expansionary monetary policies only explain a surge in funds to be reinvested. They do not explain why the extra funds ended up being lent at interest to developing-country borrowers.

Investment Uncertainty in the Industrial Countries. The major private banks could have used their new reserves to finance new capital formation in the industrial countries themselves. Investments in energy-saving equipment and techniques were an obvious target for new investments. Yet the development of energy-saving projects took time. In the wake of the first oil price shock—that is, in the mid-1970s—there was widespread pessimism about the profitability of new capital formation, either energy-saving or otherwise. For a time, then, the expanded ability of banks to lend was not absorbed by borrowers in the industrial countries, encouraging banks to look elsewhere. Attention began to shift to Third World borrowers, who had long been forced to offer higher rates of interest and dividends to attract private capital.

Resistance to Direct Foreign Investment in the 1970s. The next factor to explain is why investments in developing countries took the form of outright lending to governments and enterprises not controlled by the creditors. That is, why didn't the extra loanable reserves fuel a surge in direct foreign investment (DFI), in which the investor keeps controlling ownership of the foreign enterprises receiving the fresh capital. As it happened, the 1970s was an era of peak resistance to DFI. Populist ideological currents, valid fears about political intrigues by multinational firms, and a desire to emulate OPEC's overthrow of the power of the top international oil firms brought DFI down from about 25 percent of net financial flows to developing countries in 1960, and 20 percent in 1970, to only 10 percent by 1980.

The new policy of borrowing at interest rather than allowing direct foreign investors to control enterprises and repatriate profits from them proved to be a fateful one: when the world recession and credit squeeze hit in the early 1980s, borrowing countries were faced with real interest payments that were far heavier than the profits that would have been removed by direct investors in such profit-squeezing times. Yet outright borrowing was preferred in the mid-1970s, and this preference helps explain the surge in international loans.

The Herd Instinct among Investors. Once the rise in private lending to developing countries accelerated, it seemed to acquire a momentum of its own. Major private banks aggressively sought such lending opportunities, each showing eagerness to lend before competing banks did. Bank officers enhanced their individual careers by overruling more cautious colleagues and capturing new loans to Third World borrowers.

The lemming-like tendency to run with the herd led to a relearning of a lesson that financial history had taught before: running with the herd—or, in the other popular metaphor, jumping on the bandwagon—can be individually rational and collectively irrational when the returns from investing are not secured by any firm collateral to be seized when repayments drop off. For an individual investor, a good time to buy a risky asset is when he or she perceives that others are about to buy it. The mere perception that others will buy makes it rational—for an individual, and only for a while— to buy, knowing that later buyers will invest enough to ensure that the individual will be repaid well. The belief that the herd is on the move becomes self-fulfilling. Joining the move can be profitable for those individuals who have the wisdom or luck to participate in the early part of the move. Later investments will yield good returns only if the whole investment program is sound. That was not the case with the borrowings of Third World countries between 1974 and 1982. Much of the lending went to poorly planned projects in mismanaged economies (not unlike the investments of U.S. savings and loan institutions during the 1980s!).

OVER THE CLIFF IN 1982

In 1982, the supply of international lending dropped off, and dozens of debtor countries announced that they could not repay their previous loans. There are at least two short-run factors that help explain why the crunch came in 1982 and another commonly cited factor that does not really explain the timing of the debt crisis.

The World Depression of 1982   The year 1982 was one of worldwide depression (or, if you wish, recession) and a hard time for any debtor. World output and employment were stagnating, and inflation cooled down faster than expected. For debtors it was a time of stagnating ability to pay and a higher real interest burden. A crisis that might have come at another time thus came to a head that year.

The Investor Stampede.   Just as individual investors' enthusiasm for international lending in the 1970s had depended on their perception that others were doing it, there was a stampede to get out of such lending in 1982 largely because investors perceived that others wanted out. Once signs of depression and strain in debtor countries began to surface, all lending banks had reason to be nervous about making any new loans. Each individual lender had an incentive to stop lending and let other creditors lend the money that was crucial to assuring that he or she was repaid on schedule. Some lenders found it easier to get out than others did. In general, the smaller banks (those holding small shares of all loans) were able to bail out and demand repayment, safe in the knowledge that their individual decisions to stop lending would not cause the debtor countries to stop repaying. Large banks could not afford the same flight, however. Each knew that just trying to stop its own new loans could trigger a crisis in which a larger volume of outstanding loans, many held by itself, would not be repaid. The financial losses to lenders have thus been concentrated in the largest private international banks.

The partial stampede to stop lending in 1982 was analogous to the problem of cartel cheating discussed in Chapter 11. Individual lenders, like members of a cartel, want other members to follow a unified policy they individually abandon. That is, they are tempted to act like "free riders," leaving it to others to hold the collective arrangements together. The tendency of smaller investors to get out of lending as soon as repayments come in is just like the tendency of smaller cartel members to shave their prices and sell aggressively, forcing the larger members to cut their own output in order to prop up the cartel price.

The Doubtful Relevance of Oil Prices.
Some people have linked the difficulties of debtors at the start of the 1980s to the second oil price shock, the one hitting in 1979–80. Higher oil bills helped explain the timing of the crisis for such oil-importing nations as Brazil, Argentina, and Poland. But the same oil price hikes should have made it easier for oil exporters, such as Mexico, Venezuela, and Nigeria, to repay their debts in the early 1980s. Instead, they were in just as much trouble as the oil importers. Oil-price movements are not the reason that the debt crisis broke in 1982.

The timing of the rise and fall of international lending thus relates to a set of special circumstances. The rise of lending in the mid-1970s was prompted by a surge in private bank reserves. The bank reserves, in turn, were raised by oil-country saving and by inflationary monetary policies throughout the world. The extra reserves were channeled toward lending at interest to developing countries because investment prospects were uncertain in the leading industrial countries and because developing countries resited the inflow of direct-ownership investments. In 1982 the inflows were checked, and debtors failed to meet payments on time, partly because of the depression of that year and partly because of a speculative stampede to stop lending.

Yet the forces listed here only help explain the *timing* of the rise and fall of international lending between 1974 and 1982. Unfortunately, the press tends to concentrate on such short-run explanations of the timing of crisis without sufficient attention to a more basic fact: repayment crises are a chronic problem with international lending, especially where the borrowers are governments. It has all happened before—many times. Argentina has declared its inability to repay foreign debts at least a half-dozen times since it gained independence in the early 19th century. Guatemala has defaulted on foreign loan repayments about a dozen times. In the 1910s lenders lost vast sums in the revolutions of Mexico, Russia, and Turkey. In the early 1930s there was a worldwide wave of default involving dozens of debtor countries. The kind of crisis that has threatened the solvency of major banks in the 1980s has been a regular occurrence in modern times. Why? Why should international lending be less stable than domestic lending?

THE BASIC PROBLEM OF SOVEREIGN DEFAULT

International lending is plagued by defective property rights. The borrowers are often **sovereign,** meaning that they are legally independent. They cannot be legally forced to repay if they do not wish to do so. Especially when the borrowers are governments themselves, they can refuse to repay on time without the creditors' being able to sue them in court or seize their assets. Granted, there have been times in the past when creditors could force repayment: Britain and France were able to take over Egyptian tax collections in the latter half of the 19th century after Egypt failed to repay English and French creditors, and creditors were backed by gunboats when they demanded repayment from Venezuela at the turn of the century. But the gunboat days are over. If Brazil defaults on its debts, the United States and other lending nations cannot send gunboats to Brazil. Nor can they send thugs to beat up the Brazilian finance minister. It is possible for a debtor nation to lure foreign lending until the lending is no longer greater than the outflow of money to service the accumulated debts (i.e., to pay interest and principal), and then to default.

Of course, any experienced national leader will know how to defend the default with good moral arguments. The refusal to repay can be presented as an *inability* to repay, due to whatever has gone wrong with the economy lately—a recession, a drop in the terms of trade, a natural disaster, a war, or whatever. Typically, the governments that want to postpone or cancel repayment are not the same governments that did the earlier borrowing, leaving them the excuse that the debts were contracted by their discredited and wasteful predecessors. At the same time, both borrowing governments and their foreign creditors have a strong incentive to cover defaults with cosmetics, saying that repayments are only "rescheduled" (postponed) and not repudiated forever. But the basic problem remains: the incentive to default on borrowing is stronger when your assets cannot be seized by creditors.

The incentive to declare yourself a problem debtor may be strong if the fresh-loan period seems to be ending. If we now look back at the data in Figure 24.2, we see some behavior suggesting that countries announce repayment problems when they lose the *willingness* to repay, even if they still have the ability. As Figure 24.2 shows, an important fact about the year 1982 is that it was the year in which the flow of repayments to service the international debts of the Third World caught up with the inflows of fresh loans. It may be that debtors saw that trend continuing, strengthening their willingness to declare that they could not repay on time without new help.

The shakiness of the incentive to repay sovereign debt helps explain some features of the behavior of international lenders. One such feature is their insistence on higher interest rates when they lend to foreign governments as opposed to when they lend to ordinary private borrowers or their own governments. They demand the higher interest rates as a way of collecting what might be thought of as default-insurance premiums: for as long as there is no crisis, they collect the premiums, but they sustain a large loss when the crisis comes. Just like an insurance company, the community of international lenders between 1850 and 1980 made a good rate of return overall, with most clients (borrowers) paying premiums while a few defaulted spectacularly. Another feature tied to the sovereign status of the borrowers is wide swings in the volume of lending. Lenders first run with the herd and later flee in panic because they know they need company when lending to borrowers without effective collateral.

Being sovereign can be costly for the borrower, too. Lenders will insist on charging a higher rate of interest, or lending less, or both. Many borrowers who fully intend to repay lack a credible way to convince creditors of that. So the cost of the property-rights defect tends to be shared by the two sides.

WHEN WOULD A SOVEREIGN DEBTOR REPAY?

Can the property-rights problem of sovereign debt be solved? What could make debtor nations want to repay even if they have the power to refuse? Let us look first at the usual answer, which is false, before turning to the correct answer.

A Common Fallacy

The usual solution is to hope that debtors will repay on time to protect their own future creditworthiness. If fresh loans keep growing fast enough, the debtor countries can afford to repay an ever-growing debt service. Although the idea of relending to a problem debtor may sound correct, and this idea is still endorsed by many economists, it is flawed as a way of dealing with debtors who need the extra loans to continue to repay old ones.

The usual argument is often summarized with a steady-growth example. Let's say that if the debtor country defaults, it receives no future loans whatsoever. If the debtor behaves well and repays, it continues to receive a net inflow of resources ($I > 0$) from the rest of the world as long as its

net fresh borrowings (or increases in net debt, or Δ *D*) exceed its payments
of interest on accumulated debts (interest payments *iD*, where *i* is the interest
rate per annum and *D* is the outstanding debt):

Inflow = Fresh borrowing − Interest payments
(net of repayments of principal)

or

$$I = \Delta D - iD, \text{ so that}$$
$$I > 0 \Leftrightarrow \Delta D > iD$$

To simplify our discussion of how fast this means the new borrowings
should grow, define *r* as the growth rate of the accumulated stock of debt:
$r = \Delta D/D$, or $\Delta D = rD$. Then being a good repayer of all interest (and
principal) keeps bringing new resources into the debtor country as long as:

$$r > i$$

The orthodox discussion thus concludes hopefully that sovereign debtors
who could get away with repudiating their sovereign debt would nonetheless
continue to repay if only the international financial system keeps promising
them enough fresh loans in exchange for good behavior. Many variants of
the usual argument add that the debt service should also be an affordable
share of the debtor's exports or GNP, but this gloss is secondary.[2] The
key idea is that enough new loans will give them both the incentive and
the means to go on repaying old loans forever.

Something is drastically wrong with the usual argument. It contains a
hidden incentive for eventual default, one that makes the recurring crises
in world debt seem less accidental. Notice first that creditors *must* come
up with a stream of fresh net loans *(ΔD)* promising to be great enough to
exceed the interest payments *(iD)*, or else the debtor will have an incentive
to default. Creditors cannot use small fresh loans to persuade debtors to
repay larger amounts. If the creditors are really just lending a little in the
hope of getting greater amounts in repayment, that will probably be evident
to the debtor as well, and the debtor will still have an incentive not to
repay. No, the creditors must come up with new loans matching the debt-
service defaults to be prevented: Δ*D* must not only be positive but must,
to repeat, outweigh *iD*.

Even the generous policy of hiaving creditors repay themselves cannot

---

[2] An "affordable" debt-service ratio is often thought to mean that debt service as a share
of the borrower's GNP (or exports) should grow more slowly than the supply of new loans
as a share of GNP. In terms of our symbols, this means (retirements + *iD*)/GNP < (new
loans/GNP), which is the same thing as *iD*/GNP < Δ*D*/GNP, since Δ*D* = new loans minus
retirements. But if the debt stock is growing at the rate *r*, so that Δ*D*=*rD*, this key condition
simply turns out to be the same one as in the text: *r* > *i*. Using the GNP denominator (or
an export denominator) makes no difference.

last forever without default. As long as the period of fresh lending comes to an end someday, and the debt stops growing, debtors will see the end coming and will have an incentive to default on the remaining debt. This will be true no matter how long the period of relending continues. It is commonly supposed that the whole idea can work if creditors just keep relending long enough. Wrong. The longer they keep it up, with $I > 0$, the greater the amount of accumulated debt (D) on which debtors have an incentive to default.[3] The default incentive would grow even if the relending process continued forever. Even though it might seem that infinity is so far away that we can ignore any debt left over, there are two rebuttals: (1) notice that the idea of lending to infinity seems to work only because it assumes that an infinite debt is repudiated in the end and (2) creditor countries should have second thoughts about the financial wisdom of lending to borrowers who cannot be kept from defaulting unless the loans grow forever.

It might seem that too much has been proved. Does the above really mean that all lending to sovereign borrowers is doomed to ultimate default, making for unstable waves of overlending and underlending? No, that would overstate the case. What has been shown is that sovereign debt is subject to an ultimate default *if* the only mechanism for inducing repayments is to hold out the promise of new loans.

A Better Model of Repayment Incentives

The correct answer to the basic property-rights defect of sovereign debt is to make sure sovereign debtors borrow only up to their *collateral,* the value of the assets that the creditors could seize if the debtor fell behind on payments. Then debtors would have a stronger incentive to repay on schedule. Collateral works well in domestic lending, because national laws allow the creditor to take over assets of the nonrepaying debtor, but only in amounts tied to the value defaulted. If Donald Trump does not meet his debt payments, his U.S. creditors have the right to seize his properties. With the creditors given such security, lending takes place at a lower interest rate, with less investor jitters and less default, than if creditors had to lend without recourse against default. The debtors are more likely to borrow at a smooth sustainable pace appropriate to the flow of new productive real investments, instead of borrowing in a rush when foreign banks are getting on the bandwagon

---

[3] In fact, the longer they keep it up, the greater the value of the default incentive even when it is discounted back to the time (t_0) when lending started. As long as $r > i$, the present value of the debt left over at time t, or $D_t/(1 + i)^t = D_0(1 + r)^t/(1 + i)^t$, where D_0 is the amount of the very first loan, grows with the time span t. The greater this debt left over, the greater the amount debtors have reason to repudiate. As the text notes, continuing the process forever, until $t = \infty$, makes the present value of the ultimate default become infinite.

and being denied credit when nervous banks try to jump off the bandwagon.

There are ways to create seizable international collateral, even though they are not perfect counterparts to the collateral recognized by domestic law. Often debtor countries have assets in the creditor country that make them fear retaliation by that country. If the debtor country trades heavily with the creditor country and its close allies, the debtor country's exports and its access to revolving trade credits can depend on the goodwill of the creditor country. If the debtor country has actual gross investments in the banks and enterprises of the creditor country, it should also worry about having these seized in retaliation, the way that the United States froze Iranian assets in response to the Teheran hostage crisis in 1979–81 and several countries froze Iraqi assets after Iraq invaded Kuwait in 1990. In practice, however, the collateral mechanism is not very finely tuned: the hostage assets are being held in the creditor *country,* but not by the creditors (e.g., major banks) themselves, and the value of such assets is not necessarily in proportion to the possible default by the debtor country. Yet it is possible that such mutual dependence can give the debtor country strong reason to repay faithfully, and thereby give the creditors reason to lend at a lower interest rate.

What determines the limits of prudent lending and of borrowers' incentive to repay? The key forces are summarized in Figure 24.3. Here the stock of debt on the horizontal axis *(D)* is the lowest of three debt stocks: the leftover debt from earlier periods, the amount lenders are willing to lend, and the amount borrowers are willing to borrow. Once this is set, the borrower has agreed to pay the "debt service," or interest plus repayment of principal. To simplify, let us take a case in which the whole principal will be repaid at the end of this period, so that the debt service is iD in interest payments, where i is the real rate of interest, plus repayment of the principal D. For any given stock of debt, then, the straight line $(1 + i)D$ therefore shows the benefits of not repaying.

The debtor's cost of not repaying *(C)* also depends on the stock of debt, but only to some extent. There is a fixed cost (C_0) to making any mention of nonrepayment, regardless of the amount of debt. That fixed cost would take the form of reduced creditworthiness, a lower credit rating, from the debtor's sending the signal that nonrepayment is even being considered. Beyond C_0, the cost of not repaying unilaterally probably rises with the amount of debt not honored. Yet, as implied by the curve in Figure 24.3, that cost does not rise as fast as the stock of debt itself. This is because most of the penalty would be inflicted after even a small default, in the form of asset seizure, trade embargoes, and denial of later credits. A bigger default does not bring a much bigger penalty.

The fact that the cost of not repaying *(C)* rises more slowly with extra debt than does the debt service $(1 + i)D$ means that there is some amount of debt beyond which the willingness to repay faithfully and silently disappears. That threshold amount of debt is D_{limit} in Figure 24.3. Well-behaved

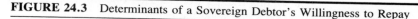

FIGURE 24.3   Determinants of a Sovereign Debtor's Willingness to Repay

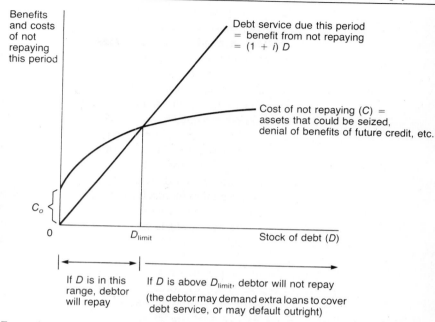

Forces that raise the danger of nonrepayment (by lowering D_{limit} or raising D):

- a rise in the real interest rate i
- a fall in the cost of nonrepayment *(C)*
  (e.g., due to a fall in the likely future loans to faithful repayers)
- a greater stock of outstanding debt *(D)* inherited from the past.

lending occurs to the left of this limit. As long as the amount lent, the stock of debt D, is less than D_{limit}, the debtor will repay faithfully and without protest, because the cost of protest or nonrepayment exceeds the amount of debt service that could be avoided. Ordinary private lending within a country usually (but not always!) operates in this prudent range.

Events could put us in the troubled range to the right of D_{limit}, as happened many times in history. A rise in the real rate of interest raises the burden of repayment (benefit of not repaying), as it did in the early 1980s. In Figure 24.3, that would be represented by an upward rotation of the benefit curve $(1 + i)D$. Or a fall in the cost of not repaying *(C)* could also change a wise level of lending into a dangerous level. That too has happened, when a sudden drop of creditors' willingness to make fresh future loans has shown debtors that there is less value in protecting their good credit rating. Such was the case in the Great Depression of the 1930s and again after the depression of 1982. Or lenders can simply overlend, driving D to the right of D_{limit} even apart from surprises in the world economy. That, too, seems to have happened.

Notice that debtors may decide it is not wise to repay quietly even if they are *able* to repay. Note also that the productivity of the real capital formation financed by past loans is absent from Figure 24.3. Bygones are bygones. How well the earlier investments paid off is not crucial to the debtor's incentive to repay debt now.

If a sovereign debtor announces that it "cannot" repay without new loans to cover the debt payments, should the lenders make the new loans? Should they buy time, hoping that conditions will make the debtor want to return to faithful repayment? Figure 24.3 suggests a negative answer. The debtor's announcement that there is a problem means that the stock of debt is already over the safe limit $(D > D_{limit})$. Starting to the right of that limit, the more the creditor extends the debt by giving a rollover loan, the greater the debtor's incentive to default sometime after that. That is, extending more loans moves us further to the right (raising D), with an even wider gap between the debtors' benefits and costs of not repaying eventually. It is hard to see how anything other than extraordinary luck could make it a good idea to make new loans to a debtor that has already revealed a willingness to throw away good credit standing if denied more loans.

WHO HAS REPAID THEIR EXTERNAL DEBTS?

Looking at experience with sovereign lending, we can find examples of countries that did repay faithfully. In each case the debtor country repaid largely because it did have assets that the creditor countries could seize in retaliation for default.

Third World Debtors since 1982?   The record since the onset of the debt crisis in 1982 is complex. On the one hand, the problem-debtor countries have suffered worse losses in GNP than other Third World countries. Yet this may be partly due to reverse causation (they became problem debtors partly because their economies suffered, not just vice versa). It also may be partly due to the sheer uncertainty about whether their governments will later impose the heavy taxes required to pay off the debt.

On the other hand, Third World debtors did not actually pay off much of their debt after 1982. The private banks who lent to them still hold sobering amounts of Third World debt, even though some debts have been written off and others have been sold to new lenders at a loss to the original banks. When one has corrected flaws in official figures showing large resource payments by Third World countries, it turns out that only Mexico, Venezuela, and Ecuador (and possibly Rumania) have made heavy repayments. What might *look* like heavy repayments by other debtors are paper "reschedulings" in which the creditors basically pay themselves in the short run, and the debt continues to rise. If one studied Figure 24.3, one would have wondered why any debtor would want to repay after incurring the credit damage of announcing a crisis, as most had done in 1982.[4] Apparently, most have not repaid much. Yet they continue to suffer the uncertainties of a debt crisis that is not resolved as long as their debts are not substantially written off.

Faithful Repayment by North America.

Before World War I, the United States and Canada were heavy net debtors to Britain and other European lenders. Those prewar debts were repaid as faithfully as ordinary private loans because the lenders generally had good collateral. Much of the lending was to private borrowers who could be dragged into North American courts, rather than to sovereign debtors. (Exceptions were the state governments in the United States, and these, especially the southern states after the Civil War, did default on loans from foreigners.) And when World War I broke out, North American nations, especially the United States, were suddenly transformed into major creditors who would certainly not default on foreign debts because they feared that foreigners would retaliate and default on the loans from America (as Britain, France, and others ultimately did by the 1930s).

The same incentive to repay faithfully exists for the heavy borrowing of the United States in the 1980s. If the United States were to repudiate its government debt to foreigners, the lending countries would surely retaliate by seizing America's vast gross assets under their jurisdiction.[5] The United States is in a peculiarly bad position when it comes to international lending. On the one hand, as a lender it may yet incur history's biggest losses on loans to developing countries. On the other, as a debtor, it may have to repay heavily. Indeed, the United States is so dominant a borrower that the more it borrows the more it drives up the real world interest rate it must repay.

East Asian Repayment.

The industrializing countries of East Asia, such as Japan before World War II or South Korea or Taiwan since, also have

---

[4] The incentives in real-world debtor countries are complex, however, and at least some parties in debtor countries would welcome the austerity that goes with having to repay foreign bankers. Austerity justified on the grounds that the foreign creditors must be repaid has at least the advantage of forcing the nation to correct the monetary inflation and overspending that contributed to the debt crisis in the first place. Yet, to repeat, it is not evident that many debtor countries have sustained large transfers of resources to creditor countries in the 1980s.

[5] It is also technically hard to default on U.S. government debt to foreigners because they could simply sell their holdings of U.S. government debt to U.S. residents, who would redeem them at face value. To default on foreign loans, a government must have such loans isolated as special illiquid direct loans, as is typical of the loans to Latin American governments today.

had a record of relatively faithful repayment of debts, even when the borrower was a sovereign government agency. Here again, the collateral model seems to apply. Industrializing East Asia is heavily dependent on its trade with its creditor countries. If it should balk at repaying debts on time, its vital export trade could be disrupted by a cessation of trade credits and perhaps also by an outbreak of retaliatory protectionism in North America and Europe. In effect, East Asia has pledged hostage assets, making it more creditworthy. The East Asian commitment to continued ties, along with its growth success, has made it a region of prompt repayment of foreign debts, official as well as private.

SUMMARY

Well-behaved international lending (or international capital flows) yields the same kinds of welfare results as international trade. Free loan markets bring welfare gains for both sides, relative to no lending. Either borrowing-country or lending-country governments can impose taxes on international lending. If the taxing country has market power (i.e., is able to affect the world interest rate), it can levy a nationally optimal tax on international lending. But if the other government retaliates with its own tax, both sides end up losing. In practice, taxes and prohibitions on international lending are hard to enforce, and evasion reduces interest-rate gaps and brings markets back closer to efficiency.

The world debt crisis, however, has shown how badly the market for sovereign debt departs from the norm of well-behaved international lending. Sovereign debt is debt that cannot be enforced in the event of nonrepayment (or debt repudiation or default) because the debtor is, or is backed by, a sovereign government. Sovereign debt leads to international inefficiencies: creditors demand higher interest rates to compensate for the likelihood of eventual default, and the volume of their lending tends to swing widely. Under these circumstances debtor countries are likely to overinvest at some times and underinvest at others. For their part the major international private lenders can suddenly be pushed to the verge of bankruptcy in a debt crisis.

Such serious consequences have already happened to a limited extent. Between 1974 and 1982 there was an unwise surge in private lending to Third World governments and enterprises whose debts had government guarantees. This surge seems to have been due to the swelling of private bank reserves by inflationary monetary policy and the accumulation of petro-dollars, to uncertainties discouraging investment in the industrial countries, and to Third World resistance to getting capital inflows in the form of direct foreign investment. In 1982, Mexico, Argentina, and Brazil gave signals that they could not repay on schedule, and investors stampeded to remove themselves from lending further, precipitating the World Debt Crisis.

Both the world depression of that year and the herd instinct of investors who lend on uncertain security contributed to the crisis.

Basic to the recurrence of international debt crises is the incentive to default on soverign debt. When debtor governments perceive that good repayment behavior no longer ensures a net inflow of funds for the future, they have an incentive to repudiate some or all of their debt in order to avoid paying out resources. The existence of the default incentive helps to explain why some Latin American countries have defaulted several times since the early 19th century, why many countries defaulted at the same time during the 1930s, and why 1982—a year in which debt service obligations caught up with fresh capital inflows—was a year in which many debtors chose to demand debt rescheduling.

What could solve the problem of default incentives on sovereign debt? Not the usually proposed solution, a combination of tiding the debtor over with fresh loans while demanding that belts be tightened. To postpone default, the fresh loans must at least match the repayments of interest and principal they were meant to induce. But if the fresh loans are that big, they raise the value of the ultimate default, regardless of how long the period of fresh lending lasts.

Rather, the correct means of overcoming the property-rights problems of sovereign debt is to write down part of the debt so that the remaining debt is within the amount that sovereign debtors have an incentive to repay. If past events have pushed debts beyond the collectible collateral, the debts must be scaled back to that collateral.

In loan contracts within a country, legally enforced collateral plays the important role of ensuring the creditor of repayment and making the debtors more creditworthy, allowing the latter to borrow at lower interest rates and on a more stable time schedule. In the past, countries that have repaid their foreign debts on schedule were those whose foreign creditors had the means to seize their assets if they did not repay on time. Mutual dependence, through trade and through lending in both directions at once, has performed the function of securing loans.

SUGGESTED READINGS

The basic welfare economics of international factor flows is extended in Grossman (*JIE*, 1984).

The literature on the world debt crisis and its causes is vast. See in particular Cline (1985); Cuddington (1989); Diaz-Alejandro (1984); Eaton and Gersovitz (1981); Eichengreen and Lindert (1989); Fishlow (1985, 1988); Frenkel, Dooley, and Wickham (1989), Lindert and Morton (1989); Niehans (1985); Sachs (1984, 1989); Smith and Cuddington (1984); Volcker (1983); and the World Bank's *World Development Report, 1985* (1985).

QUESTIONS FOR REVIEW

1. If your country absolutely had to repay all loans in full, how much would you borrow? If zero, why? If a positive amount, what determines how much you should optimally borrow?

2. If Japan's lenders cannot take foreign governments to court for debts unrepaid, should Japan lend to them at all? In not, why not? If so, how much?

3. Why was there so much private lending to developing countries in the period 1974–1982 when there had been so little from 1930 to 1974?

4. What triggered the debt crisis in 1982?

5. What forces weaken a sovereign debtor's willingness to repay?

6. The "Optimal Deadbeat" Problem: The World Bank is considering a stream of loans to Angola, to help it develop its nationalized oil fields and refineries. This is the only set of loans the World Bank would ever give Angola, and nobody else is considering lending to the country. Angola is militarily secure, and the regime cannot be overthrown. If the World Bank's streams of loans would have the effects below, would it ever be in Angola's interest to default on the loans? If not, why not? If so, why and when? State any key assumptions.

Loan effects ($ million)

Year	Inflow of Funds from World Bank	Stock of Accumulated Borrowings at End of Year	Interest to Be paid on Borrowings (at 8 percent)	Extra Oil Export Sales
1	$200	$200	0	0
2	100	300	$16	$30
3	50	350	24	30
4	0	350	28	30
5	−50 (repayment)	300	28	30
6	−50 (repayment)	250	24	30

(Repayments of $50 million each year until paid off at end of year 11.

Answer: default at the end of year 3.

▼

Direct Foreign Investment and the Multinationals

•

One of the most sensitive areas in international economics today is direct foreign investment (or DFI). Canada, Japan, and western European countries try to limit foreign investment within their borders lest their control over domestic resources be diluted by foreign ownership. Developing countries worry both that foreigners will invest in them and that they won't, fearing exploitation on the one hand and inadequate access to foreign capital and technology on the other. Governments prohibit and restrict direct foreign investments in certain lines of activity that are regarded as particularly vulnerable to foreign influence or as particularly wasteful—natural resources, banking, newspapers, and soft drinks. Governments also often stipulate that there must be local participation, training, locally purchased components, domestic research, or exports. On the other hand, some governments actively court multinational firms, whose influence and numbers slowly grow. This chapter explores why direct investment seems to occur, and whether either the source country or the host country has good reasons to try to restrict (or encourage) it.

A DEFINITION

Balance-of-payments accountants define **direct foreign investment** as any flow of lending to, or purchases of ownership in, a foreign enterprise that is largely owned by residents of the investing country. The proportions of ownership that define "largely" vary from country to country. For the United States 10 percent ownership by the investing firm suffices as an official definition of direct investment. Here are some examples of investments that do and do not fit the definition of U.S. foreign investment:

U.S. Direct Foreign Investments	*U.S. Portfolio Investments Abroad**
Alcoa's purchase of stock in a new Jamaican bauxite firm 50 percent owned by Alcoa	Alcoa's purchase of stock in a new Jamaican bauxite firm 5 percent owned by Alcoa
A loan from Ford U.S.A. to a Canadian parts-making subsidiary in which Ford holds 55 percent of shares	A loan from Ford U.S.A. to a Canadian parts-making firm in which Ford U.S.A. holds 8 percent of shares.

* As discussed in Chapter 24.

Note that direct investment consists of any investment, whether new ownership or simple lending, as long as the investing firm owns over 10 percent of the foreign firm being invested in.[1] The distinction between direct and portfolio (nondirect) investment is thus meant to focus on the issue of control.

DIRECT INVESTMENT IS NOT JUST A CAPITAL MOVEMENT

The fact that the investor has substantial control over the foreign subsidiary enterprise makes direct investment more complex in nature than portfolio investment. A controlled subsidiary often receives direct inputs of managerial skills, trade secrets, technology, rights to use brand names, and instructions about which markets to pursue and which to avoid.

In fact, direct investment is so much more than just a capital movement that in many cases it begins without any net flow of capital at all. Sometimes the parent company borrows the initial financial capital exclusively in the host country, adding only its brand name, managerial formulas, and other assets of the less tangible variety. Once the subsidiary becomes profitable, it grows from reinvested internal profits and newly borrowed funds, while sending a part of profits back to the parent whose investments were so hard to see.

Why should it often be the case that little or no financial capital initially flows in cases where the parent will ultimately build up a large equity while bringing home part of each year's profits? The main plausible explanation is that such apparently immaculate conceptions of foreign offspring are motivated by a fear of expropriation. Ever since World War I and the Russian revolution, host countries have shown willingness to seize the assets of multinationals, even without compensating the investors. Realizing the danger of expropriation, many multinationals have hedged their direct foreign

---

[1] Balance-of-payments accountants also define direct investment as any lending in, or purchase of stock in, firms owned in greater proportion by parties in the investor's home country (e.g., the United States) even if the *individual* investor does not own 10 percent of the firm being invested in.

investments in a way analogous to hedging in the foreign-exchange market. They have often matched much of their tangible assets in a host country with borrowings in that country (for which the tangible assets serve as collateral). If political change brings expropriation, the parents also can tell the host-country creditors to try to collect their repayments from their own (expropriating) government. With freedom from liabilities offsetting part or all of its asset losses in that country, the parent could not be held hostage. Its technology, market secrets, and managerial skills could typically elude expropriation. This hedging against expropriation seems to be one reason why parent firms increasingly concentrate on investing less tangible, more removable assets in their foreign subsidiaries.

WHEN AND WHERE DFI OCCURS

Direct foreign investment has been rising and falling, mainly rising, throughout the 20th century. It had its fastest growth, and took its largest share of all international investment, in the postwar generation dating roughly from the Korean War (1950–53) to the first oil shock (1973–74). During that period, international investments were dominated by investment outflows from the United States. The Americans have historically shown a greater preference for DFI and direct control than have other investing countries, particularly Britain, France, and the oil-rich nations, all of whom have channeled a greater proportion of their foreign investments into portfolio lending.[2] Thus the early postwar rise of American capital exports propelled DFI and American-based multinationals into international prominence. Since the early 1970s, DFI has grown more slowly, being eclipsed by two waves of portfolio lending—the ill-fated surge of lending to developing countries in 1974–82, which was discussed in Chapter 24, and the surge of lending to the United States in the 1980s.

Direct foreign investment has also changed direction. First, it has moved away from the Third World, where it had met with resistance and expropriations climaxing in the 1970s. Now almost half of the accumulated stock of U.S. direct investments is in Europe. Second, the United States has attracted more DFI inflows than any other nation in the early 1980s. The main direct investor in the United States as of 1980 was the Netherlands, followed by the United Kingdom, Canada, and Germany, with Japan rapidly becoming a leading investor. Almost none of the DFI in the United States is held by investors from OPEC nations. Finally, since 1978, the People's Republic of China has begun to host significant amounts of DFI, often as a partner in ownership.

---

[2] Japan has occupied an intermediate position. Much of its outward investment in the 1970s took the form of DFI, but in the 1980s, it shifted toward portfolio lending, especially lending to the U.S. government.

Auto workers add a hood to a new car manufactured in Shanghai, China, under a joint venture between China and Volkswagen. The production methods shown here are typical of multinational manufacturing: more labor intensive and less automated than in the investing and managing country (West Germany) but less labor intensive and more automated than most manufacturing in the host country (China). (J. P. Laffont/Sygma)

With these shifts has come a visible change in the character of DFI. As of the mid-1970s, the prototypical direct foreign investments were American-based extractors of minerals and other primary products, such as the Arabian-American Oil Company (Aramco) consortium in Saudi Arabia, the United Fruit Company in Central America, or Kennecott Copper in Chile. Now most DFI is in manufacturing, much of it in high-technology lines. Third World governments have switched from taxing and nationalizing DFI aggressively to wooing it with special tax breaks. Meanwhile, the United States has passed through a wave of initial shock when foreign-based firms moved into America. The same Americans who had implicitly assumed that American direct investments abroad were a boon to the host countries at the expense of American jobs now began to fear that foreign DFI in America was bad for the American hosts. Texans voiced the fear that Elf Acquitane's purchase of Texasgulf's sulfur-producing facilities might compromise America's national security. The Iowa state legislature hastily passed laws to restrict the selling of Iowa's farm land to foreign investors, lest a national legacy be lost. After a time, however, the U.S. mood became more welcoming, as states competed to attract foreign firms, and as farmers came to *hope* fervently that they could sell as much farmland as possible to wealthy foreigners.

WHAT EXPLAINS DFI?

Before we can sense what policies the source countries and host countries should adopt toward direct foreign investment, we need to survey the competing explanations for its private profitability.

Not Just Simple Competition and Portfolio Diversification

Under perfect competition, why would risk-averse firms invest so heavily in a foreign firm as to make it a largely owned subsidiary? As a rule, the variations in random luck facing competitive firms differ across firms and countries. A risk-averse investor would want to diversify his or her portfolio so as to include assets with not-so-correlated luck. Why put a large share of your net worth into a basket of investments that either pay off well together or suffer disaster together, if there are other combinations giving the same expected average return with less self-feeding risk? Thus, risk-averse investors should be expected to devote only small shares of their own portfolios to a wide range of enterprises. Such diversification is likely to steer them away from capturing controlling interests in individual enterprises.

Also, contrary to the spirit of simple models of competition, it takes some *firm-specific advantages* to explain why so much DFI occurs. One should ask what makes it possible for the direct investor to move into a foreign economy in competition with local entrepreneurs. A local company has an advantage over a foreign company, other things being equal. It is expensive to operate at a distance, expensive in travel, communication, and especially expensive in misunderstanding. To overcome the inherent native advantage of being on the ground, the firm entering from abroad must have some other advantage not shared with its local competitor. The advantage typically lies in technology or patents. It may inhere in special access to very large amounts of capital, amounts far larger than the ordinary national firm can command. The firm may have better access to markets in foreign countries merely by reason of its international status. Or, as in the case of petroleum refining or metal processing, the firm may coordinate operations and invested capital requirements at various stages in a vertical production process and, because of heavy inventory costs and its knowledge of the requirements at each stage, it may be able to economize through synchronizing operations. It may merely have differentiated products built on advertising. Or it may have truly superior management. But some special advantage is necessary for the firm to overcome the disadvantage of operating at a distance.

The firm must be able not only to make higher profits abroad than it could at home, but it also must be able to earn higher profits abroad than local firms can earn in their own markets. For all its imperfections, the international capital market would be expected to be able to transfer mere capital from one country to another better than could a firm whose major preoccupations lie in production and marketing.

DFI as Imperfect Competition: Two Views

The key role played by firm-specific advantages has led scholars to move away from models of simple competition toward perspectives associating DFI with one or another kind of special market power. Two variants, with differing policy implications, stand out.

1. The Hymer View.   A provocative thesis and book by Stephen Hymer (1976) saw the role of firm-specific advantages as a way of marrying the study of direct foreign investment with classic models of imperfect competition in product markets. To Hymer, a direct foreign investor is a monopolist or, more often, an oligopolist in product markets. It invests in foreign enterprises in order to stifle competition and protect its market power. It insists on having a controlling interest in those same enterprises, and it refuses to share ownership, in order to keep them from competing with its other branches—and also to keep its company secrets secure.

Hymer's approach does help explain the frequent pattern of "defensive investment." Major companies often seem to set up enterprises abroad that look only marginally profitable, yet do so with the stated purpose of beating their main competitors to the same national markets. Kodak may set up a foreign branch mainly because it fears that if it doesn't Fuji will. Ford and GM seem to have set up auto-making firms in the Third World in order to shut each other out. Although such defensive investment may seem like good-old competition, Hymer plausibly viewed it as oligopolistic behavior, characteristic of short-run "competition among the few" in pursuit of later market power.

If direct foreign investment really betrays power in product markets, as Hymer implied, then governments should be ready to impose controls on it. An oligopolist or monopolist that seeks to protect market power may well act against the national interest. For example, a U.S.-based subsidiary in Singapore may be told by its parent company not to sell in Thailand or India, whose markets bring high markups to its subsidiaries there. The prospective host government, here Singapore, may wish to constrain such a foreign parent to either allow more competition or stay out of Singapore, in favor of another investor who will export more aggressively from Singapore. The defensive investment pattern should also cause some concern because it implies that the company is likely to lobby the host government for special market protection, such as import barriers, which benefit the company but not the host nation as a whole.

2. The Appropriability Theory.[3]

Looked at in a different mirror, the key firm-specific advantages that seem to make DFI happen do not imply such major threats to competition in product markets. Rather, they are advantages that give firms monopoly power only in the markets for those key productive inputs themselves, such as a firm's excellent management, its superior information about buyers, its patent on a past discovery, its secret recipes, and its tricks of the trade. Seldom do these input advantages give the firm market power (i.e., control over price) in the product market. Instead, the firm typically reaps economic rents while nonetheless competing as a price-taker in its product market.

The firm-specific advantages make the firm engage in direct investment abroad for the same reasons that make it build its own facilities, instead of buying from others, at home. The economics of whether or not to engage in DFI is simply an international extension of the decision about the boundaries of the firm (whether to make or buy, whether to own or rent, etc.). In order to *appropriate* the potential gains from its advantage, the firm often finds that it is better to keep control and ownership to itself. If it did not keep tight control, and if it offered to share its foreign enterprise with other owners, its firm-specific productive advantages might be lost. For example, where production workers must be organized and supervised as only the firm knows how, efficiency and product quality might suffer if the firm were to share control with others (Japanese automakers have often feared as much about their American-subsidiary branches, though Toyota has been willing to undertake a joint production venture with General Motors). If a firm made some of its secrets freely available to partners in the host country, that knowledge might be used to compete against the firm itself, either by defecting partners or by others. (If its knowledge is protected by a patent, even in the host country, that knowledge need not be kept secret and the problem of making the fruits of productive knowledge appropriable by the discoverer is solved.)

The appropriability theory has different predictive powers from the Hymer view. Its relative strength is that it predicts both the prevalence of, and problems with, high-technology industries among direct foreign investments. DFI tends to be far heavier in high-technology industries because their dependence on complex skills and valuable knowledge makes firms in this sector especially aware of the advantages of keeping direct control of all branch enterprises. Problems arise, however, when it is difficult to guarantee that the fruits of a firm's technological advantages will be appropriated by the firm itself when it operates in some other country. If it fears it cannot

---

[3] The appropriability theory as described here is, in fact, a hybrid. As a theory of DFI and the scope of multinationals, it is copyrighted by Stephen P. Magee (1984, and sources cited there). Yet I have also mixed in traces of Ronald Coase's discussion of the nature of the firm.

keep effective control over its foreign subsidiaries, it will refrain from some productive investments, with losses to all parties (the firm itself, the host country, and the world as a whole).

The appropriability theory also has different policy implications from the Hymer view. Its emphasis on the productive nature of most of the firm-specific advantages motivating DFI favors policies that either leave DFI alone or positively encourage it with favorable government treatment. Whether DFI will be left alone or actually favored again depends on how well the firm is able to appropriate the fruits of its own productive investment. If it can do so, then the government can presumably leave it alone. if it cannot, and there are "external benefits" of its productivity that would spill over to competitors and others, the government should positively subsidize the incoming direct investment.

DFI AS TAX EVASION

The rise of direct foreign investment is in part a reaction to the rise of taxation as a share of economic life. The higher tax rates become, the greater the incentive to look for ways, both legal and otherwise, of avoiding those taxes. One obvious way is to shop around among governments and shift your firm's operations to the jurisdiction of governments offering lower tax rates.[4] Direct foreign investment does that in two ways. First, DFI allows a multinational firm to settle in countries with lower taxes. Whether this is good or bad from a world point of view depends on the uses to which tax revenues are put and whether the productivity of the investing firm is lower in the lower tax country.

Second, multinational firms can engage in *transfer pricing* and other devices for reporting most of their profits in low-tax countries, even though the profits were earned in high-tax countries. As noted briefly in Chapter 24, transfer pricing is an art form that can be practiced by accountants of any firm dealing with itself across national borders. To evade corporate income taxes, the firm can have its unit in the high-tax country be overcharged (or underpaid) for goods and services that unit buys from (sells to) the less taxed branch. That way, the unit in the high-tax country doesn't show its tax officials much profit, while the unit in the low-tax country shows high profits. Profits are clandestinely "transferred" from the branch in the high-tax country to the branch in the low-tax country. The result: net tax reduction for the multinational firm in question. Although tax officials could in principle spot and punish the evasion by proving that the prices that one branch

---

[4] Here and in what follows, we assume that higher tax rates in one nation are *not* matched by higher values of public programs in the eyes of the firm. If they were, then higher taxes would not be something to avoid. In practice, though, firms often feel that the public programs redistribute tax money toward others, and they view taxes as virtually solid losses.

charges another are far from market prices, in practice the firm can usually disguise its transfer pricing.

Governments sometimes try to retaliate against the lightfooted multinationals by changing the tax rules. A good example is the recent legal fight over the "unitary taxation" of multinational firms by California, Montana, and a few other relatively high-tax states in the United States. In levying their corporate income taxes, these states refuse to believe a multinational firm's own declaration of its profits on operations within the state. Such declarations typically show a much smaller share of profits in the high-tax states than the shares of each firm's property, payroll, or sales taking place in those states. The high-tax states turn to a unitary tax rule that assumes the multinational firm actually earned the same share of its declared world profits in the state as the average share of its world property, payroll, and sales in the state. Since 1981, Shell, Alcoa, and several foreign governments have teamed up to fight against the unitary taxes of California, Montana, and other states. A few states have yielded, allowing the multinationals to divide their reported profits between high- and low-tax areas as their accountants see fit. But the battles goes on in the remaining states. The key underlying issue is the firms' desire to shop around and choose the taxing governments they like versus some governments' desire to levy higher taxes than others levy.

SHOULD THE SOURCE COUNTRY RESTRICT DFI OUTFLOW?

To decide whether DFI should be restricted by the source (or investing) country is a difficult task. Let's approach it in four steps: (1) surveying the clear and sensible result of standard static welfare analysis, (2) noting how national welfare conclusions hinge on how we view the nationality of the multinational firm, (3) noting the special relationship of the multinational firm to international political markets, and (4) considering economic arguments for net national gains from taxing outward DFI.

The best starting point for policy judgments about DFI and multinationals is a static welfare analysis that seems to deliver most of the key lessons even though it cannot deal with much of the relevant political and economic dynamics. Look back at Figure 24.1 in Chapter 24, which gives the static-Marshallian portrayal of the effects of international lending. To apply the same framework to direct foreign investment, let the asset (or "wealth") in question become the seldom-measured bundle of managerial and financial services the parent company "invests" in the host-country branch. Let the part of the lending country be played by the source country (the country of the parent), and let the part of the borrowing country be played by the host country or countries. The rate of return becomes the rate of earnings (royalties, fees, interest, and profits) on the bundle of productive assets involved in the DFI.

With the framework of Figure 24.1 thus extended to the case of DFI, we get the standard welfare results:

the source country as a whole gains *(a + b + c)* because the gains to the investors themselves are greater than the losses to laborers and others in the source country;

and

the host country as a whole gains *(d + e + f)* because the gains to laborers and others are greater than the losses to the host-country investors who must compete against the inflow of managerial and financial assets from the source country.

The losses to laborers and others in the source country deserve further explanation. Representatives of organized labor in the United States and Canada have fought hard for restrictions on the freedom of companies based in North America to set up branches producing overseas and in Mexico, arguing that their jobs are being exported. Basically, their protest is correct, even though there are indirect ways in which DFI creates some jobs in the United States and Canada. The freedom to replace source-country production and jobs with production and jobs in other countries is particularly exercised by firms faced with strong labor organizations in the source country. But laborers are not the only ones in source countries who lose from DFI. Taxpayers in general lose because the firm's profits become harder to tax when they occur abroad, leaving other taxpayers the choice of paying more taxes or cutting back on government-financed public programs. The aggrieved taxpayers in this case are analogous to landlords who lose rents because a tenant has emigrated.

Yet for all the losses to laborers and taxpayers in the source country (like those losses to lending-country borrowers in Figure 24.1), the gains to the investors themselves are even greater. If the host country is made up of those laborers, taxpayers, and investors, there is still net gain for the country as a whole.

Here comes the second key step to understanding the welfare effects of DFI, however. To conclude from analysis like that in Figure 24.1 that the source country gains, we had to view the investors as part of the source country. But from many perspectives the nationality of the investors is not clear. They can be investors without a firm political base in any country, just like the disenfranchised migrant laborers of Chapter 23. Suppose that the source country's political debate over DFI denies the investors a voice. They might even be treated as pariahs because of their willingness to "take the money and run," leaving workers and taxpayers behind. The easiest firms to disenfranchise might be the true multinationals like Shell Petroleum N.V., who do not have a home country except as a legal technicality. If the investing firm is viewed by the source country as "them" and not as "us," the exclusively-defined source country does indeed lose from free international investment.[5]

Yet, against the possibility that multinational firms are often disenfranchised in national policy debates, we must weigh the frequent reality of the opposite case: the case in which they purchase enough lobbying voice in the political marketplace to distort the foreign policy of the source country to their own ends. Historically, the governments of the United States, Britain, and other investing nations have been involved in costly foreign conflicts in defense of investors' interests that do not align with the interests of other voters. Even though such considerations do not lend themselves to any clear quantitative accounting, the threat of foreign-policy distortion must be weighed as a factor calling for selective restraints on DFI.

There are additional economic arguments for taxing outward-bound DFI. First, a large source country like the United States or Japan might conceivably reap some slight optimal-tax gains (à la Figure 24.1) by raising the pretax returns of the restricted outflow of investments, though their power to do so as individual nations is probably declining. Second, it may well be that DFI carries external technological benefits with it. For all the firms' attempts to appropriate all the fruits of their technology, many gains may accrue to others in the place of the investment, through training and research. If so, outward DFI takes those external benefits away from the source country. A case can be made for taxing earnings from investments abroad to charge for the externalities, though in practice there is no guarantee that the tax is enforceable or set at the optimal level.

For the source country, then, a fairly clear set of qualitative results emerges:

a. the direct market effects of DFI are favorable to the source country if the investors are viewed as part of that nation, but

b. this result is reversed if the investors do not have a vote in the source country, and

c. there are political and economic drawbacks to allowing outward DFI, drawbacks that recommend restricting it to some (debatable) degree.

SHOULD THE HOST COUNTRY RESTRICT IT?

The effects of DFI on the host country, and the pros and cons of host-country restrictions on it, are symmetrical in form to those facing the source country.

---

[5] In Figure 24.1, these losses can be found, though they are not explicitly identified. The change from no investment to free investment brings the investors the markup from 2 percent to 5 percent on their entire wealth (W_j). But it costs others in the investing country the trapezoid under the marginal product curve between 2 percent and 5 percent, or $(5\%-2\%)$ W_j minus area $(a + b + c)$.

First, as noted above, the standard static analysis of international invest-ment, in the modified version of Figure 24.1 just described, finds that the host country as a whole gains *(d + e + f)* from the inflow. Laborers and suppliers employed by the new enterprises, along with national and local taxing governments, gain more than competing domestic investors lose.

Second, the host country, like the source country, needs to worry about the troubled relationship of the multinational investor to the political market-place. Multinationals can enlist the support of powerful source-country gov-ernments to pressure the host country in a confrontation. They can also buy host-country politicians and bankroll plots against the government, as International Telephone and Telegraph did against the Allende government in Chile in 1972–73. Such political realities must be weighed in the balance, even though they do not lend themselves to any quantifiable prescription for a tax on DFI.

Again, as with the source country's perspective, the host country must weigh indirect economic effects when deciding whether to tax or subsidize incoming DFI. And again the two main kinds of effects to consider relate to the possibility of an optimal tax and to technological externalities. This time, however, there may be a stronger case for encouraging the investors. The idea of an optimal tax on DFI inflows (or the private earnings derived from them) is weakened by the fact that few host countries, except perhaps Brazil, have the power to get foreign investors to take worse terms when faced with a tax. And the possibility that DFI brings technological side-benefits (training, etc.) wherever it goes argues in favor of *subsidizing* incom-ing investments to bring the country the side-benefits accompanying extra investments.

Thus, the case for taxing DFI is not as strong from the host-country perspective as from the source-country perspective. The static gains are offset by the political dangers of inviting in large multinationals, but the possibility of technological side-benefits argues for a subsidy. The case for a subsidy, while empirically uncertain, has impressed Third World govern-ments since the mid-1970s: they compete in offering special tax breaks in an attempt to woo foreign investors.

SUMMARY

Direct foreign investment (DFI) is a flow of entrepreneurial capital, in the form of some mixture of managerial skills and financial lending. Its more specific balance-of-payments accounting definition is any flow of lending to, or purchase of ownership in, a foreign enterprise that is largely owned by residents of the investing, or ''source,'' country. The returns earned by the direct investors are accordingly a mixture of interest, dividends, license fees, and managerial fees. Some DFI consists of investments in foreign branches by a parent firm clearly based in one source country. In other cases the investing firm is a true multinational, with no clear home country.

DFI grew very rapidly in the early postwar period, with the United States being the largest investing nation. Since the early 1970s, it has grown more slowly and changed direction. Less and less has been flowing to the Third World, while more and more has been flowing to the United States and the People's Republic of China. Direct investments in mineral extraction have faded, replaced by an increasing predominance of investments in manufacturing, especially in high-technology lines.

Explaining why DFI occurs requires us to go beyond the simple competitive model with portfolio diversification. What make direct investment profitable are firm-specific advantages that the firm needs to protect by directly managing production. The firm-specific advantages might be viewed in either of two ways. Hymer's view cast them in shadowy light, as embodiments of imperfect competition trying to protect company secrets and monopoly power. His view helps explain the frequent occurrence of *defensive investment* among multinational firms, who seem to be behaving like oligopolists. Hymer's view implies that the host government should restrict and regulate incoming DFI. An alternative is the *appropriability theory,* which more charitably interprets the firm-specific advantages as productive assets, the marginal products of which can be more effectively captured by the firm if it invests directly. The appropriability theory is the international counterpart to the theory of the size of the firm (i.e., when to supervise production itself instead of licensing, when to buy instead of lease, etc.). It helps account for the preponderance of technology-intensive lines in DFI, and it implies that the host government can either leave DFI inflows alone or subsidize.

Another force driving DFI is tax evasion. Shopping around the globe for the lowest cost sites involves shopping for lower tax rates as well. Part of the decision of which country to invest in therefore involves the desire to keep taxes down. Firms therefore prefer low-tax nations as ostensible bases of operation, other costs being equal. In addition, firms use *transfer pricing* to shift their reported profits to the low-tax countries.

DFI tends more and more to consist of contracts involving managerial services more than outright movements of financial capital. The most likely reason for this is the fear of expropriation. In the case of ordinary financial capital movements, the host country has an incentive to tax or expropriate once the fresh inflow stops. Anticipating this (or remembering it from past experience), the multinational firms hold back on lending capital and concentrate on dispensing managerial services on a more pay-as-you-go basis. If the host country then chooses to confiscate foreign investments, the firms will not have much in the country that can be seized.

The source (or investing) country gains from the basic market effects of DFI as long as the investors themselves continue to have voices of citizenship. If they do not have such voice, and if we therefore exclude their investment incomes from measures of the national gain, the source country then can be said to lose from DFI. It may also have other reasons to tax and restrict outward-bound DFI: the optimal tax argument, the possibility that positive external benefits accompany DFI, and the possibility of foreign-policy distortion from lobbying by multinationals.

The host country has less reason to restrict DFI than does the source country. The possibility of positive external technological and training benefits tips the scales toward subsidizing DFI inflows rather than taxing them heavily. Political dangers remain, however, in the relationship with major multinational firms.

SUGGESTED READINGS

The best single recent collection of articles surveying the economics of multinationals is the set of articles by Little, Vernon, Magee, and Drucker in Adams (1984, Part V). Stephen Hymer's theory is presented in his book (1976).

The statistical patterns of foreign investment in the United States 1979–85 support, among other things, the appropriability theory's emphasis on firm specific assets: Ray (1989).

A recent overview of the economics of multinationals in Canada in Alan. M. Rugman (1980).

QUESTIONS FOR REVIEW

1. What best explains why direct foreign investment is profitable?

2. Why is so much DFI not a financial investment (or loan) at all, but just an exchange of management services for payments of royalties and fees?

3. Review the welfare conclusions that emerge from applying Figure 24.1 to the case of direct foreign investment. Identify the likely gainers and losers.

Appendixes

▼

Factor Supply, Technology, and Production Possibilities*

•

The shape of the production-possibilities curve used so much in the theory of international trade depends on the factor supplies of the country and on the technology for combining these factors to produce outputs. The usual device for portraying the state of technology is the **production function,** which expresses the output of any one commodity as a function of its inputs. In principle, one can derive the whole shape of the production-possibilities curve just by knowing the total supplies of the factors (or inputs) and the algebraic form of each commodity's production function. In practice, it proves easy to trace out the production-possibilities curve geometrically but often impossible to solve the production-function equations for the trade-offs between one commodity and another (except by approximation, or with the help of extra limiting assumptions).

Geometrically, the production function for each commodity can be shown in two dimensions by plotting the various combinations of two factors needed to produce given amounts of the commodity in question. Figure A.1 shows several **production isoquants,** each showing the different combinations of land and labor that could yield a given level of output. The smooth isoquants Figure A.1A on the left portray a case in which land and labor are partial substitutes for one another in cloth. Starting from a point like W, it would be possible to keep the same cloth output per year (i.e., stay on the isoquant $T—T$) with less labor if one used enough more land, as at V. By contrast, in Figure A.1B, the production function has a special form (sometimes called the Leontiev production function) in which land and labor are not substitutes at all. Thus, starting from Point W, one cannot give up any labor inputs without falling to a lower output isoquant, regardless of how

---

* Appendix to Chapter 2.

FIGURE A.1A   Production Function for Cloth

much extra land is added. Thus the isoquant moves vertically up from Point *W* to points like *R* demanding the same labor inputs. Some industries are thought to resemble this special case, though the factors of production are usually partial substitutes for one another, as in Figure A.1A.

To derive the production-possibilities curves representing the greatest feasible combinations of cloth and wheat output an economy is capable of, we do not need any more economic information than that implicit in the production-function isoquants already sketched. Yet it is useful to pause briefly at this point and remember how the combinations of factors actually used are supposed to relate to factor prices in a competitive economy, since Chapters 3 through 5 will make considerable use of this relationship. The relative prices of the two factors are summarized in factor-price slopes like that of line *S—S* and *S'—S'* in Figure A.1A which are parallel. This slope shows the number of acres of land that can be traded for each hour of labor in the marketplace. Given this slope, competition would propel firms to produce at points of tangency like *W*, since such points maximize output for a given amount spent on inputs. In Figure A.1A, we have shown the often-imagined case in which any expansion of output would be achieved along the *expansion path R,* a straight line from the origin as long as the factor price ratio is still the slope *S—S*. If land became cheaper relative to labor, with a factor-price slope steeper than *S—S*, firms would tend to substitute some land for labor, shifting to points like *V*. In Figure A.1B,

FIGURE A.1B   Production Functions with Fixed Factor Proportions

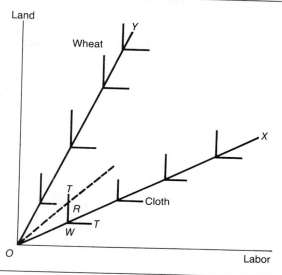

by contrast, the factor proportions would always be fixed, on the more labor-intensive expansion path *X* for cloth and the more land-intensive expansion path *Y* for wheat, regardless of the relative prices of land and labor. The relationship between production patterns and factor prices (in either direction) thus depends on the shapes of the production functions.

To know the most efficient combinations a nation can produce, we must now combine the technological possibilities represented by the production-function isoquants with the nation's total supplies of land and labor. A handy device for doing this is the so-called **Edgeworth-Bowley box diagram,** in which the dimensions of the box represent the amounts of land and labor in a country, which we shall call Britain. (See Figure A.2.) These factor supplies are assumed to be homogeneous in character and fixed in amount. The production function for cloth is drawn with its origin in the lower left-hand corner of the box at *O,* and with its isoquants, *T—T, T'—T',* and so on, moving out and up to the right. Its expansion path is *OX.* If all the labor in Britain *(OR)* were used to make cloth, only *RX* of land would be required, and *O'X* of land would be left unemployed. At *X,* the marginal physical product of land would be zero.

The production function for wheat is drawn reversed and upside down, with its origin at *O'* and extending downward and to the left. Its expansion path is *OY.* At *Y,* all the land would be employed, and *YR* of labor, but *OY* of labor would be unemployed. *OX* and *O'Y* intersect at *W,* which is the only production point in the box diagram where there can be full employ-

FIGURE A.2   Edgeworth-Bowley Box Diagram with Fixed Factor Proportions

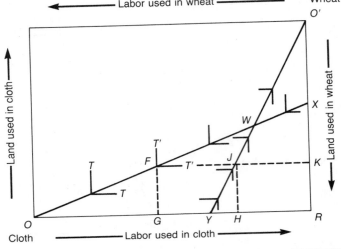

ment and positive prices for both factors. At any other point on either expansion path, say *F* on *OX,* land and labor will be able to produce at *J* on the expansion path for wheat; *OG* of labor will be engaged in cloth, and *HR* in wheat. *RK* of land will be employed in cloth, and *O'K''* in wheat. But *GH* of labor will be unemployed.

The curve *OWO',* as in Figure A.2, is in effect a transformation curve, showing the various combinations of wheat and cloth that can be produced in Britain, given the factor endowments of the country. The only point providing full employment of the two factors and positive factor prices is *W. OWO'* does not look like a transformation curve, because it is given in terms of physical units of land and labor, rather than physical units of production. If we remap the *OWO'* curve in Figure A.2 from factor space into commodity space in terms of units of wheat and cloth and turn it right side up, it appears to be a normal production-possibility curve, though kinked at *W,* as in Figure A.3.

If cloth and wheat were produced with fixed factor coefficients, and these were identical, the two expansion paths would coincide, as in A.4A, and the transformation curve becomes a straight line, as in A.4B. But this means that land and labor are always used in the same combination so that they might well be regarded as a single factor. This is equivalent to Ricardo's labor theory of value and its resultant straight-line transformation curve. A similar straight-line transformation curve would be produced by constant costs and identical production functions in the two commodities. It is vital to distinguish between constant costs and constant opportunity costs. The

FIGURE A.3 Transformation Curve Derived from Edgeworth-Bowley Box
Diagram with Fixed Factor Proportions

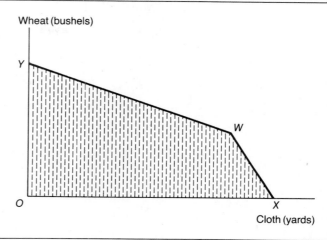

FIGURE A.4A Constant Opportunity Costs: Identical Fixed Factor Proportions

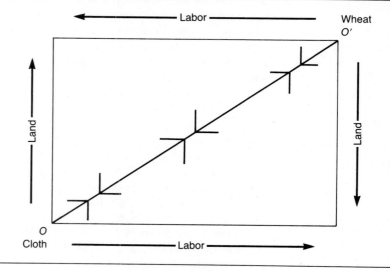

straight-line transformation curve represents constant opportunity costs. If
the production functions for the two commodities differ, the transformation
curve will exhibit curvature, even though there are constant returns to scale
in each commodity taken separately.

When the law of variable proportions holds and there is the possibility

FIGURE A.4B   Transformation Curve Derived from Figure A.4A

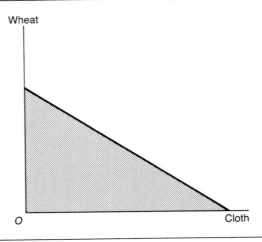

of substitution between factors in the production of a commodity, there is no unique expansion path. Instead, a separate expansion path can be drawn for any given set of factor prices, or we can draw in the isoquants for both commodities and trace out a locus of points of tangency between them. This locus represents the efficiency path, or the maximum combinations of production of the two goods which can be produced with the existing factor supply. It is shown in Figure A.5A. To see why it is an efficient path, suppose that production were to take place at W, away from the efficiency locus. W is on cloth isoquant 7, and on wheat isoquant 5. But there is a point T, also on cloth isoquant 7, which is on a higher isoquant (6) of wheat. It would therefore be possible to produce more wheat without giving up any cloth. Or there is a point T' on wheat isoquant 5 which is on cloth isoquant 8. It would be equally possible to produce more cloth and the same amount of wheat. Any point off the locus of tangencies of isoquants of the two production functions is therefore inefficient, insofar as it would be possible to get more output of one commodity without losing any of the other, by moving to the locus.

The efficiency locus is the exact analogue of the "contract curve" in exchange theory. Here the dimensions of the box are given by fixed supplies of commodities; a point off the contract curve represents initial endowments of two individuals, with utility maps measured from origins in the two corners; and the two individuals can improve their utility by moving from the initial endowment point to the contract curve.

When the Edgeworth-Bowley box is used for production, it shows not only the efficient combinations of outputs but also factor combinations and factor prices. Unlike the transformation curve (A.5B), it cannot show the

FIGURE A.5A Maximum Efficiency Locus under Variable Factor Proportions

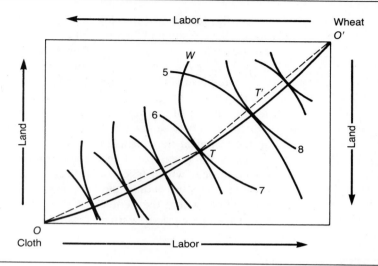

FIGURE A.5B Transformation Curve Derived from Figure A.5A

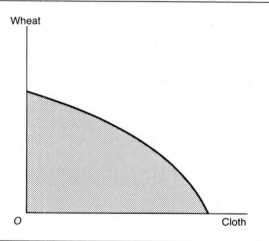

relative price of wheat and cloth. If we assume that production is at T, however, the factor proportions in cloth are represented by the slope of OT, and the factor proportions in wheat by $O'T$. It will be obvious that the indicated allocation employs all the land and all the labor. The relative price of land and labor with these outputs is represented by the slope of the tangency to the maximum efficiency locus at T.

VARIABLE FACTOR SUPPLIES

To use the Edgeworth-Bowley box approach in its usual form, one must assume that the national factor supplies are fixed. This is somewhat unrealistic because the total size of the labor force, the stock of accumulated nonhuman capital, and even the supply of improved land to respond to the rewards being offered to such factors in the marketplace.

Fortunately, the geometry can be altered to allow for a response of each factor to its rate of return. Jaroslav Vanek has demonstrated that it is possible to distinguish between two kinds of production-possibility curves, one showing the technical transformation schedules between two goods, which does not allow for reactions of the factors to changes in factor prices, and an economic one, which takes such reactions into account. The economically possible curve lies within the technically feasible curve, except at one or more points where they coincide, since the technical possibilities frontier is an envelope curve of various feasible curves.

SUGGESTED READINGS

The literature on comparative advantage and factor supply is enormous, and the student is referred to Richard E. Caves, *Trade and Economic Structure* (Cambridge, Mass.: Harvard University Press, 1960), Chapters 3, 4, and 5, for a review and bibliography. Two of the outstanding articles, R. Robinson, "Factor Proportions and Comparative Advantage," *Quarterly Journal of Economics*, May 1956, and T. M. Rybczynski, "Factor Endowment and Relative Commodity Prices," *Economica*, November 1955, are gathered in the 1967 American Economics Association, *Readings in International Economics*, Part 1.

The geometry of adding variable factor supplies to the model is sketched in Jaroslav Vanek, "An Afterthought on the 'Real Cost—Opportunity Cost Dispute' and Some Aspects of General Equilibrium under Conditions of Variable Factor Supplies," *Review of Economic Studies*, June 1959.

▼

Deriving the Offer Curve: Another Way of Modeling Trade Demand and Supply

•

The supply and demand curves introduced in Chapters 2 and 3 have several advantages. They are familiar, and they offer the easiest way of seeing how to quantify the welfare effects of trade on producer and consumer groups in each country. They are also easily extended to the task of analyzing trade effects in many different goods, each taken one at a time. Yet much of the theoretical literature uses another geometric device that gives some of the same information: the *offer curve*, showing how the export and import quantities a nation chooses will vary with the international terms of trade. The frequent use of the offer curve in the more advanced literature means that anyone seeking to master that literature needs to know how the curve is derived and used. This appendix gives the geometric derivation of the offer curve. Appendix E shows how it has been used in discussing optimal tariff policy.

A region or nation's offer curve is exactly equivalent to either its supply curve for exports or its demand curve for imports. (For examples of the latter two curves, see the center panel of Figure 3.1.) It graphs trade offers as a function of the international price ratio (the "terms of trade"). And it can be derived from the same production-possibility curves and community indifference curves used extensively in Chapter 3.

Figure B.1 shows the derivation, starting from the usual production and consumption trade-offs. For each international price ratio, the behavior of the United States produces a quantity of exports willingly offered in exchange for imports at that price ratio. At two bushels per yard, the United States does not want to trade at all, as shown at S_0. At one bushel per yard, the United States would find cloth cheaper, and wheat more valuable, than without trade. It would be willing to export 40 billion bushels and import 40 billion yards, by efficiently producing at S_1 and consuming at C_1. A price of half a bushel per yard would again induce the United States to offer 40 billion of wheat exports, but this time in exchange for 80 billion yards of cloth. Each of these offers is plotted on the lower half of Figure B.1 (as points O, O_1, and O_2), where the axes are the exports and imports to be exchanged, and the slope of any ray from the origin is a price ratio. The resulting curve O_{US} is the U.S. offer curve. A similar derivation could produce the rest of the world's offer curve, O_{RW}. Only at the equilibrium price of one bushel per yard, at point O, will the United States and the rest of the world be able to agree on how much to trade.

The offer curves have a fairly straightforward interpretation. The United States would prefer to have the foreign offer curve pushed toward the northeast (up and to the right), offering more foreign cloth for less American wheat. In fact, one can draw "trade indifference curves" such as I_2 and I_3, representing the highest levels of well-being attainable by the United States at each international price ratio.[1] Similarly, the rest of the world would just as soon have O_{US} pushed down to the southwest, giving more American wheat for less cloth.

Yet each offer curve sets a limit on the bargains the other side can get. Improvements in foreign clothmaking productivity would open up better bargains for the United States by shifting O_{RW} to the northeast. In such a case, the improvement in the terms of trade (toward cheaper imported cloth) would give the right kind of welfare hint: the United States is truly better off as the terms "improve." On the other hand, the United States gets no clear gains if the terms of trade are "improved" by a U.S. harvest failure, even though it raises the relative price of wheat in world markets. Here we are warned that welfare changes may or may not follow the terms of trade. Correct interpretation requires identifying the source of the change, and the offer curves help by distinguishing between U.S. behavior and the behavior of the rest of the world.

Within the constraints imposed by the position of the foreign offer curve, is there nothing a country can do to improve its welfare by moving its own offer curve? Not if the nation consists of large numbers of private individuals competing against each other in production and consumption with no government intervention. Such private competition merely puts us on the offer curve in the first place, and does not shift the curve. Yet if the nation acted as a single decision-making unit, there is the glimmering of a chance to squeeze more advantage out of trade in Figure B.1. Starting at the free-trade equilibrium O_1, the United States might be able to come up with a way to move a short distance to the southeast along the foreign offer curve O_{RW}, reaching somewhat higher indifference curves than at O_1. How could this be done? Through an optimal tariff of the sort discussed in Appendix E, where the offer curves reappear.

---

[1] The precise method of deriving the trade indifference curves from production blocks and community indifference curves is shown in the sixth edition of this book, Appendix B.

FIGURE B.1 Deriving the Offer Curve

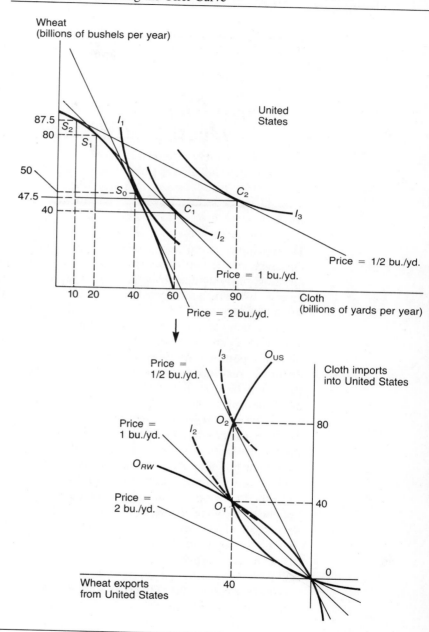

▼

A Simple General Equilibrium
Model of Trade and Growth

•

Theory improves our understanding of reality by distorting it. Every model, like every nontrivial human insight, distorts reality by simplifying it and ignoring many things that greet our eyes every day. At its best, formal theory, like art, picks just the right abstractions, the ones that show us something essential about the real world, something that mere intuition and common sense could not have established.

Formal algebraic modeling of the dependence of trade and growth on factor proportions, demand, and technology offers this sort of promise. By distorting reality constructively, it helps us see a number of relationships that were only partially established by volumes and volumes of literary and geometric illustration. Our understanding of the power and limits of the factor-proportions (or Heckscher-Ohlin) approach to explaining the links between trade and the economy has been greatly improved by a simple model of general equilibrium developed by Ronald W. Jones from diverse strands of previous theory (Jones 1965). Jones's model neatly ties together several key results presented in Part One. In a single set of equations, it links the factor-price-equalization theorem, the Stolper-Samuelson theorem, and the Rybczynski theorem of Chapter 4. More generally, it offers a coherent set of plausible testable predictions about income distribution, output growth, and prices in a trading economy. Variations on this simple model have also extended beyond trade issues to predict the effects of taxation, monopoly, and externalities in their longer-run aggregate setting.

The Jonesian model delivers these goods at theory's usual price: assumptions that obviously distort the real world. In the basic version explored here, it aggregates the world into a "two-by-two-by-two" model of just two factors of production, two countries, and two commodities that do not use each other as inputs. It also assumes perfect competition, full employment, and exogenous factor supplies. Once this sacrifice of realism has been made,

however, the model delivers insights that seem to transcend its strict assumptions.

To see how, let's trace the model from the point of view of a single small country. In this "small-country" case, trade with the rest of the world takes a very simple form at first: an exogenous price ratio fixed on world markets at a level independent of this country's behavior. Later, we shall sketch how this assumption can be relaxed by making world demand endogenous. Our country produces two goods with outputs A *and* B (e.g. let cloth = A and wheat = B), using two factors of production—the supply of labor *(L)* receiving the wage rate *(w)* and the stock of capital *(K)* receiving the rate of return *(r)*. Since there are only two goods, we only need to discuss one product price ratio, P_B, the price of the second good in units of the first good, which has a price set at unity ($P_A = 1$).

Under competition, price equals average and marginal cost in every industry. For our two sectors, this gives us two cost equations:

(1)$\qquad\qquad\qquad 1 = a_{KA}r + a_{LA}w \qquad$ and $\qquad$ **cost equations**
(2)$\qquad\qquad\qquad P_B = a_{KB}r + a_{LB}w$

where each a_{ij} is an input-output ratio for each *i*th factor and *j*th industry (e.g., a_{KA} = machine-hours of capital per yard of cloth, and a_{LB} = hours of labor per bushel of wheat). Each cost equation says that price on the left equals marginal costs on the right.

Next, we introduce factor-employment equations, which say that the total supply of each factor gets employed in one sector or another:

(3)$\qquad\qquad\qquad K = a_{KA}A + a_{KB}B \qquad$ **factor-employment**
(4)$\qquad\qquad\qquad L = a_{LA}A + a_{LB}B \qquad\qquad$ **equations**

Again, each a_{ij} is a prevailing ratio of input *i* to output in the *j*th industry, so that $a_{KA}A$ is the total amount of capital being employed in cloth production, and so forth.

Together these four equations could determine the four endogenous varia-
bles *r*, *w*, *A*, and *B*. The solution would be easy if we knew the price ratio P_B and the physical input-output ratios (the a_{ij}'s). The price ratio is no problem for now: we have made the small-country assumption that P_B is fixed on outside world markets, with our country exporting whichever goods its comparative advantage dictates at this price. The input-output ratios pose more of a problem. If we knew that all production functions were of the rigid Leontiev type, with fixed factor proportions as shown in Figures A.1B and A.2 in Appendix A, then the a_{ij}'s would be fixed numbers and we could solve the factor-employment equations to get both outputs. (That is, we would be solving for the outputs of wheat and cloth at Point W in Figures A.2 and A.3.) Fixed factor proportions seldom prevail, however. The a_{ij}'s are themselves functions of relative factor prices, or r/w. As the wage rate rises relative to the rental service price of capital, firms will try to use less labor and more capital for each level of output. We need to

decide how to represent the degree of this possible labor-capital substitution.

Most production functions that have fit the facts fairly well have assumed a constant, or approximately constant, elasticity of factor substitution. The elasticity of substitution between labor and capital in the *j*th industry is defined as

$$\sigma_j = \frac{\text{Percent rise in the capital-labor ratio } (K_j/L_j, \text{ or } a_{Kj}/a_{Lj})}{\text{Percent rise in the wage-rental ratio } (w/r)}$$

A production function holding this elasticity fixed is a constant-elasticity-of-substitution (CES) function. Special cases of the CES production function are the fixed-factor-proportions case just mentioned (for which $\sigma_j = 0$) and the venerable Cobb-Douglas production function (for which $\sigma_j = 1$ and the factor income ratio rK/wL is fixed). Given σ_A and σ_B for the wheat and cloth industries, respectively, we could in principle plug in input-output formulas of the sort $a_{ij} = a_{ij}(w,r)$, using the elasticities from the production functions in some way. There is a problem, though. These functions do not take a convenient linear form, and solving for the outputs *(A and B)* has been shown to be virtually impossible by a direct route.

Here, Jones added a clever twist that gets us back to manageable equations. His device was to convert all equations into proportionate rates of change. Once we have reexpressed Equations 1 through 4 in terms of rates of change in all variables, we can plug in the elasticities of substitution while keeping all equations conveniently linear. To do this, let us first define our proportionate rates of change. Let the "^" superscript mean the instantaneous rate of change as a proportion (or percentage/100) of the absolute level, so that for any variable X, $\hat{X} = dX/X$. Now, we are ready to rework all four equations into a linear system involving rates of change and a few key measurable elasticities and factor shares. Differentiating Equations 1 and 2 and defining some new factor cost shares yields:

(5) $\qquad\qquad 0 = \hat{r}\theta_{KA} + \hat{w}\theta_{LA} + \hat{a}_{KA}\theta_{KA} + \hat{a}_{LA}\theta_{LA}$ and

(6) $\qquad\qquad \hat{P}_B = \hat{r}\theta_{KB} + \hat{w}\theta_{LB} + \hat{a}_{KB}\theta_{KB} + \hat{a}_{LB}\theta_{LB}$

$$\underbrace{\qquad\qquad}_{\substack{price \\ changes}} \quad \underbrace{\qquad\qquad}_{\substack{factor\text{-}price \\ changes}} \quad \underbrace{\qquad\qquad\qquad}_{\substack{input\text{-}output \\ changes}}$$

where each θ_{ij} is the share of payments to factor *i* in the value of the output of the *j*th sector (e.g., $\theta_{LB} = wL_B/P_BB$). These two equations say that rates of change in product prices are determined by weighted averages of changes in factor prices and weighted averages of input-output changes. These input-output changes in turn can be relabeled as changes in overall productivity, or the ratio of outputs to inputs. Define total factor productivity T_j (or "technology," to be a little inaccurate) as a geometrically weighted average of output-input ratios, where the weights are the factor input shares of total cost. This means that $T_A = (1/a_{KA})^{\theta_{KA}} \cdot (1/a_{LA})^{\theta_{LA}}$ and $T_B = (1/a_{KB})^{\theta_{KB}} \cdot (1/a_{LB})^{\theta_{LB}}$. Differentiating again yields linear relationships in rates of change:

$$\hat{T}_A = -\hat{a}_{KA}\theta_{KA} - \hat{a}_{LA}\theta_{LA} \quad \text{and} \tag{7}$$
$$\hat{T}_B = -\hat{a}_{KB}\theta_{KB} - \hat{a}_{LB}\theta_{LB} \tag{8}$$

We can now express the cost equations in terms of these rates of progress as follows:

$$\hat{r}\theta_{KA} + \hat{w}\theta_{LA} = \hat{T}_A \tag{9}$$
$$\hat{r}\theta_{KB} + \hat{w}\theta_{LB} = \hat{T}_B + \hat{P}_B \tag{10}$$

cost-change equations

The factor-employment equations can also be converted into rate-of-change form, again by differentiating:

$$\hat{K} = \lambda_{KA}\hat{a}_{KA} + \lambda_{KA}\hat{A} + \lambda_{KB}\hat{a}_{KB} + \lambda_{KB}\hat{B} \quad \text{and} \tag{11}$$
$$\hat{L} = \lambda_{LA}\hat{a}_{LA} + \lambda_{LA}\hat{A} + \lambda_{LB}\hat{a}_{LB} + \lambda_{LB}\hat{B} \quad \text{where} \tag{12}$$

each λ_{ij} is the share of the ith factor employed in the jth sector ($\lambda_{KA} = K_A/K$, etc.). We must again convert the input-output ratios into a more useful form. It is here, with each equation focusing on changes in the use of a single factor, that we must bring in the elasticities of substitution, σ_A and σ_B. Each change in an input-output ratio, $\hat{a}_{ij}$, is the net result of two forces. The first is exogenous changes in technology. The second is induced changes in input use in response to movements in the factor-price ratio w/r. We can thus break each $\hat{a}_{ij}$ down as follows: $\hat{a}_{ij} = \hat{c}_{ij} - \hat{b}_{ij}$, where $\hat{c}_{ij}$ = the induced element and $\hat{b}_{ij}$ is an exogenous productivity (output/input) improvement. Now, using the definitions of the elasticities of substitution and Equations 7 and 8 (with the $\hat{T}$'s and $\hat{b}$'s = 0, so that $\hat{a}$'s = $\hat{c}$'s, and with each $\theta_{Lj} + \theta_{Kj} = 1$), we can derive expressions for the induced part of the input/output changes. The two sectors' elasticities of capital-labor substitution are:

$$\sigma_A = (\hat{c}_{KA} - \hat{c}_{LA})/(\hat{w} - \hat{r}) \quad \text{and} \tag{13}$$
$$\sigma_B = (\hat{c}_{KB} - \hat{c}_{LB})/(\hat{w} - \hat{r}) \tag{14}$$

The induced parts of the input/output changes become:

$$\hat{c}_{LA} = -\theta_{KA}\sigma_A(\hat{w} - \hat{r}) \tag{15} \qquad \hat{c}_{KA} = \theta_{LA}\sigma_A(\hat{w} - \hat{r}) \tag{16}$$
$$\hat{c}_{LB} = -\theta_{KB}\sigma_B(\hat{w} - \hat{r}) \tag{17} \qquad \hat{c}_{KB} = \theta_{LB}\sigma_B(\hat{w} - \hat{r}) \tag{18}$$

Each change in an input/output ratio consists of an exogenous part ($\hat{b}_{ij}$) and a part induced by changes in factor prices:

$$\hat{a}_{LA} = -\hat{b}_{LA} - \theta_{KA}\sigma_A(\hat{w} - \hat{r}) \tag{19} \qquad \hat{a}_{KA} = -\hat{b}_{KA} + \theta_{LA}\sigma_A(\hat{w} - \hat{r}) \tag{20}$$
$$\hat{a}_{LB} = -\hat{b}_{LB} - \theta_{KB}\sigma_B(\hat{w} - \hat{r}) \tag{21} \qquad \hat{a}_{KB} = -\hat{b}_{KB} + \theta_{LB}\sigma_B(\hat{w} - \hat{r}) \tag{22}$$

Using the breakdown of each input/output change into exogenous and induced parts (Equations 19–22) allows us to reexpress the two change-of-

---

FIGURE C.1   The Two-Product, Two-Factor General Equilibrium System for a
Small Open Economy, in Sketch and in Matrix Form

Sketch:

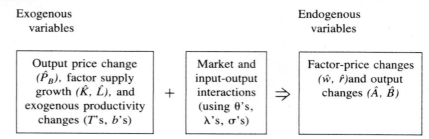

Matrix form:

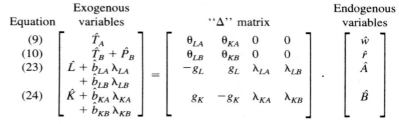

where

$$g_L = \lambda_{LA}\,\theta_{KA}\,\sigma_A + \lambda_{LB}\,\theta_{KB}\,\sigma_B \geq 0 \qquad \text{and}$$
$$g_K = \lambda_{KA}\,\theta_{LA}\,\sigma_A + \lambda_{KB}\,\theta_{LB}\,\sigma_B \geq 0$$

---

employment equations (Equations 11 and 12) as functions of exogenous
variables and the final endogenous variables $(\hat{w},\ \hat{r},\ \hat{A},\ \hat{B})$:

(23) $\hat{L} = \quad \lambda_{LA}\,[-\hat{b}_{LA}\ -\ \theta_{KA}\,\sigma_A(\hat{w}\ -\ \hat{r})]\ +\ \lambda_{LA}\hat{A}$ **employment-**
$\qquad +\ \lambda_{LB}\,[-\hat{b}_{LB}\ -\ \theta_{KB}\,\sigma_B(\hat{w}\ -\ \hat{r})]\ +\ \lambda_{LB}\hat{B}$ **change**

(24) $\hat{K} = \quad \lambda_{KA}\,[-\hat{b}_{KA}\ +\ \theta_{LA}\,\sigma_A(\hat{w}\ -\ \hat{r})]\ +\ \lambda_{KA}\hat{A}$ **equations**
$\qquad +\ \lambda_{KB}\,[-\hat{b}_{KB}\ +\ \theta_{LB}\,\sigma_B(\hat{w}\ -\ \hat{r})]\ +\ \lambda_{LB}\hat{B}$

Figure C.1 summarizes the four final equations that can now be solved
simultaneously. The four equations are the two cost-change equations (9
and 10) and the two employment-change equations (23 and 24). The four
endogenous variables are the two factor-price changes ($\hat{w}$ and $\hat{r}$) and the
two output changes ($\hat{A}$ and $\hat{B}$).

To avoid solving the four equations for four endogenous variables by
step-by-step substitution, try the slightly tidier and less tedious approach
of expressing the whole system as the matrix system in the lower panel of

FIGURE C.2   Results from the General-Equilibrium Model of a Small Open Economy

Effects of These Exogenous Shifts ↓	Effects on These Endogenous Variables = the Expressions below ÷ |Δ|:			
	Wage Change $(\hat{w})$	Rental Change $(\hat{r})$	Change in Output of A $(\hat{A})$	Change in Output of B $(\hat{B})$
Productivity growth in $A(\hat{T}_A)$:	$\theta_{KB}\|\lambda\|$	$-\theta_{LB}\|\lambda\|$	$g_L\lambda_{KB} + g_K\lambda_{LB}$	$-g_L\lambda_{KA} - g_K\lambda_{LA}$
Either productivity growth in $B(\hat{T}_B)$ or price change $(\hat{P}_B)$:	$-\theta_{KA}\|\lambda\|$	$\theta_{LA}\|\lambda\|$	$-g_L\lambda_{KB} - g_K\lambda_{LB}$	$g_L\lambda_{KA} + g_L\lambda_{KA}$
Growth in our labor supply $(\hat{L})$:	0	0	$\lambda_{KB}\|\theta\|$	$-\lambda_{KA}\|\theta\|$
Growth in our capital stock $(\hat{K})$:	0	0	$-\lambda_{LB}\|\theta\|$	$\lambda_{LA}\|\theta\|$

where

$$|\lambda| = \begin{vmatrix} \lambda_{LA} & \lambda_{LB} \\ \lambda_{KA} & \lambda_{KB} \end{vmatrix} = (\lambda_{LA} - \lambda_{KA}), \ |\theta| = \begin{vmatrix} \theta_{LA} & \theta_{KA} \\ \theta_{LB} & \theta_{KB} \end{vmatrix}$$
$$= (\theta_{LA} - \theta_{LB}), \text{ and } |\Delta| = |\lambda|\,|\theta|$$

If the *A*-sector is the more labor-intensive one, then $|\lambda|$, $|\theta|$, and $|\Delta|$ are all positive. In this case, the impacts have these signs:

	on $(\hat{w})$	on $(\hat{r})$	on $(\hat{A})$	on $(\hat{B})$
Effect of $(\hat{T}_A)$:	+	−	+	−
Effect of $(\hat{T}_B + \hat{P}_B)$:	−	+	−	+
Effect of $\hat{L}$:	0	0	+	−
Effect of $\hat{K}$:	0	0	−	+

(If the *B*-sector is more labor-intensive, the four upper-left and four lower-right signs are reversed.)

Figure C.1. The system can then be solved by devices such as Cramer's rule.

Solving the whole set of equations gives tidy and symmetrical results under the present assumptions, as shown in Figure C.2. The effects of changes in productivity, prices, and factor supplies on factor price changes and output changes all depend on how different the factor intensities of the two sectors are. That is, they depend on the values of the sectoral differences in cost shares ($\theta_{LA} - \theta_{LB}$, which also equals $\theta_{KB} - \theta_{KA}$) and the related difference in the factors' commitment to a particular sector ($\lambda_{LA} - \lambda_{KA}$, which also equals $\lambda_{KB} - \lambda_{LB}$). In what follows, we will use the case in which the *A* sector (e.g., cloth) is more labor-intensive, so that the differences just listed are all positive.

The effects of changes in productivity, prices, and factor supplies all make sense. In the top row, for example, an advance in productivity growth in the labor-intensive *A* sector raises the wage rate for labor, lowers the rental on property, and shifts output from the *B* sector to the *A* sector. A shift in productivity in the *B* (wheat) sector would have the opposite results. So would a rise in the relative price of the *B* good. Extra labor supply[1] would shift output from capital-intensive *B* to labor-intensive *A*, but have no effect on factor prices. It may seem surprising that an expansion of labor supply has no effect at all on the wage rate that labor receives. Wouldn't it bid it down, as Malthus feared? Not if it cannot affect the output price ratio *(PB)*, which is here assumed to be fixed on a world market that our economy cannot affect. If the output price ratio stays the same and productivity stays the same, the demand curve for labor is perfectly flat at a fixed wage rate regardless of shifts in labor supply. The results for shifts in the national capital supply are symmetrical with those for labor supply: accumulating more capital shifts output from labor-intensive cloth *(A)* to capital-intensive wheat *(B)*, but again has no effect on factor rewards.

THREE THEOREMS

Part of the appeal of the simple general equilibrium model is its ability to show how easily some famous theorems derive from a single model. This is worth showing, in order to underline the logical coherence of the whole Heckscher-Ohlin framework featuring factor proportions. In particular, three theorems studied in Chapter 4 can be found in Figure C.2.

The Stolper-Samuelson Theorem

Chapter 4 stressed the tension between economic classes over the trade issue, noting that Stolper and Samuelson had proved that opening trade

---

[1] Or exogenous increases in labor productivity in either sector ($-\hat{b}_{LA}$ or $-\hat{b}_{LB}$). As you might guess, there is a relationship between such labor productivities, the capital productivities ($-\hat{b}_{KA}$ and $-\hat{b}_{KB}$), and the sectors' total factor productivity growth ($\hat{T}_A$ and $\hat{T}_B$). Total-factor productivity growth is a weighted average of the growth rates in the two one-factor productivities for each sector:

$$\hat{T}_A = -\hat{b}_{LA}\theta_{LA} - \hat{b}_{KA}\theta_{KA} \quad \text{and}$$
$$\hat{T}_B = -\hat{b}_{LB}\theta_{LB} - \hat{b}_{KB}\theta_{KB}$$

These equations are consistent with Equations 7 and 8 above because each $\hat{a}_{ij} = \hat{c}_{ij} - \hat{b}_{ij}$ and each induced substitution between inputs is defined to have a zero effect on total factor productivity:

$$\hat{c}_{LA}\theta_{LA} + \hat{c}_{KA}\theta_{KA} = 0 \quad \text{and}$$
$$\hat{c}_{LB}\theta_{LB} + \hat{c}_{KB}\theta_{KB} = 0$$

would, by changing the output price ratio, bring one factor of production greater percentage gains than the price change while absolutely damaging the other class.

Figure C.2 shows this theorem in the row of results stemming from a rise in P_B, the relative price of wheat. First, the gains it brings to property owners in the form of higher rentals are:

$$(d\hat{r}/d\hat{P}_B) = \theta_{LA}|\lambda|/|\Delta| = \theta_{LA}/(\theta_{LA} - \theta_{LB}) > 1$$

The fact that this expression exceeds unity means that a 10 percent rise in the relative price of wheat would raise the rental on capital by *more* than 10 percent. Labor, on the other hand, absolutely loses from the rise in P_B:

$$(d\hat{w}/d\hat{P}_B) = -\theta_{KA}|\lambda|/|\Delta| = -\theta_{KA}/(\theta_{LA} - \theta_{LB}) < 0$$

In other words, a shift in the price ratio P_B causes a magnified shift in the relative fortunes of the two factors:

$$\hat{w} < (\hat{P}_A = 0) < \hat{P}_B < \hat{r}$$

Thus, as stated in Chapter 4, the Stolper-Samuelson theorem is an example of Jones's "magnification effect."

The Factor-Price Equalization Theorem

Chapter 4 also stated that economists had proved that opening trade would equalize the prices of each factor of production between countries, under a long list of assumptions. Figure C.2 is hiding one proof of this theorem.

Figure C.2 proves factor price equalization between countries even though it seems to show only one country. To convert Figure C.2 into an international comparison, reinterpret each change (i.e., each "^") as a rate of change *between countries* rather than as a change over time. Under the assumptions listed for the proof in Chapter 4, the two countries are the same in some key respects. They have the same price ratio because they trade freely without transport costs. Therefore, $\hat{P}_B = 0$ between countries. Assuming that the same technology prevails in both countries means that $\hat{T}_A = \hat{T}_B = 0$. The only exogenous variables left to vary between countries are the labor supply and capital supply. Suppose that our country is capital-abundant and labor-scarce. In algebraic terms, this can be viewed as saying that the differences between our factor supplies and theirs differ as follows: $\hat{L} - \hat{K} < 0$. But Figure C.2 shows that differences in factor supplies cannot affect the wage rate or the rental rate for given technology and product prices. Therefore, the international differences in factor supplies cannot cause any international differences in factor prices. The wage rate is the same between countries, and so is the rental on capital.

The Rybczynski Theorem

Chapter 4 examined the effects of factor growth on the outputs of the two sectors. It stated Rybczynski's theorem that an expansion in the supply of one factor would cause an even greater percentage output expansion in the sector that heavily used that factor, while also causing an absolute drop in the output of the other sector.

Figure C.2 agrees. Consider an expansion in the supply of labor. The third row shows that this would raise output in the labor-intensive A sector and cut output in the B sector:

$$(d\hat{A}/d\hat{L}) = \lambda_{KB}|\theta|/|\Delta| = \lambda_{KB}/(\lambda_{KB} - \lambda_{LB}) > 1 \quad \text{and}$$
$$(d\hat{B}/d\hat{L}) = -\lambda_{KA}|\theta|/|\Delta| = -\lambda_{KA}/(\lambda_{KB} - \lambda_{LB}) < 0$$

The economic logic is not hard to discover. If product prices are fixed on the world market, the way in which extra labor supply is absorbed into the system is through competition bidding labor away from the wheat *(B)* sector causing further specialization in the production of A. The effects of capital accumulation would be symmetrical: output would shift from A to B. As long as labor supply is growing faster than capital supply, we have another clear example of the Jonesian magnification effect, with the output responses being more extreme than the factor supply growth rates that cause them:

$$\hat{B} < \hat{K} < \hat{L} < \hat{A}$$

Or, if it is capital that is growing faster than labor,

$$\hat{A} < \hat{L} < \hat{K} < \hat{B}$$

In fact, the pattern of these inequalities is the exact "dual," or mirror image, of the Stolper-Samuelson theorem that $\hat{w} < \hat{P}_A < \hat{P}_B < \hat{r}$. In the Rybczynski case, exogenous factor-quantity growth rates lead to more extreme changes in output quantities; in the Stolper-Samuelson case exogenous output-price growth rates lead to more extreme changes in factor prices. The roles of outputs and factors, and the roles of prices and quantities, are reversed between the two settings.

EXPANDING THE GENERAL-EQUILIBRIUM MODEL

The 2×2 model of a small open economy has its limits as well as its logical beauty. Fortunately, improvements in computers have allowed economists to extend the model far beyond the confines shown here. The numbers of sectors and factors can easily be expanded. As long as the researcher can place reasonable bounds on the relevant elasticities, the computer can be fed numbers for every cell in a large matrix and still invert it to solve for the endogenous variables. After all, most of the parameters required by the model are just observable cost shares (the θ's) and factor use shares (the λ's).

Other features can be added. (Yes, you too can build general-equilibrium models right in your own home. Start today.) Outputs of one sector can be allowed to serve as inputs into another (e.g., by adding θ_{AB} and θ_{BA} as cost shares of wheat as an input in making cloth and of cloth as an input in growing wheat, in the cost-change equations). Taxes, subsidies, and market imperfections can also be added if one is careful with the underlying accounting identities. Perhaps most important, one can stop assuming that prices are fixed and add demand equations with demand elasticities to explain the price levels themselves. Endogenizing demand in this way allows one to quantify, for example, the adverse effect of export-biased growth (as in Chapter 4) to see if the "immiserizing growth" case looks likely.

Economists have run such "computable general equilibrium (or CGE)" models through the computer to generate fairly plausible causal inferences about macroeconomic interactions. CGE models are widely used for problems where subtle intersectoral effects are likely to emerge: the effects of changing taxes, the effects of changing trade barriers, and the determinants of movements in income distribution. For examples of studies applying such extended models, see Whalley (1984), Whalley (1985), and Williamson and Lindert (1980).

APPENDIX
D

Measuring the Effects of Protection

Figuring out who is getting how much protection from trade barriers usually requires a great deal of work. To give valuable clues about the effects of the whole structure of trade barriers, economists have developed the concept of an effective rate of protection, introduced in Chapter 6. The first part of this appendix elaborates on the algebraic formula for the effective rate, the empirical patterns it has shown, and the limitations on its usefulness as a clue to welfare effects. The second part surveys the empirical studies of the net national costs of protection.

CALCULATING THE EFFECTIVE RATE OF PROTECTION

The formula for the effective rate of protection in terms of the nominal tariff rates on the output and inputs is:

$$e_j = \frac{t_j - \Sigma_i a_{ij} t_i}{1 - \Sigma_i a_{ij}}$$

where e_j is the effective rate of protection for industry j, t_i is the nominal tariff on the output of industry j, the t_i's are the tariffs on the inputs into industry j and the a_{ij}'s are the shares of the costs of the various inputs in the value of the output of industry j, with free trade. This formula has been implicitly used in Figure 6.3, where $t_i = 0.10$, the one and only input tariff $t_i = 0.05$, and $a_{ij} = 0.73$, so that $e_j = 0.238$.

To see how this formula emerges from the definition of the effective rate, let us look at the ways in which tariffs affect value added. Without tariffs, if units are measured so that the free-trade price of the jth product is 1, then the unit value added, or v, equals $1 - \Sigma_i a_{ij}$. With tariffs, unit value added, v', equals (price of output) − (unit costs of inputs), or $(1 + t_j) - \Sigma_i a_{ij} (1 + t_i)$, assuming that all the goods are traded at fixed world prices and that the physical input-output ratios behind the a_{ij}'s do not change. From these relationships it follows that:

$$ej = v' - v = \frac{1 + t_j - \Sigma_i a_{ij} - \Sigma_i a_{ij} t_i - 1 + \Sigma_i a_{ij}}{1 - \Sigma_i a} = \frac{t_j - \Sigma_i a_{ij} t_i}{1 - \Sigma_i a_{ij}}$$

This formula confirms that the effective rate is greater than the nominal rate $(e_i > t_j)$ whenever the nominal tariff on the product is greater than the average tariff on inputs, as stated in Chapter 6.

Empirical estimates of effective rates of protection have turned up several interesting patterns. First, they show that the effective rates of protection on most industries tend to be well above the nominal rates. This is because there tends to be an "escalation" of the tariff structure over the stages of production: by and large, nominal rates tend to be higher on the more finished products than on intermediate products, both in developing and in more developed countries. This means that producers of final goods tend to receive higher effective rates of protection than do sellers of intermediate goods, as illustrated by bicycles and bicycle inputs here. There are exceptions, however. Studies have found cases in Pakistan for example, in which the complicated national structure of trade barriers gave negative effective protection to several industries, cutting their unit value added more with barriers on the importation of inputs than the protection afforded the industries on their output. The same is suspected about some industries in 19th-century Europe: it is believed that the metal-using engineering industries in Italy and Russia, and the coal-using ferrous metals industries in France, may have suffered negative effective protection due to high tariffs on their key inputs.

A set of careful studies in the 1970s showed that effective rates in developing countries are generally high, and so variable as to suggest that officials have not always realized the inter-industry complications of the trade barriers they fashioned for individual industries:

Country	Year	*Effective Rates of Protection in Manufacturing Industries* Average (percent)	Range of Rates (percent)
Brazil	1958	106	17 to 502
	1963	184	60 to 687
	1967	63	4 to 252
Chile	1967	175	−23 to 1140
Colombia	1969	19	− 8 to 140
Côte d'Ivoire	1973	41	−25 to 278
Indonesia	1971	119	−19 to 5400
Pakistan	1963/64	356	− 6 to 595
	1970/71	200	36 to 595
South Korea	1968	−1	−15 to 82
Thailand	1973	27	−43 to 236
Tunisia	1972	250	1 to 737
Uruguay	1965	384	17 to 1014

Similar measures from the 1980s show that the effective rates for Indonesia, South Korea and Thailand have converged to a somewhat narrower range than shown in the data for 1968–73, but they still vary widely.

Although it serves to underline these basic points about the incidence of protection across industries, the effective rate of protection is in some respects less helpful to a welfare evaluation of trade barriers than the demand-supply framework used in the previous sections. It does not really quantify how much any group gains or loses from a tariff or set of tariffs because it measures only impacts on value added *per unit of output,* while avoiding the important issue of how much output itself would change in response to the tariff or tariffs. It also lumps profits and other incomes within the industry together into the value-added aggregate, without showing us separately what share of the effect on unit value added goes to the managers and owners who make the decisions about how much to expand or contract the industry's output in response to tariffs. For these reasons the effective rate of protection does not directly quantify who gains or loses how much from a tariff. Measuring the gains and losses is better approached through the demand-supply framework itself, supplemented where necessary with information on how individual industries are affected by tariffs in other sectors.

EMPIRICAL STUDIES OF THE NET NATIONAL COST OF PROTECTION

Chapter 6 presented Harry Johnson's reasons for suspecting that the net national losses from trade barriers are always "small" shares of GNP. Here we look at more careful empirical estimates of those losses, and we look at the biases that are likely to creep into any such estimates.

Other empirical studies more or less confirmed Johnson's hunch. The first wave estimated Marshallian surpluses—triangles of net national gain like those shown in Table D.1. Then, from the mid-1970s on, more complex "computable general equilibrium" (CGE) methods were applied to the same task of welfare estimation. The CGE estimates were based on large computer-solved models of the economy that could pick up subtle income and price repercussions that are hidden by diagrams like those in this chapter. With either method, Marshallian or CGE, the range of welfare gains from freer trade was between − 1 percent of GNP and + 10 percent of GNP. The largest gains came when the barriers were (1) high and (2) to be removed completely, as in the studies of Brazil and Canada.

Some of the authors of the studies sketched in Table D.1 thought that the effects they measured were "small" shares of GNP. If they are right, we must ask whether the welfare effects of trade policy are large enough to be worth much political attention.

There are many reasons why one should not accept the standard measures of areas *b* plus *d* as the true measures of what tariffs do to a country's well-being. It is possible to identify several biases in the usual measures.

TABLE D.1   Some Estimates of the National Welfare Effects of Trade Barriers

Country, Year	Estimated Effect of Trade Barriers	Nature of the Estimate
A. Marshallian Surplus Measures (as in Figure 6.4):		
Hypothetical	Small shares of GNP	Hypothetical gains from removing all tariffs (i.e., losses from the tariffs) (H. G. Johnson, 1960)
United States, 1960	(a) gain or (b) loss of less than 0.11% of GNP	U.S. gains from removing all 1960 tariffs, (a) ignoring or (b) including "terms-of-trade" effects (see Chapter 7) (Stern, 1964; Basevi, 1968)
Industrial countries, 1967	Various net gains, all far below 1% of GNP	Gains to various industrial nations from the Kennedy Round tariff cuts (Balassa & Kreinin, 1967)
Developing countries, 1960s	From 9.5% of GNP (Brazil) down to −0.4% of GNP (Malaya)	Gains from removing trade barriers in six developing countries (Balassa, 1971)
United States, 1971	About 1% of GNP	U.S. gains from removing all barriers to trade, ignoring "terms of trade" effects (Magee, 1972)
B. Computable General-Equilibrium Estimates (complex variants on Appendix C):		
Canada, 1976	4.1% of GNP 8.6% of GNP	Effects of (a) unilateral Canadian and (b) worldwide tariff removal (Cox & Harris, 1985)
U.S., EC, Japan, rest of world, 1977	Gains around 1% of GNP, with losses for EC if nontariff barriers were cut	Effects of Tokyo Round liberalization on these 4 areas (Whalley, 1982)
U.S., 1984	0.6% of GNP	U.S. gains from removing all import barriers on autos, steel, and textiles and apparel (Tarr, 1989)

Past studies show the range of likely national welfare effects of tariffs and other trade barriers. Removing barriers can bring gains approaching 10 percent of GNP, but usually the gains are much smaller. In a few cases, a country actually loses because removing trade barriers can worsen its terms of trade (export prices divided by import prices), in a way considered in Chapter 7.

Although these biases are easier to state than to quantify, knowing about them allows one to decide whether a standard measure is likely to be too low or too high. As it turns out, most of the biases suggest that the usual measures underestimate the costs of trade barriers.

1. *What is "small"?* A "mere" one percent of GNP is hundreds of billions of dollars.

2. *The consumer loss is larger than the net national loss.* Most trade barriers have opposite effects on the material well-being of different groups, so that the net effect for all of these groups can look deceivingly small. In other words, trade barriers can redistribute income within a country even more than they impose a net cost on the whole country.

3. *There is an administrative cost to any trade barrier.* The basic analysis of a tariff is incomplete if it fails to recognize that a trade barrier ties up resources that society could have used in some other way. To enforce an import tariff, a country must employ customs officials at its borders. But the people administering the tariff could have been usefully employed elsewhere. To this extent, part of what is being transferred from consumers to the government does represent a social waste of resources. This means that part of area c in Figure 6.4 should be added to areas b plus d in calculating the net national loss from the tariff, even though most studies of the costs of trade barriers do not do so.

4. *Protection could slow technological progress.* The usual estimates of the cost of a tariff implicitly assume that the tariff has no effect on the tendency of domestic producers to seek and find new ways of cutting costs and shifting their marginal cost curves downward. That assumption may be incorrect.

5. *The effect of tariffs on import quantities may have been underestimated.* The measure of the net cost of a tariff depends critically on the estimate of the amount of imports it discourages. But estimates of the effect of tariffs and prices on import quantities are often biased downward, for four econometric reasons: (1) the usual statistical estimates of import-price elasticity are usually short-run elasticity estimates, which run lower than long-run elasticities; (2) the usual estimates are based on highly aggregated commodity classes, a procedure that underestimates how sensitive imports can be when the tariffs affecting their prices apply only to certain specific, and highly substitutable, commodities within these broad classes; (3) errors in the measurement of prices of imports and their domestic substitutes have been shown to cause underestimation of the price (and tariff) elasticity of imports; and finally (4) the usual estimates are beset by problems of "simultaneity bias," which again tend to cause underestimation of how much tariffs and price matter to import quantities. All these technical econometric problems mean that the effect of tariffs on imports has usually been underestimated, causing past studies to underestimate the size of the net national losses from tariffs.

6. *Foreign governments are likely to retaliate against our new trade barriers, costing us more by damaging our export markets.* So far, all six biases in the net national cost of a tariff mean that the true cost is larger than the usual estimates, such as those in Table D.1, would suggest. Not all of the possible refinements would tend to magnify the cost of the tariff, however. The following suggestions are two that might reduce it.

7. *A tariff affects the exchange rate in a way that can cut the welfare* *cost of the tariff.* The basic analysis of a tariff usually ignores any discussion of how the tariff affects the exchange rate between our currency and foreign currencies. This omission stems from the subtlety of how this relates to the welfare cost of the tariff, and from the convenience of keeping discussions of exchange rates completely separate from discussions of trade politics. Nonetheless, it is worth noting that an exchange-rate effect is linked to the cost of the tariff.

Imposing a tariff cuts the quantity of imports. It also cuts the total value spent on imports because the tariff's effect on the price paid to foreigners is either zero (as assumed in this chapter) or negative. This means that the tariff cuts the value of the foreign exchange that this country buys for the purpose of buying imported goods. As we shall see in detail in Part III, this tends to cut the price of foreign currency in terms of our own currency. That is, it tends to take more of our dollars to buy foreign currency. But this change in exchange rates will affect the quantities and dollar prices of our exports and imports. If foreigners must pay more units of their currencies to get each dollar for buying our exports, they will tend to buy less of our exports and the dollar price of our exportable goods may even decline somewhat. Similarly, residents of our country will begin to find that foreign goods will cost less than they cost originally, now that each dollar buys more units of foreign currency. So, the tariff may end up raising the dollar price of imports by less than the amount of the tariff itself. If, for example, a 10 percent tariff causes the dollar to be equal to 3 percent more of each foreign currency, the domestic dollar price of importable goods will rise only about 7 percent.

8. *Tariff changes bring displacement costs.* The net cost of a tariff is also modified by recognizing the unrealism of another assumption implicitly made by the usual basic analysis. So far, we have been assuming that the domestic supply curve was also the marginal cost curve of domestic production for the nation as well as for the private bicycle firms facing those marginal costs. This assumption was based on the further assumption that any labor or other inputs used in the domestic bicycle industry were just barely enticed away from other uses that were nearly as productive as was their use in the bicycle industry—and paid nearly as well. Thus, it was implicitly assumed that bicycle workers earning $9 an hour could also have found work elsewhere that paid them nearly $9 an hour. For this reason, the cost of bicycle labor and other inputs paid by the bicycle firms was assumed to equal the social cost of not using those inputs in other industries.

It often does not work that way. If the bicycle industry, or any other industry, were to lay off workers and other inputs, those workers would not simply move to some other productive employment with virtually the same marginal product. People's next best alternatives are well below their best ones, especially if they have become committed to their current employments by gearing their choices of residence and their personal skills to those employments. It is well known that displaced workers sustain prolonged income losses while trying to find new jobs. (Try telling displaced auto workers in Michigan that they can simply transfer to new jobs in agriculture or aircraft with no economic losses!) These displacement costs must be considered when totaling up the net effects of tariff changes.

How displacement costs affect the national loss from a tariff will depend on whether the tariff is being imposed or removed. Removing an existing tariff would clearly displace workers in import-competing industries, such as the bicycle industry in the current example. The bicycle workers would lose income for some time before finding new jobs. Similarly, managers and shareholders in the bicycle industry would experience capital losses due to the keener competition from imports. The losses suffered by those in the bicycle industry are real losses to society. These displacement costs should be subtracted from the national gains achieved by removing existing tariffs. Recent studies have shown that in some cases the estimated displacement costs have been great enough to cancel out the gains from tariff removal; in other cases, they have offset only part of the gains from freer trade.

The national losses that would result from imposing a *new* tariff, on the other hand, would not be reduced by allowing for displacement costs. If there were a new tariff on bicycles, obviously bicycle workers would not be laid off by the tariff. On the contrary, the bicycle industry would expand its output and employment in response to the new protection. If there were displacement costs to consider, they would take a subtler form and would appear in other industries. The only displacement costs to consider would be those arising from the indirect tendency of the new tariff to cause other sectors to contract. One such sector would be the whole export sector. The new tariffs on imports could make exports contract in several ways. They raise the value of our currency and, thus, could make foreigners buy less of our exports, as mentioned previously. They could provoke foreign governments into retaliating with new tariffs against our exports. So, new import tariffs can cause losses of jobs and incomes in exportable-good sectors. Reckoning the displacement costs would *raise* the estimated national losses from imposing *new* tariffs.

Economists have tried to quantify how refinements like the eight items above would change our estimates of the national losses from tariffs and other trade barriers. Some of these desirable refinements have been easier to quantify than others. So far, the last two, those that could reduce the net estimated loss from a tariff, have been quantified fairly well. It has been harder to put dollar values on some of the others. This difficulty complicates the task of deciding how bad a tariff is. But reasonable adjustments can be made. And even without being able to attach dollar numbers to each of the eight points listed, an advocate of freer trade can still use the orthodox measures of national losses from the tariff but note that important points escaping easy quantification (for example, Points 1–6 above) tend to reinforce the case against the tariff.

SUGGESTED READINGS

For a readable guide to the concept of the effective rate of protection, see Grubel (1971). For the current state of the literature on effective rates, start with the index entry for "effective rate of protection" in the Jones and Kenen *Handbook,* vol. I (1984), and work back to the discussion and sources cited there.

For a somewhat technical treatment of the statistical problems that often cause underestimation of import elasticities and the welfare costs of tariffs, see Leamer and Stern (1970, Chapters 2, 8).

APPENDIX

E

▼

The Nationally Optimal Tariff

•

DERIVING IT

It is not difficult to derive a basic formula for the tariff level that is nationally optimal for a country that can affect the foreign-supply price of imports without fear of retaliation, as in the first part of Chapter 7. This appendix does so using both the demand-supply framework of Part II and the offer-curve framework of Appendix B, showing that similar simple formulas emerge from both. An analogous formula is derived for the optimal export duty, both for a nation and for an international cartel.

We saw in the demand-supply framework in Chapter 7 that a small increase in an import tariff brings an area of gain and an area of loss to the nation. Figure E.1 compares these two areas for a tiny increase in the tariff above its initial absolute level, which is the fraction t times the initial price level, P. The extra gains come from being able to lower the foreign price on continuing imports, gaining the level of imports M times the foreign price drop dP/dt. The extra losses come from losing the extra imports (dM/dt) that were worth tP more per unit to consumers than the price (P) at which foreigners were willing to sell them to us.

The optimal tariff rate is that which just makes the extra losses and extra gains from changing the tariff equal each other. That is, the optimal tariff rate t^* as a share of initial price is the one for which:

$$\frac{\text{Extra}}{\text{gains}} - \frac{\text{Extra}}{\text{losses}} = M\frac{dP}{dt} - t^*P\frac{dM}{dt} = 0$$

so that:

$$t^* = \frac{dP/dt}{dM/dt}\frac{M}{P}$$

FIGURE E.1   The Gains and Losses from a Slight Increase in the Tariff, in a Demand-Supply Framework

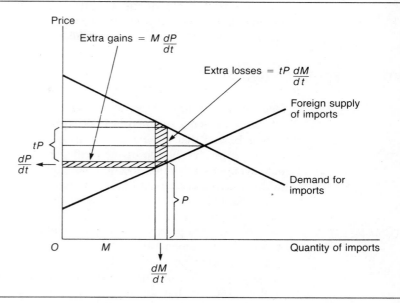

Since the foreign supply elasticity is defined as $s_m = \dfrac{dM}{dP}\dfrac{P}{M}$ along the foreign supply curve, the formula for the optimal tariff is simply $t^* = 1/s_m$, as stated in Chapter 7. If the world price is fixed beyond our control, so that $s_m = \infty$, then the optimal tariff rate is zero. The more inelastic the foreign supply, the higher the optimal tariff rate.[1]

Oddly enough, the level of the optimal tariff depends only on the foreign supply elasticity, and not at all on our own demand elasticity of imports. The same cannot be said, however, about the gains given us by the optimal

---

[1] Figure E.1 makes it easy to show that the nationally optimal tariff is lower than the tariff rate that would maximize the government's tariff revenue, even when the foreign supply curve slopes upward. The optimal tariff in Figure E.1 was one that equated the "extra gains" area with the "extra losses" area. But at this tariff rate a slight increase in the tariff still brings a net increase in government tariff revenue. By raising the tariff rate slightly, the government collects more duty on the remaining imports, M, while losing the "extra losses" area on the discouraged imports. However, its gain in revenue on M is not just the "extra gains" area already introduced, but this plus the thin unlabeled rectangle above the tP gap, which takes the form of a higher price to consumers importing M. A slight increase in the tariff would still raise revenue even when it brings no further net welfare gains to the nation. It follows that the revenue-maximizing tariff rate is higher than the optimal tariff rate. Thus a country would be charging too high a rate if it tried to find its nationally optimal tariff rate by finding out what rate seemed to maximize tariff revenues.

tariff rate. These do depend on the elasticity of our own import demand curve. For example, with a perfectly vertical import demand curve we receive no gains from the tariff as an extreme result. In this extreme case, the optimal tariff rate (or any other) simply taxes consumers, with an equal advantage accruing to government plus domestic producers.

OPTIMAL EXPORT TAXES

One can derive the optimal rate of *export* duty in the same way. Just replace all terms referring to imports with terms referring to exports, and redraw Figure E.1 so that the extra gain at the expense of foreign buyers of our exports comes at the top of the tariff gap instead of at the bottom. It turns out, symmetrically, that the optimal export duty equals the absolute value of $1/d_x$, or the reciprocal of the foreign demand elasticity for our exports.

The formula for the optimal export duty can also be used as the optimal rate of markup of an international cartel. Since both the international cartel maximizing joint profits from exports and the single nation optimally taxing its exports are monopolistic profit maximizers, it stands to reason that the formula linking optimal markup to foreign demand elasticity should hold in both cases. So, the optimal markup for an international exporting cartel is $t^* = |1/d_c|$, or the absolute value of the reciprocal of the world demand elasticity for the cartel's exports.

We can extend the formula to show how the optimal export markup for cartel members depends on the other elasticities and the market share discussed in Chapter 9's treatment of cartels like OPEC. The formula given in Chapter 9 can be derived easily here. We can link the elasticity of demand for the cartel's exports to world demand for the product, the supply of perfect substitutes from other countries, and the cartel's share of the world market by beginning with a simple identity.

$$\frac{\text{Cartel}}{\text{exports}} = \frac{\text{World}}{\text{exports}} - \frac{\begin{array}{c}\text{Other}\\\text{countries'}\\\text{exports}\end{array}}{}$$

or

$$X_c = X - X_0$$

Differentiating with respect to the cartel price yields

$$dX_c/dP = dX/dP - dX_0/dP$$

This can be reexpressed in ways that arrive at an identity involving elasticities:

$$\frac{dX_c/dP}{X} = \frac{dX/dP}{X} - \frac{dX_0/dP}{X}$$

$$\frac{dX_c}{dP}\frac{P}{X_c}\frac{X_c}{X} = \frac{dX}{dP}\frac{P}{X} - \frac{dX_0}{dP}\frac{P}{X_0}\frac{X_0}{X}$$

The cartel's share of the world market is defined as $c = X_c/X = 1 - (X_0/X)$. The elasticity of demand for the cartel's exports is defined as $d_c = (dX_c/dP)(P/X_c)$; the elasticity of world export demand for the product is $d = (dX/dP)(P/X)$; and the elasticity of noncartel countries' competing export supply of the product is $s_0 = (dX_0/dP)(P/X_0)$. Substituting these definitions into the equation above yields:

$$d_c \cdot c = d - s_0(1 - c)$$

so that:

$$d_c = \frac{d - s_0(1 - c)}{c}$$

Now since the optimal markup rate is $t^* = |1/d_c|$, this optimal cartel markup rate is:

$$t^* = \frac{c}{|d - s_0(1 - c)|}$$

As noted in Chapter 11, the optimal markup as a share of the (markup-including) price paid by buying countries is greater, the greater the cartel's market share (c), or the lower the absolute value of the world demand elasticity for exports of the product (d), or the lower the elasticity of noncartel countries' export supply (s_0). [For a generalization of this formula to cover cases in which the export supplied by noncartel countries is an imperfect substitute for the cartel's export product, see Carl van Duyne (1975).]

THE OPTIMAL TARIFF AGAIN WITH OFFER CURVES

The nationally optimal tariff on imports (or exports) can also be portrayed using the offer-curve framework of Appendix B, though this framework is less convenient for showing the *formula* for the optimal tariff. A trade-taxing country can use the tariff to move its own offer curve until it reaches the point on the foreign offer curve which maximizes the country's well-being. Figure E.2 shows this optimal tariff for a wheat-exporting country. Our country, the wheat exporter, has pushed its offer curve to the right by making the price of imported cloth in units of wheat higher within the country than the price received by our foreign cloth suppliers. At Point T domestic consumers must pay for cloth at the domestic price ratio SR/RT giving up SR in wheat for RT in cloth. The foreign suppliers receive only OR in wheat for their RT of cloth. The government has intervened to collect tariff revenue at the tariff rate SO/RT.

Figure E.2 shows that this particular tariff rate happens to be optimal, since at *Point T* the foreign offer curve is tangent to I_0, the best indifference curve we can reach through trade. The optimal tariff is positive because the foreign offer curve is not infinitely elastic. If it were infinitely elastic,

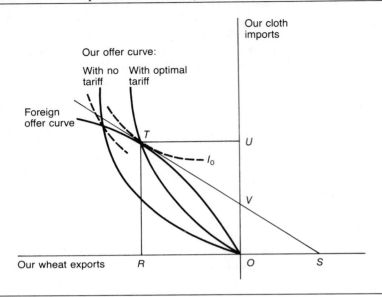

FIGURE E.2   An Optimal Tariff, Portrayed with Offer Curves

in the form of a fixed world price line coming out of the origin, our optimal tariff would be zero, since no other tariff can put us on as high an indifference curve as we can reach on our free trade, no-tariff offer curve. The same principle emerges here as in the demand-supply framework: the more elastic the foreign trading curve, the lower is our optimal tariff.

Deriving the formula for the optimal tariff rate is a little more complicated with offer curves than with demand and supply curves. The elasticity of the foreign offer curve is conventionally defined differently from a foreign supply curve, and defined in a way that is hard to identify in the offer-curve diagram itself. Any country's offer curve elasticity is conventionally defined as the ratio of the percentage response of its import demand to a percentage change in the relative price of its imports:

$$\text{Offer-curve elasticity } (e) = \frac{-(\% \text{ change in } M)}{[\% \text{ change in } (X/M)]}$$

Since the change in the price ratio X/M is not easy to spot on an offer-curve diagram like Figure E.2, let us convert this definition into a more usable equivalent:

$$e = \frac{-(\% \text{ change in } M)}{(\% \text{ change in } X) - (\% \text{ change in } M)}$$
$$= \frac{-1}{\dfrac{(\% \text{ change in } X)}{(\% \text{ change in } M)} - 1} = \frac{1}{1 - \left(\text{slope } \dfrac{\partial X}{\partial M}\right)(M/X)}$$

This last expression can be translated into a relationship among line segments in Figure E.2. We now take the foreigners' point of view, since it is their offer curve we are trying to interpret. The foreigners export cloth and import wheat. Thus the slope of their cloth exports with respect to their wheat imports at Point T is the ratio RT/RS, and the world price of their wheat imports (M/X) is RT/OR. Therefore the elasticity of their offer curve becomes

$$e = \frac{1}{1 - \dfrac{RT}{SR}\dfrac{OR}{RT}} = \frac{1}{1 - \dfrac{OR}{SR}} = \frac{SR}{SR - OR} = \frac{SR}{SO}$$

(Some authors derive an equivalent ratio on the cloth axis: $e = UO/VO$.)

We can now see the close link between the optimal tariff rate at point T and the elasticity of the foreign offer curve:

$$t^* = SO/OR = \frac{SO}{SR - SO} = \frac{1}{\dfrac{SR}{SO} - 1}$$

or

$$t^* = \frac{1}{e - 1}$$

This expression seems to differ slightly from the formula relating to the foreign supply elasticity for our imports, derived above. But the difference is only definitional. The elasticity of the foreign offer curve is defined as the elasticity of the foreigners' wheat imports with respect to the world price of cloth, not the elasticity of their cloth exports (supply of our cloth imports) with respect to the same price. Since the ratio of the foreigners' cloth exports to their wheat imports is just the world price of wheat, the offer-curve elasticity ([percent change in wheat]/[percent change in cloth/wheat]) is equal to one plus their elasticity of supply of our import, cloth. So, the expression above is equivalent to the reciprocal of the foreigners' supply elasticity of our import good, as in the demand-supply framework.[2]

---

[2] One word of caution in interpreting the optimal tariff formula relating to the foreign offer curve: the tariff rate equals the formula $1/(e - 1)$ for *any* tariff rate, not just the optimal one. To know that the rate is optimal, as at Point T, you must also know that the foreign offer curve is tangent to our indifference curve.

▼

The Monopoly Effect of a Quota

•

A significant difference between a tariff and a quota is that the conversion of a tariff into a quota that admits exactly the same volume of imports may convert a potential into an actual monopoly and reduce welfare even further. Figures F.1 and F.2 give a demonstration.

ORDINARY QUOTA VERSUS TARIFF

Figure F.1 returns us to the case of a tariff on a product for which our nation faces a fixed world price, P_0. By raising the domestic price to P_1, the tariff cuts imports to M_1 and causes deadweight welfare loses b and d, just as in Chapter 6. Figure F.1 brings out the point that this is the result of the tariff even if there is only one domestic producer. Though the tariff gives the producer some extra economic rents, represented by area a, it still leaves him a price taker, since any attempt on his part to charge a higher price than P_1 would leave buyers the option of shifting all of their demand to imports. Facing this flat demand curve, he does not charge more than P_1, and society loses only b and d from the tariff.

The quota shown in Figure F.2 is equivalent to the tariff in the sense that it also allows imports of M_1. But it plays into the hands of the sole domestic producer better than the tariff does. It leaves the domestic producer with a sloping demand curve for its product, by sharply limiting the ability of buyers to avoid it by buying abroad. Realizing this, the domestic producer will (slowly and discreetly) let its price drift up to the higher price that restricts its output back to where marginal costs and marginal revenues match. That higher price is P_2, and the more restricted domestic production level is S_2. The quota thus makes domestic output lower, and domestic price even higher, than the equivalent tariff does.

FIGURE F.1   With a Nonprohibitive Tariff, the Sole Domestic Producer Still Lacks Market Power

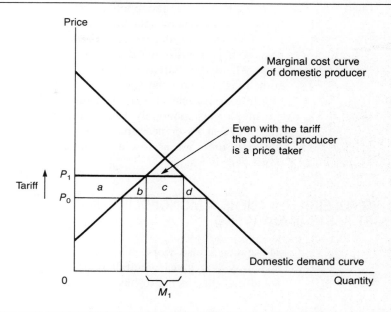

FIGURE F.2   With an Equivalent Quota, the Sole Domestic Producer Becomes a Monopolist

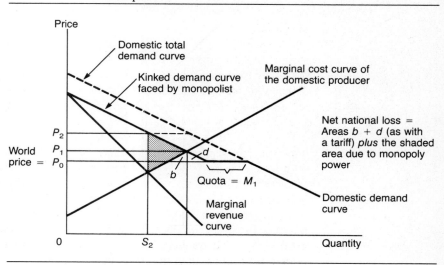

When a domestic output lower, and domestic price even higher, than the equivalent tariff does.

When a domestic monopoly is created by a quota, the nation as a whole loses *both* the deadweight loss from the reduction of imports and an extra social waste from the monopoly. In Figure F.2 the reduction of imports costs society areas b and d, and the new monopoly power costs the shaded area. All of these areas represent a lost opportunity to let consumers buy something that cost the nation less to obtain than the extra purchases were worth to consumers. By holding production back at S_2 and imports at M_1, the quota plus monopoly keeps consumers from enjoying purchases that they value at P_2 or near that even though the marginal costs of obtaining the extra units are as low as the marginal cost curve or the world price, whichever is less.

GIVING FOREIGN SUPPLIERS A MONOPOLY: THE CASE OF "VOLUNTARY EXPORT RESTRAINTS" (VERs)

The quota is also worse than the equivalent tariff when it is administered in a way that gives windfall price gains to foreign exporters, Chapter 8 noted that this seems to have been the result of the U.S. attempt to put a

---

FIGURE F.3   The Extra Cost of a Quota Enforced by (or on) Foreign Suppliers

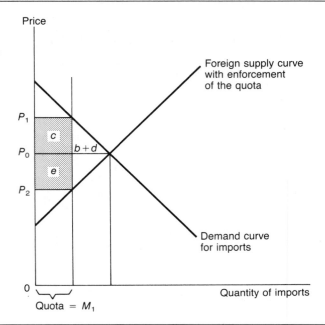

---

quantitative limit on imports of textiles and other goods while not technically administering the quotas itself. Figure F.3 shows how much more this procedure might cost an importing nation. If the government of the importing country administers an import quota of M_1, it will get the goods at the world price and somehow allocate the price-markup gains, areas c and e, among domestic residents. (As Figure F.3 is drawn here, the world price is the low level P_2 because the foreign supply curve is assumed to be upward-sloping. If the importing country faced a fixed world price, then the goods would arrive at the price P_0.) But if the quota is enforced by the foreigners, say, by their agreeing on fixed shares of this country's import market, no authority intervenes between them and buyers. Faced with this limited but prearranged import demand, they as exporters charge the highest price the traffic will bear with M_1 of imports, or the high price P_1. (The markup P_1P_2 may either remain a windfall gain for the lucky established exporters or become an additional waste of real resources spent in pursuit of the windfalls.) The importing country loses not only the triangle $b + d$ but also the price-markup rectangles c and e. These latter losses are the additional cost of having foreign exporters limit this country's imports instead of having a regular official import quota.

The Welfare Effects of Stabilizing Commodity Prices

•

If some agency could perfectly stabilize commodity prices, the world as a whole would gain. However, this ideal stabilization would have more complicated effects on the separate well-being of exporting and importing countries, as argued in Chapter 12. This appendix derives these basic results, using a simplified demand-supply model.

To analyze the effects of ideal price stabilization, we begin by simplifying the portrayal of the shocks to which world trade is subject. Let one of the two trade curves, either import demand or export supply, occupy two parallel positions in two time periods while the other trade curve stays unaltered. A demand-side variability is thus represented by two parallel demand curves, one for the period of stronger import demand (for example, an importing-country boom) and the other for the period of weaker import demand. A supply-side variability is shown by fixing the position of the import demand curves and varying the position of the competitive supply curve between two parallel positions—say, one for good-weather years and one for bad-weather years. Assume at first that the demand curves all slope downward and that the supply curves all slope upward.

If officials stabilize the price, it is assumed that they do so by correctly seeing that the trend in the good's real price is in fact zero. They stabilize by buying exactly the same amount in excess supply periods as they sell in excess demand periods, and at the same stabilized price. Their costs of maintaining the buffer stock are assumed to be zero, so that the officials make neither profits nor losses.

The well-being of a country is proxied by its net producer surplus or consumer surplus on exports or imports, respectively. For an exporting country, the net producer surplus on exports is simply the horizontal difference between producer and consumer surplus in a demand and supply diagram for the exportable good. For an importing country, similarly, the net consumer surplus on imports is obtained by subtracting the producer surplus from the consumer surplus on importables. The key element of well-being left out of these measures is just how much psychic benefit exporters and importers derive from the stability of either price or their own producer and consumer surpluses. Our procedure here is to describe how the degree of instability in these surpluses is affected by price stabilization, and to leave open the question of how much average welfare one would willingly give up to achieve a given reduction in the instability of that welfare from period to period.

Figures G.1 and G.2 and Table G.1 summarize the varied effects of commodity price stabilization. To grasp the results, let's look first at Figure G.1, which portrays a simple case of demand-side instability, such as might be experienced by the world market for metals such as tin, whose demand fluctuates with business cycles in the industrial countries. Figure G.1 condenses this instability into two parallel demand curves, D_1 for the low-

FIGURE G.1   The Effects of Price Stabilization in the Face of Demand-Side Disturbances

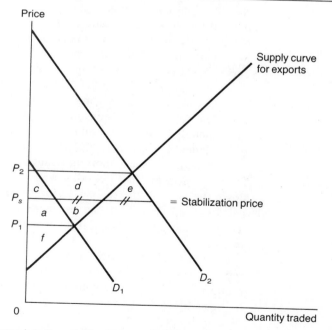

Note: this figure is patterned after the analysis in Massell (1969). For the literature that has extended and criticised Massell's framework and offered more complicated models of the stabilization issue, see Turnovsky (1978), Newbery and Stiglitz (1979), Krueger (1984, pp. 557–66), and Gardner (1987, Ch. 10).

demand troughs and D_2 for the high-demand peaks. It is assumed that officials stabilize the price of the product by buying exactly the same amount of the product in period 1 as they sell in period 2. This amount is represented by the two crosshatched line segments below areas d and e in Figure G.1. As a result of the officials' actions, the equilibrium price equals p_s in both periods instead of settling at the higher p_2 in the second period and the lower p_1 in the first.

The price stabilization appears to be a mixed blessing for the exporting countries. It makes their producer surplus on exports $a + b + f$ for both periods instead of f alone in period 1 and $a + b + c + d + f$ in period 2. This means that exporters get a more stable flow of gains across periods, which is good. Yet keeping the price at p_s has lowered their total gains over both periods, by the amount $c + d - a - b$. It has done this by keeping the exporters from pursuing the better price p_2 with the greater sales that their upward-sloping supply curve shows they would have willingly made at the higher price. By preventing the exporters from shifting their sales toward the higher-price periods, it has denied them some overall gains. Note, however, that this mixed blessing is fragile. If the supply curve were vertical in the short run, as it might be for perishable crops, then the net welfare effect on exporters would be zero ($c + d - a - b = 0$) and price stabilization would simply stabilize their gains across periods, which is only to the good. One could also show that if the two demand curves are not parallel, the mixed blessing can again fail to hold. (Consider the case in which demand fluctuates between the D_1 curve and the perfectly elastic curve at p_s: here exporters again gain unambiguously from stabilization.)

Keeping price steady in the face of the demand-side fluctuations in Figure G.1 is also a mixed blessing for importing countries. If the market had not been stabilized, the consumer surplus of the importing countries would have included the areas c and a when the price was down at p_1 and none of the lettered areas when the price was up at p_2. By contrast, keeping the price at p_s keeps the importing countries from picking up area a as part of the bargain in the first period, yet gives them areas $c + d + e$ by holding down the price in the second period, when their demand is stronger. Their gains end up greater for the two periods, by the amount $c + d + e - a$. Yet with the price fixed at p_s their gains are also more variable across the two periods.

For the world the price stabilization is a clear net gain, rather than the mixed blessing facing either side of the market. The world consumer plus producer surplus on international trade is raised by the areas $b + e$, as can be seen by adding together the net effects mentioned above. The logic behind this net gain is given in Chapter 12: the officials are acting like a merchant or arbitrageur who improves the match-up between net buyers who value a good highly and net sellers who will produce and sell it for less. They do so by matching buyers and sellers across time rather than across space.

FIGURE G.2   The Effects of Price Stabilization in the Face of Supply-Side
Disturbances

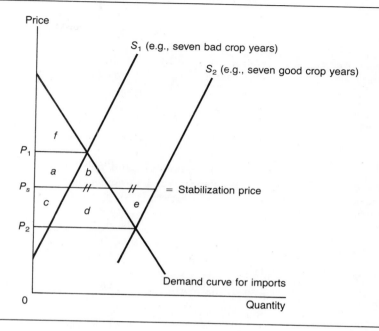

Figure G.2 pursues the opposite case of supply-side instability in parallel fashion, and Table G.1 summarizes the full set of results for the simple two-period analysis. There are patterns to the results:

1. The distribution of overall gains depends on whether instability comes from the demand side or from the supply side.
2. Any group of countries helped to higher average gains by the price stabilization is also exposed to wider fluctuations in those gains across periods.
3. The world as a whole gains from the ideal stabilization.

Subsequent scholarship has pointed out limitations of the simple and stylized Massell two-period analysis:

a. The results change as soon as we move away from the simple case of linear and parallel curves (try, for example, just making the two shift curves nonparallel and tracing the effects of a stock-preserving stabilization).
b. The results change if the two kinds of shocks (demand-side and supply-side) are either positively or negatively correlated over time.
c. The analysis exaggerates by contrasting no stabilization at all with perfect stabilization by officials. Private speculators would provide at least some

TABLE G.1   The Welfare Effects of Price Stabilization: Results of the Simple Two-Period Analysis

Group We Care about	Source of Disturbance	Effect of Price Stabilization on Producer or Consumer Surplus over Two Periods	Effect of Price Stabilization on "Risk" (that is, variance in consumer or producer surplus over two periods)
Demanders (importing countries)	Demand side	Higher welfare (gain $c + d + e - a$ in Figure G.1)	More risk
	Supply side	Lower welfare (lose $c + d - a - b$ in Figure G.2)	Less risk
Suppliers (exporting countries)	Demand side	Lower welfare (lose $c + d + a + b$ in Figure G.1	Less risk
	Supply side	Higher welfare (gain $c + d + e - a$ in Figure G.2)	More risk
Both together ("the world")	Demand side	Higher welfare (gain $b + e$ in Figure G.1)	No difference
	Supply side	Higher welfare (gain $b + e$ in Figure G.2)	No difference

Note: As stated in the text, the separate effects on demanders and suppliers are sensitive to assumptions about the slopes of the curves. The results above are based on the case of parallel shifts in straight lines, with downward-sloping demand and upward-sloping supply.

stabilization even without an official scheme, and stabilization cannot be perfect without infinite stocks.

d. If price stabilization improves private returns, private suppliers and buyers will eventually adjust their behavior to the better returns, complicating the analysis further.

Yet the simple Massell two-period analysis does the job it is assigned here: it shows the *possibility* of ideal stabilization gains, and is a starting point for other scholars' listing of the conditions under which price stabilization is likely to break down.

APPENDIX
H

The Forward Exchange Market

It is important to understand the basics of how the forward market works, what services it offers, and what difference it makes to government policy. This appendix expands on Chapter 15's coverage of the forward exchange market, providing more on private incentives, interest parity, and the relationship of exchange rates to expected inflation.

A contract to buy a currency forward is simply a written promise to sell some other currency for it at a preagreed rate of exchange. To buy £100,000 of 90-day forward sterling at $1,6430/£, a dollar holder signs an agreement to deliver $164,300 in bank deposits and buy the £100,000 in 90 days' time. If this forward contract is signed on May 9, the exchange rate at which the exchange is consummated on August 7, 90 days later, is the preagreed rate, regardless of what the spot rate of exchange turns out to be on August 7. What makes the forward market so convenient is that it involves contracts for which one must today pledge only a margin of 10 percent of the contract as security, unlike a spot exchange in which one delivers the full amount now.

MANY ROADS AROUND THE "LAKE"

The forward market offers an alternative way to hedge or speculate. No matter what asset or liability position one has in a foreign currency, there is a way of adjusting it and moving into or out of each currency through the forward market. To see how the forward market can be an alternative route for hedgers and speculators, let us consider a few examples in conjunction with Figure H.1. In Figure H.1 each position represents a way of holding one's financial assets for the short term. Movements from one side to another represent transactions in the spot and forward exchange markets:

FIGURE H.1   Spot and Forward Asset Positions in Two Currencies: The "Lake" Diagram

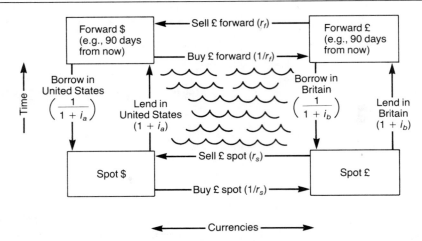

i_a = 90-day interest rate in United States.
i_b = 90-day interest rate in Britain.
r_s = spot price of the pound ($/£).
r_f = forward price of the pound ($/£).

people moving their assets from left to right are buying sterling and selling dollars, whereas those transferring from right to left are buying dollars with pounds. People moving upward in either country are lending, whereas those moving downward from forward to spot positions are either selling off interest-earning assets or actually borrowing at interest. The corresponding expressions in terms of exchange rates $(r_s$ and $r_f)$ and interest rates $(i_a$ and $i_b)$ show how the value of one's assets gets multiplied by each move.

Studying how one gets from any corner to any other for any purpose, you will find that the choice of the more profitable route always depends on the sign of a single variable. To find that variable, suppose we want to convert present dollars into future dollars (in Chapter 15 we focused on present pounds into future dollars). We could route our money through Britain, buying pounds in the spot market, investing at interest there and selling the upcoming pounds in the forward market to get an assured number of dollars in the future. This yields $(1 + i_b) \times r_f / r_s$ future dollars for every dollar invested now. Or we could simply invest our money at interest in America, getting $(1 + i_a)$ future dollars for every present dollar. Which road we should take depends on the sign of the difference between the two returns. This difference is sometimes called the **covered interest differential** (per pound) "in favor of London," or

$$CD = (1 + i_b)r_f/r_s - (1 + i_a) \tag{H.1}$$

It is not hard to see why this can be called a differential in favor of London. If it is positive, one would be better off investing in Britain, probably in London. If it is negative, with practitioners referring to a differential "against London" or "in favor of New York," one should avoid investments in Britain, lending in America instead. Why is it called *covered*? Because it shows a difference between two ways of getting from one currency to the same currency, thus covering (protecting) the investor against exchange-rate risk.

More generally, whatever one's starting and ending points, the covered differential tells which way to rotate around the lake:

If CD is *positive,* go *counterclockwise* (buying spot sterling, lending at interest in Britain, selling sterling forward, and/or borrowing in America).

If CD is *negative,* go *clockwise* (lending in America, selling dollars forward, borrowing in Britain and/or buying dollars spot).

In the literature on the forward exchange market one sometimes meets a slightly different formula for the covered differential, a handy one that can be derived from Equation H.1 using an approximation. To do so, we begin by rearranging terms in Equation H.1 as follows:

$$CD = r_f/r_s + i_b r_f/r_s - 1 - i_a \qquad \text{(H.2)}$$

Next, add and subtract the term i_b to get a more convenient expression:

$$\begin{aligned} CD &= (r_f/r_s) - 1 + i_b - i_a + i_b r_f/r_s - i_b \\ &= F + (i_b - i_a) + i_b F \end{aligned} \qquad \text{(H.3)}$$

where $F = (r_f/r_s)/r_s$ is the **forward premium** (or discount, if negative), that is, the percentage markup of the forward pound relative to the spot pound. Now, the last term in equation H.3 is a product of two small fractions, F and i_b, and can be viewed as approximately equal to zero for purposes of rough calculation. Therefore, the covered interest differential is about equal to the net premium on the forward pound plus the regular interest-rate differential:

$$CD = F + (i_b - i_a) \qquad \text{(H.4)}$$

The formula shows that the net incentive to go in one particular direction around the lake depends on how the forward premium compares with the difference between interest rates.

One *easy way to memorize* the dependence is to put it in the following intuitive form: the gain from lending in Britain is the forward premium you get on pounds plus the extra interest there.

INTEREST ARBITRAGE

The covered differential is such a handy guide to the profitable transfer of money across currencies that banks have developed the art of interest arbitrage in order to cash in on the differential. *Arbitrage* is the simultaneous buying and selling of an asset in two markets in order to profit from the price difference between the markets. ***Interest arbitrage*** is buying a country's currency spot and selling it forward, while making a net profit off the combination of higher interest rates in that country and of any forward premium on its currency. Interest arbitrage is essentially riskless, although it does tie up some assets for a while. One way of engaging in arbitrage is in fact the ultimate in hedging: one can start with dollars today and end up with a guaranteed greater amount of dollars today, by going all the way around the lake.

To see how arbitrage works, let us suppose that British and U.S. interest rates are $i_b = 4$ percent and $i_a = 3$ percent, respectively, for 90 days, and that both the spot and forward exchange rates are \$1.00/£, so that there is neither a premium nor a discount on forward sterling ($F = 0$). Seeing that this means $CD = +1$ percent, a New York arbitrageur uses the telephone and sets up a counterclockwise journey around the lake. She contracts to sell, say, \$10 million in the spot market, buying £10 million. She informs her London correspondent bank or branch bank of the purchase and instructs that bank to place the proceeds in British Treasury bills that will mature in 90 days. This means that after 90 days she will have £10.4 million × 1.04 to dispose of. Not waiting for that to happen, she contracts to sell the £10.4 million in the forward market, receiving \$10.4 million deliverable after 90 days. She could leave the matter there, knowing that her phone trip in and out of Britain will give \$10.4 million in 90 days' time, instead of the \$10.3 million she would have received by lending her original \$10 million within the United States. Or if she has excellent credit standing, she can celebrate her winnings by borrowing against the \$10.4 million in the United States at 3 percent, giving herself \$10,097,087 = \$10.4 million/(1.03) right now, or about 1 percent more than she had before she used the telephone. So, that's \$97,087 in arbitrage gains minus the cost of the telegraph communications, any transactions fees, the use of part of a credit line in the United States, and a few minutes' time. Not a bad wage. The operation is also riskless as long as nobody defaults on a contract. (The reader can confirm that if forward sterling were at a 2 percent discount ($F = -2$ percent and $r_f = \$0.98$), the New York arbitrageur would lend in the United States, buy forward sterling, borrow or sell bills in Britain, and sell pounds spot, making a net profit of about 1 percent.)

Interest arbitrage looks like the perfect money machine. It is especially attractive today, now that telecommunications and the rise of financial tax havens (the Bahamas, the Cayman Islands, etc.) have reduced transactions costs to about zero. If bankers failed to take advantage of such opportunities, we should wonder about their business acumen.

In fact, though, arbitrage is such a sure thing that it is an endangered species. Banks can program their computers to tell their traders instantly of any discrepancy in rates that would seem to allow profitable arbitrage. Such opportunities can persist only as long as other banks deal at rates that pass up arbitrage profits for themselves. Soon enough these other bank will bring their own rates back into line, removing the chance for instan money-making. Traders still make money on pure arbitrage, such as covered interest arbitrage as described here, but they have to be fast: the chance i usually gone within a minute or two.

INTEREST PARITY

John Maynard Keynes, himself an interest arbitrageur, argued that the oppor- tunities to make arbitrage profits would be self-eliminating because the for- ward exchange rate would adjust so that the covered interest differentia returned to zero. Since Keynes we have referred to the condition $CD = C$ as **interest parity,** or interest-rate parity, meaning, as the formula shows, that the forward premium has achieved parity with the interest-rate differential.[1] In his day it was a reliable tendency. Today, it is a virtual certainty, at least in the Eurocurrency markets operating through foreign countries and the offshore tax havens. Notice that interest parity is assured not only by the actions of arbitrageurs, but also the actions of hedgers and even speculators. As we have said, the different ways around the lake are open to anyone who has a large sum of money to move, regardless of either their purpose or the asset positions (corners) they start from or seek to reach. This may not be so evident in the case of speculators, whose decisions we think of as depending on expectations of exchange rates. Yet, any speculator first uses her expectations to decide what asset position to assume and then chooses her route based on the covered differential CD. This second decision makes the speculator weigh the same alternatives as an arbitrageur or hedger. *Anyone* who considers using the forward market acts in a way that drives CD toward zero, whether she is a risk-taker or risk-averter.

The persistence of interest parity has a policy implication for monetary officials trying to affect exchange rates. A currency can be supported in either the spot or forward market with similar effects. If officials buy sterling spot, for example, their raising of r_s will be partly offset by private flows responding to the fact that CD is now negative. Private parties (arbitrageurs, hedgers, and speculators) will tend to sell sterling spot, lend in the United

---

[1] To see that the condition $CD = 0$ is the same interest parity condition as the formula given in Chapter 15, note that Equation H.3 is the same thing as:

$$CD = F (1 + i_b) + (i_b - i_a), \text{ so that:}$$
$$\frac{CD}{(1 + i_b)} = F + \frac{(i_b - i_a)}{(1 + i_b)}.$$

If $CD = 0$, setting the right-hand side equal to zero gives the interest-parity formula shown in Chapter 15.

States, and buy sterling forward. If, in contrast, the officials had bought sterling forward, raising r_f, private parties would react to the now-positive value of *CD* by buying sterling spot, investing in Britain and selling sterling forward. The spot value of sterling, r_s, would again be raised. Thus, either spot or forward support of sterling tends to raise both r_s and r_f. In fact, under reasonable assumptions it can even be shown that the amount of official purchases necessary to raise both exchange rates (r_s and r_f) by the same percentage is the same whether officials buy sterling spot or buy it forward.

To illustrate this policy implication, suppose that the French government is thinking of intervening in the foreign-exchange market to bolster confidence in the franc. Suppose further that they dislike seeing the forward value of the franc 1 percent lower than its spot value, imagining this to be a sign of low speculative confidence in the future value of the franc. They could buy francs and sell dollars in either the spot or the forward market. If they somehow thought that buying the francs in the forward market would raise the forward rate more than the spot rate (and cure that look of forward discount that bothered them), they would be wrong. The interest-parity condition assures that the forward discount will stay the same as long as the interest-rate gap stays the same between countries. To get rid of the forward discount on the franc by 1 percent, they would have to lower French interest rates by 1 percent.

ARBITRAGE BETWEEN CURRENCIES AND GOODS: MANY PARITIES

The interest parity condition is rightly famous. It has become increasingly reliable since Keynes discussed it 60 years ago. There are other equilibrium tendencies produced by arbitrage, however. As long as there are different ways of selling one asset and ending up with another, the prices at which the assets can be exchanged will be closely related.

To reveal more relationships between the foreign exchange markets and such macroeconomic phenomena as inflation and real interest rates, let us think about the fact that investors can move between currencies and goods. To simplify here, let us think about uniform goods that can be bought or sold in either country. In addition to holding currencies today or in the future, you can hold goods today or in the future. Investors must always worry about price trends for goods as well as price trends for currencies. Suppose, for example, you fear more inflation in the prices of goods in Britain than in America over the next 90 days. How should your decision about where to hold your wealth relate to this fear and to the interest rates and trends in exchange rates? If others share your fear, what will happen to currency and commodity markets?

There are a number of links here, portrayed by Figure H.2. The central rectangle is just the lake diagram of Figure H.1, revisited. Now, however,

FIGURE H.2   Spot and Forward Positions in Currencies and Goods. Asset Positions: Moving with the Arrow, Multiply the Value of Your Investment by the Expression. Moving against the Arrow, Divide by It.

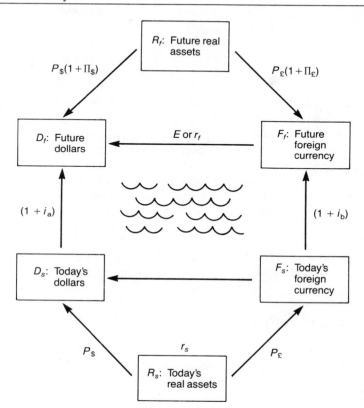

Symbols: $P_\$$, $P_\pounds$ = today's price level for real assets (wheat, soccer balls, etc.) in terms of $, £, $\pi_\$$, $\pi_\pounds$ = the expected rate of inflation in the dollar and sterling price levels, r_s, r_f = the spot and forward prices of the £ (in $/£). E = the expected future level of the spot price of the £ (not to be confused with the present forward price of it). i_a, i_b = the interest rates on widely marketed assets (e.g., treasury bills) in America and Britain. (Ignore transactions fees and ignore futures markets in real assets, such as grain futures.)

there also are ways to buy and sell goods with currencies. You can trade either currency for goods (real assets) today, at the dollar price $P_\$$ or the sterling price $P_\pounds$. If you were starting with today's dollars, your way of buying goods would depend on the relative prices shown at the bottom of Figure H.2. You might just take, say, $10,000 and buy $10,000/P_\$$ in current goods with it. Or you could take a more roundabout route, using the $10,000 to buy £10,000/$r_s$ worth of sterling and then using it to buy $10,000/r_s \, P_\pounds$

in goods today. Do whichever is cheaper. That is, you have an incentive to travel the cheaper of the two routes between today's dollars and today's real assets. The availability of this choice means that the two prices will tend to be bid into line: $P_\$ = r_s P_\pounds$. This is the purchasing-power-parity (PPP) condition discussed in Chapter 16. As argued in that chapter, it is a general tendency that works quite well over decades, but only more roughly over shorter periods, because of the costs of transactions and transportation and the underlying differences in the goods whose prices are being compared.

A version of purchasing-power parity should also hold for the future. If it doesn't, there may be unexploited chances for profitable arbitrage. Buying goods with dollars in the future should look equally cheap whether one expects to buy directly at the future dollar price or at the future pound price of goods times the dollar price of getting each pound. These different prices will depend on how much price inflation people expect between now and the future (say, 90 days from now). If people expect dollar prices to go up by the fraction $\pi_\$$, and pound prices to go up by the fraction $\pi_\pounds$, then these average expectations should be tied to what future exchange rate people expect *(E)*. Their expectations should equate the direct and indirect dollar prices of goods shown at the top of Figure H.2, or $P_\$ (1 + \pi_\$) = E P_\pounds (1 + \pi_\pounds)$. This condition can be called **expected future PPP.** It is only a rough tendency, like today's PPP, when actual changes in prices are used as measures of the expected changes $\pi_\$$ and $\pi_\pounds$.

The tendencies toward purchasing-power parity today and in our expectations about the future provide links between expected price inflation, interest rates, and exchange rates. You will recall from Chapter 15 that the forward price of the pound, or r_f, should equal E, the average expectation about the future of the spot rate. Combining the equality $E = r_f$ with the interest parity of this appendix gives further results shown in Figure H.3's summary of key parity conditions.

One result that emerges from all these arbitrage equilibria is that real interest rates should tend to be the same across countries. This is only a rough long-run tendency. In fact, expected real interest rates, as best (such) expectations can be measured, can differ noticeably between countries for years at a stretch (Blanchard & Summers, 1984, pp. 276–79). There is nonetheless a tendency toward equality.

Figure H.3 shows some of the intricacy one must expect from increasingly international financial and commodity markets. To illustrate, let us return to a question posed above: What would happen if more inflation in Britain were expected in the near future? If you alone have this new perception of higher British inflation, you can act on it by moving away from sterling into dollars or commodities over any of the routes shown in Figure H.2. As long as your fear is confirmed, you will gain from the exodus from sterling. If everyone agrees with your interpretation of the latest news, then prices and rates must change. The nominal interest rate must rise in

---

FIGURE H.3   International Parities

1. **Purchasing power parity (PPP) today:**
$$r_s P_£ = P_\$, \text{ roughly (see Chapter 16)}$$

2. **Expected future PPP:** $EP_£ (1 + \pi_\$) = P_\$ (1 + \pi_\$)$, roughly, so that $E/r_s = (1 + \pi_£)/(1 + \pi_\$)$, or, in changes from unity,

Expected		Expected $\$$		Expected £
appreciation of £ =		inflation	−	inflation

3. **Interest parity:** $(r_f/r_s) = (1 + i_a)/(1 + i_b)$ definitely.

4. **Speculators' forward equilibrium:** Forward rate measures average expected future spot rate, or $E = r_f$, we think, so that $E/r_s = r_f/r_s = (1 + i_a)/(1 + i_b) = (1 + \pi_\$)/(1 + \pi_£)$, or, in deviations from unity,

Expected £	Premium on	Difference	Expected differ-
appreciation =	forward £ =	between $\$$ =	ence between $\$$
		and £ interest	and £ inflation
		rates	rates

So we expect real interest rates to be roughly equal internationally:

5. **Real interest rate equilibrium:**

$$(1 + i_a)/(1 + \pi_\$) = (1 + i_b)/(1 + \pi_£)$$

or

$$(i_a - \pi_\$) = (i_b - \pi_£), \text{ roughly}$$

Britain and the forward premium on the pound must decline, as the parity conditions in Figure H.3 show.

The moral of Figure H.2 and Figure H.3 is that interest rates, exchange rates, and expected inflation rates are tied together. Whatever affects international differences in one is likely to affect international differences in the other two. It should be stressed, though, that one parity is much more reliable than the others. That one is the interest-parity condition described above.

SUGGESTED READINGS

An alternative presentation of the whole set of parity conditions, with some practical cautions and citations to other literature, is given in Brealey and Myers (1984, Chap. 32). The degree of precision with which the interest parity condition holds is debated by Frenkel and Levich (1975, 1977), McCormick (1979), and Rivera-Batiz and Rivera-Batiz (1985, Chap. 2).

QUESTION FOR REVIEW

You are willing to engage in interest arbitrage, and you have $100,000 in bank deposits to play with in New York. Under each of the following sets of 90-day interest rates and exchange rates, calculate the covered differential in favor of London *(CD)*, and decide whether it is more profitable to lend in London and sell pounds forward or to lend in the United States, avoiding pounds altogether:

	Interest Rate in London (i_b)	Interest Rate in New York (i_a)	Spot Price of £ (r_s)	Forward Price of £ (r_f)	Forward Premium (F)
(a)	3%	2%	$2.00	$2.00	0%
(b)	3	2	2.00	1.96	−2
(c)	4	3	2.00	1.98	−1

Answers:

(a) *CD* is 1 percent, buy sterling spot, lend in London, sell sterling forward. (b) *CD* is − 1 percent, lend in the United States. (c) *CD* is 0 you are indifferent.

▼

Devaluation and the Trade Balance

•

This appendix extends Chapter 18's explorations of the possible effects of a drop in the value of the home currency on the trade balance or, more accurately, the net balance on current account.[1] It derives a general formula for such effects, and applies it to some special cases that establish the range of possible results.

FOREIGN EXCHANGE ELASTICITIES[2]

To derive the elasticity of the trade balance with respect to the exchange rate, one must begin by linking the change in the exchange rate to elasticities of the demand for and supply of foreign exchange within the exchange market itself. To do so, we begin by differentiating the trade balance. The trade balance defined in foreign currency is:

$$TB_£ = S_£ - D_£ = V_x - V_m = P_x^£ X - P_m^£ M \tag{I.1}$$

where $S_£ = V_x$ is the supply of foreign exchange on current account, or the value of exports, and $D_£ = V_m$ is the demand for foreign exchange on current account, or the value of imports. Differentiating yields:

$$dTB_£ = dS_£ - dD_£ \tag{I.2}$$

or

$$dTB_£/V_m = dS_£/V_m - dD_£/V_m \tag{I.3}$$

---

[1] There are other determinants of the trade balance and current-account balance besides the exchange rate, of course. National income, the growth of national wealth, and interest rates at home and abroad all play roles, for example. We focus on the role of exchange-rate changes in order to illuminate Chapter 18's discussion of the possibility of unstable feedback from exchange rate to trade balance back to exchange rate.

[2] The derivation follows that given in Jaroslav Vanek (1962).

Let us define:

$$E_{tb} = \frac{dTB_\pounds/V_m}{dr/r} =$$ The elasticity of the trade balance with respect to r, the exchange rate (or price of the foreign currency, in $\$/\pounds$).

$$E_s = \frac{dS_\pounds/S_\pounds}{dr/r} =$$ The elasticity of the supply of foreign exchange, or value of exports, with respect to the exchange rate r.

$$E_d = \frac{dD_\pounds/D_\pounds}{dr/r} =$$ The elasticity of demand for foreign exchange, or the value of imports, with respect to the exchange rate r.

Then if we divide both sides of (I.3) by the proportion of change in the exchange rate *(dr/r)*, we get:

$$E_{tb} = \frac{V_x}{V_m} E_s - E_d \tag{I.4}$$

Deriving the formula for the effect of the exchange rate on the balance of trade amounts to deriving a formula relating E_{tb} to the underlying elasticities of demand and supply for exports and imports.

GOODS ELASTICITIES AND THE FOREIGN EXCHANGE ELASTICITIES

The foreign exchange supply (or demand) is linked to the export (or import) market by the fact that it is defined as the product of a trade price and a traded quantity. We therefore need to derive expressions giving the elasticities of these trade prices and quantities with respect to the exchange rate. Let us do so on the export side. There the supply, which depends on a dollar price $(P_x^\$ = P_x^\pounds \cdot r)$, must be equated with demand, which depends on a pound price. We start with the equilibrium condition in the export market, differentiate it, and keep rearranging terms until the equation takes a form relating elasticities to the change in export prices:

$$X = S_x(P_x^\pounds r) = D_x(P_x^\pounds) \tag{I.5}$$

$$dX = \frac{\partial S_x}{\partial P_x^\$} (r\, dP_x^\pounds + P_x^\pounds dr) = \frac{\partial D_x}{\partial P_x^\pounds} dP_x^\pounds \tag{I.6}$$

$$dX/X = \frac{\partial S_x}{\partial P_x^\$} \frac{1}{S_x} (r\, dP_x^\pounds + P_x^\pounds dr) = \frac{\partial D_x}{\partial P_x^\pounds} \frac{1}{D_x} dP_x^\pounds \tag{I.7}$$

Multiplying within both sides by $P_x^\$/r = P_x^\pounds$ and dividing by *dr/r* yields

$$\frac{dX/X}{dr/r} = \left[\frac{\partial S_x}{\partial P_x^\pounds} \frac{P_x^\pounds}{S_x}\right] \left(\frac{dP_x^\pounds/P_x^\pounds}{dr/r} + 1\right) = \left[\frac{\partial D_x}{\partial P_x^\pounds} \frac{P_x^\pounds}{D_x}\right] \frac{dP_x^\pounds/P_x^\pounds}{dr/r} \tag{I.8}$$

The expressions in brackets on the left and right are the elasticities of export supply *(s_x)* and demand *(d_x)*, respectively, so that

$$\frac{dX/X}{dr/r} = s_x\left(\frac{dP_x^\pounds/P_x^\pounds}{dr/r} + 1\right) = d_x\frac{dP_x^\pounds/P_x^\pounds}{dr/r} \tag{I.9}$$

and the percentage response of the pound price of exports to the exchange rate is

$$\frac{dP_x^\pounds / P_x^\pounds}{dr/r} = \frac{s_x}{d_x - s_x} \qquad (I.10)$$

This has to be negative or zero, since d_x is negative or zero and s_x is positive or zero. (The response of the dollar price of exports to the exchange rate rate equals this same expression plus one.)

Recalling that the supply of foreign exchange equals the price times the quantity of exports, or the value of exports, we can use the fact that any percentage change in this supply of foreign exchange equals the percentage price change plus the percentage quantity change:

$$E_x = \frac{dX/X}{dr/r} + \frac{dP_x^\pounds / P_x^\pounds}{dr/r} \qquad (I.11)$$

From (I.9) and (I.10), we get the relationship between the elasticity of supply of foreign exchange and the elasticities of demand and supply of exports:

$$E_s = \frac{d_x s_x}{d_x - s_x} + \frac{s_x}{d_x - s_x} = \frac{d_x + 1}{(d_x/s_x) - 1} \qquad (I.12)$$

which can be of any sign.

Going through all the same steps on the imports side yields expressions for the responses of the pound price of imports, the quantity of imports, and the demand for foreign exchange with respect to the exchange rate:

$$\frac{dP_m^\pounds / P_m^\pounds}{dr/r} = \frac{d_m}{s_m - d_m} \ (\leq 0) \qquad (I.13)$$

$$\frac{dM/M}{dr/r} = \frac{s_m d_m}{s_m - d_m} \ (\leq 0) \qquad (I.14)$$

and

$$E_d = \frac{s_m + 1}{(s_m/d_m) - 1} \ (\leq 0) \qquad (I.15)$$

THE GENERAL TRADE BALANCE FORMULA AND THE MARSHALL-LERNER CONDITION

We have now gathered all the materials we need to give the general formula for the elasticity of response of the trade balance to the exchange rate. From (I.4), (I.12), and (I.15), the formula is:

$$\text{The elasticity of the trade balance with respect to the exchange rate} = E_{tb} = \frac{V_x}{V_m} \frac{d_x + 1}{(d_x/s_x) - 1} - \frac{s_m + 1}{(s_m/d_m) - 1}. \qquad (I.16)$$

TABLE I.1 Devaluation and the Trade Balance: Applying the General Formula to Special Cases

	Assumed Elasticities	Effect of Devaluation on the Trade Balance
Case 1: Inelastic demands	$d_m = d_x = 0$	Trade balance worsens: $E_{tb} = -V_x/V_m < 0$
Case 2: Small country	$s_m = -d_x = \infty$	Trade balance improves: $E_{tb} = \dfrac{V_x}{V_m} s_x - d_m > 0$
Case 3: Prices fixed in buyer's currencies	$d_m = d_x = -\infty$	Trade balance improves: $E_{tb} = \dfrac{V_x}{V_m} s_x + s_m + 1 > 0$
Case 4: Prices fixed in sellers' currencies	$s_x = s_m = \infty$	It depends: $E_{tb} = \dfrac{V_x}{V_m}(-d_x - 1) - d_m \gtrless 0$

In Case 4, if trade was not initially in surplus, the Marshall-Lerner condition is sufficient for improvement: $|d_x + d_m| > 1$.

By studying this general formula and some of its special cases, one can determine what elasticities are crucial in making the trade-balance response stable (i.e., in making E_{tb} positive). It turns out that

> *The more elastic are import demand and export demand, the more "stable" (positive) the trade-balance response will be.*

Demand elasticities are crucial, but supply elasticities have no clear general effect on the trade-balance response. The formula is independent of whether the trade balance is expressed in dollars or in pounds.

These results can be appreciated more easily after we have considered four important special cases listed in Table I.1. The perverse result of a trade balance that worsens after the domestic currency has been devalued is the *inelastic-demand case*, already discussed in Chapter 18. As shown in Table I.1, this Case 1, in which $d_m = d_x = 0$, yields clear perversity regardless of the initial state of the trade balance. The "J curve" of Chapter 18 is based on the suspicion that this case may sometimes obtain in the short run, before demand elasticities have had a chance to rise.

A second special case, also discussed in Chapter 18, is the *small country case*, in which both export prices and imports prices are fixed in terms of foreign currencies in large outside-world markets. This Case 2 is represented in Table I.1 by infinite foreign elasticities: $s_m = -d_x = \infty$. In the small country case, devaluation or depreciation of the home currency definitely improves the trade balance, giving a stable signal back to the foreign exchange market. The small country case is realistic for so many countries—even many "large" ones are international price-takers—that its stable result is a main reason for presuming that the trade balance response eases the task of stabilizing foreign exchange markets.

Consistent with the emphasis on the importance of demand elasticities is the extreme result for Case 3. With *prices fixed in buyers' currencies,* for example, by infinitely elastic demands for imports both at home and abroad $(d_m = d_x = -\infty)$, the general formula yields the most improvement. This is a fairly realistic short-run response for many manufactures and services, where contractual commitments and the desire of sellers to avoid disrupting markets with price increases keep price tags unaffected by swings in the exchange rate.

The fourth special case considered here is one in which *prices are kept fixed in sellers' currencies.* This fits the Keynesian family of macromodels, in which supplies are infinitely elastic and prices are fixed within countries. In Case 4, the net effect of devaluation on the trade balance depends on a famous condition, the **Marshall-Lerner condition,** which says that the absolute values of the two demand elasticities must exceed unity: $|d_x + d_m| > 1$. This is sufficient for a stable result if the trade balance is not initially in surplus (i.e., if $V_x \leq V_m$, as is typical of devaluations). While the Marshall-Lerner condition strictly holds only in a narrow range of models, it is a rougher guide to the likelihood of the stabilizing result, since it reminds us of the overall pattern that higher demand elasticities give more stable results. Authors tend to argue that the Marshall-Lerner condition would be sufficient for devaluation to work as it should, even though this follows only under the assumptions of Case 4.

▼

The Keynesian Model of an Open Macroeconomy

·

Most of the policy results of Chapters 20 and 21 can be derived with a basic Keynesian model that can be presented with the help of equations or diagrams. This appendix presents a simple system of equations that captures nearly all of what Chapter 20 had to say about policy problems under fixed exchange rates, and part of what Chapter 21 concluded about floating versus fixed exchange rates. The set of equations is equivalent to a set of diagrams of our "*IS-LM-FE*" analysis.[1]

THE THREE MARKETS

National Product Market (or "IS curve")

The first of three markets to be portrayed is that for the home country's national product (Y). As in Chapters 19–21, we follow the Keynesian simplification of setting prices aside, and talking as though real and nominal national income always moved together. In accordance with the Keynesian perspective, the equilibrium level of national product is whatever level is consistent with the aggregate demand for national product:

$$Y = \frac{\text{Aggregate demand for}}{\text{our national product}} = \overset{+,-}{E(Y,i)} + \overset{-;+}{T(Y;r)}$$

Here $E(Y,i)$ represents our national expenditure on home and foreign goods (in units of the home good), which depends positively on Y and negatively on the home-country interest rate i. $T(Y;r)$ is our net current-account balance,

---

[1] For the diagrams, see Chapter 20.

or roughly our "trade balance." It depends negatively on our income because extra income makes us demand more imports, as we saw in Chapters 19 and 20. The trade balance will also be raised by a rise in the price of foreign exchange *(r)*, as long as the stability conditions of Chapter 18 and Appendix I hold. We keep this exchange-rate link stored away (behind the semicolon) until it comes in handy during the discussion of floating exchange rates.

For convenience we restate the national-product equilibrium in different terms. As noted in Chapter 19 and in textbooks of macroeconomics, the equilibrium of national product with the aggregate demand for it is equivalent to an equilibrium between national saving *(S)* and in investment:

$$\overset{+,+}{S(Y,i)} = \text{Domestic capital formation} + \text{Net foreign investment}$$
$$= \overset{+,-}{I(Y,i)} + \overset{-;+}{T(Y;r)}$$

Note that the "trade balance" *(T)* is again, more accurately, the current-account balance, or net foreign investment, as explained in Chapter 16. The trade balance is worsened by a rise in *Y* and improved by a rise in the exchange rate *r* (which represents the reciprocal of the terms of trade (rP_f/P) with the national price levels P_f and P held fixed). The equilibrium between investment and saving for equilibrium levels of *Y* and *i* is the famous "IS curve" drawn in textbooks of intermediate macroeconomics.

Our next simplification is to convert this equilibrium into a linear equation, to facilitate algebraic solutions. Let saving, investment, and the trade balance all depend on other variables according to these linear equations:

Functions	Coefficients
$S = s_0 + s_1 Y + s_2 i$	$(s_1 < 0, s_2 \leq 0)$
$I = I_0 + I_1 Y + I_2 i$	$(I_1 \geq 0, I_2 < 0)$

and

$$T = T_0 + T_1 Y + T_2 r \qquad (T_1 < 0, T_2 < 0)$$

The equilibrium condition, plotting out the "IS curve" of the macroeconomic texts, can be stated as

$$S_0 + s_1 Y + s_2 i = I_0 + I_1 Y + I_2 i + T_0 + T_1 Y + T_2 r$$

or

$$\text{Income term} + \text{Interest term} = \text{Exogenous terms}$$
$$s_1 - I_1 - T_1)Y + (s_2 - I_2)i = I_0 + T_0 - s_0 + T_2 r$$

We further assume that $(s_1 - I_1 - T_1) > 0$ *and* $(s_2 - I_2) < 0$, so that the IS curve slopes downward.

Money Market (or LM Curve)

The next market to be equilibrated, as in Chapter 20, is the market for money; that is, for the currency and checking deposits held against one country.[2] Its supply is simply M, assumed to be controlled by the central bank's monetary policy until we get to the issue of feedback from the balance of payments to the money supply. The demand for money (L) is assumed to depend on income and the rate of interest, so that the money market equilibrium (the famous LM curve) is stated as:

$$M = L_0 + L_1Y + L_2i, \qquad (L_1 > 0, L_2 < 0),$$

or

$$\text{Income term} + \text{Interest term} = \text{Exogenous term}$$
$$L_1Y \quad + \quad L_2i \quad = \quad M - L_0$$

In fact, the demand for money is best thought of as a demand for real balances (M/P) and not just as a demand for M itself. But in the Keynesian tradition, we abstract from the supply side and leave P exogenous.

The Foreign Exchange Market (FE or BP Curve)

The third market has a meaning that depends on exchange-rate institutions. If the exchange rate is fixed, as we first assume here as in Chapter 20, the third market equation records the overall balance of payments:

$$B = T + F = T_0 + T_1Y + T_2r + F_0 + F_1Y + F_2i, \quad (F_1 < 0, F_2 > 0)$$

or

$$\text{Income term} + \text{Interest term} - \text{Payments surplus} = \text{Exogenous terms}$$
$$(T_1 + F_1)Y \quad + \quad F_2i \quad - \quad B \quad = -T_0 - F_0 - T_2r$$

Here $F = F_0 + F_1Y + F_2i$ represents the net inflow of lending per year, a source of extra reserves (i.e., higher F raises B for the short run). It needs careful interpretation. Tying net *flows* of capital (lending) to interest rates and income at home and (implicitly) abroad is not to the liking of most macroeconomists. We would prefer to view the *stock* of international lending as part of portfolio decisions that allocate different investors' total net wealth stocks across countries or currencies. This stock-portfolio behavior would yield net international lending flows (like F here) only when wealth

---

[2] Here as in Chapters 19–21, I follow the usual assumption that the money claims against a country are those in its currency. As Chapter 22 stresses, however, this assumption is showing signs of severe strain in a world in which each major currency is not only held by many countries but even owed by many countries.

or rates of return or expectations are changing. When these portfolio determinants are not changing, there should be no net international flow. The present use of the lending flow F is meant to approximate the financial-flow behavior of an economy that is saving out of extra income and allocating a share of that net saving to net borrowing from abroad. [Similarly, the real investment variable $I(i)$ is meant to be a flow approximation to the part of net saving that would go into net domestic capital formation for any given structure of interest rates.] The $F(y, i)$ and $I(y, i)$ flow variables have been used in place of other, theoretically preferable, asset demand functions in order to avoid complicated differential-equations dynamics.

If the exchange rate floats, then the foreign exchange market equation has a different meaning. With officials assumed to be standing passively by, the market finds its own equilibrium exchange rate by adding a net demand for foreign exchange that is tied to the trade balance to a net demand tied to international lending flows.[3] With floating exchange rates, $B = 0$ at equilibrium and the exchange rate (r) replaces B as an endogenous variable to be determined by the macroeconomic system. The foreign exchange market equation for floating rates then becomes:

$$B = T + F = 0$$

or

Income term	Interest term	Exchange rate	Exogenous terms
$(T_1 + F_1)Y \ +$	$F_2 i \quad +$	$T_2 r \quad =$	$-T_0 - F_0$

EQUILIBRIUM WITH FIXED EXCHANGE RATES

We now have a system of three markets whose interaction determines equilibrium values of three endogenous variables: Y, i, and B in the case of fixed exchange rates, or Y, i, and r in the case of a floating rate.[4] For fixed exchange rates, the system of equations is:

---

[3] Note that this description of the foreign exchange market as a tug-of-war between *flows* again departs from our theoretical preference for thinking of demand and supply for foreign exchange as *stock* asset demands and supplies, the way we did in Chapter 16. The two approaches give qualitatively similar results, though they imply different time paths of response to any given parameter shift.

[4] Other markets are lurking in the wings. The use of interest rate implies the existence of a bond market. The real capital formation variable (I) implies a market for man-made capital goods. And we assume there is also a labor market, whose equilibrium could be a Keynesian underemployment equilibrium. All six markets (national product, money, foreign exchange, bonds, capital goods, and labor) are assumed to be in equilibrium at the same time.

$$\text{Income term} \quad \text{Interest term} \quad \overset{\text{Payments}}{\text{surplus}} \qquad \text{Exogenous terms}$$

$$(s_1 - I_1 - T_1)Y + \quad (s_2 - I_2)i \qquad\qquad = (I_0 + T_0 - s_0 + T_2r) = Z_1$$

$$\text{(J.1a)}$$

$$L_1Y \quad + \quad L_2i \qquad\qquad = \quad (M - L_0) \qquad = Z_2$$

$$\text{(J.2)}$$

$$(T_1 + F_1)Y \quad + \quad F_2i \qquad -B \quad = (-T_0 - F_0 - T_2r) \quad = Z_3$$

$$\text{(J.3a)}$$

where the Z's are just shorthand expressions for the three exogeneous terms. The same set of equations in matrix form is

$$\begin{bmatrix} (s_1 - I_1 - T_1) & (s_2 - I_2) & 0 \\ L_1 & L_2 & 0 \\ (T_1 + F_1) & F_2 & -1 \end{bmatrix} \cdot \begin{bmatrix} Y \\ i \\ B \end{bmatrix} = \begin{bmatrix} Z_1 \\ Z_2 \\ Z_3 \end{bmatrix}$$

Solving this set of equations yields expressions tying Y, i, and B to the exogenous variables alone:

$$Y = \frac{(s_2 - I_2)Z_2 - L_2Z_1}{(s_2 - I_2)L_1 - L_2(s_1 - I_1 - T_1)} \text{ (this denominator, or } \mathbf{D}, > 0) \tag{J.4}$$

$$i = \frac{L_1Z_1 - (s_1 - I_1 - T_1)Z_2}{\mathbf{D}} \tag{J.5}$$

$$B = \{Z_1[L_1F_2 - L_2(T_1 + F_1)] + Z_2[(s_1 - I_2)(T_1 + F_1) - (s_1 - I_1 - T_1)F_2] \\ + Z_3[(s_1 - I_1 - T_1)L_2 - (s_2 - I_2)L_1]\}/\mathbf{D} \tag{J.6}$$

This is the system sketched in Figure 20.1.

COMPARATIVE-STATIC RESULTS WITH FIXED EXCHANGE RATES

Using these equilibrium solutions, we can derive many of Chapter 20's conclusions about the problem of reconciling internal and external balance under fixed exchange rates.

1. The *effects of fiscal policy on the balance of payments* (Figure 20.6) can be derived by adding a shift to the national product market (the IS curve in macro texts), and differentiating the system to find the change in the payments surplus, or dB. Expansionary fiscal policy, such as a rise in government purchases, is represented in the first equation as a drop in saving, or $dG = -ds_0$. It yields an effect on the balance of payments that could be positive, negative, or zero. Using Equation (J.6) with $dZ_1 = dG$ and $dZ_2 = dZ_3 = 0$, we get

$$(dB/dG) = \begin{matrix} [(+)(+) - (-) \ (-) &] \ /(+) \\ [L_1F_2 & - L_2(T_1 + F_1)] & /\mathbf{D} \end{matrix} \tag{J.7}$$

Both of the two terms in the numerator work out to be positive, and the difference between them is of ambiguous sign. This makes sense. The first term in Equation (J.7) involves F_2, the responsiveness of our international borrowing to our interest rate. The greater this term is, the greater the short-run capital inflow (in Figure 20.6) triggered by our government's extra borrowing in the wake of its expansionary fiscal shift. The second term relates to the negative effect of our extra income on our trade balance. The greater this term, the more our expansionary policy "worsens" our balance of payments (lowers B), as discussed in connection with Figure 20.6.

2. The *effect of expansionary monetary policy on the balance of payments* (Figure 20.5) can be derived by shifting Equation (J.2) (the *LM* curve) by the change in money supply dM and solving, via Equation (J.6), for dB, the resulting change in the payments surplus:

$$
\overset{(+)}{(dB/dM)} = [\overset{(+)}{(s_2} - \overset{(-)}{I_2})\overset{-}{(T_1} + \overset{(+)}{F_1)} - \overset{(+)/(+)}{(s_1} - I_1 - T_1)F_2]/\mathbf{D} \tag{J.8}
$$

In this case, the signs line up in such a way that *(dB/dM)* is clearly negative. It should be. Expanding our money supply worsens the balance of payments in two ways. First, following either the first term in Equation (J.8) or the top set of arrows back in Figure 20.5, our income increase worsens the trade balance (and may cause some of our extra saving to spill over into capital outflow). Second, the drop in our interest rates is likely to cause further net capital outflow, again lowering B.

3. The *basic dilemma of aggregate demand policy* in an open economy with fixed exchange rates emerges just as clearly from a special use of Equations (J.7) and (J.8) as it did in Figure 20.7. The dilemma was that, if we set aside short-run, interest-rate effects on the balance of payments, either expansionary fiscal policy or expansionary monetary worsens the balance of payments. This being the case, there is a dilemma facing policymakers whose economy is beset by either unemployment-cum-payments-deficit or inflation-cum-payments-surplus, as described in connection with Figure 20.7. This result emerges from Equations (J.7) and (J.8). In either equation, set aside interest-rate effects on the balance of payments by setting $F_2 = 0$. Doing so leaves terms for either *dB/dG* or *dB/dM* that are negative, posing the dilemma just mentioned.

4. The Mundell-Fleming prescription for *monetary-fiscal mix* also emerges from a manipulation of equations (J.4), (J.7), and (J.8). The first step toward demonstrating this is straightforward: use Equation (J.4) to derive the unit impacts of expansionary fiscal and monetary policies on national product (*dY/dG* and *dY/dM*). Then, let the overall changes *dY* and *dB* be related to changes in both fiscal and monetary policies at the same time:

$$
\mathbf{D}\,dY = \overset{(+)}{(s_2} - \overset{(+)}{I_2)}\,dM - \overset{(-)}{L_2 dG} \tag{J.9}
$$

and

$$\mathbf{D}\ dB = [\overset{(+)}{(s_2 - I_2)}\overset{(-)}{(T_1 + F_1)} - \overset{(+)}{(s_1 - I_1 - T_1)}\overset{(+)}{F_2}]\ dM$$
$$+ [\overset{(+)(+)}{L_1 F_2} - \overset{(-)}{L_2}\overset{(-)}{(T_1 + F_1)}]\ dG \qquad (\text{J}.10)$$

$$\text{-----------}$$

(negative in long run)

Studying these two equations yields the Mundell-Fleming mixtures of monetary-fiscal prescriptions illustrated in Figure 20.9. To cure both excessive unemployment and a payments deficit (as at Point *A* in Figure 20.9) requires that both *dY* and *dB* be positive. This will be possible only with *dM* < 0 and *dG* > 0; that is, with a mixture of tighter monetary policy and easier fiscal policy. Correspondingly, inflation and payments surplus can be simultaneously attacked (to make *dY* and *dB* negative) with a mixture of tight fiscal policy and easy monetary policy (as prescribed for Point E in Figure 20.9). The other prescriptions of Figure 20.9 plus the assignment rule, also follow from this system of equations.

5. The effects of *perfect capital mobility* on the potency of monetary and fiscal policy can be captured by adding the right extreme parameter values to the system of equations. Perfect capital mobility means that a practically infinite amount of lending moves in or out of the country, affecting the money supply at the same time. In terms of the equations, perfect capital mobility means $F_2 = \infty$ and $L_2 = -\infty$. Plugging in these extreme values fixes the home-country interest rate and dictates national product as follows:

$$Y = Z_1/(s_1 - I_1 - T_1) \qquad (\text{J}.11)$$

National income is now determined solely by fiscal policy and the other Keynesian demand-shift parameters (within Z_1), amplified by the multiplier formula $1/(s_1 - I_1 - T_1)$. Fiscal policy (or any other shifter of Z_1) is now more powerful than in Equation (J.4) above. An expansion of government spending, for example, does not cause any rise in the interest rate, because the slightest nascent rise in the interest rate brings in enough lending from abroad to keep the rate fixed. This effectively raises the money supply in response to the extra government spending.

With perfect capital mobility, monetary policy is powerless as a regulator of the domestic economy. An attempt to increase the money supply leads only to the slightest temporary decline in the interest rate, causing the full amount of the extra money to flow abroad in search of a slightly better rate. This is shown in Equation (J.11), where the money supply plays no role in determining income.[5]

---

[5] Notice that in this treatment of the case of perfect capital mobility, we have not presented an equation for the balance-of-payments surplus, *B*. All presentations of the basic Keynesian

EQUILIBRIUM WITH FLOATING RATES

When the exchange rate floats, the foreign exchange market equation changes its nature, as noted above. It now becomes an equilibrium between demand and supply for foreign currency, and r becomes an endogenous variable in place of B, which is now set at zero. In this case, the system of equilibrium equations determining Y, i, and r becomes:

		Exchange		
Income term	Interest term	rate term	Exogenous terms	
$(s_1 - I_1 - T_1)Y +$	$(s_1 - I_2)i$	$- T_2 r$	$= (I_0 + T_0 - s_0) = Z_1$	(J.1b)
$L_1 Y +$	$L_2 i$		$= (M - L_0) = Z_2$	(J.2)
$(T_1 + F_1)Y +$	$F_2 i$	$+ T_2 r$	$= (-T_0 - F_0) = Z_3$	(J.3b)

The same set of equations can be re-expressed in matrix form as

$$\begin{bmatrix} (s_1 - I_1 - T_1) & (s_2 - I_2) & -T_2 \\ L_1 & L_2 & 0 \\ (T_1 + F_1) & F_2 & T_2 \end{bmatrix} \cdot \begin{bmatrix} Y \\ i \\ r \end{bmatrix} = \begin{bmatrix} Z_1 \\ Z_2 \\ Z_3 \end{bmatrix}$$

Solving the set of equations again yields expressions tying the endogenous variables (y, i, r) to the exogenous variables alone:

$$Y = \frac{L_2(Z_1 + Z_3) - (s_2 - I_2 + F_2)Z_2}{(s_1 - I_1 + F_1)L_2 - (s_2 - I_2 + F_2)L_1} \text{ (this denominator} = \mathbf{D'} > 0)^6$$

(J.12)

$$i = [(s_1 - I_1 + F_1)Z_2 - L_1(Z_1 + Z_3)]/\mathbf{D'}$$ (J.13)

and

$$r = \{\text{the same numerator as in equation (J.6)}\}/T_2\mathbf{D'}$$ (J.14)

This is the system sketched in Figure 21.1.

COMPARATIVE-STATIC RESULTS WITH FLOATING RATES

The conclusions of Chapter 21 follow from a comparison of the income-change condition for fixed and floating rates. We survey four such conclusions here.

---

or Mundell-Fleming model follow the same practice of finessing the B equation in order to avoid bogging down in some difficult dynamics. The case of perfect capital mobility is one in which we must drop the convenient "sterilization" assumption, the assumption that the money stock (M) is a parameter that policy can fix without regard to B. Without sterilization, there is a cumbersome dynamic relationship between B and M. B becomes a component of *change* in the money stock M. The resulting dynamic system does not lend itself easily to a static set of simultaneous equations like those used in this appendix. Hence no convenient equation for B can be presented here. The key result for perfect capital mobility and fixed exchange rates, however, is wrapped up in Equation (J.11).

[6] The term $(s_1 - I_1 + F_1)$ is positive, helping make $\mathbf{D'} < 0$, because only part of the extra saving caused by an income rise (s_1) goes into real investments (I_1) and bonds $(-F_1)$.

1. Our *monetary policy* has more impact under floating rates than under fixed. Chapter 21 explained that this was because an expansion in our money supply would cause our currency to depreciate, shifting more international demand toward the goods and services we produce, and stimulating our own aggregate demand further. The same result emerges clearly from our algebraic model when we differentiate Y with respect to the monetary shift $dM\ (= dZ_2)$:

$$(dY/dM)_{\text{float}} = \cfrac{1}{\underset{(+) - (-) \qquad (+) \quad / \qquad (+)}{L_1 - L_2(s_1 - I_1 + F_1)/(s_2 - I_2 + F_2)}} \qquad (J.15)$$

whereas from Equation (J.4) above,

$$(dY/dM)_{\text{fixed}} = \cfrac{1}{L_1 - L_2(s_1 - I_1 - T_1)/(s_2 - I_2)} \qquad (J.16)$$

The two results differ only by the roles of F_1, F_2, and T_1. Since $F_2 \geq 0$ and both F_1 and $T_1 \leq 0$, monetary policy has more effect on our national product under floating rates than under fixed rates (i.e., $(dY/dM)_{\text{float}} > (dY/dM)_{\text{fixed}}$ unless it happened that $F_1 = F_2 = T_1 = 0$). Even if capital were somehow perfectly mobile in response to the slightest nascent change in our interest rate ($L_2 = -\infty$), monetary policy would still have more effect under floating rates (i.e., the ratio $(dY/dM)_{\text{float}}/(dY/dM)_{\text{fixed}} > 1$). For better or for worse, floating exchange rates give domestic monetary policy a greater impact.

2. Our *fiscal policy* also has greater effect on our national product with floating rates than with fixed, under the plausible assumption that expansionary fiscal policy would worsen the balance of payments or raise our demand for foreign exchange. Comparing income derivatives with respect to government spending (dY/dG, where $dG = dZ_1$) brings this out clearly:

$$(dY/dG)_{\text{float}} = \cfrac{\overset{(-)}{L_2}}{\underset{(+) \quad (-)- \qquad (+) \quad (+)}{(s_1 - I_1 + F_1)L_2 - (s_2 - I_2 + F_2)L_1}} \qquad (J.17)$$

versus, form Equation (J.4) above,

$$(dY/dG)_{\text{float}} = \cfrac{\overset{(-)}{L_2}}{\underset{(+) \quad (-)- \qquad (+)}{(s_1 - I_1 - T_1)L_2 - (s_2 - I_2)L_1}} \qquad (J.18)$$

The denominator is indeed smaller, and the whole ratio larger, with floating rates than with fixed, since $F_2 \geq 0$ and F_1 and $T_1 \leq 0$.

Some authors have implied the reverse result, finding fiscal policy's impact on national product diminished with floating rates. But as mentioned in

Chapter 21, such a result would emerge only in the less likely case in which expansionary fiscal policy *improves* the balance of payments (or raises net demand for our currency) when our higher interest rates, raised by government borrowing, attract large inflows of capital from abroad. Accepting this result requires ignoring the eventual repayment of principal and interest on the borrowed capital. Note that the key role of this same condition can be found in the algebra. Back when discussing Equation (J.7) above, we noted that fiscal policy worsens the balance of payments as long as $L_1F_2 - L_2(T_1 + F_1) < 0$, as seems plausible. Notice that the same condition is the key one for making $(dY/dG)_{\text{float}} > (dY/dG)_{\text{fixed}}$ here.

3. The same algebra can be used to compare the responses of the two exchange-rate institutions to *export demand shocks*. To do so, we differentiate Equations (J.4) and (J.12) with respect to the shift toward trade-balance improvement, $dT_0 = dZ_1 = -dZ_3$. With fixed rates, Equation (J.4) implies a positive response $(dY/dT_0)_{\text{fixed}}$ equal to $(dY/dG)_{\text{fixed}}$ above. With floating rates, Equation (J.12) yields $(dY/dT_0)_{\text{float}} = 0$. That is, it implies that a shift in international demand toward our products is completely offset by our currency's appreciation, which costs us the same amount of international demand for our products. Here the model probably exaggerates. A country with a floating exchange rate probably does not get a full insulation of its national-product demand from any export-demand shifts. At the least, there should be a problem of sectoral imbalance, with the first-favored export sector expanding and raising prices, and the other tradable sectors hurt by currency appreciation experiencing cutbacks and unemployment.

4. *International capital-flow shocks,* by contrast, have an effect under floating rates that they do not have under fixed. Equation (J.12) confirms a result in Chapter 21: With the float, a surge of capital inflows from abroad will appreciate our currency and hurt aggregate demand for our tradable products. No such effect will show up with fixed rates and sterilization. Differentiating Equation (J.12) with respect to $dF_0 = -dZ_3$ yields the same absolute effect as we got for fiscal policy: $(dY/dF_0)_{\text{float}} = -(dY/dG)_{\text{float}}$. Yet the corresponding change equals zero for fixed rates with sterilization, as Equation (J.4) will confirm. The vulnerability of the economy to the effects of international flows on exchange rates is viewed as a drawback of floating rates, especially in American debates over the capital inflows and dollar appreciation of 1980–85.

SUGGESTED READINGS

The basic Keynesian open-economy model used here has often been modified and extended. Yet its basic judgments about the responses of exchange-rate regimes to different kinds of individual shocks have not yet been overturned by any new consensus view. In addition to the readings cited in Chapter 20, three important exercises in this area are *(a)* Boyer (1978), which adds an explicit social-loss-from-instabilities function and considers combinations of simultaneous shocks; *(b)* Turnovsky (1984), which adds the supply side, expectations and other important dynamic elements; and *(c)* Branson and Buiter (1984) which introduces the exchange rate and expectations about it back into the money market equation, bringing a better synthesis of the Keynesian open-economy model with our basic asset-market approach to exchange rates.

Two relatively advanced surveys of where we stand on the issue of macro-stabilization under different exchange-rate regimes are Kenen (1984) and Marston (1984).

*References**

Adams, F. G., and S. Klein, eds. *Stabilizing World Commodity Prices*. Lexington, Mass.: Lexington Books, 1978.

Adams, John, ed. *The Contemporary International Economy: A Reader*. 2d ed. New York: St. Martin's Press, 1985.

Adelman, Morris. "Politics, Economics and World Oil." *AER* 64, no. 2 (May 1974), pp. 58–67.

Aliber, Robert Z. "Speculation in the Foreign Exchanges: The European Experience, 1919–1926." *Yale Economic Essays* 2 (1962), pp. 171–245.

Allen, Polly, and Peter B. Kenen. *Asset Markets, Exchange Rates, and Economic Integration*. New York: Cambridge University Press, 1980.

Allen, Robert C. "International Competition in Iron and Steel, 1850–1913." *Journal of Economic History* 39, no. 4 (December 1979), pp. 911–38.

Amsden, Alice H. *Asia's Next Giant: South Korea and Late Industrialization*. New York: Oxford University Press, 1989.

Amuzegar, Jahangir. "The Oil Story: Facts, Fiction and Fair Play." *Foreign Affairs* 51, no. 4 (July 1973), pp. 676–89.

Anderson, Kym, and Ross Garnaut. *Australian Protectionism*. Sydney: Allen and Unwin, 1987.

Anderson, Kym, and Yujiro Hayami, with associates. *The Political Economy of Agricultural Protection*. London: Allen and Unwin, 1986.

Artus, John R., and John H. Young. "Fixed and Flexible Exchange Rates: A Renewal of the Debate." *IMF Staff Papers* 27 (December 1979), reprinted in Adams (1983, above).

---

* Some often-cited journals:
AER = American Economic Review.
JIE = Journal of International Economics.
JPE = Journal of Political Economy.

Baily, Martin Neil, and Robert J. Gordon. "The Productivity Slowdown, Measurement Issues, and the Explosion of Computer Power." *Brookings Papers in Economic Activity* 1988, 1, pp. 347–432.

Balassa, Bela. "The Purchasing-Power-Parity Doctrine." *JPE* 72, no. 6 (December 1964), pp. 584–96.

―――――. *The Structure of Protection in Developing Countries*. 1971.

―――――. *European Economic Integration*. Amsterdam: North-Holland, 1975.

Balassa, Bela, and Mordechai Kreinin. "Trade Liberalization under the Kennedy Round: The Static Effects." *Review of Economics and Statistics* 49, no. 2 (May 1967), pp. 125–37.

Baldwin, Robert E. "The Case Against Infant-Industry Protection." *JPE* 77 (1969), pp. 295–305.

―――――. "Determinants of the Commodity Structure of U.S. Trade." *AER* 61, no. 1 (March 1971), pp. 126–46.

―――――. "Trade Policies in Developed Countries." In Jones and Kenen, eds., *Handbook*, vol. I (1984).

Baldwin, Robert E., and Anne O. Krueger, eds. *The Structure and Evolution of Recent U.S. Trade Policy*. Chicago: University of Chicago Press, 1984.

Baldwin, Robert E., and J. David Richardson. *International Trade and Finance: Readings*. Boston: Little, Brown, 1981.

Bale, Malcolm, and Ernst Lutz. "Price Distortions in Agriculture and Their Effects: An International Comparison." *Amercan Journal of Agricultural Economics* 63 (February 1981), pp. 8–22.

Basevi, Georgio. "The Restrictive Effect of the U.S. Tariff and Its Welfare Value." *AER* 58, no. 4 (September 1968), pp. 840–52.

Behrman, Jere R. *Development, the International Economic Order, and Commodity Agreements*. Reading, Mass.: Addison-Wesley, 1979.

Bernhauer, Kenneth. "The Asian Dollar Market." *The Federal Reserve Bank of San Francisco Economic Review*, Winter 1983, pp. 47–63.

Bhagwati, Jagdish N. "Immiserizing Growth." Reprinted in American Economic Association, *Readings in International Economics*. Homewood, Ill.: Richard D. Irwin, 1967.

―――――. *Trade, Tariffs and Growth*. Cambridge, Mass.: MIT Press, 1969.

―――――. *The New International Economic Order*. Cambridge, Mass.: MIT Press, 1977.

Bhagwati, Jagdish N., and Anne Krueger. A series of volumes on *Foreign Trade Regimes and Economic Development*. New York: Columbia University Press for the National Bureau of Economic Research, 1973–76.

Bhandari, Jagdeep S., and Bluford H. Putnam. *Economic Interdependence and Flexible Exchange Rates*. Cambridge, Mass.: MIT Press, 1983.

Binswanger, Hans P., and Pasquale L. Scandizzo. "Patterns in Agricultural Protection." Washington, D.C.: World Bank, November 1983. *Agricultural Research Unit Discussion Paper* no. 15.

Bishop, John H. "Is the Test Score Decline Responsible for the Productivity Growth Decline?" *AER* 79, no. 1 (March 1989), pp. 178–97.

Bloomfield, Arthur I. *Monetary Policy under the International Gold Standard, 1880–1914.* New York: Federal Reserve Bank of New York, 1959.

Bordo, Michael, and Anna J. Schwartz, eds. *A Retrospect on the Classical Gold Standard, 1821–1931.* Chicago: University of Chicago Press, 1984.

Boughton, James. "Test of the Performance of Reduced-Form Exchange Rate Models." *JIE,* 1987.

Bowen, Harry P. *Changes in the International Pattern of Factor Abundance and the Composition of Trade.* Washington, D.C.: Department of Labor, 1980. Office of Foreign Economic Research, *Economic Discussion Paper* no. 8.

Bowen, Harry P., Edward E. Leamer, and Leo Sveikauskas. "Multicountry, Multi-factor tests of the Factor Abundance Theory." *AER* 77, no. 5 (December 1987).

Bowler, Ian A. *Agricultural under the Common Agricultural Policy.* Manchester: Manchester University Press, 1985.

Boyer, Russell S. "Optimal Foreign Exchange Market Intervention." *JPE* 86, no. 6 (December 1978), pp. 1045–55.

Braga, J. C., and J. A. Mendez, "Exchange Rate Risk, Exchange Rate Regime and the Volume of International Trade." *Kyklos,* 41 (1988), pp. 263–80.

Brander, James A. and Barbara J. Spencer. "Export Subsidies and International Market Share Rivalry." *JIE* 18 (1985), pp. 83–100.

Branson, William H., and Willem H. Buiter. "Monetary and Fiscal Policy with Flexible Exchange Rates." In Bhandari and Putnam (1984) above.

Brealey, Richard, and Stewart Myers. *Principles of Corporate Finance,* 2d ed. New York: McGraw-Hill, 1984.

Brecher, Richard A., and Ehsan U. Choudri. "The Leontiev Paradox, Continued." *JPE* 90, no. 4 (August 1982), pp. 820–23.

Breton, Albert. *The Economic Theory of Representative Government.* Chicago: Aldine, 1974.

Brimmer, Andrew. "Imports and Economic Welfare in the United States." Remarks before the Foreign Policy Association, New York, February 18, 1972.

Calingaert, Michael. *The 1992 Challenge from Europe.* Washington: National Planning Association, 1988.

Canzoneri, Matthew B., and Carol Ann Rogers. "Is the European Community an Optimal Currency Area? Optimal Taxation versus the Cost of Multiple Currencies." *AER* 80, no. 3 (June 1990), pp. 419–33.

Caves, Richard E. "Economic Models of Political Choice: Canada's Tariff Structure." *Canadian Journal of Economics* 4, no. 2 (May 1976), pp. 278–300.

Cecchini, Paolo. *The European Challenge, 1992: The Benefits of a Single Market.* Aldershot, Hants.: Wildwood House, 1988.

Cheh, John H. "United States Concessions in the Kennedy Round and Short-Run Labor Adjustment Costs." *JIE* 4, no. 4 (November 1974), pp. 323–40.

Cheng, Leonard K. "Assisting Domestic Industries under International Oligopoly:

The Relevance of the Nature of Competition to Optimal Policies.'' *AER* 78, no. 4 (September 1988), pp. 746–59.

Chiswick, Barry R. ''Illegal Immigration and Immigration Control.'' *Journal of Economic Perspectives*, 2, 3 (Summer 1988), pp. 101–16.

Cline, William R., ed. *Policy Alternatives for a New International Economic Order.* New York: Praeger Publishers, 1979.

————. *Exports of Manufactures from Developing Countries.* Washington, D.C.: Brookings Institution, 1984.

————. ''International Debt: From Crisis to Recovery.'' *AER* 75, no. 2 (May 1985), pp. 185–95.

Corden, W. Max. ''The Normative Theory of International Trade.'' In Jones and Kenen, eds., *Handbook,* vol. 1 (1984).

Cox, David, and Richard Harris. ''Trade Liberalization and Industrial Organization: Some Estimates for Canada.'' *JPE* 93, 1 (February 1985), pp. 115–45.

Cuddington, John T. ''The Extent and Causes of the Debt Crisis of the 1980s.'' In I. Husain and I. Diwan, eds., *Dealing with the Debt Crisis.* Washington, D.C., 1989.

Cushman, David O. ''The Effects of Real Exchange Rate Risk on International Trade.'' *JIE* 15 (February 1983), pp. 45–63.

Deardorff, Alan V. ''Testing Trade Theories and Predicting Trade Flows.'' In Jones and Kenen, eds., *Handbook,* vol. I, 1984.

Diaz-Alejandro, Carlos F. ''Latin American Debt: I Don't Think We Are in Kansas Anymore.'' *Brookings Papers in Economic Analysis 1984,* 2, pp. 335–404.

Dixit, Avinash. ''Tax Policy in Open Economies.'' In *Handbook of Public Economics,* ed. Alan Auerbach and Martin Feldstein. New York: North-Holland, 1985.

Dixit, Avinash, and Victor Norman. *The Theory of International Trade.* Welwyn: James Nisbet, 1980.

Dornbusch, Rudiger. ''Expectations and Exchange Rate Dynamics.'' *JPE* 84, no. 6 (December 1976), pp. 1161–76.

————. ''Exchange Rate Economics: Where Do We Stand?'' *Brookings Papers in Economics Analysis 1980,* 1, pp. 143–206. Also in Bhandari and Putnam (1983, above).

Downs, Anthony. *An Economic Theory of Democracy.* New York: Harper & Row, 1957.

Duke, Richard M., et. al. *The United States Steel Industry and Its International Rivals: Trends and Factors Determining International Competitiveness.* Washington, D.C.: U.S. Federal Trade Commission, November 1977.

Eaton, Jonathan, and Mark Gersovitz. ''Debt with Potential Repudiation: Theoretical and Empirical Analysis.'' *Review of Economic Studies* 48, no. 2 (April 1981), pp. 289–309.

Eaton, Jonathan, and Gene M. Grossman, ''Optimal Trade and Industrial Policy under Oligopoly,'' *QJE* 51, no. 2 (May 1986), pp. 383–406.

Eichengreen, Barry. ''International Competition in the Products of U.S. Basic Industries.'' In *The United States in the World Economy,* ed. Martin Feldstein. Chicago: University of Chicago Press for the NBER, 1988.

―――.*Golden Fetters: The Gold Standard and the Great Depression, 1919–1939.* Forthcoming.

Eichengreen, Barry, and Peter H. Lindert, eds. *The International Debt Crisis in Historical Perspective.* Cambridge, Mass.: MIT Press, 1989.

El-Agraa, Ali M., ed. *International Economic Integration.* 2d edition. New York: Macmillan, 1988.

Ethier, Wilfred J. ''Dumping.'' *JPE* 90, no. 3 (June 1982), pp. 487–506.

Feenstra, Robert C. ''Voluntary Export Restraint in U.S. Autos, 1980–81: Quality, Employment and Welfare Effects.'' In *the Structure and Evolution of Recent U.S. Trade Policy,* eds. Robet E. Baldwin and Anne O. Krueger. Chicago: University of Chicago Press for the NBER. Pp. 35–39, 1984.

―――, ed. *Empirical Methods for International Trade.* Cambridge, Mass.: MIT Press 1988.

―――. ''Auctioning U.S. Import Quotas, Foreign Response and Alternative Policies,'' *International Trade Journal* 3, no. 3 (Spring 1989), pp. 239–60. 1989a.

―――, ed. *Trade Policies for International Competitiveness.* Chicago: University of Chicago Press for the NBER, 1989b.

Finger, J. Michael, and Andrzej Olechowski. *The Uruguay Round: A Handbook for the Multilateral Trade Negotiations.* Washington, D.C. World Bank, 1987.

Fishlow, Albert. ''Lessons from the Past: Capital Markets during the Nineteenth Century and the Interwar Period.'' *International Organization,* 39, no. 3 (Summer 1985), pp. 383–439.

―――. ''External Borrowing and Debt Management.'' In *The Open Economy: Tools for Policymakers in Developing Countries,* eds. Rudiger Dornbusch, F. Leslie, C. H. Helmers. Oxford: Oxford University Press, 1988. Pp. 187–222.

Fleming, J. Marcus. ''Domestic Financial Policies under Fixed and Floating Exchange Rates,'' *IMF Staff Papers* 9 (March 1962), pp. 369–77.

Frankel, Jeffrey A. ''Tests of Monetary and Portfolio-Balance Models of Exchange Rate Determination.'' In *Exchange Rate Theory and Practice,* eds. John Bilson and Richard Marston. Chicago: University of Chicago Press, 1984.

―――. ''The Dazzling Dollar.'' *Brookings Papers in Economic Activity* 1985, 1, pp. 199–218. (1985a)

―――. ''Six Possible Meanings of 'Overvaluation': The 1981–85 Dollar.'' Princeton: Princeton University Press, December 1985. *Princeton Essays in International Finance,* no. 159. (1985b)

Frenkel, Jacob A. ''Flexible Exchange Rates, Prices, and the Role of 'News': Lessons from the 1970s.'' *JPE* 89 (1981), pp. 665–705. Also in Bhandari and Putnam (1983).

Frenkel, Jacob A., ed. *Exchange Rates and International Macroeconomics.* Chicago: University of Chicago Press, 1985.

Frenkel, Jacob A., and Harry G. Johnson, eds. *The Economics of Exchange Rates.* Reading, Mass.: Addison-Wesley, 1978.

Frenkel, Jacob A., Michael P. Dooley, and Peter Wickham, eds. *Analytical Issues in Debt.* Washington, D.C.: IMF, 1989.

Friedman, Milton. "The Case for Flexible Exchange Rates." In his *Essays in Positive Economics.* Chicago: University of Chicago Press, 1953.

————. "The Euro-Dollar Market: Some First Principles." *Federal Reserve Bank of St. Louis Review* (July 1971), pp. 375–83.

Fuss, Melvyn and Leonard Waverman. "Productivity Growth in the Auto Industry, 1970–1980: A Comparison of Canada, Japan and the United States." *NBER Working Paper* no. 1835. December, 1985.

————. "The Extent and Sources of Cost and Efficiency Differences between U.S. and Japanese Automobile Producers." *NBER Working Paper* no. 1849. March 1986.

Gallarotti, Giulio M. "Centralized versus Decentralized International Monetary Systems: The Lessons of the Classical Gold Standard." *Cato Journal,* 1989.

Gardner, Bruce L. *The Economics of Agricultural Policies.* New York: Macmillan, 1988.

Giddy, Ian. "The Foreign Exchange Option as a Hedging Tool." *New Developments in International France,* eds. J. Stern and D. Chew. Oxford: Basil Blackwell, 1988.

Gordon-Ashworth, Fiona. *International Commodity Cartels: A Contemporary History and Appraisal.* New York: St. Martin's Press, 1984.

Greenaway, David, and Chris Milner. *The Economics of Intra-Industry Trade.* Oxford: Basil Blackwell, 1986.

Greenaway, David, and P. K. M. Tharakan, eds. *Imperfect Competition and International Trade: The Policy Aspects of Intra-Industry Trade.* Atlantic Highlands, New Jersey: Humanities Press, 1986.

Gregory, Robert G. "A Sad and Sorry Story: Industry Policy for the Australian Motor Vehicle Industry." In *International Competitiveness,* eds. A. Michael Spence and Heather A. Hazard. Cambridge, Mass.: Ballinger, 1988. pp. 173–96.

Grilli, Enzo R., and Maw Cheng Yang. "Primary Commodity Prices, Manufactured Goods Prices, and the Terms of Trade of Developing Countries: What the Long Run Shows." *World Bank Economic Review* 2, no. 1 (January 1988): pp. 1–47.

Grossman, Gene M. "The Gains from International Factor Movements," *JIE* 17 (1984), pp. 73–83.

Grubel, Herbert G. "Effective Tariff Protection: A Non-specialist Introduction." In *Effective Tariff Protection,* ed. H. G. Grubel and H. G. Johnson. Geneva: GATT: 1971.

————. *International Economics.* Rev. ed. Homewood, Ill.: Richard D. Irwin, 1981.

Grubel, Herbert G., and P. J. Lloyd. *Intra-industry Trade: The Theory and Measurement of Trade in Differentiated Products.* New York: John Wiley & Sons, 1975.

Gruber, William, Dileep Mehta, and Raymond Vernon. "The R&D Factor in International Trade and International Investment of U.S. Industries." *JPE* 75, no. 1 (February 1967), pp. 20–37.

Harkness, Jon. "Factor Abundance and Comparative Advantage." *AER* 68, no. 5 (December 1978), pp. 784–800.

Havrylyshyn, O. and E. Civan, "Intra-Industry Trade and the Stage of Development: A Regression Analysis of Industrial and Developing Countries." In *Intra-Industry Trade: Empirical and Methodological Aspects,* ed. P. K. M. Tharakan. Amsterdam: North-Holland, 1983, pp. 111–40.

Hawkins, William R. "Neomercantilism: Is There a Case for Tariffs?" *National Review* April 6, 1984, pp. 25–45.

Hayes, J. P. *Economic Effects of Sanctions on Southern Africa.* Aldershot, Hants.: Gower, 1987. Thames Essay no. 53.

Heliwell, John F, and Tim Padmore. "Empirical Studies of Macroeconomic Interdependence." In Jones and Kenen, eds., *Handbook,* vol. 2, (1984), pp. 1107–51.

Helleiner, G. K. "The Political Economy of Canada's Tariff Structure: An Alternative Model." *Canadian Journal of Economics* 10, no. 2 (May 1977), pp. 318–26.

Helpman, Elhanan, and Paul R. Krugman. *Trade Policy and Market Structure.* Cambridge, Mass.: MIT Press, 1989.

Hewett, Edward A. *Foreign Trade Prices in the Council for Mutual Economic Assistance.* Cambridge: Cambridge University Press, 1974.

Hitiris, T. *European Community Economics: A Modern Introduction.* New York: Harvester Wheatsheaf, 1988.

Holden, Paul, Merle Holden, and Esther C. Suss. "The Determinants of Exchange Rate Flexibility: An Empirical Investigation." *Review of Economics and Statistics* 41, no. 3 (August 1979), pp. 327–33.

Holzman, Franklyn D. "Comecon: A 'Trade-Destroying' Customs Union?" *Journal of Comparative Economics* 9 (1985), pp. 410–23.

Hooper, Peter, and Stephen W. Kohlhagen. "The Effects of Exchange Rate Uncertainty on the Prices and Volumes of International Trade," *JIE* 8 (November 1978), pp. 483–511.

Hooper, Peter, and John E. Morton. "Fluctuations in the Dollar: A Model of Nominal and Real Exchange Rate Determination." *Journal of International Money and Finance.* 1 (1982), pp. 39–56.

Hufbauer, Gary C. "The Impact of National Characteristics and Technology on the Commodity Composition of Trade in Manufactured Goods." In *The Technology Factor in International Trade,* ed. Raymond Vernon. New York: Columbia University Press, 1970.

————. *The Free Trade Debate, a Background Paper of the Twentieth Century Fund Task Force on the Future of American Trade Policy.* New York: Priority Press Publications, 1989.

Hufbauer, Gary C., and J. J. Schott. *Economic Sanctions in Support of Foreign Policy Goals.* Washington, D.C.: Institute for International Economics, 1983.

————. *Economic Sanctions Reconsidered.* Washington, D.C.: Institute for International Economics, 1985.

Hymer, Stephen H. *The International Operation of National Firms: A Study of Direct Foreign Investment.* Cambridge, Mass.: MIT Press, 1976.

International Monetary Fund. *International Financial Statistics.* Washington, D.C.: IMF, various months and years.

Isard, Peter. "How Far Can We Push the Law of One Price?" *AER* 67, no. 5 (December 1977), pp. 942–48.

Johnson, Chalmers. *MITI and the Japanese Miracle: The Growth of Industrial Policy, 1925–1975.* Stanford: Stanford University Press, 1982.

Johnson, Harry G. "The Cost of Protection and the Scientific Tariff." *JPE* 68, no. 4 (August 1960), pp. 327–45.

————. "Optimal Trade Policy in the Presence of Domestic Distortions." In *Trade, Growth and the Balance of Payments,* ed. Robert E. Baldwin. Chicago: Rand McNally, 1965.

Jones, Ronald W., and Peter B. Kenen, eds. *Handbook of International Economics.* Two volumes. New York: North-Holland, 1984.

Karlik, John R. *Some Questions and Brief Answers about the Eurodollar Market.* A Staff Study prepared for the Joint Economic Committee, U.S. Congress. Washington, D.C.: U.S. Government Printing Office, 1977. Also excerpted in Baldwin and Richardson (1981), cited above.

Katz, Lawrence F., and Lawrence H. Summers. "Industry Rents: Evidence and Implications." *Brookings Papers in Economic Analysis,* "Microeconomics," 1989, pp. 209–90.

Keesing, Donald B. "The Impact of Research and Development on United States Trade." *JPE* 75, no. 2 (February 1967), pp. 38–48.

Kenen, Peter B. "Macroeconomic Theory and Policy: How the Closed Economy Was Opened." In Jones and Kenen, eds., *Handbook,* vol. II (1984).

Kindleberger, Charles P. *International Money.* London: George Allen & Unwin, 1981.

Krause, Lawrence B. "How Much of Current Unemployment Did We Import?" *Brookings Papers in Economic Analysis,* 1971, 1.

Krueger, Anne O. "The Political Economy of a Rent-Seeking Society." *AER* 64, no. 3 (June 1974), pp. 291–303.

————. *The Benefits and Costs of Import Substitution in India: A Microeconomic Study.* Minneapolis: University of Minnesota Press, 1975.

————. "Trade Policies in Developing Countries." In Jones and Kenen, eds., *Handbook,* vol. I (1984).

Krueger, Anne O., Maurice Schiff, and Alberto Valdés, eds Forthcoming. *The Political Economy of Agricultural Price Policies.* Oxford: Oxford University Press.

Krugman, Paul R. "Increasing Returns, Monopolistic Competition, and International Trade." *JIE* 9 (1979), pp. 469–79.

————, ed. *Strategic Trade Policy and the New International Economics.* Cambridge, Mass.: MIT Press, 1986.

Lancaster, Kelvin. "Intra-Industry Trade Under Perfect Monopolistic Competition." *JIE* 10 (1980), pp. 151–75.

Lavergne, Real P. *The Political Economy of U.S. Tariffs*. New York: Academic Press, 1983.

Lawrence, Robert Z. *Can America Compete?* Washington, D.C.: Brookings Institution, 1984.

Leamer, Edward E. "The Leontiev Paradox, Reconsidered." *JPE* 88, no. 3 (June 1980), pp. 495–503.

————. *Sources of International Comparative Advantage: Theory and Evidence.* Cambridge, Mass.: MIT Press, 1984.

Leamer, Edward E., and Stern, Robert M. *Quantitative International Economics.* Chicago: Aldine, 1970.

Leontiev, Wassily. "Factor Proportions and the Structure of American Trade: Further Theoretical and Empirical Analysis." *Review of Economics and Statistics* 38, no. 4 (November 1956), pp. 386–407.

Levich, Richard M. "Empirical Studies of Exchange Rates: Price Behavior, Rate Determination and Market Efficiency." In Jones and Kenen, eds., *Handbook,* Vol. II (1984).

————. "Financial Innovations in International Financial Markets." In *The United States in the World Economy,* ed. Martin Feldstein. Chicago: University of Chicago Press, 1988.

Lindert, Peter H. *Key Currencies and Gold, 1900–1913.* Princeton, N.J.: Princeton University Press, 1969.

————. "Historical Patterns in Agricultural Policy." In *Agricultural and the State: Growth, Employment and Poverty in Developing Countries,* ed. C. Peter Timmer. Ithaca, N.Y.: Cornell University Press, Forthcoming.

Lindert, Peter H., and Peter J. Morton. "How Sovereign Debt Has Worked." In Jeffrey D. Sachs (1989).

Magee, Stephen P. "The Welfare Effects of Restrictions on U.S. Trade." *Brookings Papers in Economic Analysis* 1972, 3, pp. 645–707.

————. "Twenty Paradoxes in International Trade Theory." In *International Trade and Agriculture: Theory and Policy,* ed. Jimmye Hillman and Andrew Schmitz. Boulder, Colo.: Westview Press, 1979, pp. 91–116.

Magee, Stephen P., William Brock, and Leslie Young. *Black Hole Tariffs and Endogenous Policy Theory.* Cambridge: Cambridge University Press, 1989.

Markusen, J. R., and J. R. Melvin. "Trade, Factor Prices, and Gains from Trade with Increasing Returns to Scale." *Canadian Journal of Economics* 14 (1981), pp. 450–69.

Marston, Richard C. "Stabilization Policies in Open Economies." In Jones and Kenen, eds., *Handbook,* vol. II (1984).

Massell, Benton F. "Price Stabilization and Welfare." *Quarterly Journal of Economics* 83, no. 2 (May 1969), pp. 284–98.

McCalla, Alex F., and Timothy E. Josling. *Agricultural Policies and World Markets.* New York: Macmillan, 1985.

McCulloch, Rachel. "Unexpected Real Consequences of Floating Exchange Rates." In Adams (1985).

McKinnon, Ronald. *Money in International Exchange.* New York: Oxford University Press, 1979.

_____. "The Exchange Rate and Macroeconomic Policy: Changing Postwar Perceptions." *Journal of Economic Literature* 19, no. 2 (June 1981), pp. 531–57.

_____. "Currency Substitution and Instability in the World Dollar Market," *AER* 72, no. 3 (June 1982), pp. 320–33.

_____. "Optimum Currency Areas." *AER* 53, no. 1 (March 1963), pp. 717–25.

Meade, James. *Trade and Welfare.* Oxford: Oxford University Press, 1955.

Meese, Richard. "Currency Fluctuations in the Post-Bretton Woods Era." *JIE,* 4, no. 1 (Winter 1990), pp. 117–34.

Meese, Richard, and Kenneth Rogoff. "Empirical Exchange Rate Models of the Seventies: How Well Do They Fit Out of Sample?" *JIE* 14 (February 1983), pp. 3–24.

Meier, Gerald M. *Problems of a World Monetary Order.* 2d ed. New York: Oxford University Press, 1982.

Miller, Marcus H., and John E. Spencer. "The Static Economic Effects of the UK Joining the EEC: A General Equilibrium Approach." *Review of Economic Studies* 44 (1977), pp. 71–94.

Morici, Peter. *Meeting the Competitive Challenge: Canada and the United States in the Global Economy.* Washington, D.C.: Canadian-American Committee, 1988a.

_____. *Reassessing American Competitiveness.* Washington, D.C.: National Planning Association, 1988b.

_____, *Making Free Trade Work: The Canada-U.S. Agreement.* New York: Council on Foreign Relations, 1990.

Moyer, H. Wayne, and Timothy E. Josling. *Agricultural Policy Reform.* Ames: Iowa State University Press, 1990.

Mundell, Robert. *International Economics.* New York: Macmillan, 1968.

Mussa, Michael. "Tariffs and the Distribution of Income." *JPE* 82, no. 6 (December 1974), pp. 1191–204.

Mutoh, Hiromichi, Sueo Sekiguchi, Kotaro Suzumura, and Ippei Yamazawa. *Industrial Policies for Pacific Economic Growth.* Sydney: Allen and Unwin, 1986.

Mutti, John, and Peter Morici. *Changing Patterns of U.S. Industrial Activity and Comparative Advantage.* Washington, D.C.: National Planning Association, 1983.

Newbery, D. M. G., and J. E. Stiglitz. "The Theory of Commodity Price Stabilization Rules: Welfare Impacts and Supply Responses." *Economic Journal* 89 (1979), pp. 799–817.

Niehans, Jurg. "International Debt with Unenforceable Claims." *San Francisco Federal Reserve Bank Review* (February 1985), pp. 64–79.

Niehans, Jurg, and John Hewson. "The Eurodollar Market and Monetary Theory." *Journal of Money, Credit and Banking* 8 (February 1976), pp. 1–27.

Officer, Lawrence. "The Purchasing Power Parity Theory of Exchange Rates: A Review Article." *IMF Staff Papers* 23 (March 1976).

Olson, Mancur. *The Logic of Collective Action.* Cambridge, Mass.: Harvard University Press, 1965.

Oswald, Rudy. "Statement of U.S. Aims at the World Trade Ministers' Meeting: A Labor View." In Adams (1985).

Parkin, J. Michael. *Macroeconomics.* Englewood Cliffs, N.J.: Prentice-Hall, 1984.

Peterson, E. Wesley F., and Clare B. Lyons. "The Perpetual Agricultural Policy Crisis in the European Community." *Agriculture and Human Values* 6, nos. 1–2 (Winter-Spring 1989), pp. 11–21.

Pincus, Jonathon J. "Pressure Groups and the Pattern of Tariffs." *JPE* 83, no. 4 (July/August 1975), pp. 757–77.

Pomfret, Richard. *Unequal Trade: The Economics of Discriminatory International Trade Policies.* Oxford: Basil Blackwell, 1988.

Porter, Michael E. *The Competitive Advantage of Nations.* New York: Free Press, 1990.

Postner, Harry. *The Factor Content of Canada's Foreign Trade.* Ottawa: Economic Council of Canada, 1975.

Ray, Edward John. "The Determinants of Tariff and Nontariff Trade Restrictions in the United States." *JPE* 89, no. 1 (February 1981), pp. 105–21.

————. "The Determinants of Foreign Direct Investment in the United States, 1979–85." In *Trade Policies for International Competitiveness,* ed. Robert C. Feenstra. Chicago: University of Chicago Press for NBER, 1989. pp. 53–84.

Ray, Edward John, and Howard P. Marvel. "The Patterns of Protection in the Industrialized World." *Review of Economics and Statistics* 66, no. 3 (August 1984), pp. 452–58.

Reynolds, Clark W., and Robert K. McCleery. "Modeling U.S.-Mexico Economic Linkages *AER* 72, 2 (May 1985), pp. 217–22.

————. "The Political Economy of Immigration Law: Impact of Simpson-Rodino on the United States and Mexico," *Journal of Economic Perspectives,* 2, no. 3 (Summer 1988), pp. 117–132.

Rivera-Batiz, Francisco L., and Lius Rivera-Batiz. *International Finance and Open Economy Macroeconomics.* New York: Macmillan, 1985.

Rosefielde, Steven. "Factor Proportions and Economic Rationality in Soviet International Trade, 1955–1968." *AER* 64, no. 4 (September 1974), pp. 670–81.

Rueff, Jacques. Translated 1972. *The Monetary Sin of the West.* New York: Macmillan.

Ruffin, Roy J. "The Missing Link: The Ricardian Approach to the Factor Endowments Theory of Trade." *AER* 78, no. 4 (September 1988), pp. 759–72.

Rugman, Alan M. *Multinationals in Canada.* Boston: Martinus Nijhoff, 1980.

Sachs, Jeffrey D. *Theoretical Issues in International Borrowing.* Princeton, N.J.: Princeton Univerity Press, 1984. Princeton Studies in International Finance no. 54.

_____. *Developing Country Debt, Volume 1: The World Financial System*. Chicago: University of Chicago Press for the NBER, 1989.

Saunders, R. S. "The Political Economy of Effective Protection in Canada's Manufacturing Sector." *Canadian Journal of Economics* 13, no. 2 (May 1980), pp. 340–48.

Scandizzo, Pasquale L., and Dimitris Diakosawas. *Instability in the Terms of Trade of Primary Commodities, 1900–1982*. Rome: UN, FAO 1987.

Schafer, Jeffrey R., and Bonnie E. Loopesko. "Floating Exchange Rates after Ten Years." *Brookings Papers in Economic Analysis 1983*, 1, pp. 1–86.

Scherer, Frederick M. *Industrial Market Structure and Economic Performance*. Chicago: Rand-McNally, 1971.

Simon, Julian L. *The Economic Consequences of Immigration*. Oxford: Basil Blackwell, 1989.

Smith, Gordon M., and John T. Cuddington, eds. *International Debt and the Developing Countries*. Washington, D.C.: World Bank, 1984.

Solomon, Robert. *The International Monetary System, 1945–1976*. New York: Harper & Row, 1977.

Somanath, V. S. "Efficient Exchange Rate Forecasts: Lagged Models Better than the Random Walk." *Journal of International Money and Finance*. 1986, pp. 195–220.

Stegemann, Klaus. "Policy Rivalry among Industrial States: What Can We Learn from Models of Strategic Trade Policy?" *International Organization* 43, 1 (Winter 1989), pp. 73–100.

Stern, J., and D. Chew, eds *New Developments in International Finance*. Oxford: Basil Blackwell, 1988.

Stern, Robert M. "The U.S. Tariff and the Efficiency of the U.S. Economy." *AER* 54, no. 2 (May 1964), pp.

_____. *The Balance of Payments*. Chicago: Aldine, 1973.

Stern, Robert M., and Keith E. Maskus. "Determinants of the Structure of U.S. Foreign Trade, 1958–76." *JIE* 11, no. 2 (May 1981), pp. 207–24.

Stigler, George J. "A Theory of Oligopoly." *JPE*, February 1964. Reprinted as Chapter 5 of his *The Organization of Industry*. Homewood, Ill.: Richard D. Irwin, 1968.

Summers, Robert and Alan Heston. 1988. "A New Set of International Comparisons of Real Product and Price Levels: Estimates for 130 Countries, 1950–1985." *Review of Income and Wealth*, Series 34, no. 1 (March), pp. 1–25 and attached diskettes.

Suslow, Valerie Y. "Stability in International Cartels: An Empirical Survey." Stanford University, Hoover Institution, *Working Paper in Economics* E-88-7. February 1988.

Tarr, David G. *A General Equilibrium Analysis of the Welfare and Employment Effects of U.S. Quotas in Textiles, Autos, and Steel*. Washington, D.C.: U.S. Federal Trade Commission, February 1989. Bureau of Economics Staff Report.

Taylor, Dean. "Official Intervention in the Foreign Exchange Market, or, Bet against the Central Bank." *JPE* 90, no. 2 (April 1982), pp. 356–68.

Temin, Peter. "The Relative Decline of the British Steel Industry, 1880–1913." In *Industrialization in Two Systems*, ed. Henry Rosovsky. New York: John Wiley & Sons, 1966.

Tharakan, P. K. M., ed. *Intra-Industry Trade: Empirical and Methodological Aspects*. Amsterdam: North-Holland, 1983.

Triffin, Robert. *Gold and the Dollar Crisis*. New Haven, Conn.: Yale University Press, 1960.

Tsiang, S. C. "Fluctuating Exchange Rates in Countries with Relatively Stable Economies: Some European Experiences after World War I." *IMF Staff Papers* 7 (October 1959), pp. 244–73.

Turnovsky, Stephen J. "The Distribution of Welfare Gains from Price Stabilization: A Survey of Some Theoretical Issues." In F. G. Adams and S. Klein (1978).

—————. "Exchange Market Interventions in a Small Open Economy." In Bhandari and Putnam (1984) above.

Tyers, Rodney and Kym Anderson. *Distortions in World Food Markets*. Cambridge: Cambridge University Press for the Trade Policy Research Centre. Forthcoming.

U.S. Department of Agriculture, Economic Research Service. *Embargoes, Surplus Disposal and U.S. Agriculture*. Washington, D.C.: Government Printing Office, December 1986. Agricultural Economic Report no. 564. Edited by Alex F. McCalla, T. Kelley White and Kenneth Clayton.

Van Duyne, Carl. "Commodity Cartels and the Theory of Derived Demand." *Kyklos*, 28, no. 3 (1975), pp. 597–611.

Vanek, Jaroslav. *International Trade: Theory and Economic Policy*. Homewood, Ill.: Richard D. Irwin, 1962.

Vernon, Raymond G. "International Investment and International Trade in the Product Cycle." *Quarterly Journal of Economics* 80, no. 2 (May 1966), pp. 190–207.

—————. "The Product Cycle Hypotheses in a New International Environment." *Oxford Bulletin of Economics and Statistics* 41 (November 1979), pp. 255–67.

Vernon, Raymond G., ed. *The Oil Crisis*. New York: W. W. Norton, 1976.

Volcker, Paul L. "How Serious Is U.S. Bank Exposure?" *Challenge*, May–June 1983, pp. 11–19.

Weintraub, Sidney, "U.S.-Canada Free Trade: What's In It for the U.S.?" *Journal of Interamerican Studies and World Affairs*. 26 (1984), pp. 225–44.

Whalley, John. "An Evaluation of the Tokyo Round Trade Agreement Using General Equilibrium Computation Methods." *Journal of Policy Modeling* 4 (1982), pp. 341–61.

Whitney, William G. "The Structure of the American Economy in the Later Nineteenth Century." Unpublished Ph.D. dissertation, Harvard University, 1968.

Williamson, Jeffrey G., and Peter H. Lindert. *American Inequality: A Macroeconomic History*. New York: Academic Press, 1980.

Williamson, John. "The Case for Managed Exchange Rates." In Adams (1983), cited above.

Wonnacott, Paul, and Ronald J. Wonnacott. "Free Trade between the United States and Canada: Fifteen Years Later." *Canadian Public Policy*, October 1982, supplement.

Wonnacott, Ronald J., and Paul Wonnacott. *Free Trade between the United States and Canada: The Potential Economic Effects*. Cambridge, Mass.: Harvard University Press, 1967.

Woo, Wing T. "The Monetary Approach to Exchange Rate Determination under Rational Expectations: The Dollar-Deutschemark Rate." *JIE* 18 (1985), pp. 1–16.

Wright, Gavin. "The Origins of American Industrial Success, 1879–1940," *AER*, 80, no. 4 (September 1990), pp. 651–68.

Yamamura, Kozo. "Caveat Emptor: The Industrial Policy of Japan," in P. Krugman (1986).

Yeager, Leland B. "A Rehabilitation of Purchasing-Power-Parity." *JPE* 66, no. 6 (December 1958), pp. 516–30.

————. *International Monetary Relations*. New York: Harper and Row, 1976.

Index